Contents

Supporting resources

Visit **www.pearsoned.co.uk/wood** to find valuable online resources

Companion Website for students

- Learning objectives for each chapter
- Multiple choice questions to help you test your learning
- Review questions and answers
- Links to relevant sites on the web
- Searchable online glossary
- Flashcards to test your knowledge of key terms and definitions

For instructors

- Complete, downloadable Solutions Manual
- PowerPoint slides that can be downloaded and used for presentations
- Testbank of question material

Also: The Companion Website provides the following features:

- Search tool to help locate specific items of content
- E-mail results and profile tools to send results of quizzes to instructors
- Online help and support to assist with website usage and troubleshooting

For more information please contact your local Pearson Education sales representative or visit **www.pearsoned.co.uk/wood**

Guided tour of the book

Part opening

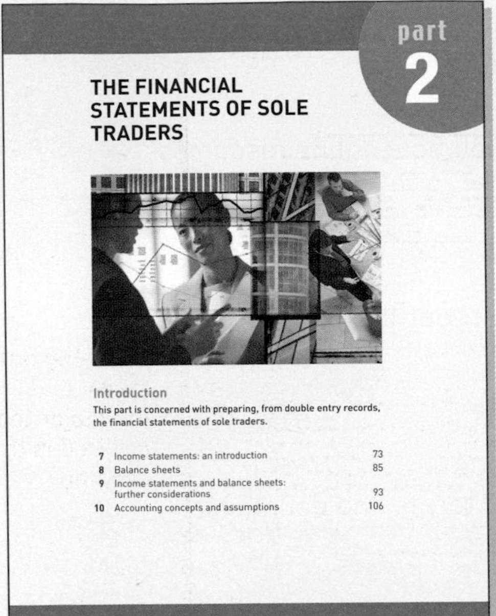

part 2

THE FINANCIAL STATEMENTS OF SOLE TRADERS

Introduction

This part is concerned with preparing, from double entry records, the financial statements of sole traders.

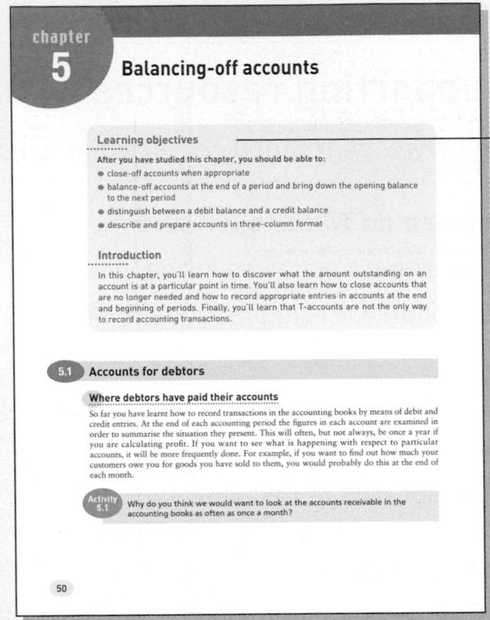

chapter 5

Balancing-off accounts

Learning objectives

After you have studied this chapter, you should be able to:

- close-off accounts when appropriate
- balance-off accounts at the end of a period and bring down the opening balance to the next period
- distinguish between a debit balance and a credit balance
- describe and prepare accounts in three-column format

Introduction

In this chapter, you'll learn how to discover what the amount outstanding on an account is at a particular point in time. You'll also learn how to close accounts that are no longer needed and how to record appropriate entries in accounts at the end and beginning of periods. Finally, you'll learn that T-accounts are not the only way to record accounting transactions.

5.1 Accounts for debtors

Where debtors have paid their accounts

So far you have learnt how to record transactions in the accounting books by means of debit and credit entries. At the end of each accounting period the figures in each account are examined in order to summarise the situation they present. This will often, but not always, be once a year if you are calculating profit. If you want to see what is happening with respect to particular accounts, it will be more frequently done. For example, if you want to find out how much your customers owe you for goods you have sold to them, you would probably do this at the end of each month.

Activity 5.1 Why do you think we would want to look at the accounts receivable in the accounting books as often as once a month?

50

Learning objectiv[es] outline what you v[will] need to have learn[t] by the end of the chapter.

Exhibits offer clear examples of accounting practice and methodology.

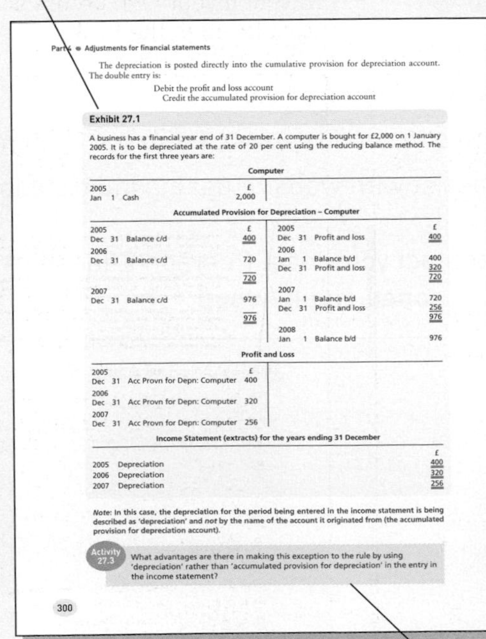

Part 4 • Adjustments for financial statements

The depreciation is posted directly into the cumulative provision for depreciation account. The double entry is:

Debit the profit and loss account
Credit the accumulated provision for depreciation account

Exhibit 27.1

A business has a financial year end of 31 December. A computer is bought for £2,000 on 1 January 2005. It is to be depreciated at the rate of 20 per cent using the reducing balance method. The records for the first three years are:

Computer

			£				£
2005							
Jan	1	Cash	2,000				

Accumulated Provision for Depreciation – Computer

			£				£
2005				2005			
Dec	31	Balance c/d	400	Dec	31	Profit and loss	400
2006				2006			
Dec	31	Balance c/d	720	Jan	1	Balance b/d	400
				Dec	31	Profit and loss	320
			720				720
2007				2007			
Dec	31	Balance c/d	976	Jan	1	Balance b/d	720
				Dec	31	Profit and loss	256
			976				976
				2008			
				Jan	1	Balance b/d	976

Profit and Loss

			£	
2005				
Dec	31	Acc Provn for Depn: Computer	400	
2006				
Dec	31	Acc Provn for Depn: Computer	320	
2007				
Dec	31	Acc Provn for Depn: Computer	256	

Income Statement (extracts) for the years ending 31 December

		£
2005	Depreciation	400
2006	Depreciation	320
2007	Depreciation	256

Note: In this case, the depreciation for the period being entered in the income statement is being described as 'depreciation' and *not* by the name of the account it originated from (the accumulated provision for depreciation account).

Activity 27.3 What advantages are there in making this exception to the rule by using 'depreciation' rather than 'accumulated provision for depreciation' in the entry in the income statement?

300

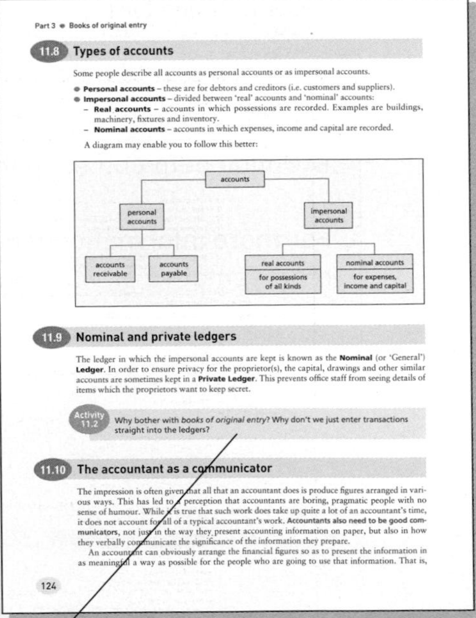

Part 3 • Books of original entry

11.8 Types of accounts

Some people describe all accounts as personal accounts or as impersonal accounts.

- **Personal accounts** – these are for debtors and creditors (i.e. customers and suppliers).
- **Impersonal accounts** – divided between 'real' accounts and 'nominal' accounts:
  - **Real accounts** – accounts in which possessions are recorded. Examples are buildings, machinery, fixtures and inventory.
  - **Nominal accounts** – accounts in which expenses, income and capital are recorded.

A diagram may enable you to follow this better:

11.9 Nominal and private ledgers

The ledger in which the impersonal accounts are kept is known as the **Nominal** (or 'General') **Ledger**. In order to ensure privacy for the proprietor(s), the capital, drawings and other similar accounts are sometimes kept in a **Private Ledger**. This prevents office staff from seeing details of items which the proprietors want to keep secret.

Activity 11.2 Why bother with *books of original entry*? Why don't we just enter transactions straight into the ledgers?

11.10 The accountant as a communicator

The impression is often given that all that an accountant does is produce figures arranged in various ways. This has led to a perception that accountants are boring, pragmatic people with no sense of humour. While it is true that such work does take up quite a lot of an accountant's time, it does not account for all of a typical accountant's work. **Accountants also need to be good communicators**, not just in the way they present accounting information on paper, but also in how they verbally communicate the significance of the information they prepare.

An accountant can obviously arrange the financial figures so as to present the information in as meaningful a way as possible for the people who are going to use that information. That is,

124

Activities occur frequently throughout the book to test your understanding of new concepts.

Worked examples are provided to guide you through more difficult concepts.

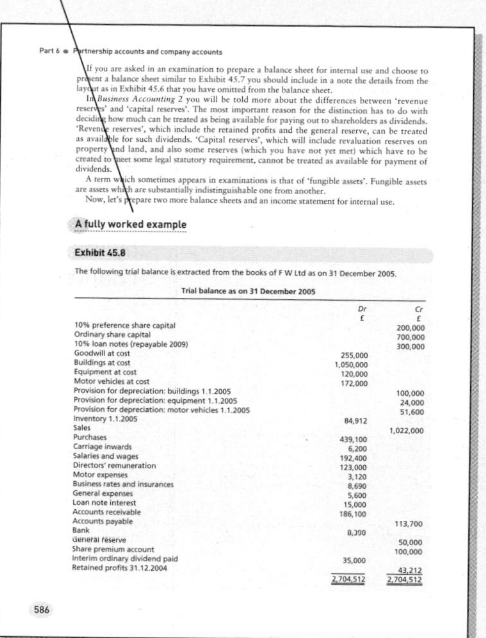

Part 6 ● Partnership accounts and company accounts

If you are asked in an examination to prepare a balance sheet for internal use and choose to present a balance sheet similar to Exhibit 45.7 you should include in a note the details from the layout as in Exhibit 45.6 that you have omitted from the balance sheet.

In *Business Accounting 2* you will be told more about the differences between 'revenue reserves' and 'capital reserves'. The most important reason for the distinction has to do with deciding how much can be treated as being available for paying out to shareholders as dividends. 'Revenue reserves', which include the retained profits and the general reserve, can be treated as available for such dividends. 'Capital reserves', which will include revaluation reserves on property and land, and also some reserves (which you have not yet met) which have to be created to meet some legal statutory requirement, cannot be treated as available for payment of dividends.

A term which sometimes appears in examinations is that of 'fungible assets'. Fungible assets are assets which are substantially indistinguishable one from another.

Now, let's prepare two more balance sheets and an income statement for internal use.

A fully worked example

Exhibit 45.8

The following trial balance is extracted from the books of F W Ltd as on 31 December 2005.

Trial balance as on 31 December 2005

	Dr £	*Cr* £
10% preference share capital		200,000
Ordinary share capital		700,000
10% loan notes (repayable 2009)		300,000
Goodwill at cost	255,000	
Buildings at cost	1,050,000	
Equipment at cost	120,000	
Motor vehicles at cost	172,000	
Provision for depreciation: buildings 1.1.2005		100,000
Provision for depreciation: equipment 1.1.2005		24,000
Provision for depreciation: motor vehicles 1.1.2005		51,600
Inventory 1.1.2005	84,912	
Sales		1,022,000
Purchases	439,100	
Carriage inwards	6,200	
Salaries and wages	192,400	
Directors' remuneration	123,000	
Motor expenses	3,120	
Business rates and insurances	8,690	
General expenses	5,600	
Loan note interest	15,000	
Accounts receivable	186,100	
Accounts payable		113,700
Bank	8,390	
General reserve		50,000
Share premium account		100,000
Interim ordinary dividend paid	35,000	
Retained profits 31.12.2004		43,212
	2,704,512	2,704,512

586

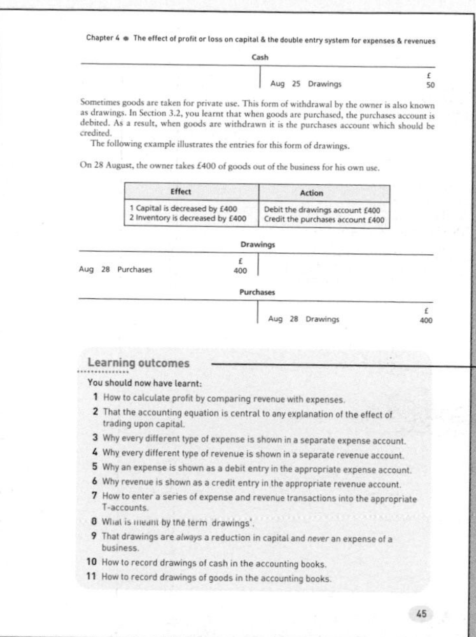

Chapter 4 ● The effect of profit or loss on capital & the double entry system for expenses & revenues

Cash

			£
		Aug 25 Drawings	50

Sometimes goods are taken for private use. This form of withdrawal by the owner is also known as drawings. In Section 3.2, you learnt that when goods are purchased, the purchases account is debited. As a result, when goods are withdrawn it is the purchases account which should be credited.

The following example illustrates the entries for this form of drawings.

On 28 August, the owner takes £400 of goods out of the business for his own use.

Effect	Action
1 Capital is decreased by £400 2 Inventory is decreased by £400	Debit the drawings account £400 Credit the purchases account £400

Drawings

	£		
Aug 28 Purchases	400		

Purchases

			£
		Aug 28 Drawings	400

Learning outcomes

You should now have learnt:

1 How to calculate profit by comparing revenue with expenses.
2 That the accounting equation is central to any explanation of the effect of trading upon capital.
3 Why every different type of expense is shown in a separate expense account.
4 Why every different type of revenue is shown in a separate revenue account.
5 Why an expense is shown as a debit entry in the appropriate expense account.
6 Why revenue is shown as a credit entry in the appropriate revenue account.
7 How to enter a series of expense and revenue transactions into the appropriate T-accounts.
8 What is meant by the term 'drawings'.
9 That drawings are *always* a reduction in capital and *never* an expense of a business.
10 How to record drawings of cash in the accounting books.
11 How to record drawings of goods in the accounting books.

45

Learning outcomes revisit and reinforce the major topics covered in the chapter.

Each chapter ends with a selection of **practice questions** to prepare you for your examinations.

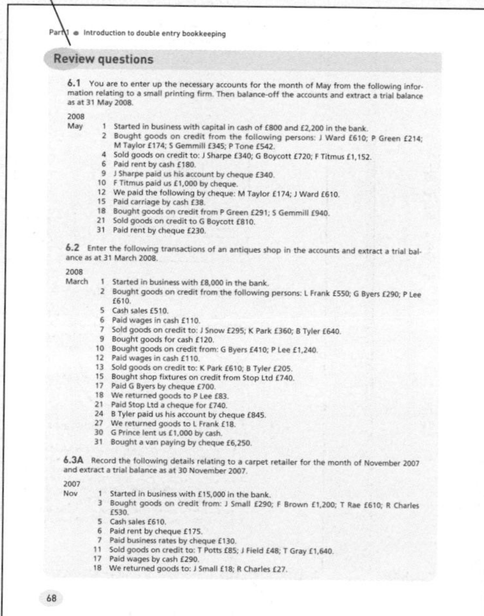

Part 1 ● Introduction to double entry bookkeeping

Review questions

6.1 You are to enter up the necessary accounts for the month of May from the following information relating to a small printing firm. Then balance-off the accounts and extract a trial balance as at 31 May 2008.

2008
May
1 Started in business with capital in cash of £800 and £2,200 in the bank.
2 Bought goods on credit from the following persons: J Ward £610; P Green £214; M Taylor £174; S Gemmill £345; P Tone £542.
4 Sold goods on credit to: J Sharpe £340; G Boycott £720; F Titmus £1,152.
6 Paid rent by cash £180.
9 J Sharpe paid us his account by cheque £340.
10 F Titmus paid us £1,000 by cheque.
12 We paid the following by cheque: M Taylor £174; J Ward £610.
15 Paid carriage by cash £38.
18 Bought goods on credit from P Green £291; S Gemmill £940.
21 Sold goods on credit to G Boycott £810.
31 Paid rent by cheque £230.

6.2 Enter the following transactions of an antiques shop in the accounts and extract a trial balance as at 31 March 2008.

2008
March
1 Started in business with £8,000 in the bank.
2 Bought goods on credit from the following persons: L Frank £550; G Byers £290; P Lee £610.
5 Cash sales £510.
6 Paid wages in cash £110.
7 Sold goods on credit to: J Snow £295; K Park £360; B Tyler £640.
9 Bought goods for cash £120.
10 Bought goods on credit from: G Byers £410; P Lee £1,240.
12 Paid wages in cash £110.
13 Sold goods on credit to: K Park £610; B Tyler £205.
15 Bought shop fixtures on credit from Stop Ltd £740.
17 Paid G Byers by cheque £700.
18 We returned goods to P Lee £83.
21 Paid Stop Ltd a cheque for £740.
24 B Tyler paid us his account by cheque £845.
27 We returned goods to L Frank £18.
30 G Prince lent us £1,000 by cash.
31 Bought a van paying by cheque £6,250.

6.3A Record the following details relating to a carpet retailer for the month of November 2007 and extract a trial balance as at 30 November 2007.

2007
Nov
1 Started in business with £15,000 in the bank.
3 Bought goods on credit from: J Small £290; F Brown £1,200; T Rae £610; R Charles £530.
5 Cash sales £610.
6 Paid rent by cheque £175.
7 Paid business rates by cheque £130.
11 Sold goods on credit to: T Potts £85; J Field £48; T Gray £1,640.
17 Paid wages by cash £290.
18 We returned goods to: J Small £18; R Charles £27.

68

Five sets of **multiple choice questions** allow you a quick and easy method of checking your own progress as you work through the book.

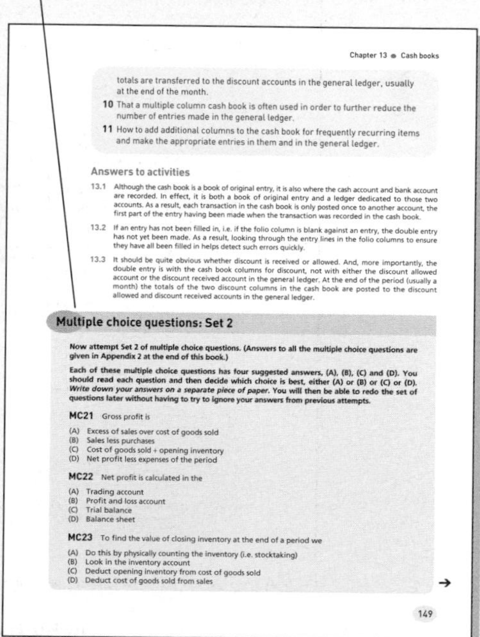

Chapter 13 ● Cash books

totals are transferred to the discount accounts in the general ledger, usually at the end of the month.
10 That a multiple column cash book is often used in order to further reduce the number of entries made in the general ledger.
11 How to add additional columns to the cash book for frequently recurring items and make the appropriate entries in them and in the general ledger.

Answers to activities

13.1 Although the cash book is a book of original entry, it is also where the cash account and bank account are recorded. In effect, it is both a book of original entry and a ledger dedicated to those two accounts. As a result, each transaction in the cash book is only posted once to another account, the first part of the entry having been made when the transaction was recorded in the cash book.

13.2 If an entry has not been filled in, i.e. if the folio column is blank against an entry, the double entry has not yet been made. As a result, looking through the entry lines in the folio columns to ensure they have all been filled in helps detect such errors quickly.

13.3 It should be quite obvious whether discount is received or allowed. And, more importantly, the double entry is with the cash book columns for discount, not with either the discount allowed account or the discount received account in the general ledger. At the end of the period (usually a month) the totals of the two discount columns in the cash book are posted to the discount allowed and discount received accounts in the general ledger.

Multiple choice questions: Set 2

Now attempt Set 2 of multiple choice questions. (Answers to all the multiple choice questions are given in Appendix 2 at the end of this book.)

Each of these multiple choice questions has four suggested answers, (A), (B), (C) and (D). You should read each question and then decide which choice is best, either (A) or (B) or (C) or (D). *Write down your answers on a separate piece of paper.* You will then be able to redo the set of questions later without having to try to ignore your answers from previous attempts.

MC21 Gross profit is

(A) Excess of sales over cost of goods sold
(B) Sales less purchases
(C) Cost of goods sold + opening inventory
(D) Net profit less expenses of the period

MC22 Net profit is calculated in the

(A) Trading account
(B) Profit and loss account
(C) Trial balance
(D) Balance sheet

MC23 To find the value of closing inventory at the end of a period we

(A) Do this by physically counting the inventory (i.e. stocktaking)
(B) Look in the inventory account
(C) Deduct opening inventory from cost of goods sold
(D) Deduct cost of goods sold from sales

→

149

Notes for teachers and lecturers

This textbook has been written so that a very thorough introduction to accounting is provided in two volumes. The split into two volumes is a recognition of the fact that many students will find that Volume 1 contains all that they require. Volume 2 takes the studies of the remainder of the readers to a more advanced stage.

This textbook is suitable for anyone who wants to obtain a good grounding in financial accounting under international GAAP and for those studying accounting where there is an option to use international GAAP terminology, for whatever purpose. This could include those embarking on their studies for the Open University Certificate in Accounting, or for qualifications from the Association of Accounting Technicians, the Institute of Secretaries and Administrators, or any of the six UK and Irish Chartered Accountancy bodies. The financial accounting requirements for National Vocational Qualifications are also fully covered.

The book has the following features:

1 Each chapter:
   - starts with Learning Objectives;
   - contains Activities designed to broaden and reinforce students' understanding of the concepts being covered and, in some cases, to introduce new concepts in such a way that they do not come as a surprise when introduced formally later in the book;
   - ends with Learning Outcomes that can be mapped back to the Learning Objectives, reinforcing the major topics and concepts covered in the chapter;
   - contains answers to all the Activities immediately after the Learning Outcomes.
2 The book has an alphabetical Glossary (Appendix 3) of all the significant terms introduced. Each entry is referenced back to the chapter in which it appeared.
3 Five sets of twenty multiple choice questions are positioned in the book (in Chapters 6, 13, 27, 33 and 45) at the point at which they should be attempted, rather than as a group at the end of the book. All the answers are at the back of the book in Appendix 2.
4 At the end of Part 4 (Adjustments for financial statements), there are five Scenario Questions which are designed to reinforce learning of the adjustments through their application in the preparation of financial statements previously learnt in Parts 1–3.
5 A set of Notes for Students appears at the front of the book. This covers how to use this book, how to tackle the end-of-chapter Review Questions, and how to study for and sit examinations. It should be read by students before they start working through the main text.
6 Blue is used in the text so as to enhance readability and bring out key points in the text.

Some changes have been made to the content of the book:

- The text has been amended to base it on International GAAP.
- Depreciation is now dealt with in Chapters 26 and 27. The material on additional methods of depreciation that was part of Chapter 37 has been moved into Chapter 26.
- All dates are now 'real' dates, such as 2008, rather than the artificial 20X8.
- The sequence in the balance sheet has been amended to reflect the norms of International GAAP.

The general public has tended to view accounting as a traditional, never-changing subject. This is not true; despite appearances, accounting is a dynamic subject. The big change, begun in 2005 and ongoing for the next few years, is the move in the UK from domestic accounting rules to international rules. Specifically, the rules that have been developed in the UK since 1970, known as Statements of Standard Accounting Practice (SSAPs) and Financial Reporting Standards (FRSs), are effectively being phased out. In their place are International Financial Reporting Standards (IFRSs) and International Accounting Standards (IASs).

This change is being introduced gradually, with all companies across the European Union, including the UK, that are listed on a stock exchange in the EU using the international set of standards from 2005 (later in the case of some stock exchanges). Other companies, broadly some small and medium-sized ones, will continue to use the old UK standards for the time being. However, it seems likely that all companies will move to using international standards in the medium term and the UK standards will then presumably wither away. Indeed, the UK's standard-setters are currently working on convergence of UK and international rules.

This means that UK accounting is currently in the middle of a major transition, and this book reflects that. The book is now based on the terminology and rules of international generally accepted accounting standards. However, we have retained reference to the equivalent UK GAAP terminology where it is appropriate to do so. For example, what has traditionally been known as the **profit and loss account** in the UK is now called the **income statement.**

You will find below a very simple comparative table that provides an 'at a glance' view of the key terminology changes from UK to international standards. Also, when a key international term first appears in the text you will sometimes see the UK equivalent placed next to it in colour and in bold to make it clear how the terminology has changed (**profit and loss account**).

International	**Traditional UK**
Accounts payable	Creditors
Accounts receivable	Debtors
Allowance for doubtful debts	Provision for doubtful debts
Income statement	Profit and loss account
Inventory	Stock(s)
Loan note	Debenture
Non-current assets	Fixed assets
Non-current liabilities	Long-term liabilities
Retained profits	Profit and loss account (on balance sheet)
Revenue	Turnover
No equivalent	Exceptional item
No equivalent	Extraordinary item

Review questions and their solutions have been amended to reflect international GAAP.

We hope that you find these changes helpful and appropriate and would welcome comments on these and any other changes you feel ought to be made in future editions. You can contact Alan Sangster by email at **a.j.a.sangster@btinternet.com** or by letter via the publishers.

We would like to thank all those teachers and lecturers who gave us their advice as to the changes they would like to see incorporated in this edition. Above all, we would like to acknowledge the assistance we have received from Graeme C Reid, FCA FCCA, lecturer in Financial Accounting, Auditing and Entrepreneurship at the University of Hull, who contributed questions for Chapters 6, 7, 8, 9, 13, 15, 18, 24, 25, 26, 27, 28, 30, 31, 32, 33, 34, 35, 37, 41, 43 and 45, plus the five Scenario Questions at the end of Part 4.

Frank Wood and Alan Sangster

Notes for students

This textbook is organised to provide you with what has been found to be the most appropriate sequencing of topics as you build the foundations of your accounting knowledge. You will find that a number of features of the book, properly used, will enhance your understanding and extend your ability to cope with what will possibly appear, at first, to be a mystifying array of rules and procedures.

To make best use of this resource, you should consider the following as being a proven path to success:

- At the start of each chapter, **read the Learning Objectives**. Then, while you work through the material, try to detect when you have achieved each of these objectives.
- At the end of each chapter **check what you have learnt against the Learning Outcomes** that follow the main text.
- If you find that you cannot say 'yes, I have learnt that' to any of the Learning Outcomes, look back through the chapter and reread the topic you have not yet learnt.
- **Learn the meaning of each new term as it appears.** Do not leave learning what terms mean until you are revising for an exam. Accounting is best learnt as a series of building blocks. If you don't remember what terms mean, your knowledge and ability to 'do' accounting will be very seriously undermined, in much the same way as a wall built without mortar is likely to collapse the first time someone leans against it.
- Attempt each of the Activities in the book ***at the point at which they appear***. This is *very* important. They will reinforce your learning and help set in context some of the material that may otherwise appear very artificial and distant from the world you live in. The answers are at the end of each chapter. **Do not look at the answers before you attempt the questions – you'll just be cheating yourself.** Once you have answered one, check your answer against the answer provided in the book and be sure you understand it before moving on.
- Attempt each of the sets of multiple choice questions when you reach them in the book. There are five sets of twenty questions, one at the end of each of Chapters 6, 13, 27, 33 and 45. The answers are in Appendix 2 at the back of the book. **Do not look at the answers before you attempt the questions – you'll just be cheating yourself**. If you get any wrong, be sure you understand why before moving on to new material.
- Attempt the Scenario Questions at the end of Part 4. They will help you see how the items covered in Part 4 affect the preparation of financial statements.
- **Learn the *accounting equation* when you first come across it in Chapter 1.** It is *the* key to understanding many of the aspects of accounting that students find difficult. Make sure that you learn it in both the forms presented to you or that you can rearrange it to produce the alternate form when appropriate.
- Do not be disillusioned by the mystery of double entry. The technique has been in common use for over 500 years and is probably the most tried and trusted technique for doing anything you are ever likely to encounter. It really is not difficult, so long as you remember the accounting equation and can distinguish between things that you own and things that you owe. Like riding a bike, once you understand it, you'll never forget it and, the more you do it, the easier it gets.
- Because of time pressure, some teachers and lecturers will need to omit Chapter 40 (*Joint Venture Accounts*). Make sure that you work through it on your own before you look at the material in Chapter 41, the first chapter on accounting for partnerships. This is very important, as accounting for joint ventures bridges the gap between accounting for sole traders and

accounting for partnerships and will make it much easier for you to understand the differences between them.

- Above all, remember that accounting is a vehicle for providing financial information in a form that assists decision-making. Work hard at presenting your work as neatly as possible and remember that pictures (in this case, financial figures) only carry half the message. When you are asked for them, words of explanation and insight are essential in order to make an examiner appreciate what you know and that you actually understand what the figures mean.

There are two subjects we would like you to consider very carefully – making best use of the end-of-chapter Review Questions, and your examination technique.

Review questions: the best approach

We have set review questions at the end of most chapters for you to gauge how well you understand and can apply what you have learnt. **If you simply read the text without attempting the questions then we can tell you now that you will not pass your examinations.** You should first attempt each question, then check your answer fully against the answers at the back of the book.

What you should not do is perform a 'ticking' exercise. By this we mean that you should not simply compare the question with the answer and tick off the bits of the answer against the relevant part of the question. No one ever learnt to do accounting properly that way. It is tempting to save time in so doing but, believe us, you will regret it eventually. We have deliberately had the answers printed using a different page layout to try to stop you indulging in a 'ticking' exercise.

Need for practice

You should also try to find the time to answer as many exercises as possible. Our reasons for saying this are as follows:

1 Even though you may think you understand the text, when you come to answer the questions you may often find your understanding incomplete. The true test of understanding is whether or not you can tackle the questions competently.
2 It is often said that practice makes perfect, a sentiment we don't fully agree with. There is, however, enough sense in it in that, if you don't do quite a lot of accounting questions, you will almost certainly not become good at accounting.
3 You simply have to get up to a good speed in answering questions: you will always fail accounting examinations if you are a very slow worker. The history of accountancy examinations so far has always been that a ridiculously large amount of work has been expected from a student during a short time. However, examining boards maintain that the examination could be completed in the time by an adequately prepared student. You can take it for granted that *adequately prepared students* are those who not only have the knowledge, but have also been trained to work quickly and, at the same time, maintain accuracy and neatness.
4 Speed itself is not enough. You also have to be neat and tidy, and follow all the proper practices and procedures while working at speed. Fast but really scruffy work can also mean failing the exam. Why? At this level, the examiner is very much concerned with your practical ability in the subject. Accounting is a practical subject, and your practical competence is being tested. The examiner will, therefore, expect the answers to be neat and well set out. Untidy work with numbers spread over the page in a haphazard way, badly written numbers, and columns of figures in which the vertical columns are not set down in straight lines, will incur the examiner's displeasure.
5 Appropriate presentation of information is important. Learn how to present the various financial statements you may need to produce in an examination. Examiners expect to see the items in income statements, balance sheets, and cash flow statements in the correct order and

will probably deduct marks if you don't do this. Practise by writing down examples of these statements without any numbers until you always get the layout correct. One exam trick most students overlook is that the layout of a financial statement is often included in an examination paper as part of one question while another question asks you to produce a financial statement. **The one you need to produce will contain different numbers but the general layout should be very similar.**

Need for headings

The next thing is that work should not only be neat but well laid out. Headings should always be given, and any dates needed should be inserted. The test you should apply is to imagine that you are a partner in a firm of professional accountants and you are away on holiday for a few weeks. During that time your assistants have completed all sorts of work including reports, drafting final accounts, various forms of other computations and so on. All of this work is deposited on your desk while you are away. When you return you look at each item in the pile awaiting your attention. Suppose the first item looks like a balance sheet as at 31 December in respect of one of your clients. When you look at it you can see that it is a balance sheet, but you don't know for which client, neither do you know which year it is for. Would you be annoyed with your staff? Of course you would. So, in an examination, why should the examiner accept as a piece of your work a balance sheet answer without the date or the name of the business or the fact that it is a balance sheet written clearly across the top? If proper headings are not given you will lose a lot of marks. Always put in the headings properly. Don't wait until your examination to start this correct practice. Similar attention should be paid to sub-totals which need showing, e.g. for Non-current assets or for Current assets.

We will be looking at examination technique in the next section.

The examiner

What you should say to yourself is: 'Suppose I were in charge of an office, doing this type of accounting work, what would I say if one of my assistants put on my desk a sheet of paper with accounting entries on it written in the same manner as my own efforts in attempting this question?' Just look at some of the work you have done in the past. Would you have told your assistant to go back and do the work again because it is untidy? If you say that about your own work, why should the examiner think any differently?

Anyone who works in accounting knows that untidy work leads to completely unnecessary errors. Therefore, the examiner's insistence on clear, tidy, well laid out work is not an outdated approach. Examiners want to ensure that you are not going to mess up the work of an accounting department. Imagine going to the savings bank and the manager saying to you: 'We don't know whether you've got £5 in the account or £5,000. You see, the work of our clerks is so untidy that we can never sort out exactly how much is in anybody's account.' We would guess that you would not want to put a lot of money into an account at that bank. How would you feel if someone took you to court for not paying a debt of £100 when, in fact, you owed them nothing? This sort of thing would happen all the time if we simply allowed people to keep untidy accounts. The examiner is there to ensure that the person to whom they give a certificate will be worthy of it, and will not continually mess up the work of any firm at which they may work in the future.

We can imagine quite a few of you groaning at all this, and if you do not want to pass the examination please give up reading here. If you do want to pass, and your work is untidy, what can you do about it? Well, the answer is simple enough: start right now to be neat and orderly in your work. Quite a lot of students have said to us over the years: 'I may be giving you untidy work now but, when I actually get into the exam room, I will then do my work neatly enough.' This is as near impossible as anything can be. You cannot suddenly become able to do accounting work neatly, and certainly not when you are under the stress and strain of an examination. Even the neatest worker may well find in an examination that their work may not be of its usual standard as nervousness will cause them to make mistakes. If this is true, and you are an untidy worker now, your work in an examination is likely to be even more untidy. Have we convinced you yet?

The structure of the questions

We have tried to build up the review questions in a structured way, starting with the easiest and then going on to more difficult ones. We would like to have omitted all the difficult questions, on the basis that you may well spend a lot of time doing them without adding very much to your knowledge about accounting. However, if all the questions were straightforward, the shock of meeting more complicated questions for the first time in an examination could lead you to fail it. We have, therefore, tried to include a mixture of straightforward and complicated questions to give you the maximum benefit.

The answers

At the back of the book, you will find answers to approximately half of the Review Questions. The answers to the other review questions (indicated by the letter 'A' after the question number) are only available to you from your teacher or lecturer. Don't worry if you are studying this subject on your own. There are still more than sufficient review questions to ensure you know and understand the material in the book.

Examination technique

As authors, we can use the first person here, as we want to put across to you a message about examinations, and we want you to feel that we are writing this for you as an individual rather than simply as one of the considerable number of people who have read this book.

By the time you sit your first examination, you will have spent a lot of hours trying to master such things as double entry, balance sheets, final adjustments, and goodness knows what else. Learning accounting/bookkeeping does demand a lot of discipline and practice. Compared with the many hours learning the subject, most students spend very little time actually considering in detail how to tackle the examination. You may be one of them, and we would like you to start planning now for the day when you will need to be able to demonstrate that you have learnt and understood, and can apply, the material in this book.

Understanding examiners

Let's start by saying that if you want to understand anything about examinations then you have got to understand examiners, so let us look together at what these peculiar creatures get up to in an examination. The first thing is that when they set an examination they are looking at it on the basis that they want good students to get a pass mark. Obviously anyone who doesn't achieve the pass mark will fail, but the object of the exercise is to find those who will pass, not find the failures. This means that if you have done your work properly, and if you are not sitting for an examination well above your intellectual capabilities, you should manage to get a pass mark. It is important for us to stress this before we get down to the details of setting about the task.

There are, however, quite a large number of students who will fail, not because they haven't put in enough hours on their studies, nor because they are unintelligent, but simply because they throw away marks unnecessarily by poor examination technique. If you can read the rest of this piece, and then say honestly that you wouldn't have committed at least one of the mistakes that we are going to mention, then you are certainly well outside the ordinary range of students.

Punctuality

Before thinking about the examination paper itself, let us think about how you are going to get to the examination room. If it is at your own college then you have no problems as to how you will get there. On the other hand, it may be an external centre. Do you know exactly where the place is? If not, you had better have a trip there if possible. How are you going to get there? If you are going by bus or train, do you know which bus or train to catch? Will it be the rush hour when it may well take you much longer than if it were held at midday?

Quite a large proportion of students lose their way to the examination room, or else arrive, breathless and flustered, at the very last minute. They then start off the attempt at the examination in a somewhat nervous state: a recipe for disaster for a lot of students. So plan how you are going to get there and give yourself enough time.

Last-minute learning for your examination will be of little use to you. The last few days before the examination should not be spent cramming. You can look at past examination papers and rework some of them. This is totally different from trying to cram new facts into your head.

On your way to the examination, if you can, try relaxation exercises. Deep breathing exercises in particular will put you into a relaxed mood. If you can't do anything like this, try reading the newspaper. Granted, you will need some adrenalin to spur you into action when you actually start answering the examination paper, but you do not want to waste it before the examination instead and then put yourself into a highly nervous state.

Read the rubric carefully and follow its instructions

The rubric appears at the start of the examination paper, and says something such as:

> 'Attempt five questions only: the *three* questions in Section A and *two* from Section B.'

That instruction from the examiner is to be followed exactly. The examinee (i.e. you) cannot change the instruction – it means what it says.

Now you may think that is so simple that it is not worthwhile our forcibly pointing it out to you. We wish that was the case for all students. However, you would be amazed at the quite high percentage of students who do not follow the instructions given in the rubric. Having been examiners for many years for examining bodies all over the world we can assure you that we are not overstating the case. Let us look at two typical examples where students have ignored the rubric above:

(*a*) A student answered *two* questions from Section A and *three* from Section B. Here the examiners will mark the two Section A answers plus the first two answers shown on the examinee's script in respect of Section B. They will not read any part of the third displayed answer to Section B. The student can therefore only get marks for four answers.

(*b*) A student answered *three* questions from Section A and *three* from Section B. Here the examiners will mark the three answers to Section A plus the first two displayed answers to Section B. They will not look at the third answer to Section B.

In the case of (*b*), the student may have done it that way deliberately, thinking that the examiner would mark all three Section B answers, and then award the student the marks from the best two answered questions. Most examiners will not waste time marking an extra answer. Students have argued that examiners would do that, but they are simply deluding themselves.

If you have time and want to give an extra answer, thinking that you will get better marks than one answered previously, then do so. If you do, make certain that the examiner is fully aware that you have deleted the answer that you do not want to have marked. Strike lines right through it, and also state that you wish to delete it. Otherwise it is possible that the first answers only will be marked and your new answer ignored.

Always remember in examinations that you should try to make life easier for the examiner. Give examiners what they want, in the way that they want it. If you do, you will get better marks. Make their job harder than it needs to be and you will suffer. Examiners are only human beings after all!

Time planning

We must now look at the way in which you should tackle the examination paper. One of the problems with bookkeeping/accounting examinations is that students are expected to do a lot of work in a relatively short time. We have campaigned against this attitude, but the tradition is longstanding and here to stay. It will be the same for every other student taking your examination, so it is not unfair so far as any one student is concerned. Working at speed does bring various disadvantages, and makes the way you tackle the examination of even greater importance than for examinations where the pace is more leisurely.

Time per question

The marks allotted to each question will indicate how long you should take in tackling the question. Most examinations are of three hours' duration, i.e. 180 minutes. This means that in a normal examination, with 100 marks in total, a 20-mark question should be allocated 20 per cent of the time, i.e. 20% × 180 = 36 minutes. Similarly, a question worth 30 marks should take up 30 per cent of the time, i.e. 30% × 180 = 54 minutes, and so on. Alternatively it is 1.8 minutes for each mark awarded for the question.

If the question is in parts, and the marks awarded are shown against each part, then that will give you a clue as to the time to be spent on each part. If part of the question asks for a description, for instance, and only three marks are awarded to that part, then you should not spend twenty minutes on a long and detailed description. Instead a brief description, taking about five minutes, is what is required.

Do the easiest questions first

Always tackle the easiest question first, then the next easiest question and so on. Leave the most difficult question as the last one to be attempted. Why is this good advice? The fact is, most examiners usually set what might be called 'warm-up' questions. These are usually fairly short, and not very difficult questions, and the examiner will expect you to tackle these first.

You may be able to do the easiest question in less than the time allocated. The examiner is trying to be kind to you. The examiner knows that there is a certain amount of nervousness on the part of a student taking an examination, and wants to give you the chance to calm down by letting you tackle these short, relatively easy questions first of all, and generally settle down to your work.

Even where all the questions are worth equal marks, you are bound to find some easier than others. It is impossible for an examiner to set questions which are exactly equal in difficulty. So, remember, start with the easiest question. This will give you a feeling of confidence. It is very desirable to start off in this way.

Do not expect that these 'warm-up' questions will be numbered 1 and 2 on your examination paper. Most accounting examinations start off with a rather long question, worth quite a lot of marks, as question number 1 on the paper. Over the years we have advised students not to tackle these questions first. A lot of students are fascinated by the fact that such a question is number 1, that it is worth a lot of marks, and their thinking runs: 'If I do this question first, and make a good job of it, then I am well on the way to passing the examination.'

There is no doubt that a speedy and successful attempt at such a question could possibly lead to a pass. The trouble is that this doesn't usually happen, and many students have admitted afterwards that their failure could be put down to simply ignoring this advice. What happens very often is that the student starts off on such a question, things don't go very well, a few mistakes are made, the student then looks at the clock and sees that they are not 'beating the clock' in terms of possible marks, and then panic descends on them. Leaving that question very hastily, the student then proceeds to the next question, which normally might have been well attempted but, because of the state of mind, a mess is made of that one as well, and so students fail an examination which they had every right to think they could pass.

Attempt every required question

The last point concerning time allocation which we want to get through is that you should attempt each and every question as required. On each question the first few marks are the easiest to get. For instance, on an essay question it is reasonably easy to get, say, the first five marks in a 20-mark question. Managing to produce a perfect answer to get the last five marks, from 15 to 20, is extremely difficult. This applies also to computational questions.

This means that in an examination of, say, five questions with 20 marks possible for each question, there is not much point in tackling three questions only and trying to make a good job of them. The total possible marks would be 60, and if you had not achieved full marks for each question, in itself extremely unlikely, you could easily fall below the pass mark of, say, 50 marks. It is better to leave questions unfinished when your allotted time, calculated as shown earlier, has expired, and to then go on immediately to the other questions. It is so easy, especially in an accounting examination, to find that one has exceeded the time allowed for a question by a considerable margin. So, although you may find it difficult to persuade yourself to do so, move on to the next question when your time for a question has expired.

Computations

When you sit an examination, you should be attempting to demonstrate how well you know the topics being examined. In accounting examinations, there are three things in particular to remember. If you fail to do so, you will probably earn less marks than your knowledge deserves. One of these things has already been mentioned – be neat and tidy. The other two have to do with computations: *show all your workings* and *don't worry if your balance sheet does not balance*.

Workings

One golden rule which should *always* be observed is to **show all of your workings**. Suppose you have been asked to work out the Cost of Goods Sold, not simply as part of a Trading Account but for some other reason. On a scrap of paper you work out the answers below:

	£
Opening inventory	4,000
Add Purchases	11,500
	15,500
Less Closing inventory	(3,800)
	12,700

You put down the answer as £12,700. The scrap of paper with your workings on it is then crumpled up by you and thrown in the wastepaper basket as you leave the room. You may have noticed in reading this that in fact the answer should have been 11,700 and not 12,700 (the arithmetic was incorrect). The examiner may well have allocated, say, four marks for this bit of the question. What will he do when he simply sees your answer as £12,700? Will he say: 'I should imagine that the candidate mis-added to the extent of £1,000 and, as I am not unduly penalising for arithmetic, I will give the candidate 3½ marks'? Unfortunately the examiner cannot do this.

The candidate got the wrong answer, there is no supporting evidence, and so the examiner gives a mark of nil. If you had only attached the workings to your answer, then we have no doubt that you would have got $3^1/_2$ marks at least.

It is often better to put the workings on the face of the final accounts, if appropriate. For instance, if rent paid is £1,900 and £300 of it has been paid in advance, you can show it on the face of the income statement as:

Rent (1,900 – 300)	£1,600

By showing the workings in brackets you are demonstrating that you realise that they would not be shown on the published accounts. It also makes it easier for the examiner to mark.

Do balance sheets have to balance?

Many students ask: 'What should I do if my balance sheet doesn't balance?' The answer is quite simple: leave it alone and get on with answering the rest of the examination paper.

One of the reasons for this is to try and ensure that you answer the required number of questions. You might take twenty minutes to find the error, which might save you one mark. In that time you might have gained, say, ten marks if, instead, you had tackled the next question, for which you would not have had time if you had wasted it by searching for the error(s). That assumes that you actually find the error(s)! Suppose you don't, you have spent twenty minutes looking for it, have not found it, so how do you feel now? The answer is, of course: quite terrible. You may make an even bigger mess of the rest of the paper than you would have done if you had simply ignored the fact that the balance sheet did not balance. In any case, it is quite possible to get, say, 29 marks out of 30 even though the balance sheet does not balance. The error may be a very minor one for which the examiner deducts one mark only.

Of course, if you have finished all the questions, then by all means spend the rest of your time tracing the error and correcting it. Be certain, however, that your corrections are carried out neatly. Untidy crossings-out can result in the loss of marks. So, sometimes, an error found can get back one mark, which is then lost again because the corrections make an untidy mess of your paper, and examiners often deduct marks, quite rightly so, for untidy work. It might be better to write against the error 'see note', indicating exactly where the note is shown. You can then illustrate to the examiner that you know what the error is and how to correct it.

Essay questions

Until a few years ago, there were not many essay questions in accounting examinations at this level. This has changed, and you therefore need to know the approach to use in answering such questions.

Typical questions

Before discussing these, we want you to look at two recent examination questions. Having done that, visualise carefully what you would write in answer to them. Here they are:

(*a*) You are employed as a bookkeeper by G Jones, a trader. State briefly what use you would make of the following documents in relation to your bookkeeping records.

- (*i*) A bank statement.
- (*ii*) A credit note received to correct an overcharge on an invoice.
- (*iii*) A pay-in slip.
- (*iv*) A petty cash voucher.

(*b*) Explain the term 'depreciation'. Name and describe briefly two methods of providing for depreciation of non-current assets.

Now we can test whether or not you would have made a reasonably good attempt at the questions. With question (*a*) a lot of students would have written down what a bank statement is, what a pay-in slip is, what a petty cash voucher is, and so on. Marks gained by you for an answer like that would be . . . virtually nil. Why is this? Well, you simply have not read the question properly. The question asked what *use* you would make of the documents, not to *describe* what the documents were. The bank statement would be used to check against the bank column in the Cash Book or cash records to see that the bank's entries and your own are in accordance with one another, with a bank reconciliation statement being drawn up to reconcile the two sets of records. The petty cash voucher would be used as a basis for entering up the payments columns in the Petty Cash Book. The *use* of the items was asked for, not the *descriptions* of the items.

Let us see if you have done better on question (*b*). Would you have written down how to calculate two methods of depreciation, probably the reducing balance method and the straight line method? But have you remembered that the question also asked you to *explain the term depreciation*? In other words, what is depreciation generally? A fair number of students will have omitted that part of the question. Our guess is that far more students would have made perhaps a poor attempt at question (*a*) rather than doing question (*b*).

Underline the key words

We have already illustrated that a large percentage of students fail to answer the question set, instead answering the question they imagine it to be. Too many students write down everything they know about a topic, rather than what the examiner has asked for.

To remedy this defect, *underline the key words* in a question. This brings out the meaning so that it is difficult to misunderstand the question. For instance, let us look at the following question:

'Discuss the usefulness of departmental accounts to a business.'

Many students will write down all they know about departmental accounts, how to draw them up, how to apportion overheads between departments, how to keep columnar sales and purchases journals to find the information, etc.

Number of marks gained . . . virtually nil.

Now underline the key words. They will be:

Discuss usefulness departmental accounts

The question is now seen to be concerned not with *describing* departmental accounts, but instead discussing the *usefulness* of departmental accounts.

Lastly, if the question says 'Draft a report on . . .' then the answer should be in the form of a *report*; if it says 'List the . . .' then the answer should consist of a *list*. Similarly 'Discuss . . .' asks for a *discussion*. 'Describe . . .' wants you to *describe* something, and so on.

You should therefore ensure that you are going to give the examiners

(*i*) what they are asking for

and

(*ii*) in the way that they want it.

If you do not comply with (*i*) you may lose all the marks. If you manage to fulfil (*i*) but do not satisfy the examiner on (*ii*) you will still lose a lot of marks.

It is also just as important in computational questions to underline the key words to get at the meaning of a question, and then answer it in the manner required by the examiner. With computational questions it is better to look at what is required first before reading all of the rest of the question. That way, when you are reading the rest of the question, you are able to decide how to tackle it.

Never write out the question

Often – too often – students spend time writing out the text of essay questions before they set about answering them. This is a complete waste of time. It will not gain marks and should *never* be done.

Running out of time?

If your plans don't work out, you may find yourself with a question you could answer, but simply do not have the time to do it properly. It is better to write a short note to the examiner to that effect, and put down what you can of the main points in an abbreviated fashion. This will show that you have the knowledge and should gain you some marks.

Summary

Remember:

1. **Read the instructions.**
2. **Plan your time before you start.**
3. **Tackle the easiest questions first.**
4. **Finish off answering each question when your time allocation for the question is up.**
5. **Hand in all your workings.**
6. **Do remember to be neat, and to include all proper headings, dates, sub-totals, etc. A lot of marks can be lost if you don't.**
7. **Only answer as many questions as you are asked to tackle by the examiner. Extra answers will not normally be marked and certainly won't get credit.**
8. **Underline the *key* words in each question to ensure that you answer the question set, and not the question you wrongly take it to be.**
9. **Never write out the text of essay questions.**

Best of luck with your examination. We hope you get the rewards you deserve!

Frank Wood and Alan Sangster

Publisher's acknowledgements

We are very grateful to teachers of accounting in many schools, colleges of further education and universities whose generous advice has contributed to the development of this new edition. We wish to thank, in particular:

Ann-Marie Ward, Queens University, Belfast
Bhagwan Moorjani, University of Westminster
Georgios Iatridis, Manchester University
Chris McMahon, Liverpool John Moores University
Adil Mahmood, Bradford College
Graeme Reid, Hull University
Rohan Chambers, University of Technology, Jamaica
Mike Rogers, Basingstoke College of Technology
Lindsay Whitlow, Dudley College
Paul Wertheim, Solihull College
David Gilding, Park Lane College, Leeds
Malcolm Rynn, Greencroft School, County Down
Eric Edwards, University of Northumberland
Helen Khoo, Sunway College, Petaling Jaya, Malaysia
Caroline Teh Swee Gaik, Inti College, Nilai, Malaysia.
Christopher Foo, St George's School, Malaysia
Dave Knight, Leeds Met
Patrick Devlin, Glasgow Cale
Sally Nower, Colchester
Pushpa Kalu, Silpa
Penny Gardner, Napier
Sarah Knight, Huntingdon

We are grateful to the following for permission to reproduce examination questions:

Association of Accounting Technicians (AAT); Assessment and Qualifications Alliance (NEAB/AQA, SEB/AQA and AEB/AQA); Scottish Qualifications Authority (SQA); Association of Chartered Certified Accountants (ACCA); Oxford, Cambridge and RSA Examinations (MEG/OCR); Institute of Chartered Secretaries and Administrators (ICSA); London Qualifications Ltd trading as Edexcel and the Sage Group plc for Exhibit 23.1.

All answers to questions are the authors' own work and have not been supplied by any of the examining bodies.

part 1

INTRODUCTION TO DOUBLE ENTRY BOOKKEEPING

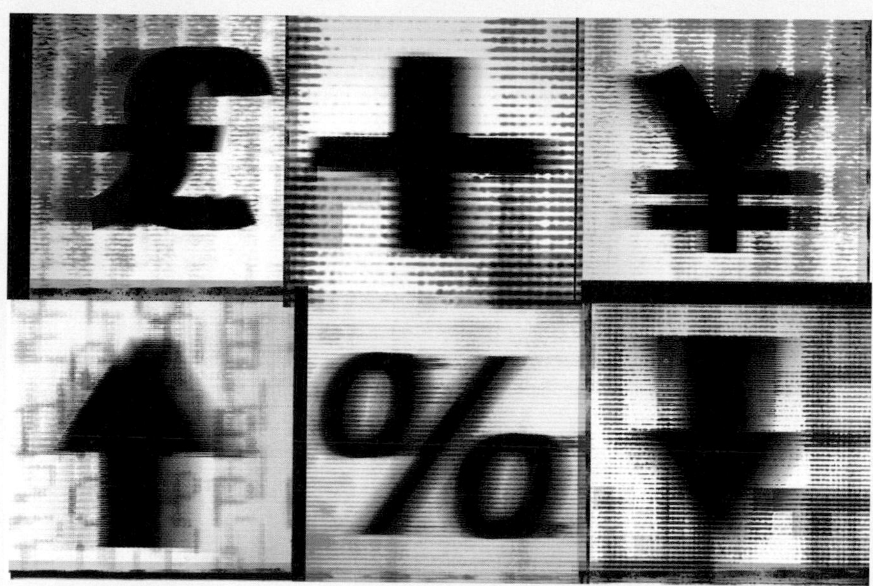

Introduction

This part is concerned with the basic principles underlying the double entry system of bookkeeping.

chapter 1

The accounting equation and the balance sheet

Learning objectives

After you have studied this chapter, you should be able to:

- explain what accounting is about
- briefly describe the history of accounting
- explain the relationship between bookkeeping and accounting
- list the main users of accounting information and what accounting information they are interested in
- present and explain the accounting equation
- explain the relationship between the accounting equation and the layout of the balance sheet
- explain the meaning of the terms assets, capital, liabilities, accounts receivable (**debtors**), and creditors accounts payable (**creditors**)
- describe how accounting transactions affect the items in the accounting equation
- draw up balance sheets after different accounting transactions have occurred

Introduction

In this chapter, you will learn: what accounting is; what led to its development into what it is today; who uses accounting information; and the relationship between the various components that, together, comprise what is known as the 'accounting equation'.

1.1 What is accounting?

What do *you* think of when you read or hear the word, 'accounting'? What do *you* believe it means or represents?

If you have already attended some accounting classes or if you have spoken with someone who knows something about accounting, you will probably have a fairly good idea of what accounting is and what it is used for. If not, you may find it useful to have this knowledge before you start studying the subject. During the course of the next few pages, let's see if you can gain that knowledge and learn what accounting is.

Accounting can be defined as 'the process of identifying, measuring, and communicating economic information to permit informed judgements and decisions by users of the information'. A bit of a mouthful really, but what it means is that accounting involves deciding what amounts of money are, were, or will be involved in transactions (often buying and selling transactions) and then organising the information obtained and presenting it in a way that is useful for decision-making.

Despite what some people think, accounting is not a branch of mathematics, although the man credited with writing the first book to be printed on the subject, Fra Luca Pacioli (c. 1445–1517), was a mathematician and teacher. He wrote on the topic 'in order that the subjects of the most gracious Duke of Urbino [his sponsor or benefactor] may have complete instructions in the conduct of business', and to 'give the trader without delay information as to his assets and liabilities'. ('Assets' are things that you own; 'liabilities' are things that you owe.)

What Pacioli wrote is contained in 27 pages of a school textbook and reference manual for merchants on business and mathematics (*Summa de arithmetica, geometria, proportioni et proportionalita – Everything about Arithmetic, Geometry and Proportion*) which was first published in Italy in 1494. The bookkeeping treatise has been translated into many languages, including English, and is acknowledged as the chief reason why we maintain accounts in the way we do today.

Accounting may not require a knowledge of mathematics but you do need to be able to add, subtract, multiply and divide – things you need to be able to do in your daily life anyway. Otherwise, you would not know how much money you had with you, how much you would have if you spent some of it, or whether the change you received was correct. So, let's remove one big misconception some people have concerning accounting: you do not need to be good at arithmetic to be good at accounting, though you will find it easier to 'do' accounting if you are.

The history of accounting

Accounting began because people needed to:

- record business transactions,
- know if they were being financially successful, and
- know how much they owned and how much they owed.

It is known to have existed in one form or another since at least 3500 BC (records exist which indicate its use at that time in Mesopotamia). There is also considerable evidence of accounting being practised in ancient times in Egypt, China, India, Greece, and Rome. In England, the 'Pipe Roll', the oldest surviving accounting record in the English language, contains an annual description of rents, fines and taxes due to the King of England, from 1130 to 1830.

However, it was only when Pacioli wrote about it in 1494 or, to be more precise, wrote about a branch of accounting called 'bookkeeping', that accounting began to be standardised and recognised as a process or procedure.

No standard system for maintaining accounting records had been developed before this because the circumstances of the day did not make it practicable for anyone to do so – there was little point, for example, in anyone devising a formal system of accounting if the people who would be required to 'do' accounting did not know how to read or write.

One accounting scholar (A. C. Littleton) suggested that seven key ingredients which were required before a formal system could be developed existed when Pacioli wrote his treatise:

- *Private property*. The power to change ownership exists and there is a need to record the transaction.
- *Capital*. Wealth is productively employed such that transactions are sufficiently important to make their recording worthwhile and cost-effective.
- *Commerce*. The exchange of goods on a widespread level. The volume of transactions needs to be sufficiently high to motivate someone to devise a formal organised system that could be applied universally to record transactions.
- *Credit*. The present use of future goods. Cash transactions, where money is exchanged for goods, do not require that any details be recorded of who the customer or supplier was. The existence of a system of buying and selling on credit (i.e. paying later for goods and services

purchased today) led to the need for a formal organised system that could be applied universally to record credit transactions.
- *Writing*. A mechanism for making a permanent record in a common language. Writing had clearly been around for a long time prior to Pacioli but it was, nevertheless, an essential element required before accounting could be formalised.
- *Money*. There needs to be a common denominator for exchange. So long as barter was used rather than payment with currency, there was no need for a bookkeeping system based upon transactions undertaken using a uniform set of monetary values.
- *Arithmetic*. As with writing, this has clearly been in existence far longer than accounting. Nevertheless, it is clearly the case that without an ability to perform simple arithmetic, there was no possibility that a formal organised system of accounting could be devised.

When accounting information was being recorded in the Middle Ages it sometimes simply took the form of a collection of invoices (which each show the details of a transaction) and receipts (which each confirm that a payment has been made) which were used by the owner to calculate the profit or loss of the business up to some point in time. This practice persists to this day in many small businesses.

The accountant of the Middle Ages would be someone who had learnt how to convert the financial transaction data (i.e. the data recorded on invoices and receipts, etc.) into accounting information. Quite often, it would be the owner of the business who performed all the accounting tasks. Otherwise, an employee would be given the job of maintaining the accounting records.

As businesses grew in size, so it became less common for the owner to personally maintain the accounting records and more usual for someone to be employed as an accounts clerk. Then, as companies began to dominate the business environment, managers became separated from owners – the owners of companies (shareholders) often have no involvement in the day-to-day running of the business. This led to a need for some monitoring of the managers. Auditing of the financial records became the norm and this, effectively, established the accounting profession.

The first national body of accountants, the Institute of Chartered Accountants of Scotland, was formed in 1854 and other national bodies began to emerge gradually throughout the world, with the English Institute of Chartered Accountants being formed in 1880 and the first US national accounting body being formed in 1887.

If you wish to discover more about the history of accounting, you will find that it is readily available on the World Wide Web. Perform a search on either of the terms 'history of accounting' or 'accounting history' and you should find more information than you could ever realistically read on the subject.

The objectives of accounting

Accounting has many objectives, including letting people and organisations know:

- if they are making a profit or a loss;
- what their business is worth;
- what a transaction was worth to them;
- how much cash they have;
- how wealthy they are;
- how much they are owed;
- how much they owe to someone else;
- enough information so that they can keep a financial check on the things they do.

However, the primary objective of accounting is to provide information for decision-making. The information is usually financial, but can also be given in volumes, for example the number of cars sold in a month by a car dealership or the number of cows in a farmer's herd.

So, for example, if a business recorded what it sold, to whom, the date it was sold, the price at which it was sold, and the date it received payment from the customer, along with similar data concerning the purchases it made, certain information could be produced summarising what had taken place. The profitability of the business and the financial status of the business could also be identified, at any particular point in time. It is the primary objective of accounting to take such information and convert it into a form that is useful for decision-making.

People and businesses

Accounting is something that affects people in their personal lives just as much as it affects very large businesses. We all use accounting ideas when we plan what we are going to do with our money. We have to plan how much of it we will spend and how much we will save. We may write down a plan, known as a **budget**, or we may simply keep it in our minds.

Recording accounting data

However, when people talk about accounting, they are normally referring to accounting as used by businesses and other organisations. The owners cannot remember all the details so they have to keep records of it.

Organisations not only record cash received and paid out. They will also record goods bought and sold, items bought to use rather than to sell, and so on. This part of accounting is usually called the *recording of data*.

Classifying and summarising

When the data is being recorded it has to be organised so as to be most useful to the business. This is known as *classifying* and *summarising* data.

Following such classifications and summaries it will be possible to work out how much profit or loss has been made by the business during a particular period. It will also be possible to show what resources are owned by the business, and what is owed by it, on the closing date of the period.

Communicating information

From the data, people skilled in accounting should be able to tell whether or not the business is performing well financially. They should be able to ascertain the strengths and weaknesses of the business.

Finally, they should be able to tell or *communicate* their results to the owners of the business, or to others allowed to receive this information.

Accounting is, therefore, concerned with:

- recording data;
- classifying and summarising data;
- communicating what has been learnt from the data.

1.2 What is bookkeeping?

Until about one hundred years ago all accounting data was *kept* by being recorded manually in *books*, and so the part of accounting that is concerned with recording data is often known as **bookkeeping**.

Nowadays, although handwritten books may be used (particularly by smaller organisations), most accounting data is recorded electronically and stored electronically using computers.

Bookkeeping is the process of recording data relating to accounting transactions in the accounting books.

1.3 Accounting is concerned with . . .

Accounting is concerned with the uses which accountants might make of the bookkeeping information given to them. This book will cover many such uses.

1.4 Users of accounting information

Possible users of accounting information include:

- *Managers*. These are the day-to-day decision-makers. They need to know how well things are progressing financially and about the financial status of the business.
- *Owner(s) of the business*. They want to be able to see whether or not the business is profitable. In addition they want to know what the financial resources of the business are.
- *A prospective buyer*. When the owner wants to sell a business the buyer will want to see such information.
- *The bank*. If the owner wants to borrow money for use in the business, then the bank will need such information.
- *Tax inspectors*. They need it to be able to calculate the taxes payable.
- *A prospective partner*. If the owner wants to share ownership with someone else, then the would-be partner will want such information.
- *Investors*, either existing ones or potential ones. They want to know whether or not to invest their money in the business.

There are many other users of accounting information – suppliers and employees, for example. One obvious fact is that without properly recorded accounting data a business would have many difficulties providing the information these various users (often referred to as '**stakeholders**') require.

However, the information produced by accounting needs to be a compromise – so many different groups of stakeholders make it impossible to produce accounting information at a reasonable cost in a form that suits them all. As a result, accounting focuses on producing information for owners. The other stakeholder groups often find the accounting information provided fails to tell them what they really want to know. However, if organisations made the effort to satisfy the information needs of all stakeholders, accounting would be a very costly exercise indeed!

1.5 The accounting equation

By adding up what the accounting records say belongs to a business and deducting what they say the business owes, you can identify what a business is worth according to those accounting records. The whole of financial accounting is based upon this very simple idea. It is known as the *accounting equation*.

It can be explained by saying that if a business is to be set up and start trading, it will need resources. Let's assume first that it is the owner of the business who has supplied all of the resources. This can be shown as:

Resources supplied by the owner = Resources in the business

In accounting, special terms are used to describe many things. The amount of the resources supplied by the owner is called **capital**. The actual resources that are then in the business are called **assets**. This means that when the owner has supplied all of the resources, the accounting equation can be shown as:

Capital = Assets

Usually, however, people other than the owner have supplied some of the assets. **Liabilities** is the name given to the amounts owing to these people for these assets. The accounting equation has now changed to:

Capital = Assets – Liabilities

This is the most common way in which the accounting equation is presented. It can be seen that the two sides of the equation will have the same totals. This is because we are dealing with the same thing from two different points of view – the value of the owners' investment in the business and the value of what is owned by the owners.

Activity 1.1

What piece of useful information that is available from these three items is not directly shown by this equation? (*Hint*: you were introduced to it at the start of this section.)

Unfortunately, with this form of the accounting equation, we can no longer see at a glance what value is represented by the resources in the business. You can see this more clearly if you switch assets and capital around to produce the alternate form of the accounting equation:

Assets = Capital + Liabilities

This can then be replaced with words describing the resources of the business:

Resources: what they are = Resources: who supplied them
(Assets) (Capital + Liabilities)

It is a fact that no matter how you present the accounting equation, the totals of both sides will *always* equal each other, and that this will *always* be true no matter how many transactions there may be. The actual assets, capital and liabilities may change, but the total of the assets will always equal the total of capital + liabilities. Or, reverting to the more common form of the accounting equation, the capital will always equal the assets of the business minus the liabilities.

Assets consist of property of all kinds, such as buildings, machinery, inventories (**stocks**) of goods and motor vehicles. Other assets include debts owed by customers and the amount of money in the organisation's bank account.

Liabilities include amounts owed by the business for goods and services supplied to the business and for expenses incurred by the business that have not yet been paid for. They also include funds borrowed by the business.

Capital is often called the owner's **equity** or net worth. It comprises the funds invested in the business by the owner plus any profits retained for use in the business less any share of profits paid out of the business to the owner.

Activity 1.2

What else would affect capital? (*Hint*: this item causes the value of capital to fall.)

1.6 The balance sheet and the effects of business transactions

The accounting equation is expressed in a financial position statement called the **balance sheet**.

Activity 1.3 Without looking back, write down the commonly used form of the accounting equation.

The balance sheet shows the financial position of an organisation at a point in time. In other words, it presents a snapshot of the organisation at the date for which it was prepared. The balance sheet is not the first accounting record to be made, nor the first that you will learn how to do, but it is a convenient place to start to consider accounting.

Let's now look at how a series of transactions affects the balance sheet.

1 The introduction of capital

On 1 May 2007, B Blake started in business and deposited £60,000 into a bank account opened specially for the business. The balance sheet would show:

B Blake
Balance sheet as at 1 May 2007

	£
Assets: Cash at bank	60,000
Capital	60,000

Note how the top part of the balance sheet contains the assets and the bottom part contains the capital. This is always the way the information is presented in a balance sheet.

2 The purchase of an asset by cheque

On 3 May 2007, Blake buys a small shop for £32,000, paying by cheque. The effect of this transaction on the balance sheet is that the cash at the bank is decreased and the new asset, building, is added:

B Blake
Balance sheet as at 3 May 2007

Assets	£
Shop	32,000
Cash at bank	28,000
	60,000
Capital	60,000

Note how the two parts of the balance sheet 'balance'. That is, their totals are the same. This is always the case with balance sheets.

3 The purchase of an asset and the incurring of a liability

On 6 May 2007, Blake buys some goods for £7,000 from D Smith, and agrees to pay for them some time within the next two weeks. The effect of this is that a new asset, **inventory**, is acquired, and a liability for the goods is created. A person to whom money is owed for goods is known in accounting language as a **creditor**, and is described in the balance sheet as an **account payable**. The balance sheet becomes:

B Blake
Balance sheet as at 6 May 2007

Assets	£
Shop	32,000
Inventory	7,000
Cash at bank	28,000
	67,000
Less: Account payable	(7,000)
	60,000
Capital	60,000

Note how the liability (the account payable) is shown as a deduction from the assets. This is exactly the same calculation as is presented in the most common form of the accounting equation.

Why do you think the £7,000 value for account payable is shown in brackets?

Now, let's return to our example.

4 Sale of an asset on credit

On 10 May 2007, goods which cost £600 were sold to J Brown for the same amount, the money to be paid later. The effect is a reduction in the stock of goods and the creation of a new asset. A person who owes the business money is known in accounting language as a **debtor**, and is described in the balance sheet as an **account receivable**. The balance sheet is now:

B Blake
Balance sheet as at 10 May 2007

Assets	£
Shop	32,000
Inventory	6,400
Account receivable	600
Cash at bank	28,000
	67,000
Less: Account payable	(7,000)
	60,000
Capital	60,000

5 Sale of an asset for immediate payment

On 13 May 2007, goods which cost £400 were sold to D Daley for the same amount. Daley paid for them immediately by cheque. Here one asset, inventory, is reduced, while another asset, cash at bank, is increased. The balance sheet becomes:

B Blake
Balance sheet as at 13 May 2007

Assets	£
Shop	32,000
Inventory	6,000
Account receivable	600
Cash at bank	28,400
	67,000
Less: Account payable	(7,000)
	60,000
Capital	60,000

6 The payment of a liability

On 15 May 2007, Blake pays a cheque for £3,000 to D Smith in part payment of the amount owing. The asset of cash at bank is therefore reduced, and the liability to the creditor is also reduced. The balance sheet is now:

B Blake
Balance sheet as at 15 May 2007

Assets	£
Shop	32,000
Inventory	6,000
Account receivable	600
Cash at bank	25,400
	64,000
Less: Account payable	(4,000)
	60,000
Capital	60,000

Note how the total of each part of the balance sheet has not changed. The business is still worth £60,000 to the owner.

7 Collection of an asset

J Brown, who owed Blake £600, makes a part payment of £200 by cheque on 31 May 2007. The effect is to reduce one asset, account receivable, and to increase another asset, cash at bank. The balance sheet becomes:

B Blake
Balance sheet as at 31 May 2007

Assets	£
Shop	32,000
Inventory	6,000
Account receivable	400
Cash at bank	25,600
	64,000
Less: Account payable	(4,000)
	60,000
Capital	60,000

1.7 Equality of the accounting equation

It can be seen that every transaction has affected two items. Sometimes it has changed two assets by reducing one and increasing the other. In other cases, the effect has been different. However, in each case other than the very first (when the business was started by the owner injecting some cash into it), no change was made to the total of either section of the balance sheet and the equality between their two totals has been maintained. The accounting equation has held true throughout the example, and it always will. The effect of each of these seven accounting transactions upon the two sections of the balance sheet is shown below:

Number of transaction as above	Assets	Capital and Liabilities	Effect on balance sheet totals
1	+	+	Each side added to equally
2	+ −		A *plus* and a *minus* both on the assets side *cancelling each other out*
3	+	+	Each side has equal additions
4	+ −		A *plus* and a *minus* both on the assets side *cancelling each other out*
5	+ −		A *plus* and a *minus* both on the assets side *cancelling each other out*
6	−	−	Each side has equal deductions
7	+ −		A *plus* and a *minus* both on the assets side *cancelling each other out*

These are not the only types of accounting transactions that can take place. Two other examples arise when the owner withdraws resources from the business for his or her own use; and where the owner pays a business expense personally.

A summary of the effect upon assets, liabilities and capital of each type of transaction you've been introduced to so far is shown below:

Example of transaction	Effect	
(1) Owner pays capital into the bank	↑ Increase asset (Bank)	↑ Increase capital
(2) Buy inventory by cheque	↓ Decrease asset (Bank)	↑ Increase asset (Inventory)
(3) Buy inventory on credit	↑ Increase asset (Inventory)	↑ Increase liability (Accounts payable)
(4) Sale of inventory on credit	↓ Decrease asset (Inventory)	↑ Increase asset (Accounts receivable)
(5) Sale of inventory for cash (cheque)	↓ Decrease asset (Inventory)	↑ Increase asset (Bank)
(6) Pay creditor	↓ Decrease asset (Bank)	↓ Decrease liability (Accounts payable)
(7) Debtor pays money owing by cheque	↑ Increase asset (Bank)	↓ Decrease asset (Accounts receivable)
(8) Owner takes money out of the business bank account for own use	↓ Decrease asset (Bank)	↓ Decrease capital
(9) Owner pays creditor from private money outside the firm	↓ Decrease liability (Accounts payable)	↑ Increase capital

These last two types of transactions do cause the totals of each part of the balance sheet to change (as did the very first, when capital was introduced to the business by the owner). When the capital changes, the totals of the two parts of the balance sheet both change.

1.8 More detailed presentation of the balance sheet

Let's now look at the balance sheet of B Blake as at 31 May 2007, presented in line with how you will learn to present the information later in the book:

B Blake
Balance sheet as at 31 May 2007

	£	£
Non-current assets		
Shop		32,000
Current assets		
Inventory	6,000	
Account receivable	400	
Cash at bank	25,600	
		32,000
Total assets		64,000
Less Current liabilities		
Account payable		(4,000)
Net assets		60,000
Capital		60,000

You will have noticed in this balance sheet the terms 'non-current assets', 'current assets' and 'current liabilities'. **Chapter 8** contains a full explanation of these terms. At this point we will simply say:

- **Non-current assets** (**fixed assets**) are assets which have a long life bought with the intention to use them in the business and not with the intention to simply resell them, e.g. buildings, machinery, fixtures, motor vehicles.
- **Current assets** are assets consisting of cash, goods for resale or items having a short life (i.e. no more than a year remaining on the date of the balance sheet). For example, the value of inventory in hand goes up and down as it is bought and sold. Similarly, the amount of money owing to us by debtors will change quickly, as we sell more to them on credit and they pay their debts. The amount of money in the bank will also change as we receive and pay out money.
- **Current liabilities** are those liabilities which have to be paid within no more than a year from the date on the balance sheet, e.g. accounts payable for goods purchased.

Don't forget that there is a Glossary of accounting terms at the back of the book.

Learning outcomes

You should now have learnt:

1 Accounting is concerned with the recording, classifying and summarising of data, and then communicating what has been learnt from it.

2 Accounting has existed for at least 5,500 years but a formal, generally accepted method of recording accounting data has only been in existence for the last 500 years.

→

3. It may not only be the owner of a business who will need the accounting information. It may need to be shown to others, e.g. the bank or the Inspector of Taxes.
4. Accounting information can help the owner(s) of a business to plan for the future.
5. The accounting equation is: Capital = Assets − Liabilities.
6. The two sides of the accounting equation are represented by the two parts of the balance sheet.
7. The total of one part of the balance sheet should always be equal to the total of the other part.
8. Every transaction affects two items in the accounting equation. Sometimes that may involve the same item being affected twice, once positively (going up) and once negatively (going down).
9. Every transaction affects two items in the balance sheet.

***Note*: Generally, the values used in exhibits and exercises have been kept down to relatively small amounts. This has been done deliberately to make the work of the student that much easier. Constantly handling large figures does not add anything to the study of the principles of accounting. It simply wastes a lot of the student's time, and he/she will probably make far more errors if larger figures are used.**

Doing this may lead to the authors being accused of not being 'realistic' with the figures given, but we believe that it is far more important to make learning easier for the student.

Answers to activities

1.1 Who supplied the resources of the business.

1.2 Capital will be reduced if a business makes a loss. The loss means that assets have been reduced and capital is reduced by the same amount so as to maintain the balance in the accounting equation.

1.3 Capital = Assets − Liabilities

1.4 It is a negative number. In accounting, we *always* use brackets to indicate negative numbers.

Review questions

If you haven't already started answering them, you now have a set of graded review questions to try. 'Graded' means that they get more difficult as you go through them. Ideally, they should be done in the sequence they appear. *However, don't forget that the questions with an 'A' after the question number do not have any answers provided in this book*. Your teacher or lecturer will be able to provide you with the answers to those questions but be sure to attempt them first before asking for the answers! The answers to the other questions can be found at the back of the book.

We realise that you would like to have *all* the answers in the book. However, teachers and lecturers would not then be able to test your knowledge with questions from this book, as you would already possess the answers. It is impossible to please everyone, and the compromise reached is that of putting a large number of review questions in the book.

This means that appropriate reinforcement of what you have learnt can take place, even if you are studying on your own and have to miss out all the 'A' questions because you have no access to the answers.

Multiple choice questions. In addition to these Review Questions, there are questions relating to the material in this chapter among a bank of multiple choice questions at the end of Chapter 6. You should wait and attempt them when you reach them, not before.

1.1 Complete the gaps in the following table:

	Assets	*Liabilities*	*Capital*
	£	£	£
(*a*)	12,500	1,800	?
(*b*)	28,000	4,900	?
(*c*)	16,800	?	12,500
(*d*)	19,600	?	16,450
(*e*)	?	6,300	19,200
(*f*)	?	11,650	39,750

1.2A Complete the gaps in the following table:

	Assets	*Liabilities*	*Capital*
	£	£	£
(*a*)	55,000	16,900	?
(*b*)	?	17,200	34,400
(*c*)	36,100	?	28,500
(*d*)	119,500	15,400	?
(*e*)	88,000	?	62,000
(*f*)	?	49,000	110,000

1.3 Which of the items in the following list are liabilities and which of them are assets?

(*a*) Loan to C Shirley
(*b*) Bank overdraft
(*c*) Fixtures and fittings
(*d*) Computers
(*e*) We owe a supplier for inventory
(*f*) Warehouse we own

1.4A Classify the following items into liabilities and assets:

(*a*) Motor vehicles
(*b*) Premises
(*c*) Accounts payable for inventory
(*d*) Inventory
(*e*) Accounts receivable
(*f*) Owing to bank
(*g*) Cash in hand
(*h*) Loan from D Jones
(*i*) Machinery

1.5 State which of the following are wrongly classified:

Assets	*Liabilities*
Loan from C Smith	Inventory
Cash in hand	Accounts receivable
Machinery	Money owing to bank
Accounts payable	
Premises	
Motor vehicles	

→

1.6A Which of the following are shown under the wrong headings?

Assets	*Liabilities*
Cash at bank	Loan from J Graham
Fixtures	Machinery
Accounts payable	Motor vehicles
Building	
Inventory	
Accounts receivable	
Capital	

1.7 B Wise is setting up a new business. Before actually selling anything, he bought a van for £4,500, a market stall for £2,000 and an inventory of goods for £1,500. He did not pay in full for his inventory of goods and still owes £1,000 in respect of them. He borrowed £5,000 from C Fox. After the events just described, and before trading starts, he has £400 cash in hand and £1,100 cash at bank. Calculate the amount of his capital.

1.8A F Flint is starting a business. Before actually starting to sell anything, he bought fixtures for £1,200, a van for £6,000 and an inventory of goods for £2,800. Although he has paid in full for the fixtures and the van, he still owes £1,600 for some of the inventory. B Rub lent him £2,500. After the above, Flint has £200 in the business bank account and £175 cash in hand. You are required to calculate his capital.

1.9 Draw up G Putty's balance sheet from the following information as at 31 December 2008:

	£
Capital	9,700
Accounts receivable	1,200
Van	3,800
Accounts payable	1,600
Fixtures	1,800
Inventory	4,200
Cash at bank	300

1.10A Draw up M Kelly's balance sheet as at 30 June 2006 from the following items:

	£
Capital	10,200
Equipment	3,400
Accounts payable	4,100
Inventory	3,600
Accounts receivable	4,500
Cash at bank	2,800

1.11 Complete the columns to show the effects of the following transactions:

		Effect upon	
	Assets	*Liabilities*	*Capital*
(*a*) We pay a creditor £70 in cash.			
(*b*) Bought fixtures £200 paying by cheque.			
(*c*) Bought goods on credit £275.			
(*d*) The proprietor introduces another £500 cash into the business.			
(*e*) J Walker lends the business £200 in cash.			
(*f*) A debtor pays us £50 by cheque.			
(*g*) We return goods costing £60 to a supplier whose bill we had not paid.			
(*h*) Bought additional shop premises paying £5,000 by cheque.			

1.12A Complete the columns to show the effects of the following transactions:

		Effect upon	
	Assets	*Liabilities*	*Capital*
(*a*) Bought a van on credit £8,700.			
(*b*) Repaid by cash a loan owed to F Duff £10,000.			
(*c*) Bought goods for £1,400 paying by cheque.			
(*d*) The owner puts a further £4,000 cash into the business.			
(*e*) A debtor returns to us goods worth £150. We agree to make an allowance for them.			
(*f*) Bought goods on credit £760.			
(*g*) The owner takes out £200 cash for his personal use.			
(*h*) We pay a creditor £1,150 by cheque.			

1.13 G Brown has the following items in her balance sheet as on 30 April 2008: Capital £18,400; Accounts payable £2,100; Fixtures £2,800; Car £3,900; Inventory £4,550; Accounts receivable £2,780; Cash at bank £6,250; Cash in hand £220.

During the first week of May 2008

(*a*) She bought extra inventory for £400 on credit.
(*b*) One of the debtors paid her £920 by cheque.
(*c*) She bought a computer by cheque £850.

You are asked to draw up a balance sheet as on 7 May 2008 after the above transactions have been completed.

1.14A J. Hill has the following assets and liabilities as on 30 November 2009: Accounts payable £2,800; Equipment £6,200; Car £7,300; Inventory £8,100; Accounts receivable £4,050; Cash at bank £9,100; Cash in hand £195.

You are not given the capital amount at that date.

During the first week of December 2009

(*a*) Hill bought extra equipment on credit for £110.
(*b*) Hill bought extra inventory by cheque £380.
(*c*) Hill paid creditors by cheque £1,150.
(*d*) Debtors paid Hill £640 by cheque and £90 by cash.
(*e*) Hill put an extra £1,500 into the business, £1,300 by cheque and £200 in cash.

You are to draw up a balance sheet as on 7 December 2009 after the above transactions have been completed.

You can find a range of additional self-test questions, as well as material to help you with your studies, on the website that accompanies this book at www.pearsoned.co.uk/wood.

chapter 2

The double entry system for assets, liabilities and capital

Learning objectives

After you have studied this chapter, you should be able to:

- explain what is meant by 'double entry'
- explain how the double entry system follows the rules of the accounting equation
- explain why each transaction is recorded into individual accounts
- describe the layout of a 'T-account'
- explain what is meant by the terms debit and credit
- explain the phrase 'debit the receiver and credit the giver'
- prepare a table showing how to record increases and decreases of assets, liabilities and capital in the accounts
- enter a series of transactions into T-accounts

Introduction

In this chapter, you will learn how the double entry system is used to record financial transactions and how to use T-accounts, the traditional way to make such entries under the double entry system.

2.1 Nature of a transaction

In Chapter 1, you saw how various events had changed two items in the balance sheet. Events which result in such changes are known as 'transactions'. This means that if the proprietor asks the price of some goods, but does not buy them, then there is no transaction. If the proprietor later asks the price of some other goods, and then buys them, then there would be a transaction, and two balance sheet items would then have to be altered.

2.2 The double entry system

We have seen that every transaction affects two items. We need to show these effects when we first record each transaction. That is, when we enter the data relating to the transaction in the accounting books we need to ensure that the items that were affected by the transaction, and only those items, are shown as having changed. This is the bookkeeping stage of accounting and the process we use is called **double entry**. You will often hear it referred to as **double entry bookkeeping**. Either term is correct.

Activity 2.1 Why do you think it is called 'double entry'?

If we want to show the double effect of every transaction when we are doing our bookkeeping, we have to show the effect of each transaction on each of the two items it affects. For each transaction this means that a bookkeeping entry will have to be made to show an increase or decrease of one item, and another entry to show the increase or decrease of the other item. From this description, you will probably see that the term 'double entry bookkeeping' is a good one, as each entry is made twice (double entry).

At this point, you may be wondering why you can't just draw up a new balance sheet after each transaction, and so provide all the information required.

Activity 2.2 Why can't we just adjust the balance sheet and forget about making entries in any of the accounting books?

Instead of constantly drawing up balance sheets after each transaction what we have instead is the 'double entry' system. The basis of this system is that the transactions which occur are entered in a set of **accounts** within the accounting books. An account is a place where all the information referring to a particular asset or liability, or to capital, is recorded.

Thus, there will be an account where all the information concerning office equipment will be entered. Similarly, there will be an account for buildings, where all the information concerned with buildings will be shown. This will be extended so that every asset, every liability and capital will each have its own account for transactions involving that item.

2.3 The accounts for double entry

Each account should be shown on a separate page in the accounting books. The double entry system divides each page into two halves. The left-hand side of each page is called the **debit** side, while the right-hand side is called the **credit** side. The title of each account is written across the top of the account at the centre.

This is the layout of a page of an accounts book:

Title of account written here

Left-hand side of the page This is the 'debit' side.	*Right-hand side of the page* This is the 'credit' side.

Do you see how the shape resembles a 'T'? Not surprisingly, these are commonly referred to as **T-accounts**:

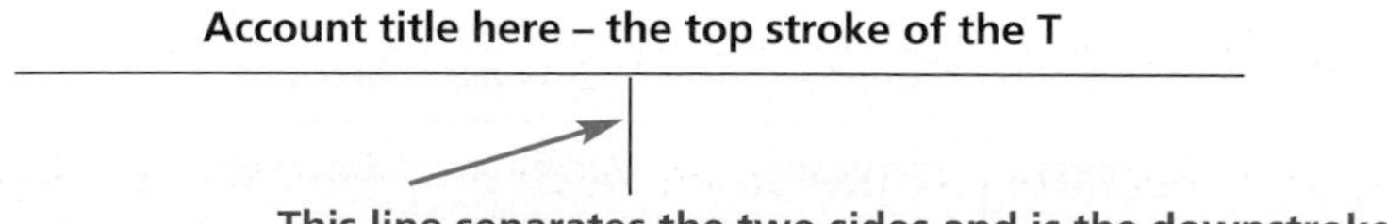
Account title here – the top stroke of the T
This line separates the two sides and is the downstroke of the T

Many students find it very difficult to make correct entries in the accounts because they forget that *debit* and *credit* have special accounting meanings. Don't fall into that trap. You must not confuse any other meanings you know for these two terms with the accounting ones.

You describe the entries in the accounts by saying something like 'debit account "x" with £z and credit account "y" with £z', inserting the names of the accounts and the actual amount in place of x, y and z. So, for example, if you paid £10 by cheque for a kettle, you could say 'debit the kettle account with £10 and credit the bank account with £10'.

To actually make this entry, you enter £10 on the left-hand (i.e. debit) side of the kettle account and on the right-hand (i.e. credit) side of the bank account.

Kettle account

£	
10	

Bank account

	£
	10

You learnt in Chapter 1 that transactions increase or decrease assets, liabilities or capital. In terms of the assets, liabilities and capital:

- to **increase** an **asset** we make a DEBIT entry
- to **decrease** an **asset** we make a CREDIT entry
- to **increase** a **liability/capital** account we make a CREDIT entry
- to **decrease** a **liability/capital** account we make a DEBIT entry.

Placing these in a table organised by type of item, the double entry rules for bookkeeping are:

Accounts	To record	Entry in the account
Assets	an increase a decrease	Debit Credit
Liabilities	an increase a decrease	Credit Debit
Capital	an increase a decrease	Credit Debit

Let's look once again at the accounting equation:

	Capital =	Assets –	Liabilities
To increase each item	Credit	Debit	Credit
To decrease each item	Debit	Credit	Debit

The double entry rules for liabilities and capital are the same, but they are the opposite of those for assets. Looking at the accounts the rules will appear as:

Capital account

Decreases	*Increases*
–	+

Any asset account

Increases	*Decreases*
+	–

Any liability account

Decreases	*Increases*
–	+

In a real business, at least one full page would be taken for each account in the accounting books. However, as we have not enough space in this textbook to put each account on a separate page, we will list the accounts under each other.

2.4 Worked examples

The entry of a few transactions can now be attempted.

1 The owner starts the business with £10,000 in cash on 1 August 2008.

The effects of this transaction are entered as follows:

Effect	Action
1 Increases the *asset* of cash 2 Increases the capital	Debit the cash account Credit the capital account

Cash

2008	£			
Aug 1	10,000			

Capital

		2008	£
		Aug 1	10,000

The date of the transaction has already been entered. (**Never forget to enter the date of each transaction.**) Now there remains the description (often referred to as the 'narrative') which is to be entered alongside the amount. This is completed by a cross-reference to the title of the other account in which the double entry is completed. The double entry to the item in the cash account is completed by an entry in the capital account. Therefore the word 'Capital' will appear as the narrative in the cash account:

Cash

2008	£		
Aug 1 **Capital**	10,000		

Similarly, the double entry to the item in the capital account is completed by an entry in the cash account, so the word 'Cash' will appear in the capital account:

Capital

		2008	£
		Aug 1 Cash	10,000

2 A van is bought for £4,500 cash on 2 August 2008.

Effect	Action
1 Increases the *asset* of van 2 Decreases the *asset* of cash	Debit the van account Credit the cash account

Van

2008	£		
Aug 2 Cash	4,500		

Cash

			2008		£
			Aug 2	Van	4,500

3 Fixtures (e.g. shelves) are bought on credit from Shop Fitters for £1,250 on 3 August 2008.

Effect	Action
1 Increases the *asset* of fixtures	Debit the fixtures account
2 Increases the *liability* to Shop Fitters	Credit the Shop Fitters account

Fixtures

2008		£			
Aug 3	Shop Fitters	1,250			

Shop Fitters

			2008		£
			Aug 3	Fixtures	1,250

Note how the liability of accounts payable is split in the accounting books so that a separate account is maintained for each account payable.

4 Paid the amount owing to Shop Fitters in cash on 17 August 2008.

Effect	Action
1 Decreases the *liability* to Shop Fitters	Debit the Shop Fitters account
2 Decreases the *asset* of cash	Credit the cash account

Shop Fitters

2008		£			
Aug 17	Cash	1,250			

Cash

			2008		£
			Aug 17	Shop Fitters	1,250

5 Transactions to date.

Combining all four of these transactions, the accounts now contain:

Cash

2008		£	2008		£
Aug 1	Capital	10,000	Aug 2	Van	4,500
			17	Shop Fitters	1,250

Capital

			2008		£
			Aug 1	Cash	10,000

Van

		£			£
2008					
Aug 2	Cash	4,500			

Shop Fitters

		£			£
2008			2008		
Aug 17	Cash	1,250	Aug 3	Fixtures	1,250

Fixtures

		£			£
2008					
Aug 3	Shop Fitters	1,250			

Note how you enter each transaction in an account in date order and how, once you open an account (e.g. Shop Fitters), you continue to make entries in it rather than opening a new account for every entry.

Before you read further, work through Review Questions 2.1 and 2.2A.

2.5 A further worked example

Have you noticed how each column of figures is headed by a '£' sign? This is important. You always need to indicate what the figures represent. In this case, it is pounds; in other cases you will meet during this book, the figures may be thousands of pounds (represented by '£000') or they could be in a different currency altogether. **Always include appropriate column headings.**

Now you have actually made some entries in accounts, go carefully through the following example. Make certain you can understand every entry and, if you have any problems, reread the first four sections of this chapter until you are confident that you know and understand what you are doing.

First, here is a table showing a series of transactions, their effects and the double entry action to take:

Transactions	Effect	Action
2008 May 1 Started a household machines business putting £25,000 into a business bank account.	↑ Increases *asset* of bank. ↑ Increases *capital* of owner.	Debit bank account. Credit capital account.
3 Bought equipment on credit from House Supplies £12,000.	↑ Increases *asset* of equipment. ↑ Increases *liability* to House Supplies.	Debit equipment account. Credit House Supplies account.
4 Withdrew £150 cash from the bank and placed it in the cash box.	↑ Increases *asset* of cash. ↓ Decreases *asset* of bank.	Debit cash account. Credit bank account.

→

Transactions		Effect	Action
2008 May 7	Bought a van paying by cheque, £6,800.	↑ Increases *asset* of van. ↓ Decreases *asset* of bank.	Debit van account. Credit bank account.
10	Sold some equipment that was not needed at cost of £1,100 on credit to J Rose.	↑ Increases *asset* of money owing from J Rose. ↓ Decreases *asset* of equipment.	Debit J Rose account. Credit equipment account.
21	Returned some of the equipment costing £2,300 to House Supplies.	↓ Decreases *liability* to House Supplier. ↓ Decreases *asset* of equipment.	Debit House Supplies. Credit equipment account.
28	J Rose pays the amount owing, £1,100, by cheque.	↑ Increases *asset* of bank. ↓ Decreases *asset* of money owing by J Rose.	Debit bank account. Credit J Rose account.
30	Bought another van paying by cheque £4,300.	↑ Increases *asset* of vans. ↓ Decreases *asset* of bank.	Debit van account. Credit bank account.
31	Paid £9,700 to House Supplies by cheque.	↓ Decreases *liability* to House Supplies. ↓ Decreases *asset* of bank.	Debit House Supplies. Credit bank account.

You may find it worthwhile trying to enter all these transactions in T-accounts before reading any further. You will need to know that, similarly to accounts payable, the asset of accounts receivable is split in the accounting books so that a separate account is maintained for each debtor. You will need accounts for Bank, Cash, Capital, Equipment, Vans, House Supplies and J Rose.

In T-account form this is shown:

Bank

2008			£	2008			£
May	1	Capital	25,000	May	4	Cash	150
					7	Van	6,800
	28	J Rose	1,100		30	Van	4,300
					31	House Supplies	9,700

Cash

2008			£				
May	4	Bank	150				

Capital

2008				2008			£
				May	1	Bank	25,000

Equipment

2008			£	2008			£
May	3	House Supplies	12,000	May	10	J Rose	1,100
					21	House Supplies	2,300

Vans

2008			£				
May	7	Bank	6,800				
	30	Bank	4,300				

House Supplies

2008			£	2008			£
May	21	Equipment	2,300	May	3	Equipment	12,000
	31	Bank	9,700				

J Rose

2008			£	2008			£
May	10	Equipment	1,100	May	28	Bank	1,100

If you tried to do this before looking at the answer, be sure you understand any mistakes you made before going on.

2.6 Abbreviation of 'limited'

In this book, when we come across transactions with limited companies the letters 'Ltd' are used as the abbreviation for 'Limited Company'. So, if you see that the name of a business is 'W Jones Ltd', it is a limited company. In our accounting books, transactions with W Jones Ltd will be entered in the same way as for any other customer or supplier. It will be seen later that some limited companies use plc (which stands for 'public limited company') instead of Ltd.

2.7 Value Added Tax (VAT)

You may have noticed that VAT has not been mentioned in the examples covered so far. This is deliberate, so you are not confused as you learn the basic principles of accounting. In Chapter 19, you will be introduced to VAT and shown how to make the entries relating to it.

Learning outcomes

You should now have learnt:

1. That double entry follows the rules of the accounting equation.
2. That double entry maintains the principle that every debit has a corresponding credit entry.
3. That double entries are made in accounts in the accounting books.
4. Why each transaction is entered into accounts rather than directly into the balance sheet.

5 How transactions cause increases and decreases in asset, liability and capital accounts.

6 How to record transactions in T-accounts.

Answers to activities

2.1 Each transaction is entered twice. In an accounting transaction, something always 'gives' and something 'receives' and both aspects of the transaction must be recorded. In other words, there is a double entry in the accounting books – each transaction is entered twice.

2.2 A balance sheet is a financial statement that summarises the financial position of an organisation at a point in time. It does not present enough information about the organisation to make it appropriate to enter each transaction directly on to the balance sheet. It does not, for instance, tell us who the debtors are or how much each one of them owes the organisation, nor who the creditors are or the details of the amounts owing to each of them. We need to maintain a record of each individual transaction so that (a) we know what occurred and (b) we can check to see that it was correctly recorded.

Review questions

2.1 Complete the following table:

		Account to be debited	*Account to be credited*
(*a*)	Bought office machinery on credit from D Isaacs Ltd.		
(*b*)	The proprietor paid a creditor, C Jones, from his private funds.		
(*c*)	A debtor, N Fox, paid us in cash.		
(*d*)	Repaid part of loan from P Exeter by cheque.		
(*e*)	Returned some of office machinery to D Isaacs Ltd.		
(*f*)	A debtor, N Lyn, pays us by cheque.		
(*g*)	Bought van by cash.		

2.2A Complete the following table:

		Account to be debited	*Account to be credited*
(*a*)	Bought lorry for cash.		
(*b*)	Paid creditor, T Lake, by cheque.		
(*c*)	Repaid P Logan's loan by cash.		
(*d*)	Sold lorry for cash.		
(*e*)	Bought office machinery on credit from Ultra Ltd.		
(*f*)	A debtor, A Hill, pays us by cash.		
(*g*)	A debtor, J Cross, pays us by cheque.		
(*h*)	Proprietor puts a further amount into the business by cheque.		
(*i*)	A loan of £200 in cash is received from L Lowe.		
(*j*)	Paid a creditor, D Lord, by cash.		

2.3 Write up the asset and liability and capital accounts to record the following transactions in the records of F Murray.

2007
July 1 Started business with £15,000 in the bank.
2 Bought office furniture by cheque £1,200.

3 Bought machinery £1,400 on credit from Trees Ltd.
5 Bought a van paying by cheque £6,010.
8 Sold some of the office furniture – not suitable for the business – for £150 on credit to D Twig & Sons.
15 Paid the amount owing to Trees Ltd £1,400 by cheque.
23 Received the amount due from D Twig & Sons £150 in cash.
31 Bought more machinery by cheque £650.

2.4 You are required to open the asset and liability and capital accounts and record the following transactions for June 2008 in the records of P Bernard.

2008
June 1 Started business with £12,000 in cash.
2 Paid £11,700 of the opening cash into a bank account for the business.
5 Bought office furniture on credit from Dream Ltd for £1,900.
8 Bought a van paying by cheque £5,250.
12 Bought equipment from Pearce & Sons on credit £2,300.
18 Returned faulty office furniture costing £120 to Dream Ltd.
25 Sold some of the equipment for £200 cash.
26 Paid amount owing to Dream Ltd £1,780 by cheque.
28 Took £130 out of the bank and added to cash.
30 F Brown lent us £4,000 – giving us the money by cheque.

2.5A Write up the asset, capital and liability accounts in the books of D Gough to record the following transactions:

2009
June 1 Started business with £16,000 in the bank.
2 Bought van paying by cheque £6,400.
5 Bought office fixtures £900 on credit from Old Ltd.
8 Bought van on credit from Carton Cars Ltd £7,100.
12 Took £180 out of the bank and put it into the cash till.
15 Bought office fixtures paying by cash £120.
19 Paid Carton Cars Ltd a cheque for £7,100.
21 A loan of £500 cash is received from B Berry.
25 Paid £400 of the cash in hand into the bank account.
30 Bought more office fixtures paying by cheque £480.

2.6A Write up the accounts to record the following transactions:

2007
March 1 Started business with £750 cash and £9,000 in the bank.
2 Received a loan of £2,000 from B Blane by cheque.
3 Bought a computer for cash £600.
5 Bought display equipment on credit from Clearcount Ltd £420.
8 Took £200 out of the bank and put it in the cash till.
15 Repaid part of Blane's loan by cheque £500.
17 Paid amount owing to Clearcount Ltd £420 by cheque.
24 Repaid part of Blane's loan by cash £250.
31 Bought a printer on credit from F Jones for £200.

You can find a range of additional self-test questions, as well as material to help you with your studies, on the website that accompanies this book at www.pearsoned.co.uk/wood.

chapter 3

Inventory

Learning objectives

After you have studied this chapter, you should be able to:

- explain why it is inappropriate to use an inventory account to record increases and decreases in inventory
- describe the two causes of inventory increasing
- describe the two causes of inventory decreasing
- explain the difference between a purchase account and a returns inwards account
- explain the difference between a sales account and a returns outwards account
- explain how to record increases and decreases of inventory in the appropriate accounts
- explain the meanings of the terms 'purchases' and 'sales' as used in accounting
- explain the differences in recording purchases on credit as compared to recording purchases that are paid for immediately in cash
- explain the differences in recording sales on credit as compared to recording sales that are paid for immediately in cash

Introduction

In this chapter, you will learn how to record movements in inventory in the appropriate ledger accounts and how to record purchases and sales on credit, as opposed to purchases and sales for cash.

3.1 Inventory movements

In the examples in Chapter 1, inventory was sold at the same price at which it was bought. This is, of course, extremely unusual. In fact, any new business doing this wouldn't last terribly long. Businesses need to make profits to survive, as many 'dot.com' Internet companies discovered in 2000 when their bubble burst and all the losses they had been making took effect.

Normally, goods and services are sold above cost price, the difference being **profit**. As you know, when goods and services are sold for less than their cost, the difference is a **loss**.

Let's think about the double entry implications if all sales were at cost price. Fill in the blanks in the following:

As we did in Chapter 1, it would be possible to have an inventory account with goods purchased being ________ to the inventory account (as purchases represent __ ________ in the asset, inventory) and goods sold being ________ to it (as sales represent __ ________ in the asset, inventory).

The difference between the two sides of the inventory account would then represent the cost of the goods unsold at that date. (We'll ignore things like wastage, obsolescence and losses of inventory for now.)

However, most sales are not priced at cost and, therefore, the sales figures include elements of profit or loss. Because of this, in most cases, the difference between the two sides of the inventory account would not represent the cost of the inventory. Maintaining an inventory account on this basis would therefore serve no useful purpose.

To address this, we subdivide the way inventory is reported into several accounts, each one showing a movement of inventory. Firstly, we must distinguish between transactions that cause inventory to increase and those that cause it to decrease. Let's deal with each of these in turn.

1 **Increase in inventory.** This can be due to one of two causes:

(*a*) The purchase of additional goods.

(*b*) The return into the business of goods previously sold. The reasons for this are numerous. The goods may have been the wrong type; they may, for example, have been surplus to requirements or faulty.

To distinguish the two aspects of the increase of inventory, two accounts are opened:

(*i*) **a Purchases Account** – in which purchases of goods are entered; and

(*ii*) **a Returns Inwards Account** – in which goods being returned into the business are entered. (Another name for this account is the **Sales Returns Account.**)

So, for *increases* in inventory, we need to choose which of these two accounts to use to record the *debit* side of the transaction.

2 **Decrease in inventory.** Ignoring things like wastage and theft, this can be due to one of two causes:

(*a*) The sale of goods.

(*b*) Goods previously bought by the business now being returned to the supplier.

Once again, in order to distinguish the two aspects of the decrease of inventory, two accounts are opened:

(*i*) **a Sales Account** – in which sales of goods are entered; and

(*ii*) **a Returns Outwards Account** – in which goods being returned out to a supplier are entered. (This is also known as the **Purchases Returns Account.**)

So, for *decreases* in inventory, we need to choose which of these two accounts to use to record the *credit* side of the transaction.

As inventory is an asset, and these four accounts are all connected with this asset, the double entry rules are those used for assets.

Activity 3.2

What are the double entry rules for assets?

Accounts	To record	Entry in the account
Assets	an increase a decrease	________ ________

We shall now look at some entries in the following sections.

3.2 Purchase of inventory on credit

On 1 August 2008, goods costing £165 are bought on credit from D Henry. First, the two-fold effect of the transaction must be considered so that the bookkeeping entries can be worked out.

1 The asset of inventory is increased. An increase in an asset needs a debit entry in an account. Here the account is one designed for this type of inventory movement. It is clearly a 'purchase' movement so that the account to use must be the purchases account.
2 There is an increase in a liability. This is the liability of the business to D Henry because the goods bought have not yet been paid for. An increase in a liability needs a credit entry. In this case, it would be a credit entry to D Henry's account.

These two entries appear in the accounts as:

Purchases

2008			£				
Aug	1	D Henry	165				

D Henry

				2008			£
				Aug	1	Purchases	165

Note that these entries look identical to those you would make if you were using an inventory account rather than a purchases account. (The word 'inventory' would replace 'purchases' if an inventory account were being used.)

3.3 Purchases of inventory for cash

On 2 August 2008, goods costing £310 are bought, cash being paid for them immediately at the time of purchase.

1 As before, it is the asset of inventory that is increased, so a debit entry will be needed. The movement of inventory is that of a 'purchase', so the purchases account needs to be debited.
2 The asset of cash is decreased. To reduce an asset a credit entry is called for, and the asset is cash, so we need to credit the cash account.

Purchases

2008			£				
Aug	2	Cash	310				

Cash

				2008			£
				Aug	2	Purchases	310

3.4 Sales of inventory on credit

On 3 August 2008, goods were sold on credit for £375 to J Lee.

1 An asset account is increased. The increase in the asset of debtors requires a debit and the debtor is J Lee, so that the account concerned is that of J Lee.
2 The asset of inventory is decreased. For this a credit entry to reduce an asset is needed. The movement of inventory is clearly the result of a 'sale' and so it is the sales account that needs to be credited.

J Lee

2008		£			
Aug 3	Sales	375			

Sales

			2008		£
			Aug 3	J Lee	375

3.5 Sales of stock for cash

On 4 August 2008, goods are sold for £55, cash being received immediately at the time of sale.

1 The asset of cash is increased, so the cash account must be debited.
2 The asset of inventory is reduced. The reduction of an asset requires a credit and the movement of inventory is represented by 'sales'. Thus the entry needed is a credit in the sales account.

Cash

2008		£			
Aug 4	Sales	55			

Sales

			2008		£
			Aug 4	Cash	55

So far, so good. Apart from replacing the inventory account with the purchases account for inventory increases and the sales account for inventory decreases, you've done nothing different in your entries to the accounts compared with what you learnt in Chapters 1 and 2.

Go back to Chapters 1 and 2, and refresh your understanding of account entries.

Now let's look at the other inventory-related transactions that cause inventory to increase and decrease – returns inwards (sales that are being returned) and returns outwards (purchases that are being returned to the supplier).

3.6 Returns inwards

On 5 August 2008, goods which had been previously sold to F Lowe for £29 are now returned *to the business*. This could be for various reasons such as:

- we sent goods of the wrong size, the wrong colour or the wrong model;
- the goods may have been damaged in transit;
- the goods are of poor quality.

1 The asset of inventory is increased by the goods returned. Thus, a debit representing an increase of an asset is needed. This time, the movement of inventory is that of 'returns inwards'. The entry required is a debit in the *Returns Inwards Account.*
2 There is a decrease in an asset. The debt of F Lowe to the business is now reduced. A credit is needed in F Lowe's account to record this.

Returns inwards

2008			£	2008			£
Aug	5	F Lowe	29				

F Lowe

2008			£	2008			£
				Aug	5	Returns inwards	29

(Remember, another name for the Returns Inwards account is the 'Sales Returns account'.)

3.7 Returns outwards

On 6 August 2008, goods previously bought for £96 are returned *by the business* to K Howe.

1 The liability of the business to K Howe is decreased by the value of the goods returned. The decrease in a liability needs a debit, this time in K Howe's account.
2 The asset of inventory is decreased by the goods sent out. Thus, a credit representing a reduction in an asset is needed. The movement of inventory is that of 'returns outwards' so the entry will be a credit in the *Returns Outwards Account.*

K Howe

2008			£	2008			£
Aug	6	Returns outwards	96				

Returns outwards

2008			£	2008			£
				Aug	6	K Howe	96

(Remember, another name for the Returns Outwards account is the 'Purchases Returns account'.)

You're probably thinking this is all very straightforward. Well, let's see how much you have learnt by looking at two review questions.

Before you read further, work through Review Questions 3.1 and 3.2.

3.8 A worked example

2009
May 1 Bought goods on credit £220 from D Small.
2 Bought goods on credit £410 from A Lyon & Son.
5 Sold goods on credit to D Hughes for £60.
6 Sold goods on credit to M Spencer for £45.

10	Returned goods £15 to D Small.
11	Goods sold for cash £210.
12	Goods bought for cash £150.
19	M Spencer returned £16 goods to us.
21	Goods sold for cash £175.
22	Paid cash to D Small £205.
30	D Hughes paid the amount owing by him £60 in cash.
31	Bought goods on credit £214 from A Lyon & Son.

You may find it worthwhile trying to enter all these transactions in T-accounts before reading any further. You will need the following accounts: Purchases, Sales, Returns Outwards, Returns Inwards, D Small, A Lyon & Son, D Hughes, M Spencer and Cash.

Purchases

2009			£				
May	1	D Small	220				
	2	A Lyon & Son	410				
	12	Cash	150				
	31	A Lyon & Son	214				

Sales

				2009			£
				May	5	D Hughes	60
					6	M Spencer	45
					11	Cash	210
					21	Cash	175

Returns outwards

				2009			£
				May	10	D Small	15

Returns inwards

2009			£				
May	19	M Spencer	16				

D Small

2009			£	2009			£
May	10	Returns outwards	15	May	1	Purchases	220
	22	Cash	205				

A Lyon & Son

				2009			£
				May	2	Purchases	410
					31	Purchases	214

D Hughes

2009			£	2009			£
May	5	Sales	60	May	30	Cash	60

M Spencer

2009			£	2009			£
May	6	Sales	45	May	19	Returns inwards	16

Cash

2009			£	2009			£
May	11	Sales	210	May	12	Purchases	150
	21	Sales	175		22	D Small	205
	30	D Hughes	60				

If you tried to do this before looking at the answer, be sure you understand any mistakes you made before going on.

3.9 Special meaning of 'sales' and 'purchases'

You need to remember that 'sales' and 'purchases' have a special meaning in accounting when compared to ordinary language usage.

Purchases in accounting means the *purchase of those goods which the business buys with the intention of selling*. Obviously, sometimes the goods are altered, added to, or used in the manufacture of something else, but it is the element of resale that is important. To a business that deals in computers, for instance, computers constitute purchases.

If something else is bought *which the business does not intend to sell*, such as a van, such an item cannot be called 'purchases', even though in ordinary language you would say that a van has been purchased. The van was bought to be used and *not* for resale.

Similarly, **sales** means the *sale of those goods in which the business normally deals and which were bought with the prime intention of resale*. The word 'sales' must never be given to the disposal of other items, such as vans or buildings that were purchased to be used and *not* to be sold.

If we did not keep to these meanings, we would find it very difficult to identify which of the items in the purchases and sales accounts were inventory and which were assets that had been bought to be used.

Let's now look at another of the small complications accountants need to deal with – the differences between the treatment of cash transactions and credit transactions.

3.10 Comparison of cash transactions and credit transactions for purchases and sales

As you saw in the last example, when goods are purchased for cash, the entries are:

- **Debit the purchases account**
- **Credit the cash account.**

On the other hand the complete set of entries for the purchase of goods on credit can be broken down into two stages: first, the purchase of the goods, and second, the payment for them.

The first part is:

- **Debit the purchases account**
- **Credit the supplier's account.**

The second part is:

- **Debit the supplier's account**
- **Credit the cash account.**

What is the difference between the treatment of cash purchases and credit purchases?

A study of cash sales and credit sales reveals a similar difference in treatment:

Cash sales	Credit sales
Complete entry: Debit cash account Credit sales account	First part: Debit customer's account Credit sales account Second part: Debit cash account Credit customer's account

Learning outcomes

You should now have learnt:

1. That it is *not* appropriate to use an inventory account to record increases and decreases in inventory because inventory is normally sold at a price greater than its cost.
2. That inventory increases either because some inventory has been purchased or because inventory that was sold has been returned by the buyer.
3. That inventory decreases either because some inventory has been sold or because inventory previously purchased has been returned to the supplier.
4. That a purchase account is used to record purchases of inventory (as debit entries in the account) and that a returns inwards account is used to record inventory returned by customers (as debit entries in the account).
5. That a sales account is used to record sales of inventory (as credit entries in the account) and that a returns outwards account is used to record inventory returned to suppliers (as credit entries in the account).
6. How to record increases and decreases of inventory in the appropriate accounts.
7. That in accounting, the term 'purchases' refers to purchases of inventory. Acquisitions of any other assets, such as vans, equipment and buildings, are *never* described as purchases.
8. That in accounting, the term 'sales' refers to sales of inventory. Disposals of any other assets, such as vans, equipment and buildings, are *never* described as sales.
9. That purchases for cash are *never* entered in the supplier's account.
10. That purchases on credit are *always* entered in the supplier's (creditor's) account.
11. That sales for cash are *never* entered in the customer's account.
12. That sales on credit are *always* entered in the customer's (debtor's) account.

Answers to activities

3.1 As we did in Chapter 1, it would be possible to have an inventory account with goods purchased being DEBITED to the inventory account (as purchases represent AN INCREASE in the asset, inventory) and goods sold being CREDITED to it (as sales represent A DECREASE in the asset, inventory).

3.2

Accounts	To record	Entry in the account
Assets	an increase a decrease	Debit Credit

3.3 With cash purchases, no entry is made in the supplier's account. This is because cash passes immediately and therefore there is no need to keep a check of how much money is owing to that supplier. On the other hand, with credit purchases, the records should show to whom money is owed until payment is made and so an entry is always made in the supplier's (creditor's) account.

Review questions

3.1 Complete the following table:

	Account to be debited	*Account to be credited*
(*a*) Goods bought on credit from J Reid.		
(*b*) Goods sold on credit to B Perkins.		
(*c*) Vans bought on credit from H Thomas.		
(*d*) Goods sold, a cheque being received immediately.		
(*e*) Goods sold for cash.		
(*f*) Goods purchased by us returned to supplier, H Hardy.		
(*g*) Machinery sold for cash.		
(*h*) Goods sold returned to us by customer, J Nelson.		
(*i*) Goods bought on credit from D Simpson.		
(*j*) Goods we returned to H Forbes.		

3.2A Complete the following table:

	Account to be debited	*Account to be credited*
(*a*) Goods bought on credit from T Morgan.		
(*b*) Goods returned to us by J Thomas.		
(*c*) Machinery returned to L Jones Ltd.		
(*d*) Goods bought for cash.		
(*e*) Van bought on credit from D Davies Ltd.		
(*f*) Goods returned by us to I Prince.		
(*g*) D Picton paid us his account by cheque.		
(*h*) Goods bought by cheque.		
(*i*) We paid creditor, B Henry, by cheque.		
(*j*) Goods sold on credit to J Mullings.		

3.3 You are to write up the following in the books:

2008		
July	1	Started in business with £750 cash.
	3	Bought goods for cash £110.
	7	Bought goods on credit £320 from F Herd.
	10	Sold goods for cash £64.
	14	Returned goods to F Herd £46.
	18	Bought goods on credit £414 from D Exodus.
	21	Returned goods to D Exodus £31.
	24	Sold goods to B Squire £82 on credit.
	25	Paid F Herd's account by cash £274.
	31	B Squire paid us his account in cash £82.

3.4A Enter the following transactions in the appropriate accounts:

2006		
Aug	1	Started in business with £7,400 cash.
	2	Paid £7,000 of the opening cash into the bank.
	4	Bought goods on credit £410 from J Watson.
	5	Bought a van by cheque £4,920.
	7	Bought goods for cash £362.
	10	Sold goods on credit £218 to L Less.
	12	Returned goods to J Watson £42.
	19	Sold goods for cash £54.
	22	Bought fixtures on credit from Firelighters Ltd £820.
	24	F Holmes lent us £1,500 paying us the money by cheque.
	29	We paid J Watson his account by cheque £368.
	31	We paid Firelighters Ltd by cheque £820.

3.5 Enter the following transactions in the accounts of L Linda:

2007		
July	1	Started in business with £20,000 in the bank.
	2	R Hughes lent us £5,000 in cash.
	3	Bought goods on credit from B Brown £1,530 and I Jess £4,162.
	4	Sold goods for cash £1,910.
	6	Took £200 of the cash and paid it into the bank.
	8	Sold goods on credit to H Rise £1,374.
	10	Sold goods on credit to P Taylor £341.
	11	Bought goods on credit from B Brown £488.
	12	H Rise returned goods to us £65.
	14	Sold goods on credit to G Pate £535 and R Sim £262.
	15	We returned goods to B Brown £94.
	17	Bought van on credit from Aberdeen Cars Ltd £4,370.
	18	Bought office furniture on credit from J Winter Ltd £1,800.
	19	We returned goods to I Jess £130.
	20	Bought goods for cash £390.
	24	Goods sold for cash £110.
	25	Paid money owing to B Brown by cheque £1,924.
	26	Goods returned to us by G Pate £34.
	27	Returned some of office furniture costing £180 to J Winter Ltd.
	28	L Linda put a further £2,500 into the business in the form of cash.
	29	Paid Aberdeen Cars Ltd £4,370 by cheque.
	31	Bought office furniture for cash £365.

→

→ **3.6A** Enter the following transactions in the accounts:

2009		
May	1	Started in business with £18,000 in the bank.
	2	Bought goods on credit from B Hind £1,455.
	3	Bought goods on credit from G Smart £472.
	5	Sold goods for cash £210.
	6	We returned goods to B Hind £82.
	8	Bought goods on credit from G Smart £370.
	10	Sold goods on credit to P Syme £483.
	12	Sold goods for cash £305.
	18	Took £250 of the cash and paid it into the bank.
	21	Bought a printer by cheque £620.
	22	Sold goods on credit to H Buchan £394.
	23	P Syme returned goods to us £160.
	25	H Buchan returned goods to us £18.
	28	We returned goods to G Smart £47.
	29	We paid Hind by cheque £1,373.
	31	Bought machinery on credit from A Cobb £419.

You can find a range of additional self-test questions, as well as material to help you with your studies, on the website that accompanies this book at www.pearsoned.co.uk/wood.

hapter 4

The effect of profit or loss on capital and the double entry system for expenses and revenues

Learning objectives

After you have studied this chapter, you should be able to:

- calculate profit by comparing revenue with expenses
- explain how the accounting equation is used to show the effects of changes in assets and liabilities upon capital after goods or services have been traded
- explain why separate accounts are used for each type of expense and revenue
- explain why an expense is entered as a debit in the appropriate expense account
- explain why an item of revenue is entered as a credit in the appropriate revenue account
- enter a series of expense and revenue transactions into the appropriate T-accounts
- explain how the use of business cash and business goods for the owner's own purposes are dealt with in the accounting records

Introduction

In this chapter, you will learn how to calculate profits and losses and how to enter expense and revenue transactions into the ledger. You will also learn about drawings (i.e. amounts withdrawn from the business by the owner), and how to record them.

4.1 The nature of profit or loss

To an accountant, **profit** means the amount by which **revenue** is greater than **expenses** for a set of transactions. The term revenue means the sales value of goods and services that have been supplied to customers. The term expenses means the cost value of all the assets that have been used up to obtain those revenues.

If, therefore, we supplied goods and services valued for sale at £100,000 to customers, and the expenses incurred by us in order to supply those goods and services amounted to £70,000 the result would be a profit of £30,000:

		£
Revenue:	goods and services supplied to our customers for the sum of	100,000
Less Expenses:	value of all the assets used up to enable us to supply these goods and services	(70,000)
Profit is therefore:		30,000

On the other hand, it is possible for our expenses to exceed our revenues for a set of transactions. In this case the result is a **loss**. For example, a loss would be incurred given the following:

		£
Revenue:	what we have charged to our customers in respect of all the goods and services supplied to them	60,000
Less Expenses:	value of all the assets used up to supply these goods and services to our customers	(80,000)
Loss is therefore:		(20,000)

In each of these two examples, a different explanation was given for the terms 'revenue' and 'expenses'. What is the difference between the two explanations given for 'revenue'? What is the difference between the two explanations given for 'expenses'?

4.2 The effect of profit and loss on capital

Businesses exist to make a profit and so increase their capital. Let's look at the relationship between profit and capital in an example.

On 1 January the assets and liabilities of a business are:

Assets: Fixtures £10,000; Inventory £7,000; Cash at the bank £3,000.
Liabilities: Accounts payable £2,000.

The capital is found from the accounting equation:

Capital = Assets – Liabilities

In this case, capital is £10,000 + £7,000 + £3,000 – £2,000 = £18,000.

During January, the whole of the £7,000 inventory is sold for £11,000 cash. On 31 January the assets and liabilities have become:

Assets: Fixtures £10,000; Inventory nil; Cash at the bank £14,000.
Liabilities: Accounts payable £2,000.

The capital is now £22,000:

Assets (£10,000 + £14,000) – Liabilities £2,000

So capital has increased by £4,000 from £18,000 to £22,000. It has increased by £4,000 because the £7,000 inventory was sold at a profit of £4,000 for £11,000. Profit, therefore, increases capital:

Old capital + Profit = New capital

£18,000 + £4,000 = £22,000

A loss, on the other hand, would reduce the capital:

Old capital – Loss = New capital

4.3 Profit or loss and sales

Profit will be made when goods or services are sold for more than they cost, while the opposite will result in a loss.

(You will learn later that there are different types of profit, some of which you may have heard of, such as 'gross profit' and 'net profit'. For now, we're not going to complicate things by going into that level of detail so, whatever you may already know about these different types of profit, try to focus for the time being on the simple definition of profit presented here.)

4.4 Profit or loss and expenses

Once profits or losses have been calculated, you can update the capital account. How often this will be done will depend on the business. Some only attempt to calculate their profits and losses once a year. Others do it at much more frequent intervals. Generally speaking, the larger the business, the more frequently profits are calculated.

In order to calculate profits and losses, revenue and expenses must be entered into appropriate accounts. All the expenses could be charged to one Expenses Account, but you would be able to understand the calculations of profit better if full details of each type of expense were shown in those profit calculations. The same applies to each type of revenue.

For this reason, a separate account is opened for each type of expense and for each type of revenue. For example, accounts in use may include:

Commissions account	Subscriptions account	Rent account
Bank interest account	Motor expenses account	Postages account
Royalties receivable account	Telephone account	Stationery account
Rent receivable account	General expenses account	Wages account
Overdraft interest account	Audit fees account	Insurance account

It is purely a matter of choice in a business as to the title of each expense or revenue account. For example, an account for postage stamps could be called 'Postage stamps account', 'Postages account', 'Communication expenses account', and so on. Also, different businesses amalgamate expenses, some having a 'Rent and telephone account', others a 'Rent, telephone and insurance account', etc. Infrequent or small items of expense are usually put into a 'Sundry expenses account' or a 'General expenses account'.

Most organisations use names for their accounts that make it obvious which accounts are for revenue and which accounts are for expenses. However, some don't. When in doubt as to whether an account is for revenue or expenses, you have two obvious indicators to consult. The first is on which side the entries are mainly appearing in the accounts. If it is the debit side, the account is almost certainly an expense account. The other indicator is the nature of the business. For example, a commission account in the accounting books of a firm of stockbrokers is almost certainly a revenue account.

Identify which of the accounts listed in the table above are expense accounts and which ones are revenue accounts.

4.5 Debit or credit

You need to know whether expense accounts should be debited or credited with the amounts involved. You know that assets involve expenditure by the business and are shown as debit entries. Expenses also involve expenditure by the business and should, therefore, also be debit entries. Why? Because assets and expenses must ultimately be paid for. This payment involves a credit to the bank account (or to the cash account) so the original entry in the asset account or in the expense account must be a debit.

Even where an expense is incurred on credit, the creditor must eventually be paid. The first entry will be to credit the supplier's (i.e. creditor's) account and debit the expense account. When payment is made to the supplier, the bank account is credited and the supplier's account is debited.

For example, if you pay rent of £500 in cash, the asset cash is decreased by £500. The accounting equation tells you that this means that the capital is reduced by each expense – if assets decrease, so does capital; if liabilities increase, capital decreases (otherwise the accounting equation won't balance). Expense accounts contain debit entries for expenses. The second part of the entry will either be a credit against an asset account, such as cash, or it will be a credit against a liability account, such as creditors.

Activity 4.3

Some students find this explanation involving the capital account very difficult to understand, so try this example to ensure you have followed it. Write down the accounting equation and see if you can work out what happens to it if (a) a business spends £30 in cash hiring a van for a day and (b) if a business hires a van for a day at a cost of £30 and is given 1 month to pay the bill. Assume in each case that the business has assets of £200, liabilities of £80 and capital of £120 before the transaction. What happens to capital in each case?

Revenue is the opposite of expenses and is, therefore, treated in the opposite way – revenue entries appear on the credit side of the revenue accounts. You've already seen this when you've entered sales figures as credits into the sales account. Thus, revenue is collected together in appropriately named accounts, where it is shown as a credit until it is transferred to the profit calculations at the end of the period.

Consider too the use of funds to pay for expenses which are used up in the short term, or assets which are used up in the long term, both for the purpose of getting revenue. Both of these forms of transactions are entered on the debit side of the appropriate accounts (expense accounts or asset accounts respectively), while the revenue which they generate is shown on the credit side of the appropriate revenue accounts.

So, to summarise, profit belongs to the owners. Revenues increase profits, so they increase capital, and that makes them credits. Expenses decrease profits, so they reduce capital, and that makes them debits. The treatment of expenses is the same as the treatment of assets. Increases in expenses result in debit entries to the appropriate expense accounts, while decreases (such as refunds for overpayment of an electricity bill) result in credit entries to those same accounts. Revenue is treated the same as liabilities. Increases in revenue are credited to the appropriate revenue accounts, while decreases are debited to the same accounts.

In other words:

Debit	Credit
Expenses	Revenues
Losses	Profits
Assets	Liabilities
	Capital

4.6 Double entries for expenses and revenues

Let's look at some examples that demonstrate the double entry required:

1 Rent of £200 is paid in cash.
Here the twofold effect is:

(*a*) The total of the expenses of rent is increased. As expense entries are shown as debits, and the expense is rent, the action required is to debit the rent account with £200.
(*b*) The asset of cash is decreased. This means the cash account must be credited with £200 to show the decrease of the asset.

Summary: Debit the *rent account* with £200.
Credit the *cash account* with £200.

2 Motor expenses of £355 are paid by cheque.
The twofold effect is:

(*a*) The total of the motor expenses paid is increased. The amount in expense accounts is increased through debit entries, so the action required is to debit the motor expenses account with £355.
(*b*) The asset of funds in the bank is decreased. This means the bank account must be credited with £355 to show the decrease of the asset.

Summary: Debit the *motor expenses account* with £355.
Credit the *bank account* with £355.

3 £60 cash is received for commission earned by the business.

(*a*) The asset of cash is increased. This needs a debit entry of £60 in the cash account to increase the asset.
(*b*) The revenue account, commissions received, is increased. Revenue is shown by a credit entry, so, to increase the revenue account, the commissions received account is credited with £60.

Summary: Debit the *cash account* with £60.
Credit the *commissions received account* with £60.

Now look at some more transactions and their effect upon the accounts in the following table:

			Increase	Action	Decrease	Action
June	1	Paid for postage stamps by cash £50	Expense of postage	Debit postage account	Asset of cash	Credit cash account
	2	Paid for electricity by cheque £229	Expense of electricity	Debit electricity account	Asset of bank	Credit bank account
	3	Received rent in cash £138	Asset of cash Revenue of rent	Debit cash account Credit rent received account	No decrease to record	No action to take
	4	Paid insurance by cheque £142	Expense of insurance	Debit insurance account	Asset of bank	Credit bank account

Entering these four examples into the appropriate accounts results in:

Cash

			£				£
June	3	Rent received	138	June	1	Postage	50

Bank

							£
				June	2	Electricity	229
					4	Insurance	142

Electricity

			£				
June	2	Bank	229				

Insurance

			£				
June	4	Bank	142				

Postage

			£				
June	1	Cash	50				

Rent received

							£
				June	3	Cash	138

4.7 Drawings

Sometimes the owners will want to take cash out of the business for their private use. This is known as **drawings**. Any money taken out as drawings will reduce capital. Drawings are *never* expenses of a business. An increase in drawings is a debit entry in the drawings account, with the credit being against an asset account, such as cash or bank.

In theory, the debit entry should be made in the capital account (as drawings decrease capital). However, to prevent the capital account becoming full of lots of small transactions, drawings are not entered in the capital account. Instead, a *drawings account* is opened, and the debits are entered there.

The following example illustrates the entries for drawings:

On 25 August, the owner takes £50 cash out of the business for his own use.

Effect	Action
1 Capital is decreased by £50 2 Cash is decreased by £50	Debit the drawings account £50 Credit the cash account £50

Drawings

			£				
Aug	25	Cash	50				

Cash

			£
		Aug 25 Drawings	50

Sometimes goods are taken for private use. This form of withdrawal by the owner is also known as drawings. In Section 3.2, you learnt that when goods are purchased, the purchases account is debited. As a result, when goods are withdrawn it is the purchases account which should be credited.

The following example illustrates the entries for this form of drawings.

On 28 August, the owner takes £400 of goods out of the business for his own use.

Effect	Action
1 Capital is decreased by £400 2 Inventory is decreased by £400	Debit the drawings account £400 Credit the purchases account £400

Drawings

	£		
Aug 28 Purchases	400		

Purchases

			£
		Aug 28 Drawings	400

Learning outcomes

You should now have learnt:

1. How to calculate profit by comparing revenue with expenses.
2. That the accounting equation is central to any explanation of the effect of trading upon capital.
3. Why every different type of expense is shown in a separate expense account.
4. Why every different type of revenue is shown in a separate revenue account.
5. Why an expense is shown as a debit entry in the appropriate expense account.
6. Why revenue is shown as a credit entry in the appropriate revenue account.
7. How to enter a series of expense and revenue transactions into the appropriate T-accounts.
8. What is meant by the term 'drawings'.
9. That drawings are *always* a reduction in capital and *never* an expense of a business.
10. How to record drawings of cash in the accounting books.
11. How to record drawings of goods in the accounting books.

Answers to activities

4.1 There is no difference between either the two meanings given for revenue or the two meanings given for expenses. In each case, you are being given a slightly different wording so as to help you understand what the two terms mean.

4.2

Expense accounts	*Revenue accounts*
Rent account	Subscriptions account
Postages account	Rent receivable account
Commissions account	Royalties receivable account
Stationery account	
Wages account	
Insurance account	
Bank interest account	
Motor expenses account	
Telephone account	
General expenses account	
Overdraft interest account	
Audit fees account	

Note that the answer has assumed that *unless* words like 'received' or 'receivable' follow the name of an account, the account is an expense. For example, the Commission Account and the Bank Interest Account could easily be for revenue rather than expenses. However, accounting practice is that as most accounts are for expenses, where there may be some confusion as to whether an account is for revenue or expenses, the name of the revenue account should make it clear that it is for revenue, not expenses. You can see an example in this question if you compare the names of the two rent accounts. Accounts like Subscriptions tend to appear mainly in the accounting books of clubs and societies and so there is no need in that case to indicate in the name that it is a revenue account. You can tell whether subscriptions are revenue or expenditure items from the type of organisation whose accounting books you are looking at. The same would apply, but even more so, to Audit Fees which are only ever revenue accounts in the accounting books of a firm of accountants. In all other cases, they are expense accounts.

4.3 The accounting equation is Capital = Assets – Liabilities. In this example, it starts as £120 = £200 – £80. Each transaction is entered twice. In both cases, the debit entry is £30 to a van hire expense account. The credit in (a) is to the cash account. In (b) it is to the car hire company's account (the creditor's account). In order for the accounting equation to balance, in (a) an asset (i.e. cash) has been reduced by £30 so capital must be reduced by the same amount, £30. In the case of (b) liabilities (i.e. the van hire company's account) have increased by £30 and so capital must be also be reduced by that amount, £30. In the case of (a) the accounting equation becomes £90 = £170 – £80. In (b) it becomes £90 = £200 – £110. The effect on capital in both cases is that it decreases by the amount of the expense.

Review questions

4.1 Enter the following transactions, completing the double entry in the books for the month of May 2007:

2007		
May	1	Started in business with £9,000 in the bank and £1,000 in cash.
	2	Purchased goods £290 on credit from D James.
	3	Bought fixtures and fittings £1,150 paying by cheque.
	5	Sold goods for cash £140.
	6	Bought goods on credit £325 from C Monty.
	10	Paid rent by cash £200.
	12	Bought stationery £45, paying in cash.
	18	Goods returned to D James £41.
	21	Received rent of £25 by cheque for sublet of corner space.
	23	Sold goods on credit to G Cross for £845.

24 Bought a van paying by cheque £4,100.
30 Paid the month's wages by cash £360.
31 The proprietor took cash for his own personal use £80.

4.2 Write up the following transactions in the books of P Hewitt:

2008

March	1	Started in business with cash £8,500.
	2	Bought goods on credit from W Young £420.
	3	Paid rent by cash £210.
	4	Paid £6,000 of the cash of the business into a bank account.
	5	Sold goods on credit to D Unbar £192.
	7	Bought stationery £25 paying by cheque.
	11	Cash sales £81.
	14	Goods returned by us to W Young £54.
	17	Sold goods on credit to J Harper £212.
	20	Paid for repairs to the building by cash £78.
	22	D Unbar returned goods to us £22.
	27	Paid W Young by cheque £366.
	28	Cash purchases £470.
	29	Bought a van paying by cheque £3,850.
	30	Paid motor expenses in cash £62.
	31	Bought fixtures £840 on credit from B Coal.

4.3A Prepare the double entries (*not* the T-accounts) for the following transactions using the format:

Date		Dr	Cr
	Account name	£x	
	Account name		£x

July	1	Started in business with £5,000 in the bank and £1,000 cash.
	2	Bought stationery by cheque £75.
	3	Bought goods on credit from T Smart £2,100.
	4	Sold goods for cash £340.
	5	Paid insurance by cash £290.
	7	Bought a computer on credit from J Hott £700.
	8	Paid expenses by cheque £32.
	10	Sold goods on credit to C Biggins £630.
	11	Returned goods to T Smart £550.
	14	Paid wages by cash £210.
	17	Paid rent by cheque £225.
	20	Received cheque £400 from C Biggins.
	21	Paid J Hott by cheque £700.
	23	Bought stationery on credit from News Ltd £125.
	25	Sold goods on credit to F Tank £645.
	31	Paid News Ltd by cheque £125.

4.4A Write up the following transactions in the T-accounts of F Fernandes:

Feb	1	Started in business with £11,000 in the bank and £1,600 cash.
	2	Bought goods on credit: J Biggs £830; D Martin £610; P Lot £590.
	3	Bought goods for cash £370.
	4	Paid rent in cash £75.
	5	Bought stationery paying by cheque £62.
	6	Sold goods on credit: D Twigg £370; B Hogan £290; K Fletcher £410.
	7	Paid wages in cash £160.
	10	We returned goods to D Martin £195.

→

11 Paid rent in cash £75.
13 B Hogan returns goods to us £35.
15 Sold goods on credit to: T Lee £205; F Sharp £280; G Rae £426.
16 Paid business rates by cheque £970.
18 Paid insurance in cash £280.
19 Paid rent by cheque £75.
20 Bought van on credit from B Black £6,100.
21 Paid motor expenses in cash £24.
23 Paid wages in cash £170.
24 Received part of amount owing from K Fletcher by cheque £250.
28 Received refund of business rates £45 by cheque.
28 Paid by cheque: J Biggs £830; D Martin £415; B Black £6,100.

4.5 From the following statements which give the cumulative effects of individual transactions, you are required to state as fully as possible what transaction has taken place in each case. That is, write descriptions similar to those given in questions 4.1–4.4. There is no need to copy out the table. The first column of data gives the opening position. Each of the other columns represents a transaction. It is these transactions (A–I) that you are to describe.

Transaction:		*A*	*B*	*C*	*D*	*E*	*F*	*G*	*H*	*I*
Assets	*£000*	*£000*	*£000*	*£000*	*£000*	*£000*	*£000*	*£000*	*£000*	*£000*
Land and buildings	450	450	450	450	575	575	275	275	275	275
Motor vehicles	95	100	100	100	100	100	100	100	100	100
Office equipment	48	48	48	48	48	48	48	48	48	48
Inventory	110	110	110	110	110	110	110	110	110	93
Accounts receivable	188	188	188	188	188	108	108	108	108	120
Bank	27	22	22	172	47	127	427	77	77	77
Cash	15	15	11	11	11	11	11	11	3	3
	933	933	929	1,079	1,079	1,079	1,079	729	721	716
Liabilities										
Capital	621	621	621	621	621	621	621	621	621	616
Loan from Lee	200	200	200	350	350	350	350	–	–	–
Accounts payable	112	112	108	108	108	108	108	108	100	100
	933	933	929	1,079	1,079	1,079	1,079	729	721	716

Note: the sign *£000* means that all the figures shown underneath it are in thousands of pounds, e.g. Office Equipment book value is £48,000. It saves constantly writing out 000 after each figure, and is done to save time and make comparison easier.

4.6A The following table shows the cumulative effects of a succession of separate transactions on the assets and liabilities of a business. The first column of data gives the opening position.

Transaction:		*A*	*B*	*C*	*D*	*E*	*F*	*G*	*H*	*I*
Assets	*£000*	*£000*	*£000*	*£000*	*£000*	*£000*	*£000*	*£000*	*£000*	*£000*
Land and buildings	500	500	535	535	535	535	535	535	535	535
Equipment	230	230	230	230	230	230	230	200	200	200
Inventory	113	140	140	120	120	120	120	120	119	119
Trade accounts receivable	143	143	143	173	160	158	158	158	158	158
Prepaid expenses*	27	27	27	27	27	27	27	27	27	27
Cash at bank	37	37	37	37	50	50	42	63	63	63
Cash on hand	9	9	9	9	9	9	9	9	9	3
	1,059	1,086	1,121	1,131	1,131	1,129	1,121	1,112	1,111	1,105
Liabilities										
Capital	730	730	730	740	740	738	733	724	723	717
Loan	120	120	155	155	155	155	155	155	155	155
Trade accounts payable	168	195	195	195	195	195	195	195	195	195
Accrued expenses*	41	41	41	41	41	41	38	38	38	38
	1,059	1,086	1,121	1,131	1,131	1,129	1,121	1,112	1,111	1,105

Required:
Identify clearly and as fully as you can what transaction has taken place in each case. Give two possible explanations for transaction I. Do not copy out the table but use the reference letter for each transaction.

(*Association of Accounting Technicians*)

******Authors' note*: You have not yet been told about 'prepaid expenses' and 'accrued expenses'. Prepaid expenses are expenses that have been paid in advance, the benefits of which will only be felt by the business in a later accounting period. Because the benefit of having incurred the expense will not be received until a future time period, the expense is not included in the calculation of profit for the period in which it was paid. As it was not treated as an expense of the period when profit was calculated, the debit in the account is treated as an asset when the balance sheet is prepared, hence the appearance of the term 'prepaid expenses' among the assets in the question. Accrued expenses, on the other hand, are expenses that have not yet been paid for benefits which have been received. In F, £8,000 was paid out of the bank account of which £3,000 was used to pay off some of the accrued expenses.**

You can find a range of additional self-test questions, as well as material to help you with your studies, on the website that accompanies this book at www.pearsoned.co.uk/wood.

chapter 5

Balancing-off accounts

Learning objectives

After you have studied this chapter, you should be able to:

- close-off accounts when appropriate
- balance-off accounts at the end of a period and bring down the opening balance to the next period
- distinguish between a debit balance and a credit balance
- describe and prepare accounts in three-column format

Introduction

In this chapter, you'll learn how to discover what the amount outstanding on an account is at a particular point in time. You'll also learn how to close accounts that are no longer needed and how to record appropriate entries in accounts at the end and beginning of periods. Finally, you'll learn that T-accounts are not the only way to record accounting transactions.

5.1 Accounts for debtors

Where debtors have paid their accounts

So far you have learnt how to record transactions in the accounting books by means of debit and credit entries. At the end of each accounting period the figures in each account are examined in order to summarise the situation they present. This will often, but not always, be once a year if you are calculating profit. If you want to see what is happening with respect to particular accounts, it will be more frequently done. For example, if you want to find out how much your customers owe you for goods you have sold to them, you would probably do this at the end of each month.

Why do you think we would want to look at the accounts receivable in the accounting books as often as once a month?

Let's look at the account of one of our customers, K Tandy, for transactions in August 2008:

K Tandy

2008			£	2008			£
Aug	1	Sales	144	Aug	22	Bank	144
	19	Sales	300		28	Bank	300

If you add up the figures on each side, you will find that they both sum to £444. In other words, during the month we sold a total of £444 worth of goods to Tandy, and have been paid a total of £444 by her. This means that at the end of August she owes us nothing. As she owes us nothing, we do not need her account to prepare the balance sheet (there is no point in showing a figure for debtors of zero in the balance sheet). We can, therefore, **close off** her account on 31 August 2008. This is done by inserting the totals on each side:

K Tandy

2008			£	2008			£
Aug	1	Sales	144	Aug	22	Bank	144
	19	Sales	300		28	Bank	300
			444				444

Notice that totals in accounting are always shown with a single line above them, and a double line underneath. As shown in the following completed account for C Lee, totals on accounts at the end of a period are always shown on a level with one another, even when there are less entries on one side than on the other.

Now, let's look at the account for C Lee.

C Lee

2008			£	2008			£
Aug	11	Sales	177	Aug	30	Bank	480
	19	Sales	203				
	22	Sales	100				
			480				480

In this account, C Lee also owed us nothing at the end of August 2008, as he had paid us for all the sales we made to him.

***Note*: In handwritten accounts, you will often see this layout enhanced by two intersecting lines, one horizontal and one diagonal on the side which has less entries. If this were done, C Lee's account would look like this:**

C Lee

2008			£	2008			£
Aug	11	Sales	177	Aug	30	Bank	480
	19	Sales	203				
	22	Sales	100				
			480				480

We won't use this layout in this book, but your teacher or lecturer may want you to use it whenever you are preparing T-accounts.

Why do you think we would want to draw these two extra lines onto the handwritten account?

If an account contains only one entry on each side and they are equal, you don't need to include totals. For example:

K Wood

2008			£	2008			£
Aug	6	Sales	214	Aug	12	Bank	214

Now let's look at what happens when the two sides do not equal each other.

Where debtors still owe for goods

It is unlikely that everyone will have paid the amounts they owe us by the end of the month. In these cases, the totals of each side would not equal one another. Let's look at the account of D Knight for August 2008:

D Knight

2008			£	2008			£
Aug	1	Sales	158	Aug	28	Bank	158
	15	Sales	206				
	30	Sales	118				

If you add the figures you will see that the debit side adds up to £482 and the credit side adds up to £158. You should be able to see what the difference of £324 (i.e. £482 – £158) represents. It consists of the last two sales of £206 and £118. They have not been paid for and so are still owing to us on 31 August 2008.

In double entry, we only enter figures as totals if the totals on both sides of the account agree. We do, however, want to **balance-off** the account for August showing that Knight owes us £324. (While there would be nothing wrong in using the term 'close off', 'balance-off' is the more appropriate term to use when there is a difference between the two sides of an account.)

If Knight owes us £324 at close of business on 31 August 2008, then the same amount will be owed to us when the business opens on 1 September 2008.

Balancing the accounts is done in five stages:

1 Add up both sides to find out their totals. Note: do not write anything in the account at this stage.
2 Deduct the smaller total from the larger total to find the balance.
3 Now enter the balance on the side with the smallest total. This now means the totals will be equal.
4 Enter totals level with each other.
5 Now enter the balance on the line below the totals on the *opposite* side to the balance shown above the totals.

Against the balance above the totals, complete the date column by entering the last day of that period – for August, this will always be '31' even if the business was shut on that date because it fell on a weekend or was a holiday. Below the totals, show the first day of the next period against the balance – this will always be the day immediately after the last day of the previous period, in this case, September 1. The balance above the totals is described as the **balance *carried down*** (often this is abbreviated to 'balance c/d'). The balance below the total is described as the **balance *brought down*** (often abbreviated to 'balance b/d').

Knight's account when 'balanced-off' will appear as follows:

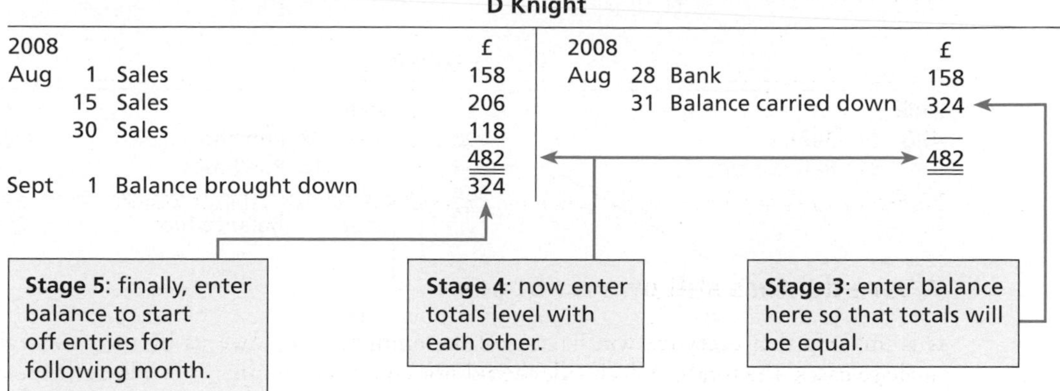

D Knight

2008			£	2008			£
Aug	1	Sales	158	Aug	28	Bank	158
	15	Sales	206		31	Balance carried down	324
	30	Sales	118				
			482				482
Sept	1	Balance brought down	324				

Stage 5: finally, enter balance to start off entries for following month.
Stage 4: now enter totals level with each other.
Stage 3: enter balance here so that totals will be equal.

Note for students

- From now on, we will use the abbreviations 'c/d' and 'b/d'.
- The date given to balance c/d is the last day of the period which is finishing, and balance b/d is given the opening date of the next period.
- As the total of the debit side originally exceeded the total of the credit side, **the balance is said to be a 'debit balance'**. This being a personal account (for a person), the person concerned is said to be a debtor – the accounting term for anyone who owes money to the business.

Just as when the two sides each have only one entry and the two sides are equal, if an account contains only one entry it is unnecessary to enter the total after entering the balance carried down (because the balance becomes the only entry on the other side and it is equal to the other entry). A double line ruled under the entry will mean that the entry is its own total. For example:

B Walters

2008			£	2008			£
Aug	18	Sales	51	Aug	31	Balance c/d	51
Sept	1	Balance b/d	51				

***Note*: T-accounts should *always* be closed off at the end of each period, even when they contain only one entry.**

5.2 Accounts for creditors

Exactly the same principles will apply when the balances are carried down to the credit side. **This balance is known as a 'credit balance'.** We can look at the accounts of two of our suppliers which are to be balanced-off:

E Williams

2008			£	2008			£
Aug	21	Bank	100	Aug	2	Purchases	248
					18	Purchases	116

K Patterson

2008			£	2008			£
Aug	14	Returns outwards	20	Aug	8	Purchases	620
	28	Bank	600		15	Purchases	200

We now add up the totals and find the balance, i.e. Stages 1 and 2. When balanced-off, these will appear as:

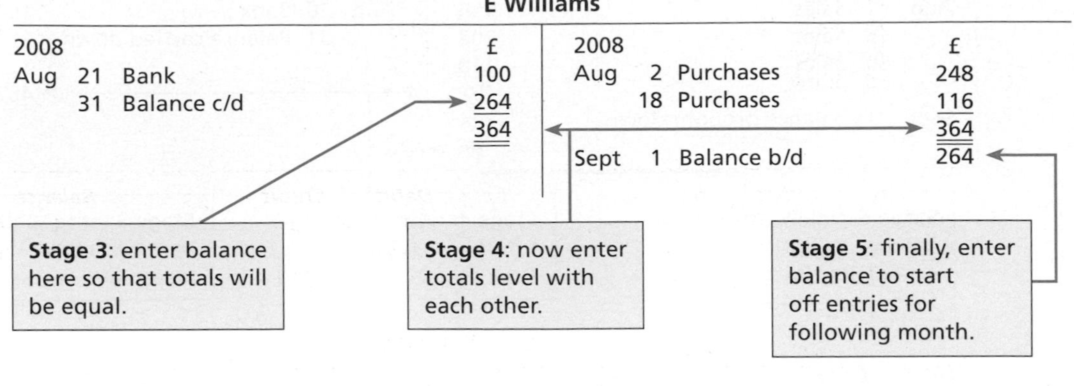

E Williams

			£				£
2008				2008			
Aug	21	Bank	100	Aug	2	Purchases	248
	31	Balance c/d	264		18	Purchases	116
			364				364
				Sept	1	Balance b/d	264

Stage 3: enter balance here so that totals will be equal.
Stage 4: now enter totals level with each other.
Stage 5: finally, enter balance to start off entries for following month.

K Patterson

			£				£
2008				2008			
Aug	14	Returns outwards	20	Aug	8	Purchases	620
	28	Bank	600		15	Purchases	200
	31	Balance c/d	200				
			820				820
				Sept	1	Balance b/d	200

The accounts of E Williams and K Patterson have credit balances. They are 'creditors' – the accounting term for someone to whom money is owed.

Before you read further attempt Review Questions 5.1 and 5.2.

5.3 Three-column accounts

Through the main part of this book, the type of account used is the T-account, where the left-hand side of the account is the debit side, and the right-hand side is the credit side. However, when computers are used the style of the ledger account is sometimes different. It appears as three columns of figures, one column for debit entries, another column for credit entries, and the last column for the balance. If you have a current account at a bank your bank statements will normally be shown using this three-column format.

The accounts used in this chapter will now be redrafted to show the ledger accounts drawn up in this way.

K Tandy

			Debit	*Credit*	*Balance* (and whether debit or credit)	
2008			£	£	£	
Aug	1	Sales	144		144	Dr
	19	Sales	300		444	Dr
	22	Bank		144	300	Dr
	28	Bank		300	0	

C Lee

			Debit	Credit	Balance	
2008			£	£	£	
Aug	11	Sales	177		177	Dr
	19	Sales	203		380	Dr
	22	Sales	100		480	Dr
	30	Bank		480	0	

K Wood

			Debit	Credit	Balance	
2008			£	£	£	
Aug	6	Sales	214		214	Dr
	12	Bank		214	0	

D Knight

			Debit	Credit	Balance	
2008			£	£	£	
Aug	1	Sales	158		158	Dr
	15	Sales	206		364	Dr
	28	Bank		158	206	Dr
	31	Sales	118		324	Dr

B Walters

			Debit	Credit	Balance	
2008			£	£	£	
Aug	18	Sales	51		51	Dr

E Williams

			Debit	Credit	Balance	
2008			£	£	£	
Aug	2	Purchases		248	248	Cr
	18	Purchases		116	364	Cr
	21	Bank	100		264	Cr

K Patterson

			Debit	Credit	Balance	
2008			£	£	£	
Aug	8	Purchases		620	620	Cr
	14	Returns	20		600	Cr
	15	Purchases		200	800	Cr
	28	Bank	600		200	Cr

Note how the balance is calculated after every entry. This can be done quite simply when using a computer because the software can automatically calculate the new balance as soon as an entry is made.

When manual methods are being used it is often too much work to have to calculate a new balance after each entry. Also, the greater the number of calculations, the greater the possibility of errors. For these reasons, it is usual for students to use T-accounts *except* when required to use three-column accounts in an exam! However, it is important to note that there is no difference in principle – the final balances are the same using either method.

Learning outcomes

You should now have learnt:

1. How to close off accounts upon which there is no balance oustanding.
2. How to balance-off accounts at the end of a period.
3. How to bring down the opening balance on an account at the start of a new period.
4. That when an opening balance on an account is a debit, that account is said to have a debit balance. It also has a debit balance during a period whenever the total of the debit side exceeds the total of the credit side.
5. That when an opening balance on an account is a credit, that account is said to have a credit balance. It also has a credit balance during a period whenever the total of the credit side exceeds the total of the debit side.
6. That 'debtors' are people or organisations whose account in your accounting books has a greater value on the debit side. They owe you money. They are included in the amount shown for accounts receivable in the balance sheet.
7. That 'creditors' are people or organisations whose account in your accounting books has a greater value on the credit side. You owe them money. They are included in the amount shown for accounts payable in the balance sheet.
8. That T-accounts and three-column accounts disclose the same balance, given identical information about transactions.
9. That three-column accounts update and show the balance on the account after every transaction.
10. How to prepare three-column accounts.

Answers to activities

5.1 In order to survive, businesses must, in the long term, make profits. However, even profitable businesses go 'bust' if they do not have enough funds to pay their bills when they are due. Debtors represent a resource that is not yet in the form of funds (e.g. cash) that can be used to pay bills. By regularly monitoring the position on the account of each debtor, a business can tell which debtors are being slow to pay and, very importantly, do something about it.

5.2 The purpose is to prevent any more entries being made in the account. The entries would *always* be made in ink, so as to prevent their being erased and replaced with different entries. In a computerised accounting system, there is no need for measures such as these, because the controls and checks built into the computerised system prevent such things from happening.

Review questions

5.1 Enter the following items in the appropriate debtors' accounts (i.e. your customers' accounts) only; do *not* write up other accounts. Then balance-off each of these personal accounts at the end of the month. (Keep your answer; it will be used as a basis for Review Question 5.3.)

2008

May	1	Sales on credit to B Flyn £810; G Goh £763; T Fey £392.
	4	Sales on credit to F Start £480; B Flyn £134.
	10	Returns inwards from B Flyn £93; T Fey £41.
	18	G Goh paid us by cheque £763.
	20	T Fey paid us £351 by cheque.
	24	B Flyn paid us £500 by cash.
	31	Sales on credit to F Start £240.

5.2 Enter the following in the appropriate creditors' accounts (i.e. your suppliers' accounts) only. Do *not* write up the other accounts. Then balance-off each of these personal accounts at the end of the month. (Keep your answer; it will be used as the basis for Review Question 5.4.)

2008

June	1	Purchases on credit from J Saville £240; P Todd £390; J Fry £810.
	3	Purchases on credit from P Todd £470; J Mehan £1,450.
	10	We returned goods to J Fry £82; J Saville £65.
	15	Purchases on credit from J Saville £210.
	19	We paid J Mehan by cheque £1,450.
	28	We paid J Saville by cash £300.
	30	We returned goods to P Todd £39.

5.3 Redraft each of the accounts given in your answer to 5.1 in three-column style.

5.4 Redraft each of the accounts given in your answer to 5.2 in three-column style.

5.5 Enter the following in the personal accounts (i.e. the creditor and debtor accounts) only. Do *not* write up the other accounts. Balance-off each personal account at the end of the month. After completing this, state which of the balances represent debtors and which represent creditors.

2008

Sept	1	Sales on credit to J Bee £520; T Day £630; J Soul £240.
	2	Purchases on credit D Blue £390; F Rise £510; P Lee £280.
	8	Sales on credit to T Day £640; L Hope £418.
	10	Purchases on credit from F Rise £92; R James £870.
	12	Returns inwards from J Soul £25; T Day £190.
	17	We returned goods to F Rise £12; R James £84.
	20	We paid D Blue by cheque £390.
	24	J Bee paid us by cheque £400.
	26	We paid R James by cheque £766.
	28	J Bee paid us by cash £80.
	30	L Hope pays us by cheque £418.

5.6A Enter the following transactions in personal accounts only. Bring down the balances at the end of the month. After completing this, state which of the balances represent debtors and which represent creditors.

2007

May	1	Credit sales G Wood £310; K Hughes £42; F Dunn £1,100; M Lyons £309.
	2	Credit purchases from T Sim £190; J Leech £63; P Tidy £210; F Rock £190.
	8	Credit sales to K Hughes £161; F Dunn £224.

→

9 Credit purchases from J Leech £215; F Rock £164.
10 Goods returned to us by F Dunn £31; M Lyons £82.
12 Cash paid to us by M Lyons £227.
15 We returned goods to T Sim £15; F Rock £21.
19 We received cheques from F Dunn £750; G Wood £310.
21 We sold goods on credit to G Wood £90; K Hughes £430.
28 We paid by cheque the following: T Sim £175; F Rock £100; P Tidy £180.
31 We returned goods to F Rock £18.

5.7A Redraft each of the accounts given in your answer to 5.6A in three-column style.

You can find a range of additional self-test questions, as well as material to help you with your studies, on the website that accompanies this book at www.pearsoned.co.uk/wood.

chapter

6

The trial balance

Learning objectives

After you have studied this chapter, you should be able to:

- prepare a trial balance from a set of accounts
- explain why the debit and credit trial balance totals should equal one another
- explain why some of the possible errors that can be made when double entries are being entered in the accounts do not prevent the trial balance from 'balancing'
- describe uses for a trial balance other than to check for double entry errors

Introduction

In this chapter, you'll learn how to prepare a trial balance from the accounts in the accounting books. You'll discover that the alternate version of the accounting equation can be a useful guide to understanding why a trial balance must balance if all the double entries in the accounts are correct. You'll also learn that the trial balance is no guarantee that the double entries have all been recorded correctly. Finally, at the end of the chapter, you'll have the opportunity to do twenty multiple choice questions covering the material in Chapters 1–6.

6.1 Total debit entries = Total credit entries

You've learnt that under double entry bookkeeping

- for each debit entry there is a credit entry
- for each credit entry there is a debit entry.

Let's see if you can remember the basics of double entry.

Activity 6.1

What is the double entry for each of the following transactions:

(*a*) Purchase of a new van for £9,000 which was paid in full by cheque

Dr		£	
	Cr		£

(*b*) Goods which cost £40 taken out by the owner for her own use

Dr		£	
	Cr		£

The total of all the items recorded in all the accounts on the debit side should equal the total of all the items recorded on the credit side of the accounts.

Do you remember the alternate form of the accounting equation you were shown in Chapter 1? What does it tell you has happened when it does not balance?

We need to check that for each debit entry there is also an equal credit entry. In order to check that there is a matching credit entry for every debit entry, we prepare something called a **trial balance**.

A type of trial balance could be drawn up by listing all the accounts and then entering the total of all the debit entries in each account in one column and the total of all the credit entries in each account into another column. Finally, you would add up the two columns of figures and ensure they are equal. Using the worked example in Section 3.8, this trial balance would be:

Trial balance as at 31 May 2009

	Dr	*Cr*
	£	£
Purchases	994	
Sales		490
Returns outwards		15
Returns inwards	16	
D Small	220	220
A Lyon & Son		624
D Hughes	60	60
M Spencer	45	16
Cash	445	355
	1,780	1,780

6.2 Total debit balances = Total credit balances

The method described in Section 6.1 is *not* the accepted method of drawing up a trial balance, but it is the easiest to understand at first. The form of trial balance used by accountants is a list of account balances arranged according to whether they are debit balances or credit balances.

Let's balance-off the accounts you saw in Section 3.8. The new entries are highlighted so that you can see the entries required to arrive at the closing balances that are used in the trial balance.

You may find it worthwhile trying to balance these accounts yourself before reading any further.

Purchases

2009			£	2009			£
May	1	D Small	220	May	31	**Balance c/d**	**994**
	2	A Lyon & Son	410				
	12	Cash	150				
	31	A Lyon & Son	214				
			994				**994**
June	**1**	**Balance b/d**	**994**				

Sales

			£				£
2009				2009			
May	31	Balance c/d	490	May	5	D Hughes	60
					6	M Spencer	45
					11	Cash	210
					21	Cash	175
			490				490
				June	11	Balance b/d	490

Returns outwards

			£				£
2009				2009			
May	31	Balance c/d	15	May	10	D Small	15
				June	1	Balance b/d	15

Returns inwards

			£				£
2009				2009			
May	19	M Spencer	16	May	31	Balance c/d	16
June	1	Balance b/d	16				

D Small

			£				£
2009				2009			
May	10	Returns outwards	15	May	1	Purchases	220
	22	Cash	205				
			220				220

A Lyon & Son

			£				£
2009				2009			
May	31	Balance c/d	624	May	2	Purchases	410
					31	Purchases	214
			624				624
				June	1	Balance b/d	624

D Hughes

			£				£
2009				2009			
May	5	Sales	60	May	30	Cash	60

M Spencer

			£				£
2009				2009			
May	6	Sales	45	May	19	Returns inwards	16
					31	Balance c/d	29
			45				45
June	1	Balance b/d	29				

Cash

			£				£
2009				2009			
May	11	Sales	210	May	12	Purchases	150
	21	Sales	175		22	D Small	205
	30	D Hughes	60		31	Balance c/d	90
			445				445
June	1	Balance b/d	90				

If you tried to do this before looking at the answer, be sure you understand any mistakes you made before going on.

If the trial balance was drawn up using the closing account balances, it would appear as follows:

Trial balance as at 31 May 2009		
	Dr	*Cr*
	£	£
Purchases	994	
Sales		490
Returns outwards		15
Returns inwards	16	
A Lyon & Son		624
M Spencer	29	
Cash	90	
	1,129	1,129

The trial balance always has the date of the *last* day of the accounting period to which it relates. It is a snapshot of the balances on the ledger accounts at that date.

Just like the trial balance you saw in Section 6.1, the two sides of this one also 'balance'. However, the totals are lower. This is because the £220 in D Small's account, £60 in D Hughes' account, £16 in M Spencer's account and £355 in the cash account have been cancelled out from each side of these accounts by taking only the *balances* instead of the *totals*. As equal amounts have been cancelled from each side, £651 in all, the new totals should still equal one another, as in fact they do at £1,129. (You can verify this if you subtract the new total of £1,129 from the previous one of £1,780. The difference is £651 which is the amount cancelled out from both sides.)

This form of trial balance is the easiest to extract when there are more than a few transactions during the period and it is the one accountants use.

Note that a trial balance can be drawn up at any time. However, it is normal practice to prepare one at the end of an accounting period before preparing an 'income statement' and 'balance sheet'. The income statement shows what profit has been earned in a period. (You will be looking at income statements in the next chapter.) The balance sheet shows what the assets and liabilities of a business are at the end of a period.

Go back to Chapter 1 to refresh your understanding of the balance sheet.

What advantages are there in preparing a trial balance when you are about to prepare an income statement and balance sheet?

As you've just learnt from Activity 6.3, trial balances are not just done to find errors.

6.3 Trial balances and errors

Many students new to accounting assume that when the trial balance 'balances', the entries in the accounts must be correct. **This assumption is incorrect.** While it means that certain types of error have not been made (such as forgetting to enter the credit side of a transaction), there are several types of error that will not affect the balancing of a trial balance – omitting a transaction altogether, for example.

Examples of the errors which would be revealed, provided there are no compensating errors which cancel them out, are addition errors, using one figure for the debit entry and another figure for the credit entry, and entering only one side of a transaction.

We shall consider addition errors in greater detail in Chapter 33.

Activity 6.4

If a trial balance fails to agree, what steps would you take in order to find the cause of the difference?

6.4 Multiple choice self-test questions

A growing practice of examining boards is to set multiple choice questions in accounting. In fact, this has become so popular with examiners that all the largest professional accounting bodies now use them, particularly in their first-level examinations.

Multiple choice questions give an examiner the opportunity to cover large parts of the syllabus briefly, but in detail. Students who omit to study areas of the syllabus will be caught out by an examiner's use of multiple choice questions. It is no longer possible to say that it is highly probable a certain topic will not be tested – the examiner can easily cover it with a multiple choice question.

We have deliberately included sets of twenty multiple choice questions at given places in this textbook, rather than a few at the end of each chapter. Such questions are relatively easy to answer a few minutes after reading the chapter. Asking the questions later is a far better test of your powers of recall and understanding. It also gives you practice at answering questions covering a range of topics in one block, as in an examination.

Each multiple choice question has a 'stem' (a part which poses the problem), a 'key' (which is the one correct answer), and a number of 'distractors', i.e. incorrect answers. The key plus the distractors are known as the 'options'.

If you do not know the answer, you should guess. You may be right by chance, or you may remember something subconsciously. In any event, unless the examiner warns otherwise, you will be expected to guess if you don't know the answer.

Read through the Learning Outcomes for this chapter and then attempt Multiple Choice Set 1.

Answers to all the multiple choice questions are given in Appendix 2 at the end of this book.

6.5 Closing inventory

Inventory at the end of a period is not usually to be found in an account in the ledger. It has to be found from stock records and physical stocktaking. As it is not generally to be found in the ledger, it does not generally appear among the balances in a trial balance. However, opening inventory is often recorded in a ledger account, in which case the inventory balance at the start of a period would be included in trial balance prepared at the end of that period.

Learning outcomes

You should now have learnt:

1. How to prepare a trial balance.
2. That trial balances are one form of checking the accuracy of entries in the accounts.
3. That errors can be made in the entries to the accounts that will not be shown up by the trial balance.
4. That the trial balance is used as the basis for preparing income statements and balance sheets.

Answers to activities

6.1 (*a*) Dr Van account £9,000
Cr Bank account £9,000
(*b*) Dr Drawings account £40
Cr Purchases account £40

6.2 The alternate form of the accounting equation is Assets = Capital + Liabilities. All the accounts with debit balances are assets and all the accounts with credit balances are either capital or liabilities. This means that so long as you enter a debit for every credit, the alternate accounting equation must always balance. If the alternate accounting equation does not balance, you've made an error somewhere, either in your double entries, or in your arithmetic within the individual accounts. Virtually all occurrences where the accounting equation does not balance that arise in practice are the result of double entry errors.

6.3 Firstly, you can verify whether the total of the debit balances equals the total of the credit balances. They need to be equal, or your income statement and balance sheet will be incorrect and your balance sheet will not balance. (That is, the accounting equation will not balance.) Secondly, you need to know what the balance is on every account so that you can enter the appropriate figures into the income statement and balance sheet. If you don't prepare a trial balance, you will find it much more difficult to prepare these two accounting statements.

6.4 You need to check each entry to verify whether or not it is correct but firstly, it is best to start by checking that the totals in the trial balance have been correctly summed. Then, check that no account has been omitted from the trial balance. Then, check each account in turn.

Multiple choice questions: Set 1

Now attempt Set 1 of multiple choice questions. (Answers to all the multiple choice questions are given in Appendix 2 at the end of this book.)

Each of these multiple choice questions has four suggested answers, (A), (B), (C) and (D). You should read each question and then decide which choice is best, either (A) or (B) or (C) or (D). ***Write down your answers on a separate piece of paper.*** **You will then be able to redo the set of questions later without having to try to ignore your answers.**

MC1 Which of the following statements is **incorrect**?

(A) Assets – Capital = Liabilities
(B) Liabilities + Capital = Assets
(C) Liabilities + Assets = Capital
(D) Assets – Liabilities = Capital

MC2 Which of the following is **not** an asset?

(A) Buildings
(B) Cash balance
(C) Accounts receivable
(D) Loan from K Harris

MC3 Which of the following is a liability?

(A) Machinery
(B) Accounts payable for goods
(C) Motor vehicles
(D) Cash at bank

MC4 Which of the following is **incorrect**?

	Assets	Liabilities	Capital
	£	£	£
(A)	7,850	1,250	6,600
(B)	8,200	2,800	5,400
(C)	9,550	1,150	8,200
(D)	6,540	1,120	5,420

MC5 Which of the following statements is correct?

		Effect upon	
		Assets	*Liabilities*
(A)	We paid a creditor by cheque	−Bank	−Accounts payable
(B)	A debtor paid us £90 in cash	+Cash	+Accounts receivable
(C)	J Hall lends us £500 by cheque	+Bank	−Loan from Hall
(D)	Bought goods on credit	+Inventory	+Capital

MC6 Which of the following are correct?

	Accounts	*To record*	*Entry in the account*
(*i*)	Assets	an increase	Debit
		a decrease	Credit
(*ii*)	Capital	an increase	Debit
		a decrease	Credit
(*iii*)	Liabilities	an increase	Credit
		a decrease	Debit

(A) (*i*) and (*ii*)
(B) (*ii*) and (*iii*)
(C) (*i*) and (*iii*)
(D) (*i*), (*ii*) and (*iii*)

MC7 Which of the following are correct?

		Account to be debited	*Account to be credited*
(*i*)	Bought office furniture for cash	Office furniture	Cash
(*ii*)	A debtor, P Sangster, pays us by cheque	Bank	P Sangster
(*iii*)	Introduced capital by cheque	Capital	Bank
(*iv*)	Paid a creditor, B Lee, by cash	B Lee	Cash

(A) (*i*), (*ii*) and (*iii*) only
(B) (*ii*), (*iii*) and (*iv*) only
(C) (*i*), (*ii*) and (*iv*) only
(D) (*i*) and (*iv*) only

MC8 Which of the following are **incorrect**?

		Account to be debited	*Account to be credited*
(*i*)	Sold van for cash	Cash	Van
(*ii*)	Returned some of Office Equipment to Suppliers Ltd	Office Equipment	Suppliers Ltd
(*iii*)	Repaid part of loan from C Charles by cheque	Loan from C Charles	Bank
(*iv*)	Bought machinery on credit from Betterways Ltd	Betterways Ltd	Machinery

→

(A) (*ii*) and (*iv*) only
(B) (*iii*) and (*iv*) only
(C) (*ii*) and (*iii*) only
(D) (*i*) and (*iii*) only

MC9 Which of the following best describes the meaning of 'Purchases'?

(A) Items bought
(B) Goods bought on credit
(C) Goods bought for resale
(D) Goods paid for

MC10 Which of the following should not be called 'Sales'?

(A) Office fixtures sold
(B) Goods sold on credit
(C) Goods sold for cash
(D) Sale of item previously included in 'Purchases'

MC11 Of the following, which are correct?

		Account to be debited	*Account to be credited*
(*i*)	Goods sold on credit to R Williams	R Williams	Sales
(*ii*)	S Johnson returns goods to us	Returns inwards	S Johnson
(*iii*)	Goods bought for cash	Cash	Purchases
(*iv*)	We returned goods to A Henry	A Henry	Returns inwards

(A) (*i*) and (*iii*) only
(B) (*i*) and (*ii*) only
(C) (*ii*) and (*iv*) only
(D) (*iii*) and (*iv*) only

MC12 Which of the following are **incorrect**?

		Account to be debited	*Account to be credited*
(*i*)	Goods sold for cash	Cash	Sales
(*ii*)	Goods bought on credit from T Carter	Purchases	T Carter
(*iii*)	Goods returned by us to C Barry	C Barry	Returns outwards
(*iv*)	Van bought for cash	Purchases	Cash

(A) (*i*) and (*iii*) only
(B) (*iii*) only
(C) (*ii*) and (*iv*) only
(D) (*iv*) only

MC13 Given the following, what is the amount of Capital? Assets: Premises £20,000; Inventory £8,500; Cash £100. Liabilities: Accounts payable £3,000; Loan from A Adams £4,000

(A) £21,100
(B) £21,600
(C) £32,400
(D) £21,400

MC14 Which of the following is correct?

(A) Profit does not alter capital
(B) Profit reduces capital
(C) Capital can only come from profit
(D) Profit increases capital

MC15 Which of the following are correct?

		Account to be debited	Account to be credited
(*i*)	Received commission by cheque	Bank	Commission received
(*ii*)	Paid rates by cash	Rates	Cash
(*iii*)	Paid motor expenses by cheque	Motor expenses	Bank
(*iv*)	Received refund of insurance by cheque	Insurance	Bank

(A) (*i*) and (*ii*) only
(B) (*i*), (*ii*) and (*iii*) only
(C) (*ii*), (*iii*) and (*iv*) only
(D) (*i*), (*ii*) and (*iv*) only

MC16 Of the following, which are **incorrect**?

		Account to be debited	Account to be credited
(*i*)	Sold van for cash	Cash	Sales
(*ii*)	Bought stationery by cheque	Stationery	Bank
(*iii*)	Took cash out of business for private use	Cash	Drawings
(*iv*)	Paid general expenses by cheque	General expenses	Bank

(A) (*ii*) and (*iv*) only
(B) (*i*) and (*ii*) only
(C) (*i*) and (*iii*) only
(D) (*ii*) and (*iii*) only

MC17 What is the balance on the following account on 31 May 2008?

C De Freitas

2008			£	2008			£
May	1	Sales	205	May	17	Cash	300
	14	Sales	360		28	Returns	50
	30	Sales	180				

(A) A credit balance of £395
(B) A debit balance of £380
(C) A debit balance of £395
(D) There is a nil balance on the account

MC18 What would have been the balance on the account of C De Freitas in MC17 on 19 May 2008?

(A) A debit balance of £265
(B) A credit balance of £95
(C) A credit balance of £445
(D) A credit balance of £265

MC19 Which of the following best describes a trial balance?

(A) Shows the financial position of a business
(B) It is a special account
(C) Shows all the entries in the books
(D) It is a list of balances on the books

MC20 Is it true that the trial balance totals should agree?

(A) No, there are sometimes good reasons why they differ
(B) Yes, except where the trial balance is extracted at the year end
(C) Yes, always
(D) No, because it is not a balance sheet

Review questions

6.1 You are to enter up the necessary accounts for the month of May from the following information relating to a small printing firm. Then balance-off the accounts and extract a trial balance as at 31 May 2008.

2008		
May	1	Started in business with capital in cash of £800 and £2,200 in the bank.
	2	Bought goods on credit from the following persons: J Ward £610; P Green £214; M Taylor £174; S Gemmill £345; P Tone £542.
	4	Sold goods on credit to: J Sharpe £340; G Boycott £720; F Titmus £1,152.
	6	Paid rent by cash £180.
	9	J Sharpe paid us his account by cheque £340.
	10	F Titmus paid us £1,000 by cheque.
	12	We paid the following by cheque: M Taylor £174; J Ward £610.
	15	Paid carriage by cash £38.
	18	Bought goods on credit from P Green £291; S Gemmill £940.
	21	Sold goods on credit to G Boycott £810.
	31	Paid rent by cheque £230.

6.2 Enter the following transactions of an antiques shop in the accounts and extract a trial balance as at 31 March 2008.

2008		
March	1	Started in business with £8,000 in the bank.
	2	Bought goods on credit from the following persons: L Frank £550; G Byers £290; P Lee £610.
	5	Cash sales £510.
	6	Paid wages in cash £110.
	7	Sold goods on credit to: J Snow £295; K Park £360; B Tyler £640.
	9	Bought goods for cash £120.
	10	Bought goods on credit from: G Byers £410; P Lee £1,240.
	12	Paid wages in cash £110.
	13	Sold goods on credit to: K Park £610; B Tyler £205.
	15	Bought shop fixtures on credit from Stop Ltd £740.
	17	Paid G Byers by cheque £700.
	18	We returned goods to P Lee £83.
	21	Paid Stop Ltd a cheque for £740.
	24	B Tyler paid us his account by cheque £845.
	27	We returned goods to L Frank £18.
	30	G Prince lent us £1,000 by cash.
	31	Bought a van paying by cheque £6,250.

6.3A Record the following details relating to a carpet retailer for the month of November 2007 and extract a trial balance as at 30 November 2007.

2007		
Nov	1	Started in business with £15,000 in the bank.
	3	Bought goods on credit from: J Small £290; F Brown £1,200; T Rae £610; R Charles £530.
	5	Cash sales £610.
	6	Paid rent by cheque £175.
	7	Paid business rates by cheque £130.
	11	Sold goods on credit to: T Potts £85; J Field £48; T Gray £1,640.
	17	Paid wages by cash £290.
	18	We returned goods to: J Small £18; R Charles £27.

19 Bought goods on credit from: R Charles £110; T Rae £320; F Jack £165.
20 Goods were returned to us by: J Field £6; T Potts £14.
21 Bought van on credit from Turnkey Motors £4,950.
23 We paid the following by cheque: J Small £272; F Brown £1,200; T Rae £500.
25 Bought another van, paying by cheque immediately £6,200.
26 Received a loan of £750 cash from B Bennet.
28 Received cheques from: T Potts £71; J Field £42.
30 Proprietor brings a further £900 into the business, by a payment into the business bank account.

6.4A Record the following transactions for the month of January of a small finishing retailer, balance-off all the accounts, and then extract a trial balance as at 31 January 2008.

2008
Jan 1 Started in business with £10,500 cash.
2 Put £9,000 of the cash into a bank account.
3 Bought goods for cash £550.
4 Bought goods on credit from: T Dry £800; F Hood £930; M Smith £160; G Low £510.
5 Bought stationery on credit from Buttons Ltd £89.
6 Sold goods on credit to: R Tong £170; L Fish £240; M Singh £326; A Tom £204.
8 Paid rent by cheque £220.
10 Bought fixtures on credit from Chiefs Ltd £610.
11 Paid salaries in cash £790.
14 Returned goods to: F Hood £30; M Smith £42.
15 Bought van by cheque £6,500.
16 Received loan from B Barclay by cheque £2,000.
18 Goods returned to us by: R Tong £5; M Singh £20.
21 Cash sales £145.
24 Sold goods on credit to: L Fish £130; A Tom £410; R Pleat £158.
26 We paid the following by cheque: F Hood £900; M Smith £118.
29 Received cheques from: R Pleat £158; L Fish £370.
30 Received a further loan from B Barclay by cash £500.
30 Received £614 cash from A Tom.

6.5 **Note, this question should not be attempted until cash discounts and trade discounts have been covered (see Chapters 13 and 14). It should also be noted that this is an example of the exception to the rule that closing inventory does not generally appear in a trial balance.**

On 1 October 2009, the owner of the USS Enterprise, Mr Kirk, decides that he will boldly go and keep his records on a double entry system. His assets and liabilities at that date were:

	£
Fixtures and equipment	20,000
Inventory including weapons	15,000
Balance at Universe Bank	17,500
Cash	375
Accounts payable – Spock	3,175
– Scott	200
– McCoy	500

Kirk's transactions during October were as follows:

1 Sold faulty phasers, original cost £500, to Klingon Corp, for cash £5,000
2 Bought Photon Torpedoes (weapons), on credit from Central Council £2,500
3 Sold goods to Aardvarks, original cost £250, on credit, £1,500
4 Bought Cloaking Device (Fixture and Fittings) from Klingon Corp £3,500
5 Paid the balance owed to Spock at 1 October less a 5% cash discount
6 Paid Central Council full amount due by cheque

→

7 Received full amount due from Aardvarks by cheque
8 Paid Klingon Corp by cheque after deducting 20% trade discount
9 Paid, by bankers order, £10,000 for repairs to Enterprise following disagreement over amount owing to Klingon Corp and faculty phasers.

Required:
Open Enterprise's ledger accounts at 1 October, record all transactions for the month, balance the ledger accounts, and prepare a trial balance as at 31 October.

You can find a range of additional self-test questions, as well as material to help you with your studies, on the website that accompanies this book at www.pearsoned.co.uk/wood.

part

2

THE FINANCIAL STATEMENTS OF SOLE TRADERS

Introduction

This part is concerned with preparing, from double entry records, the financial statements of sole traders.

chapter 7

Income statements: an introduction

Learning objectives

After you have studied this chapter, you should be able to:

- explain why income statements are not part of the double entry system
- explain why profit is calculated
- calculate cost of goods sold, gross profit, and net profit
- explain the difference between gross profit and net profit
- explain the relationship between the trading account and the profit and loss account
- explain how the trading account and the profit and loss account fit together to create the income statement
- explain how to deal with closing inventory when preparing the trading account section of an income statement
- close down the appropriate accounts and transfer the balances to the trading account
- close down the appropriate accounts and transfer the balances to the profit and loss account
- prepare an income statement from information given in a trial balance
- make appropriate double entries to incorporate net profit and drawings in the capital account

Introduction

In this chapter, you will learn how to close down revenue and expenditure accounts in order to calculate profit and prepare an income statement. You will learn how to adjust purchases with inventory and arrive at the cost of goods sold, and will discover the difference between gross profit and net profit. You will learn how to prepare an income statement, and, finally, you will learn how to transfer net profit and drawings to the capital account at the end of a period.

7.1 Purpose of income statements

The main reason why people set up businesses is to make profits. Of course, if the business is not successful, it may well incur losses instead. The calculation of such profits and losses is probably the most important objective of the accounting function. The owners will want to know how the actual profits compare with the profits they had hoped to make. Knowing what profits are being made helps businesses to do many things, including:

- planning ahead
- obtaining loans from banks, from other businesses, or from private individuals
- telling prospective business partners how successful the business is
- telling someone who may be interested in buying the business how successful the business is
- calculating the tax due on the profits so that the correct amount of tax can be paid to the tax authorities.

Chapter 4 dealt with the grouping of revenue and expenses prior to bringing them together to compute profit. In the case of a trader (someone who is mainly concerned with buying and selling goods), the profits are calculated by drawing up an **income statement**.

When it is shown in detail rather than in summary form (as is the case for the published income statements of companies), it contains something called the **trading account**. The trading account is prepared in order to arrive at a figure for **gross profit**.

Below the trading account is shown a summary of another account – the **profit and loss account**. The profit and loss account is prepared so as to arrive at the figure for **net profit**.

It is these two accounts that together comprise the income statement. Both the trading account and the profit and loss account are part of the double entry system. At the end of a financial period, they are closed off. They are then summarised and the information they contain is then copied into an income statement. **Income statements are not part of the double entry system.**

7.2 Gross profit

One of the most important uses of income statements is that of comparing the results obtained with the results expected. In a trading organisation, a lot of attention is paid to how much profit is made, before deducting expenses, for every £1 of sales revenue. As mentioned in Section 7.1, so that this can easily be seen in the profit calculation, the statement in which profit is calculated is split into two sections – one in which the gross profit is found (**this is the trading account section of the statement**), and the next section in which the **net profit** is calculated (**this is the 'profit and loss account' section of the statement**).

Gross profit is the excess of sales revenue over the **cost of goods sold**. Where the cost of goods sold is greater than the sales revenue, the result is a **gross loss**. By taking the figure of sales revenue less the cost of goods sold to generate that sales revenue, it can be seen that the accounting custom is to calculate a trader's profits **only on goods that have been sold.**

Activity 7.1

What does this tell you about the costs and revenues that are included in the calculation of gross profit? (*Hint*: what do you not include in the calculation?)

To summarise:

Gross profit (calculated in the **trading account**)	is the excess of sales revenue over the cost of goods sold in the period.

Activity 7.2

Calculate the gross profit or gross loss of each of the following businesses:

	Cost of goods purchased	*Sales*	*Gross profit/(Gross loss)*
	£	£	£
A	9,820	10,676	________
B	7,530	14,307	________
C	10,500	19,370	________
D	9,580	9,350	________
E	8,760	17,200	________

7.3 Net profit

Net profit, found in the profit and loss account, consists of the gross profit plus any revenue other than that from sales, such as rents received or commissions earned, less the total costs used up during the period other than those already included in the 'cost of goods sold'. Where the costs used up exceed the gross profit plus other revenue, the result is said to be a **net loss**. Thus:

Net profit (calculated in the profit and loss account)	is what is left of the gross profit after all other expenses have been deducted.

Activity 7.3

Using the answer to Activity 7.2, complete the following table:

	Other revenues	*Expenses*	*Net profit/(Net loss)*
	£	£	£
A	–	2,622	________
B	4,280	2,800	________
C	500	2,500	________
D	–	1,780	________
E	3,260	2,440	________

7.4 Information needed

Before drawing up an income statement you should prepare the trial balance. This contains nearly all the information needed. (Later on in this book you will see that certain adjustments have to be made, but we will ignore these at this stage.)

We can now look at the trial balance of B Swift, drawn up as on 31 December 2008 after the completion of his first year in business.

Exhibit 7.1

B Swift Trial balance as at 31 December 2008	Dr	Cr
	£	£
Sales		38,500
Purchases	29,000	
Rent	2,400	
Lighting expenses	1,500	
General expenses	600	
Fixtures and fittings	5,000	
Accounts receivable	6,800	
Accounts payable		9,100
Bank	15,100	
Cash	200	
Drawings	7,000	
Capital		20,000
	67,600	67,600

***Note*: To make this easier to follow, we shall assume that purchases consist of goods that are resold without needing any further work. You'll learn later that these are known as 'finished goods' but, for now, we'll simply refer to them as 'goods'.**

We have already seen that gross profit is calculated as follows:

Sales – Cost of goods sold = Gross profit

It would be easier if all purchases in a period were always sold by the end of the same period. In that case, cost of goods sold would always equal purchases. However, this is not normally the case and so we have to calculate the cost of goods sold as follows:

What we bought in the period:	Purchases
Less Goods bought but not sold in the period:	(Closing inventory)
	= Cost of goods sold

In Swift's case, there are goods unsold at the end of the period. However, there is no record in the accounting books of the value of this unsold inventory. The only way that Swift can find this figure is by checking his inventory at the close of business on 31 December 2008. To do this he would have to make a list of all the unsold goods and then find out their value. The value he would normally place on them would be the cost price of the goods, i.e. what he paid for them. Let's assume that this is £3,000.

The cost of goods sold figure will be:

	£
Purchases	29,000
Less Closing inventory	(3,000)
Cost of goods sold	26,000

Based on the sales revenue of £38,500 the gross profit can be calculated:

Sales – Cost of goods sold = Gross profit
£38,500 – £26,000 = £12,500

We now have the information we need to complete the trading account section of the income statement. Next, we need to close off the sales and purchases accounts at the end of the period so that they start the next period with no balance. To do so, we need to create a trading account (this is *not* the same as the trading part of the income statement, though it does produce the same gross profit figure) and then make the following entries:

(**A**) The balance of the sales account is transferred to the trading account by:

1 Debiting the sales account (thus closing it)
2 Crediting the trading account.

(**B**) The balance of the purchases account is transferred to the trading account by:

1 Debiting the trading account
2 Crediting the purchases account (thus closing it).

(**C**) There is, as yet, no entry for the closing inventory in the double entry accounts. This is achieved as follows:

1 Debit a closing inventory account with the value of the closing inventory.
2 Credit the trading account (thus completing the double entry).

The trading account will look like this:

Trading

2008				£	2008				£
Dec	31	Purchases	(B)	29,000	Dec	31	Sales	(A)	38,500
						31	Closing inventory	(C)	3,000

We now close off the trading account in the normal way. In this case, revenues exceed costs so we describe the balance as 'gross profit'.

Trading

2008				£	2008				£
Dec	31	Purchases	(B)	29,000	Dec	31	Sales	(A)	38,500
	31	Gross profit		12,500		31	Closing inventory	(C)	3,000
				41,500					41,500

Note that the balance shown on the trading account is described as 'gross profit' rather than being described as a balance. Also, note that the balance (i.e. the gross profit) is not brought down to the next period. The other accounts used in these double entries appear as shown below. (Note that there is no detail of the entries prior to the end of the period as all the information we have been given is the closing balances. These closing balances are simply described here as 'balance'.)

Sales

2008			£	2008			£
Dec	31	Trading	38,500	Dec	31	Balance	38,500

Purchases

2008			£	2008			£
Dec	31	Balance	29,000	Dec	31	Trading	29,000

Closing inventory

2008			£	2008			£
Dec	31	Trading	3,000	Dec	31	Balance	3,000

The entry of the closing inventory on the credit side of the trading account is, in effect, a deduction from the purchases on the debit side. As you will see when we look later at the trading account part of the income statement, the closing inventory is shown as a deduction from the purchases and the figure then disclosed is described as 'cost of goods sold'.

It must be remembered that we are concerned here with the very first year of trading when, for obvious reasons, there is no opening inventory. In Chapter 9, we will examine how to account for inventory in the later years of a business.

We can now draw up a profit and loss account (which is an 'account' opened so that the end-of-period double entries can be completed). Double entries are then prepared, firstly transferring the gross profit from the trading account to the credit of the profit and loss account. To do this, you would change the entry in the trading account to read 'Gross profit transferred to profit and loss':

Trading

2008			£	2008			£
Dec	31	Purchases	29,000	Dec	31	Sales	38,500
	31	Gross profit transferred to Profit and loss	12,500		31	Closing inventory	3,000
			41,500				41,500

Then, any revenue account balances, other than sales (which have already been dealt with in the trading account), are transferred to the credit of the profit and loss account. Typical examples are commissions received and rent received. In the case of B Swift, there are no such revenue accounts.

The costs used up in the year, in other words, the expenses of the year, are then transferred to the debit of the profit and loss account. (It may also be thought, quite rightly, that, as the fixtures and fittings have been used during the year with subsequent deterioration of the assets, something should be charged for this use. **This charge is known as 'depreciation'**. The methods for calculating this are left until Chapter 26.)

The profit and loss account will now appear as follows:

Profit and loss

2008			£	2008			£
Dec	31	Rent	2,400	Dec	31	Gross profit transferred from Trading	12,500
	31	Lighting expenses	1,500				
	31	General expenses	600				
	31	Net profit	8,000				
			12,500				12,500

The expense accounts closed off will now appear as:

Rent

2008			£	2008			£
Dec	31	Balance	2,400	Dec	31	Profit and loss	2,400

Lighting expenses

2008			£	2008			£
Dec	31	Balance	1,500	Dec	31	Profit and loss	1,500

General expenses

2008			£	2008			£
Dec	31	Balance	600	Dec	31	Profit and loss	600

You now have all the information you need in order to prepare the income statement for the year ending 31 December 2008. It looks like this:

Exhibit 7.2

B Swift
Income statement for the year ending 31 December 2008

	£	£
Sales		38,500
Less Cost of goods sold:		
Purchases	29,000	
Less Closing inventory	(3,000)	
		(26,000)
Gross profit		12,500
Less Expenses		
Rent	2,400	
Lighting expenses	1,500	
General expenses	600	
		(4,500)
Net profit		8,000

Note: 'Revenue' is often used instead of 'sales' in this statement.

7.5 Effect on the capital account

Although the net profit has been calculated at £8,000 and is shown as a balancing figure on the debit side of the profit and loss account, no credit entry has yet been made to complete the double entry. In other accounts, the credit entry would normally be the 'balance b/d' at the start of the next period. However, as net profit increases the capital of the owner, the credit entry must be made in the capital account by transferring the net profit from the profit and loss account. (You would change the entry in the profit and loss account from 'net profit' to read 'net profit transferred to capital'.)

The trading account and the profit and loss account, and, indeed, all the revenue and expense accounts, can thus be seen to be devices whereby the capital account is saved from being concerned with unnecessary detail. Every sale made at a profit increases the capital of the proprietor, as does each item of revenue, such as rent received. On the other hand, each sale made at a loss, or each item of expense, decreases the capital of the proprietor.

Instead of altering the capital after each transaction, the respective bits of profit and loss, and of revenue and expense, are collected together using suitably described accounts. Then all the balances are brought together in one financial statement, the 'income statement', and the increase in the capital, i.e. the net profit, is determined. Alternatively, in the case of a net loss, the decrease in the capital is ascertained.

The fact that a separate drawings account has been in use can now also be seen to have been in keeping with the policy of avoiding unnecessary detail in the capital account. There will, therefore, only be one figure for drawings entered in the debit side of the capital account – the total of the drawings for the whole of the period.

The capital account, showing these transfers, and the drawings account now closed are as follows:

Capital

2008			£	2008			£
Dec	31	Drawings	7,000	Jan	1	Cash	20,000
	31	Balance c/d	21,000	Dec	31	Net profit	8,000
			28,000				28,000
				2006			
				Jan	1	Balance b/d	21,000

Drawings

2008			£	2008			£
Dec	31	Balance	7,000	Dec	31	Capital	7,000

Bertram Quigley opened a pet shop on 1 January 2008. He invested £10,000 in the business. The following information was obtained from his accounting records at the end of the year: Purchases of goods for resale £7,381; Sales £13,311; Expenses £1,172; Drawings £800; Inventory £410. What is the balance on Bertram Quigley's capital account at 31 December 2008?

7.6 The balances still in our books

It should be noticed that not all the items in the trial balance have been used in the income statement. The remaining balances are assets or liabilities or capital, they are not expenses or revenue. These will be used later when a balance sheet is drawn up. (You'll remember learning in Chapter 1 that assets, liabilities and capital are shown in balance sheets.)

Go back to Chapter 1 to refresh your understanding of assets, liabilities and capital.

Exhibit 7.3 shows the trial balance after the entries to the trading account and the profit and loss account have been made and the income statement prepared. All the accounts that were closed off in that process have been removed, and drawings and net profit have been transferred to the capital account. Notice also that the inventory account, which was not originally in the trial balance, is in the redrafted trial balance, as the item was not created as a balance in the books until the trading account was prepared. We will be using this trial balance when we start to look at balance sheets in the next chapter.

***Note*: As the income statement was prepared using all this information, the trial balance shown in Exhibit 7.3 can also be described as having been prepared following preparation of the income statement.**

Exhibit 7.3

B Swift **Trial balance as at 31 December 2008** (after the trading account and the profit and loss account have been completed and the income statement prepared and the capital account adjusted for net profit and drawings)	*Dr*	*Cr*
	£	£
Fixtures and fittings	5,000	
Accounts receivable	6,800	
Accounts payable		9,100
Inventory	3,000	
Bank	15,100	
Cash	200	
Capital		21,000
	30,100	30,100

Note for students: Now that you have learnt how to prepare a T-account for the trading account and a T-account for the profit and loss account, we will only rarely ask you to prepare them again. You should remember how they are used to calculate gross profit and net profit and the typical entries they may contain. From now on, we will concentrate on producing the financial statement that combines these two accounts: the income statement.

Note also that under UK GAAP (i.e. UK accounting rules) the income statement was called the 'profit and loss account'. This confusing use of the same title for a financial statement and for an account in the ledger caused many problems. However, even though we now use the term 'income statement' for the financial statement you may sometimes see such a statement with the old title, or you may even be asked to prepare a financial statement using that title. If so, remember that it is the same as the one we call an income statement.

Learning outcomes

You should now have learnt:

1 Why income statements are not part of the double entry system.
2 Why profit is calculated.
3 How to calculate cost of goods sold, gross profit and net profit.
4 The double entries required in order to close off the relevant expense and revenue accounts at the end of a period and post the entries to the trading account and to the profit and loss account.
5 How to deal with inventory at the end of a period.
6 How to prepare an income statement from a trial balance.
7 How to transfer the net profit and drawings to the capital account at the end of a period.
8 That balances on accounts not closed off in order to prepare the income statement are carried down to the following period, that these balances represent assets, liabilities and capital, and that they are entered in the balance sheet.

Answers to activities

7.1 You only include the costs that were incurred in creating those goods that were sold. These costs include the cost of buying those goods and any costs incurred in converting goods purchased into the goods that were sold – for example, the costs of converting raw materials into finished goods. The only costs you include are those that relate to the goods sold. The costs relating to goods that have not yet been sold are not included. You do not include other costs of the business, such as postage, motor expenses, office expenses, salaries of managers, and advertising costs. Nor do you include any costs relating to the purchase or use of any assets, such as motor vehicles, computers, machinery, fixtures and fittings, and buildings.

7.2

	Cost of goods purchased	Sales	Gross profit/(Gross loss)
	£	£	£
A	9,820	10,676	856
B	7,530	14,307	6,777
C	10,500	19,370	8,870
D	9,580	9,350	(230)
E	8,760	17,200	8,440

7.3

	Other revenues	Expenses	Net profit/(Net loss)
	£	£	£
A	–	2,622	(1,766)
B	4,280	2,800	8,257
C	500	2,500	6,870
D	–	1,780	(2,010)
E	3,260	2,440	9,260

7.4 £14,368. That is, £10,000 + £13,311 – (£7,381 – £410) – £1,172 – £800.

Review questions

7.1 From the following trial balance of A Moore, extracted after one year's trading, prepare an income statement for the year ending 31 December 2008. A balance sheet is not required.

Trial balance as at 31 December 2008

	Dr	*Cr*
	£	£
Sales		190,576
Purchases	119,832	
Salaries	56,527	
Motor expenses	2,416	
Rent	1,894	
Insurance	372	
General expenses	85	
Premises	95,420	
Motor vehicles	16,594	
Accounts receivable	26,740	
Accounts payable		16,524
Cash at bank	16,519	
Cash in hand	342	
Drawings	8,425	
Capital		138,066
	345,166	345,166

Inventory at 31 December 2008 was £12,408.

(Keep your answer; it will be used later in Review Question 8.1.)

7.2 From the following trial balance of B Lane after his first year's trading, you are required to draw up an income statement for the year ending 30 June 2008. A balance sheet is not required.

Trial balance as at 30 June 2008

	Dr	*Cr*
	£	£
Sales		265,900
Purchases	154,870	
Rent	4,200	
Lighting and heating expenses	530	
Salaries and wages	51,400	
Insurance	2,100	
Buildings	85,000	
Fixtures	1,100	
Accounts receivable	31,300	
Sundry expenses	412	
Accounts payable		15,910
Cash at bank	14,590	
Drawings	30,000	
Vans	16,400	
Motor running expenses	4,110	
Capital		114,202
	396,012	396,012

Inventory at 30 June 2008 was £16,280.

(Keep your answer; it will be used later in Review Question 8.2.)

7.3A From the following trial balance of B Morse drawn up on conclusion of his first year in business, draw up an income statement for the year ending 31 December 2008. A balance sheet is not required.

Trial balance as at 31 December 2008

	Dr	*Cr*
	£	£
General expenses	305	
Business rates	2,400	
Motor expenses	910	
Salaries	39,560	
Insurance	1,240	
Purchases	121,040	
Sales		235,812
Car	4,300	
Accounts payable		11,200
Accounts receivable	21,080	
Premises	53,000	
Cash at bank	2,715	
Cash in hand	325	
Capital		23,263
Drawings	23,400	
	270,275	270,275

Inventory at 31 December 2008 was £14,486.

(Keep your answer; it will be used later in Review Question 8.3A.)

→ **7.4A** Extract an income statement for the year ending 30 June 2008 for G Graham. The trial balance as at 30 June 2008 after his first year of trading was as follows:

	Dr	*Cr*
	£	£
Equipment rental	940	
Insurance	1,804	
Lighting and heating expenses	1,990	
Motor expenses	2,350	
Salaries and wages	48,580	
Sales		382,420
Purchases	245,950	
Sundry expenses	624	
Lorry	19,400	
Accounts payable		23,408
Accounts receivable	44,516	
Fixtures	4,600	
Shop	174,000	
Cash at bank	11,346	
Drawings	44,000	
Capital		194,272
	600,100	600,100

Inventory at 30 June 2008 was £29,304.

(Keep your answer; it will be used later in Review Question 8.4A.)

7.5 Henry York is a sole trader who keeps records of his cash and bank transactions. His transactions for the month of March were as follows:

March

1 Cash in hand £100, Cash at bank £5,672.
4 York received a cheque for £1,246 from W Abbot which was paid directly into the bank. This represented sales.
6 Paid wages in cash £39.
8 Sold goods for cash £152.
10 Received cheque from G Smart for £315, in full settlement of a debt of £344; this was paid directly into the bank.
11 Paid sundry expenses in cash £73.
14 Purchased goods by cheque for £800.
18 Paid J Sanders a cheque of £185 in full settlement of a debt of £201.
23 Withdrew £100 from the bank for office purposes.
24 Paid wages in cash £39.
26 Sold goods for cash £94.
28 Paid salaries by cheque £230.
31 Retained cash amounting to £150 and paid the remainder into the bank.

Required:

(*a*) Enter the above transactions within T-accounts and bring down the balances.

(*b*) Assuming no opening accounts receivable, accounts payable, or inventory, prepare an income statement for the month ended 31 March.

You can find a range of additional self-test questions, as well as material to help you with your studies, on the website that accompanies this book at www.pearsoned.co.uk/wood.

chapter 8

Balance sheets

Learning objectives

After you have studied this chapter, you should be able to:

- explain why balance sheets are not part of the double entry system
- explain why it is important that account balances are shown under appropriate headings in the balance sheet
- explain the meanings of the terms non-current asset, current asset, current liability, and non-current liability
- describe the sequence in which each of the five main categories of items appear in the balance sheet
- describe the sequence in which each non-current asset is entered in the balance sheet
- describe the sequence in which each current asset is entered in the balance sheet
- draw up a balance sheet from information given in a trial balance

Introduction

In this chapter, you'll learn how to present asset, liability and capital balances in a balance sheet and of the importance of adopting a consistent and meaningful layout.

8.1 Contents of the balance sheet

In Chapter 1, you learnt that balance sheets contain details of assets, liabilities and capital. The items and amounts to be entered in the balance sheet are found in the accounting books. As shown in the previous chapter, they comprise those **accounts with balances** that were *not* included in the income statement. All these accounts that continue to have balances must be assets, capital or liabilities.

Why have the accounts entered into the income statement been removed from the trial balance? (*Hint*: it is *not* just because they were entered in that statement.)

8.2 Drawing up a balance sheet

Let's look again at the post-income-statement trial balance of B Swift (from Exhibit 7.3):

Exhibit 8.1

B Swift
Trial balance as at 31 December 2008
(after the trading account and the profit and loss account have been completed and the income statement prepared and the capital account adjusted for net profit and drawings)

	Dr	*Cr*
	£	£
Fixtures and fittings	5,000	
Accounts receivable	6,800	
Accounts payable		9,100
Inventory	3,000	
Bank	15,100	
Cash	200	
Capital		21,000
	30,100	30,100

You'll probably remember seeing examples of balance sheets in Chapter 1. If not, this would be a good time to spend a few minutes reading that chapter again.

Based on what you learnt in Chapter 1, let's now draw up the balance sheet for B Swift as at 31 December 2008.

Exhibit 8.2

B Swift
Balance sheet as at 31 December 2008

	£
Assets	
Fixtures and fittings	5,000
Inventory	3,000
Accounts receivable	6,800
Bank	15,100
Cash	200
Total assets	30,100
Liabilities	
Accounts payable	(9,100)
Net assets	21,000
Capital	21,000

8.3 No double entry in balance sheets

After the way we used the double entry system in the previous chapter to prepare the information we needed in order to draw up the income statement, it should not surprise you to learn that **balance sheets are also not part of the double entry system.**

Activity 8.2 Why do you think it is that the balance sheet is not part of the double entry system?

When we draw up accounts such as a cash account, a rent account, a sales account, a trading account, or a profit and loss account, we are preparing them as part of the double entry system. We make entries on the debit side and the credit side of these accounts.

In drawing up a balance sheet, we do not enter anything in the various accounts. We do not actually transfer the fixtures and fittings balance or the accounts payable balance, or any of the other balances, to the balance sheet.

All we do is to *list* the asset, capital and liabilities balances so as to form a balance sheet. This means that none of these accounts have been closed off. *Nothing is entered in the ledger accounts.*

When the next accounting period starts, these accounts are still open and they all contain balances. As a result of future transactions, entries are then made in these accounts that add to or deduct from these opening balances using double entry.

If you see the word 'account', you will know that what you are looking at is part of the double entry system and will include debit and credit entries. If the word 'account' is not used, it is not part of double entry. For instance, the following items are not 'accounts', and are therefore *not* part of the double entry:

Trial balance:	this is simply a list of the debit and credit balances in the accounts.
Income statement:	this is a lot of revenues and expenditures arranged so as to produce figures for gross profit and net profit for a specific period of time.
Balance sheet:	this is a list of balances arranged according to whether they are assets, capital or liabilities and so depict the financial situation on a specific date.

8.4 Balance sheet layout

Have you ever gone into a shop and found that the goods you were interested in were all mixed up and not laid out in a helpful or consistent way? You can see an example of this in most large shops specialising in selling CDs. They mix up some of their inventory, particularly anything on 'special offer', so that you need to search through everything in order to find what you want. In the process of doing so, the shop hopes that you will come across other things that you will buy that you would otherwise never have thought of. Some of Richard Branson's first Virgin music shops in the early 1970s used this technique and it seems to have developed from there as an effective way to sell music.

Unfortunately, this mix-up presentation technique would be of no benefit to the users of the balance sheet. They would never find anything they didn't set out to find, but they would still have to go through the hassle of sorting through all the information in order to produce a meaningful balance sheet for themselves. Because the balance sheet is intended to be helpful and informative, we take great care in ensuring that it portrays the information it contains in a consistent and meaningful way.

As a result, not only can a user who is only interested in looking at the balance sheet of one organisation find it easy to find information without it, other users who look at lots of different balance sheets, such as bank managers, accountants and investors, find it straightforward making comparisons between different balance sheets.

While the balance sheet layout used in Exhibit 8.2 could be considered useful, it can be improved. Let's look at how we can do this. Firstly, we'll look at how assets could be presented in a more helpful and more meaningful way.

Assets

We are going to show the assets under two headings, non-current assets and current assets.

Non-current assets

Non-current assets are assets that

1 were not bought primarily to be sold; but
2 are to be used in the business; and
3 are expected to be of use to the business for a long time.

Examples: buildings, machinery, motor vehicles, fixtures and fittings.

Non-current assets are listed first in the balance sheet starting with those the business will keep the longest, down to those which will not be kept so long. For instance:

Non-current assets
1 Land and buildings 2 Fixtures and fittings 3 Machinery 4 Motor vehicles

Current assets

Current assets are assets that are likely to change in the short term and certainly within twelve months of the balance sheet date. They include items held for resale at a profit, accounts receivable, cash in the bank, and cash in hand.

These are listed in increasing order of liquidity – that is, starting with the asset furthest away from being turned into cash, and finishing with cash itself. For instance:

Current assets
1 Inventory 2 Accounts receivable 3 Cash at bank 4 Cash in hand

Some students feel that accounts receivable should appear before inventory because, at first sight, inventory would appear to be more easily realisable (i.e. convertible into cash) than accounts receivable. In fact, accounts receivable can normally be more quickly turned into cash – you can often **factor** them by selling the rights to the amounts owed by debtors to a finance company for an agreed amount.

As all retailers would confirm, it is not so easy to quickly turn inventory into cash. Another advantage of using this sequence is that it follows the order in which full realisation of the assets in a business takes place: before there is a sale, there must be an inventory of goods which, when sold on credit, turns into accounts receivable and, when payment is made by the debtors, turns into cash.

Liabilities

There are two categories of liabilities, current liabilities and non-current liabilities.

Current liabilities

Current liabilities are items that have to be paid within a year of the balance sheet date.

Examples: bank overdrafts, accounts payable resulting from the purchase on credit of goods for resale.

Non-current liabilities

Non-current liabilities are items that have to be paid more than a year after the balance sheet date.

Examples: bank loans, loans from other businesses.

8.5 A properly drawn up balance sheet

Exhibit 8.3 shows Exhibit 8.2 drawn up in a more appropriate way. **You should also read the notes following the exhibit.**

Exhibit 8.3

B Swift
Balance sheet as at 31 December 2008

	£	£
Non-current assets		
Fixtures and fittings		5,000
Current assets		
Inventory	3,000	
Accounts receivable	6,800	
Bank	15,100	
Cash	200	
		25,100
Total assets		30,100
Current liabilities		
Accounts payable		(9,100)
Net assets		21,000
Capital		
Cash introduced		20,000
Add Net profit for the year		8,000
		28,000
Less Drawings		(7,000)
		21,000

Notes:

(*a*) There are four categories of entries shown in this balance sheet. In practice, the fifth, non-current liabilities, often appears. It is positioned after the current liabilities; and its total is added to the total of current liabilities to get the figure for total liabilities. Exhibit 8.4 shows where this would be if B Swift had any long-term liabilities.

(*b*) The figure for each item within each category should be shown and a total for the category produced. An example of this is the £25,100 total of current assets. The figures for each asset are listed, and the total is shown below them.

(*c*) The total for non-current assets is added to the total for current assets and the total is labelled 'total assets'.

(*d*) The total for current liabilities is added to the total for non-current liabilities and the total is labelled 'total liabilities'.

(*e*) The total liabilities amount is subtracted from the total assets to get an amount labelled 'net assets'. This amount will be the same as the total capital (which, in company financial statements, is called 'total equity').

(*f*) You do not write the word 'account' after each item.

(*g*) The owners will be most interested in their capital and the reasons why it has changed during the period. To show only the final balance of £21,000 means that the owners will not know how it was calculated. So we show the full details of the capital account.

(*h*) Look at the date on the balance sheet. Now compare it with the dates put on the top of the income statement in the previous chapter. The balance sheet is a position statement – it is shown as being at one point in time, e.g. '*as at* 31 December 2008'. The income statement is different. It is for a period of time, in this case for a whole year, and so it uses the phrase 'for the year ending'.

***Note*: the difference between current assets and total liabilities is known as 'net current assets' or 'working capital' and is the amount of resources the business has in a form that is readily convertible into cash. This figure is not shown in the balance sheet but is easy to produce from a completed balance sheet.**

Exhibit 8.4

B Swift
Balance sheet as at 31 December 2008
(showing the position of non-current liabilities)

	£	£
Non-current assets		
Fixtures and fittings		5,000
Current assets		
Inventory	3,000	
Account receivable	6,800	
Bank	15,100	
Cash	200	
		25,100
Total assets		30,100
Current liabilities		
Accounts payable	9,100	
Non-current liabilities	–	
Total liabilities		(9,100)
Net assets		21,000
Capital		
Cash introduced		20,000
Add Net profit for the year		8,000
		28,000
Less Drawings		(7,000)
Total capital		21,000

Learning outcomes

You should now have learnt:

1 That all balances remaining on a trial balance after the income statement for a period has been drawn up are displayed in a balance sheet dated 'as at' the last day of the period.

2 That the balance sheet is *not* part of double entry.

3 That the balance sheet starts with non-current assets at the top, then current assets, then current liabilities, then non-current liabilities, then capital.

4 The meanings of the terms non-current asset, current asset, current liability, and non-current liability.

5 That you list non-current assets in descending order starting with those that will remain in use in the business for the longest time.

6 That you list current assets from top to bottom in increasing order of liquidity.

7 That current assets less current liabilities are known as 'net current assets' or 'working capital'.

8 Why the figure for net current assets is very important.

Answers to activities

8.1 All these accounts should have been closed off when the trading account and the profit and loss account were completed and the income statement prepared. Only accounts with balances appear in a trial balance.

8.2 A balance sheet is a financial statement that summarises the position at the end of a period. It contains all the balances on the accounts held in the accounting books at that time. As it is prepared after the income statement, all the accounts have already been balanced-off. All we do with the balance sheet is lift the balances carried forward from the accounts and place them in an appropriate position in the statement.

Review questions

8.1 Return to Review Question 7.1 and prepare a balance sheet as at 31 December 2008.

8.2 Return to Review Question 7.2 and prepare a balance sheet as at 30 June 2008.

8.3A Return to Review Question 7.3A and prepare a balance sheet as at 31 December 2008.

8.4A Return to Review Question 7.4A and prepare a balance sheet as at 30 June 2008.

8.5 G. Hope started in business on 1 July 2007, with £40,000 capital in cash. During the first year he kept very few records of his transactions.

The assets and liabilities of the business at 30 June 2008 were:

	£
Freehold premises	76,000
Mortgage on the premises	50,000
Inventory	24,000
Accounts receivable	2,800
Cash and bank balances	5,400
Accounts payable	7,600

→

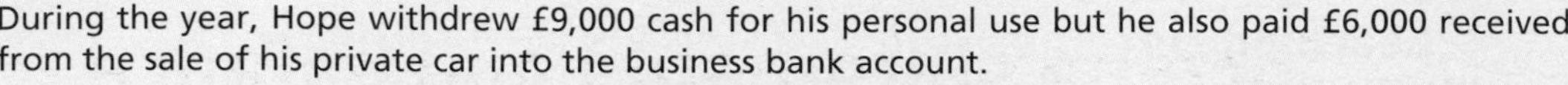

During the year, Hope withdrew £9,000 cash for his personal use but he also paid £6,000 received from the sale of his private car into the business bank account.

Required:
From the above information, prepare a balance sheet showing the financial position of the business at 30 June 2008 and indicating the net profit for the year.

8.6A The following information relates to A Trader's business:

Assets and liabilities at	1 January 2009	31 December 2009
	£	£
Fixtures	18,000	16,200
Account receivable	4,800	5,800
Inventory	24,000	28,000
Accounts payable	8,000	11,000
Cash	760	240
Balance at bank	15,600	4,600
Loan from B Burton	6,000	2,000
Motor vehicle	–	16,000

During the year, Trader had sold private investments for £4,000 which he paid into the business bank account, and he had drawn out £200 weekly for private use.

Required:
Prepare a balance sheet as at 31 December 2009 and give the net profit as at that date.

You can find a range of additional self-test questions, as well as material to help you with your studies, on the website that accompanies this book at www.pearsoned.co.uk/wood.

Chapter 9

Income statements and balance sheets: further considerations

Learning objectives

After you have studied this chapter, you should be able to:

- explain the terms returns inwards, returns outwards, carriage inwards and carriage outwards
- record returns inwards and returns outwards in the income statement
- explain the difference between the treatment of carriage inwards and carriage outwards in the income statement
- explain why carriage inwards is treated as part of the cost of purchasing goods
- explain why carriage outwards is *not* treated as part of the cost of purchasing goods
- prepare an inventory account showing the entries for opening and closing inventory
- prepare an income statement and a balance sheet containing the appropriate adjustments for returns, carriage and other items that affect the calculation of the cost of goods sold
- explain why the costs of putting goods into a saleable condition should be charged to the trading account

Introduction

This chapter contains material that *many* students get wrong in examinations. Take care as you work through it to understand and learn the points as they are presented to you.

In this chapter, you'll learn how to treat goods returned from customers and goods returned to suppliers in the trading account. You'll also learn how to deal with the costs of transporting goods into and out of a business. You will learn how to record inventory in an inventory account and then carry it forward in the account to the next period. You'll also learn how to enter opening inventory in the trading account. You'll learn that there are other costs that must be added to the cost of goods in the trading account. Finally, you'll learn how to prepare an income statement and a balance sheet when any of these items are included in the list of balances at the end of a period.

9.1 Returns inwards and returns outwards

In Chapter 3, the idea of different accounts for different movements of inventory was introduced. There are four accounts involved. The sales account and the **returns inwards account** deal with goods sold and goods returned by customers. The purchases account and the **returns outwards account** deal with goods purchased and goods returned to the supplier respectively. In our first look at the preparation of a trading account in Chapter 7, returns inwards and returns outwards were omitted. This was done deliberately, so that your first sight of income statements would be as straightforward as possible.

Why do you think organisations bother with the two returns accounts? Why don't they just debit sales returned to the sales account and credit purchases returned to the purchases account?

Just as you may have done yourself, a large number of businesses return goods to their suppliers (**returns outwards**) and will have goods returned to them by their customers (**returns inwards**). When the gross profit is calculated, these returns will have to be included in the calculations.

Let us look again at the trial balance shown in Exhibit 7.1:

Exhibit 7.1 (extract)

B Swift Trial balance as at 31 December 2008	*Dr*	*Cr*
	£	£
Sales		38,500
Purchases	29,000	

Now, suppose that in Exhibit 7.1 the trial balance of B Swift, rather than simply containing a sales account balance of £38,500 and a purchases account balance of £29,000 the balances included those for returns inwards and outwards:

Exhibit 9.1

B Swift Trial balance as at 31 December 2008 (extract)	*Dr*	*Cr*
	£	£
Sales		40,000
Purchases	31,200	
Returns inwards	1,500	
Returns outwards		2,200

Comparing these two exhibits reveals that they amount to the same thing as far as gross profit is concerned. Sales were £38,500 in the original example because returns inwards had already been deducted in arriving at the amount shown in Exhibit 7.1. In the amended version, returns inwards should be shown separately in the trial balance and then deducted on the face of the income statement to get the correct figure for goods sold to customers and *kept* by them, i.e. £40,000 – £1,500 = £38,500. Purchases were originally shown as being £29,000. In the new version, returns outwards should be deducted to get the correct figure of purchases *kept* by Swift. Both the returns accounts are included in the calculation of gross profit, which now becomes:

(Sales *less* Returns inwards) – (Cost of goods sold *less* Returns outwards) = Gross profit

The gross profit is therefore unaffected and is the same as in Chapter 7: £12,500.

The trading account section of the income statement will appear as in Exhibit 9.2:

Exhibit 9.2

B Swift
Trading account section of the income statement for the year ending 31 December 2008

	£	£
Sales		40,000
Less Returns inwards		(1,500)
		38,500
Less Cost of goods sold:		
Purchases	31,200	
Less Returns outwards	(2,200)	
	29,000	
Less Closing Inventory	(3,000)	
		(26,000)
Gross profit		12,500

9.2 Carriage

If you have ever purchased anything by telephone, by letter or over the Internet, you have probably been charged for 'postage and packing'. When goods are delivered by suppliers or sent to customers, the cost of transporting the goods is often an additional charge to the buyer. In accounting, this charge is called 'carriage'. When it is charged for delivery of goods purchased, it is called **carriage inwards.** Carriage charged on goods sent out by a business to its customers is called **carriage outwards.**

When goods are purchased, the cost of carriage inwards may either be included as a hidden part of the purchase price, or be charged separately. For example, suppose your business was buying exactly the same goods from two suppliers. One supplier might sell them for £100 and not charge anything for carriage. Another supplier might sell the goods for £95, but you would have to pay £5 to a courier for carriage inwards, i.e. a total cost of £100. In both cases, the same goods cost you the same total amount. It would not be appropriate to leave out the cost of carriage inwards from the 'cheaper' supplier in the calculation of gross profit, as the real cost to you having the goods available for resale is £100.

As a result, in order to ensure that the true cost of buying goods for resale is *always* included in the calculation of gross profit, carriage inwards **is *always* added to the cost of purchases in the trading account.**

Carriage outwards is not part of the selling price of goods. Customers could come and collect the goods themselves, in which case there would be no carriage outwards expense for the seller to pay or to recharge customers. **Carriage outwards is *always* entered in the profit and loss account section of the income statement. It is *never* included in the calculation of gross profit.**

Suppose that in the illustration shown in this chapter, the goods had been bought for the same total figure of £31,200 but, in fact, £29,200 was the figure for purchases and £2,000 for carriage inwards. The trial balance extract would appear as in Exhibit 9.3.

Exhibit 9.3

B Swift
Trial balance as at 31 December 2008 (extract)

	Dr	*Cr*
	£	£
Sales		40,000
Purchases	29,200	
Returns inwards	1,500	
Returns outwards		2,200
Carriage inwards	2,000	

The trading account section of the income statement would then be as shown in Exhibit 9.4:

Exhibit 9.4

B Swift
Trading account section of the income statement for the year ending 31 December 2008

	£	£
Sales		40,000
Less Returns inwards		(1,500)
		38,500
Less Cost of goods sold:		
Purchases	29,200	
Less Returns outwards	(2,200)	
	27,000	
Carriage inwards	2,000	
	29,000	
Less Closing inventory	(3,000)	
		(26,000)
Gross profit		12,500

It can be seen that the three versions of B Swift's trial balance have all been concerned with the same overall amount of goods bought and sold by the business, at the same overall prices. Therefore, in each case, the same gross profit of £12,500 has been found.

Before you proceed further, attempt Review Questions 9.1 and 9.2A.

9.3 The second year of a business

At the end of his second year of trading, on 31 December 2009, B Swift draws up another trial balance.

Exhibit 9.5

B Swift
Trial balance as at 31 December 2009

	Dr	*Cr*
	£	£
Sales		67,000
Purchases	42,600	
Lighting and heating expenses	1,900	
Rent	2,400	
Wages: shop assistant	5,200	
General expenses	700	
Carriage outwards	1,100	
Buildings	20,000	
Fixtures and fittings	7,500	
Accounts receivable	12,000	
Accounts payable		9,000
Bank	1,200	
Cash	400	
Drawings	9,000	
Capital		31,000
Inventory (at 31 December 2008)	3,000	
	107,000	107,000

Adjustments needed for stock

So far, we have been looking at new businesses only. When a business starts, it has no inventory brought forward. B Swift started in business in 2008. Therefore, when we were preparing Swift's income statement for 2008, there was only closing inventory to worry about.

When we prepare the income statement for the second year we can see the difference. If you look back to the income statement in Exhibit 9.4, you can see that there was closing inventory of £3,000. This is, therefore, the opening inventory figure for 2009 that we will need to incorporate in the trading account. It is also the figure for inventory that you can see in the trial balance at 31 December 2009.

The closing inventory for one period is *always* brought forward as the opening inventory for the next period.

Swift checked his inventory at 31 December 2009 and valued it at that date at £5,500.

We can summarise the opening and closing inventory account positions for Swift over the two years as follows:

Trading account for period →	**Year to 31 December 2008**	**Year to 31 December 2009**
Opening inventory 1.1.2008	None	
Closing inventory 31.12.2008	£3,000	
Opening inventory 1.1.2009		£3,000
Closing inventory 31.12.2009		£5,500

Inventory account

Before going any further, let's look at the inventory account for both years:

Inventory

			£				£
2008				2008			
Dec	31	Trading	3,000	Dec	31	Balance c/d	3,000
2009				2009			
Jan	1	Balance b/d	3,000	Dec	31	Trading	3,000
Dec	31	Trading	5,500		31	Balance c/d	5,500
			8,500				8,500

You can see that in 2009 there is both a debit and a credit double entry made at the end of the period to the trading account. First, the inventory account is credited with the opening inventory amount of £3,000 and the trading account is debited with the same amount. Then, the inventory account is debited with the closing inventory amount of £5,500 and the trading account is credited with the same amount.

Thus, while the first year of trading only includes one inventory figure in the trading account, for the second year of trading both opening and closing inventory figures will be in the calculations.

Let's now calculate the cost of goods sold for 2009:

	£
Inventory of goods at start of year	3,000
Add Purchases	42,600
Total goods available for sale	45,600
Less What remains at the end of the year (i.e. closing inventory)	(5,500)
Therefore the cost of goods that have been sold is	40,100

We can look at a diagram to illustrate this:

Exhibit 9.6

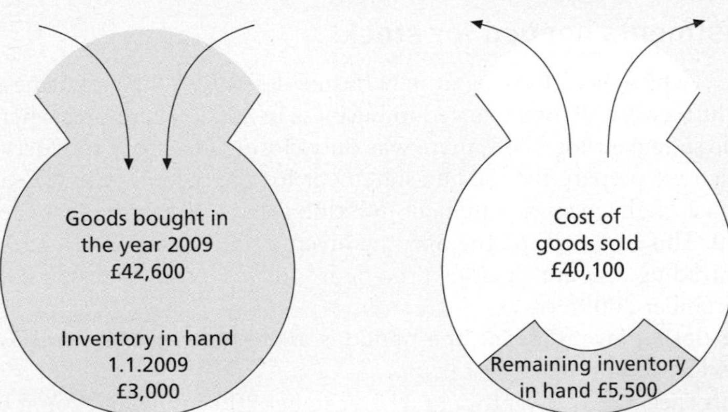

You can see that the left-hand container in the exhibit contains all the inventory available to be sold during the year. In the right-hand container, the closing inventory at the end of the year is now lying at the bottom and the empty space above it must, therefore, represent the inventory that has been sold.

The calculation of gross profit can now be done. You know from the trial balance that sales were £67,000 and from the calculation above that the cost of goods sold was £40,100. Gross profit is, therefore, £26,900.

Now the income statement and the balance sheet can be drawn up, as shown in Exhibits 9.7 and 9.8:

Exhibit 9.7

B Swift
Income statement for the year ending 31 December 2009

	£	£
Sales		67,000
Less Cost of goods sold:		
Opening inventory	3,000	
Add Purchases	42,600	
	45,600	
Less Closing inventory	(5,500)	
		(40,100)
Gross profit		26,900
Less Expenses:		
Wages	5,200	
Lighting and heating expenses	1,900	
Rent	2,400	
General expenses	700	
Carriage outwards	1,100	
		(11,300)
Net profit		15,600

Exhibit 9.8

B Swift
Balance sheet as at 31 December 2009

	£	£
Non-current assets		
Buildings		20,000
Fixtures and fittings		7,500
		27,500
Current assets		
Inventory	5,500	
Accounts receivable	12,000	
Bank	1,200	
Cash	400	
		19,100
Total assets		46,600
Current liabilities		
Accounts payable		(9,000)
Net assets		37,600
Capital		
Balance at 1 January 2009		31,000
Add Net profit for the year		15,600
		46,600
Less Drawings		(9,000)
Total capital		37,600

Financial statements

Financial statements is the term given to all the summary statements that accountants produce at the end of accounting periods. They are often called **'final accounts'**, but this term is quite misleading (as none of the financial statements are 'accounts' in the accounting sense). Nevertheless, some do still refer to them as the 'final accounts' or simply as **the accounts** of a business. You will, therefore, need to be aware of these terms, just in case you read something that uses these terms, or your teacher or lecturer, or an examiner, uses them at some time.

Other expenses in the trading account

You already know that carriage inwards is added to the cost of purchases in the trading account. You also need to add to the cost of goods in the trading account any costs incurred in converting purchases into goods for resale. In the case of a trader, it is very unusual for any additional costs to be incurred getting the goods ready for sale.

What costs do you think a trader may incur that would need to be added to the cost of the goods in the trading account?

For goods imported from abroad it is usual to find that the costs of import duty and insurance are treated as part of the cost of the goods, along with any costs incurred in repackaging the goods. Any such additional costs incurred in getting goods ready for sale are debited to the trading account.

Note: Students often find it difficult to remember how to treat returns and carriage when preparing the income statement. You need to be sure to learn and remember that all returns, inwards and outwards, and carriage inwards appear in the calculation of gross profit. Carriage outwards appears as an expense in the profit and loss account section of the income statement.

9.4 A warning

Students lose a lot of marks on the topics covered in this chapter because they assume that the topics are easy and unlikely to be things that they will forget. Unfortunately, they are fairly easy to understand, and that is why they are easily forgotten and confused. You would be wise to make sure that you have understood and learnt everything presented to you in this chapter before you go any further in the book.

9.5 Review questions: the best approach

Before you attempt the review questions at the end of this chapter, you should read the section on review questions in the Notes for Students (pp. xv–xxiv).

Learning outcomes

You should now have learnt:

1. That returns *inwards* should be deducted from sales in the *trading* account.
2. That returns *outwards* should be deducted from purchases in the *trading* account.
3. That carriage *inwards* is shown as an expense item in the *trading* account.
4. That carriage *outwards* is shown as an expense in the *profit and loss* account.
5. How to prepare the inventory account and carry forward the balance from one period to the next.
6. That in the second and later years of a business, both opening and closing inventory are brought into the trading account.
7. That it is normal practice to show cost of goods sold as a separate figure in the trading account.
8. How to prepare an income statement that includes the adjustments for carriage inwards and both opening and closing inventory in the trading section and carriage outwards as an expense in the profit and loss section.
9. That expense items concerned with getting goods into a saleable condition are charged in the trading account.
10. That where there is import duty or insurance charged on goods purchased, these costs are treated as part of the cost of goods sold.

Answers to activities

9.1 Organisations want to know how much they sold as a separate item from how much of those goods sold were returned. The same goes for purchases and the goods sent back to the supplier. It is useful to know what proportion of goods sold are returned and whether there is any pattern in which customers are returning them. On the purchases side, knowing how many times goods have been returned and the proportion of purchases from individual suppliers that are being returned helps with monitoring the quality of the goods being purchased. While this information could be gathered if returns accounts were not used, it would be a more complicated task obtaining it. Most of all, however, the sales account is a revenue account. Entering returns inwards amounts in the sales account is contrary to the nature of the sales account. The same holds for returns outwards and the purchases account, which is an expense account.

9.2 In the case of a trader, it is very unusual for any additional costs to be incurred getting the goods ready for sale. However, a trader who sells clocks packed in boxes might buy the clocks from one supplier, and the boxes from another. Both of these items would be charged in the trading account as purchases. In addition, if someone was paid to pack the clocks into the boxes, then the wages paid for that to be done would also be charged in the trading account as part of the cost of those goods. Be careful not to confuse this with the wages of shop assistants who sell the clocks. Those wages *must* be charged in the profit and loss account because they are selling costs rather than extra costs incurred getting the goods ready for sale. The wages of the person packing the clocks would be the only wages in this case that were incurred while 'putting the goods into a saleable condition'.

Review questions

9.1 From the following information, draw up the trading account section of the income statement of J Bell for the year ending 31 December 2007, which was his first year in business:

	£
Carriage inwards	980
Returns outwards	840
Returns inwards	1,290
Sales	162,918
Purchases	121,437
Inventory of goods: 31 December 2007	11,320

9.2A The following information is available for the year ending 31 March 2008. Draw up the trading account section of the income statement of P Frank for that year.

	£
Inventory: 31 March 2008	52,400
Returns inwards	16,220
Returns outwards	19,480
Purchases	394,170
Carriage inwards	2,490
Sales	469,320

9.3 From the following trial balance of G Still, draw up an income statement for the year ending 30 September 2009, and a balance sheet as at that date.

	Dr	*Cr*
	£	£
Inventory: 1 October 2008	41,600	
Carriage outwards	2,100	
Carriage inwards	3,700	
Returns inwards	1,540	
Returns outwards		3,410
Purchases	188,430	
Sales		380,400
Salaries and wages	61,400	
Warehouse rent	3,700	
Insurance	1,356	
Motor expenses	1,910	
Office expenses	412	
Lighting and heating expenses	894	
General expenses	245	
Premises	92,000	
Motor vehicles	13,400	
Fixtures and fittings	1,900	
Accounts receivable	42,560	
Accounts payable		31,600
Cash at bank	5,106	
Drawings	22,000	
Capital		68,843
	484,253	484,253

Inventory at 30 September 2009 was £44,780.

...tracted from the books of F Sorley on 30 April 2007. From ...e his income statement for the year ending 30 April 2007,

	Dr	Cr
	£	£
		210,420
	108,680	
	9,410	
	1,115	
	840	
	4,900	
		3,720
	41,800	
	912	
	6,800	
	318	
	14,400	
	912	
	23,200	
		14,100
	4,100	
	240	
	29,440	
		18,827
	247,067	247,067

...of T Owen as at 31 March 2009. Draw up a set of financial ...2009.

	Dr	Cr
	£	£
	52,800	
		276,400
	141,300	
	1,350	
	5,840	
		2,408
	63,400	
	3,800	
	714	
	1,930	
	1,830	
	208	
Buildings	125,000	
Accounts receivable	45,900	
Accounts payable		24,870
Fixtures	1,106	
Cash at bank	31,420	
Cash in hand	276	
Drawings	37,320	
Capital		210,516
	514,194	514,194

Inventory at 31 March 2009 was £58,440.

→

9.6A F Brown drew up the following trial balance as at 30 September 2008. You are to draft the income statement for the year ending 30 September 2008 and a balance sheet as at that date.

	Dr	*Cr*
	£	£
Capital		49,675
Drawings	28,600	
Cash at bank	4,420	
Cash in hand	112	
Accounts receivable	38,100	
Accounts payable		26,300
Inventory: 30 September 2007	72,410	
Van	5,650	
Office equipment	7,470	
Sales		391,400
Purchases	254,810	
Returns inwards	2,110	
Carriage inwards	760	
Returns outwards		1,240
Carriage outwards	2,850	
Motor expenses	1,490	
Rent	8,200	
Telephone charges	680	
Wages and salaries	39,600	
Insurance	745	
Office expenses	392	
Sundry expenses	216	
	468,615	468,615

Inventory at 30 September 2008 was £89,404.

9.7 Enter the following transactions in the ledger of A Baker and prepare a trial balance at 31 May, together with a calculation of the profit for the month and a balance sheet at 31 May.

May	1	Started in business with £1,500 in the bank and £500 cash.
	2	Purchased goods to the value of £1,750 from C Dunn, agreeing credit terms of 60 days.
	3	Bought fixtures and fittings for the bakery for £150, paying by cheque.
	6	Bought goods on credit from E Farnham for £115.
	10	Paid rent of £300 paying cash.
	12	Bought stationery – cash book and invoices – for £75 – paying by cash.
	14	Sold goods on credit, value £125, to G Harlem.
	20	Bought an old van for deliveries for £2,000 on credit from I Jumpstart.
	30	Paid wages of £450 net for the month by cheque.
	31	Summarised cash sales for the month and found them to be £2,500. Took a cheque for £500 as own wages for the month. Banked £2,000 out of the cash sales over the month.
	31	Closing inventory was £500.

9.8A Ms Porter's business position at 1 July was as follows:

	£
Inventory	5,000
Equipment	3,700
Creditor (OK Ltd)	500
Debtor (AB Ltd)	300
Bank balance	1,200

During July, she:

	£
Sold goods for cash – paid to bank	3,200
Sold goods to AB Limited	600
Bought goods from OK Ltd on credit	3,900
Paid OK Ltd by cheque	3,000
Paid general expenses by cheque	500
AB Ltd paid by cheque	300

Inventory at 31 July was £6,200

Required:

(*a*) Open ledger accounts (including capital) at 1 July
(*b*) Record all transactions
(*c*) Prepare a trial balance
(*d*) Prepare an income statement for the period
(*e*) Prepare a balance sheet as at 31 July

9.9 From the following trial balance of Kingfire, extracted after one year of operations, prepare an income statement for the year ending 30 June 2008, together with a balance sheet as at that date.

	£	£
Sales		35,800
Purchases	14,525	
Salaries	2,325	
Motor expenses	9,300	
Rent and business rates	1,250	
Insurances – building	750	
– vehicles	1,200	
Motor vehicles	10,000	
Fixtures	17,500	
Cash in hand	500	
Cash at bank		1,250
Drawings	12,000	
Long-term loan		15,000
Capital		19,275
Accounts receivable	11,725	
Accounts payable		9,750
	81,075	81,075

Inventory on 30 June 2008 was £3,000.

You can find a range of additional self-test questions, as well as material to help you with your studies, on the website that accompanies this book at www.pearsoned.co.uk/wood.

chapter 10

Accounting concepts and assumptions

Learning objectives

After you have studied this chapter, you should be able to:

- describe the assumptions which are made when recording accounting data
- explain why one set of financial statements has to serve many purposes
- explain the implications of objectivity and subjectivity in the context of accounting
- explain what accounting standards are and why they exist
- explain the underlying concepts of accounting
- explain how the concepts and assumptions of materiality, going concern, comparability through consistency, prudence, accruals, separate determination, substance over form and other concepts and assumptions affect the recording and adjustment of accounting data and the reporting of accounting information

Introduction

What you have been reading about so far has been concerned with the recording of transactions in the books and the subsequent preparation of trial balances, income statements, and balance sheets. Such recording has been based on certain assumptions. Quite deliberately, these assumptions were not discussed in detail at the time. This is because it is much easier to look at them with a greater understanding *after* basic double entry has been covered. These assumptions are known as the *concepts of accounting*.

The income statements and balance sheets shown in the previous chapters were drawn up for the owner of the business. As shown later in the book, businesses are often owned by more than just one person and these accounting statements are for the use of all the owners.

If the financial statements were solely for the use of the owner(s), there would be no need to adopt a common framework for the preparation and presentation of the information contained within them. However, as you learnt at the start of this book, there are a lot of other people who may be interested in seeing these financial statements, and they need to be able to understand them. It is for this reason that there has to be a commonly established practice concerning how the information in the financial statements is prepared and presented.

In this chapter, you will learn about some of the agreed practices that underpin the preparation of accounting information, and about some of the regulations that have been developed to ensure that they are adhered to.

10.1 Objective of financial statements

Financial statements should provide information about the financial position, performance and changes in the financial position of an entity that is useful to a wide range of users in making economic decisions. In order to achieve this objective, financial statements are prepared on the basis of a number of established concepts and assumptions and must adhere to the rules and procedures set down in accounting standards.

10.2 One set of financial statements for all purposes

If it had always been the custom to draft different financial statements for different purposes, so that one version was given to a banker, another to someone wishing to buy the business, etc., then accounting would be very different from what it is today. However, this has not occurred. Identical copies of the financial statements are given to all the different external stakeholders, irrespective of why they wish to look at them.

This means that the banker, the prospective buyer of the business, shareholders, etc. all see the same income statement and balance sheet. This is not an ideal situation as the interests of each party are different and each party seeks different kinds of information from those wanted by the others. For instance, bank managers would really like to know how much the assets would sell for if the business ceased trading. They could then see what the possibility would be of the bank obtaining repayment of its loan or the overdraft. Other people would also like to see the information in the way that is most useful to them.

Activity 10.1

This doesn't sound very ideal for anyone, does it? What benefits do you think there may be that outweigh these disadvantages of one set of financial statements for all?

Because everyone receives the same income statement and balance sheet, in order to be of any use, all the various stakeholders have to believe that the assumptions upon which these financial statements are based are valid and appropriate. If they don't, they won't trust the financial statements.

Assume that you are in a class of students and that you have the problem of valuing your assets, which consist of four textbooks. The first value you decide is based upon how much you could sell them for. Your own guess is £60, but the other members of your class suggest they should be valued at anything from £30 to £80.

Suppose that you now decide to put a value on their use to you. You may well think that the use of these textbooks will enable you to pass your examinations and that you'll then be able to get a good job. Another person may have the opposite idea concerning the use of the textbooks. The use value placed on the textbooks by others in the class will be quite different. Your value may be higher than those of some of your colleagues and lower than others.

Finally, you decide to value them by reference to cost. You take out the receipts you were given when you purchased the textbooks, which show that you paid a total of £120 for them. If the rest of the class does not think that you have altered the receipts, then they will all agree with you that the value of the books, expressed at original cost, is £120. At last, you have found a way of valuing the textbooks where everyone agrees on the same figure. As this is the only valuation that you can all agree upon, each of you decides to use the idea of valuing the asset of textbooks at their cost price so that you can have a meaningful discussion about what you are worth (in terms of your assets, i.e. your textbooks) compared with everyone else in the class. It probably won't come as a surprise to you to learn that this is precisely the basis upon which the assets of a business are valued. Accountants call it the **historical cost concept**.

10.3 Objectivity and subjectivity

The use of a method which arrives at a value that everyone can agree to *because it is based upon a factual occurrence* is said to be **objective**. Valuing your textbooks at their cost is, therefore, objective – you are adhering to and accepting the facts. You are not placing your own interpretation on the facts. As a result, everyone else knows where the value came from and can see that there is very good evidence to support its adoption.

If, instead of being objective, you were **subjective**, you would use your own judgement to arrive at a cost. This often results in the value you arrive at being biased towards your own views and preferences – as in the example above when the usefulness of the textbooks to you for examinations was the basis of their valuation. Subjective valuations seem right to the person who makes them, but many other people would probably disagree with the value arrived at, because it won't appear to them to be objectively based.

The desire to provide the same set of financial statements for many different parties, and so provide a basis for measurement that is generally acceptable, means that objectivity is sought in financial accounting. If you are able to understand this desire for objectivity, then many of the apparent contradictions in accounting can be understood, because objectivity is at the heart of the financial accounting methods we all use.

Financial accounting, therefore, seeks objectivity and it seeks consistency in how information is prepared and presented. To achieve this, there must be a set of rules which lay down the way in which the transactions of the business are recorded. These rules have long been known as 'accounting concepts'. A group of these have become known as 'fundamental accounting concepts' or 'accounting principles' and have been enforced through their incorporation in accounting standards issued on behalf of the accountancy bodies by accounting standards boards, and by their inclusion in the relevant legislation governing companies.

10.4 Accounting Standards and Financial Reporting Standards in the UK

At one time, there used to be quite wide differences in the ways that accountants calculated profits. In the late 1960s a number of cases led to a widespread outcry against this lack of uniformity in accounting practice.

In response, the UK accounting bodies formed the Accounting Standards Committee (ASC). It issued a series of accounting standards, called *Statements of Standard Accounting Practice* (SSAPs). The ASC was replaced in 1990 by the Accounting Standards Board (ASB), which also issued accounting standards, this time called *Financial Reporting Standards* (FRSs). Both forms of accounting standards are compulsory, enforced by company law.

By the end of 2007, 27 FRSs and seven SSAPs were in force. From time to time, the ASB also issues *Urgent Issue Task Force Abstracts* (UITFs). These are generally intended to be in force only while a standard is being prepared or an existing standard amended to cover the topic dealt with in the UITF. Of course, some issues do not merit a full standard and so 2 of the 45 UITFs issued to date are still in force. UITFs carry the same weight as accounting standards and their application is compulsory for financial statements prepared under UK GAAP.

SSAPs and FRSs were generally developed with the larger company in mind. In an effort to make adherence to standards more manageable for smaller companies, in 1997 the ASB issued a third category of standard – the *Financial Reporting Standard for Smaller Entities* (FRSSE). It is, in effect, a collection of some of the rules from virtually all the other accounting standards. Small entities could choose whether to apply it or continue to apply all the other accounting standards.

The authority, scope and application of each document issued by the ASB is announced when the document is issued. Thus, even though each accounting standard and UITF must be applied by anyone preparing financial statements under UK GAAP, in some cases certain classes of organisations are exempted from applying some or all of the rules contained within them. You can find out more about the work of the ASB and the standards and UITFs currently in issue at its website (**www.frc.org.uk/asb/technical/standards/accounting.cfm**).

The use of accounting standards does not mean that two identical businesses will show exactly the same revenue, expenditure and profits year by year in their financial statements. It does, however, considerably reduce the possibilities of very large variations in financial reporting.

In 2005, most companies whose shares were quoted on the stock exchange were required to switch to International Accounting Standards and other companies could do so if they wished.

10.5 International Accounting Standards

The Accounting Standards Board deals with the United Kingdom and Ireland. Besides this and other national accounting boards, there is an international organisation concerned with accounting standards. The International Accounting Standards Committee (IASC) was established in 1973 and changed its name to the International Accounting Standards Board (IASB) in 2000.

The need for an IASB has been said to be mainly due to:

(*a*) The considerable growth in international investment. This means that it is desirable to have similar accounting methods the world over so that investment decisions are more compatible.
(*b*) The growth in the number of multinational organisations. These organisations have to produce financial statements covering a large number of countries. Standardisation between countries makes the accounting work that much easier, and reduces costs.
(*c*) As quite a few countries now have their own standard-setting bodies, it is desirable that their efforts should be harmonised.
(*d*) The need for accounting standards in countries that cannot afford a standard-setting body of their own.

The work of the IASB is overseen by 22 trustees, six from Europe, six from the USA, and six from Asia/Pacific. The remaining four can be from anywhere so long as geographical balance is retained. The IASB has 12 full-time members and two part-time members. Its members must reflect an appropriate balance of auditors, financial statement preparers, users of financial statements and academics.

The IASC issued International Accounting Standards (IASs) and the IASB issues International Financial Reporting Standards (IFRSs). When the IASC was founded, it had no formal authority and IASs were entirely voluntary and initially intended for use in countries that either did not have their own accounting standards or would have had considerable logistical difficulty in establishing and maintaining the infrastructure necessary to sustain a national accounting standards board.

Up until 2005, SSAPs and FRSs had precedence over IASs in the UK. All this has changed. From 2005, it is mandatory for all listed companies within the European Union preparing consolidated financial statements (i.e. the financial statements of a group of companies of which they are the overall parent company) to publish them in accordance with IASs and IFRSs.

This means that there is now a dual set of standards in force in the UK, some of which apply to a small number of large companies (IASs and IFRSs), and the rest (SSAPs and FRSs) which apply to all other entities. (Companies that prefer to apply International GAAP may also do so.) While the ASB has been at pains to ensure that most of the provisions of the relevant IASs are incorporated in existing SSAPs or FRSs and each FRS indicates the level of compliance with the relevant IAS, there do remain some differences between the two sets of standards. This textbook describes and discusses the contents of International Accounting Standards, and the terminology used throughout the book is that typically used under those standards.

10.6 Accounting standards and the legal framework

Accounting standards are given legal status under the Companies Acts and comply with European Union Directives. This ensures that there is no conflict between the law and accounting standards. Anyone preparing financial statements which are intended to show a 'true and fair view' (i.e. truly reflect what has occurred and the financial position of the organisation) must observe the rules laid down in the accounting standards.

10.7 Underlying accounting concepts

A number of accounting concepts have been applied ever since financial statements were first produced for external reporting purposes. These have become second nature to accountants and are not generally reinforced, other than through custom and practice.

The historical cost concept

The need for this has already been described in the textbook valuation example. It means that assets are normally shown at cost price, and that this is the basis for valuation of the assets.

The money measurement concept

Accounting information has traditionally been concerned only with those facts covered by (*a*) and (*b*) which follow:

(*a*) it can be measured in monetary units, and
(*b*) most people will agree to the monetary value of the transaction.

This limitation is referred to as the **money measurement concept**, and it means that accounting can never tell you everything about a business. For example, accounting does not show the following:

(*c*) whether the business has good or bad managers,
(*d*) whether there are serious problems with the workforce,
(*e*) whether a rival product is about to take away many of the best customers,
(*f*) whether the government is about to pass a law which will cost the business a lot of extra expense in future.

The reason that (*c*) to (*f*) or similar items are not recorded is that it would be impossible to work out a monetary value for them which most people would agree to.

Some people think that accounting and financial statements tell you everything you want to know about a business. The above shows that this is not the case.

The business entity concept

The **business entity concept** implies that the affairs of a business are to be treated as being quite separate from the non-business activities of its owner(s).

The items recorded in the books of the business are, therefore, restricted to the transactions of the business. No matter what activities the proprietor(s) get up to outside the business, they are completely disregarded in the books kept by the business.

The only time that the personal resources of the proprietor(s) affect the accounting records of a business is when they introduce new capital into the business, or take drawings out of it.

The dual aspect concept

This states that there are two aspects of accounting, one represented by the assets of the business and the other by the claims against them. The concept states that these two aspects are always equal to each other. In other words, this is the alternate form of the accounting equation:

Assets = Capital + Liabilities

As you know, double entry is the name given to the method of recording transactions under the **dual aspect concept**.

The time interval concept

One of the underlying principles of accounting, the **time interval concept**, is that financial statements are prepared at regular intervals of one year. Companies which publish further financial statements between their annual ones describe the others as 'interim statements'. For internal management purposes, financial statements may be prepared far more frequently, possibly on a monthly basis or even more often.

10.8 Underlying assumptions

The IASB framework lists two assumptions that must be applied if financial statements are to meet their objectives: the **accrual basis** (also called the **accruals concept**) and the **going concern concept**.

Accrual basis

The effects of transactions and other events are recognised when they occur and they are recorded in the books and reported in the financial statements of the period to which they relate.

Net profit is the difference between revenues and the expenses incurred in generating those revenues, i.e.

Revenues – Expenses = Net Profit

Determining the expenses used up to obtain the revenues is referred to as *matching* expenses against revenues. The key to the application of the concept is that all income and charges relating to the financial period to which the financial statements relate should be taken into account without regard to the date of receipt or payment.

This concept is particularly misunderstood by people who have not studied accounting. To many of them, actual payment of an item in a period is taken as being matched against the revenue of the period when the net profit is calculated. The fact that expenses consist of the assets used up in a particular period in obtaining the revenues of that period, and that cash paid in a period and expenses of a period are usually different, as you will see later, comes as a surprise to a great number of them.

Going concern

It is assumed that the business will continue to operate for at least twelve months after the end of the reporting period.

Suppose, however, that a business is drawing up its financial statements at 31 December 2008. Normally, using the historical cost concept, the assets would be shown at a total value of

£100,000. It is known, however, that the business will be forced to close down in February 2009, only two months later, and the assets are expected to be sold for only £15,000.

In this case it would not make sense to keep to the going concern concept, and so we can reject the historical cost concept for asset valuation purposes. In the balance sheet at 31 December 2008 the assets will therefore be shown at the figure of £15,000. Rejection of the going concern concept is the exception rather than the rule.

Examples where the going concern assumption should be rejected are:

- if the business is going to close down in the near future;
- where shortage of cash makes it almost certain that the business will have to cease trading;
- where a large part of the business will almost certainly have to be closed down because of a shortage of cash.

10.9 Qualitative characteristics of financial statements

These are the attributes that make the information provided in financial statements useful to users. There are four principal qualitative characteristics: understandability, relevance, reliability and comparability.

Understandability

Information in financial statements should be readily understandable by users.

Relevance

Information in financial statements must be relevant to the decision-making needs of users. To be relevant, information must influence the economic decisions of users by helping them evaluate past, present or future events or confirming, or correcting, their past evaluation.

Materiality

Information is **material** if its omission or misstatement could influence the economic decisions of users. Materiality depends on the size of the item or error judged in the particular circumstances of its omission or misstatement.

Everything that appears in a financial accounting statement should be 'material'. That is, it should be of interest to the stakeholders, those people who make use of financial accounting statements. It need not be material to every stakeholder, but it must be material to a stakeholder before it merits inclusion.

Accounting does not serve a useful purpose if the effort of recording a transaction in a certain way is not worthwhile. Thus, if a box of paper-clips was bought it would be used up over a period of time, and this cost is used up every time someone uses a paper-clip. It is possible to record this as an expense every time a paper-clip is used but, obviously, the price of a paper-clip is so small that it is not worth recording it in this fashion, nor is the entire box of paper-clips. The paper-clips are not a material item and, therefore, the box would be charged as an expense in the period when it was bought, irrespective of the fact that it could last for more than one accounting period. In other words, **do not waste your time in the elaborate recording of trivial items.**

Similarly, the purchase of a cheap metal ashtray would also be charged as an expense in the period when it was bought because it is not a material item, even though it may in fact last for twenty years. A lorry would, however, be deemed to be a material item in most businesses, and so, as will be seen in Chapter 26, an attempt is made to charge each period with the cost consumed in each period of its use.

Which fundamental accounting concept is what is being described in the previous paragraph an example of?

Businesses fix all sorts of arbitrary rules to determine what is material and what is not. There is no law that lays down what these should be – the decision as to what is material and what is not is dependent upon judgement. A business may well decide that all items under £100 should be treated as expenses in the period in which they were bought, even though they may well be in use in the business for the following ten years. Another business, especially a large one, may fix the limit at £1,000. Different limits may be set for different types of item.

It can be seen that the size and the type of business will affect the decisions as to which items are material. With individuals, an amount of £1,000 may well be more than you, as a student, possess. For a multi-millionaire, what is a material item and what is not will almost certainly not be comparable. Just as individuals vary, then, so do businesses. Some businesses have a great deal of machinery and may well treat all items of machinery costing less than £1,000 as not being material, whereas another business which makes about the same amount of profit, but has very little machinery, may well treat a £600 machine as being a material item as they have fixed their materiality limit at £250.

Reliability

To be useful, information must also be reliable. To be reliable, information must be free from material error and bias and able to be depended upon by users to represent faithfully what it claims to represent.

Faithful representation

A balance sheet should represent faithfully the transactions and other events that result in assets, liabilities and equity of the entity at the reporting date.

Substance over form

Transactions and other events must be accounted for and presented in accordance with their substance and economic reality and not merely their legal form. This is referred to as **substance over form.**

The legal form of a transaction can differ from its real substance. Where this happens, accounting should show the transaction in accordance with its real substance which is, basically, how the transaction affects the economic situation of the business. This means that accounting in this instance will not reflect the exact legal position concerning that transaction.

You have not yet come across the best and easiest illustration of this concept. Later in your studies you may have to learn about accounting for fixed assets being bought on hire purchase. We will take a car as an example.

- From a legal point of view, the car does not belong to the business until all the hire purchase instalments have been paid, and an option has been taken up whereby the business takes over legal possession of the car.
- From an economic point of view, you have used the car for business purposes, just as any other car owned by the business which was paid for immediately has been used. In this case, the business will show the car being bought on hire purchase in its ledger accounts and balance sheet as though it were legally owned by the business, but also showing separately the amount still owed for it.

In this way, therefore, the substance of the transaction has taken precedence over the legal form of the transaction.

Neutrality

Information in financial statements must be free of bias.

Prudence

This is the inclusion of a degree of caution in the exercise of the judgement needed in making the estimates required under conditions of uncertainty (e.g. decisions relating to bad debts and allowances for doubtful debts), such that assets and income are not overstated and liabilities and expenses are not understated.

Very often accountants have to use their judgement to decide which figure to take for an item. Suppose a debt has been owing for quite a long time, and no one knows whether it will ever be paid. Should the accountant be optimistic and think that it will be paid, or be more pessimistic?

It is the accountant's duty to see that people get the proper facts about a business. The accountant should make certain that assets are not valued too highly. Similarly, liabilities should not be shown at values that are too low. Otherwise, people might inadvisedly lend money to a business, which they would not do if they had been provided with the proper facts.

The accountant should always exercise caution when dealing with uncertainty while, at the same time, ensuring that the financial statements are neutral – that gains and losses are neither overstated nor understated – and this is known as **prudence**.

It is true that, in applying the prudence concept, an accountant will normally make sure that all losses are recorded in the books, but that profits and gains will not be anticipated by recording them before they should be recorded. Although it emphasises neutrality, many people feel that the prudence concept means that accountants will normally take the figure relating to unrealised profits and gains which will understate rather than overstate the profit for a period. That is, they believe that accountants tend to choose figures that will cause the capital of the business to be shown at a lower amount rather than at a higher amount.

Do you agree with this view that the prudence concept results in accountants producing financial statements that understate profits and gains and therefore present a value for capital that is lower than it should be? Justify your answer.

The recognition of profits at an appropriate time has long been recognised as being in need of guidelines and these have long been enshrined in what is known as the **realisation concept**. This is not so much a separate concept as a part of the broader concept of prudence.

The realisation concept holds to the view that profit and gains can only be taken into account when realisation has occurred and that realisation occurs only when the ultimate cash realised is capable of being assessed (i.e. determined) with reasonable certainty. Several criteria have to be observed before realisation can occur:

- goods or services are provided for the buyer;
- the buyer accepts liability to pay for the goods or services;
- the monetary value of the goods or services has been established;
- the buyer will be in a situation to be able to pay for the goods or services.

Notice that it is not the time

- when the order is received; or
- when the customer pays for the goods.

However, **it is only when you can be reasonably certain as to how much will be received that you can recognise profits or gains.**

Of course, recognising profits and gains now that will only be 100 per cent known in future periods is unlikely to ever mean that the correct amount has been recognised. Misjudgements can arise when, for example, profit is recognised in one period, and later it is discovered that this was incorrect because the goods involved have been returned in a later period because of some deficiency. Also, where services are involved rather than goods, the services might turn out to be subject to an allowance being given in a later period owing to poor performance.

What do you think the accountant should do about these possibilities when applying the realisation concept?

The accountant needs to take every possibility into account yet, at the same time, **the prudence concept requires that the financial statements are 'neutral', that is, that neither gains nor losses should be overstated or understated.**

As you will see if you take your studies to a more advanced stage, there are times other than on completion of a sale when profit may be recognised. These could include profits on long-term contracts spanning several years, such as the building of a hotel or a very large bridge. In this case, profit might be calculated for each year of the contract, even though the work is not finished at that date.

Completeness

To be reliable, information in financial statements must be complete within the bounds of materiality and cost.

Comparability

Comparability requires **consistency**. The measurement and display of the financial effect of similar transactions and other events must be done in a consistent way throughout an entity and over time for that entity, and in a consistent way for different entities. Users must be informed of the accounting policies used in the preparation of the financial statements. They must be informed of any changes in those policies and of the effects of such changes. Financial statements must include corresponding information for the preceding periods.

10.10 Constraints on relevant and reliable information

Timeliness

Information must be reported in a timely manner.

Balance between benefit and cost

The benefits of information should exceed the costs of obtaining it.

Balance between qualitative characteristics

The aim should be to achieve a balance among the characteristics that best meets the objective of financial statements – see Section 10.1.

10.11 Other assumptions

Separate determination

In determining the aggregate amount of each asset or liability, the amount of each individual asset or liability should be determined separately from all other assets and liabilities. This is called **separate determination**. For example, if you have three machines, the amount at which machinery is shown in the balance sheet should be the sum of the values calculated individually for each of the three machines. Only when individual values have been derived should a total be calculated.

Stability of currency

Accounting follows the historical cost concept, so assets are normally shown at their original cost. This has the effect of distorting the financial statements if inflation has caused the value of money to change over time – assets purchased twenty years ago for £50,000 would cost considerably more today, yet they would appear at that cost, not at the equivalent cost today. Users of financial statements need to be aware of this. There are techniques for eliminating these distortions, and they are covered in *Business Accounting 2*.

10.12 Accounting concepts and assumptions in action

This is too early a stage in your studies for you to be able to appreciate more fully how these concepts and assumptions work in practice. It is far better left towards the end of this book and, therefore, we consider this topic further in Chapter 47.

Learning outcomes

You should now have learnt:

1 Why one set of financial statements has to serve many purposes.

2 Why the need for general agreement has given rise to the concepts and conventions that govern accounting.

3 The implications of objectivity and subjectivity in the context of accounting.

4 What accounting standards are and why they exist.

5 The assumptions which are made when recording accounting data.

6 The underlying concepts of accounting.

7 How the concepts and assumptions of materiality, going concern, comparability through consistency, prudence, accruals, separate determination, substance over form, and other concepts and assumptions affect the recording and adjustment of accounting data and the reporting of accounting information.

8 That an assumption is made that monetary measures remain stable, i.e. that accounts are not normally adjusted for inflation or deflation.

Answers to activities

10.1 Although this is hardly ideal, at least everyone receives the same basic financial information concerning an organisation and, because all financial statements are prepared in the same way, comparison between them is reasonably straightforward. Also, some of the users of these financial statements have other sources of information, financial and otherwise, about a business – the banker, for example, will also have access to the financial statements produced for use by the managers of the business. These 'management accounts' are considerably more detailed than the financial statements and most bankers insist upon access to them when large sums of money are involved. (The financial statements produced for internal use are dealt with in Chapter 45.) The banker will also have information about other businesses in the same industry and about the state of the market in which the business operates, and will thus be able to compare the performance of the business against that of its competitors.

10.2 The accruals concept.

10.3 Although accountants do include all the losses that have been identified in the financial statements, they also include all the gains that can be identified with reasonable certainty. In effect, by doing so, an accountant is being neutral and so, in practice, the amount of capital shown in the balance sheet should be a true reflection of the position as known when the financial statements were produced.

10.4 When applying the realisation concept, the accountant will endeavour to estimate as accurately as possible the returns or allowances that are reasonably likely to arise and will build that information into the calculation of the profit and gains to be recognised in the period for which financial statements are being prepared.

Review questions

10.1 What is meant by the 'money measurement concept'?

10.2 Explain the concept of prudence in relation to the recognition of profits and losses.

10.3 Explain the term 'materiality' as it is used in accounting.

10.4 'The historical cost convention looks backwards but the going concern convention looks forwards.'

Required:

(*a*) Explain clearly what is meant by:
  (*i*) the historical cost convention;
  (*ii*) the going concern convention.

(*b*) Does traditional financial accounting, using the historical cost convention, make the going concern convention unnecessary? Explain your answer fully.

(*c*) Which do you think a shareholder is likely to find more useful – a report on the past or an estimate of the future? Why?

(*Association of Chartered Certified Accountants*)

You can find a range of additional self-test questions, as well as material to help you with your studies, on the website that accompanies this book at www.pearsoned.co.uk/wood.

part 3

BOOKS OF ORIGINAL ENTRY

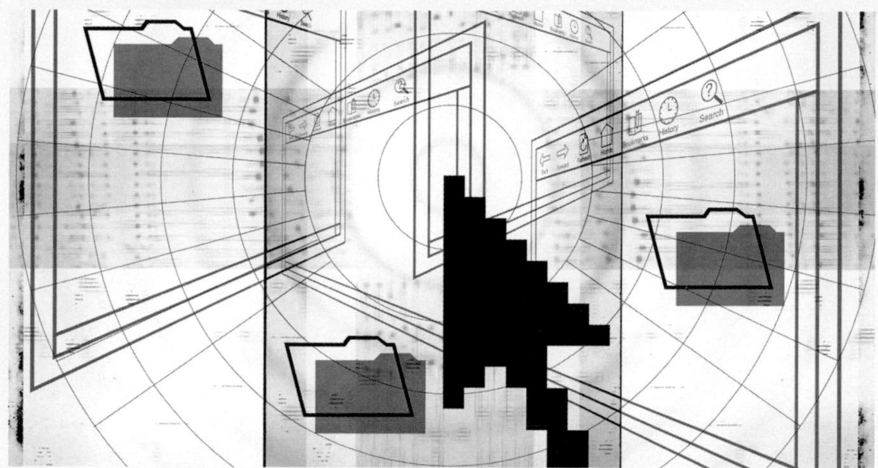

Introduction

This part is concerned with the books into which transactions are first entered; it also includes chapters on VAT, the banking system in the UK, employees' pay, computers and computerised accounting systems.

chapter 11

Books of original entry and ledgers

Learning objectives

After you have studied this chapter, you should be able to:

- justify the need for books of original entry
- explain what each book of original entry is used for
- describe the process of recording transactions in a book of original entry and then recording a summary of the transactions involving similar items in a ledger
- distinguish between personal and impersonal accounts
- list the ledgers most commonly used and distinguish between those that are used for personal accounts and those that are used for impersonal accounts
- explain the broader role of an accountant, the communicator role that lies beyond the recording and processing of data about transactions

Introduction

In this chapter, you will learn about the books in which details of accounting transactions are recorded. You will learn that Day Books and Journals are used to record all transactions made on credit and that the Cash Book is used to record all cash and bank transactions. Then, you will learn that these entries are transferred from the books of original entry to a set of books called Ledgers and that each Ledger is for a particular type of item and that, by having a set of Ledgers, entries in accounts of items of a similar nature are recorded in the same place.

11.1 The growth of the business

When a business is very small, all the double entry accounts can be kept in one book, which we would call a 'ledger'. As the business grows it would be impossible just to use one book, as the large number of pages needed for a lot of transactions would mean that the book would be too big to handle. Also, suppose we have several bookkeepers. They could not all do their work properly if there were only one ledger.

The answer to this problem is for us to use more books. When we do this, we put similar types of transactions together and have a book for each type. In each book, we will not mix together transactions which are different from one another.

11.2 Books of original entry

When a transaction takes place, we need to record as much as possible of the details of the transaction. For example, if we sold four computers on credit to a Mr De Souza for £1,000 per computer, we would want to record that we sold four computers for £1,000 each to Mr De Souza on credit. We would also want to record the address and contact information of Mr De Souza and the date of the transaction. Some businesses would also record information like the identity of the person who sold them to Mr De Souza and the time of the sale.

Books of original entry are the books in which we first record transactions, such as the sale of the four computers. We have a separate book for each kind of transaction.

Thus, the nature of the transaction affects which book it is entered into. Sales will be entered in one book, purchases in another book, cash in another book, and so on. We enter transactions in these books, recording

- the date on which each transaction took place – the transactions should be shown in date order – and
- details relating to the sale (as listed in the computer example above), which are entered in a 'details' column.

Also,

- a folio column entry is made cross-referencing back to the original 'source document', e.g. the invoice, and
- the monetary amounts are entered in columns included in the books of original entry for that purpose.

11.3 Types of books of original entry

Books of original entry are known as either 'journals' or '**day books**'. However, in the case of the last book of original entry shown below, it is always a 'journal' and the second last is always known as the 'cash book'. The term 'day book' is, perhaps, more commonly used, as it more clearly indicates the nature of these books of original entry – entries are made to them every day. The commonly used books of original entry are:

- **Sales day book** (or *Sales journal*) – for credit sales.
- **Purchases day book** (or *Purchases journal*) – for credit purchases.
- **Returns inwards day book** (or *Returns inwards journal*) – for returns inwards.
- **Returns outwards day book** (or *Returns outwards journal*) – for returns outwards.
- **Cash book** – for receipts and payments of cash and cheques.
- General journal (or **journal** if the term 'day book' is used for the other books of original entry) – for other items.

Most students find it less confusing if 'day book' is used rather than 'journal', as it makes it very clear what is meant when someone refers to 'the journal'. **During the remainder of this book, we will use the term 'day book'. However, never forget that the term 'journal' can always be substituted for the term 'day book'. Be sure to remember this. Examiners may use either term.**

11.4 Using more than one ledger

Entries are made in the books of original entry. The entries are then summarised and the summary information is entered, using double entry, to accounts kept in the various ledgers of the business. One reason why a set of ledgers is used rather than just one big ledger is that this makes it easier to divide the work of recording all the entries between different bookkeepers.

Why else do you think we have more than one ledger?

11.5 Types of ledgers

The different types of ledgers most businesses use are:

- **Sales ledger**. This is for customers' personal accounts.
- **Purchases ledger**. This is for suppliers' personal accounts.
- **General ledger**. This contains the remaining double entry accounts, such as those relating to expenses, non-current assets, and capital.

11.6 A diagram of the books commonly used

All business transactions

Classify – put same types of transactions together

Credit sales	Credit purchases	Returns inwards	Returns outwards	Cash receipts and payments	Other types
Enter in Sales Day Book	Enter in Purchases Day Book	Enter in Returns Inwards Day Book	Enter in Returns Outwards Day Book	Enter in Cash Book	Enter in Journal

Enter in double entry accounts in the various ledgers
- Sales Ledger
- Purchases Ledger
- General Ledger

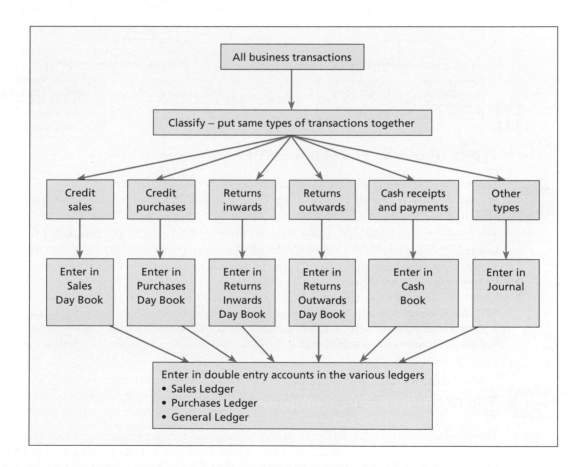

11.7 Description of books used

In the next few chapters we will look at the books used in more detail.

11.8 Types of accounts

Some people describe all accounts as personal accounts or as impersonal accounts.

- **Personal accounts** – these are for debtors and creditors (i.e. customers and suppliers).
- **Impersonal accounts** – divided between 'real' accounts and 'nominal' accounts:
  - **Real accounts** – accounts in which possessions are recorded. Examples are buildings, machinery, fixtures and inventory.
  - **Nominal accounts** – accounts in which expenses, income and capital are recorded.

A diagram may enable you to follow this better:

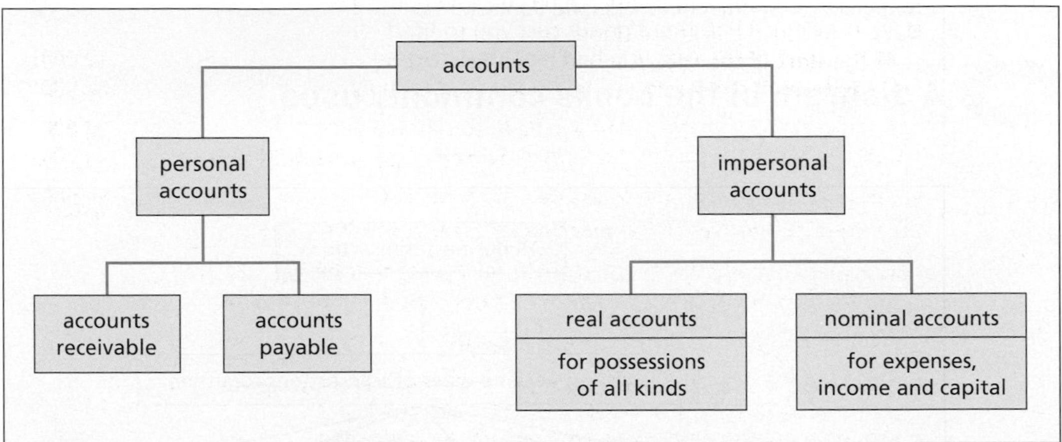

11.9 Nominal and private ledgers

The ledger in which the impersonal accounts are kept is known as the **Nominal** (or 'General') **Ledger**. In order to ensure privacy for the proprietor(s), the capital, drawings and other similar accounts are sometimes kept in a **Private Ledger**. This prevents office staff from seeing details of items which the proprietors want to keep secret.

Why bother with *books of original entry*? Why don't we just enter transactions straight into the ledgers?

11.10 The accountant as a communicator

The impression is often given that all that an accountant does is produce figures arranged in various ways. This has led to a perception that accountants are boring, pragmatic people with no sense of humour. While it is true that such work does take up quite a lot of an accountant's time, it does not account for all of a typical accountant's work. **Accountants also need to be good communicators**, not just in the way they present accounting information on paper, but also in how they verbally communicate the significance of the information they prepare.

An accountant can obviously arrange the financial figures so as to present the information in as meaningful a way as possible for the people who are going to use that information. That is, after all, what accountants are trained to do. If the financial figures are to be given to several people, all of whom are very knowledgeable about accounting, an accountant will simply apply all the conventions and regulations of accounting in order to present the information in the 'normal' accounting way, knowing full well that the recipients of the information will understand it.

On the other hand, accounting figures may well be needed by people who have absolutely no knowledge at all of accounting. In such a case, a typical accounting statement would be of little or no use to them. They would not understand it. In this case, an accountant might set out the figures in a completely different way to try to make it easy for them to grasp. For instance, instead of preparing a 'normal' income statement, the accountant might show the information as follows:

	£	£
In the year ended 31 December 2009 you sold goods for		100,000
Now, how much had those goods cost you to buy?		
At the start of the year you had inventory costing	12,000	
+ You bought some more goods in the year costing	56,000	
So altogether you had goods available to sell that cost	68,000	
– At the end of the year, you had inventory of goods unsold that cost	(6,000)	
So, the goods you had sold in the year had cost you	62,000	
Let us deduct this from what you had sold the goods for		(62,000)
This means that you had made a profit on buying and selling goods, before any other expenses had been paid, amounting to		38,000
(We call this type of profit the ***gross*** **profit**)		
But, during the year, you suffered other expenses such as wages, rent and electricity. The amount of these expenses, not including anything you took for yourself, amounted to		(18,000)
So, in this year your sales value exceeded all the costs involved in running the business (so that the sales could be made) by		20,000
(We call this type of profit the ***net*** **profit**)		

An accountant is failing to perform his or her role appropriately and effectively if the figures are not arranged so as to make them meaningful to the recipient. The accountant's job is not just to produce figures for the accountant's own consumption, it is to communicate the results to other people, many of whom know nothing about accounting.

Reconcile this observation with the standardisation of the presentation of financial accounting information as contained in accounting standards and the Companies Acts.

Nowadays, communication skills are a very important part of the accountant's role. Very often, the accountant will have to talk to people in order to explain the figures, or send a letter or write a report about them. The accountant will also have to talk or write to people to find out exactly what sort of accounting information is needed by them, or to explain to them what sort of information could be provided.

If accounting examinations contained only computational questions, they would not test the ability of candidates to communicate in any way other than writing down accounting figures and, as a result, the examinations would fail to examine these other important aspects of the job.

In recent years much more attention has been paid by examining boards to these other aspects of an accountant's work.

Learning outcomes

You should now have learnt:

1 That transactions are classified and details about them are entered in the appropriate book of original entry.

2 That the books of original entry are used as a basis for posting the transactions in summary form to the double entry accounts in the various ledgers.

3 That there is a set of books of original entry, each of which serves a specific purpose.

4 That there is a set of ledgers, each of which serves a specific purpose.

5 That accountants need to be good communicators.

Answers to activities

11.1 The most important reason is to aid analysis by keeping similar items together.

11.2 Books of original entry contain all the important information relating to a transaction. Ledgers just contain a summary. In fact, some of the entries in the ledgers are often just one-line entries covering an entire month of transactions.

11.3 There really is no conflict so far as financial information prepared for internal use is concerned. Financial statements produced for consumption by users outside the business do have to conform to the conventions relating to content and layout. However, those prepared for internal use do not. There is no reason why they could not be prepared along the lines of the unconventionally laid-out income statement shown on page 125. External stakeholders will never receive their financial statements in this highly user-friendly form. It is simply too much work to customise the financial statement for every class of stakeholder.

You can find a range of additional self-test questions, as well as material to help you with your studies, on the website that accompanies this book at www.pearsoned.co.uk/wood.

hapter 12

The banking system in the UK

Learning objectives

After you have studied this chapter, you should be able to:

- describe the changes that have occurred in the UK since the late 1960s in the ways payments can be made
- describe the many alternatives to cheques and cash that currently exist
- describe the cheque clearing system
- write a cheque
- explain the effect of various kinds of crossings on cheques
- explain how to endorse a cheque over to someone else
- complete bank pay-in slips
- explain the timing differences between entries in a cash book and those on a bank statement

Introduction

In this chapter, you'll learn about the current UK system for payment of money out of and into bank accounts. You'll learn about the range of plastic cards in use and about various alternatives to cheques that have arisen since the 1960s. You will also learn about the cheque clearing system and how to prepare cheques and bank pay-in slips.

12.1 Twenty-first-century banking

Until quite recently, if individuals wanted money out of their bank accounts, they had to go to their local branch and use a cheque to withdraw the amount they needed. Now they can go into their bank, hand over their **debit card** and withdraw money from their account. Alternatively, they can use virtually any cash machine to do the same thing.

This alternative to cheques first started in 1967 when Barclays Bank introduced the first 'automatic teller machines' (ATMs) or 'cash machines'. These early ATMs gave cash in exchange for tokens. In the early 1970s, **plastic cards** were introduced with magnetic strips that enabled the ATMs to read the account details and process transactions directly with the accounts held in the bank. This marked the start of the plastic card revolution in banking and transaction payment.

By the mid 1970s a number of banks had ATMs in the wall outside major branches where cash could be withdrawn using a **Personal Identification Number** or 'PIN'.

At that time, ATMs offered a very limited service – some, for example, only allowed you to withdraw £10, no matter how much you had in your bank account.

Why do you think they only offered a limited service at that time?

Gradually, cash machines became more common and by the mid 1980s the facilities they offered began to include the options to print a mini statement, provide a receipt, and vary the amount you wished to withdraw. However, you could only use the machines at some of the branches of your own bank.

ATM facilities now are very much better than thirty years ago. In addition to allowing withdrawal of funds and informing customers of the balance on their accounts, some ATMs also allow customers to order cheque books, change their PIN, request statements, pay bills, deposit funds and order mini statements; and most ATMs allow access to funds '24/7', i.e. 24 hours a day, 7 days a week. And, for some time, many banks and building societies have allowed their customers access to their accounts via cash machines owned by other institutions, principally through the Link network (**www.link.co.uk**), of which thirty-eight UK financial institutions and thirteen non-financial institutions are members.

It is hardly surprising that nearly half of all personal cash withdrawals from bank accounts are now done through an ATM and that over 75 per cent of all cash in circulation comes from an ATM. In fact, over 35 million people make an average of six withdrawals, each of an average of £66, from one of the UK's 61,000 ATMs each month. In a move towards widening accessibility, over a quarter of ATMs are *not* located at banks, but in places such as shopping centres, supermarkets, railway stations and airports where obtaining money quickly is important.

Outside the UK, customers of many UK banks can continue to use their plastic cards in ATMs through the Visa 'Plus' and Mastercard 'Cirrus' network.

Cash is still the most popular method of making payments, but use of debit and credit cards is growing. **Direct debits** are the most popular form of non-cash payment and debit cards are the most popular form of payment by plastic card. The situation is changing significantly, as can be seen by the way it changed between 2002 and 2005, shown in Exhibit 12.1:

Exhibit 12.1

Payment transactions by medium in 2005	Number (billion)	% change on 2002
Debit card purchases	4.08	36.4
Credit and charge card purchases	1.92	14.0
Store cards (estimate)	0.08	(41.7)
Plastic card withdrawals at ATMs and branch counters	2.81	19.9
Direct debits, standing orders, direct credits and CHAPS	5.38	36.8
Cheques	1.93	(19.3)
Total non-cash (plastic card, automated and paper)	***16.21***	***20.2***
Cash payments (estimate)	23.97	(10.0)
Post Office order book payments and passbook withdrawals	0.26	(62.6)
TOTAL	40.43	(0.9)

How many different forms of plastic cards do you think there are? Think about this for a minute and then list as many forms of plastic card as you can. (Note: this is *not* a question about how many different credit cards there are. It is about different forms of plastic cards, of which a credit card is but one example.)

Now let's look in more detail at some of the features of the UK banking and payments system.

12.2 Debit cards

Debit cards were first introduced into the UK in 1967. The most basic debit cards have an ATM facility. However, many also serve as cheque guarantee cards and as **Switch** cards. Switch is a debit card system that is rapidly replacing cheques as a way to pay for in-store purchases. It allows holders to pay for purchases and, in some shops, withdraw cash at the checkout till. Similarly to cheques, the money spent is automatically withdrawn from the shopper's bank account within three days. More than half the adults in the UK use a debit card. The use of these cards increased by over 500 per cent between 1993 (660 million transactions) and 2005 (4.08 billion transactions).

12.3 Direct debits

Direct debits are the most popular form of non-cash payment and their use was forecast to double by the end of the decade. They were introduced as a paper-based system in 1967. The scheme is managed by BACS Limited, the UK's automated clearing house. They enable payments to be made automatically into a bank account for whatever amount the recipient requests. (This differs from another similar payment medium, the **standing order**, which pays only an amount agreed by the payer.)

12.4 Internet banking

Increasingly, people are making non-cash payments by using credit cards on the Internet. Individuals can also operate their bank accounts in this way, with most banks now offering a 24/7 facility to check account balances, set up standing orders, view direct debits, pay bills and transfer funds between current accounts and savings accounts. In 2006, 42 per cent of 28 million UK adults who used the Internet accessed their current accounts in this way.

12.5 Clearing

Clearing involves the transmission and settlement of cheque payments between accounts held at different banks and different branches of the same bank. Clearing generally takes three working days:

Day 1 Cheques are processed by the bank into which they were paid. Information about each cheque is then sent electronically through a secure data exchange network (the Inter Bank Data Exchange) to the clearing centre of the bank on which the cheque is drawn.

Day 2 Each cheque is physically delivered to an Exchange Centre, where each bank collects all the cheques drawn on accounts held with it.

Day 3 Bank staff review the cheques presented for payment and decide whether to authorise payment; and the banks pay each other the net value of the cheques transferred between them.

APACS

The Association for Payment Clearing Services was set up in 1985. It is the umbrella body for the UK payments industry and it oversees the major UK payment clearing systems and maintains their operational efficiency and financial integrity.

Cheque and Credit Clearing Company

The Cheque and Credit Clearing Company is responsible for the bulk clearing of cheques and paper credits throughout Great Britain. Cheque and credit payments in Northern Ireland are processed locally.

Members of the Cheque and Credit Clearing Company, under the umbrella of APACS, are individually responsible for processing cheques drawn by or credited to the accounts of their customers. In addition, several hundred other institutions, such as smaller building societies, provide cheque facilities for their customers and obtain indirect access to the cheque clearing mechanisms by means of commercially negotiated agency arrangements with one of the full members of APACS.

You can find further information about many of the topics so far covered in this chapter at the APACS website (www.apacs.org.uk) and at the National Statistics website (www.statistics.gov.uk).

Let's look now at the types of bank account typically in use and at how cheque payments are made.

12.6 Types of account

There are two main types of bank account: current accounts and deposit accounts.

Current accounts

Current accounts may be used for regular payments into and out of a bank account. A **cheque book** will be given by the bank to the holder of the account. The cheque book will be used by the account holder to make payments out of the current account.

So that the account holder can pay money into his/her current account, the holder may also be given a pay-in book.

Holders of current accounts are usually also given a multiple use plastic card incorporating a cheque guarantee card, debit card and ATM card.

Many years ago, banks discovered that customers normally don't change banks once they have opened accounts. Their initial response in the 1970s was to encourage students to do so by offering free gifts, such as loose-leaf folders and note pads. Things have moved on a lot and they now offer reduced facility current accounts to children, young adults and students, often with free gifts such as toys, personal organisers, calculators, discount vouchers to be used in retail stores, and even cash.

Current accounts often earn little or no interest. To gain more interest on funds deposited in a bank, it is necessary to also open a **deposit account**.

Deposit accounts

These accounts generally earn more interest than current accounts and are intended for funds that will not be accessed on a frequent or regular basis. However, this is now changing with many banks linking current accounts to deposit accounts (also known as 'savings accounts') so that funds can be transferred from one to the other whenever it is appropriate. Some banks operate this automatically but most leave it to the account holder to notify the bank, often by telephone, that a transfer should be made between the accounts.

12.7 Cheques

Use of cheques peaked in 1990, since when debit cards and direct debits have swiftly established themselves as favourite alternatives among private individuals. Nevertheless, they remain the most common form of payment used by businesses.

Activity 12.3 Why do you think businesses still prefer to use cheques?

The cheque system

1 When the bank has agreed to let someone open a current account it obtains a copy of the new customer's signature. This allows the bank to verify that cheques used are, in fact, signed by the customer. The bank then normally issues the new customer with a cheque book. (Note: some current accounts only offer a debit card and customers have to request a cheque book in addition if they intend writing cheques.)
2 The cheques can then be used to make payments out of the account. Account holders need to ensure that they do not make out a cheque for more than they have in their account – post-dating cheques (i.e. putting a future date on them when sufficient funds will be available) is not permitted and banks will not process such cheques. If a customer wishes to pay out more money than is available they should contact the bank first and request an **overdraft**. The bank is not obliged to grant an overdraft, though many grant all their customers a minimal one – perhaps £100 – when they open the current account that they can use if they wish. (Businesses often have very large overdrafts as this is a cheaper way of financing short-term borrowing than taking out a formal **bank loan**.)
3 The person filling in the cheque and using it for payment is known as the **drawer**. The person to whom the cheque is paid is known as the **payee**.

Activity 12.4 Why do you think an overdraft is cheaper than a bank loan?

The features of a cheque

Exhibit 12.2 shows a blank cheque before it is filled in.

On the face of the cheque are various sets of numbers. These are:

914234 Every cheque printed for the Cheshire Bank for your account will be given a different number, so that individual items can be traced.

09-07-99 Each branch of every bank in the United Kingdom has a different number given to it. Thus this branch has a 'code' number 09-07-99.

058899 Each account with the bank is given a different number. This particular number is kept only for the account of J Woodstock at the Stockport branch.

Exhibit 12.2

Counterfoil	Cheque
______ 20__	09-07-99
	Cheshire Bank Ltd. ______ 20__
PAYEE ______	Stockport Branch
	324 Low Road, Stockport, Cheshire SK6 8AP
	PAY ______ OR ORDER
	______ £
	J. WOODSTOCK
£	
914234	**914234 09-07-99′: 058899**

This part is the counterfoil

If a cheque has a counterfoil attached, it can be filled in at the same time as the cheque, showing the information that was entered on the cheque. The counterfoil is then kept as a note of what was paid, to whom, and when. (Many cheque books don't have counterfoils. Instead they contain separate pages where the details can be entered.)

We can now look at the completion of a cheque. Let's assume that we are paying seventy-two pounds and eighty-five pence to K Marsh on 22 May 2007. Exhibit 12.3 shows the completed cheque.

Exhibit 12.3

Counterfoil	Cheque
22 May 20 *07*	09-07-99
	Cheshire Bank Ltd. *22 May* 20 *07*
PAYEE	Stockport Branch
K. Marsh	324 Low Road, Stockport, Cheshire SK6 8AP
	PAY *K. Marsh* OR ORDER
	Seventy-two pounds 85p £ *72.85*
	J. WOODSTOCK
£ *72.85*	*J. Woodstock*
914234	**914234 09-07-99′: 058899**

In Exhibit 12.3, the drawer is J Woodstock, and the payee is K Marsh.

The two parallel lines across the face of the cheque are drawn as a safeguard. If this had not been done, the cheque would have been an 'uncrossed cheque'. If this cheque had not been crossed, a thief could have gone to the Stockport branch of the Cheshire Bank and obtained cash in exchange for the cheque. When the cheque is crossed it *must* be paid into a bank account. Normally, a more secure type of crossing is used.

Cheque crossings

Cheques can be further safeguarded by using a specific crossing, i.e. writing a form of instruction within the crossing on the cheques as shown in Exhibit 12.4:

Exhibit 12.4

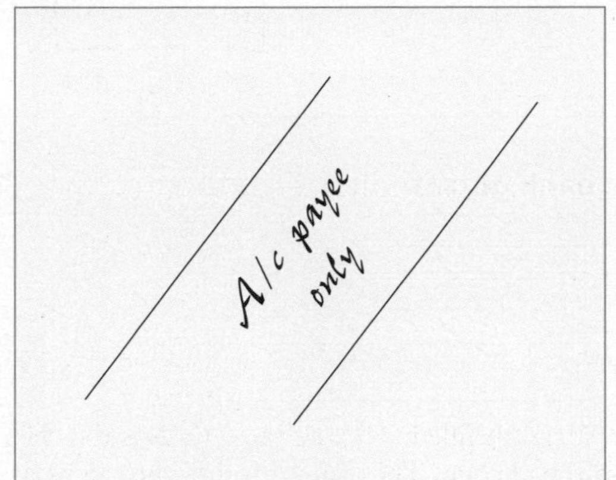

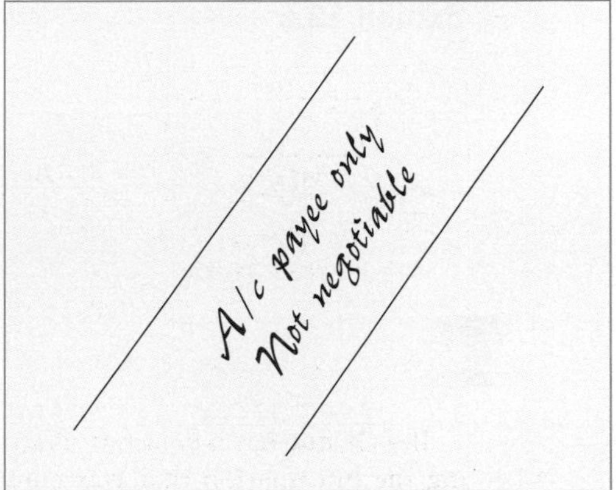

These both mean the same thing. They are specific instructions to the banks about the use of the cheque. There is a third, more common crossing that also means the same thing, '**Account Payee**'. As it is shorter, it is the one most commonly used. The use of any of these three crossings means the cheques should be paid only into the account of the payee named. If cheques (whether crossed or not) are lost or stolen, the drawer must advise their bank immediately and the cheques will be 'stopped', i.e. payment will not be made on these cheques, provided the drawer acts swiftly. In addition, if a crossed cheque is lost or stolen it will be of no use to the thief or finder. This is because it is impossible for this cheque to be paid into any bank account other than that of the named payee. For obvious reasons, cheques are often printed with the 'Account Payee' crossing on them.

Cheque endorsements

Cheques with the above crossings can only be paid into the bank account of the payee. However, if the crossing does not contain any of these three terms, a cheque received by someone can be endorsed over to someone else. The person then receiving the cheque could bank it. This means that if Adam Smith receives a cheque from John Wilson, he can 'endorse' the cheque and hand it to Petra Jones as payment of money by Smith to Jones. Jones can then pay it into her bank account.

To endorse the cheque, Smith would write the words 'Pay P Jones or order' on the reverse side of the cheque and then sign underneath it. Jones would then usually bank the cheque, but she could endorse it over to someone else by adding yet another **endorsement** and signing it.

A cheque which has been paid to someone, and has passed through their bank account or been endorsed over by that person to someone else, is legal proof of the fact that payment had been made. However, cheques do not indicate what the payment was for, and so do not legally carry the same weight as a receipt.

12.8 Pay-in slips

When we want to pay money into a current account, either cash or cheques, or both, we use a **pay-in slip**. When the payment is into an account held in a different bank, the form is called a **bank giro credit**. The two types of form are virtually identical. A bank giro credit can be used instead of a pay-in slip, but not the other way around, as the details of the other bank need to be entered on the bank giro credit. Exhibit 12.5 shows a completed bank giro credit.

Exhibit 12.5

Face of bank giro credit

Counterfoil:

Date *22 May 2007*
Cashier's stamp and initials

A/c *J. WOODSTOCK*

Cash	*23.92*
Cheques PO's etc	*249.59*
£	*273.51*

Counterfoil retained by Woodstock

Bank giro credit:

Date *22 May 2007*
Cashier's stamp and initials

bank giro credit
Destination Branch Code number *09-07-99*
Bank *Cheshire Bank*
Branch *Stockport*

	pounds	pence
£5 notes and over	*20*	
£1 coins	*3*	
50p coins		*50*
Other silver		*30*
Bronze coins		*12*
Total cash	*23*	*92*
Cheques, PO's etc. (see over)	*249*	*59*
	273	*51*

Account Name (Block letters) & A/c. No *J. WOODSTOCK 058899*

Paid in by *J Woodstock*

Details for advice to recipient

Bank giro credit and cash and cheques handed in to bank

Reverse side of bank giro credit

Details of Cheques, POs etc

for cheques please specify Drawer's name	and Bank Code Number as shown in top right corner				
E. KANE & SON	*02-58-76*	*184*	*15*	*184*	*15*
J. GALE	*05-77-85*	*65*	*44*	*65*	*44*
In view of the risk of loss in course of clearing, customers are advised to keep an independent record of the drawers of cheques.	Total carried over £	*249*	*59*	*249*	*59*

Reverse of counterfoil

J Woodstock has banked the following items:

Four	£5 notes		
Three	£1 coins		
One	50p coin		
Other silver	30p		
Bronze coins	12p		
Cheques received from:			Code numbers:
E Kane & Son		£184.15	02-58-76
J Gale		£65.44	05-77-85

12.9 Cheque clearing

In Section 12.5, you learnt about the cheque clearing system. Let's now look at an example of how cheques paid from one person's bank account pass into another person's bank account. We'll use the cheque from Exhibit 12.3.

2007
May 22 Woodstock, in Stockport, sends the cheque to K Marsh, who lives in Leeds. Woodstock enters the payment in his cash book.
23 Cheque received by Marsh. He deposits it the same day in his bank account at Barclays Bank in Leeds. Marsh shows the cheque in his cash book as being received and banked on 23 May.
24 The Exchange Centre in London receives it, where the Cheshire Bank collects it. The Cheshire Bank sends the cheque to their Stockport branch.
25 Staff at the Stockport branch of the Cheshire Bank examine the cheque. If there is nothing wrong with it, the cheque can now be debited by the bank to J Woodstock's account.

In Chapter 30, we'll be looking at bank reconciliation statements.

What we have looked at so far:

2005
May 22 the day on which Woodstock has made the entry in his cash book
25 the day when the bank makes an entry in Woodstock's account in respect of the cheque

will become an important part of your understanding of such statements.

Learning outcomes

You should now have learnt:

1. That the banking sector has been revolutionised by the developments in computers and information technology over the last forty years.
2. That where previously payments could usually only be made by cash or cheque, there is now a wide range of alternatives, ranging from plastic cards to direct debits and direct transfers into bank accounts.
3. That the use of cheques is falling but that they are still a very common form of payment in business.
4. That cheque clearing is the way in which a cheque goes through the banking system and is credited to its rightful owner and charged against the drawer's bank account.

→

5 That it usually takes three days for a cheque payment to reach the account of the payee.

6 That it usually takes three days for a debit card payment to reach the account of the payee.

7 That cash is still the most common form of medium for payments.

8 That holders of a current account will be normally be issued with a cheque book and a multiple use plastic card incorporating a cheque guarantee card, debit card and ATM card.

9 How to write a cheque.

10 That crossings on cheques indicate that they must be banked before cash can be collected for them.

11 That special crossings on cheques act as instructions to the banker, and are usually used to ensure that the cheque cannot be used by anyone other than its rightful owner.

12 That cheque endorsements enable the rightful owner of the cheque to give it to someone else.

13 How to complete a bank pay-in slip.

14 How to complete a bank giro credit.

Answers to activities

12.1 Computers were still very limited in what they could do, particularly in terms of the size of computer needed for even the smallest task. Without the sophisticated programming flexibility of modern computers, these first age cash machines could only have very limited facilities. There was also the fairly obvious point that cash machines were a new invention and no one knew at that time whether the general public would actually use them!

12.2 There are many varieties of plastic cards. A list based on one produced by the Association for Payment Clearing Services (APACS) is listed below:

- **Affinity card**. A credit card where the card issuer makes a donation to an organisation (often a charity) every time the card is used.
- **ATM card**. A plastic card used in an ATM for cash withdrawals and other bank services.
- **Business card**. Also known as a company or corporate card. A card which companies issue to staff to pay for business expenses like travel costs.
- **Charge card**. A payment card that requires the cardholder to settle the account in full at the end of a specified period, such as American Express and Diners cards. Holders have to pay an annual fee for the card. (Compare this to a credit card.)
- **Cheque guarantee card**. A card that guarantees settlement of cheques of up to a specified amount.
- **Credit card**. A card enabling the holder to make purchases and to draw cash up to a pre-arranged limit. The credit granted in a period can be settled in full or in part by the end of a specified period. Many credit cards carry no annual fee. (Compare this to a charge card.)
- **Debit card**. A card linked to a bank or building society account and used to pay for goods and services by debiting the holder's account. Debit cards are usually combined with other facilities such as ATM and cheque guarantee functions.
- **Electronic purse**. Also known as a prepayment card. This card has a stored cash value which can be used to purchase goods and services – it is an alternative to cash. The card can be disposable or re-loadable. Examples include Mondex and VisaCash.
- **Loyalty card**. Cards issued by retailers to promote customer loyalty. Holders earn cash back, vouchers or discounts. Examples include the Tesco Clubcard and the Boots Advantage card.

- **Payment card**. A generic term for any plastic card (credit, debit, charge, etc.) which may be used on its own to pay for goods and services or to withdraw cash.
- **Purchasing card**. A payment card issued to businesses, companies or government departments to make supplier and/or trade payments.
- **Smart card**. A card that holds details on a computer chip instead of a traditional magnetic stripe. (This is expected to be the normal form of all credit and debit cards in the future.)
- **Shareholder card**. A special form of store card issued to shareholders that operates like a credit card but gives the holder a discount off all purchases charged to the card. These cards can only be used in shops owned by the company that issued the card. An example is the Arcadia Group card.
- **Store card**. Also known as a retailer card. A plastic payment card that can be used only in a specified retailer or group of retailers. An example is the John Lewis Partnership card.
- **Travel & entertainment card**. A plastic payment card which operates similarly to a charge card.

12.3 Businesses can't send employees round to all their suppliers with debit cards. Nor can they insist that one-off suppliers allow them to pay by direct transfer into the supplier's bank account. Cheques remain more convenient in many cases, though there is a definite shift towards using more modern methods. The most obvious indicator of this is the attempt by many companies to encourage shareholders to accept their dividend payments as electronic transfers into the shareholders' bank accounts.

Customers also still often use cheques, particularly for postal payments for goods purchased by telephone or mail order and to send deposits on, for example, holidays – and to pay credit card bills!

12.4 It is not because the rate of interest is lower on overdrafts, it isn't, it is higher! It is because interest on overdrafts is charged daily on the amount of the overdraft on that date. Bank loans are for fixed amounts and interest is paid on the full amount each day whether or not the money has been spent. With an overdraft, customers have the freedom to use as much or as little of the overdraft as they wish (and so incur interest only on the amount they are overdrawn). In many cases, they will never actually use the overdraft facility. Also, bank loans must be repaid on a stated date. Overdrafts are only payable to the bank when the bank demands repayment, which is rare, unless the individual or business looks likely to have problems paying back the overdraft at some future date. Thus, overdrafts are cheaper to use than bank loans, they are more flexible, and the borrower doesn't have to look regularly for other funds to replace them.

You can find a range of additional self-test questions, as well as material to help you with your studies, on the website that accompanies this book at www.pearsoned.co.uk/wood.

chapter 13

Cash books

Learning objectives

After you have studied this chapter, you should be able to:

- explain the format of two-column and three-column cash books
- enter up and balance-off cash books
- use folio columns for cross-referencing purposes
- make the entries for discounts allowed and discounts received both in the cash book and, at the end of a period, in the discount accounts in the general ledger
- make similar entries in separate columns in the cash book for other recurring items

Introduction

In this chapter, you'll learn how businesses record cash and cheque transactions in the cash book. You'll learn that a memorandum column, called the 'folio column', is included in the cash book; and you'll learn the reasons why this is done. You will learn how to make the necessary entries in the cash book and how to include entries for discounts received from creditors and allowed to debtors, both in the cash book and in the general ledger.

13.1 Drawing up a cash book

The cash book consists of the cash account and the bank account put together in one book. We used to show these two accounts on different pages of the ledger. Now it is easier to put the two sets of account columns together. This means that we can record all money received and paid out on a particular date on the same page.

In the cash book, the debit column for cash is put next to the debit column for bank. The credit column for cash is put next to the credit column for bank.

Exhibit 13.1 shows how a cash account and a bank account would appear if they had been kept separately. In Exhibit 13.2, they are shown as if the transactions had, instead, been kept in a cash book.

The bank column contains details of the payments made by cheque and direct transfer from the bank account and of the money received and paid into the bank account. The bank will have a copy of the account in its own books.

Periodically, or on request from the business, the bank sends a copy of the account in its books to the business. This document is known as the **bank statement**. When the business receives the bank statement, it checks it against the bank columns in its cash book to ensure that there are no errors.

Exhibit 13.1

Cash

2008			£	2008			£
Aug	2	T Moore	33	Aug	8	Printing	20
	5	K Charles	25		12	C Potts	19
	15	F Hughes	37		28	Office stationery	25
	30	H Howe	18		31	Balance c/d	49
			113				113
Sept	1	Balance b/d	49				

Bank

2008			£	2008			£
Aug	1	Capital	10,000	Aug	7	Rent	205
	3	W P Ltd	244		12	F Small Ltd	95
	16	K Noone	408		26	K French	268
	30	H Sanders	20		31	Balance c/d	10,104
			10,672				10,672
Sept	1	Balance b/d	10,104				

Exhibit 13.2

Cash book

			Cash	*Bank*				*Cash*	*Bank*
2008			£	£	2008			£	£
Aug	1	Capital		10,000	Aug	7	Rent		205
	2	T Moore	33			8	Printing	20	
	3	W P Ltd		244		12	C Potts	19	
	5	K Charles	25			12	F Small Ltd		95
	15	F Hughes	37			26	K French		268
	16	K Noone		408		28	Office stationery	25	
	30	H Sanders		20		31	Balances c/d	49	10,104
	30	H Howe	18						
			113	10,672				113	10,672
Sept	1	Balances b/d	49	10,104					

13.2 Cash paid into the bank

In Exhibit 13.2, the payments into the bank were cheques received by the business. They have been banked immediately upon receipt. We must now consider cash being paid into the bank.

1 Let's look at the position when customers pay their account in cash and, later, a part of this cash is paid into the bank. The receipt of the cash is debited to the cash column on the date received, the credit entry being in the customer's personal account. The cash banked has the following effect needing action:

Effect	Action
1 Asset of cash is decreased	Credit the asset account, i.e. the cash account which is represented by the cash column in the cash book.
2 Asset of bank is increased	Debit the asset account, i.e. the bank account which is represented by the bank column in the cash book.

A cash receipt of £100 from M Davies on 1 August 2008 which was followed by the banking on 3 August of £80 of this amount would appear in the cash book as follows:

Cash book					
	Cash	*Bank*		*Cash*	*Bank*
2008	£	£	2008	£	£
Aug 1 M Davies	100		Aug 3 Bank	80	
3 Cash		80			

The details column shows entries against each item stating the name of the account in which the completion of double entry has taken place. Against the cash payment of £80 appears the word 'bank', meaning that the debit of £80 is to be found in the bank column, and the opposite applies.

2 Where the whole of the cash received is banked immediately the receipt can be treated in exactly the same manner as a cheque received, i.e. it can be entered directly into the bank column.

3 If the business requires cash, it may withdraw cash from the bank. Assuming this is done by use of a cheque, the business would write out a cheque to pay itself a certain amount in cash. The bank will give cash in exchange for the cheque over the counter. It could also be done using a cash card. The effect on the accounts is the same.

The twofold effect and the action required is:

Effect	Action
1 Asset of bank is decreased	Credit the asset account, i.e. the bank column in the cash book.
2 Asset of cash is increased	Debit the asset account, i.e. the cash column in the cash book.

A withdrawal of £75 cash on 1 June 2008 from the bank would appear in the cash book as:

Cash book					
	Cash	*Bank*		*Cash*	*Bank*
2008	£	£	2008	£	£
June 1 Bank	75		June 1 Cash		75

Both the debit and credit entries for this item are in the same book. When this happens it is known as a **contra** item.

13.3 The use of folio columns

As you have already seen, the details column in an account contains the name of the account in which the other part of the double entry has been entered. Anyone looking through the books should, therefore, be able to find the other half of the double entry in the ledgers.

However, when many books are being used, just to mention the name of the other account may not be enough information to find the other account quickly. More information is needed, and this is given by using **folio columns**.

In each account and in each book being used, a folio column is added, always shown on the left of the money columns. In this column, the name of the other book and the number of the page in the other book where the other part of the double entry was made is stated against each and every entry.

So as to ensure that the double entry is completed, **the folio column should only be filled in when the double entry has been completed.**

An entry for receipt of cash from C Kelly whose account was on page 45 of the sales ledger, and the cash recorded on page 37 of the cash book, would have the following folio column entries:

- in the cash book, the folio column entry would be SL 45
- in the sales ledger, the folio column entry would be CB 37.

Note how each of the titles of the books is abbreviated so that it can fit into the space available in the folio column. Each of any contra items (transfers between bank and cash) being shown on the same page of the cash book would use the letter '¢' (for 'contra') in the folio column. There is no need to also include a page number in this case.

The act of using one book as a means of entering transactions into the accounts, so as to perform or complete the double entry, is known as **posting**. For example, you 'post' items from the sales day book to the appropriate accounts in the sales ledger and to the sales account and you 'post' items from the cash book to the appropriate accounts in the sales ledger.

Activity 13.1

Why do you think only one account is posted to from the cash book rather than two, which is what happens with postings from the other day books (i.e. the other books of original entry)?

13.4 Advantages of folio columns

As described in Section 13.3, folio entries speed up the process of finding the other side of the double entry in the ledgers.

Activity 13.2

What other advantage can you think of for using a folio column?

13.5 Example of a cash book with folio columns

The following transactions are written up in the form of a cash book. The folio columns are filled in as though all the double entries had been completed to other accounts.

2008			£
Sept	1	Proprietor puts capital into a bank account for the business.	10,940
	2	Received cheque from M Boon.	315
	4	Cash sales.	802
	6	Paid rent by cash.	135
	7	Banked £50 of the cash held by the business.	50
	15	Cash sales paid direct into the bank.	490
	23	Paid cheque to S Wills.	277
	29	Withdrew cash from bank for business use.	120
	30	Paid wages in cash.	518

Cash book *(page 1)*

			Folio	*Cash*	*Bank*				*Folio*	*Cash*	*Bank*
2008				£	£	2008				£	£
Sept	1	Capital	GL1		10,940	Sept	6	Rent	GL65	135	
	2	M Boon	SL98		315		7	Bank	¢	50	
	4	Sales	GL87	802			23	S Wills	PL23		277
	7	Cash	¢		50		29	Cash	¢		120
	15	Sales	GL87		490		30	Wages	GL39	518	
	29	Bank	¢	120			30	Balances	c/d	219	11,398
				922	11,795					922	11,795
Oct	1	Balances	b/d	219	11,398						

The abbreviations used in the folio column are:

GL = general ledger SL = sales ledger ¢ = contra PL = purchases ledger

13.6 Cash discounts

Businesses prefer it if their customers pay their accounts quickly. A business may accept a smaller sum in full settlement if payment is made within a certain period of time. The amount of the reduction of the sum to be paid is known as a '*cash discount*'. The term 'cash discount' thus refers to the allowance given for quick payment. It is still called cash discount, even if the account is paid by cheque or by direct transfer into the bank account.

The rate of cash discount is usually stated as a percentage. Full details of the percentage allowed, and the period within which payment is to be made, are quoted on all sales documents by the seller. A typical period during which discount may be allowed is one month from the date of the original transaction.

***Note*: Cash discounts *always* appear in the profit and loss section of the income statement. They are not part of the cost of goods sold. Nor are they a deduction from selling price. Students often get this wrong in examinations – be careful!**

13.7 Discounts allowed and discounts received

A business may have two types of cash discounts in its books. These are:

1 **Discounts allowed:** cash discounts allowed by a business to its customers when they pay their accounts quickly.

2 **Discounts received**: cash discounts received by a business from its suppliers when it pays what it owes them quickly.

We can now see the effect of discounts by looking at two examples.

Example 1

W Clarke owed us £100. He pays us in cash on 2 September 2008, which is within the time limit applicable for a 5 per cent cash discount. He pays £100 – £5 = £95 in full settlement of his account.

Effect	Action
1 Of cash: Cash is increased by £95. Asset of accounts receivable is decreased by £95.	 Debit cash account, i.e. enter £95 in debit column of cash book. Credit W Clarke £95.
2 Of discounts: Asset of accounts receivable is decreased by £5. (After the cash was paid there remained a balance of £5. As the account has been paid, this asset must now be cancelled.) Expense of discounts allowed increased by £5.	 Credit W Clarke £5. Debit discounts allowed account £5.

Example 2

The business owed S Small £400. It pays him by cheque on 3 September 2008, which is within the time limit laid down by him for a $2^1/_2$ per cent cash discount. The business will pay £400 – £10 = £390 in full settlement of the account.

Effect	Action
1 Of cheque: Asset of bank is reduced by £390. Liability of accounts payable is reduced by £390.	 Credit bank, i.e. entry in the credit bank column for £390. Debit S Small's account £390.
2 Of discounts: Liability of accounts payable is reduced by £10. (After the cheque was paid, a balance of £10 remained. As the account has been paid the liability must now be cancelled.) Revenue of discounts received increased by £10.	 Debit S Small's account £10. Credit discounts received account £10.

The entries made in the business's books would be:

Cash book							*(page 32)*
	Folio	*Cash*	*Bank*		*Folio*	*Cash*	*Bank*
2008		£	£	2008		£	£
Sept 2 W Clarke	SL12	95		Sept 3 S Small	PL75		390

Discounts received (General Ledger *page 18*)

	Folio	£		Folio	£
			2008 Sept 2 S Small	PL75	10

Discounts allowed (General Ledger *page 17*)

	Folio	£		Folio	£
2008 Sept 2 W Clarke	SL12	5			

W Clarke (Sales Ledger *page 12*)

	Folio	£		Folio	£
2008 Sept 1 Balance	b/d	100	2008 Sept 2 Cash	CB32	95
			2 Discount	GL17	5
		100			100

S Small (Purchases Ledger *page 75*)

	Folio	£		Folio	£
2008 Sept 3 Bank	CB32	390	2008 Sept 1 Balance	b/d	400
3 Discount	GL18	10			
		400			400

It is the accounting custom to enter the word 'Discount' in the personal accounts without stating whether it is a discount received or a discount allowed.

Why do you think it is accounting custom only to enter the word 'Discount' in the personal accounts?

13.8 Discounts columns in cash book

The *discounts allowed account* and the *discounts received account* are in the general ledger along with all the other revenue and expense accounts. It has already been stated that every effort should be made to avoid too many entries in the general ledger. To avoid this, we add two columns for discount in the cash book.

An extra column is added on each side of the cash book in which the amounts of discounts are entered. Discounts received are entered in the discounts column on the credit side of the cash book, and discounts allowed in the discounts column on the debit side of the cash book.

The cash book entries for the two examples so far dealt with would be:

Cash book *(page 32)*

	Folio	Discount	Cash	Bank		Folio	Discount	Cash	Bank
2008		£	£	£	2008		£	£	£
Sept 2 W Clarke	SL12	5	95		Sept 3 S Small	PL75	10		390

There is no alteration to the method of showing discounts in the personal accounts.

To make entries in the discounts accounts in the general ledger

At the end of the period:

Total of discounts column on receipts side of cash book	Enter on **debit** side of discounts allowed account.
Total of discounts column on payments side of cash book	Enter on **credit** side of discounts received account.

13.9 A worked example

2008			£
May	1	Balances brought down from April:	
		Cash balance	29
		Bank balance	654
		Accounts receivable accounts:	
		B King	120
		N Campbell	280
		D Shand	40
		Accounts payable accounts:	
		U Barrow	60
		A Allen	440
		R Long	100
	2	B King pays us by cheque, having deducted $2^1/_2$ per cent cash discount £3.	117
	8	We pay R Long his account by cheque, deducting 5 per cent cash discount £5.	95
	11	We withdrew £100 cash from the bank for business use.	100
	16	N Campbell pays us his account by cheque, deducting $2^1/_2$ per cent discount £7.	273
	25	We paid office expenses in cash.	92
	28	D Shand pays us in cash after having deducted 5 per cent cash discount.	38
	29	We pay U Barrow by cheque less 5 per cent cash discount £3.	57
	30	We pay A Allen by cheque less $2^1/_2$ per cent cash discount £11.	429

Folio numbers have been included in the solution to make the example more realistic.

Cash book *(page 64)*

	Folio	*Discount*	*Cash*	*Bank*		*Folio*	*Discount*	*Cash*	*Bank*
2008		£	£	£	2008		£	£	£
May 1 Balance	b/d		29	654	May 8 R Long	PL58	5		95
2 B King	SL13	3		117	11 Cash	¢			100
11 Bank	¢		100		25 Office expenses	GL77		92	
16 N Campbell	SL84	7		273					
28 D Shand	SL91	2	38		29 U Barrow	PL15	3		57
					30 A Allen	PL98	11		429
					31 Balances	c/d		75	363
		12	167	1,044			19	167	1,044
Jun 1 Balances	b/d		75	363					

Sales ledger

B King *(page 13)*

2008		*Folio*	£	2008		*Folio*	£
May 1	Balance	b/d	120	May 2	Bank	CB64	117
				2	Discount	CB64	3
			120				120

N Campbell *(page 84)*

2008		Folio	£	2008		Folio	£
May	1 Balance	b/d	280	May	16 Bank	CB64	273
					16 Discount	CB64	7
			280				280

D Shand *(page 91)*

2008		Folio	£	2008		Folio	£
May	1 Balance	b/d	40	May	28 Cash	CB64	38
					28 Discount	CB64	2
			40				40

Purchases ledger

U Barrow *(page 15)*

2008		Folio	£	2008		Folio	£
May	29 Bank	CB64	57	May	1 Balance	b/d	60
	29 Discount	CB64	3				
			60				60

R Long *(page 58)*

2008		Folio	£	2008		Folio	£
May	8 Bank	CB64	95	May	1 Balance	b/d	100
	8 Discount	CB64	5				
			100				100

A Allen *(page 98)*

2008		Folio	£	2008		Folio	£
May	30 Bank	CB64	429	May	1 Balance	b/d	440
	30 Discount	CB64	11				
			440				440

General ledger

Office expenses *(page 77)*

2008		Folio	£				
May	25 Cash	CB64	92				

Discounts received *(page 88)*

				2008		Folio	£
				May	31 Total for the month	CB64	19

Discounts allowed *(page 89)*

2008		Folio	£				
May	31 Total for the month	CB64	12				

Is the above method of entering discounts correct?

You can easily check. See the following:

Discounts in ledger accounts	Debits		Credits	
		£		
Discounts received	U Barrow	3	Discounts received	£19
	R Long	5		
	A Allen	11		
		19		
				£
Discounts allowed	Discounts allowed	£12	B King	3
			N Campbell	7
			D Shand	2
				12

You can see that proper double entry has been carried out. Equal amounts, in total, have been entered on each side of the two discount accounts.

13.10 Bank overdrafts

A business may borrow money from a bank by means of a bank **overdraft**. This means that the business is allowed to pay more out of its bank account than the total amount it has deposited in the account.

Up to this point, the bank balances have all been money at the bank, so they have all been assets, i.e. debit balances. When the bank account is overdrawn, the business owes money to the bank, so the account is a liability and the balance becomes a credit one.

Taking the cash book last shown, suppose that the amount payable to A Allen was £1,429 instead of £429. The amount in the bank account, £1,044, is exceeded by the amount withdrawn. We will take the discount for Allen as being £11. The cash book would appear as follows:

Cash book *(page 64)*

	Discount	*Cash*	*Bank*		*Discount*	*Cash*	*Bank*
2008	£	£	£	2008	£	£	£
May 1 Balances b/d		29	654	May 8 R Long	5		95
2 B King	3		117	11 Cash			100
11 Bank		100		25 Office expenses		92	
16 N Campbell	7		273				
28 D Shand	2	38		29 U Barrow	3		57
31 Balance c/d				30 A Allen	11		1,429
			637	31 Balance c/d		75	
	12	167	1,681		19	167	1,681
Jun 1 Balance b/d		75		Jun 1 Balance b/d			637

On a balance sheet, a bank overdraft is shown as an item included under the heading 'current liabilities'.

13.11 Bank cash books

In the United Kingdom, except for very small organisations, three-column cash books are not usually used. All receipts, whether of cash or cheques, will be banked daily. A 'petty cash book' will be used for payments of cash. As a result, there will be no need for cash columns in the cash book itself.

This move towards only recording bank transactions in the cash book is not yet evident in countries where banking systems are not as developed or as efficient as in the UK.

13.12 Multiple column cash book

In Chapter 18, you will learn how to prepare an analytical (or multiple column) petty cash book. Cash books are often prepared with multiple columns where additional columns are added for each ledger account to which many entries may be made in a period. As with columns for discount, this has the advantage of reducing the number of entries made in the accounts in the general ledger.

Learning outcomes

You should now have learnt:

1. That a cash book consists of a cash account and a bank account put together into one book.
2. How to enter up and balance a two-column cash book, i.e. one containing a debit and a credit column for the bank account, and a debit and a credit column for the cash account.
3. That the bank columns in the cash book are for cheques and any other transfers of funds that have been made into or out of the bank account.
4. That a folio column is included in the cash book so as to help trace entries made into accounts in the ledgers and so as to provide assurance that the double entries have been made.
5. That cash discounts are given to encourage people to pay their accounts within a stated time limit.
6. That 'cash discount' is the name given for discount for quick payment even where the payment was made by cheque or by direct transfer into the bank account, rather than by payment in cash.
7. That cash discounts appear in the profit and loss part of the income statement.
8. How to enter up and balance a three-column cash book, i.e. one containing a debit and a credit column for the bank account, a debit and a credit column for the cash account, and a debit and a credit column for discount.
9. That the discounts columns in the cash book make it easier to enter up the books. They act as a collection point for discounts allowed and discounts received, for which double entry into the general ledger is completed when the

totals are transferred to the discount accounts in the general ledger, usually at the end of the month.

10 That a multiple column cash book is often used in order to further reduce the number of entries made in the general ledger.

11 How to add additional columns to the cash book for frequently recurring items and make the appropriate entries in them and in the general ledger.

Answers to activities

13.1 Although the cash book is a book of original entry, it is also where the cash account and bank account are recorded. In effect, it is both a book of original entry and a ledger dedicated to those two accounts. As a result, each transaction in the cash book is only posted once to another account, the first part of the entry having been made when the transaction was recorded in the cash book.

13.2 If an entry has not been filled in, i.e. if the folio column is blank against an entry, the double entry has not yet been made. As a result, looking through the entry lines in the folio columns to ensure they have all been filled in helps detect such errors quickly.

13.3 It should be quite obvious whether discount is received or allowed. And, more importantly, the double entry is with the cash book columns for discount, not with either the discount allowed account or the discount received account in the general ledger. At the end of the period (usually a month) the totals of the two discount columns in the cash book are posted to the discount allowed and discount received accounts in the general ledger.

Multiple choice questions: Set 2

Now attempt Set 2 of multiple choice questions. (Answers to all the multiple choice questions are given in Appendix 2 at the end of this book.)

Each of these multiple choice questions has four suggested answers, (A), (B), (C) and (D). You should read each question and then decide which choice is best, either (A) or (B) or (C) or (D). ***Write down your answers on a separate piece of paper.*** **You will then be able to redo the set of questions later without having to try to ignore your answers from previous attempts.**

MC21 Gross profit is

(A) Excess of sales over cost of goods sold
(B) Sales less purchases
(C) Cost of goods sold + opening inventory
(D) Net profit less expenses of the period

MC22 Net profit is calculated in the

(A) Trading account
(B) Profit and loss account
(C) Trial balance
(D) Balance sheet

MC23 To find the value of closing inventory at the end of a period we

(A) Do this by physically counting the inventory (i.e. stocktaking)
(B) Look in the inventory account
(C) Deduct opening inventory from cost of goods sold
(D) Deduct cost of goods sold from sales

→

→ **MC24** The credit entry for net profit is on the credit side of

(A) The trading account
(B) The profit and loss account
(C) The drawings account
(D) The capital account

MC25 Which of these best describes a balance sheet?

(A) An account proving the books balance
(B) A record of closing entries
(C) A listing of balances
(D) A statement of assets

MC26 The descending order in which current assets should be shown in the balance sheet is

(A) Inventory, Accounts receivable, Bank, Cash
(B) Cash, Bank, Accounts receivable, Inventory
(C) Accounts receivable, Inventory, Bank, Cash
(D) Inventory, Accounts receivable, Cash, Bank

MC27 Which of these best describes non-current assets?

(A) Items bought to be used in the business
(B) Items which will not wear out quickly
(C) Expensive items bought for the business
(D) Items having a long life and not bought specifically for resale

MC28 Carriage inwards is charged to the trading account because

(A) It is an expense connected with buying goods
(B) It should not go in the balance sheet
(C) It is not part of motor expenses
(D) Carriage outwards goes in the profit and loss account

MC29 Given figures showing: Sales £8,200, Opening inventory £1,300, Closing inventory £900, Purchases £6,400, Carriage inwards £200, the cost of goods sold figure is

(A) £6,800
(B) £6,200
(C) £7,000
(D) Another figure

MC30 The costs of putting goods into a saleable condition should be charged to

(A) The trading account
(B) The profit and loss account
(C) The balance sheet
(D) None of these

MC31 Suppliers' personal accounts are found in the

(A) Nominal ledger
(B) General ledger
(C) Purchases ledger
(D) Sales ledger

MC32 The sales day book is best described as

(A) Part of the double entry system
(B) Containing customers' accounts
(C) Containing real accounts
(D) A list of credit sales

MC33 Which of the following are personal accounts?

(*i*) Buildings
(*ii*) Wages
(*iii*) Accounts receivable
(*iv*) Accounts payable

(A) (*i*) and (*iv*) only
(B) (*ii*) and (*iii*) only
(C) (*iii*) and (*iv*) only
(D) (*ii*) and (*iv*) only

MC34 When Lee makes out a cheque for £50 and sends it to Young, then Lee is known as

(A) The payee
(B) The banker
(C) The drawer
(D) The creditor

MC35 If you want to make sure that your money will be safe if cheques sent are lost in the post, you should

(A) Not use the postal service
(B) Always pay by cash
(C) Always take the money in person
(D) Cross your cheques 'Account Payee only, Not Negotiable'

MC36 When depositing money in your current account you should always use

(A) A cheque book
(B) A paying-in slip
(C) A cash book
(D) A general ledger

MC37 A debit balance of £100 in a cash account shows that

(A) There was £100 cash in hand
(B) Cash has been overspent by £100
(C) £100 was the total of cash paid out
(D) The total of cash received was less than £100

MC38 £50 cash taken from the cash till and banked is entered

(A) Debit cash column £50: Credit bank column £50
(B) Debit bank column £50: Credit cash column £50
(C) Debit cash column £50: Credit cash column £50
(D) Debit bank column £50: Credit bank column £50

→

→ **MC39** A credit balance of £200 on the cash columns of the cash book would mean

(A) We have spent £200 more than we have received
(B) We have £200 cash in hand
(C) The bookkeeper has made a mistake
(D) Someone has stolen £200 cash

MC40 'Posting' the transactions in bookkeeping means

(A) Making the first entry of a double entry transaction
(B) Entering items in a cash book
(C) Making the second entry of a double entry transaction
(D) Something other than the above

Review questions

13.1 Write up a two-column cash book for a pine furniture shop from the following details, and balance it off as at the end of the month:

2008
May 1 Started in business with capital in cash £1,000.
2 Paid rent by cash £230.
3 G Broad lent us £2,000, paid by cheque.
4 We paid J Fine by cheque £860.
5 Cash sales £190.
7 F Love paid us by cheque £34.
9 We paid A Moore in cash £92.
11 Cash sales paid direct into the bank £151.
15 P Hood paid us in cash £96.
16 We took £100 out of the cash till and paid it into the bank account.
19 We repaid R Onions £500 by cheque.
22 Cash sales paid direct into the bank £122.
26 Paid motor expenses by cheque £75.
30 Withdrew £200 cash from the bank for business use.
31 Paid wages in cash £320.

13.2A Write up a two-column cash book for a second-hand bookshop from the following:

2009
Nov 1 Balance brought forward from last month: Cash £295; Bank £4,240.
2 Cash sales £310.
3 Took £200 out of the cash till and paid it into the bank.
4 F Bell paid us by cheque £194.
5 We paid for postage stamps in cash £80.
6 Bought office equipment by cheque £310.
7 We paid L Root by cheque £94.
9 Received business rates refund by cheque £115.
11 Withdrew £150 from the bank for business use.
12 Paid wages in cash £400.
13 Cash sales £430.
14 Paid motor expenses by cheque £81.
16 J Bull lent us £1,500 in cash.
20 K Brown paid us by cheque £174.
28 We paid general expenses in cash £35.
30 Paid insurance by cheque £320.

13.3 A three-column cash book for a wine wholesaler is to be written up from the following details, balanced-off, and the relevant discount accounts in the general ledger shown.

2008
Mar 1 Balances brought forward: Cash £620; Bank £7,142.
2 The following paid their accounts by cheque, in each case deducting 5 per cent cash discounts: G Slick £260; P Fish £320; T Old £420 (all amounts are pre-discount).
4 Paid rent by cheque £430.
6 F Black lent us £5,000 paying by cheque.
8 We paid the following accounts by cheque in each case deducting a $2^1/_2$ per cent cash discount: R White £720; G Green £960; L Flip £1,600 (all amounts are pre-discount).
10 Paid motor expenses in cash £81.
12 J Pie pays his account of £90, by cheque £88, deducting £2 cash discount.
15 Paid wages in cash £580.
18 The following paid their accounts by cheque, in each case deducting 5 per cent cash discount: A Pony £540; B Line & Son £700; T Owen £520 (all amounts are pre-discount).
21 Cash withdrawn from the bank £400 for business use.
24 Cash drawings £200.
25 Paid W Peat his account of £160, by cash £155, having deducted £5 cash discount.
29 Bought fixtures paying by cheque £720.
31 Received commission by cheque £120.

13.4A Enter the following in the three-column cash book of an office supply shop. Balance-off the cash book at the end of the month and show the discount accounts in the general ledger.

2008
June 1 Balances brought forward: Cash £420; Bank £4,940.
2 The following paid us by cheque, in each case deducting a 5 per cent cash discount: S Braga £820; L Pine £320; G Hodd £440; M Rae £1,040.
3 Cash sales paid direct into the bank £740.
5 Paid rent by cash £340.
6 We paid the following accounts by cheque, in each case deducting $2^1/_2$ per cent cash discount: M Peters £360; G Graham £960; F Bell £400.
8 Withdrew cash from the bank for business use £400.
10 Cash sales £1,260.
12 B Age paid us their account of £280 by cheque less £4 cash discount.
14 Paid wages by cash £540.
16 We paid the following accounts by cheque: R Todd £310 less cash discount £15; F Dury £412 less cash discount £12.
20 Bought fixtures by cheque £4,320.
24 Bought lorry paying by cheque £14,300.
29 Received £324 cheque from A Line.
30 Cash sales £980.
30 Bought stationery paying by cash £56.

13.5 On 1 September, V Duckworth, a bar manager and entrepreneur, has the following financial position relating to her activities as a corporate function organiser:

	£
Balance at bank	1,000
Accounts receivable – M Baldwin	2,500
– A Roberts	900
– G Platt	250
Inventory	750
Accounts payable – Newton and Ridley	4,500
– J Duckworth	125

→

During September the following events occur:

1 M Baldwin settles his account after taking a cash discount of 20%.
2 A Roberts is declared bankrupt and no payments are anticipated in respect of the debt.
3 G Platt pays in full.
4 All accounts payable are paid. Newton and Ridley had indicated that, because of the speed of payment, a 10% quick settlement discount may be deducted from the payment.

Required:

(*a*) Use T-accounts to open a bank account and the accounts for the accounts receivable and accounts payable at 1 September.
(*b*) Record the above transactions for September.
(c) Balance-off the accounts at the end of the month.

13.6A At 1 September the financial position of Sara Young's business was:

	£
Cash in hand	80
Balance at bank	900
Accounts receivable: AB	200
CD	500
EF	300
Inventory	1,000
Accounts payable: GH	600
IJ	1,400

During September:

1 The three debtors settled their accounts by cheque subject to a cash discount of 4%.
2 A cheque for £100 was cashed for office use.
3 GH was paid by cheque less 7.5% cash discount.
4 IJ's account was settled, subject to a discount of 5%, by cheque.
5 Wages of £130 were paid in cash.

Required:

(*a*) Open a three-column cash book and the accounts for the accounts receivable and accounts payable at 1 September.
(*b*) Record the above transactions for September.

You can find a range of additional self-test questions, as well as material to help you with your studies, on the website that accompanies this book at www.pearsoned.co.uk/wood.

hapter 14

Sales day book and sales ledger

Learning objectives

After you have studied this chapter, you should be able to:

- distinguish between a cash sale and a credit sale and between the way they are recorded in the accounting books
- explain why, when credit card payments are received at the time of sale, details of the customer are not recorded even though a debtor is created at the same time
- draw up a sales invoice
- explain why multiple copies are often made of each sales invoice
- make the appropriate entries relating to credit sales in a sales day book
- make the correct postings from the sales day book to the sales ledger and general ledger
- explain how trade discounts differ from cash discounts, both in nature and in the way they are treated in the accounting books
- describe measures that may be taken to exercise credit control over debtors

Introduction

In Chapter 11, you learnt that, rather than having only one book of original entry and only one ledger, most businesses use a set of day books (or journals) and a set of ledgers. In this chapter, you'll learn more about the sales day book (or sales journal) and the sales ledger. You'll also learn how cash and credit sales are entered in these books, and about trade discounts and how to record them.

14.1 Cash sales

As you have already learnt, when goods are paid for immediately they are described as 'cash sales', even where the payment has been made by cheque or transfer of funds from the customer's bank account into the seller's bank account. For accounting purposes, in such cases we do not need to know the names and addresses of customers nor what has been sold to them and, as a result, there is no need to enter such sales in the sales day book. **The sales day book (and all the other day books) are *only* used for credit transactions.**

Other than for accounting purposes, can you think of anything a business might want to record somewhere outside the accounting records concerning these transactions?

Credit card payments

When customers pay immediately by credit card, so far as recording details of the customer is concerned, this is treated as if it were a payment made by cash. No record is required for accounting purposes concerning the contact details of the customer. However, it is still a credit transaction and it does result in a debtor being created – the credit card company. The double entry would be a credit to the sales account and a debit to the credit card company's account in the sales ledger.

14.2 Credit sales

In all but the smallest business, most sales will be made on credit. In fact, the sales of many businesses will consist entirely of credit sales. The only major exceptions to this are Internet businesses (such as Amazon) and retailers (e.g. corner shops and supermarkets), where all sales are paid for at the time of sale.

For each credit sale, the selling business will give or send a document to the buyer showing full details of the goods sold and the prices of the goods. This document is an 'invoice'. It is known to the buyer as a 'purchase invoice' and to the seller as a **sales invoice**. The seller will keep one or more copies of each sales invoice for his or her own use.

What uses would the seller have for these copies of the sales invoice?

Exhibit 14.1 is an example of an invoice:

Exhibit 14.1

Your Purchase Order: 10/A/980

INVOICE No 16554

J Blake
7 Over Warehouse
Leicester LE1 2AP
1 September 2009

To: D Poole & Co
45 Charles Street
Manchester M1 5ZN

	Per unit	Total
	£	£
21 cases McBrand Pears	20	420
5 cartons Kay's Flour	4	20
6 cases Joy's Vinegar	20	120
		560
Terms $1\frac{1}{4}$% cash discount if paid within one month		

You must not think that all invoices will look exactly like the one shown in Exhibit 14.1. Each business will have its own design. All invoices will be uniquely numbered, usually sequentially, and they will contain the names and addresses of both the supplier and the customer. In this case, the supplier is J Blake and the customer is D Poole. (A 'purchase order' – there's one referred to in the top left-hand corner of this sales invoice – is the record or document drawn up by the customer that the customer referred to or gave the seller when the order was placed with the seller. It is used by the buyer to check the details of the order against the invoice and against the goods delivered.)

14.3 Copies of sales invoices

As soon as the sales invoices for the goods being sold have been prepared, they are given or sent to the customer. The copies kept by the seller are created at the same time as the original.

14.4 Making entries in the sales day book

From the copy of the sales invoice, the seller enters up the transaction in the sales day book. This book is merely a list of details relating to each credit sale:

- date
- name of customer
- invoice number
- folio column
- final amount of invoice.

There is no need to show details of the goods sold in the sales day book. This can be found by looking at copy invoices.

We can now look at Exhibit 14.2, which shows page 26 of a sales day book, starting with the record of the sales invoice already shown in Exhibit 14.1. (These could have been on any page. In this example, we are assuming they have been entered on page 26 as pages 1–25 have been filled with details of earlier transactions.)

Exhibit 14.2

Sales Day Book				*(page 26)*
		Invoice No	*Folio*	*Amount*
2009				£
Sept	1 D Poole	16554		560
	8 T Cockburn	16555		1,640
	28 C Carter	16556		220
	30 D Stevens & Co	16557		1,100
				3,520

14.5 Posting credit sales to the sales ledger

Instead of having one ledger for all accounts, we now have a separate sales ledger for credit sale transactions. This was described in Chapter 11.

1 The credit sales are now posted, one by one, to the debit side of each customer's account in the sales ledger.
2 At the end of each period the total of the credit sales is posted to the credit of the sales account in the general ledger.

This is now illustrated in Exhibit 14.3.

Exhibit 14.3 Posting credit sales

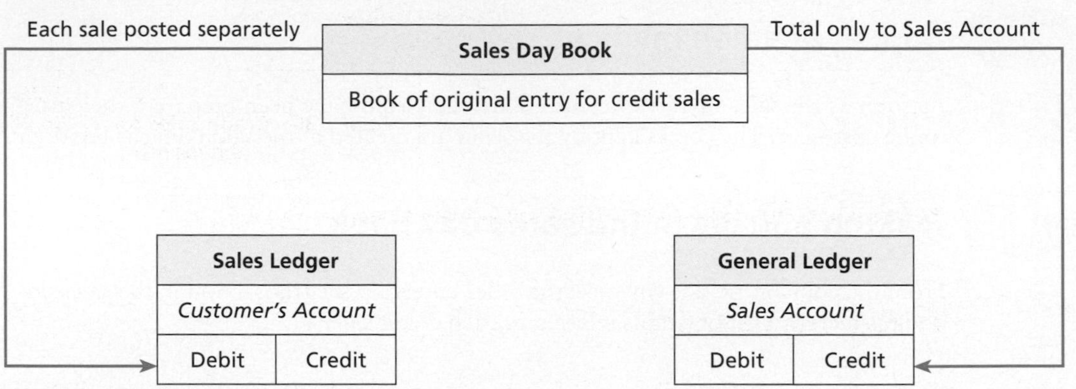

14.6 An example of posting credit sales

The sales day book in Exhibit 14.2 is now shown again. This time, posting is made to the sales ledger and the general ledger. Notice the completion of the folio columns with the reference numbers.

Sales Day Book			*(page 26)*
	Invoice No	*Folio*	*Amount*
2009			£
Sept 1 D Poole	16554	SL 12	560
8 T Cockburn	16555	SL 39	1,640
28 C Carter	16556	SL 125	220
30 D Stevens & Co	16557	SL 249	1,100
Transferred to Sales Account		GL 44	3,520

Sales Ledger

D Poole *(page 12)*

	Folio	£	
2009			
Sept 1 Sales	SB 26	560	

T Cockburn *(page 39)*

	Folio	£	
2009			
Sept 8 Sales	SB 26	1,640	

C Carter (page 125)

	Folio	£	
2009			
Sept 28 Sales	SB 26	220	

D Stevens & Co (page 249)

	Folio	£	
2009			
Sept 30 Sales	SB 26	1,100	

General Ledger

Sales (page 44)

		Folio	£
	2009		
	Sept 30 Credit sales for the month	SB 26	3,520

Before you continue you should attempt Review Question 14.1.

14.7 Trade discounts

Suppose you are the proprietor of a business. You are selling to three different kinds of customer:

1 traders who buy a lot of goods from you.
2 traders who buy only a few items from you.
3 the general public (direct).

The traders themselves have to sell the goods to the general public in their own areas. They have to make a profit to help finance their businesses, so they will want to pay you less than the retail price (i.e. the price at which the goods are sold to the general public).

The traders who buy in large quantities will not want to pay as much as those traders who buy in small quantities. You want to attract large customers like these, so you are happy to sell to these traders at a lower price than the price you charge the other customers.

This means that your selling prices are at three levels:

1 to traders buying large quantities,
2 to traders buying small quantities, and
3 to the general public.

Let's use an example to illustrate this. You sell a food mixing machine. The basic price is £200. The traders who buy in large quantities are given 25 per cent trade discount. The other traders are given 20 per cent, and the general public get no trade discount. The price paid by each type of customer would be:

		Trader 1		Trader 2	General Public
		£		£	£
Basic price		200		200	200
Less Trade discount	(25%)	(50)	(20%)	(40)	nil
Price to be paid by customer		150		160	200

You could deal with this by having three price lists, and many businesses do. However, some use trade discounts instead. This involves having only one price list but giving a **trade discount** to traders so that they are invoiced for the correct price.

Exhibit 14.4 is an example of an invoice for a food manufacturer and retailer that shows how trade discount is presented clearly and the trade discounted price easily identified. It is for the same items as were shown in Exhibit 14.1 as having been sold to D Poole. In that example, the seller operated a different price list for each category of customer. This time the seller is R Grant and trade discount is used to adjust the selling price to match the category of customer.

Exhibit 14.4

Your Purchase Order: 11/A/G80 To: D Poole & Co 45 Charles Street Manchester M1 5ZN	**INVOICE No 30756**	R Grant Higher Side Preston PR1 2NL 2 September 2009 Tel (01703) 33122 Fax (01703) 22331	
		Per unit	Total
		£	£
21 cases McBrand Pears		25	525
5 cartons Kay's Flour		5	25
6 cases Joy's Vinegar		25	150
			700
Less 20% trade discount			(140)
			560

By comparing Exhibits 14.1 and 14.4, you can see that the amount paid by D Poole was the same. It is simply the method of calculating it that is different.

14.8 No double entry for trade discounts

As trade discount is simply a way of calculating sales prices, no entry for trade discount should be made in the double entry records, nor in the sales day book. The recording of Exhibit 14.4 in R Grant's sales day book and D Poole's personal account will be:

Sales Day Book			*(page 87)*
	Invoice No	*Folio*	*Amount*
2009			£
Sept 2 D Poole	30756	SL 32	560

Sales Ledger
D Poole *(page 32)*

	Folio	£	
2009			
Sept 2 Sales	SB 87	560	

To compare with cash discounts:

- Trade discounts: *never* shown in double entry accounts, nor in the income statement.
- Cash discounts: *always* shown in double entry accounts and in the profit and loss part of the income statement.

Be very careful about this topic. Students often get confused between the treatment of trade discount and the treatment of cash discount. Remember, it is trade discount that is not entered anywhere in either the ledger accounts or the financial statements. Cash discount appears in the cash book and is always shown in the financial statements.

14.9 Manufacturer's recommended retail price

Looking at an item displayed in a shop window, you will frequently see something like the following:

50 inch HD LCD TV	
Manufacturer's Recommended Retail Price	£2,300
less discount of 20 per cent	(460)
You pay only	£1,840

Very often the manufacturer's recommended retail price is a figure above what the manufacturer would expect the public to pay for its product. In the case of the TV, the manufacturer would probably have expected the public to pay around £1,840 for the TV.

The inflated figure used for the 'manufacturer's recommended retail price' is simply a sales gimmick. Most people like to feel they are getting a bargain. Most people feel happier about making a purchase like this if they are told they are getting '20 per cent discount' and pay £1,840 than when they are told that the price is £1,840 and that they cannot get any discount.

14.10 Credit control

Any organisation which sells goods on credit should keep a close check to ensure that debtors pay their accounts on time. If this is not done properly, the amount of accounts receivables can grow to a level that will make the business short of cash. Businesses that grow too short of cash will fail, no matter how profitable they may be.

The following procedures should be carried out:

1 A credit limit should be set for each debtor. Debtors should not be allowed to owe more than their credit limit. The amount of the limit will depend on the circumstances. Such things as the size of the customer's business and the amount of business done with it, as well as its past record of payments, will help guide the choice of credit limit. Credit rating agencies may be used to assess the credit worthiness of customers before credit is granted.

2 As soon as the payment date set by the seller has been reached, a check should be made to verify whether the debtor has paid the amount due. Failure to pay on time may trigger a refusal to supply any more goods to the customer until payment is received, even if the customer's credit limit has not been reached.

3 Where payment is not forthcoming, after investigation it may be necessary to take legal action to sue the customer for the debt. This will depend on the circumstances.

4 It is important that the customer is aware of what will happen if the amount due is not paid by the deadline set by the seller.

Learning outcomes

You should now have learnt:

1. That 'sales day book' and 'sales journal' are different names for the same book.
2. That cash sales are not entered in the sales day book.
3. That when credit card payments are received at the time of sale, details of the customer are not recorded even though a debtor is created at the same time.
4. That the sales day book (or sales journal) contains information relating to each credit sale made in each period.
5. That the sales day book is used for posting credit sales to the sales ledger.
6. That the total of the sales day book for the period is posted to the credit of the sales account in the general ledger.
7. How to make the appropriate entries relating to credit sales in a sales day book and make the correct postings from it to the sales ledger and general ledger.
8. How to prepare a sales invoice.
9. Why multiple copies are often made of each sales invoice.
10. That no entry is made for trade discounts in the double entry accounts.
11. That all businesses should operate a sound system of credit control over their debtors.
12. Some measures that may be taken to exercise credit control over debtors.

Answers to activities

14.1 A business may want to know the contact details of cash customers for marketing purposes. In fact, most businesses of any size would like to keep records in a database of all their cash customers for this reason. Businesses may also want to encourage cash customers to open credit accounts with the business so that they may be more likely to buy from the business in future. Also, where the goods sold are to be delivered to the customer, the customer's contact details will need to be recorded, but this will be in a record held elsewhere than in the accounting books.

14.2 Sellers keep copies of sales invoices for a number of reasons including: to prove that a sale took place; to enable the entries in the books to be correctly recorded and checked; to pass to the inventory department so that the correct goods can be selected for shipping to the customer; to pass to the delivery department, so that the correct goods will be shipped to the customer and to the correct address, and to enable the goods to be shipped accompanied by a copy of the sales invoice so that the customer can acknowledge receipt of the correct goods.

Review questions

14.1 You are to enter up the Sales Day Book from the following details. Post the items to the relevant accounts in the Sales Ledger and then show the transfer to the sales account in the General Ledger.

2006			
Mar	1	Credit sales to B Hope	£310
	3	Credit sales to T Fine	£285
	6	Credit sales to L Moore	£38
	10	Credit sales to B Hope	£74

	17	Credit sales to H Tor	£534
	19	Credit sales to J Young	£92
	27	Credit sales to T Most	£44
	31	Credit sales to R Best	£112

14.2A Enter up the Sales Day Book from the following details. Post the items to the relevant accounts in the Sales Ledger and then show the transfer to the sales account in the General Ledger.

2008			
Mar	1	Credit sales to I Hood	£520
	3	Credit sales to S Bell	£318
	5	Credit sales to J Smart	£64
	7	Credit sales to K Byers	£165
	16	Credit sales to T Todd	£540
	23	Credit sales to W Morris	£360
	30	Credit sales to F Lock	£2,040

14.3 F Benjamin of 10 Lower Street, Plymouth, is selling the following items at the recommended retail prices as shown: white tape £10 per roll, green felt at £4 per metre, blue cotton at £6 per sheet, black silk at £20 per dress length. He makes the following sales:

2007

May 1 To F Gray, 3 Keswick Road, Portsmouth: 3 rolls white tape, 5 sheets blue cotton, 1 dress length black silk. Less 25 per cent trade discount.

4 To A Gray, 1 Shilton Road, Preston: 6 rolls white tape, 30 metres green felt. Less $33^1/_3$ per cent trade discount.

8 To E Hines, 1 High Road, Malton: 1 dress length black silk. No trade discount.

20 To M Allen, 1 Knott Road, Southport: 10 rolls white tape, 6 sheets blue cotton, 3 dress lengths black silk, 11 metres green felt. Less 25 per cent trade discount.

31 To B Cooper, 1 Tops Lane, St Andrews: 12 rolls white tape, 14 sheets blue cotton, 9 metres green felt. Less $33^1/_3$ per cent trade discount.

You are to (*a*) draw up a sales invoice for each of the above sales, (*b*) enter them up in the Sales Day Book and post to the personal accounts, and (*c*) transfer the total to the sales account in the General Ledger.

14.4A J Fisher, White House, Bolton, is selling the following items at the retail prices as shown: plastic tubing at £1 per metre, polythene sheeting at £2 per length, vinyl padding at £5 per box, foam rubber at £3 per sheet. She makes the following sales:

2009

June 1 To A Portsmouth, 5 Rockley Road, Worthing: 22 metres plastic tubing, 6 sheets foam rubber, 4 boxes vinyl padding. Less 25 per cent trade discount.

5 To B Butler, 1 Wembley Road, Colwyn Bay: 50 lengths polythene sheeting, 8 boxes vinyl padding, 20 sheets foam rubber. Less 20 per cent trade discount.

11 To A Gate, 1 Bristol Road, Hastings: 4 metres plastic tubing, 33 lengths of polythene sheeting, 30 sheets foam rubber. Less 25 per cent trade discount.

21 To L Mackeson, 5 Maine Road, Bath: 29 metres plastic tubing. No trade discount is given.

30 To M Alison, Daley Road, Box Hill: 32 metres plastic tubing, 24 lengths polythene sheeting, 20 boxes vinyl padding. Less $33^1/_3$ per cent trade discount.

Required:

(*a*) Draw up a sales invoice for each of the above sales.
(*b*) Enter them up in the Sales Day Book and post to the personal accounts.
(*c*) Transfer the total to the sales account in the General Ledger.

You can find a range of additional self-test questions, as well as material to help you with your studies, on the website that accompanies this book at www.pearsoned.co.uk/wood.

chapter 15

Purchases day book and purchases ledger

Learning objectives

After you have studied this chapter, you should be able to:

- make the appropriate entries relating to credit purchases in a purchases day book
- make the correct postings from the purchases day book to the purchases ledger and general ledger
- explain the differences between the processes of recording credit sales and credit purchases in the books

Introduction

In this chapter, you'll continue your look at the day books and ledgers by looking in more detail at the purchases day book (or purchases journal) and the purchases ledger. Having already looked at the sales side of transactions in Chapter 14, you're now going to look at them from the side of purchases. Much of what you will learn in this chapter is virtually identical to what you learnt in Chapter 14. This shouldn't come as a surprise. After all, you're looking once more at how transactions are processed in day books and ledgers and the process ought to be similar as you move from the sales side to the purchases side of similar transactions. If it weren't, accounting would be a far more complex subject than it is.

15.1 Purchases invoices

In Chapter 14, you learnt that an invoice is called a 'sales invoice' when it is entered in the books of the seller. When an invoice is entered in the books of the buyer, it is called a '**purchases invoice**'. For example, in Exhibit 14.1, the first invoice you looked at in Chapter 14,

- in the books of J Blake, the seller, it is a sales invoice, and
- in the books of D Poole, the buyer, it is a purchases invoice.

15.2 Making entries in the purchases day book

From the purchases invoices for goods bought on credit, the purchaser enters the details in the purchases day book (or purchases journal).

Think back to what you learnt about the list of items contained in the sales day book. What do you think is the list of items recorded in the purchases day book?

There is no need to show details of the goods bought in the purchases day book. This can be found by looking at the invoices themselves. Exhibit 15.1 is an example of a purchases day book.

Exhibit 15.1

Purchases Day Book					(page 49)
			Invoice No	*Folio*	*Amount*
2009					£
Sept	1	J Blake	9/101		560
	8	B Hamilton	9/102		1,380
	19	C Brown	9/103		230
	30	K Gabriel	9/104		510
					2,680

Note the entry for 1 September and compare it to the entry on the same date shown in the sales day book of J Blake in Exhibit 14.2. What differences are there between the entries in the two day books? Why do you think these differences arise?

15.3 Posting credit purchases to the purchases ledger

We now have a separate purchases ledger. The double entry is as follows:

1 The credit purchases are posted one by one, to the credit of each supplier's account in the purchases ledger.
2 At the end of each period the total of the credit purchases is posted to the debit of the purchases account in the general ledger. This is now illustrated in Exhibit 15.2.

Exhibit 15.2 Posting credit purchases

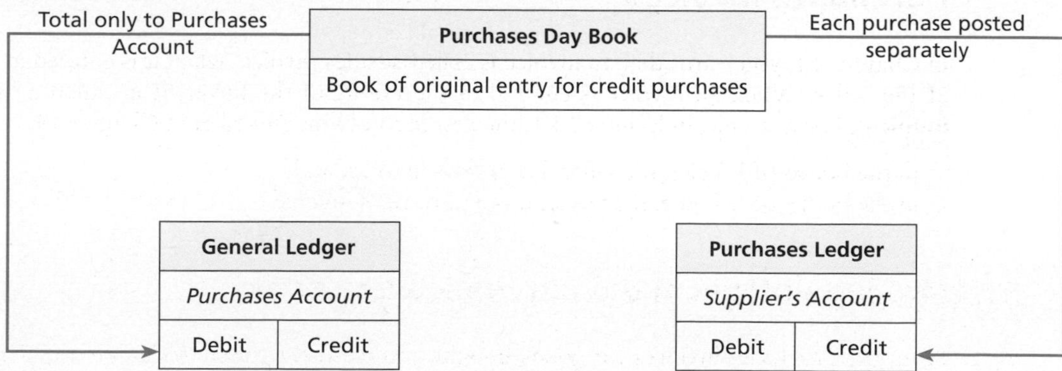

15.4 An example of posting credit purchases

The purchases day book in Exhibit 15.1 is now shown again in Exhibit 15.3 but, this time, posting is made to the purchases ledger and the general ledger. Note the completion of the folio columns indicating that the posting had been completed.

Exhibit 15.3

Purchases Day Book *(page 49)*

			Invoice No	*Folio*	*Amount*
2009					£
Sept	1	J Blake	9/101	PL 16	560
	8	B Hamilton	9/102	PL 29	1,380
	19	C Brown	9/103	PL 55	230
	30	K Gabriel	9/104	PL 89	510
Transferred to Purchases Account				GL 63	2,680

Purchases Ledger

J Blake *(page 16)*

					Folio	£
	2009					
	Sept	1	Purchases		PB 49	560

B Hamilton *(page 29)*

					Folio	£
	2009					
	Sept	8	Purchases		PB 49	1,380

C Brown *(page 55)*

					Folio	£
	2009					
	Sept	19	Purchases		PB 49	230

K Gabriel *(page 89)*

					Folio	£
	2009					
	Sept	30	Purchases		PB 49	510

General Ledger

Purchases *(page 63)*

			Folio	£	
2009					
Sept	30	Credit purchases for the month	PB 49	2,680	

Learning outcomes

You should now have learnt:

1. That 'purchases day book' and 'purchases journal' are different names for the same book.
2. That cash purchases are not entered in the purchases day book.
3. That the purchases day book is a list of all credit purchases.
4. That the purchases day book is used to post the items to the personal accounts in the purchases ledger.
5. That the total of credit purchases for the period is posted from the purchases day book to the debit of the purchases account in the general ledger.
6. How to make the appropriate entries relating to credit purchases in a purchases day book and make the correct postings from it to the purchases ledger and general ledger.
7. That the process of making entries in the books of the purchaser is very similar to that of making those in the books of the seller.

Answers to activities

15.1 Similarly to the sales day book, the purchases day book is merely a list of details relating to each credit purchase. The list of items is virtually identical to those recorded in the sales day book, the only differences being that it is the name of the supplier that is recorded, not the purchaser, and that the invoice number is replaced with the buyer's own internally generated reference number:

- date
- name of supplier
- the reference number of the invoice
- folio column
- final amount of invoice.

15.2 Apart from the name of the day books, there are two differences. Firstly, the description of the entry in each case contains the name of the other party to the transaction. This is the personal account in the respective ledger (sales or purchases) where details of the transaction will be entered. The second difference is in the entry in the Invoice Number column. In the case of the seller, Blake, the number entered in Chapter 14 was the number of the invoice that Blake gave to the invoice and is the invoice number shown on the invoice in Exhibit 14.1. In the case of the buyer, Poole, the invoice number is one Poole gave the invoice when it was received from the seller, Blake. As with the number assigned to it by the seller, the buyer also gives each purchase invoice a unique number relating to its place in the sequence of purchase invoices that the buyer has received so far in the period. '9/101' probably means 'month nine' (9), 'purchase invoice' (1) 'number one' (01).

Review questions

15.1 A Jack has the following purchases for the month of May 2008:

2008
May 1 From D Pope: 4 DVDs at £60 each, 3 mini hi-fi units at £240 each. Less 25 per cent trade discount.
3 From F Lloyd: 2 washing machines at £280 each, 5 vacuum cleaners at £80 each, 2 dishwashers at £200 each. Less 20 per cent trade discount.
15 From B Sankey: 1 hi-fi unit at £600, 2 washing machines at £320 each. Less 25 per cent trade discount.
20 From J Wilson: 6 CD/radios at £45 each. Less $33^1/_3$ per cent trade discount.
30 From R Freer: 4 dishwashers at £240 each. Less 20 per cent trade discount.

Required:
(*a*) Draw up a purchases invoice for each of the above purchases.
(*b*) Enter up the purchases day book for the month.
(*c*) Post the transactions to the suppliers' accounts.
(*d*) Transfer the total to the purchases account.

15.2A J Glen has the following purchases for the month of June 2009:

2009
June 2 From F Day: 2 sets golf clubs at £800 each, 5 footballs at £40 each. Less 25 per cent trade discount.
11 From G Smith: 6 cricket bats at £60 each, 6 ice skates at £35 each, 4 rugby balls at £30 each. Less 20 per cent trade discount.
18 From F Hope: 6 sets golf trophies at £90 each, 4 sets golf clubs at £900. Less $33^1/_3$ per cent trade discount.
25 From L Todd: 5 cricket bats at £52 each. Less 25 per cent trade discount.
30 From M Moore: 8 goal posts at £80 each. Less 40 per cent trade discount.

Required:
(*a*) Enter up the purchases day book for the month.
(*b*) Post the items to the suppliers' accounts.
(*c*) Transfer the total to the purchases account.

15.3 C Phillips, a sole trader specialising in material for Asian clothing, has the following purchases and sales for March 2009:

Mar 1 Bought from Smith Stores: silk £40, cotton £80. All less 25 per cent trade discount.
8 Sold to A Grantley: lycra goods £28, woollen items £44. No trade discount.
15 Sold to A Henry: silk £36, lycra £144, cotton goods £120. All less 20 per cent trade discount.
23 Bought from C Kelly: cotton £88, lycra £52. All less 25 per cent trade discount.
24 Sold to D Sangster: lycra goods £42, cotton £48. Less 10 per cent trade discount.
31 Bought from J Hamilton: lycra goods £270. Less $33^1/_3$ per cent trade discount.

Required:
(*a*) Prepare the purchases and sales day books of C Phillips from the above.
(*b*) Post the items to the personal accounts.
(*c*) Post the totals of the day books to the sales and purchases accounts.

15.4A A Henriques has the following purchases and sales for May 2006:

2006
May 1 Sold to M Marshall: brass goods £24, bronze items £36. Less 25 per cent trade discount.
7 Sold to R Richards: tin goods £70, lead items £230. Less 33$^1/_3$ per cent trade discount.
9 Bought from C Clarke: tin goods £400. Less 40 per cent trade discount.
16 Bought from A Charles: copper goods £320. Less 50 per cent trade discount.
23 Sold to T Young: tin goods £50, brass items £70, lead figures £80. All less 20 per cent trade discount.
31 Bought from M Nelson: brass figures £100. Less 50 per cent trade discount.

Required:

(*a*) Write up the sales and purchases day books.
(*b*) Post the items to the personal accounts.
(*c*) Post the totals of the day books to the sales and purchases accounts.

15.5 A Jones has the following credit purchases and credit sales for May:

May 1 Sold to M Marshall: brass goods £24, bronze items £36. All less 25 per cent trade discount.
Sold to R Richards: tin goods £70, lead items £230. All less 33$^1/_3$ per cent trade discount.
9 Bought from C Clarke: tin goods £400 less 40 per cent trade discount.
16 Bought from A Charles: copper goods £320 less 50 per cent trade discount.
23 Sold to T Young: tin goods £50, brass items £70, lead figures £80. All less 20 per cent trade discount.
31 Bought from M Nelson: brass figures £100 less 50 per cent trade discount.

Required:

(*a*) Write up sales and purchases day books.
(*b*) Post the items to the personal accounts.
(*c*) Post the totals of the day books to the sales and purchases accounts.
(*d*) What are the books of prime entry within a business and why are they so called? Illustrate your answer with suitable examples.

You can find a range of additional self-test questions, as well as material to help you with your studies, on the website that accompanies this book at www.pearsoned.co.uk/wood.

chapter 16

Returns day books

Learning objectives

After you have studied this chapter, you should be able to:

- make the appropriate entries relating to returns outwards in the returns outwards day book
- make the appropriate entries relating to returns inwards in the returns inwards day book
- make the correct postings from the returns day books to the purchases ledger, sales ledger and general ledger
- explain the differences between a credit note and a debit note
- describe how a debtor should use statements received from suppliers
- enter up the accounts for credit card transactions
- explain the need for internal checks on all sales and purchases invoices and credit notes
- describe what use may be made of factoring

Introduction

In this chapter, you'll continue your look at the day books and ledgers by looking in more detail at the two day books that are used to record returns – the returns inwards day book (or returns inwards journal) and the returns outwards day book (or returns outwards journal). Having already looked at the sales side of transactions in Chapter 14 and the purchases side in Chapter 15, you'll find that much of what you will learn in this chapter is very similar. In fact, postings from the returns day books to the personal accounts are the mirror image of the ones you learnt to make for sales and purchases.

16.1 Returns inwards and credit notes

You know that businesses allow customers to return goods they've bought. You've probably done so yourself at some time or other. Some retail businesses give every customer the right to do so within a few days of the sale and won't ask why they are being returned. It is a means of assuring the customer that the seller believes that the goods are of good quality and will do what the customer wants. Whatever the rights of return granted by the seller, in the UK there are also legal rights of return that permit retail customers to return goods for a refund should the goods prove to have been unfit for the purpose that was intended.

Businesses that deal with trade customers may operate a similar policy, but that would be more unusual and would normally include a proviso that the customer had a justifiable and reasonable reason for returning the goods.

List as many reasons as you can think of why (a) retail customers and (b) trade customers may return goods to the seller.

Sometimes sellers may agree to keep the goods returned, even when they don't normally do so, but won't provide a full refund. Sometimes buyers will agree to keep goods they had wanted to return if the seller offers to refund some of the price they paid.

When the seller agrees to take back goods and refund the amount paid, or agrees to refund part or all of the amount the buyer paid, a document known as a **credit note** will be sent to the customer, showing the amount of the allowance given by the seller.

It is called a credit note because the customer's account will be credited with the amount of the allowance, to show the reduction in the amount owed.

Referring back to Exhibit 14.4, if D Poole returns two of the cases of McBrand Pears, a credit note like the one shown in Exhibit 16.1 would be issued by R Grant, the seller.

Exhibit 16.1

R Grant
Higher Side
Preston PR1 2NL
8 September 2009

Tel (01703) 33122
Fax (01703) 22331

To: D Poole & Co
45 Charles Street
Manchester M1 5ZN

CREDIT NOTE No 9/37

	Per unit	Total
	£	£
2 cases McBrand Pears	25	50
Less 20% trade discount		(10)
		40

To stop them being mistaken for invoices, credit notes are often printed in red.

16.2 Returns inwards day book

The credit notes are listed in a returns inwards day book (or returns inwards journal). This is then used for posting the items, as follows:

1 Sales ledger: credit the amount of credit notes, one by one, to the accounts of the customers in the ledger.
2 General ledger: at the end of the period the total of the returns inwards day book is posted to the debit of the returns inwards account.

16.3 Example of a returns inwards day book

Exhibit 16.2 presents an example of a returns inwards day book showing the items to be posted to the sales ledger and the general ledger followed by the entries in the ledger accounts.

Exhibit 16.2

Returns Inwards Day Book *(page 10)*

	Note No	*Folio*	*Amount*
2009			£
Sept 8 D Poole	9/37	SL 12	40
17 A Brewster	9/38	SL 58	120
19 C Vickers	9/39	SL 99	290
29 M Nelson	9/40	SL 112	160
Transferred to Returns Inwards Account		GL 114	610

Sales Ledger

D Poole *(page 12)*

	2009	*Folio*	£
	Sept 8 Returns inwards	RI 10	40

A Brewster *(page 58)*

	2009	*Folio*	£
	Sept 17 Returns inwards	RI 10	120

C Vickers *(page 99)*

	2009	*Folio*	£
	Sept 19 Returns inwards	RI 10	290

M Nelson *(page 112)*

	2009	*Folio*	£
	Sept 29 Returns inwards	RI 10	160

General Ledger

Returns Inwards *(page 114)*

2009	*Folio*	£	
Sept 30 Returns for the month	RI 10	610	

The returns inwards day book is sometimes known as the sales returns day book, because it is goods that were sold that are being returned.

16.4 Returns outwards and debit notes

If the supplier agrees, goods bought previously may be returned. When this happens a **debit note** is sent by the customer to the supplier giving details of the goods and the reason for their return.

The credit note received from the supplier will simply be evidence of the supplier's agreement, and the amounts involved.

Also, an allowance might be given by the supplier for any faults in the goods. Here also, a debit note should be sent to the supplier. Referring back to Exhibit 16.1, Exhibit 16.3 shows an example of the debit note that Poole, the buyer, may have sent to Grant, the seller.

Exhibit 16.3

D Poole & Co
45 Charles Street
Manchester M1 5ZN
7 September 2009

Tel (0161) 488 2142
Fax (0161) 488 2143

To: R Grant
Higher Side
Preston PR1 2NL

DEBIT NOTE No 9.22

	Per Unit	Total
	£	£
2 cases McBrand Pears damaged in transit	25	50
Less 20% trade discount		(10)
		40

Note the differences between this debit note and the credit note in Exhibit 16.1: the names and addresses have swapped places and the document is described as 'Debit Note No 9.22' rather than 'Credit Note No 9/37', because Poole uses its own debit note numbering sequence. Also, the dates are different. In this case, it is assumed that Poole raised the debit note on 7 September and sent it and the goods to Grant. Grant received the goods on 8 September and raised the credit note on that date. Finally, the reason for the return of the goods is given.

16.5 Returns outwards day book

The debit notes are listed in a returns outwards day book (or returns outwards journal). This is then used for posting the items, as follows:

1 Purchases ledger: debit the amounts of debit notes, one by one, to the personal accounts of the suppliers in the ledger.
2 General ledger: at the end of the period, the total of the returns outwards day book is posted to the credit of the returns outwards account.

16.6 Example of a returns outwards day book

Exhibit 16.4 presents an example of a returns outwards day book showing the items to be posted to the purchases ledger and the general ledger followed by the entries in the ledger accounts.

Exhibit 16.4

Returns Outwards Day Book *(page 7)*

			Note No	*Folio*	*Amount*
2009					£
Sept	7	R Grant	9.22	PL 29	40
	16	B Rose	9.23	PL 46	240
	28	C Blake	9.24	PL 55	30
	30	S Saunders	9.25	PL 87	360
Transferred to Returns Outwards Account				GL 116	670

Purchases Ledger

R Grant *(page 29)*

			Folio	£	
2009			*Folio*	£	
Sept	7	Returns outwards	RO 7	40	

B Rose *(page 46)*

			Folio	£	
2009			*Folio*	£	
Sept	16	Returns outwards	RO 7	240	

C Blake *(page 55)*

			Folio	£	
2009			*Folio*	£	
Sept	28	Returns outwards	RO 7	30	

S Saunders *(page 87)*

			Folio	£	
2009			*Folio*	£	
Sept	30	Returns outwards	RO 7	360	

General Ledger

Returns Outwards *(page 116)*

				Folio	£
	2009			*Folio*	£
	Sept	30	Returns for the month	RO 7	670

The returns outwards day book is sometimes known as the purchases returns day book, because it is goods that were purchased that are being returned.

16.7 Double entry and returns

Exhibit 16.5 shows how the entries are made for returns inwards and returns outwards.

Exhibit 16.5 Posting returns inwards and returns outwards

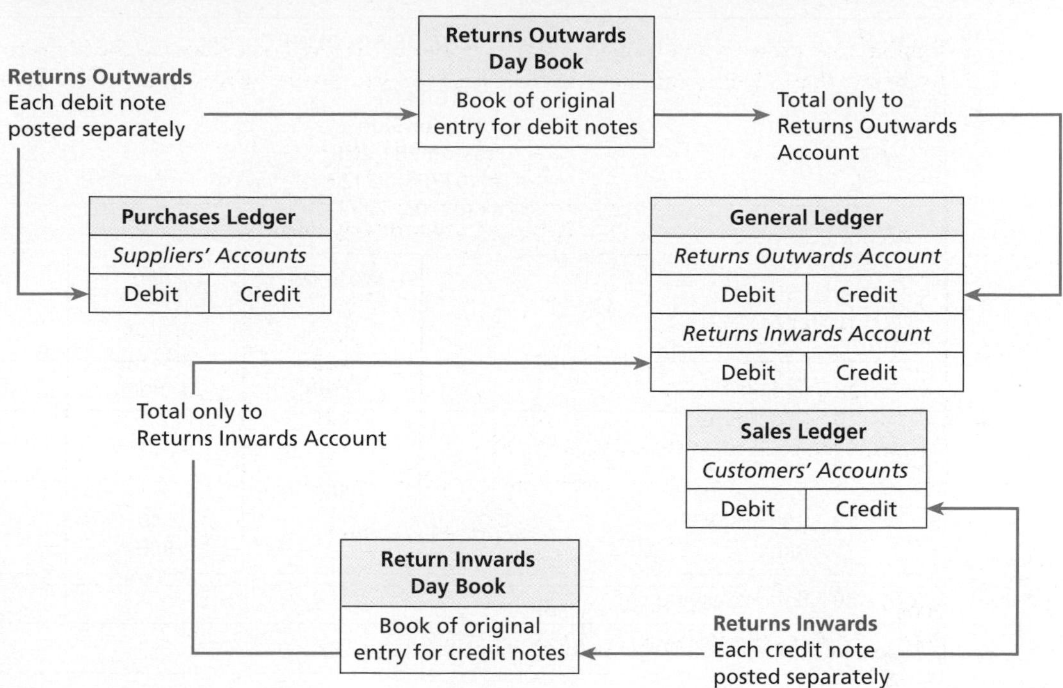

16.8 Statements

At the end of each month, a **statement** should be sent to each debtor who owes money on the last day of the month. It is really a copy of the debtor's account in the seller's books. It should show:

1 the amount owing at the start of the month;
2 the amount of each sales invoice sent to the debtor during the month;
3 credit notes sent to the debtor in the month;
4 cash and cheques received from the debtor during the month; and, finally,
5 the amount due from the debtor at the end of the month.

Exhibit 16.6 on the next page shows an example of a statement.

Debtors will check to see if the account in their accounting records agrees with the statement. If the statement shows that they owe £520, but their records show a different amount due, they will investigate the difference in order to see whether either the statement or their records is incorrect. If they discover that there has been an error in their books, they will correct it. If they find that there is an error in the statement, they will contact the seller.

Activity 16.2 What sort of things could result in the statement and the account held in the books of the debtor showing different balances?

Exhibit 16.6

STATEMENT OF ACCOUNT

R GRANT
Higher Side
Preston PR1 2NL
Tel (01703) 33122
Fax (01703) 22331

Accounts Dept
D Poole & Co
45 Charles Street
Manchester M1 5ZN

Date		*Details*	*Debit*	*Credit*	*Balance*
2009			£	£	£
Sept	1	Balance b/d			880
	2	Invoice 30756	560		1,440
	8	Returns 9/37		40	1,400
	25	Bank		880	520
Sept	30	Balance owing c/d			520
All accounts due and payable within 1 month					

Apart from enabling debtors to check the amount due, the statement also acts as a reminder to debtors that they owe the seller money, and shows the date by which they should make payment. Sellers who are contacted by a debtor querying a statement will benefit from having any errors identified in their records.

16.9 Sales and purchases via credit cards

Various banks, building societies and other financial institutions issue credit cards to their customers. The most common examples are Visa and MasterCard. The holder of the credit card purchases goods or services without giving cash or cheques, but simply signs a credit card voucher. The customer is given a copy and the other copy is filed by the seller. Such sales are very rarely sales to anyone other than the general public.

The seller is paid later by the credit card company for all the credit card transactions in the period since the last payment made to the seller. This payment is subject to a deduction of commission by the credit card company.

Once a month, the customer pays the credit card company for all of the payments charged to the credit card during the previous month.

As far as the purchaser is concerned, he has seen goods and has received them (or received the service he requested). In the eyes of the customer, they were paid for at the time of purchase and a loan has been granted by the credit card company in order to do so.

Once the customer has the goods, or has received the appropriate services, the customer does not become a debtor needing an entry in a sales ledger and so (as mentioned in Chapter 14), similarly to a cash sale, no ledger account is maintained for the customer. All the selling company is then interested in, from a recording point of view, is collecting the money from the credit card company.

The double entry needed is:

Sale of items via credit cards:	Dr: Credit card company Cr: Sales
Receipt of money from credit card company:	Dr: Bank Cr: Credit card company
Commission charged by credit card company:	Dr: Selling expenses Cr: Credit card company

***Note*: the commission is *not* a deduction from the selling price. It is treated in the same way as cash discounts. That is, it is a selling expense and is entered in the profit and loss account section of the income statement.**

16.10 Internal check

When sales invoices are prepared, they should be very carefully checked. A system is usually set up so that each stage of the preparation of an invoice is checked by someone other than the person whose job is to send out the invoice.

Activity 16.3

What sort of things could occur that make checking of all invoices, both those for sales and those for purchases, something that all businesses should do?

A system should, therefore, be set up whereby invoices are checked at each stage by someone other than the person who sends out the invoices or is responsible for paying them.

For purchase invoices, checks should be established, such as using a rubber stamp to stamp each incoming invoice with a mini form with spaces for ticks as each stage of the check on them is completed. The spaces in the stamp will be filled in by the people responsible for making each of the checks on the purchase invoices received, e.g.:

- one person certifying that the goods were actually received;
- a second person certifying that the goods were ordered;
- a third person certifying that the prices and calculations on the invoice are correct, and in accordance with the order originally placed and agreed;
- a fourth person certifying that the goods are in good condition and suitable for the purpose for which ordered.

Naturally, in a small business, simply because the office staff might be quite small, this cross-check may be in the hands of only one person other than the person who will pay the invoice.

A similar sort of check will be made in respect of sales invoices being sent out and on credit notes, both those being sent out and those being received.

16.11 Factoring

You've already learnt that one of the problems that many businesses face is the time taken by debtors to pay their accounts. Few businesses have so much cash available to them that they do not mind how long debtors take to pay. It is a rather surprising fact that a lot of businesses which fail do so not because the business is not making a profit, but because it has run out of cash funds. Once that happens, confidence in the business evaporates, and the business then finds that very few people will supply it with goods. It also cannot pay its employees. Closure of the business then happens fairly quickly in many cases.

As mentioned in Chapter 8, in the case of accounts receivable, the cash flow problem may be alleviated by using the services of a financial intermediary called a factor.

Factoring is a financial service designed to improve the cash flow of healthy, growing companies, enabling them to make better use of management time and the money tied up in trade credit to customers.

In essence, factors provide their clients with three closely integrated services covering sales accounting and collection; credit management, which can include protection against bad debts; and the availability of finance against sales invoices.

16.12 E&OE

On some invoices and other documents you will see 'E&OE' printed at the bottom. This abbreviation stands for 'Errors and Omissions Excepted'. Basically, this is a warning that there may possibly be errors or omissions which could mean that the figures shown could be incorrect, and that the recipient should check carefully the figures before taking any action concerning them.

Learning outcomes

You should now have learnt:

1. That 'returns inwards day book', 'returns inwards journal', 'sales returns journal' and 'sales returns day book' are different names for the same book.
2. That 'returns outwards day book', 'returns outwards journal', 'purchases returns journal' and 'purchases returns day book' are different names for the same book.
3. That goods returned by customers are all entered in a returns inwards day book.
4. That the returns inwards day book is used to post each item to the credit of the personal account of the customer in the sales ledger.
5. That the total of the returns inwards day book is debited at the end of the period to the returns inwards account in the general ledger.
6. That goods returned to suppliers are all entered in a returns outwards day book.
7. What the difference is between a credit note and a debit note.
8. That the returns outwards day book is used to debit the personal account of each supplier in the purchases ledger.
9. That the total of the returns outwards day book is credited at the end of the period to the returns outwards account in the general ledger.
10. How to make the appropriate entries relating to returns in the returns inwards and returns outwards day books and make the correct postings from them to the purchases ledger, sales ledger and general ledger.
11. That the process of making entries for returns in the books of purchasers and sellers is the mirror image of those made in their books for purchases and sales.

12 That statements are used by debtors to check the entries made in their books.

13 Of a range of causes for differences that can arise between statements and the seller's account in the debtor's purchases ledger and that such differences may not all be the result of an error.

14 How credit card transactions are recorded in the books and how commission charged to sellers by the credit card companies is treated in the income statement.

15 Why an effective system of invoice checking should be used by all businesses.

16 Why factoring is an attractive option for some businesses.

Answers to activities

16.1 In either case, the reasons why goods may be returned include:

- they were of the wrong type (e.g. the wrong model number of replacement remote control for a TV)
- the item purchased was one that was already owned by the customer (e.g. a CD)
- they were the wrong colour (e.g. paint doesn't match the existing colour)
- they were the wrong size (e.g. a pair of trousers was too tight)
- they were faulty (e.g. a computer kept crashing)
- a customer bought more than was needed (newsagents returning unsold newspapers)
- a customer changed her mind (e.g. hire purchase agreement on a DVD player)
- a customer saw the same goods elsewhere at a cheaper price
- a customer found the goods too difficult to use (e.g. the instructions for setting up and operating a video recorder were too complicated)
- (for trade customers) a customer had returned a faulty item to them and they were now returning it to their supplier
- items had been received in a damaged condition by the customer (e.g. fruit delivered to a supermarket)
- the seller had asked all customers to return a specific item (e.g. when an electrical good or a child's toy was found to be dangerous).

16.2 Differences could be due to a number of things having occurred, including the following:

- a purchase had been omitted from the books of either the seller or the debtor
- a purchase had been incorrectly entered in the books of either the seller or the debtor
- a purchase had been made at the end of the month but only entered in the books of either the seller or the debtor in the following month
- goods returned had been entered in the books of the seller but not in the books of the debtor
- goods returned had been incorrectly entered in the books of either the seller or the debtor
- the debtor had entered goods as having been returned in the books when, in fact, the goods were not returned to the seller
- a purchase had been recorded in the books of the seller in the debtor's account when it should have been entered in the account of another customer
- a purchase had been recorded in the books of the debtor in the seller's account when it should have been entered in the account of another seller
- a payment made to the supplier and entered in the books of the debtor had not yet been received by the seller
- goods had been despatched by the seller and entered in the books of the seller but had not yet been received by the debtor.

16.3 If this were not done then it would be possible for someone inside a business to send out an invoice at a price less than the true price. Any difference could then be split between that person and the outside business. For example, if an invoice was sent to Ivor Twister & Co for £2,000 but the invoice clerk made it out deliberately for £200 then, if there was no cross-check, the difference of £1,800 could be split between the invoice clerk and Ivor Twister & Company.

Similarly, outside businesses could send invoices for goods which were never received by the business. This might be in collaboration with an employee within the business, but there are businesses sending false invoices which rely on the businesses receiving them being inefficient and paying for items never received. There have been cases of businesses sending invoices for such items as advertisements which have never been published. The cashier of the business receiving the invoice, if the business is an inefficient one, might possibly think that someone in the business had authorised the advertisements and would pay the bill. Besides these there are, of course, genuine errors that an invoice checking system helps to avoid.

Review questions

16.1 You are to enter up the Purchases Day Book and the Returns Outwards Day Book from the following details, then to post the items to the relevant accounts in the Purchases Ledger and to show the transfers to the General Ledger at the end of the month.

2007
May 1 Credit purchase from F Bean £324.
4 Credit purchases from the following: A Clerk £216; B Lock £322; F Turner £64; G Rill £130.
7 Goods returned by us to the following: F Bean £56; A Clerk £28.
10 Credit purchase from B Lock £140.
18 Credit purchases from the following: J Top £230; I Gray £310; F Low £405; P Able £180.
25 Goods returned by us to the following: I Gray £140; B Lock £34.
31 Credit purchases from: F Turner £174; T Burns £230.

16.2A Enter up the Sales Day Book and the returns inwards day book from the following details. Then post to the customers' accounts and show the transfers to the General Ledger.

2008
June 1 Credit sales to: B Dock £240; M Ryan £126; G Soul £94; F Trip £107.
6 Credit sales to: P Coates £182; L Job £203; T Mann £99.
10 Goods returned to us by: B Dock £19; F Trip £32.
20 Credit sales to B Uphill £1,790.
24 Goods returned to us by L Job £16.
30 Credit sales to T Kane £302.

16.3 You are to enter up the sales, purchases, returns inwards and returns outwards day books from the following details, then to post the items to the relevant accounts in the sales and purchases ledgers. The totals from the day books are then to be transferred to the accounts in the General Ledger.

2009
May 1 Credit sales: T Thompson £56; L Rodriguez £148; K Barton £145.
3 Credit purchases: P Potter £144; H Harris £25; B Spencer £76.
7 Credit sales: K Kelly £89; N Mendes £78; N Lee £257.
9 Credit purchases: B Perkins £24; H Harris £58; H Miles £123.
11 Goods returned by us to: P Potter £12; B Spencer £22.
14 Goods returned to us by: T Thompson £5; K Barton £11; K Kelly £14.
17 Credit purchases: H Harris £54; B Perkins £65; L Nixon £75.
20 Goods returned by us to B Spencer £14.
24 Credit sales: K Mohammed £57; K Kelly £65; O Green £112.
28 Goods returned to us by N Mendes £24.
31 Credit sales: N Lee £55.

16.4A You are to enter the following items in the books, post to personal accounts, and show the transfers to the General Ledger.

2009		
July	1	Credit purchases from: K Hill £380; M Norman £500; N Senior £106.
	3	Credit sales to: E Rigby £510; E Phillips £246; F Thompson £356.
	5	Credit purchases from: R Morton £200; J Cook £180; D Edwards £410; C Davies £66.
	8	Credit sales to: A Green £307; H George £250; J Ferguson £185.
	12	Returns outwards to: M Norman £30; N Senior £16.
	14	Returns inwards from: E Phillips £18; F Thompson £22.
	20	Credit sales to: E Phillips £188; F Powell £310; E Lee £420.
	24	Credit purchases from: C Ferguson £550; K Ennevor £900.
	31	Returns inwards from: E Phillips £27; E Rigby £30.
	31	Returns outwards to: J Cook £13; C Davies £11.

You can find a range of additional self-test questions, as well as material to help you with your studies, on the website that accompanies this book at www.pearsoned.co.uk/wood.

chapter

17

The journal

Learning objectives

After you have studied this chapter, you should be able to:

- explain the purpose of having a journal
- enter up the journal
- post from the journal to the ledgers
- complete opening entries for a new set of accounting books in the journal and make the appropriate entries in the ledgers
- describe and explain the accounting cycle

Introduction

In this chapter, you will learn about the book of original entry that sweeps up all the transactions that have not been entered fully in the other five books of original entry – the journal. You'll learn about the sort of transactions that are entered in the journal and how to make those entries. You'll also learn how to transfer those entries to the accounts in the ledgers. Finally, you will learn what the accounting cycle consists of and see how it links all the material you have learnt so far in this book.

17.1 Main books of original entry

We have seen in earlier chapters that most transactions are entered in one of the following books of original entry:

- cash book
- sales day book
- purchases day book
- returns inwards day book
- returns outwards day book.

These books are each devoted to a particular form of transaction. For example, all credit sales are in the sales day book. To trace any of the transactions entered in these five books would be relatively easy, as we know exactly which book of original entry would contain the information we are looking for.

17.2 The journal: the other book of original entry

The other items which do not pass through these five books are much less common, and sometimes much more complicated. It would be easy for a bookkeeper to forget the details of these transactions if they were made directly into the ledger accounts from the source documents and, if the bookkeeper left the business, it could be impossible to understand such bookkeeping entries.

If these five books are used to record all cash and bank transactions, and all credit purchase and sales items, what are these other items that need to be recorded in a sixth book of original entry?

What is needed is a form of diary to record such transactions, before the entries are made in the double entry accounts. This book is called the **journal**. For each transaction it will contain:

- the date
- the name of the account(s) to be debited and the amount(s)
- the name of the account(s) to be credited and the amount(s)
- a description and explanation of the transaction (this is called a **narrative**)
- a folio reference to the source documents giving proof of the transaction.

The use of a journal makes fraud by bookkeepers more difficult. It also reduces the risk of entering the item once only instead of having double entry. Despite these advantages there are many businesses which do not have such a book.

17.3 Typical uses of the journal

Some of the main uses of the journal are listed below. It must not be thought that this is a complete list.

1 The purchase and sale of fixed assets on credit.
2 Writing off bad debts.
3 The correction of errors in the ledger accounts.
4 Opening entries. These are the entries needed to open a new set of books.
5 Adjustments to any of the entries in the ledgers.

The layout of the journal is:

The Journal				
Date	*Details*	*Folio*	*Dr*	*Cr*
	The name of the account to be debited. The name of the account to be credited. The narrative.			

On the first line in the entry is the account to be debited. The second line gives the account to be credited. It is indented so as to make it obvious that it is the credit part of the double entry. The final line is a description of what is being done and provides a permanent record of the reason(s) for the entry.

You should remember that the journal is not a double entry account. It is a form of diary, just as are the day books you learnt about in Chapters 14 to 16. Entering an item in the journal is not the same as recording an item in an account. Once the journal entry is made, the entry in the double entry accounts can then be made.

Note for students: The vertical lines have been included above in order to illustrate how the paper within the journal may be printed. You may find it useful to rule your paper according to this layout when attempting examples and questions on this topic.

17.4 Journal entries in examination questions

If you were to ask examiners what type of bookkeeping and accounting questions are always answered badly by students they would certainly include 'questions involving journal entries'. This is not because they are difficult, but because many students seem to suffer some sort of mental block when doing such questions. The authors, who have been examiners for a large number of accounting bodies around the world, believe that this occurs because students fail to view the journal as a document containing instructions, three per transaction:

1 The account(s) to be debited.
2 The account(s) to be credited.
3 A description of the transaction.

To help you avoid this sort of problem with journal entries, you'll first of all see what the entries are in the accounts, and then be shown how to write up the journal for each of these entries. Let's now look at a few examples.

In practice, the folio reference entered in the T-accounts is often that of the other account involved in the transaction, rather than that of a journal entry. However, this is done when no journal entry has been prepared. When a journal entry has been prepared, it is always the journal entry folio reference that appears in the T-accounts.

Purchase and sale on credit of non-current assets

1 A milling machine is bought on credit from Toolmakers Ltd for £10,550 on 1 July 2008.

The transaction involves the acquisition of an asset matched by a new liability. From what you have learnt in earlier chapters, you will know that the acquisition of an asset is represented by a debit entry in the asset account. You will also know that a new liability is recorded by crediting a liability account. The double entries would be:

Machinery Folio GL1

2008				£					
July	1	Toolmakers Ltd	J1	10,550					

Toolmakers Ltd Folio PL55

					2008				£
					July	1	Machinery	J1	10,550

Activity 17.2

All the folio numbers have been entered in these ledger accounts. You do need to enter them at some time so that you can trace the other side of the entries, but why have they already been entered?

Now what we have to do is to record those entries in the journal. Remember, the journal is simply a kind of diary, not in account form but in ordinary written form. It says which account has to been debited, which account has been credited, and then gives the narrative which simply describes the nature of the transaction. For the transaction above, the journal entry will appear as follows:

The Journal				(page 1)
Date	*Details*	*Folio*	*Dr*	*Cr*
2008			£	£
July 1	Machinery	GL 1	10,550	
	Toolmakers Ltd	PL55		10,550
	Purchase of milling machine on credit,			
	Purchases invoice No 7/159			

2 Sale of van no longer required for £800 on credit to K Lamb on 2 July 2008.

Here again it is not difficult to work out what entries are needed in the double entry accounts. They are as follows:

K Lamb Folio SL79

2008			£				
July 2	Van	J2	800				

Van Folio GL51

				2008			£
				July 2	K Lamb	J2	800

The journal entry will appear as follows:

The Journal				(page 2)
Date	*Details*	*Folio*	*Dr*	*Cr*
2008			£	£
July 2	K Lamb	SL79	800	
	Van	GL51		800
	Sales of van no longer required			
	See letter ref. KL3X8g			

Bad debts

A debt of £78 owing to us from H Mander is written off as a bad debt on 31 August 2008.

As the debt is now of no value we have to stop showing it as an asset. This means that we will credit H Mander to cancel it out of his account. A bad debt is an expense, and so we will debit it to a bad debts account. The double entry for this is shown as:

Bad Debts Folio GL16

2008			£				
Aug 31	H Mander	J3	78				

H Mander Folio SL99

				2008			£
				Aug 31	Bad debts	J3	78

The journal entry is:

The Journal				(page 3)
Date	*Details*	*Folio*	*Dr*	*Cr*
2008			£	£
Aug 31	Bad debts	GL16	78	
	H Mander	SL99		78
	Debt written off as bad. See letter in file HM2X8			

Correction of errors

This is explained in detail in Chapters 32 and 33.

However, the same procedures are followed as in the case of these other types of journal entries.

Opening entries

J Brew, after being in business for some years without keeping proper records, now decides to keep a double entry set of books. On 1 July 2008 he establishes that his assets and liabilities are as follows:

Assets: Van £3,700; Fixtures £1,800; Inventory £4,200;
Accounts receivable – B Young £95, D Blake £45; Bank £860; Cash £65.
Liabilities: Accounts payable – M Quinn £129, C Walters £410.

The Assets therefore total £3,700 + £1,800 + £4,200 + £95 + £45 + £860 + £65 = £10,765; and the Liabilities total £129 + £410 = £539.

The Capital consists of Assets – Liabilities, i.e. £10,765 – £539 = £10,226.

1 July 2008 will be the first day of the accounting period, as that is the date on which all the asset and liability values were established.

We start the writing up of the books on 1 July 2008. To do this we:

1 Open the journal and make the journal entries to record the opening assets, liabilities and capital.
2 Open asset accounts, one for each asset. Each opening asset is shown as a debit balance.
3 Open liability accounts, one for each liability. Each opening liability is shown as a credit balance.
4 Open an account for the capital. Show it as a credit balance.

The journal records what you are doing, and why. Exhibit 17.1 shows:

- The journal
- The opening entries in the double entry accounts.

Exhibit 17.1

The Journal				(page 5)
Date	*Details*	*Folio*	*Dr*	*Cr*
2008			£	£
July 1	Van	GL1	3,700	
	Fixtures	GL2	1,800	
	Inventory	GL3	4,200	
	Accounts receivable – B Young	SL1	95	
	D Blake	SL2	45	
	Bank	CB1	860	
	Cash	CB1	65	
	Accounts payable – M Quinn	PL1		129
	C Walters	PL2		410
	Capital	GL4		10,226
	Assets and liabilities at this date entered to open the books.		10,765	10,765

General Ledger

Van *(page 1)*

2008			Folio	£				
July	1	Balance	J 5	3,700				

Fixtures *(page 2)*

2008			Folio	£				
July	1	Balance	J 5	1,800				

Inventory *(page 3)*

2008			Folio	£				
July	1	Balance	J 5	4,200				

Capital *(page 4)*

					2008			Folio	£
					July	1	Balance	J 5	10,226

Sales Ledger

B Young *(page 1)*

2008			Folio	£				
July	1	Balance	J 5	95				

D Blake *(page 2)*

2008			Folio	£				
July	1	Balance	J 5	45				

Purchases Ledger

M Quinn *(page 1)*

					2008			Folio	£
					July	1	Balance	J 5	129

C Walters *(page 2)*

					2008			Folio	£
					July	1	Balance	J 5	410

Cash Book

(page 1)

2008			Folio	*Cash* £	*Bank* £	
July	1	Balances	J 5	65	860	

Once these opening balances have been recorded in the books, the day-to-day transactions can be entered in the normal manner.

At the elementary level of examinations in bookkeeping, questions are often asked which require you to open a set of books and record the day-by-day entries for the ensuing period.

Do you think you will ever need to do this again for this business? (Hint: think about the entries to be made at the start of the next accounting period.)

Adjustments to any of the entries in the ledgers

These can be of many types and it is impossible to write out a complete list. Several examples are now shown:

1 K Young, a debtor, owed £2,000 on 1 July 2009. He was unable to pay his account in cash, but offers a five-year-old car in full settlement of the debt. The offer is accepted on 5 July 2009.

The personal account has now been settled and needs to be credited with the £2,000. On the other hand, the business now has an extra asset, a car, resulting in the car account needing to be debited with the £2,000 value that has been placed upon the new car.

The double entry recorded in the ledgers is:

Car GL171

2009				£				
July 5	K Young	J6		2,000				

K Young SL333

2009				£	2009			£
July 1	Balance b/d			2,000	July 5	Motor car	J6	2,000

The journal entry is:

The Journal *(page 6)*

Date	*Details*	*Folio*	*Dr*	*Cr*
2009			£	£
July 5	Car	GL171	2,000	
	K Young	SL333		2,000
	Accepted car in full settlement of debt per letter dated 5/7/2009			

2 T Jones is a creditor. On 10 July 2009 his business is taken over by A Lee to whom the debt of £150 is now to be paid.

Here one creditor is just being exchanged for another one. The action needed is to cancel the amount owing to T Jones by debiting his account, and to show it owing to Lee by opening an account for Lee and crediting it.

The entries in the ledger accounts are:

T Jones SL92

2009				£	2009			£
July 10	A Lee	J7		150	July 1	Balance b/d		150

A Lee SL244

					2009			£
					July 10	T Jones	J7	150

The journal entry is:

The Journal				(page 7)
Date	Details	Folio	Dr	Cr
2009			£	£
July 10	T Jones	SL 92	150	
	A Lee	SL244		150
	Transfer of indebtedness as per letter ref G/1335			

3 We had not yet paid for an office printer we bought on credit for £310 because it was not working properly when installed. On 12 July 2009 we returned it to the supplier, RS Ltd. An allowance of £310 was offered by the supplier and accepted. As a result, we no longer owe the supplier anything for the printer.

The double entry in the ledger accounts is:

RS Ltd PL124

2009				£	2009				£
July	12	Office machinery	J8	310	July	1	Balance b/d		310

Office Machinery GL288

2009				£	2009				£
July	1	Balance b/d		310	July	12	RS Ltd	J8	310

The journal entry is:

The Journal				(page 8)
Date	Details	Folio	Dr	Cr
2009			£	£
July 12	RS Ltd	PL124	310	
	Office machinery	GL288		310
	Faulty printer returned to supplier.			
	Full allowance given. See letter 10/7/2009.			

17.5 Examination guidance

Later on in your studies, especially in *Business Accounting 2*, you may find that some of the journal entries become rather more complicated than those you have seen so far. The best plan for nearly all students is to follow this advice:

1 **On your examination answer paper write a heading 'Workings'. Then show the double entry accounts under that heading.**
2 **Now put a heading 'Answer', and show the answer in the form of the Journal, as shown in this chapter.**

If the question asks for journal entries you must *not* fall into the trap of just showing the double entry accounts, as you could get no marks at all *even though your double entry records are correct*. The examiner wants to see the journal entries, and you *must* show those in your answer.

17.6 The basic accounting cycle

Now that we have covered all aspects of bookkeeping entries, we can show the whole **accounting cycle** in the form of the diagram in Exhibit 17.2.

Note that the 'accounting cycle' refers to the sequence in which data is recorded and processed until it becomes part of the financial statements at the end of the period.

Exhibit 17.2 The accounting cycle for a profit-making organisation

Source documents

Where original information is to be found

- Sales and purchases invoices
- Debit and credit notes for returns
- Bank pay-in slips and cheque counterfoils
- Receipts for cash paid out and received
- Correspondence containing other financial information

Original entry

What happens to it

Classified and then entered in books of original entry:

- The cash books*
- Sales and purchases day books
- Returns inwards and outwards day books
- The journal

Double entry

How the dual aspect of each transaction is recorded

Double entry accounts

General ledger	*Sales ledger*	*Purchases ledger*	*Cash books**
Real and nominal accounts	Accounts receivable	Accounts payable	Cash book and petty cash book

(**Note*: Cash books fulfil the roles both of books of original entry and double entry accounts)

Check arithmetic

Checking the arithmetical accuracy of double entry accounts

Trial balance

Profit or loss

Calculation of profit or loss for the accounting period shown in a financial statement

Income statement

Closing financial position

Financial statement showing liabilities, assets and capital at the end of the accounting period

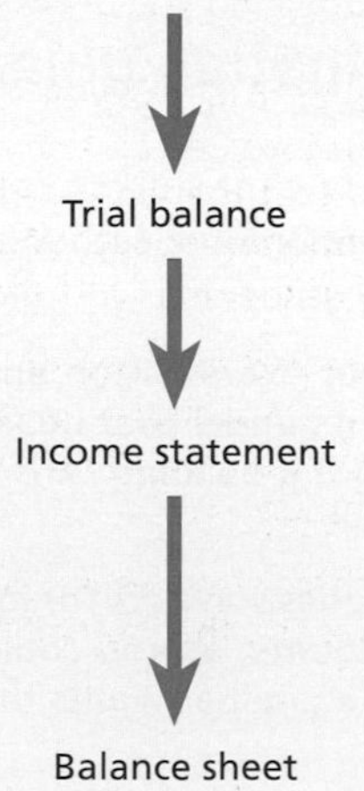

Balance sheet

Activity 17.4 What are the six books of original entry?

Learning outcomes

You should now have learnt:

1 What the journal is used for.

2 That the journal is the collection place for items that do not pass fully through the other five books of original entry.

3 That there is a range of possible types of transactions that must be entered in the journal.

4 That the opening double entries made on starting a set of books for the first time are done using the journal.

5 How to make the opening entries for a new set of books in the journal and in the ledger accounts.

6 That the main parts of the accounting cycle are as follows:

(*a*) Collect source documents.
(*b*) Enter transactions in the books of original entry.
(*c*) Post to ledgers.
(*d*) Extract trial balance.
(*e*) Prepare the income statement.
(*f*) Draw up the balance sheet.

Answers to activities

17.1 All transactions relating to non-current assets. Also, entries have to be recorded somewhere when errors in the books have to be corrected, or when any figures in the ledger accounts need to be changed. Also, any transfers involving the Capital Account, such as when funds are set aside from the Capital Account to provide resources should a building need to be repaired or replaced.

17.2 You are looking at the ledger accounts after the details have been entered in them from the journal and you always enter the folio number in the ledger account as you make each entry, not afterwards. The check that the entries has been completed is made by only entering the folio numbers *in the journal* as each entry is written in the appropriate ledger account. You could, therefore, see an entry in the journal that has no folio numbers entered against it. This would signify that the journal entry has not yet been fully recorded in the appropriate ledger accounts. As mentioned above, you should *never* see this in a ledger account as the folio number is always entered *at the same time* as the rest of the details from the journal are entered.

17.3 The need for opening entries will not occur very often. They will not be needed each year as the balances from the previous period will have been brought forward. They will only be required a second time if the business goes through a change in status, for example, if it becomes a limited company.

17.4 Cash book, sales day book, purchases day book, returns inwards day book, returns outwards day book and the journal.

Review questions

17.1 You are to show the journal entries necessary to record the following items which occured in 2008:

(*a*) May 1 Bought a van on credit from Deedon Garage for £5,395.
(*b*) May 3 A debt of £81 owing from P Knight was written off as a bad debt.
(*c*) May 8 Office furniture bought by us for £610 was returned to the supplier Timewas Ltd, as it was unsuitable. Full allowance will be given to us.
(*d*) May 12 We are owed £320 by R Twig. He is declared bankrupt and we received £51 in full settlement of the debt.
(*e*) May 14 We take goods costing £22 out of the business inventory without paying for them.
(*f*) May 28 Some time ago we paid an insurance bill thinking that it was all in respect of the business. We now discover that £62 of the amount paid was in fact insurance of our private house.
(*g*) May 28 Bought machinery for £1,260 on credit from Electrotime Ltd.

17.2A Show the journal entries necessary to record the following items:

2007
Apr 1 Bought fixtures on credit from Bell and Co £1,153.
4 We take goods costing £340 out of the business inventory without paying for them.
9 £68 of the goods taken by us on 4 April is returned back into inventory by us. We do not take any money for the return of the goods.
12 H Cowes owes us £640. He is unable to pay his debt. We agree to take some computer equipment from him at that value and so cancel the debt.
18 Some of the fixtures bought from Bell and Co, £42 worth, are found to be unsuitable and are returned to them for full allowance.
24 A debt owing to us by P Lees of £124 is written off as a bad debt.
30 Office equipment bought on credit from Furniture Today Ltd for £1,710.

17.3 You are to open the books of F Polk, a trader, via the journal to record the assets and liabilities, and are then to record the daily transactions for the month of May. A trial balance is to be extracted as on 31 May 2009.

2009
May 1 *Assets*: Premises £34,000; Van £5,125; Fixtures £810; Inventory £6,390; Accounts receivable: P Mullen £140, F Lane £310; Cash at bank £6,240; Cash in hand £560.
Liabilities: Accounts payable: S Hood £215, J Brown £460.
1 Paid storage costs by cheque £40.
2 Goods bought on credit from: S Hood £145; D Main £206; W Tone £96; R Foot £66.
3 Goods sold on credit to: J Wilson £112; T Cole £164; F Syme £208; J Allen £91; P White £242; F Lane £90.
4 Paid for motor expenses in cash £47.
7 Cash drawings by proprietor £150.
9 Goods sold on credit to: T Cole £68; J Fox £131.
11 Goods returned to Polk by: J Wilson £32; F Syme £48.
14 Bought another van on credit from Abel Motors Ltd £4,850.
16 The following paid Polk their accounts by cheque less 5 per cent cash discount: P Mullen; F Lane; J Wilson; F Syme.
19 Goods returned by Polk to R Foot £6.
22 Goods bought on credit from: L Mole £183; W Wright £191.
24 The following accounts were settled by Polk by cheque less 5 per cent cash discount: S Hood; J Brown; R Foot.
27 Salaries paid by cheque £480.
30 Paid business rates by cheque £132.
31 Paid Abel Motors Ltd a cheque for £4,850.

You can find a range of additional self-test questions, as well as material to help you with your studies, on the website that accompanies this book at www.pearsoned.co.uk/wood.

hapter 18

The analytical petty cash book and the imprest system

Learning objectives

After you have studied this chapter, you should be able to:

- explain why many organisations use a petty cash book
- make entries in a petty cash book
- transfer the appropriate amounts from the petty cash book to the ledgers at the end of each period
- explain and operate the imprest system for petty cash
- explain why some organisations use a bank cash book
- make entries in a bank cash book

Introduction

You may remember that you learnt in Chapter 13 that there is a second type of cash book, called the **petty cash book**, which many businesses use to record small amounts paid for in cash. (It was included in the accounting cycle shown in Exhibit 17.2.) In this chapter, you'll learn of the type of items that are recorded in the petty cash book, and how to make the entries to it. You'll also learn how to transfer financial data from the petty cash book into the ledgers. Finally, you will learn about bank cash books and how they differ from the cash books you learnt about in Chapter 13.

18.1 Division of the cash book

As businesses continue to grow, some now having a commercial value in excess of that of many smaller countries, you have learnt that, for many, it has become necessary to have several books instead of just one ledger. In fact, nowadays all but the very smallest organisations use sets of ledgers and day books.

Activity 18.1 Why do we have day books? Why don't we just enter every transaction directly into the appropriate ledger accounts?

The cash book became a book of original entry so that all cash and bank transactions could be separated from the rest of the accounts in the general ledger. It is for much the same reason that many organisations use a petty cash book. Every business has a number of transactions of very small value which, were they all recorded in the cash book, would only serve to make it more difficult to identify the important transactions that businesses need to keep a close eye upon. **Just like the cash book, the petty cash book is both a book of original entry and a ledger account.**

The advantages of using a petty cash book can be summarised as follows:

- The task of handling and recording small cash payments can be given by the cashier (the person responsible for recording entries in the cash book) to a junior member of staff. This person is known as the 'petty cashier'. The cashier, who is a more senior and, consequently, higher paid member of staff would be saved from routine work.
- If small cash payments were entered into the main cash book, these items would then need posting one by one to the ledgers. For example, if travelling expenses were paid to staff on a daily basis, this could mean approximately 250 postings to the staff travelling expenses account during the year, i.e. 5 days per week × 50 working weeks per year. However, if a petty cash book is used, it would only be the monthly totals for each period that need posting to the general ledger. If this were done, only twelve entries would be needed in the staff travelling expenses account instead of approximately 250.

When a petty cashier makes a payment to someone, then that person will have to fill in a voucher showing exactly what the payment was for. They usually have to attach bills, e.g. for petrol, to the petty cash voucher. They would sign the voucher to certify that their expenses had been received from the petty cashier.

18.2 The imprest system

It is all very well having a petty cash book, but where does the money paid out from it come from? The **imprest system** is one where the cashier gives the petty cashier enough cash to meet the petty cash needs for the following period. Then, at the end of the period, the cashier finds out the amounts spent by the petty cashier, by looking at the entries in the petty cash book. At the same time, the petty cashier may give the petty cash vouchers to the cashier so that the entries in the petty cash book may be checked. The cashier then passes cash to the value of the amount spent on petty cash in the period to the petty cashier. In other words, the cashier tops up the amount remaining in petty cash to bring it back up to the level it was at when the period started. This process is the imprest system and this topped-up amount is known as the petty cash **float**.

Exhibit 18.1 shows an example of this method.

Exhibit 18.1

		£
Period 1	The cashier gives the petty cashier	100
	The petty cashier pays out in the period	(78)
	Petty cash now in hand	22
	The cashier now gives the petty cashier the amount spent	78
	Petty cash in hand at the end of Period 1	100
Period 2	The petty cashier pays out in the period	(84)
	Petty cash now in hand	16
	The cashier now gives the petty cashier the amount spent	84
	Petty cash in hand at the end of Period 2	100

It may be necessary to increase the petty cash float to be held at the start of each period. In the above case, if we had wanted to increase the float at the end of the second period to £120, then the cashier would have given the petty cashier an extra £20, i.e. £84 + £20 = £104.

In some small organisations, no petty cash book is kept. Instead, at the end of each period, the amount left in petty cash is reconciled (i.e. checked and verified as correct) with the receipts held by the petty cashier. The amount spent is then given to the petty cashier in order to restore the float to its agreed level. However, this is not an ideal method to adopt. Businesses need to control the uses of all their resources, including petty cash, and so virtually every organisation that operates a petty cash float maintains a petty cash book. The most common format adopted is the 'analytical petty cash book'.

18.3 Illustration of an analytical petty cash book

An analytical petty cash book is shown in Exhibit 18.2. This example shows one for a nursery school.

Exhibit 18.2

Petty Cash Book *(page 31)*

Receipts	*Folio*	*Date*	*Details*	*Voucher No*	*Total*	*Motor Expenses*	*Staff Travelling Expenses*	*Postage*	*Cleaning*	*Ledger Folio*	*Ledger Accounts*
£				£	£	£	£	£		£	
300	CB 19	Sept 1	Cash								
		2	Petrol	1	16	16					
		3	J Green	2	23		23				
		3	Postage	3	12			12			
		4	D Davies	4	32		32				
		7	Cleaning	5	11				11		
		9	Petrol	6	21	21					
		12	K Jones	7	13		13				
		14	Petrol	8	23	23					
		15	L Black	9	5		5				
		16	Cleaning	10	11				11		
		18	Petrol	11	22	22					
		20	Postage	12	12			12			
		22	Cleaning	13	11				11		
		24	G Wood	14	7		7				
		27	C Brown	15	13					PL18	13
		29	Postage	16	12	—	—	12	—		—
					244	82	80	36	33		13
						GL	GL	GL	GL		
244	CB 22	30	Cash			17	29	44	64		
—		30	Balance	c/d	300						
544					544						
300		Oct 1	Balance	b/d							

The receipts column is the debit side of the petty cash book. On giving £300 to the petty cashier on 1 September, the credit entry is made in the cash book while the debit entry is made in the petty cash book. A similar entry is made on 30 September for the £244 paid by the headteacher to the petty cashier. As this amount covers all the expenses paid by the petty cashier, the float is now restored to its earlier level of £300. The credit side is used to record all the payments made by the petty cashier.

The transactions that were recorded in the petty cash book were:

2008		Voucher number		£
Sept	1	–	The headteacher gives £300 as float to the petty cashier	
			Payments out of petty cash during September:	
	2	1	Petrol: School bus	16
	3	2	J Green – travelling expenses of staff	23
	3	3	Postage	12
	4	4	D Davies – travelling expenses of staff	32
	7	5	Cleaning expenses	11
	9	6	Petrol: School bus	21
	12	7	K Jones – travelling expenses of staff	13
	14	8	Petrol: School bus	23
	15	9	L Black – travelling expenses of staff	5
	16	10	Cleaning expenses	11
	18	11	Petrol: School bus	22
	20	12	Postage	12
	22	13	Cleaning expenses	11
	24	14	G Wood – travelling expenses of staff	7
	27	15	Settlement of C Brown's account in the Purchases Ledger	13
	29	16	Postage	12
	30	–	The headteacher reimburses the petty cashier the amount spent in the month.	

The process followed during the period that led to these entries appearing in the petty cash book as shown in Exhibit 18.2 is:

1 Enter the date and details of each payment. Put the amount paid in the Total column.
2 Put the same amount in the column for that type of expense.
3 At the end of each period, add up the Total column.
4 Add up each of the expense columns. The total found in step 3 should equal the total of all the expense columns. In Exhibit 18.2 this is £244.
5 Enter the amount reimbursed to make up the float in the Receipts column.
6 Balance-off the petty cash book, carrying down the petty cash in hand balance to the next period.

To complete the double entry for petty cash expenses paid:

1 The total of each expense column is debited to the appropriate expense account in the general ledger.
2 The folio number of each expense account in the general ledger is entered under the appropriate expense column in the petty cash book. (This signifies that the double entry to the ledger account has been made.)
3 The last column in the petty cash book is a Ledger column. It contains entries for items paid out of petty cash which need posting to a ledger other than the general ledger. (This might arise, for example, if a purchases ledger account was settled out of petty cash.)

Where is the other side of the double entry for all these expense postings to the ledgers recorded?

The double entries for all the items in Exhibit 18.2 are shown in Exhibit 18.3.

Exhibit 18.3

Cash Book
(Bank and Folio columns only) *(page 19)*

				Folio	£
			2008		
			Sept 1 Petty cash	PCB 31	300
			30 Petty cash	PCB 31	244

General Ledger
School Bus Expenses *(page 17)*

	Folio	£			
2008					
Sept 30 Petty cash	PCB 31	82			

Staff Travelling Expenses *(page 29)*

	Folio	£			
2008					
Sept 30 Petty cash	PCB 31	80			

Postage *(page 44)*

	Folio	£			
2008					
Sept 30 Petty cash	PCB 31	36			

Cleaning *(page 64)*

	Folio	£			
2008					
Sept 30 Petty cash	PCB 31	33			

Purchases Ledger
C Brown *(page 18)*

	Folio	£			£
2008			2008		
Sept 30 Petty cash	PCB 31	13	Sept 1 Balance	b/d	13

Note how the Folio column is used to enter 'b/d'. You may have noticed previously that this is done for both 'b/d' and 'c/d' in all ledger accounts and in the cash book where contra entries are also indicated in the folio column by use of the symbol '¢'.

18.4 Bank cash book

Nowadays, many businesses have only a small number of sales that are paid for with cash. The rest of the 'cash' sales are actually paid using credit cards, cheques and direct transfers into the business bank account using systems like Switch (which, as you learnt in Chapter 12, is operated by UK banks and involves a customer's bank card being swiped into a special machine in the same way that credit card payments are processed). Switch is used in retail transactions and results in the payment being transferred immediately from the customer's bank account into the business bank account.

Organisations which have only a small number of sales for cash may use a different form of cash book from the one you learnt about in Chapter 13. If they do, they will use a petty cash book and a **bank cash book**. The bank cash book is given this name because *all* payments in cash are entered in the petty cash book, and the bank cash book contains *only* bank columns and discount columns.

In a bank cash book (it could also be done in an 'ordinary' cash book), an extra column may be added. The extra column would show the details of the cheques and direct transfers banked, with just the total of the banking being shown in the total column.

Exhibit 18.4 shows the receipts side of a bank cash book containing this extra column. The totals of the deposits made into the bank on each of the three days were £192, £381 and £1,218. The details column shows what the bankings are made up of.

Exhibit 18.4

Bank Cash Book (Receipts side)

Date		*Details*	*Discount*	*Items*	*Total Banked*
2009			£	£	£
May	14	G Archer	5	95	
	14	P Watts	3	57	
	14	C King		40	192
	20	K Dooley	6	114	
	20	Cash Sales		55	
	20	R Jones		60	
	20	P Mackie	8	152	381
	31	J Young		19	
	31	T Broome	50	950	
	31	Cash Sales		116	
	31	H Tiller	7	133	1,218

Learning outcomes

You should now have learnt:

1. That the petty cash book saves (*a*) the cash book and (*b*) the ledger accounts from containing a lot of trivial detail.
2. That the use of the petty cash book enables the cashier or a senior member of staff to delegate this type of work to a more junior member of staff.
3. That the cashier should periodically check the work performed by the petty cashier.
4. That all payments made by the petty cashier should have petty cash vouchers as evidence of proof of expense.
5. How to enter petty cash transactions into the petty cash book.
6. How to transfer the totals for each expense recorded in the petty cash book to the appropriate ledger accounts.
7. How to operate a float system for petty cash.
8. The difference between a cash book and a bank cash book.
9. Why some organisations use a bank cash book instead of a cash book.

Answers to activities

18.1 One reason why we have day books is to avoid too much detail being entered in the ledgers.

18.2 In the petty cash book. Like the cash book, the petty cash book is not only a book of original entry, it is also an account that would otherwise appear in the general ledger.

Review questions

18.1 The following is a summary of the petty cash transactions of Jockfield Ltd for May 2008.

			£
May	1	Received from Cashier £300 as petty cash float	
	2	Postage	18
	3	Travelling	12
	4	Cleaning	15
	7	Petrol for delivery van	22
	8	Travelling	25
	9	Stationery	17
	11	Cleaning	18
	14	Postage	5
	15	Travelling	8
	18	Stationery	9
	18	Cleaning	23
	20	Postage	13
	24	Delivery van 5,000 mile service	43
	26	Petrol	18
	27	Cleaning	21
	29	Postage	5
	30	Petrol	14

You are required to:

(*a*) Rule up a suitable petty cash book with analysis columns for expenditure on cleaning, motor expenses, postage, stationery, travelling.

(*b*) Enter the month's transactions.

(*c*) Enter the receipt of the amount necessary to restore the imprest and carry down the balance for the commencement of the following month.

(*d*) State how the double entry for the expenditure is completed.

(*Association of Accounting Technicians*)

18.2

(*a*) Why do some businesses keep a petty cash book as well as a cash book?

(*b*) Kathryn Rochford keeps her petty cash book on the imprest system, the imprest being £25. For the month of April 2009 her petty cash transactions were as follows:

			£
Apr	1	Petty cash balance	1.13
	2	Petty cashier presented vouchers to cashier and obtained cash to restore the imprest	23.87
	4	Bought postage stamps	8.50
	9	Paid to Courtney Bishop, a creditor	2.35
	11	Paid bus fares	1.72
	17	Bought envelopes	0.70
	23	Received cash for personal telephone call	0.68
	26	Bought petrol	10.00

(*i*) Enter the above transactions in the petty cash book and balance the petty cash book at 30 April, bringing down the balance on 1 May.

(*ii*) On 1 May Kathryn Rochford received an amount of cash from the cashier to restore the imprest. Enter this transaction in the petty cash book.

(*c*) Open the ledger accounts to complete the double entry for the following:

(*i*) The petty cash analysis columns headed *Postage and Stationery* and *Travelling Expenses*;

(*ii*) The transactions dated 9 and 23 April 2009.

(*Northern Examinations and Assessment Board: GCSE*)

→

→ **18.3A** Rule up a petty cash book with analysis columns for office expenses, motor expenses, cleaning expenses and casual labour. The cash float is £600 and the amount spent is reimbursed on 30 June.

2007			£
June	1	F Black – casual labour	18
	2	Letterheadings	41
	2	Abel Motors – motor repairs	67
	3	Cleaning materials	4
	6	Envelopes	11
	8	Petrol	22
	11	P Lyon – casual labour	16
	12	T Upton – cleaner	8
	12	Paper clips	3
	14	Petrol	19
	16	Adhesive tape	2
	16	Petrol	25
	21	Motor taxation	95
	22	F Luck – casual labour	19
	23	T Upton – cleaner	14
	24	J Lamb – casual labour	27
	25	Copy paper	8
	26	Lively Cars – motor repairs	83
	29	Petrol	24
	30	F Tred – casual labour	21

18.4 Oakhill Printing Cost Ltd operates its petty cash account on the imprest system. It is maintained at a figure of £80, with the balance being restored to that amount on the first day of each month. At 30 April 2006 the petty cash box held £19.37 in cash.

During May 2006, the following petty cash transactions arose:

			£
May	1	Cash received to restore imprest (to be derived)	?
	1	Bus fares	0.41
	2	Stationery	2.35
	4	Bus fares	0.30
	7	Postage stamps	1.70
	7	Trade journal	0.95
	8	Bus fares	0.64
	11	Tippex	1.29
	12	Typewriter ribbons	5.42
	14	Parcel postage	3.45
	15	Paper-clips	0.42
	15	Newspapers	2.00
	16	Photocopier repair	16.80
	19	Postage stamps	1.50
	20	Drawing pins	0.38
	21	Train fare	5.40
	22	Photocopier paper	5.63
	23	Display decorations	3.07
	23	Tippex	1.14
	25	Wrapping paper	0.78
	27	String	0.61
	27	Sellotape	0.75
	27	Biro pens	0.46

			£
	28	Typewriter repair	13.66
	30	Bus fares	2.09
June	1	Cash received to restore imprest (to be derived)	?

Required:

(*a*) Open and post the company's analysed petty cash book for the period 1 May to 1 June 2006 inclusive.

(*b*) Balance the account at 30 May 2006.

(*c*) Show the imprest reimbursement entry on June 1.

You can find a range of additional self-test questions, as well as material to help you with your studies, on the website that accompanies this book at www.pearsoned.co.uk/wood.

chapter 19

Value added tax

Learning objectives

After you have studied this chapter, you should be able to:

- enter up VAT in all the necessary books and accounts
- distinguish between taxable businesses and other businesses
- make out sales invoices including charges for VAT
- fill in a VAT Return form

Introduction

In this chapter, you'll learn about the UK system of Value Added Tax. You will learn about how the concept that *the final consumer pays all* underlies the system and of how VAT is collected in stages as goods pass their way down the supply chain. You'll learn about the different rates of VAT and of the different ways VAT has to be recorded as a result. Finally, you will learn how to prepare a VAT Account and complete a VAT Return.

19.1 What is VAT?

Value Added Tax (VAT) is a tax charged on the supply of most goods and services in the United Kingdom. Some goods and services are not taxable, for example postal services. In addition some persons and businesses are exempted, such as those with low levels of turnover. Value Added Tax is administered in the UK by HM Revenue and Customs.

The concept underlying VAT is that the tax is paid by the ultimate consumer of the goods or services *but* that everyone in the supply chain must account for and settle up the net amount of VAT they have received in the VAT tax period, usually three months. If they have received more in VAT than they have paid out in VAT, they must send that difference to HM Revenue and Customs. If they have paid out more than they have received, they will be reimbursed the difference.

Goods typically pass through at least two sellers (the manufacturer and the retailer) before they are finally sold to the consumer. These intermediate-stage VAT payments will be cancelled out when the final stage in the chain is reached and the good or service is sold to its ultimate consumer.

Exhibit 19.1 shows, through an example, how the system works.

Exhibit 19.1

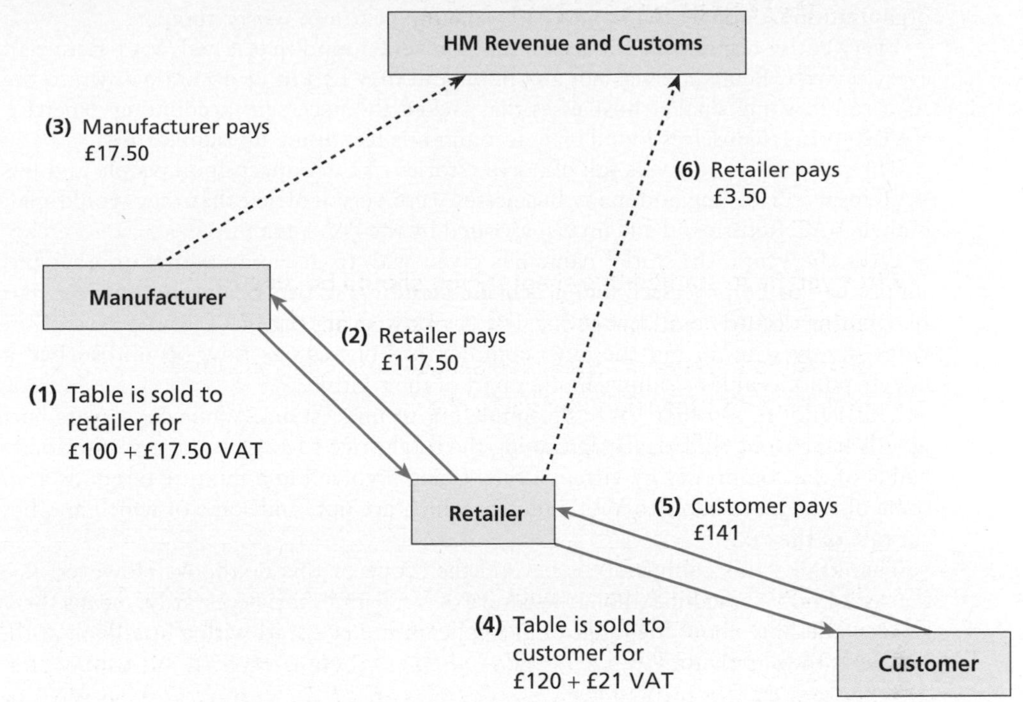

In the example in Exhibit 19.1:

1 A manufacturer sells a table to a retailer for £100 plus VAT of £17.50.
2 The retailer pays the manufacturer £117.50 for the table.
3 The VAT on that sale (£17.50) is sent by the manufacturer to HM Revenue and Customs.
4 The retailer sells the goods to the customer (i.e. the consumer) for £120 plus VAT of £21.
5 The customer pays £141 to the retailer for the table.
6 The amount of VAT paid for the goods by the retailer to the manufacturer (£17.50) is deducted from the VAT received by the retailer from the customer (£21) and the difference of £3.50 is then sent to HM Revenue and Customs.

Only the ultimate consumer has actually paid any VAT. Unfortunately, everyone in the chain has to send the VAT charged at the step when they were in the role of seller.

In theory, the amount received in stages by HM Revenue and Customs will equal the amount of VAT paid by the ultimate consumer in the final stage of the supply chain.

Can you think of any circumstances where this may not be the case?

19.2 Background

When VAT was first introduced in 1973 as a result of the entry of the UK into the EU, it came as quite a shock to the business community and to many accountants. The previous tax on goods,

Purchase Tax, had only applied to manufacturers and wholesalers whose goods were liable to the tax. VAT, on the other hand, applied to virtually all goods and services and all but a few organisations suddenly found they had something extra to worry about.

Every entity responsible for accounting for VAT found that it had 'VAT Returns' to complete every quarter. Being late was not an option and they had to be accurate down to the last penny. As a result, some smaller businesses that lacked the necessary accounting expertise to do their VAT Returns themselves found their accountant's fees going up significantly.

The press of the day was full of horror stories of the impact upon people and businesses of a VAT inspector calling and many businesses were very worried that they would make a mistake in their VAT Return and end up being visited by the 'VAT man'.

Over the years, the initial panic has given way to acceptance that another piece of paper simply has to be processed and a debt outstanding settled or an amount receivable received. Accounting records and accounting systems now deal with VAT routinely and the additional work involved in all but the most complex businesses has now been absorbed and become largely unnoticeable as simply another part of the routine.

This is not to say that VAT is a simple tax to understand. While consumers hardly notice it (goods have to be sold clearly indicating the total price to pay), some organisations suffer at the hands of the complexity by virtue of their being involved in a mixture of goods and/or services, some of which are liable to VAT, some of which are not, and some of which are, but at a different rate of the tax.

Thankfully, this complexity is beyond the scope of this textbook. However, it is important that you know something about the nature of VAT and that, necessarily, means that you need to know something about the range of its application. Let's start with a brief look at the VAT rates and what they apply to.

19.3 VAT rates

The **standard rate** of VAT is decided by Parliament. It has been changed from time to time. At the time of writing it is 17.5 per cent. There is also currently a **reduced rate** of 5 per cent on domestic fuel and power, one of 5 per cent on the installation of some energy-saving materials, and a **zero rate** on items like food sold in a supermarket.

19.4 Standard-rated businesses

You've already seen an example in Exhibit 19.1 of what happens to the VAT when a manufacturer sells to a retailer who then sells to a consumer. Another common example involves a business selling its own product direct to the final consumer.

Imagine that Trader A (a farmer) sells some of the plants they have grown to the general public.

Trader A sells goods to Jones for £100 + VAT of 17.5%:

		£
The sales invoice is for:	Price	100.00
	+ VAT 17.5%	17.50
	= Total price	117.50

Trader A will then pay the £17.50 they have collected to the Revenue and Customs.

***Note*: VAT has to be recorded and included in the VAT Return *to the penny*.**

In both this example and the one shown in Exhibit 19.1, you can see that the full amount of VAT has fallen on the person who finally buys the goods. The sellers have merely acted as unpaid collectors of the tax for HM Revenue and Customs.

The value of goods sold and/or services supplied by a business is known as the **outputs**. VAT on such items is called **output tax**. The value of goods bought in and/or services supplied to a business is known as the **inputs**. The VAT on these items is, therefore, called **input tax**.

19.5 Exempted businesses

Some businesses are exempted from accounting for VAT. They do not add VAT to the amount at which they sell their products or supply their services, nor do they get a refund of the VAT they have themselves paid on goods and services bought by them.

The types of businesses exempted can be listed under two headings:

1 Nature of business. Various types of business do not have to add VAT to charges for goods or services. A bank, for instance, does not have to add VAT on to its bank charges, nor do credit card companies.
2 Small businesses. If small businesses do register for VAT then they will have to keep full VAT records in addition to charging out VAT. To save very small businesses the costs and effort of keeping such records, provided that their turnover is below a certain amount (at the time of writing, £64,000 in a 12-month period), they don't need to register unless they want to. They can also deregister if their turnover falls below a certain level (at the time of writing, £62,000).

Apart from not having to keep VAT records, what advantages might there be for a business that does not register for VAT?

19.6 Zero-rated businesses

This special category of business

1 does not have to add VAT on to the selling price of products, and
2 can obtain a refund of all VAT paid on the purchase of goods or services.

If, therefore, £100,000 worth of goods are sold by the business, nothing has to be added for VAT but, if £8,000 VAT had been paid by it on goods or services bought, then the business would be able to claim a full refund of the £8,000 paid.

It is 2 above which distinguishes it from an exempted business. A zero-rated business is, therefore, in a better position than an exempted business. Examples of zero-rated businesses are those selling young children's clothing and shoes.

19.7 Partly exempt businesses

Some businesses sell some goods which are exempt, some that are zero-rated, and others that are standard-rated. These traders will have to apportion their turnover accordingly, and follow the rules already described for each separate part of their turnover.

19.8 Different methods of accounting for VAT

If a business is exempted from registering for VAT (an **unregistered business**), it need not keep any VAT records. The amount it enters in its accounting records relating to expenditure would be the total amount paid to suppliers including any VAT. For example, if it purchased goods for £235 that included £35 for VAT, it would enter £235 in its purchases account and make no separate entries for the £35 VAT. It would not charge VAT on its sales. As a result, VAT will not appear anywhere in its accounting records or in its financial statements.

The VAT account

All **registered businesses** must account for VAT on all the taxable supplies they make and all the taxable goods and services they receive. This includes standard-rated, reduced rate and zero-rated supplies. They must also keep records of any exempt supplies they make. They must also keep a summary (called a 'VAT account') of the totals of input tax and output tax for each VAT tax period. All these records must be kept up-to-date.

Exhibit 19.2 shows an example of a 'VAT account'* in the format suggested by HM Revenue and Customs in Notice 700/21.

Exhibit 19.2

2008	£	2008	£
Input Tax: January	1,000.10	Output Tax: January	1,645.40
February	1,240.60	February	2,288.15
March	845.85	March	1,954.80
	3,086.55		5,888.35
VAT allowable on acquisitions	45.10	VAT due on acquisitions	45.10
Net overclaim of input tax from previous returns	(130.65)	Net understatement of output tax on previous returns	423.25
Bad debt relief	245.90	Annual adjustment: Retail Scheme D	91.69
Sub-total	3,246.90	Sub-total	6,448.39
Less: VAT on credits received from suppliers	(18.20)	*Less*: VAT on credits allowed to customers	(14.90)
Total tax deductible	3,228.70	Total tax payable	6,433.49
		Less total tax deductible	(3,228.70)
		Payable to Revenue and Customs	3,204.79

***Note*: Although this is described as a 'VAT account' and it is set-out with two sides like a T-account, it is not ruled off in the way that T-accounts are ruled off. It is a memorandum item and is *not* part of the double entry system.**

VAT in the ledger accounts and financial statements

How VAT appears in the ledger accounts and in the financial statements depends on which of the following categories businesses fall into:

1 **Exempted businesses.** Do not record VAT. VAT does not appear in the financial statements.
2 **Standard-rated businesses.** Need to record all output and input VAT. VAT will not appear in the profit and loss account, though it will appear in the balance sheet among either current assets or current liabilities.
3 **Partially exempt businesses.** Need to record all output and input VAT. In the case of input VAT, they must distinguish between (a) expenditure relating to taxable supplies and (b) expenditure relating to exempt supplies. Only (a) can be reclaimed; (b) is added to the net cost to arrive at the cost of each item of expenditure of type (b) to enter in the financial statements.

   VAT will not appear in the profit and loss account, though it will appear in the balance sheet among either current assets or current liabilities.

4 **Zero-rated businesses**. Need to record all *input* VAT. VAT will not appear as an expense in the profit and loss account, though it will appear in the balance sheet among the current assets.

The following discussion of the accounting entries needed will, therefore, distinguish between these two types of business: those which can recover VAT paid, and those which cannot get refunds of VAT paid.

***Note*: For simplicity, most of the examples in this book use a VAT rate of 10 per cent.**

19.9 Entries for businesses which can recover VAT paid

1 Standard-rated and reduced-rated businesses

Value Added Tax and sales invoices

Standard-rated and reduced-rated businesses have to add VAT to the value of the sales invoices. It must be pointed out that this is based on the amount of the invoice *after* any trade discount has been deducted. Exhibit 19.3 is an invoice drawn up from the following details:

On 2 March 2008, W Frank & Co, Hayburn Road, Stockport, sold the following goods to R Bainbridge Ltd, 267 Star Road, Colchester. Bainbridge's Order Number was A/4/559, for the following items:

200 Rolls T56 Black Tape at £6 per 10 rolls
600 Sheets R64 Polythene at £10 per 100 sheets
7,000 Blank Perspex B49 Markers at £20 per 1,000

All of these goods are subject to VAT at the rate of 10 per cent. A trade discount of 25 per cent is given by Frank & Co. The sales invoice is numbered 8851.

Exhibit 19.3

W Frank & Co
Hayburn Road
Stockport SK2 5DB
VAT No: 454 367 821

To: R Bainbridge Ltd
267 Star Road
Colchester CO1 1BT

INVOICE No: 8851

Date: 2 March 2008
Your order no A/4/559

	£
200 Rolls T56 Black Tape @ £6 per 10 rolls	120
600 Sheets R64 Polythene @ £10 per 100 sheets	60
7,000 Blank Perspex B49 Markers @ £20 per 1,000	140
	320
Less Trade Discount 25%	(80)
	240
Add VAT 10%	24
	264

Note how VAT is calculated on the price *after* deducting trade discount.

The sales day book will normally have an extra column for the VAT contents of the sales invoice. This is needed to make it easier to account for VAT. Let's now look at the entry of several sales invoices in the sales day book and in the ledger accounts.

Example

W Frank & Co sold the following goods during the month of March 2008:

			Total of invoice, after trade discount deducted but before VAT is added	*VAT 10%*
2008			£	£
March	2	R Bainbridge Ltd (see Exhibit 19.3)	240	24
	10	S Lange & Son	300	30
	17	K Bishop	160	16
	31	R Andrews	100	10

Sales Day Book *(page 58)*

			Invoice No	*Folio*	*Net*	*VAT*	*Gross*
2008					£	£	£
March	2	R Bainbridge Ltd	8851	SL 77	240	24	264
	10	S Lange & Son	8852	SL 119	300	30	330
	17	K Bishop	8853	SL 185	160	16	176
	31	R Andrews	8854	SL 221	100	10	110
Transferred to General Ledger					800	80	880
					GL76	GL90	

Now that the sales day book has been written up, the next task is to enter the amounts of the invoices in the individual customers' accounts in the sales ledger. These are simply charged with the full amounts of the invoices including VAT.

In this example, K Bishop is shown as owing £176. When she pays her account she will pay £176. It is the responsibility of W Frank & Co to ensure that the figure of £16 VAT in respect of this item is included in the total amount payable to the Revenue and Customs.

Sales Ledger

R Bainbridge Ltd *(page 77)*

			Folio	£	
2008					
Mar	2	Sales	SB 58	264	

S Lange & Son *(page 119)*

			Folio	£	
2008					
Mar	10	Sales	SB 58	330	

K Bishop *(page 185)*

			Folio	£	
2008					
Mar	17	Sales	SB 58	176	

R Andrews *(page 221)*

			Folio	£	
2008					
Mar	31	Sales	SB 58	110	

In total, therefore, the personal accounts have been debited with £880, this being the total of the amounts which the customers will have to pay. The actual 'sales' of the business are not £880, but £800. The other £80 is the VAT that W Frank & Co are collecting on behalf of HM Revenue and Customs. The double entry is made in the general ledger:

1 Credit the sales account with the sales content only, i.e. £800.
2 Credit the Value Added Tax account* with the VAT content only, i.e. £80.

***Note*: This is *not* the same as the VAT Account required to be prepared by Revenue and Customs, which you saw an example of in Section 19.8.**

These are shown as

General Ledger

Sales *(page 76)*

					Folio	£
		2008				
		Mar	31	Credit sales	SB 58	800

Value Added Tax *(page 90)*

					Folio	£
		2008				
		Mar	31	Sales Day Book: VAT	SB 58	80

Value Added Tax and purchases invoices

In the case of a taxable business, it has to add VAT to its sales invoices, but it will *also* be able to get a refund of the VAT which it pays on its purchases.

As you saw in Exhibit 19.1, instead of paying VAT on sales to the Revenue and Customs, and then claiming a refund of the VAT on purchases, the business sets off the amount paid as VAT on purchases against the amount paid as VAT on sales. This means that only the difference has to be paid to the Revenue and Customs. It is shown as:

		£
(*a*)	VAT collected on sales invoices	xxx
(*b*)	*Less* VAT paid on purchases	(xxx)
(*c*)	Net amount to be paid to the Revenue and Customs	xxx

In the (unusual) event that (*a*) is less than (*b*), it would be the Revenue and Customs that would refund the difference (*c*) to the business. These settlements between businesses and the Revenue and Customs normally take place every three months, when the VAT Return is completed and submitted by the business to the Revenue and Customs.

Why do you think it is rare for input VAT (i.e. VAT on purchases) to be greater than output VAT (i.e. VAT on sales)? When might this be most likely to occur?

The recording of purchases in the purchases book and purchases ledger follows a similar method to that of sales, but with the personal accounts being credited instead of debited.

We can now look at the records of purchases for the same business whose sales have been dealt with, W Frank & Co. The business made the following purchases for March 2008:

			Total of invoice, after trade discount deducted but before VAT is added	*VAT 10%*
2008			£	£
Mar	1	E Lyal Ltd (see Exhibit 19.4)	180	18
	11	P Portsmouth & Co	120	12
	24	J Davidson	40	4
	29	B Cofie & Son Ltd	70	7

Before looking at the recording of these in the purchases records, compare the first entry for E Lyal Ltd with Exhibit 19.4 to ensure that the correct amounts have been shown.

Exhibit 19.4

Date: 1/3/2008
Your Order No: BB/667

E Lyal Ltd
College Avenue
St Albans
Hertfordshire ST2 4JA
VAT No: 214 634 816

To: W Frank & Co
Hayburn Road
Stockport

INVOICE No K453/A

Terms: Strictly net 30 days

	£
50 metres of BYC plastic 1 metre wide × £3 per metre	150
1,200 metal tags 500 mm × 10p each	120
	270
Less Trade discount at $33\frac{1}{3}$%	(90)
	180
Add VAT 10%	18
	198

The purchases day book entries can now be made:

Purchases Day Book *(page 38)*

			Folio	*Net*	*VAT*	*Gross*
2008				£	£	£
March	1	E Lyal Ltd	PL 15	180	18	198
	11	P Portsmouth	PL 70	120	12	132
	24	J Davidson	PL 114	40	4	44
	29	B Cofie Ltd	PL 166	70	7	77
Transferred to General Ledger				410	41	451
				GL 54	GL 90	

These transactions are entered in the purchases ledger and the total net purchases and total VAT are entered in the general ledger. Once again, there is no need for the VAT to be shown as separate amounts in the accounts of the suppliers.

Purchases Ledger

E Lyal Ltd *(page 15)*

				Folio	£
	2008				
	Mar	1	Purchases	PB 38	198

P Portsmouth *(page 70)*

				Folio	£
	2008				
	Mar	11	Purchases	PB 38	132

J Davidson *(page 114)*

				Folio	£
	2008				
	Mar	24	Purchases	PB 38	44

B Cofie Ltd *(page 166)*

				2008			Folio	£
				Mar	29	Purchases	PB 38	77

The personal accounts have been credited with a total of £451, this being the total of the amounts which W Frank & Co will have to pay to them.

The actual cost of purchases is not, however, £451. You can see that the correct amount is £410. The other £41 is the VAT which the various businesses are collecting for the Revenue and Customs. This amount is also the figure for VAT which is reclaimable from the Revenue and Customs by W Frank & Co. The debit entry in the purchases account is, therefore, £410, as this is the actual cost of the goods to the business. The other £41 is entered on the debit side of the VAT account.

Notice that there is already a credit of £80 in the VAT account in respect of the VAT added to sales.

General Ledger

Purchases *(page 54)*

2008			Folio	£					
Mar	31	Credit purchases	PB 38	410					

Value Added Tax *(page 90)*

2008			Folio	£	2008			Folio	£
Mar	31	Purchases Day Book: VAT	PB 38	41	Mar	31	Sales Day Book: VAT	SB 58	80
	31	Balance c/d		39					
				80					80
					Apr	1	Balance b/d		39

In the financial statements of W Frank & Co, the following entries would be made:

Trading account for the month ended 31 March 2008:
Debited with £410 as a transfer from the purchases account
Credited with £800 as a transfer from the sales account

Balance sheet as at 31 March 2008:
The balance of £39 (credit) on the VAT account would be shown as a current liability, as it represents the amount owing to the Revenue and Customs for VAT.

2 Zero-rated businesses

Zero-rated businesses

1 do not have to include VAT on their sales invoices, as their rate of VAT is zero or nil
2 can, however, reclaim from the Revenue and Customs any VAT paid on goods or services bought.

Accordingly, because of 1, no VAT is entered in the sales day book. VAT on sales does not exist. Because of 2, the purchases day book and purchases ledger will appear in exactly the same manner as for standard-rated businesses, as already shown in the case of W Frank & Co.

The VAT account will only have debits in it, being the VAT on purchases. Any balance on this account will be shown in the balance sheet as a debtor.

19.10 VAT and cash discounts

Where a cash discount is offered for speedy payment, VAT is calculated on an amount represented by the value of the invoice less such a discount. Even if the cash discount is lost because of late payment, the VAT will not change.

Exhibit 19.5 shows an example of such a sales invoice, assuming a cash discount offered of 2.5 per cent and the VAT rate at 10 per cent.

Exhibit 19.5

Date: 1.3.2008 Your Order No: TS/778 To: R Noble Belsize Road Edgeley Stockport	**ATC Ltd** **18 High Street** **London WC2 E9AN** VAT No: 967 425 735 **INVOICE No ZT48910**	
		£
80 paper dispensers @ £20 each		1,600
Less Trade discount at 25%		400
		1,200
Add VAT 10%		117*
		1,317
Terms: Cash discount 2.5% if paid within 30 days		

**Note*: The VAT has been calculated on the net price £1,200 less cash discount 2.5 per cent, i.e. £30, giving £1,170, 10% of which is £117.

19.11 Entries for businesses which cannot get refunds of VAT paid

As these businesses do not include VAT in the prices they charge, there is obviously no entry for VAT either in the sales day book or in the sales ledger. They do not get a refund of VAT on purchases. This means that there will not be a VAT account. All that will happen is that VAT paid is included as part of the cost of the goods bought.

Assume that the only purchase made in a month was of goods for £120 + VAT £12 from D Oswald Ltd. The entries relating to it will appear as:

Purchases Day Book *(page 11)*

	Folio	£
2008		
May 16 D Oswald Ltd	PL 14	132
Transferred to General Ledger		132
		GL 17

Purchases Ledger
D Oswald Ltd *(page 14)*

	2008			Folio	£
	May	16	Purchases	PB11	132

General Ledger
Purchases *(page 17)*

2008			*Folio*	£	
May	31	Purchases Day Book	PB11	132	

Trading Account for the month ending 31 May 2008 (extract)

	£	£
Sales		xxx
Less Cost of goods sold		
Purchases	132	

19.12 VAT included in gross amount

You will often know only the gross amount of an item. This figure is made up of the net amount plus VAT. To find the amount of VAT which has been added to the net amount, a formula capable of being used with any rate of VAT can be used. It is:

$$\frac{\text{\% rate of VAT}}{100 + \text{\% rate of VAT}} \times \text{Gross amount} = \text{VAT}$$

Suppose that the gross amount of sales was £1,650 and the rate of VAT was 10 per cent. To find the amount of VAT and the net amount before VAT was added, you insert this information into the formula:

$$\frac{10}{100 + 10} \times £1{,}650 = \frac{10}{110} \times £1{,}650 = £150$$

Therefore, the net amount was £1,500 which, with VAT of £150 added, becomes £1,650 gross.

Given a VAT rate of 17.5 per cent, to find the amount of VAT in a gross price of £705, the calculation is:

$$\frac{17.5}{100 + 17.5} \times £705 = \frac{7}{47} \times £705 = £105$$

19.13 VAT on items other than sales and purchases

VAT is not just paid on purchases of raw materials and goods for resale. It is also payable on many expense items and on the purchase of non-current assets.

Businesses which *can* get refunds of VAT paid will not include VAT as part of the cost recorded in the ledger account of the expense or non-current asset. Businesses which *cannot* get refunds of VAT paid will include the VAT in the cost recorded in the ledger account of the expense or non-current asset. For example, businesses buying similar items would make the following debit entries in their ledger accounts:

	Business which can reclaim VAT		*Business which cannot reclaim VAT*	
Buys Machinery	Debit Machinery	£200	Debit Machinery	£220
£200 + VAT £20	Debit VAT Account	£20		
Buys Stationery	Debit Stationery	£150	Debit Stationery	£165
£150 + VAT £15	Debit VAT Account	£15		

19.14 Relief from VAT on bad debts

It is possible to claim relief on any debt which is more than six months old and has been written off in the ledger accounts. You can see an example of this in the VAT Account shown in Exhibit 19.2. Should the debt later be paid, the VAT refunded will then have to be paid back to the Revenue and Customs.

19.15 Purchase of cars

Normally, the VAT paid on a car bought for a business is not reclaimable.

19.16 VAT owing

VAT owing by or to the business can be included with accounts receivable or accounts payable, as the case may be. There is no need to show the amount(s) owing as separate items.

19.17 Columnar day books and VAT

The use of columns for VAT in both sales and purchases day books is shown in Chapter 20.

19.18 VAT return forms

At the end of each VAT tax period, a VAT Return has to be filled in and sent to the Revenue and Customs. The most important part of the form is concerned with boxes 1 to 9 which are shown in Exhibit 19.6. For illustration, we have entered some figures in the form and have assumed a VAT rate of 10 per cent.

The contents of the boxes on the VAT Return are now explained:

1 This box contains the VAT due on sales and other outputs. We have charged our customers £8,750 VAT on our sales invoices for the period.
2 This box would show the VAT due (but not paid) on all goods and related services acquired in this period from other EU member states. In this case there were no such transactions.
3 This box contains the total of Boxes 1 and 2. This is the total output tax due.
4 This box contains the total of the input tax you are entitled to reclaim for the period. We have made purchases and incurred expenses during the period on which we have been charged £6,250 VAT.
5 This is the difference between the figures in Boxes 3 and 4. If the amount in Box 3 is greater than the amount in Box 4, the amount in Box 5 is the amount payable to the Revenue and Customs. If the amount in Box 3 is less than the amount in Box 4, the amount in Box 5 is owing to you by HM Revenue and Customs. As we have collected £8,750 VAT from our customers, but only suffered £6,250 on all purchases and expenses, we owe the Revenue and Customs £2,500, i.e. £8,750 – £6,250.
6 In Box 6 you enter the total sales/outputs excluding any VAT. Our total value of sales for the period was £97,500.
7 In Box 7 you enter the total purchases/inputs excluding any VAT. Our total value of purchases and expenses was £71,900, but some of these expenses were not subject to a charge for VAT.

8 This box contains the total value of all supplies of goods to other EU member states. Of the sales included in Box 6, £10,000 was to other countries within the European Union. VAT was not charged on these sales.

9 This box contains the total value of all acquisitions of goods from other EU member states, including any goods acquired by you from another member state. Of the total purchases included in Box 7, £1,450 was from other countries within the European Union.

Exhibit 19.6

		£	
1	VAT due in this period on **sales** and other outputs	8,750	–
2	VAT due in this period on **acquisitions** from other **EU member states**	–	–
3	Total VAT due **(the sum of boxes 1 and 2)**	8,750	–
4	VAT reclaimed in this period on **purchases** and other inputs (including acquisitions from the EU)	6,250	–
5	Net VAT to be paid to Revenue and Customs or reclaimed by you (difference between boxes 3 and 4)	2,500	–
6	Total value of **sales** and all other outputs excluding any VAT. **Include your box 8 figure**	97,500	–
7	Total value of **purchases** and all other inputs excluding any VAT. **Include your box 9 figure**	71,900	–
8	Total value of all supplies of goods and related services, excluding any VAT, to other **EU member states**	10,000	–
9	Total value of all acquisitions of goods and related services, excluding any VAT, from other **EU member states**	1,450	–

Only Boxes 1 to 5 are used to determine how much is due to or from Revenue and Customs. Boxes 6 to 9 are for statistical purposes so that the UK government can assess the performance of the economy and similar matters.

19.19 VAT on goods taken for private use

If a trader takes some goods out of his own business stock for his own private use, then he should be charged with any VAT incurred when the business acquired the goods.

For instance, suppose that Smith, a furniture dealer, takes a table and chairs out of stock for permanent use in his own home. In the business accounting records, both the net cost and VAT relating to the table and chairs were recorded and the VAT will have been reclaimed from HM Revenue and Customs. You can't just charge the drawings account with the net cost of the table. That would mean that too much VAT had been reclaimed. You need to charge the proprietor's drawings with both the net cost price of the goods *and* the VAT.

The double entry to be made if the table and chairs cost £1,000 + VAT at 10 per cent would, therefore, be:

	£	£
Dr Drawings	1,100	
Cr Purchases		1,000
VAT		100

There can sometimes be complicating circumstances, outside the scope of this book, which might influence the amount of VAT to be charged on such drawings.

19.20 HM Revenue and Customs Guides and Notices

All the rules relating to VAT are contained in 'Notices' issued by HM Revenue and Customs. These are all available at the HM Revenue and Customs website: **www.hmrc.gov.uk** (there is an excellent introduction to VAT entitled 'Introduction to VAT' within the VAT section of the Revenue and Customs webpages).

For more detailed information, one of the most useful Notices is the one that tells you all about the VAT system, *Notice 700, The VAT Guide*. Anyone wishing to know if they should be registered for VAT should look at *Notice 700/1, Should I be registered for VAT?* and the updates to 700/1.

Up-to-date registration and deregistration limits and VAT rates in general, can be found on the HM Revenue and Customs website, usually within hours of changes being announced.

Learning outcomes

You should now have learnt:

1 That very small businesses with a low turnover (at the time of writing, below £70,000 in a 12-month period) do *not* have to register for VAT. They can, however, do so if they wish.

2 How to prepare a VAT Account as recommended by HM Revenue and Customs.

3 That the VAT Account should show the balance owing to, or by, HM Revenue and Customs.

4 That the VAT Account prepared for HM Revenue and Customs is a memorandum item that is not part of the double entry system and is *not* the same as the ledger account for VAT.

5 That if a business cannot get a refund of VAT on its costs, then the VAT will be included in the costs transferred to the trading and profit and loss accounts, or be included in the cost of non-current assets in the balance sheet. VAT does not appear as a separate item in either financial statement.

6 That although businesses show VAT separately on sales invoices, the VAT is not regarded as part of the sales figure in the trading account.

7 That VAT is calculated on the sales value less any cash discount offered.

8 How to complete a VAT Return.

Answers to activities

19.1 Strictly speaking it should always work that way. Even if goods are never sold by the retailer and have to be scrapped, the system still works. The retailer becomes the final consumer. As a result, it is the retailer who ends up having to pay the full amount of VAT, albeit on the price paid to the manufacturer, rather than on the price at which the goods were being offered for sale.

19.2 The price consumers pay for goods and services from unregistered businesses should be lower than they pay registered businesses for the same items. This should help unregistered businesses compete against their larger competitors, which is good for the unregistered business and for the consumer. As a result, many unregistered businesses go to great lengths – some not exactly legal, such as doing work and being paid in cash so that nothing gets entered in the books – to ensure that their turnover does not exceed the registration limit.

19.3 Goods and services are normally sold at a higher amount than was paid for them when purchased. Input VAT may be greater than output VAT when a business is new and has purchased a large amount of inventory. It often takes time for a business to become established and for sales to reach their 'normal' level.

Review questions

19.1 On 1 May 2007, F Marr Ltd, 2 Frank Lane, Manchester, sold the following goods on credit to M Low & Son, Byron Golf Club, Cheesham, Notts:

Order No A/496
3 sets 'Tiger Gold' golf clubs at £810 per set.
150 Rose golf balls at £20 per 10 balls.
4 Daly golf bags at £270 per bag.

Trade discount is given at the rate of $33\frac{1}{3}$%.
All goods are subject to VAT at 10%.

(*a*) Prepare the sales invoice to be sent to M Low & Son. The invoice number will be 2094.
(*b*) Show the entries in the personal ledgers of F Marr Ltd and M Low & Son.

19.2A On 1 March 2006, A Duff, Middle Road, Paisley, sold the following goods on credit to R Wilson, 24 Peter Street, Loughborough, Order No 943:

20,000 Coils Sealing Tape	@ £6.10 per 1,000 coils
40,000 Sheets Bank A5	@ £4.60 per 1,000 sheets
24,000 Sheets Bank A4	@ £8.20 per 1,000 sheets

All goods are subject to VAT at 10%.

(*a*) Prepare the sales invoice to be sent to R Wilson.
(*b*) Show the entries in the personal ledgers of R Wilson and A Duff.

19.3 The following sales have been made by F Rae Ltd during the month of June 2009. All the figures are shown net after deducting trade discount, but before adding VAT at the rate of 10%.

2009			
August	1	to G Clark Ltd	£210
	8	to P Main	£430
	19	to W Roy	£120
	31	to F Job	£60

You are required to enter up the Sales Day Book, Sales Ledger and General Ledger in respect of the above items for the month.

→

→ **19.4** The following sales and purchases were made by J Flan Ltd during the month of May 2006.

			Net	*VAT added*
2006			£	£
May	1	Sold goods on credit to A Bell & Co	220	22
	4	Sold goods on credit to D Player and Co	380	38
	10	Bought goods on credit from:		
		F Loy and Partners	510	51
		R Dixon Ltd	270	27
	14	Bought goods on credit from G Melly	90	9
	16	Sold goods on credit to D Player and Co	80	8
	23	Bought goods on credit from E Flynn	140	14
	31	Sold goods on credit to P Green	30	3

Enter up the Sales and Purchases Day Books, Sales and Purchases Ledgers and the General Ledger for the month of May 2006. Carry the balance down on the VAT account.

19.5A The credit sales and purchases for the month of December 2007 in respect of G Bain & Co were:

			Net, after trade discount	*VAT 10%*
2007			£	£
Dec	1	Sales to H Impey Ltd	180	18
	4	Sales to B Volts	410	41
	5	Purchases from G Sharpe and Co	90	9
	8	Purchases from R Hood and Associates	150	15
	14	Sales to L Marion	190	19
	18	Purchases from F Tuckley Ltd	130	13
	28	Sales to B Volts	220	22
	30	Purchases from R Hood and Associates	350	35

Write up all of the relevant books and ledger accounts for the month.

19.6 Louise Baldwin commenced business as a wholesaler on 1 March 2009.

Her sales on credit during March 2009 were:

March 9 Neville's Electrical
4 computer monitors list price £180 each, less 20% trade discount

March 17 Maltby plc
20 computer printers list price £200 each, less 25% trade discount

March 29 Neville's Electrical
Assorted software list price £460, less 20% trade discount

All transactions are subject to Value Added Tax at 10%.

(*a*) Rule up a Sales Day Book and head the main columns as follows.

Date	*Name and Details*	*List price less trade discount £–p*	*VAT £–p*	*Total £–p*

Enter the above information in the Sales Day Book, totalling and ruling off at the end of March 2009.

(*b*) Make the necessary postings from the Sales Day Book to the personal and nominal accounts in the ledger.

(*c*) Prepare a trial balance as at 31 March 2009.

(Edexcel Foundation, London Examinations: GCSE)

19.7A Mudgee Ltd issued the following invoices to customers in respect of credit sales made during the last week of May 2007. The amounts stated are all net of Value Added Tax. All sales made by Mudgee Ltd are subject to VAT at 15%.

Invoice No	*Date*	*Customer*	*Amount*
			£
3045	25 May	Laira Brand	1,060.00
3046	27 May	Brown Bros	2,200.00
3047	28 May	Penfold's	170.00
3048	29 May	T Tyrrell	460.00
3049	30 May	Laira Brand	1,450.00
			£5,340.00

On 29 May Laira Brand returned half the goods (in value) purchased on 25 May. An allowance was made the same day to this customer for the appropriate amount.

On 1 May 2007 Laira Brand owed Mudgee Ltd £2,100.47. Other than the purchases detailed above Laira Brand made credit purchases (including VAT) of £680.23 from Mudgee Ltd on 15 May. On 21 May Mudgee Ltd received a cheque for £2,500 from Laira Brand.

Required:

(*a*) Show how the above transactions would be recorded in Mudgee Ltd's Sales Day Book for the week ended 30 May 2007.

(*b*) Describe how the information in the Sales Day Book would be incorporated into Mudgee Ltd's double entry system.

(*c*) Reconstruct the personal account of Laira Brand as it would appear in Mudgee Ltd's ledger for May 2007.

(Association of Accounting Technicians)

You can find a range of additional self-test questions, as well as material to help you with your studies, on the website that accompanies this book at www.pearsoned.co.uk/wood.

chapter

20 Columnar day books

Learning objectives

After you have studied this chapter, you should be able to:

- explain why organisations use columnar day books
- decide which basis is to be used for the selection of analysis columns for columnar day books
- write up columnar day books for sales, purchases or for any other aspect of an organisation
- write up columnar day books that include a column for VAT
- explain the advantages of maintaining columnar day books compared to 'normal' day books
- explain why the advantages of maintaining day books far outweigh the disadvantages of doing so

Introduction

In this chapter, you'll learn why many organisations use columnar day books rather than the form of day book that you have learnt about in earlier chapters of this book. You'll learn how to prepare and make entries into columnar day books, and how to make the appropriate entries from them to the ledgers. In addition, you will learn about how to record VAT in columnar day books and of the advantages of using columnar day books rather than the form of day book you learnt about earlier.

20.1 Columnar purchases day books

So far, you may have assumed that the purchases day book was solely for recording the original entry of purchases on credit and that all other expenditure was first entered in the journal. There are many organisations which operate their purchases day book in this way. However, many use only one book (the purchases day book) to record all items obtained on credit. This will include transactions involving purchases, stationery, non-current assets, motor expenses, and so on. All credit invoices for any expense will be entered in this book.

However, although only one book is used, all of the various types of items are not simply lumped together. The business needs to know how much was for purchases, how much for stationery, how much for motor expenses, etc., so that the relevant ledger accounts can have the correct amount of expenditure entered in them. This is achieved by having a set of analysis columns in the book, in the same way as you have analysis columns in cash books and petty cash books. All of the items are entered in a total column, but then they are analysed as between the different sorts of expenditure.

Exhibit 20.1 shows such a **Columnar Purchases Day Book** (or Purchases Analysis Book) drawn up for a month from the following list of items obtained on credit. For the purposes of this example, we shall assume the business is not registered for VAT.

2009			£
May	1	Bought goods from D Watson Ltd on credit	2,960
	3	Bought goods on credit from W Donachie & Son	760
	5	Van repaired, received invoice from Barnes Motors Ltd	1,120
	6	Bought packaging material from J Corrigan & Co	650
	8	Bought goods on credit from C Bell Ltd	2,120
	14	Lorry serviced, received invoice from Barnes Motors Ltd	390
	23	Bought packaging material on credit from A Hartford & Co	350
	26	Bought goods on credit from M Doyle Ltd	2,430
	30	Received invoice for carriage inwards on goods from G Owen	58

Exhibit 20.1

Columnar Purchases Day Book *(page 105)*

Date	*Name of business*	*PL Folio*	*Total*	*Purchases*	*Stationery*	*Motor expenses*	*Carriage inwards*
2009			£	£	£	£	£
May 1	D Watson Ltd	129	2,960	2,960			
3	W Donachie & Son	27	760	760			
5	Barnes Motors Ltd	55	1,120			1,120	
6	J Corrigan & Co	88	650		650		
8	C Bell Ltd	99	2,120	2,120			
14	Barnes Motors Ltd	55	390			390	
23	A Hartford & Co	298	350		350		
26	M Doyle Ltd	187	2,430	2,430			
30	G Owen	222	58				58
			10,838	8,270	1,000	1,510	58
				GL 77	GL 97	GL 156	GL 198

Exhibit 20.1 shows that the figure for each item is entered in the Total column, and is then also entered in the column for the particular type of expense. At the end of the month the arithmetical accuracy of the additions can be checked by comparing the total of the Total column with the sum of totals of all of the other columns.

It can be seen that the total of purchases for the month of May was £8,270. This can be debited to the purchases account in the general ledger. Similarly, the total of stationery bought on credit in the month can be debited to the packaging material account in the general ledger, and so on. The folio number of the page to which the relevant total has been debited is shown immediately under the total figure for each column, e.g. under the column for motor expenses is GL 156, meaning that this item has been entered on page 156 of the general ledger.

Note for students: The vertical lines have been included above in order to illustrate how the paper within the purchases analysis book may be printed. You may find it useful to rule your paper according to this layout when attempting examples and questions on this topic. If you do, remember that the number of columns required will vary according to the circumstances.

Think for a moment about a computerised accounting system – that is, one where all the entries are made on computer and the books are electronic documents. Can you think of any reason why the folio number in such cases would not represent a specific page in a ledger?

The entries in the ledgers can now be shown:

General Ledger

Purchases *(page 77)*

2009			£	
May	31	Purchases analysis PB 105	8,270	

Stationery *(page 97)*

2009			£	
May	31	Purchases analysis PB 105	1,000	

Motor Expenses *(page 156)*

2009			£	
May	31	Purchases analysis PB 105	1,510	

Carriage Inwards *(page 198)*

2009			£	
May	31	Purchases analysis PB 105	58	

The individual accounts of the creditors, whether they are for goods or for expenses such as stationery or motor expenses, can be kept together in a single purchases ledger. However, there is no need for the purchases ledger to have accounts only for creditors for purchases. Perhaps there is a slight misuse of the name purchases ledger where this happens, but it is common practice amongst a lot of businesses. Many businesses will give it the more correct title in that case of the **Bought Ledger**.

To carry through the double entry involved with Exhibit 20.1 the purchases ledger is now shown.

Purchases Ledger

W Donachie & Son *(page 27)*

	2009				£
	May	3	Purchases	PB 105	760

Barnes Motors Ltd *(page 55)*

	2009				£
	May	5	Purchases	PB 105	1,120
		14		PB 105	390

J Corrigan & Co *(page 88)*

	2009				£
	May	6	Purchases	PB 105	650

C Bell Ltd *(page 99)*

	2009				£
	May	8	Purchases	PB 105	2,120

	D Watson Ltd				(*page 129*)
	2009				£
	May	1	Purchases	PB 105	2,960

	M Doyle Ltd				(*page 187*)
	2009				£
	May	26	Purchases	PB 105	2,430

	G Owen				(*page 222*)
	2009				£
	May	30	Purchases	PB 105	58

	A Hartford & Co				(*page 298*)
	2009				£
	May	23	Purchases	PB 105	350

If the business were split up into departments or sections, instead of having one *Purchases* column it would be possible to have one column for *each* of the departments. In this way, the total purchases for each department for the accounting period could be ascertained. In fact, you could have as many columns as you wanted in this book. It all depends how extensively you want to analyse the credit expenditure recorded in the book. You might, for example, wish to keep all entries for credit purchases made from one supplier in one column dedicated to that supplier and so only post the total purchases from that supplier each month to the supplier's personal account in the purchases ledger.

20.2 Columnar sales day books

A similar approach can be adopted with the sales day book. You may, for example, wish to know the sales for each section or department of the business. The 'normal' sales day book shows only the total of sales for the accounting period. In this case, you could use a **Columnar Sales Day Book** (or Sales Analysis Book). For a business which is not registered for VAT that sells sports goods, household goods and electrical items, it might appear as in Exhibit 20.2:

Exhibit 20.2

Columnar Sales Day Book

Date	*Name of business*	*SL Folio*	*Total*	*Sports Dept*	*Household Dept*	*Electrical Dept*
2009			£	£	£	£
May 1	N Coward Ltd	87	190		190	
5	L Oliver	76	200	200		
8	R Colman & Co	157	300	102		198
16	Aubrey Smith Ltd	209	480			480
27	H Marshall	123	220	110	45	65
31	W Pratt	66	1,800		800	1,000
			3,190	412	1,035	1,743

Note for students: As with the Columnar Purchases Day Book, the vertical lines have been included above in order to illustrate how the paper within the Columnar Sales Day Book may be

printed. You may find it useful to rule your paper according to this layout when attempting examples and questions on this topic. If you do, remember that the number of columns will vary according to the circumstances.

20.3 Columnar day books and VAT

In the UK, if a business is 'exempted' for Value Added Tax (VAT), it doesn't charge customers VAT and so does not add VAT on to the value of its sales invoices and cannot reclaim VAT on its purchases. When a business sells 'zero-rated' goods, it does not charge VAT on such sales but will do so on sales of other goods and services unless it is either exempted from doing so or not registered for VAT. As you learnt in Chapter 19, items that are zero-rated include most food (but not meals in restaurants and cafés or hot take-away food and drink), books and newspapers, young children's clothing and shoes, prescriptions, and many aids for disabled people.

(You can find out more about VAT at the UK Revenue and Customs website: www.hmrc.gov.uk.)

Both Exhibits 20.1 and 20.2 have been prepared on the basis that the business is not registered for VAT, which has the same effect as being exempted for VAT. Let's imagine that the business in Exhibit 20.2 was registered for VAT. The Columnar Sales Day Book should include a column for VAT.

In Exhibit 20.3, the debtors are shown charged with the gross amounts (selling price net of VAT plus VAT), e.g. N Coward Ltd with £209 (i.e. £190 plus VAT of £19). The VAT account would be credited with £319 being the total of the VAT column. The sales account would be credited with the sales figures of £412, £1,035 and £1,743. (For ease of calculation, we're using a VAT rate of 10 per cent.)

Exhibit 20.3

Columnar Sales Day Book

Date	Name of business	SL Folio	Total	VAT	Sports Dept	Household Dept	Electrical Dept
2009			£	£	£	£	£
May 1	N Coward Ltd	87	209	19		190	
5	L Oliver	76	220	20	200		
8	R Colman & Co	157	330	30	102		198
16	Aubrey Smith Ltd	209	528	48			480
27	H Marshall	123	242	22	110	45	65
31	W Pratt	66	1,980	180	—	800	1,000
			3,509	319	412	1,035	1,743

Note how all the columns to the right of the VAT column contain the same information as in the example in Exhibit 20.2 which ignored VAT.

Activity 20.2

Why is the total amount received for each sale not inserted in each of the department columns?

Hint: students often suggest that the total amount relating to each transaction represents the value of the sale and so it is the total amount that needs to be recorded in the General Ledger in order that the figure for sales in the Income Statement is not understated.

Similarly, a Columnar Purchases Day Book would include a VAT column if the business was not zero-rated. In this case, the total of the VAT column would be debited to the VAT account. The total of the Purchases column would be debited to the purchases account with the total of each expense column debited to the various expense accounts in the general ledger.

20.4 Advantages of columnar day books

The advantages of columnar day books are that they provide exactly the information an organisation needs, at the time when it is wanted, in a place which is convenient and easy to find, and they avoid cluttering up the ledgers with lots of detailed transaction data. Different businesses have different needs and, therefore, analyse their day books in different ways.

Columnar day books enable us to do such things as:

1 Calculate the profit or loss made by each part of a business.
2 Draw up control accounts for the sales and purchases ledgers (see Chapter 31).
3 Keep a check on the sales of each type of goods sold.
4 Keep a check on goods sold in different locations, departments or sections.
5 Identify purchasers of each type of good offered for sale.

List as many things as you can that could be analysed in a separate column in a columnar day book that would enable an organisation to do something far more easily than when a 'normal' day book is used.

20.5 Books as collection points

You have learnt so far that the sales and purchases day books, and the day books for returns, are simply collection points for the data to be entered in the accounts of the double entry system. There is nothing in the law or accounting standards that says that, for instance, a Sales Day Book has to be maintained. We could just look at the sales invoices and enter the debits in the customers' personal accounts from them. Then we could keep all the sales invoices together in a file. At the end of the month we could add up the amounts of the sales invoices, and then enter that total to the credit of the sales account in the general ledger, but we wouldn't want to! Would we?

Spend one minute listing as many advantages as you can for *not* using books of original entry for purchases, sales and returns transactions. Then spend another minute listing as many disadvantages as you can think of.

While, there is, strictly speaking, no need for columnar day books to be used if entries are made directly into the ledger accounts from the source documents, it is considered good practice to do so, particularly when the accounting records are not computerised.

Learning outcomes

You should now have learnt:

1 That columnar day books and analysis books are two names for the same thing.
2 That columnar day books are used in order to show the value of each of the various types of items bought and sold so that the relevant accounts may have the correct amount entered into them.

→

3 That the columns in a columnar day book are chosen on the basis of what type of information an organisation wishes to be highlighted as, for example, in the case of a department or a major supplier.

4 How to prepare a columnar day book for entry of the relevant data.

5 How to make entries in columnar day books and transfer the balances at the end of a period to the appropriate ledger accounts.

6 How to include VAT in a columnar day book.

7 That the advantages of maintaining day books far outweigh the disadvantages of doing so.

Answers to activities

20.1 This convention that the folio number represents a page in a ledger is really only applicable to handwritten manual accounting systems. In many organisations, the folio number is the number of the *account* in the ledger, rather than the *page* in the ledger. This is particularly the case in computerised accounting systems, when page numbers, as such, do not exist.

20.2 VAT does not increase sales revenue. It is a tax on sales and the money received in respect of it is passed directly to HM Revenue and Customs. VAT does not appear in the income statement.

20.3 There are many other things columnar day books can enable an organisation to do far more easily than when a 'normal' day book is used. For example, they can be used to:

- record the details of all sales to a major customer in a book other than the General Ledger
- record the details of all purchases from a major supplier in a book other than the General Ledger
- identify which supplier(s) each type of good offered for sale was purchased from
- identify which types of goods offered for sale are purchased by a particular supplier.

20.4 There is probably only one advantage of not using these day books – that no one needs to write entries in them if they don't exist. There are many, many disadvantages. The most obvious concerns what happens when an invoice is lost from the box before it is recorded in the ledger, or even after it has been recorded in the ledger. How can you verify the transaction took place or was for the amount of money entered in the ledger? And how can you tell what was actually bought or sold without the original (source) document? All businesses really ought to use day books.

Review questions

20.1 R Bright, an electrical goods wholesaler, has three departments: (*a*) Music, (*b*) TV and (*c*) Kitchen. The following is a summary of Bright's sales invoices during the week 1 to 7 February 2007.

	Customer	*Invoice No*	*Department*	*List price less trade discount*	*VAT*	*Total invoice price*
				£	£	£
Feb 1	M Long	403	TV	3,900	390	4,290
2	F Ray	404	Music	1,100	110	1,210
3	M Tom	405	TV	980	98	1,078
5	T John	406	Kitchen	410	41	451
7	F Ray	407	TV	1,660	166	1,826
7	M Long	408	Music	2,440	244	2,684

The VAT rate was 10 per cent.

(*a*) Record the above transactions in a columnar book of original entry and post to the general ledger in columnar form.

(*b*) Write up the personal accounts in the appropriate ledger.
NB Do not balance-off any of your ledger accounts.

20.2 Enter up a columnar purchases day book with columns for the various expenses for F Wayne for the month from the following information on credit items.

2006			£
July	1	Bought goods from G Hope	560
	3	Bought goods from B Smith	420
	4	Received electricity bill (lighting & heating from Scottish Gas)	91
	5	Bought goods from F Loy	373
	6	Van repaired, received bill from Bright Body Shop	192
	8	Bought stationery from Light Letters	46
	10	Van serviced, bill from Pope Garage	124
	12	Gas bill received from Scottish Gas (lighting & heating)	88
	15	Bought goods from B Bill	265
	17	Bought light bulbs (lighting & heating) from G Fyfe	18
	18	Goods bought from T Tully	296
	19	Invoice for carriage inwards from Rapid Flight Ltd	54
	21	Bought stationery from K Frank	14
	23	Goods bought from F Loy	218
	27	Received invoice for carriage inwards from Couriers Ltd	44
	31	Invoice for motor spares supplied during the month received from Pope Garage	104

20.3 Enter up the relevant accounts in the purchases and general ledgers from the columnar purchases day book you completed for Question 20.2.

20.4A Enter up a columnar purchases day book with columns for the various expenses for G Graham for the month from the following information on credit items.

2008			£
June	1	Bought goods from J Syme	108
	4	Bought goods from T Hill	210
	7	Bought goods from F Love	195
	8	Truck repaired, received bill from Topp Garages	265
	9	Received phone bill from BT	65
	9	Bought stationery from Gilly Shop	19
	17	Bought goods from G Farmer	181
	19	Bought fluorescent light bulb (lighting & heating) from B&T Ltd	13
	21	Goods bought from T Player	222
	22	Invoice for carriage inwards from Overnight Couriers Ltd	46
	23	Bought stationery from J Moore	12
	24	Car serviced, bill from Topp Garages	364
	25	Electricity bill received from PowerNorth Ltd (lighting & heating)	39
	25	Goods bought from H Noone	193
	28	Received invoice for carriage inwards from PMP Ltd	38
	30	Invoice for replacement car tyre received from Topp Garages	66

20.5A Enter up the relevant accounts in the purchases and general ledgers from the columnar purchases day book you completed for Question 20.4A.

You can find a range of additional self-test questions, as well as material to help you with your studies, on the website that accompanies this book at www.pearsoned.co.uk/wood.

chapter 21

Employees' pay

Learning objectives

After you have studied this chapter, you should be able to:

- explain the basic system of PAYE income tax
- explain the difference between employee's and employer's National Insurance Contributions
- calculate the net pay of an employee given details of his or her gross pay and PAYE income tax and other deductions
- calculate the amount of the employer's National Insurance Contribution that would have to be paid on behalf of an employee given details of the employee's gross pay and PAYE income tax and other deductions
- explain how basic pensions and additional pensions are determined

Introduction

In this chapter, you'll learn about the calculation of pay and the deductions that are made from it by an employer for tax and National Insurance. You'll also learn about two forms of state pensions that an employee may be eligible for upon retirement, and about a number of items that reduce an employee's liability to income tax. You'll learn about some benefits that employees can receive as a result of their having made National Insurance Contributions. Finally, you'll learn how to calculate the net payment received by employees after adjusting their gross pay by the reliefs available and deductions, both statutory and voluntary, that have to be made.

21.1 Pay

Employees are paid either a wage or a salary. If you see an advert for a job and it mentions that the rate of pay will be £8 per hour, that is an example of a wage. If, on the other hand, an advert refers to an annual amount, that is a salary. In the UK, we normally talk about wages per hour or per week, and salaries per year.

Write down what you think would be good definitions for the term 'wage' and the term 'salary'.

In the UK, every employee is taxed under a system called **PAYE (Pay As You Earn)**. This means that for every employee, employers are required by law to make various deductions for tax and National Insurance (effectively a contribution towards some of the benefits people who have made these contributions receive from the state, such as money paid by the state to someone who is out of work or retired). As a result, a distinction is made between

- **gross pay**, which is the amount of wages or salary *before* deductions are made, and
- **net pay**, which is the amount of wages or salary *after* deductions.

Many employees talk about 'take-home pay'. This is, in fact, the same as their net pay.

Activity 21.2 What other deductions might be made from gross pay by an employer?

21.2 Methods of calculating gross pay

The methods employers use to calculate gross pay vary widely, not just between employers but also for employees in the same organisation. The main methods are:

- a fixed amount per period of time, usually a year;
- piece rate: pay based on the number of units produced by the employee;
- commission: a percentage based on the value of sales made by the employee;
- basic hourly rate: a fixed rate multiplied by number of hours worked.

Arrangements for rewarding people for working overtime (time exceeding normal hours worked) will vary widely. The rate will usually be in excess of that paid during normal working hours. Many people who are being paid salaries are not paid for working overtime.

In addition, bonuses may be paid on top of these 'normal' earnings. Bonus schemes will also vary widely, and may depend on the amount of net profit made by the company, or on the amount of work performed, or on the quality of performance by the employee, or on production levels achieved, either by the whole company or by the department in which the employee works. In some cases, these bonuses can amount to many times an employee's 'normal' salary.

Activity 21.3 Can you think of any examples where these extremely high bonuses have been paid?

21.3 Income tax deductions

In the UK, the wages and salaries of all employees are liable to have income tax deducted from them. This does not mean that everyone will pay income tax – some may not earn enough to be liable for any tax. However, if income tax is found to be payable, under the PAYE system the employer deducts the tax due from the employee's wages or salary and sends it to HM Revenue and Customs, the government department in charge of the collection of income tax.

Each person in the UK is allowed to subtract various amounts called 'allowances' from their earnings when calculating how much they are liable to pay in income tax. Many people pay no tax because they earn less than their total allowance. The amounts given for each person depend upon his or her personal circumstances, but everyone is entitled to a personal allowance. For the tax year ending on 5 April 2008, that allowance was £5,225.

An extra allowance is given to blind people. Anyone aged over 65 receives an additional allowance, and there is a married couple's allowance if at least one person in a marriage or civil partnership was born before 6 April 1935. Other allowances available may depend on the type of job. For example, some people can claim allowances for special clothing they need for their job. The totals of these allowances are known as a person's 'personal reliefs' or **personal allowances.** Once these have been deducted, any balance of income remaining will have to suffer income tax. However, contributions to superannuation (or pension) schemes are also deducted before arriving at the amount upon which tax is due – you'll learn about superannuation contributions later in this chapter.

The calculation is, therefore:

	£
Gross pay	xxx
Less: reliefs	(xxx)
Pay which is taxable	xxx

Two people may, therefore, earn the same wages, but if one of them gets more allowances than the other, he or she will have less taxable pay, and so will pay less income tax than the other person.

Each year in the Budget, the Chancellor of the Exchequer announces what the rates of income tax are going to be for the following year, and also how much is to be deducted in respect of each allowance.

Because of the annual changes in tax rates and allowances, the rates of income tax shown from here onwards are for illustration only, and are not necessarily the actual rates of income tax at the time you are reading this book.

Let's assume that the rates of income tax (on the amount actually exceeding the allowances for each person) are:

On the first £3,000	Income tax at 20%
On the next £24,000	Income tax at 25%
On the remainder	Income tax at 40%

The income tax payable by each of four people can now be calculated:

1 Miss Brown earns £3,800 per annum. Her personal reliefs amount to £4,000. Income tax payable = Nil.

2 Mr Green earns £8,760 per annum. His personal reliefs amount to £4,000. Income tax is therefore payable on the excess of £4,760. This amounts to:

		£
On first £3,000 at 20%	=	600
On remaining £1,760 at 25%	=	440
Total income tax for the year		1,040

3 Mr Black earns £10,700 per annum. His personal reliefs amount to £5,300. Income tax is therefore payable on the excess of £5,400. This amounts to:

		£
On first £3,000 at 20%	=	600
On remaining £2,400 at 25%	=	600
Total income tax for the year		1,200

4 Mr White earns £39,700 per annum. His personal allowances amount to £5,200. Income tax is therefore payable on the excess of £34,500. This amounts to:

		£
On first £3,000 at 20%	=	600
On next £24,000 at 25%	=	6,000
On remaining £7,500 at 40%	=	3,000
Total income tax for the year		9,600

Let's assume that Miss Brown and Mr Green are paid weekly, and Mr Black and Mr White are paid monthly. If each payment to them during the year was of equal amounts, then we can calculate the amount of PAYE deducted from each payment of earnings.

PAYE deducted on a weekly basis:

1 Miss Brown. Tax for year = nil. Tax each week = nil.
2 Mr Green. Tax for year = £1,040. Tax each week £1,040 ÷ 52 = £20.

PAYE deducted on a monthly basis:

3 Mr Black. Tax for year = £1,200. Tax each month £1,200 ÷ 12 = £100.
4 Mr White. Tax for year = £9,600. Tax each month £9,600 ÷ 12 = £800.

These examples were deliberately made easy to understand. In real life, earnings may change part-way through a tax year, the amounts paid each week or month may be different, etc. HM Revenue and Customs issues employers with tax tables to help calculate the PAYE code numbers used to deal with the different allowances employees may have, and we shall look at these next.

21.4 PAYE code numbers

We have already seen that personal reliefs, which are deducted from gross pay to find taxable pay, will vary between employees.

When employers come to use tax tables they need an easy method of knowing the amount of personal reliefs to which each of their employees is entitled. The Revenue and Customs solve this for employers by giving each employee a tax code number and giving the employer books of tax code tables that show what tax to deduct.

The **tax code** will incorporate all the tax reliefs to which the employee is entitled. This means that should the worker receive extra reliefs for special clothing, or for being blind, these extra reliefs will be incorporated into the tax code.

To find the tax code, the total of all the reliefs is first calculated. The tax code will consist of the total reliefs excluding the final digit. The number will be followed by a letter. For example:

L means a code incorporating the basic personal allowance.
P is for a tax code with the full personal allowance for those aged 65–74.

In the case of the employees given in Section 21.3

- Miss Brown's personal reliefs amounted to £4,000. Her tax code will be 400L.
- Mr Green's personal reliefs amounted to £4,000. His tax code will be 400L.
- Mr Black is aged 66. His personal tax reliefs amounted to £5,300. His tax code will be 530P.
- Mr White is aged 69. His personal tax reliefs amounted to £5,200. His tax code will be 520P.

21.5 National Insurance

In the UK, National Insurance Contributions have to be paid for and by each employee. In return, the employee may claim benefits from the state, if and when required, e.g. for retirement or when unemployed. The actual benefits available in return for these contributions are:

- Incapacity Benefit
- Jobseeker's Allowance
- Maternity Allowance
- Retirement Pension
- Widowed Mother's Allowance
- Widow's Payment
- Widow's Pension
- Bereavement Benefit
- Additional State Pension.

National Insurance Contributions are split into two parts:

(*a*) the part that employees have to suffer by it being deducted from their pay;
(*b*) the part that the employer has to suffer. This is not deductible from pay.

The rates change from time to time but, assuming a total National Insurance rate of 19 per cent, of which the employee's contribution is 9 per cent and the employer's contribution 10 per cent, then £38 total contribution will have to be paid in respect of an employee who has earned £200 in the period, i.e. £200 × 19% = £38.

Of this, £18 (9%) can be deducted from the employee's pay, whilst £20 (10%) is a cost to the employer.

Pensions

Paying National Insurance Contributions results in employees receiving a state pension when they retire. Where an employee qualifies for a 'basic pension', the pension paid is based upon the number of years in which the 'minimum amount' of contributions were paid. This minimum amount is based on employees needing to have paid contributions on earnings of at least 52 times the weekly lower earnings limit during a tax year. If the weekly lower earnings limit is £100, the employee would need to have earned £5,200 in the year for that year to be included in the calculation of the basic pension. The number of years when this occurred is then multiplied by the basic pension per year to arrive at the amount of basic pension the individual will receive.

Where employees pay more than the minimum amount required for a basic pension, they will be entitled to an extra pension on top of their basic pension. This is known as 'additional pension' (AP). It is based upon earnings during the employee's working life from the year 1978–79 to that ending before the one in which the employee reaches retirement age.

Where an employee belongs to a contracted-out (superannuation or) occupational pension scheme (one operated by or on behalf of their employer) or a personal pension scheme (one run by, for example, an insurance company to which the employee makes contributions out of net pay), that scheme will provide a pension wholly or partly in place of any additional pension the individual may have otherwise been eligible to receive.

21.6 Other deductions from pay

Pensions contributions

An employee may belong to a company's occupational pension scheme. The money paid into the fund will be paid partly by the company and partly by the employee. For example, the employee's contribution could be 6 per cent, with the company paying whatever is necessary to give the employee the agreed amount of pension.

The amount of the contribution payable by employees will, therefore, be deducted in calculating the net pay due to them.

Voluntary contributions

These include items such as charitable donations, subscriptions to the business's social club, union subscriptions and payments under a 'Save as You Earn' (SAYE) Scheme.

21.7 Statutory Sick Pay and Statutory Maternity Pay

1 Statutory Sick Pay (SSP) is a payment made to employees when they are ill and absent from work. At present, it is not paid for the first three days of illness, and is limited to a total of 28 weeks' maximum.

2 Statutory Maternity Pay (SMP) is a payment made for up to 39 weeks to an employee away from work on maternity leave.

SSP and SMP are paid to employees in the same way as ordinary wages. They are both liable to have income tax and National Insurance deducted from them.

21.8 Calculation of net wages/salary payable

UK students who need to know how to use PAYE tax and National Insurance tables will need to study this further.

For general guidance for all readers, and for those who do not want to know about the use of income tax and National Insurance tables, we can look at two general examples of the calculation of net pay. The percentages used are for illustrative purposes only.

(A) G Jarvis:

	£
Gross earnings for the week ended 8 May 2008	500
Income tax: found by consulting tax tables and employee's code number	60
National Insurance: 9% of gross pay	45

G Jarvis: Payslip week ended 8 May 2008

	£	£
Gross pay for the week		500
Less Income tax	60	
National Insurance	45	
		(105)
Net pay		395

(B) H Reddish:

	£
Gross earnings for the month of May 2008	6,000
Income tax (from tax tables)	1,120
Superannuation: 6% of gross pay	360
National Insurance: 9% of gross pay	540

H Reddish: Payslip month ended 31 May 2008

	£	£
Gross pay for the month		6,000
Less Income tax	1,120	
Superannuation	360	
National Insurance	540	
		(2,020)
Net pay		3,980

The total costs to the employer in each of the above cases will be as follows, assuming the employer's part of National Insurance Contributions to be £50 for Jarvis and £600 for Reddish:

	G Jarvis	*H Reddish*
	£	£
Gross pay	500	6,000
Employer's share of National Insurance	50	600
Total cost to the employer	550	6,600

It will be the figures of £550 and £6,600 that will be incorporated in the income statement as expenses shown under wages and salaries headings.

You can find out more about income tax and National Insurance Contributions at the Revenue and Customs website (www.hmrc.gov.uk).

Learning outcomes

You should now have learnt:

1 That the PAYE system ensures that employees pay tax on their earnings.

2 That the amount of tax paid varies between employees and depends on their eligibility for the various reliefs available.

3 That tax codes are used by employers to calculate tax due by employees.

4 That National Insurance Contributions are deducted from earnings at the same time as income tax.

5 That superannuation (i.e. pension) contributions are deducted from earnings to find taxable pay.

6 That the level of state pension is dependent upon the individual having paid sufficient employee's National Insurance Contributions before reaching retirement age.

7 That employees who are members of a superannuation (or occupational pension) scheme pay lower levels of National Insurance Contributions.

8 That employers pay an employer's National Insurance Contribution on behalf of each employee.

9 How to calculate net pay given the gross pay, PAYE and NIC amounts.

Answers to activities

21.1 There is no exact definition of 'wage' or of 'salary'. In general, it is accepted that wages are earnings paid on a weekly basis, whilst salaries are paid monthly. In accounting, you will see this distinction taken a step further when you look at types of costs in Chapter 37. In effect, accounting assumes that salaries are fixed amounts paid monthly and that people who are paid a salary do not receive any extra payment should they happen to work extra hours in the month. Those who earn wages are assumed to be paid extra when they work extra hours.

21.2 Other deductions include contributions to a superannuation scheme (i.e. a pension scheme), charitable contributions (where the employee has agreed to give some of the wage or salary to a charity and has asked the employer to deduct the money from the amount earned), and subscriptions to a trade union (where the employer has asked that this be done). None of these are compulsory, but they all affect the amount the employee is left with as 'take-home pay'.

21.3 People working as traders in the financial markets can earn huge amounts in bonus payments – figures in excess of £1 million are not unusual – if they or their business have had a particularly successful year. However, very few people perform this type of work, and some of those who do receive very small bonuses if, indeed, they receive any bonus at all.

Review questions

***Note*: These questions are for general use only. They have been designed to be able to be done without the use of tax and National Insurance tables. The National Insurance given is the employee's part only.**

21.1 H Smith is employed at a rate of £5 per hour. During the week to 18 May 2009 he worked his basic week of 40 hours. According to the requisite tables the income tax due on his wages was £27, and National Insurance £16. Calculate his net wages.

21.2 B Charles has a basic working week of 40 hours, paid at the rate of £4 per hour. For hours worked in excess of this he is paid $1\frac{1}{2}$ times basic rate. In the week to 12 March 2006 he worked 45 hours. The first £80 per week is free of income tax, on the next £50 he pays at the 20% rate and above that he pays at the 25% rate. National Insurance amounted to £17. Calculate his net wages.

21.3 B Croft has a job as a car salesman. He is paid a basic salary of £200 per month, with a commission extra of 2% on the value of his car sales. During the month of April 2006 he sells £30,000 worth of cars. The first £450 per month is free of income tax, on the next £50 he pays at the 20% rate and above that he pays at the 25% rate. He also pays National Insurance for the month of £66. Calculate his net pay for the month.

21.4 T Penketh is an accountant with a salary of £2,000 per month plus bonus, which for May 2006 was £400. He pays superannuation contributions of 5% of gross pay, and these are allowed as reliefs against income tax. In addition to this he has further reliefs of £430. The taxable pay is taxed at the rate of 20% on the first £250, whilst the remainder suffers the 25% tax rate. In addition he pays National Insurance of £190. Calculate his net pay for the month.

21.5A K Blake is employed at the rate of £6 per hour. During the week to 25 May 2006 he works 35 hours. According to the tax and National Insurance tables he should pay income tax £28 and National Insurance £18. Calculate his net wages.

21.6A R Kennedy is a security van driver. He has a wage of £200 per week, plus danger money of £2 per hour extra spent in transporting gold bullion. During the week ended 15 June 2006 he spends 20 hours taking gold bullion to London Airport. The first £90 per week of his pay is free of income tax, whilst on the next £50 he pays at the 20% rate, and at the 25% rate above that figure. He pays National Insurance for the week of £19. Calculate his net pay for the week.

21.7A Mrs T Hulley is paid monthly. For part of April 2006 she earns £860 and then goes on maternity leave, her maternity pay for April being £90. She has pay free of tax £320, whilst on the next £250 she pays at the 20% tax rate, and 25% above that. She pays £79 National Insurance. Calculate her net pay for the month.

21.8A P Urmston is paid monthly. For June 2006 he earns £1,500 and also receives statutory sick pay of £150. He pays £90 superannuation which is allowed as a relief against income tax and he has further reliefs (free pay) of £350. The taxable pay is taxed at the rate of 20% on the first £250 and 25% thereafter. He pays National Insurance of £130 for the month. Calculate his net pay for the month.

You can find a range of additional self-test questions, as well as material to help you with your studies, on the website that accompanies this book at www.pearsoned.co.uk/wood.

chapter 22

Computers and accounting

Learning objectives

After you have studied this chapter, you should be able to:

- explain that different computer hardware configurations are used, depending largely upon company size
- explain why financial accounting packages tend to be bought 'off-the-shelf', possibly customised to the business, or the software (particularly in larger companies) may be commissioned from computer software specialists either within the business or from external agencies
- explain why accountants use spreadsheets to write many of their own computer programs, particularly for managerial accounting purposes
- explain that an accounting information system is just one part of the management information system
- describe the structure and flexibility of spreadsheets
- explain why a database package is a useful tool
- explain the importance of backing up data in a computerised environment
- explain the importance of and benefits of the use of passwords
- describe the requirements and implications of the Data Protection Act 1998

Introduction

In this chapter, you'll learn about how computers can be used to input and process data and produce output from an accounting system that can be used for decision-making. You'll learn about how computers are linked together and of the differences between buying ready-made accounting software and writing the accounting program from scratch. You'll be introduced to spreadsheets and database packages and you will learn of the importance of backing up data and using passwords. Finally, you will learn about the regulations relating to the storage of personal data on computer.

22.1 Background

Nowadays, there are very few businesses which do not use a computer for at least some of their data processing tasks. In some cases, this may simply involve the accountant using a spreadsheet as an extended trial balance, the data being input having been obtained, in the first place, from the manually maintained ledgers. Once the final adjustments to the trial balance have been made, the spreadsheet would then be used to produce the financial statements. (You will be learning about these accounting activities in the next few chapters.)

In other cases, computers may be used for most, or even all, of the accounting tasks. Whatever the level of use of computers in accounting, accountants need to be able to understand how data is being entered and processed so that they can understand and have faith in the reliability of the figures produced. It has been suggested, for example, that over 60 per cent of spreadsheet programs have errors. This is something accountants need to guard against.

Auditors have special computer programs designed to test the reliability of computerised accounting systems but it is obviously better to ensure that the computers are being used appropriately and correctly in the first place, rather than relying on an auditor to discover that some aspect of the system is not operating correctly – you would not, for example, wish to discover that for the previous year you have been giving all your customers a 10 per cent cash discount, even when they haven't paid you the amount they owe you! Thus, when computers are used in accounting, the accountant involved needs to ensure that they are being used appropriately and that the records they are creating and the output they produce is both valid and meaningful.

22.2 Large versus small systems

The technology when computers are used in an accounting system will vary in size to meet the volume of data processing required by the business. Very large businesses may use a large and extremely powerful central computer for handling bulk data and workstations and/or standalone PCs for a number of purposes such as data entry, producing departmental accounts and **financial modelling** (i.e. **forecasting** and **'what if'** or **sensitivity analysis**). Other businesses will use PCs for all accounting purposes.

Whatever the hardware used, where more than one person is using the computerised part of the accounting system some mechanism has to be in place to enable data to be entered and accessed by everyone who is responsible for that aspect of the system. This is unlikely to be done by sharing the same PC, so some appropriate organisation of the hardware is required.

Networks

When a central computer is used, the **workstations** used to interrogate the data held on the central computer may be **dumb terminals** – i.e. they have no processing capabilities of their own – or PCs. In either case, they need to be networked (i.e. linked together through wires that run from their workstations to the central computer; or via phone lines over the Internet; or connected using a wireless network).

In some cases, these groupings of a central computer with workstations will be a **local area network** (LAN) (i.e. internal to the location). In other cases, they will be part of a **wide area network** (WAN) (i.e. connected outside the location of the workstation to, for example, a computer located at the business's head office in another city). It is quite common for a workstation to be connected to both a local area network and a wide area network.

Being linked together has the advantage that data and information can be passed directly from one computer to another. Thus, although they can operate independently of any other computer, PC-based systems may also be connected together on a local area network, and have links to wide area networks.

Special forms of these networks emerged over the past few years as a result of the extension of the Internet. It is now becoming increasingly common for businesses to have an '**intranet**', a network based on Internet technologies where data and information private to the business is made available to employees of the business. Some also have **extranets**, where data and information private to the business is made available to a specific group of outsiders, for example making a company's stock records available online to major customers. Of course, most now have **websites** where they place information for the use of anyone who happens to want to look at it. In many cases, these contain copies of the latest financial statements of the business and a part of the website is devoted to promoting and selling goods and services.

Software

The software used may be developed in-house (by employees) or written under contract with an outside business or agency. Such systems are tailored to exactly what the business wants and are sometimes referred to as 'bespoke' systems. A large supermarket chain, for example, could have software developed incorporating the EPOS (electronic point of sale) system and you see this being used when barcodes on goods are scanned at supermarket check-outs. Not only do these check-out systems keep an accurate check on what is sold, in the form of an electronic cash book, but such information can be fed into the central computer to assist the process of reordering inventory from warehouses, and to keep a check on cash sales. They also provide data for inventory analysis and marketing purposes.

Expensive, specially designed software (often called 'customised' software) of this type will be used, generally, only by large businesses. Many medium-sized and smaller businesses will not require such special solutions, and will rely on 'off-the-shelf' software packages, most of which are flexible enough to be adapted to meet the major needs of most businesses.

Most financial accounting and bookkeeping programs are purchased off-the-shelf and then developed in-house, often by the accountants working, in the case of ledger systems, with their organisation's IT department.

Besides the main accounting system, the part used for recording transactions, making adjustments and producing financial statements, accountants also use the accounting system to tackle other problems not yet discussed in this textbook. These will include matters such as forecasting the cash flows of a business (i.e. how much money will leave the organisation and how much will be received), stock ordering, deciding on capital expenditure investment, how to find the sales volume at which the business moves into profit (breakeven analysis) and costing.

For such purposes, irrespective of the size of the business, accountants can use PC-based spreadsheets (see Section 22.5), such as Excel, and databases, such as Access. Such systems will change fairly rapidly over the years as new ones are developed.

The cost of computer hardware and software has been falling in real terms for many years – it has been suggested that had the same relative cost reduction applied to a Rolls-Royce car, it would now be cheaper to throw the car away once it ran out of petrol than to fill up the petrol tank! Consequently, computerisation is now affordable for all businesses. In fact, such has been the increase in data processing and power and range of analysis available as a result of businesses seeking to maximise the use of their computing power that many businesses now process such large volumes of data that they would find it impossible to revert to a manual system.

22.3 Benefits from computers

Time-saving with respect to transaction processing, increased accuracy and the production of a whole series of reports are obvious desirable and realistic benefits when computers are used for accounting. The basic principle of any accounting system is depicted in Exhibit 22.1.

Computers can be used in all aspects of the accounting system. When computers are used for some or all of these activities they can do everything that can be done with a manual system, but computers often do them faster, more accurately, and more efficiently.

Exhibit 22.1

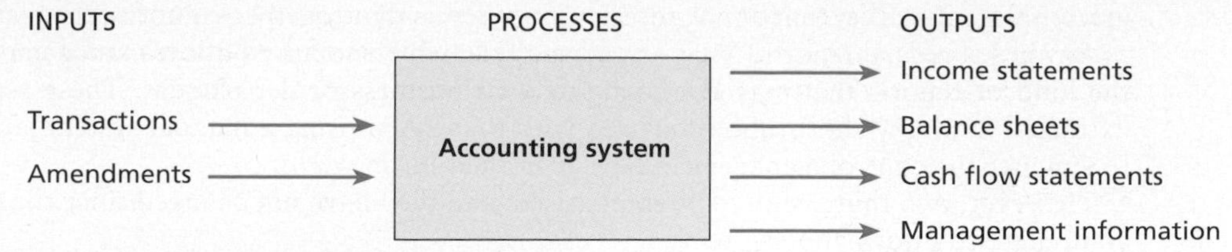

Increased job satisfaction

Increased job satisfaction and more effective use of operator time can be added bonuses of computerisation. For example, if a business computerises its inventory records, an operator's job of keeping records properly maintained will be much the same as in the manual system. However, with instant reporting facilities available, such as a list of all inventory items that may be in short supply, the operator can produce details almost instantly. This will allow an operator the facility of keeping a much closer check on inventory levels. Also, if time can be saved in producing inventory reports, the operator may have more time to chase up suppliers who are not delivering on time, or to shop around the market for better suppliers and products. Obviously, these are more interesting tasks than entering data into the accounting records and then ploughing through them in order to produce the reports.

Is it always going to be the case that employees experience greater satisfaction from working in a computerised environment?

Overall

Many more benefits of computerisation tend to become apparent as businesses develop their systems. It is worth noting that the extent of the benefits will vary from business to business, with each one deriving different benefits. It may well be the case that a business can derive no benefit at all from computerisation.

Some benefits bring problems of their own. For example, once computers are being used effectively in an accounting system, managers will often find themselves extracting reports that under a manual system could not be achieved within a timescale that would serve a useful purpose. The improved reporting and analysis that can be achieved by computerisation should improve the whole decision-making process within a business, but it can also lead to information overload as decision-makers find they have too much information and cannot fully understand or apply it.

22.4 Management information systems

All computer systems, whether purchased off-the-shelf or custom-made for a particular business, will need to supply information in a form that management can use to assist in its decision-making. Whether the output is on paper, via computer screens, on disk or available online, the information system centred upon the computer is generally referred to as the 'management information system' (MIS). The MIS contains far more information than the accounting information system – production data and marketing statistics, for example, would be included in the MIS. The accounting information system is a component within the MIS, and must be capable of integration with the other functional information systems that together comprise the rest of the MIS.

Beyond standard reports, MISs are normally flexible enough to allow management to extract the kind of reports that may be unique to their business or department. These reports can be extracted in a very short time compared with that taken using a manual system, and they serve to enhance the control management have over their business.

However, two things should be emphasised, and they have not changed since the early days of computerised information systems:

1 The reports and information extracted from a computer can only be as good as the data placed into it – the well-known 'garbage in, garbage out' situation. If the full benefits of computerisation are to be enjoyed, regular checks need to be made to ensure that the data input is accurate and timely.
2 Computerisation allows infinite instant access to data. It is a straightforward way of designing and producing a new report, and it can be easier to print all possible types of reports across all functions than to limit the reports produced to those actually needed by the people they are sent to. If report generation is not controlled, information overload will occur and decision-makers may have difficulty seeing the wood because of all the trees.

22.5 Use of spreadsheets

The spreadsheet is the software tool most used by accountants. Spreadsheets first appeared in 1979 and within only a handful of years surveys were showing that of those accountants who had access to PCs, virtually 100 per cent were using them for some task or other. The name derives from the appearance of the computer *spreading* data across a *sheet*, allowing the user to directly enter numbers, formulae or text into the cells. Exhibit 22.2 shows an example of an empty spreadsheet.

As you can see, the screen is divided into vertical columns and horizontal rows to form a grid of cells. Each cell is referred to by its co-ordinate, like a map reference or a point on a graph. For example, cell C12 is in column C row 12. Formulae can be entered to link cells. An example of linking cells is where a cell entry reads:

=B5*C12

(Note the use of an asterisk to represent a multiplication sign.)

This expression makes the value of the contents of the cell it is in equal to the value of cell B5 multiplied by the value of cell C12. Thus, if the formula was entered in cell D16 and B5 contained the number 6 and C12 contained the number 4, D16 would display the value 24. A spreadsheet is, effectively, a very powerful screen-based calculator and report generator whose output, both text and graphs, can be printed or electronically transmitted to another computer.

Any item in a spreadsheet can be changed at any time and the new results will instantly and automatically be shown. This makes it very easy to perform 'what if' or sensitivity analysis (for example, what would the result be if sales were to increase by 10 per cent?) and has led to a far higher level of understanding of the effects of decisions than was ever possible when all such recalculations could involve several days' work. It is this facility of being able to quickly recalculate formulae that makes the spreadsheet a powerful, useful and popular analytical tool.

Spreadsheets can be used in order to seek goals, such as specific profit figures. For example, spreadsheets can depict the sales and costs of a business and the goal-seeking function can then be used to determine what selling price will be required in order to achieve a specific net profit.

Spreadsheets tend to be written by accountants for their own use, rather than by computer programmers. Some other examples of uses for spreadsheets include:

Exhibit 22.2

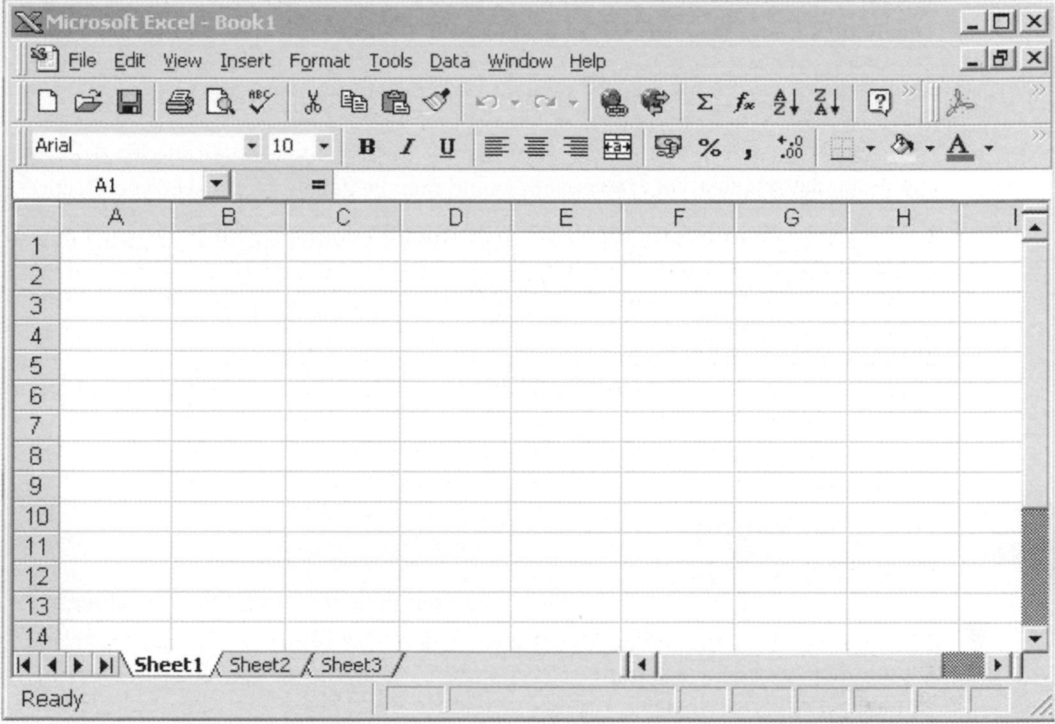

Screenshot reprinted by permission from Microsoft Corporation.

- financial plans and budgets can be represented as a table, with columns for time periods (e.g. months) and rows for different elements of the plan (e.g. costs and revenue);
- tax, investment and loan calculations can be made with ease;
- statistics using built-in functions such as averages, standard deviations, time series and regression analysis can be calculated;
- consolidation – merging branch or departmental accounts to form overall company (consolidated) financial statements;
- multi-dimensional spreadsheets can be created, enabling far deeper analysis of data – the 'sheet' tabs at the foot of the spreadsheet in Exhibit 22.2 can each be a 'dimension' that can be linked to other sheets, thus permitting views to be developed across various dimensions of a business activity. Even without this facility, the number of rows and columns available in a spreadsheet make this type of data modelling relatively simple for all but the most complex of scenarios;
- currency conversion is simple – useful for an organisation with overseas interests such as a multinational company;
- timetabling and roster planning of staff within organisations or departments can be performed.

It is hardly surprising that spreadsheets are so widely used by accountants.

Why do you think that accountants frequently write their own spreadsheet programs rather than having them written by an IT specialist?

22.6 Use of databases

Instead of being specifically designed for the types of task that accountants perform a lot, databases are designed for a more general purpose. A database is organised into a collection of related files into which go records. For example, an inventory system could be developed where an inventory file contains a record for each item of inventory. The records are further broken down into fields. Hence, there could be a field for reference, one for description, a quantity, reordering level and so on. The system would then be developed to keep such records updated.

This application is favoured by many businesses as it tends to be more flexible than an accounting package and easier and cheaper to put together than a set of programs specifically written for the business.

Such database packages require a little more computing expertise and a sound knowledge of the accounting system in order to create something appropriate. In such instances, while many would be written by an accountant, it is possible that computing and accounting personnel would work together on the development, particularly where the accountant had no previous experience of using the database software.

22.7 Data back-ups

One of the most important principles in computing is the discipline of backing up data held on computer. Backing up is now performed easily by simply copying the relevant files to another computer or onto a storage medium, such as a CD or even a floppy disk.

This serves the purpose that, if anything ever goes wrong with the data, then the business can always revert to a back-up copy of the data. If, for example, a company backs up its data at midday and there is a loss of data later that afternoon, then the worst that could happen is that the company has to restore the data from the midday back-up and then re-enter the data since that time. Clearly, therefore, the more often a business backs up its data, the less work is needed in the event of data loss.

Many of the software packages routinely used by accountants, such as spreadsheets, can be programmed to automatically back up work every few minutes so that it is not all lost should the computer or program crash.

22.8 Passwords

When computers are being used along with an accounting package, it is normally possible for passwords to be set up to restrict which personnel have access to certain parts of the computerised elements of the accounting system. This assists management in maintaining tighter control on the system and avoids over-complicating operations for operators. It ensures that operators do not have access to parts of a wider system than they need in order to do their job adequately, and avoids the risks inherent in exposing all parts of the system to all operators. As an extra benefit, if the functions available to operators are limited, it becomes easier and quicker to train the operators.

Activity 22.3 What has happened in recent years to make the use of passwords more important than ever?

22.9 Data security and the Data Protection Act 1998

Most businesses that make extensive use of computers for accounts, payroll, and any other applications that involve personal details of individuals, need to register with the **Information Commissioner's Office.**

The Data Protection Act defines a **data controller** as someone who determines how and for which purposes **personal data** is used. A **data subject** is anyone on whom data is held on a computer that can be identified as relating to them. Such data on a computer has to be processed by the computer's software before it can serve the purpose of information. It is this information that the **Information Commissioner** wants to know about.

Essentially, data users must declare what information they have access to on data subjects and the uses they will put that information to. The main objective of the Act is to ensure that individuals are aware of what is being held about them on business computers and allow them access to this information.

If a business is only using the Sales Ledger or Purchases Ledger for preparing and sending invoices and statements and does not use the comment details for a contact name then registration may not be necessary. Also, if customers and suppliers are companies, and individuals cannot be identified in the data, registration is not necessary. In the same way, if all a business does with payroll data is to pay wages and prepare statutory returns, registration is not necessary.

If customer and supplier lists are used for sending out sales promotions, the business must register. Likewise, registration is required if a business uses data on the payroll for management information about staff sickness or any form of staff monitoring.

Forms for registration require the business to reveal the kind of data it holds on individuals and the purpose for which it wants to use it. The business must also give details on how data subjects can find out what data is held on computer about them.

In addition to the possible need to register, businesses must comply with certain practices with regard to holding personalised data on computer. Many of these legal requirements simply define good computing practice and should be applied, where applicable, to all data used on a computer. These legal principles are contained in Schedule I of the Act:

1 Personal data shall be processed fairly and lawfully and, in particular, shall not be processed unless certain conditions contained in Schedules 2 and 3 of the Act have been met.
2 Personal data shall be obtained only for one or more specified and lawful purposes, and shall not be further processed in any manner incompatible with that purpose or those purposes.
3 Personal data shall be adequate, relevant and not excessive in relation to the purpose or purposes for which they are processed.
4 Personal data shall be accurate and, where necessary, kept up to date.
5 Personal data processed for any purpose or purposes shall not be kept for longer than is necessary for that purpose or those purposes.
6 Personal data shall be processed in accordance with the rights of data subjects under this Act.
7 Appropriate technical and organisational measures shall be taken against unauthorised or unlawful processing of personal data and against accidental loss or destruction of, or damage to, personal data.
8 Personal data shall not be transferred to a country or territory outside the European Economic Area unless that country or territory ensures an adequate level of protection for the rights and freedoms of data subjects in relation to the processing of personal data.

The website of the Information Commissioner's Office can be found at www.ico.gov.uk and the text of the Data Protection Act 1998 can be found at www.opsi.gov.uk/acts/acts1998/19980029.htm.

Learning outcomes

You should now have learnt that:

1. Computers can be and normally are linked together when they are used as part of the accounting system.
2. Software may be written from scratch or bought 'off-the-shelf'.
3. Software bought 'off-the-shelf' is often customised to fit the needs of the organisation.
4. Accounting information systems are just one part of an overall management information system.
5. Output can be excessive and cause information overload if not controlled to ensure it is useful to the person who receives it.
6. Spreadsheets are in general use by accountants who commonly develop their own software applications with them.
7. Databases are well suited to recording facts such as names, addresses and stock levels.
8. Backing up data is an essential task in a computerised environment.
9. Use of passwords assists in limiting access to parts of an information system and to the system as a whole and should not be ignored, particularly as the Internet has opened up the possibility of information systems being penetrated by outsiders.
10. The Data Protection Act 1998 must be observed when personal data is held on computer.

Answers to activities

22.1 No, there are many negative impacts on individuals. For example, a job may have been interesting previously because it involved searching about for information. Now it is routine and, therefore, less interesting. Also, computers and software can have faults that make it frustrating to use them, such as a PC crash where all data entered is lost or a network failure that means no work can be done.

22.2 There are many reasons, including:

Pragmatic reasons:

- Accountants understand accounting better than IT specialists so may spend a lot of the time instructing IT specialists in how to perform accounting tasks rather than in telling them what is required.
- A spreadsheet written by an IT specialist may contain logic errors arising from a lack of knowledge of accounting.
- Accountants known what they want, IT specialists need to be told, and telling someone something does not necessarily mean (a) that they understand what you want, (b) that they agree with what you want to the extent that they think it is worthwhile providing it, and (c) that what they produce will actually be what was requested. (For example, an accountant may ask for a spreadsheet to prepare financial statements from a trial balance and the IT specialist may produce one where all the items within the balance sheet categories have been put in alphabetic order and some of the headings have been changed to make them more 'normal'.)
- All but the very complex spreadsheet programs can be written in a few hours, some in minutes. It may take longer to explain what is required than to actually write it.

- IT specialists have other work to do and it may take them days, weeks, even months, to produce the spreadsheet, by which time the accountant wants something else instead.
- Some spreadsheet applications that an accountant writes will be needed immediately and will not be used again. There is no time to brief anyone on what is required.

Risk aversion reasons:

- A lack of willingness on the part of the accountant to appear unable to perform what many accountants would consider to be a trivial skill effectively enough to produce their own spreadsheets.
- The '*not invented here syndrome*', whereby people do not generally like to use someone else's idea of what is required. They prefer to use one they made themselves, even if it is technically and operationally inferior, and takes more time and effort to do than can be justified by the benefits that result.
- A desire not to use a spreadsheet in the first place, possibly arising from a low level of personal IT literacy.

22.3 This has become a far more important aspect of information systems in recent years, because of the many ways in which outsiders can hack into company information systems through the company's Internet links.

Review questions

22.1 What are the legal principles underlying the protection of personal information kept on computers?

22.2 What benefits can flow from processing sales details on a computer?

22.3 For what type of activities in accounting is the use of spreadsheets particularly suitable?

You can find a range of additional self-test questions, as well as material to help you with your studies, on the website that accompanies this book at www.pearsoned.co.uk/wood.

chapter 23

Computerised accounting systems

Learning objectives

After you have studied this chapter, you should be able to:

- explain how computerised accounting systems mimic manual accounting systems and can do everything that is done by a manual accounting system
- describe how computerised accounting systems automate most of the entries required in a manual accounting system including, in some cases, the initial entry for each transaction
- describe and explain the advantages and pitfalls of using a computerised accounting system
- explain the importance of fully integrating a computerised accounting system
- explain the importance of full compatibility between the various components of a computerised accounting system
- explain the need to take great care when converting from a manual accounting system to a computerised one

Introduction

In this chapter, you'll learn about the differences between manual and computerised accounting information systems and about the benefits of using computerised accounting systems to produce output for decision-making. You will also learn of the variety of output that can be produced by a computerised information system. In addition, you will learn of the importance of integration and compatibility of all the components of a computerised accounting system and of the need to take great care when switching from a manual system to a computerised one.

23.1 Background

Most businesses, except the very smallest, now use computers to handle their accounting data. When businesses switch to computerised accounting, they soon discover that bookkeeping and accounting skills are more important than computing ones. This is because users of many computerised accounting systems have very little to learn in order to use them. In Windows-based software, as you can see from the entry screen of the *Sage Instant Accounting 2000* accounting package shown in Exhibit 23.1, the interfaces look fairly familiar – the file menu is usually in the top left, for example, and many of the icons are the same and have the same meanings across a whole range of software produced by different companies.

Exhibit 23.1

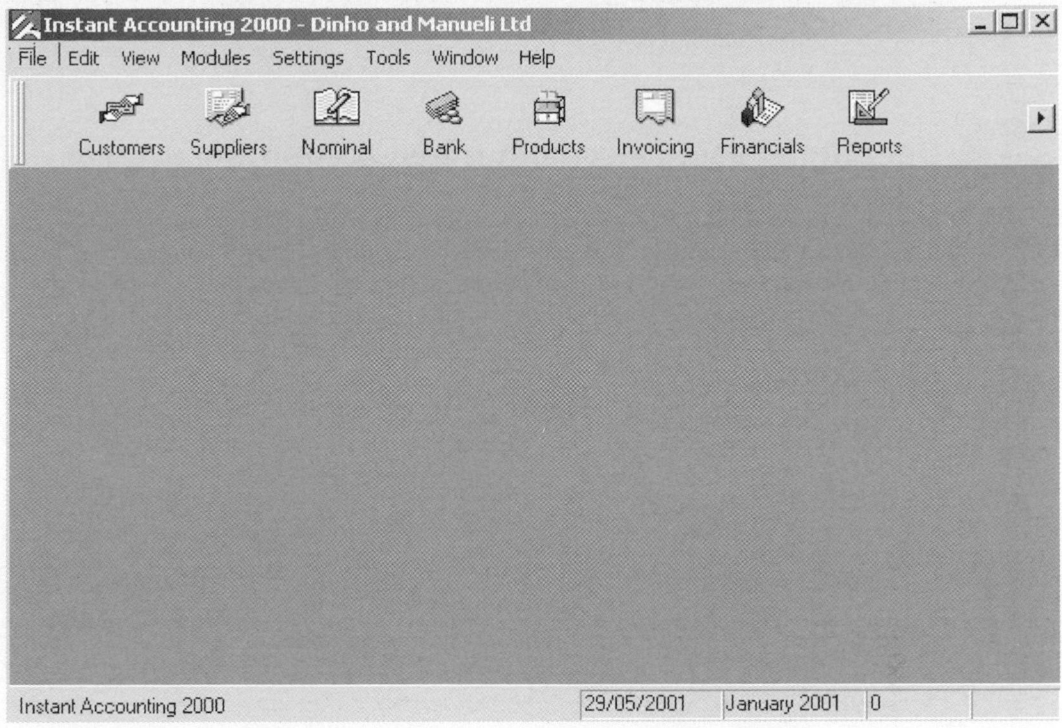

Screenshot reprinted by courtesy of the Sage Group plc.

Not very long ago, only the largest businesses used computers to handle their accounting data. Why do you think the situation is so different now?

The methods adopted in computer-based accounting adhere to the fundamental principles of accounting covered in this and other accounting textbooks. No matter how sophisticated and easy to use a computerised accounting system is, it will not overcome the need for bookkeeping and accounting knowledge by those in control. Imagine, for example, how anyone who does not know how to prepare journal entries could correct an error in an original entry correctly from an accounting point of view and, just as importantly, understand why it is important not to erase the original entry.

Apart from a need for knowledge of accounting principles in order to best convert a business from manual to computer-based accounting, some accounting knowledge is required to help understand the significance of many of the outputs from a computerised accounting system, just as it is required in respect of output from a manual accounting system.

Thus, computerised accounting systems do not remove the need for some accounting knowledge among those responsible for key accounting tasks or from those who use the output from the accounting systems. In fact, some accountants working in practice would tell you that they believe there is an even greater need for accounting knowledge among those who record the transactions in a computerised accounting system than among those using a manual one.

What do you think? Is there an even greater need for accounting knowledge among those that record the transactions in a computerised accounting system? Why?/Why not?

23.2 Benefits of using a computerised accounting system

As you learnt in Chapter 22, there are many benefits of using a computerised accounting system. Overall, probably the greatest benefit comes from the fact that a computerised accounting system can do the same things as a manual system, but does them better. Thus all the features in a manual system, such as the one shown in Exhibit 23.2, can be replicated in a computerised accounting system which not only does them quicker, more accurately, and 100 per cent consistently, but can also do them more frequently *and* do other things as well.

Exhibit 23.2

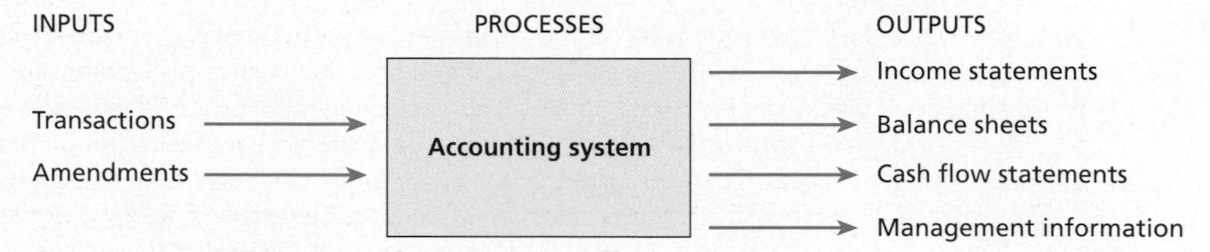

Let's look at some of these benefits in more detail.

Speed and accuracy

The main aim of computerising an accounting system is to perform the processing stage electronically, much more quickly, consistently and accurately than if it were done manually. However, transactions and amendment details have to be input into the process (1) in the correct form, (2) in the correct order, and (3) in a timely manner. Although there is scope to use electronic methods of entering some of this information (e.g. EPOS systems and document scanning), it requires a good deal of initiative and an organised way of doing things in order to do so. Nevertheless, improved accuracy is one of the more obvious benefits of any kind of computerised accounting system.

Further time-saving can be achieved by immediate output of reports, such as customer statements, purchase analysis, cash and bank statements, and details about whether the business is meeting sales targets. Such reports and statements can be produced both on request and, automatically, by the computer searching through information generated and saved within the accounting system and then producing whatever report is required.

Error detection

Effective error detection improves the decision-making process. For example, a computerised accounting system should be capable of detecting when a customer appears to be running up excessive debts with the business, so offering the chance for the credit controller to take remedial action.

Another area is the need to remain within budgets. Many business expenses can get out of hand if they are not checked at regular intervals. A computerised accounting system should be capable of an activity called **exception reporting**, a process of issuing a warning message to decision-makers when something unexpected is happening: for example, when expenditure against a budget is higher than it should be. In a manual accounting system, the situation can occur that errors or unwanted transactions go unnoticed until it is too late, resulting in unnecessary costs being incurred by the business.

Enhanced reporting

For many businesses, the task of producing reports on a regular basis, such as VAT Returns, payroll processing, cash flow analysis, and financial statements, can be time-consuming, tedious and unrewarding. The use of a computerised accounting system speeds up the process to the point, in some cases, where it is done automatically thus reducing the monotony of producing lengthy reports requiring extensive preparatory analysis of data. In many cases, such as VAT Returns and payslips, businesses find that they can use computer printouts or electronic output, e.g. on computer disks, instead of having to manually complete official or standard forms.

23.3 Computerised accounting records

Many businesses now make good use of accounting packages which are readily available and have been well tested. Such packages are commonly modularised with, typically, the sales ledger, purchases ledger, general ledger, inventory control, sales invoicing, sales order processing, purchases order processing, non-current assets, payroll, bill of materials, and job costing all being offered as separate modules in their own right. When a business decides to computerise its accounting system, it acquires only the modules it needs. For example, a sole trader would have no use for a payroll module.

The various ledgers and accounts maintained in a computerised accounting system mimic those kept in a manual system. The general ledger, for example, will adhere to the basic rules of double entry bookkeeping in that each debit entry has a corresponding credit entry – if a customer is issued with an invoice, the transaction giving precise details of the invoice will be stored in the credit sales records to form part of the customer history and then the double entry is made by crediting sales accounts and debiting a debtor's account.

The difference lies in the method of entry – each transaction is entered only once (accountants refer to this as a 'single entry' system) and the software automatically completes the double entry. This has a downside, however: some computerised accounting packages will post various amounts into suspense accounts when it is unclear where postings are to be made. These require manual intervention and journal entries to remove each item from the suspense account and complete the original double entry.

(Suspense accounts are the topic of Chapter 33.)

Flexibility

The information stored in a computerised accounting system is available instantly and can be used to produce statements, ledger account details, analysis of how long debts have been outstanding, etc. immediately it is requested. For example, the computerised sales ledger will hold all details about customers. The starting point would be to enter the details concerning the customer (name, address, etc.) along with the balance brought forward from the manual system (if such a transfer is occurring; otherwise, if it is a new customer, an opening zero balance will be created automatically by the software).

All transactions relating to a customer, such as the issue of an invoice or receipt of payment, are entered into the system and automatically posted to the customer's account. Customers can, at any time, be issued with a statement of their account, and the business can always obtain an up-to-date and complete history of trading with any particular customer. The purchases ledger will operate in exactly the same way in that supplier details are held and, once entered through the purchases module, all transactions relating to individual purchasers will automatically be posted to the appropriate account.

Bank payments and receipts are a central feature of computerised accounting systems. The modules can be operated by someone with virtually no bookkeeping knowledge. For example, if an electricity bill is paid, the system will prompt for the details of the transaction that are required to process and record the double entry. The system will not assume any knowledge of double entry on the part of the individual making the entries.

Account codes

In order to use a computerised accounting system efficiently and effectively, someone with both accounting skills and a good knowledge of the business will be required to organise the accounts and ledgers in the first instance. Some of these packages are not written for specific businesses and need to be 'tailored' to the one that is going to use it. Most require businesses to define what accounts they are to have in their general ledger and how such accounts are to be grouped.

For example, accounts for non-current assets may have account references commencing with 'N', while expense accounts commence with 'E'. The package will probably have its own default set of **account codes** (the computerised equivalent of the folio references in a manual system), and it may be necessary to override the defaults in the accounting package in order to use the business's own account code list (also known as the '**chart of accounts**'). In addition, part of the setting-up of a computer system will require the tailoring of the package for certain reports such as the income statement and balance sheet.

Knowledge of double entry

Most packages are capable of allowing businesses to set up their preferred methods for dealing with depreciation of non-current assets and regular payments of, for example, rent and rates. However, as you saw with the need to correct entries in a suspense account arising from the computer not knowing how to complete a double entry, such packages do require a good 'knowledge' of double entry so that adjustments can be made through their journal entries. For example, the computer will not overcome some errors and omissions, such as the operator misreading an amount on an invoice or crediting a payment to the wrong customer account. Anyone correcting these errors will require a full knowledge of the relevant part of the accounting system as well as knowledge of bookkeeping and accounting principles.

23.4 Computerised inventory control and modular integration

Automation of much of the data processing can be taken further when integrating other modules. Inventory control offers the benefit of keeping very close tabs on inventory levels. If an invoicing package is also in use, then an invoice can be generated in such a way that an operator can collect the details of the business or person to invoice from the sales ledger and details of all inventory to be invoiced from the inventory files. Once the invoice has been raised, the recorded inventory levels fall accordingly, the sales ledger is updated and the nominal entries are made by crediting sales and debiting accounts receivable control (a topic which will be covered in Chapter 31).

Sales order processing

Sales order processing allows an order to be placed into the system which can then be used at a later stage to generate an invoice. Sales order processing is important to many businesses as it gives them an indication about what inventory levels are required. Having sales orders on computer also offers the advantage of being able to monitor sales orders outstanding and so ensure that they are supplied on time to the customers. Computers can produce outstanding order reports and such things as 'picking lists' (a list of items to be taken out of storage and given or shipped to customers) very quickly.

Purchase order processing

Purchase order processing allows an operator to print an order to send off to a supplier or, in some more advanced systems, to transmit it over a direct link into the supplier's accounting system where it will be recorded and converted into an issue from inventory. The computerised purchase order system also serves the useful purpose of allowing instant access to information about what is on order. This prevents duplicate orders arising.

Modular integration

The full use of all modules in this integrated manner allows a business to access inventory details and get a complete profile on its status in terms of what is left in stock, what is on order, and what has been ordered by customers. Furthermore, most packages keep a history of inventory movements so helping the business to analyse specific inventory turnovers. When integrated in this fashion, the processing structure may be as depicted in Exhibit 23.3.

Exhibit 23.3 An integrated computerised accounting system

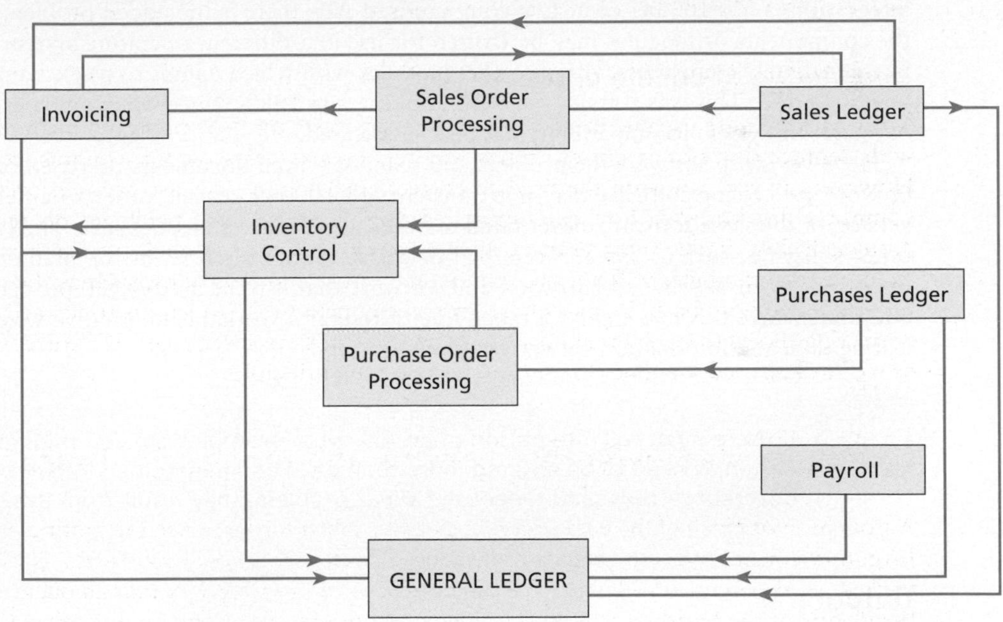

Exhibit 23.3 includes a payroll module. Businesses with a large number of employees would find this particularly useful as payroll systems require a good deal of regular processing. Again, a reasonable knowledge of payroll is required in order to set up the system in the first place.

23.5 Accounting information systems

An **accounting information system (AIS)** is the total suite of components that, together, comprise all the inputs, storage, transaction processing, collating and reporting of financial transaction data. It is, in effect, the infrastructure that supports the production and delivery of accounting information.

The objective of an accounting information system is to collect and store data about accounting transactions so as to generate meaningful output for decision-making. The combination of a shoebox containing receipts for all purchases and a cheque book being kept by the corner shopkeeper is, in itself, an accounting system, as is the set of day books and ledgers kept by the local department store and the integrated computerised accounting system of a large company.

There is no need for an AIS to be computerised in order to be described in this way. Computerisation may only have been introduced on some of the accounting tasks, such as the accounting books, the payroll system or the inventory control system. When the entire suite of accounting tasks and records is computerised, the benefits are clearly greater than when only parts of the AIS are computerised. **Most people assume you are talking about a *fully* computerised accounting system when you refer to an AIS and *this is how we shall use the term in the rest of this chapter*.** However, much of what follows, apart from the benefits of full integration, is also applicable to partially computerised AISs.

Full integration and compatibility

For an AIS to be fully effective, *all* the components need to be integrated with each other, otherwise information gets lost, misentered from one record to another, or duplicated (often incorrectly as each version of it is updated at different times). Major errors may ultimately arise if integration is not 100 per cent. In a computerised AIS, there is the added problem that some of the components or modules may be written for use in a different operating system and may not be immediately compatible with the other modules with which data is to be exchanged, retrieved or transferred. This was a major problem until the late 1980s, since when much of the difficulty of operating system incompatibility has been eradicated.

However, with software the problem still remains – even documents prepared on one version of word processing software may not transfer with 100 per cent accuracy to an earlier or later version of the same software, never mind to other word processing packages. The same holds for other software, such as spreadsheets and database files. Therefore, at the planning stage, it is important to ensure that all hardware and software that is to be used is 100 per cent compatible and that, where it is not, steps are taken to ensure that a workable alternative way of communicating data and information between modules is found.

If there is not full integration of an AIS, what examples can you think of where data may need to be entered more than once and maintained in two or more different records simultaneously? What problems may result from this?

Outputs

An AIS, computerised or manual, can, of course, produce whatever reports you wish, so long as the relevant data is stored within the AIS or accessible to the AIS. Where a fully computerised AIS is clearly superior is in the range of reports it can produce virtually instantly and in the way it can be programmed to produce periodic reports precisely when they are scheduled to be available. There is no need for decision-makers to wait two weeks for the summary of the previous month's business activities – a delay that was commonplace in manual accounting systems. It is now available as soon as business closes at the end of the last day of the month.

Some of the other reports produced by most manual AISs can also take a very long time to produce. Some only take an hour or two to prepare manually. However, a computerised AIS can produce these reports in seconds, and as often as the decision-makers wish. These include aged debtors reports (a list of debtors showing how much they each owe, and for how long the amounts have been outstanding); price lists; inventory levels and quantities for reordering; lists of invoices and credit notes; and audit trail information to enable errors to be traced and corrected (whereby the route a transaction took through the accounting records to the financial statements is revealed). The savings in personnel and time and, therefore, costs that can result from fully computerising the AIS cannot be understated, even for smaller businesses that wish to maximise their efficiency.

When computers were first used in this way, many decision-makers were far from pleased. Why?

In the early days of computerised AISs, all the output was on paper. Now, much of it is electronic.

Electronic dissemination

One of the major benefits of a computerised AIS is that output generated from it need not be in hard copy. It can be visual on a computer screen, or distributed electronically on DVD, CD or floppy disk, or by direct file transfer to another computer over a LAN, WAN, intranet or extranet or the Internet.

While many organisations still require that information be passed to them on their own forms, the IT revolution of the past few years has led to many organisations being willing to accept printout generated from a computer, emailed electronic documents, or disks containing the document, instead of having their own forms completed and returned. For example, fairly standard and repetitive information generation, such as VAT receipts and payments, are common to most businesses, and the Revenue and Customs accept computer-generated VAT returns, computer-generated payroll data and computer-generated tax returns.

In fact, the Revenue and Customs currently (2008) accepts all the following documents electronically:

- annual tax returns (income tax and corporation tax);
- starter/leaver details (forms P45, P46, P160);
- daily coding (form P6);
- PAYE return;
- annual and budget code number updates (form P9);
- pension and works number updates;
- end-of-year returns (forms P35, P38A and P14);
- expenses and benefits (form P11D);
- construction industry vouchers CIS23 and CIS25;
- tax credit notices (form TC700 series);
- student declaration (form P38s);
- student loan deductions (forms SL1 and SL2).
- VAT Return (form 100)

and is moving towards compulsory electronic filing for some, including VAT and Corporation Tax.

Benefits of electronic filing of documents

Among the recognised benefits of electronic submission of documents and hence, potentially, of a computerised AIS are:

- speed;
- improved accuracy in that what is sent is what was intended to be sent;

- improved accuracy in that what is sent is received, and in the form intended;
- lower administration costs;
- greater security;
- less use of paper;
- immediate acknowledgement of receipt.

Benefits of electronic transmission of funds

Of course, if electronic submission of documents is a recent phenomenon, electronic transmission of funds has been around a good deal longer. Among the benefits attributed to it and again, potentially, to a computerised AIS are:

- certainty of payment on a specific date;
- certainty that exactly the amount due to be paid is paid;
- immediate acknowledgement of receipt;
- lower administration costs;
- lower bank charges;
- greater security.

Benefits of linking AISs

Another significant recent change brought about by computerisation of AISs is the growth in electronic data exchange between supplier and customer. Some very large companies now insist that their suppliers link their inventory systems to the customer's AIS. The customer can then interrogate the inventory records of the supplier to see if items are available and place orders directly into the supplier's AIS without any need for physical transmission of an order document. This has helped the growth of just-in-time inventory keeping by customers who, rather than holding their own inventory, simply order it from their suppliers when required.

Among the benefits attributed to linking AISs and again, potentially, to a computerised AIS are:

- speed;
- lower administration costs;
- greater awareness of the current position;
- improved control of related risks;
- greater security of a continuing relationship between the parties.

23.6 Issues to consider when introducing a fully computerised AIS

When you computerise an accounting system, you have some decisions to make. These include:

1. Deciding whether to mimic what you have been doing manually or start from scratch and redesign everything. For example, you may only have been using one ledger in the manual system, but may choose to use three or four in the computerised system. You may have had a two-column cash book in the manual system but decide to have a columnar cash book in the computerised system.
2. Deciding whether to buy a general accounting package 'off-the-shelf' or create one from scratch. Depending on the size of the business, creating one from scratch may be done using a spreadsheet and a database package or it may involve having computer programmers writing the entire system.
3. If you decide to buy one off-the-shelf, you need to decide how much to customise it, if at all.
4. If you decide not to customise it, or aren't able to customise parts of it, you may need to change the terminology you use when referring to parts of the accounting system. For example, you may need to refer to the Nominal Ledger rather than the General Ledger and to the Purchases

Journal rather than the Purchases Day Book. For example, *Sage* uses the term 'Customers Module' rather than Sales Ledger and 'Suppliers Module' instead of a Purchases Ledger.

5 You need to decide who is going to be responsible for overseeing the project.
6 You need to decide how long you are going to allow for the new system to be developed and make plans to introduce it accordingly.
7 You need to decide who is to be trained in using it and when.
8 You need to decide how long you will run the new system in parallel with the existing manual system before you stop using the manual system.
9 You need to identify the hardware you will need and ensure that it is in place at the appropriate time.
10 You need to identify who is going to test the new system and what data is to be used to do so.
11 You need to weigh up the costs and benefits of computerising the accounting system and decide whether it is actually worth doing it.

These are just some of the issues you need to deal with. Many more will appear as each of these questions is answered and many more will materialise as the project proceeds.

The most popular software used by small and medium-sized businesses in the UK is *Sage*. However, you should look at a range of available alternatives, such as *Pegasus*, *Quickbooks* and *Microsoft Dynamics GP*, before proceeding to purchase the package you intend using. Factors to consider obviously include price, but they also include capacity, hardware requirements, ease of use, reliability, appropriateness of the way data is entered, stored and secured, and the range and style of reports that can be produced. You also need to consider compatibility of the package with any other systems or packages you might wish to link it to if that is, in fact, a possibility in the first place. Accountants are not normally the most knowledgeable people to answer these technical questions and guidance from an IT specialist is often advisable.

Once the package is installed and fully operational, you need to monitor its effectiveness and reliability and need to have contingency plans in place should it ultimately prove to have been a mistake. (In other words, you need to ensure you can revert to the previous system if necessary.)

When you come to review your hardware or operating system with a view to upgrading it, you need to ensure that the package will continue to run without any problems when you upgrade. You also need to consider carefully before committing to an upgrade of the accounting package, in case things that used to work no longer function or need to be done in very different ways.

You also need to ensure that the data stored in the system is backed up regularly and that password or other security devices are in place in order to prevent unauthorised access to it.

Overall, you need to think the whole thing through very carefully before committing to the switch and you need to ensure you have all the controls over the system in place before it starts to be used.

Nevertheless, although great care and a lot of effort must be expended when converting to a computerised accounting system, there is no doubt that the benefits of having an appropriate one will vastly improve the quality and reliability of the accounting data and information produced.

Learning outcomes

You should now have learnt that:

1 Bookkeeping and accounting skills and knowledge are more important than computing skills and knowledge when a switch is made from a manual accounting system to a computerised accounting system.

2 The user interface of an accounting package often looks similar to those of other frequently used Windows-based software packages.

→

3 Computerised accounting systems can do everything a manual accounting system can do, but does them quicker, more accurately, more consistently, and with greater flexibility.

4 A considerably enhanced ability to obtain reports is available from a computerised accounting system compared to a manual accounting system.

5 The various records maintained in a computerised accounting system mimic those in a manual accounting system, though the names of some of the records may be different.

6 Acccount codes are used in computerised accounting systems instead of folio numbers.

7 Maximised integration of the various components in a computerised accounting system generates the maximum benefits.

8 Compatibility between the various components in a computerised accounting system is essential if it is to operate effectively.

9 One of the major benefits of computerised accounting systems is the ability to generate electronic output.

10 Implementing a switch to a computerised accounting system is a non-trivial task that should never be done lightly and needs to be done with the greatest of care.

Answers to activities

23.1 This question can be answered from many perspectives including:

- vastly lower relative cost of computer technology and IT in general
- greater ease of use thanks to a graphical rather than a text-based visual interface (this only really became the norm in the mid 1990s)
- wide range of available software to choose from
- the current high flexibility in (even off-the-shelf) software enabling customisation to suit the needs of the business
- a vastly greater level of IT literacy
- pressure from accountants to modernise methods and so increase control over the accounting records
- greater financial awareness among business people generally (e.g. the enormous growth in MBA holders over the past twenty years)
- pressures from the authorities to maintain up-to-date accounting records (e.g. VAT)
- pressure from competitors (i.e. the need to keep up)
- deeper insight that can be gained by using computers and information technology to present views of the business and business opportunities virtually instantly when they could only be produced manually after weeks of effort
- a desire to appear 'modern and up-to-date'.

23.2 Most accountants would disagree with the comment in a general sense but agree with it in the context of (a) knowing the accounts to use, (b) knowing whether an entry looks correct and, most importantly, (c) knowing how to make appropriate entries when an error has occurred.

23.3 One example would be where the inventory control system is not integrated with the Sales Ledger. A customer could return goods that were recorded in the inventory control system immediately. However, it might take a few hours, even days, for the credit entry to be made in the customer's account in the Sales Ledger. During the delay period, the customer might be refused credit because the account showed that the customer's credit limit had been reached when, in fact, the customer had no outstanding debt to the business as a result of having returned the items purchased. The customer might also be sent a statement of the account that did not show the credit entry but was accompanied by a letter demanding immediate payment as the account was now overdue. If the reverse happened and the first entry was made in the Sales Ledger, orders from other customers for the same items might be rejected because the inventory records showed a zero amount of those items in inventory when, in fact, the ones returned by the customer were in the warehouse.

Another problem of non-integration relates to customer details. If they are changed, for example by a change of address, and only entered in the Sales Ledger and not in the records maintained by the delivery department, goods ordered by the customer could be sent to the wrong address.

If the Cash Book is not fully integrated with the Sales Ledger, customers may pay their accounts but still be shown as debtors when the system is asked to print an aged list of debtors in the middle of a month. Time and effort might then be expended chasing a debt that didn't exist and, of course, the customer would not be exactly pleased either.

23.4 There were a number of issues at that time:

- The output was sometimes inaccurate, mainly due to the inexperience of the people who were keying data into the AIS, but also due to errors in programming. Also, until the late 1970s, much of the input was by punched card and cards in a batch had to be entered into the computer in the same order as they were produced. If a batch of cards was dropped before being put into the card reader that then transferred the data into the computer, all sorts of nonsense could result. This type of situation gave rise to the phrase 'garbage in, garbage out' which was often used by those who favoured traditional manual systems when explaining why computers were 'useless'. It still applies today, but for different reasons, such as the original data being incorrect or out-of-date.
- Many early AISs were developed by computer specialists, not accountants. They often produced reports that were less meaningful than they might have been, frequently omitting key information. The decision-makers did not know what rules had been followed in generating numbers in the reports and so would sometimes reach a decision assuming the data meant one thing when, in fact, it meant something else. (For example, the scrap value of a non-current asset may have been ignored when calculating whether it should be used for one more year or replaced.) They also often gave everything possible to the decision-makers, resulting in huge piles of reports being received of which only a few pages were actually of any interest.

In other words, the output from early computerised AISs was often less than useful and often could not be relied upon.

Review questions

23.1 What benefits for the whole accounting system can follow from using a computer for accounting work?

23.2 Why is the need for accounting skills and knowledge important when the accounting system is computerised?

23.3 Why is the need to fully integrate a computerised accounting system so important?

23.4 What issues need to be considered when making the switch from a manual accounting system to a computerised accounting system?

You can find a range of additional self-test questions, as well as material to help you with your studies, on the website that accompanies this book at www.pearsoned.co.uk/wood.

part 4

ADJUSTMENTS FOR FINANCIAL STATEMENTS

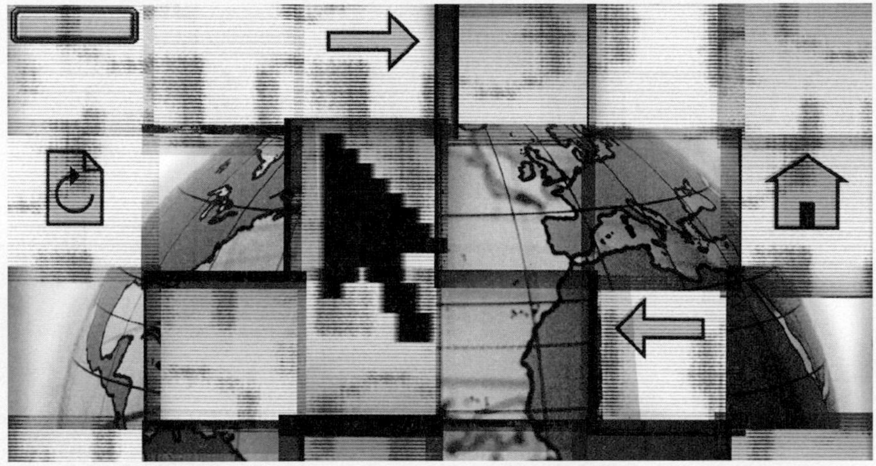

Introduction

This part is concerned with all the adjustments that have to be made before financial statements can be prepared.

The Scenario Questions take the knowledge you have acquired in Parts 1 to 3 and apply it to what you have learnt in Part 4.

hapter 24

Capital expenditure and revenue expenditure

Learning objectives

After you have studied this chapter, you should be able to:

- distinguish between expenditure that is capital in nature and that which is revenue expenditure
- explain why some expenditure is a mixture of capital expenditure and revenue expenditure
- explain the effect on the financial statements and the profits shown there, if revenue expenditure is wrongly treated as being capital expenditure, and vice versa

Introduction

In this chapter, you'll learn about the difference between capital expenditure and revenue expenditure. You will learn how to split expenditure that is a mixture of both capital and revenue expenditure and to make the appropriate entries in the ledgers and in the financial statements. You will also learn why organisations generally prefer to treat as much expenditure as possible as capital expenditure, how to deal with loan interest relating to acquisition of a non-current asset, and how to classify and deal with the income generated when a non-current asset is sold.

24.1 Capital expenditure

Before you start this topic, you need to be aware that 'capital expenditure' has nothing to do with the owner's Capital Account. The two terms happen to start with the same first word, and they are both things that are likely to be around the business for quite a long time. While both are, in a sense, long-term investments, one made by the business, the other made by the owner, they are, by definition, two very different things.

Capital expenditure is incurred when a business spends money either to:

- buy non-current assets, or
- add to the value of an existing non-current asset.

Included in such amounts should be spending on:

- acquiring non-current assets
- bringing them into the business
- legal costs of buying buildings
- carriage inwards on machinery bought
- any other cost needed to get a non-current asset ready for use.

24.2 Revenue expenditure

Expenditure which is not spent on increasing the value of non-current assets, but is incurred in running the business on a day-to-day basis, is known as **revenue expenditure**.

The difference between revenue expenditure and capital expenditure can be seen clearly with the total cost of using a van for a business. Buying a van is an example of capital expenditure. The van will be in use for several years and is, therefore, a non-current asset.

Paying for petrol to use in the van is revenue expenditure. This is because the expenditure is used up in a short time and does not add to the value of non-current assets.

Why do you think a business might want to treat an item of expenditure as capital rather than as revenue? (Hint: where does an item of capital expenditure *not* appear in the financial statements?)

24.3 Differences between capital and revenue expenditure

The examples listed in Exhibit 24.1 demonstrate the difference in classification.

Exhibit 24.1

Expenditure	*Type of Expenditure*
1 Buying van	**Capital**
2 Petrol costs for van	Revenue
3 Repairs to van	Revenue
4 Putting extra headlights on van	**Capital**
5 Buying machinery	**Capital**
6 Electricity costs of using machinery	Revenue
7 We spent £1,500 on machinery: £1,000 was for an item (improvement) added to the machine; and £500 was for repairs	**Capital £1,000** Revenue £500
8 Painting outside of new building	**Capital**
9 Three years later – repainting outside of building in (8)	Revenue

You already know that revenue expenditure is chargeable to the income statement, while capital expenditure will result in increased figures for non-current assets in the balance sheet. Getting the classification wrong affects the profits reported and the capital account and asset values in the financial statements. It is, therefore, important that this classification is correctly done.

24.4 Capital expenditure: further analysis

As mentioned earlier, capital expenditure not only consists of the cost of purchasing a non-current asset, but also includes other costs necessary to get the non-current asset operational.

Spend a minute listing some examples of these other costs like the ones you've already learnt about.

24.5 Joint expenditure

Sometimes one item of expenditure will need to be divided between capital and revenue expenditure – there was an example in Exhibit 24.1 when £1,500 spent on machinery was split between capital and revenue.

Exhibit 24.2

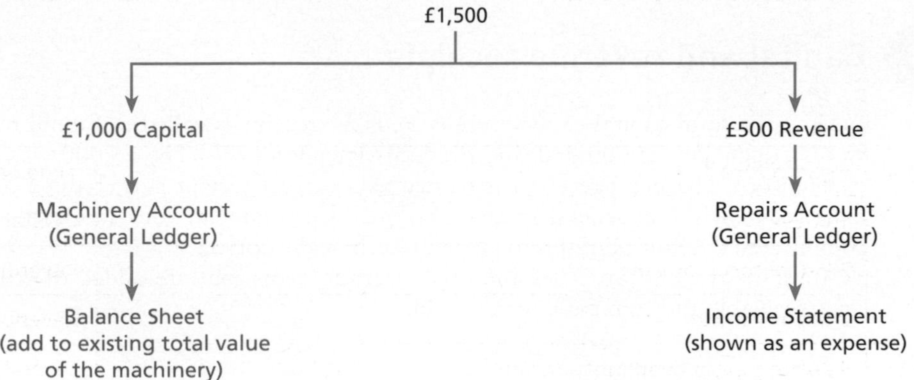

Activity 24.3

A builder was engaged to tackle some work on your premises, the total bill being for £3,000. If one-third of this was for repair work and two-thirds for improvements, where should the two parts be entered in the accounting books and where would they appear in the financial statements?

24.6 Incorrect treatment of expenditure

If one of the following occurs:

1 capital expenditure is incorrectly treated as revenue expenditure, or
2 revenue expenditure is incorrectly treated as capital expenditure,

then both the balance sheet figures and the income statement figures will be incorrect.

This means that the net profit figure will be incorrect and, if the expenditure affects items in the trading account part of the income statement, the gross profit figure will also be incorrect.

Activity 24.4 Can you think of an example where an item may have been treated wrongly as revenue expenditure and charged in the trading account when it should have been treated as capital expenditure?

24.7 Treatment of loan interest

If money is borrowed to finance the purchase of a non-current asset, interest will have to be paid on the loan. Most accountants would argue that the loan interest is *not* a cost of acquiring the asset, but is simply a cost of *financing* its acquisition. This meant that loan interest was revenue expenditure and *not* capital expenditure. In 1993, this changed and it is now compulsory to capitalise interest incurred in *constructing* a non-current asset.

Activity 24.5 Why shouldn't the interest on the funds borrowed to finance *acquisition* of a non-current asset be included in its cost?

24.8 Capital and revenue receipts

When an item of capital expenditure is sold, the receipt is called a 'capital receipt'. Suppose a van is bought for £5,000 and sold five years later for £750. The £5,000 was treated as capital expenditure. The £750 received is treated as a capital receipt and credited to the non-current asset account in the General Ledger. (You will learn later in your studies that it is a bit more complicated than this, but this treatment is technically correct.)

'Revenue receipts' are sales and other revenue items that are added to gross profit, such as rent receivable and commissions receivable.

24.9 Finally

Students generally find this topic very difficult to grasp. Trying to remember when something should be treated as capital expenditure and when something should be treated as revenue expenditure seems just too difficult to remember correctly.

In fact, the rules are *very* simple:

1. **If expenditure is *directly* incurred in bringing a non-current asset into use for the first time, it is capital expenditure.**
2. **If expenditure improves a non-current asset (by making it superior to what it was when it was first owned by the organisation, e.g. building an extension to a warehouse), it is capital expenditure.**
3. **All other expenditures are revenue expenditure.**

So, faced with having to decide, ask if (1) is true in this case. If it isn't, ask if (2) is true in this case. If it isn't, it is revenue expenditure. If either (1) or (2) is true, it is capital expenditure. Try it on the items in Exhibit 24.1 – it works!

Learning outcomes

You should now have learnt:

1 How to distinguish between capital expenditure and revenue expenditure.

2 That some items are a mixture of capital expenditure and revenue expenditure, and the total outlay need to be apportioned accordingly.

3 That if capital expenditure or revenue expenditure is mistaken one for the other, then gross profit and/or net profit will be incorrectly stated, as will the capital account and non-current assets in the balance sheet.

4 That if capital receipts or revenue receipts are mistaken one for the other, then gross profit and/or net profit will be incorrectly stated, as will the capital account and non-current assets in the balance sheet.

Answers to activities

24.1 Capital expenditure appears in the balance sheet whereas revenue expenditure appears in the income statement. If expenditure is treated as revenue expenditure, it reduces profit immediately by the amount spent. If it is treated as capital expenditure, there is no immediate impact upon profit. Profit is only affected when a part of the expenditure is charged against income during the time the item purchased is in use, and those charges (called 'depreciation') spread the cost of the item over a number of years. As a result, profits in the period in which the expenditure took place are lower if an item of expenditure is treated as revenue expenditure. Businesses like to show that they are being as profitable as possible, so they tend to want to treat everything possible as a capital expense. Doing this also makes the business look more wealthy as the non-current assets are at a higher value than they would have been had the expenditure been treated as revenue. (You'll learn about depreciation in Chapter 26.)

24.2 Some of the other possible additional costs are: (*a*) installation costs; (*b*) inspection and testing the asset before use; (*c*) architects' fees for building plans and for supervising construction of buildings; (*d*) demolition costs to remove something before new building can begin.

24.3 The debit entries would be Repairs £1,000 and Premises £2,000. The credit entry would be Accounts Payable 'Builder' £3,000. The £1,000 will, therefore, appear in the income statement (in the profit and loss part) as revenue expenditure. The £2,000 identified as capital expenditure will appear in the balance sheet as part of the figure for Premises.

24.4 When goods are being manufactured from raw materials, employees will be being paid wages. Those wages will be part of the cost of the inventory of finished goods. It sometimes happens that employees do other work in periods when their normal work is not keeping them busy. Imagine some employees were moved temporarily to help build an extension to the premises – for example, by helping to build a small garage to hold the company chairman's car while he was working in his office. If their wages for that period were mistakenly included as usual in the cost of goods produced, that would be an example of capital expenditure being wrongly classified as revenue expenditure and would result in gross profit being understated.

24.5 Organisations have a number of sources of funds, only one of which is borrowing. The non-current asset could have been paid for using existing funds already held by the organisation. The funds borrowed to pay for it could just as easily have been used to buy raw materials while the funds already available for purchase of raw materials could have been used to finance the new non-current asset. How could anyone be sure that the funds borrowed were actually used to purchase it, and why should they be tied so strongly to it when other funds could have been used instead? It is a very circuitous argument but, in the end, the funds borrowed entered the pool of all the organisation's funds. Just because an amount equal to the amount borrowed was then used to pay for the non-current asset is not sufficient reason to include the interest costs in the cost of the non-current asset. The interest costs are simply part of the costs of financing all the assets of the organisation.

However, this changed in 1993 when an accounting standard was issued (IAS 23 *Borrowing costs*) that allows interest directly attributable to the construction of a tangible non-current asset to be capitalised as part of the cost of that asset. In 2007, the standard was amended making it compulsory to capitalise such borrowing costs. Note that it *does not* permit capitalisation of interest incurred on the funds used to purchase a non-current asset, only interest incurred *on the construction* of one.

Review questions

24.1

(*a*) What is meant by 'capital expenditure' and by 'revenue expenditure'?
(*b*) Some of the following items should be treated as capital and some as revenue. For each of them state which classification applies:

(*i*) The purchase of machinery for use in the business.
(*ii*) Carriage paid to bring the machinery in (*i*) above to the works.
(*iii*) Complete redecoration of the premises at a cost of £1,500.
(*iv*) A quarterly account for heating.
(*v*) The purchase of a soft drinks vending machine for the canteen with a stock of soft drinks.
(*vi*) Wages paid by a building contractor to his own workmen for the erection of an office in the builder's stockyard.

24.2A Indicate which of the following would be revenue items and which would be capital items in a wholesale bakery:

(*a*) Purchase of a new van.
(*b*) Purchase of replacement engine for existing van.
(*c*) Cost of altering interior of new van to increase carrying capacity.
(*d*) Cost of motor tax for new van.
(*e*) Cost of motor tax for existing van.
(*f*) Cost of painting business's name on new van.
(*g*) Repair and maintenance of existing van.

24.3 State the type of expenditure, capital or revenue, incurred in the following transactions:

(*a*) Breakdown van purchased by a garage.
(*b*) Repairs to a fruiterer's van.
(*c*) The cost of installing a new machine.
(*d*) Cost of hiring refrigeration plant in a butcher's shop.
(*e*) Twelve dozen sets of cutlery, purchased by a catering firm for a new dining-room.
(*f*) A motor vehicle bought for resale by a motor dealer.
(*g*) The cost of acquiring patent rights.

24.4A On what principles would you distinguish between capital and revenue expenditure? Illustrate your answer by reference to the following:

(*a*) The cost of repairs and an extension to the premises.
(*b*) Installation of a gas central heating boiler in place of an oil-fired central heating boiler.
(*c*) Small but expensive alterations to a cigarette manufacturing machine which increased the machine's output by 20%.

24.5 Explain clearly the difference between capital expenditure and revenue expenditure. State which of the following you would classify as capital expenditure, giving your reasons:

(*a*) Cost of building extension to factory.
(*b*) Purchase of extra filing cabinets for sales office.
(*c*) Cost of repairs to accounting machine.
(*d*) Cost of installing reconditioned engine in delivery van.
(*e*) Legal fees paid in connection with factory extension.

24.6A The data which follows was extracted from the books of account of H Kirk, an engineer, on 31 March 2006, his financial year end.

		£
(*a*)	Purchase of extra milling machine (includes £300 for repair of an old machine)	2,900
(*b*)	Rent	750
(*c*)	Electrical expenses (includes new wiring £600, part of premises improvement)	3,280
(*d*)	Carriage inwards (includes £150 carriage on new cement mixer)	1,260
(*e*)	Purchase of extra drilling machine	4,100

You are required to allocate each or part of the items above to either 'capital' or 'revenue' expenditure.

24.7 For the business of J Charles, wholesale chemist, classify the following between 'capital' and 'revenue' expenditure:

(*a*) Purchase of an extra van.
(*b*) Cost of rebuilding warehouse wall which had fallen down.
(*c*) Building extension to the warehouse.
(*d*) Painting extension to warehouse when it is first built.
(*e*) Repainting extension to warehouse three years later than that done in (*d*).
(*f*) Carriage costs on bricks for new warehouse extension.
(*g*) Carriage costs on purchases.
(*h*) Carriage costs on sales.
(*i*) Legal costs of collecting debts.
(*j*) Legal charges on acquiring new premises for office.
(*k*) Fire insurance premium.
(*l*) Costs of erecting new machine.

24.8A For the business of H Ward, a food merchant, classify the following between 'capital' and 'revenue' expenditure:

(*a*) Repairs to meat slicer.
(*b*) New tyre for van.
(*c*) Additional shop counter.
(*d*) Renewing signwriting on shop.
(*e*) Fitting partitions in shop.
(*f*) Roof repairs.
(*g*) Installing thief detection equipment.
(*h*) Wages of shop assistant.
(*i*) Carriage on returns outwards.
(*j*) New cash register.
(*k*) Repairs to office safe.
(*l*) Installing extra toilet.

24.9

(*a*) Distinguish between capital and revenue expenditure.
(*b*) Napa Ltd took delivery of a PC and printer on 1 July 2006, the beginning of its financial year. The list price of the equipment was £4,999 but Napa Ltd was able to negotiate a price of £4,000 with the supplier. However, the supplier charged an additional £340 to install and test the equipment. The supplier offered a 5% discount if Napa Ltd paid for the equipment and the additional installation costs within seven days. Napa Ltd was able to take advantage of this additional discount. The installation of special electrical wiring for the computer cost £110. After initial testing certain modifications costing £199 proved necessary. Staff were sent on special training courses to operate the PC and this cost £990. Napa Ltd insured the machine against fire and theft at a cost of £49 per annum. A maintenance agreement was entered into

→

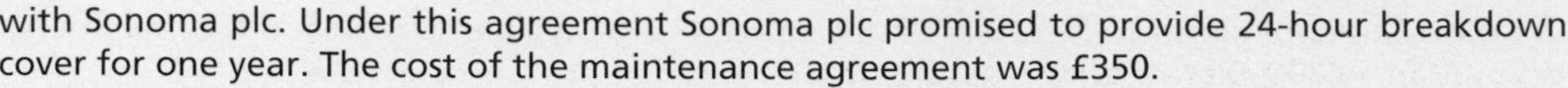

with Sonoma plc. Under this agreement Sonoma plc promised to provide 24-hour breakdown cover for one year. The cost of the maintenance agreement was £350.

Required:
Calculate the acquisition cost of the PC to Napa Ltd.

(*c*) The following costs were also incurred by Napa Ltd during the financial year ended 30 June 2007:

(*1*) Interest on loan to purchase PC.
(*2*) Cost of software for use with the PC.
(*3*) Cost of customising the software for use in Napa Ltd's business.
(*4*) Cost of paper used by the computer printer.
(*5*) Wages of computer operators.
(*6*) Cost of ribbons used by the computer printer.
(*7*) Cost of adding extra memory to the PC.
(*8*) Cost of floppy disks used during the year.
(*9*) Costs of adding a manufacturer's upgrade to the PC equipment.
(*10*) Cost of adding air conditioning to the computer room.

Required:
Classify each of the above as capital expenditure or revenue expenditure.

(*Association of Accounting Technicians*)

24.10A Classify the following items as either revenue or capital expenditure:

(*a*) An extension to an office building costing £24,000.
(*b*) The cost of replacement valves on all the labelling machines in a canning factory.
(*c*) Repairs to the warehouse roof.
(*d*) Annual service costs for a courier firm's fleet of vans.
(*e*) Replacement of rubber tread on a printing press with a plastic one that has resulted in the useful economic life of the printing press being extended by three years.
(*f*) A new bicycle purchased by a newsagent for use by the newspaper delivery boy.
(*g*) Repairs to a refrigeration system of a meat wholesaler.
(*h*) Repainting of the interior of a bar/restaurant which has greatly improved the potential for finding a buyer for the bar/restaurant as a going concern.
(*i*) Wages paid to employees who worked on the construction of their company's new office building.

24.11 A Bloggs, a building contractor, had a wooden store shed and a brick-built office which have balances b/d in the books of £850 and £179,500 respectively. During the year, the wooden shed was pulled down at a cost of £265, and replaced by a brick building. Some of the timber from the old store shed was sold for £180 and the remainder, valued at £100, was used in making door frames, etc., for the new store. The new brick-built store was constructed by the builder's own employees, the expenditure thereon being materials (excluding timber from the old store shed) £4,750; wages £3,510; and direct expenses of £85.

At about the same time, certain repairs and alterations were carried out to the office, again using the builder's own materials, the cost of which was: wages £290 and materials £460. It was estimated that £218 of this expenditure, being mainly that incurred on providing additional windows, represented improvements, 50% of this being wages, 50% materials.

Required:
Prepare the following four ledger accounts as they would appear after giving effect to all the above matters:

(*a*) Wooden store shed account
(*b*) Office buildings account
(*c*) New store account
(*d*) Office buildings repairs account

24.12 At the beginning of the financial year on 1 April 2005, a company had a balance on plant account of £372,000 and on provision for depreciation of plant account of £205,400.

The company's policy is to provide depreciation using the reducing balance method applied to the non-current assets held at the end of the financial year at the rate of 20% per annum.

On 1 September 2005 the company sold for £13,700 some plant which it had acquired on 31 October 2001 at a cost of £36,000. Additionally, installation costs totalled £4,000. During 2003 major repairs costing £6,300 had been carried out on this plant and, in order to increase the capacity of the plant, a new motor had been fitted in December 2003 at a cost of £4,400. A further overhaul costing £2,700 had been carried out during 2004.

The company acquired new replacement plant on 30 November 2005 at a cost of £96,000, inclusive of installation charges of £7,000.

Required:
Calculate:
(*a*) the balance of plant at cost at 31 March 2006
(*b*) the provision for depreciation of plant at 31 March 2006
(*c*) the profit or loss on disposal of the plant.

(*Association of Chartered Certified Accountants*)

24.13A Sema plc, a company in the heavy engineering industry, carried out an expansion programme in the 2006 financial year, in order to meet a permanent increase in contracts.

The company selected a suitable site and commissioned a survey and valuation report, for which the fee was £1,500. On the basis of the report the site was acquired for £90,000.

Solicitors' fees for drawing up the contract and conveyancing were £3,000.

Fees of £8,700 were paid to the architects for preparing the building plans and overseeing the building work. This was carried out partly by the company's own workforce (at a wages cost of £11,600), using company building materials (cost £76,800), and partly by subcontractors who charged £69,400, of which £4,700 related to the demolition of an existing building on the same site.

The completed building housed two hydraulic presses.

The cost of press A was £97,000 (ex-works), payable in a single lump sum two months after installation. Sema was given a trade discount of 10% and a cash discount for prompt payment of 2%. Hire of a transporter to collect the press and to convey it to the new building was £2,900. Installation costs were £2,310, including hire of lifting gear, £1,400.

Press B would have cost £105,800 (delivered) if it had been paid in one lump sum. However, Sema opted to pay three equal annual instalments of £40,000, starting on the date of acquisition. Installation costs were £2,550, including hire of lifting gear, £1,750.

The whole of the above expenditure was financed by the issue of £500,000 7% Loan notes (on which the annual interest payable was £35,000).

Before the above acquisitions were taken into account, the balances (at cost) on the non-current asset accounts for premises and plant were £521,100 and £407,500 respectively.

Required:
(*a*) Using such of the above information as is relevant, post and balance the premises and plant accounts for the 2006 financial year.
(*b*) State, with reasons, which of the given information you have not used in your answer to (*a*) above.

(*Association of Chartered Certified Accountants*)

24.14 Why is the distinction between classifying something as capital expenditure and classifying it as revenue expenditure so important to the users of financial statements?

24.15A John Boggis saw a computer for sale in a local store for £1,499. This was much cheaper than he'd seen it for sale elsewhere. He needed five of these PCs and also needed the cabling to →

network them. Following negotiations with the retailer, he obtained the machines for a total of £7,000. However, the cost of the cabling was £300 and the supplier was going to charge £500 to install the network. If John paid the total amount due before installation, he would receive a discount of $2\frac{1}{2}$ per cent. He liked this idea and paid immediately.

Subsequently, he purchased three printers costing £125 each and software costing £350, together with CDs and other consumables costing a total of £250. The supplier gave a discount of £50 on the consumables due to the size of the order.

All of John's staff were sent on a customised training course organised by the retailer at a total cost of £500.

Required:

(*a*) Calculate the amount capitalised in the balance sheet and also the amount to be charged to revenue accounts.

(*b*) 'Materiality' is a concept which sometimes has an effect on the capitalisation of amounts within a balance sheet. Give examples of how this may be done.

You can find a range of additional self-test questions, as well as material to help you with your studies, on the website that accompanies this book at www.pearsoned.co.uk/wood.

Chapter 25

Bad debts, allowance for doubtful debts, and provisions for discounts on accounts receivable

Learning objectives

After you have studied this chapter, you should be able to:

- explain and show how bad debts are written-off
- explain why allowances for doubtful debts are made
- make the necessary entries to record an allowance for doubtful debts in the books
- calculate and make provisions for discounts on accounts receivable
- make all the entries in the income statement and balance sheet for bad debts, allowances for doubtful debts, and provisions for cash discount

Introduction

In this chapter, you'll learn how businesses deal with bad debts and how they provide for the possibility that other debts will not be paid. You'll learn how to record increases and decreases in the allowance for doubtful debts. Finally, you'll learn how to make and adjust provisions for cash discounts.

25.1 Bad debts

With many businesses a large proportion, if not all, of the sales are on credit. The business is therefore taking the risk that some of the customers may never pay for the goods sold to them on credit. This is a normal business risk and such **bad debts** are a normal business expense. They must be charged to the income statement as an expense when calculating the net profit or loss for the period. The other thing that needs to be done is to remove the bad debt from the asset account. Usually, this will mean closing the debtor's account.

When a debt is found to be 'bad', the asset as shown by the debt in the debtor's account is worthless. It must be eliminated from the account. If doing so reduces the balance to zero, the debtor's account is closed.

To record a bad debt, you credit the debtor's account to cancel the asset and increase the expense account by debiting it to the bad debts account.

Activity 25.1

What circumstances might lead you to write-off a debt as bad and *not* close the debtor's account?

There are a range of possible scenarios that may exist concerning a bad debt. The first two were discussed in the answer to Activity 25.1:

- the debtor may be refusing to pay one of a number of invoices;
- the debtor may be refusing to pay part of an invoice;
- the debtor may owe payment on a number of invoices and have indicated that only a proportion of the total amount due will ever be paid because the debtor's business has failed;
- the debtor's business has failed and nothing is ever likely to be received.

Whatever the reason, once a debt has been declared 'bad', the journal entry is the same. You debit the bad debt account with the amount of the bad debt and credit the debtor's account in the sales ledger to complete the double entry.

At the end of the period, the total of the bad debts account is transferred to the income statement.

An example of debts being written off as bad is shown in Exhibit 25.1:

Exhibit 25.1

C Bloom

2008			£	2008			£
Jan	8	Sales	520	Dec	31	Bad debts	520

R Shaw

2008			£	2008			£
Feb	16	Sales	375	Aug	17	Cash	125
				Dec	31	Bad debts	250
			375				375

Bad Debts

2008			£	2008			£
Dec	31	C Bloom	520	Dec	31	Profit and loss	770
		R Shaw	250				
			770				770

Income Statement (extract) for the year ending 31 December 2008

	£
Gross profit	xxx
Less Expenses:	
Bad debts	(770)

25.2 Allowance for doubtful debts

Why allowances are needed

When we are drawing up our financial statements, we want to achieve the following objectives:

- to charge as an expense in the income statement for that year an amount representing debts that will never be paid;
- to show in the balance sheet a figure for accounts receivable as close as possible to the true value of accounts receivable at the balance sheet date.

Debts declared bad are usually debts that have existed for some time, perhaps even from previous accounting periods.

However, how about other debts that have not been paid by the year end? These may not have been owing for so long, in which case it will be more difficult to determine which of them will be bad debts. Nevertheless, as all businesses experience bad debts at some time, it is likely that at least some of these other debts will ultimately prove to be bad. The prudence concept – you learnt about this in Chapter 10 – says that this possibility needs to be provided for in the current period, otherwise both the accounts receivable balance reported in the balance sheet and the profit reported in the income statement will almost certainly be overstated.

It is impossible to determine with absolute accuracy at the year end what the true amount is in respect of debtors who will never pay their accounts. So, how do you decide on the amount of a provision (i.e. an allowance) against the possibility of some of the remaining debts (after removing those which have been written off as bad) proving bad in a future period?

In order to arrive at a figure for doubtful debts, a business must first consider that some debtors will never pay any of the amount they owe, while others will pay a part of the amount owing only, leaving the remainder permanently unpaid. The estimated figure can be made:

(*a*) by looking at each debt, and deciding to what extent it will be bad;
(*b*) by estimating, on the basis of experience, what percentage of the total amount due from the remaining debtors will ultimately prove to be bad debts.

It is well known that the longer a debt is owing, the more likely it is that it will become a bad debt. Some businesses draw up an 'ageing schedule', showing how long debts have been owing. Older debtors need higher percentage estimates of bad debts than do newer debtors. The percentages chosen should reflect the actual pattern of bad debts experienced in the past. Exhibit 25.2 gives an example of an ageing schedule.

Exhibit 25.2

Ageing Schedule for Doubtful Debts

Period debt owing	*Amount*	*Estimated percentage doubtful*	*Allowance for doubtful debts*
	£	%	£
Less than 1 month	5,000	1	50
1 month to 2 months	3,000	3	90
2 months to 3 months	800	4	32
3 months to 1 year	200	5	10
Over 1 year	160	20	32
	9,160		214

Most businesses don't go to this level of detail. Instead, they apply a percentage to the overall balance of accounts receivable (after deducting the bad debts). The percentage will be one the business has established over the years as being the most appropriate.

Now, let's look at how the allowance for doubtful debts is entered in the books.

Accounting entries for allowances for doubtful debts

The accounting entries needed for the **allowance for doubtful debts** are:

Year in which the allowance is *first* made:

1 Debit the profit and loss account with the amount of the allowance (i.e. deduct it from gross profit as an expense).
2 Credit the *Allowance for Doubtful Debts Account*.

Exhibit 25.3 shows the entries needed for the initial allowance for doubtful debts.

Exhibit 25.3

At 31 December 2008, the accounts receivable figure after deducting bad debts was £10,000. It is estimated that 2 per cent of debts (i.e. £200) will eventually prove to be bad debts, and it is decided to make a provision for these. The accounts will appear as follows:

Profit and Loss

			£				
2008			£				
Dec	31	Allowance for doubtful debts	200				

Allowance for Doubtful Debts

				2008			£
				Dec	31	Profit and loss	200

In the financial statements, the allowance is shown as follows:

Income Statement (extract) for the year ending 31 December 2008

	£
Gross profit	xxx
Less Expenses:	
Allowance for doubtful debts	(200)

Balance Sheet (extract) as at 31 December 2008

	£	£
Current assets		
Accounts receivable	10,000	
Less Allowance for doubtful debts	(200)	
		9,800

As shown, in the balance sheet, the balance on the allowance for doubtful debts is deducted from the accounts receivable total.

You'll have noticed that we are using two different accounts to make the two different types of adjustments to accounts receivable. This is done in order to make it clear how much is (*a*) being written-off as bad debts, and how much is (*b*) being treated as an allowance for doubtful debts:

1 **Bad debts account:** This expense account is used when a debt is believed to be irrecoverable and is written-off.
2 **Allowance for doubtful debts account:** This account is used only for estimates of the amount of debt remaining at the year end ***after** the debts have been written off* that are likely to finish up as bad debts. (This account is also known as the 'allowance for *bad* debts account'.)

By charging both (1) and (2) in the income statement, we present the full picture of the amounts provided for in respect of both bad and doubtful debts. As you've already seen in Exhibits 25.1 and 25.3, these amounts are shown as deductions from the gross profit.

By showing (2) as a deduction from the figure of accounts receivable in the balance sheet, we get a net figure, which represents a more accurate figure of the value of accounts receivable than the total of all the accounts receivable balances in the sales ledger. It may not be absolutely accurate – only time will tell which debts will turn out to be bad – but it is better than not attempting to make an estimate.

When you look at depreciation in Chapter 26, you will see that it bears similarities to the allowance for doubtful debts. Depreciation is charged as a debit to the profit and loss account and as a credit against non-current asset accounts in the ledger. It represents an estimate of how much of the overall economic usefulness of a non-current asset has been used up in each accounting period. Like the allowance for doubtful debts, it can never be completely accurate since only in several years' time, when the asset is put out of use, can it be determined whether or not the provisions made have been appropriate. Having to make estimates where absolute accuracy is impossible is a part of accounting.

Activity 25.2 Why do accountants have to make these allowances?

25.3 Increasing the allowance

Let us suppose that for the same business as in Exhibit 25.3, at the end of the following year, 31 December 2009, the allowance for doubtful debts needed to be increased. This was because the allowance was kept at 2 per cent, but the accounts receivable figure had risen to £12,000. An allowance of £200 had been brought forward from the *previous* year, but we now want a total allowance of £240 (i.e. 2 per cent of £12,000). All that is now needed is a provision for an extra £40. The double entry will be:

1 Debit Profit and Loss Account with the increase in the allowance (i.e. deduct it from gross profit as an expense).
2 Credit the Allowance for Doubtful Debts Account.

These entries are illustrated in Exhibit 25.4.

Exhibit 25.4

Profit and Loss

			£					
2009			£					
Dec	31	Allowance for doubtful debts	40					

Allowance for Doubtful Debts

2009			£	2009			£
Dec	31	Balance c/d	240	Jan	1	Balance b/d	200
				Dec	31	Profit and loss	40
			240				240
				2010			
				Jan	1	Balance b/d	240

Income Statement (extract) for the year ending 31 December 2009

	£
Gross profit	xxx
Less Expenses	
Allowance for doubtful debts (increase)	(40)

Balance Sheet (extract) as on 31 December 2009

	£	£
Current assets		
Accounts receivable	12,000	
Less Allowance for doubtful debts	(240)	
		11,760

Why do you only need to create an expense for the difference between the provisions of the two years?

25.4 Reducing the allowance

To reduce the allowance, you simply do the opposite to what you did to increase it. The allowance for doubtful debts has a credit balance. Therefore, to reduce it we would need a debit entry in the allowance account. The credit would be in the profit and loss account. Let's assume that at 31 December 2010, the figure for accounts receivable had fallen to £10,500 but the allowance remained at 2 per cent, i.e. £210 (2 per cent of £10,500).

As the allowance had previously been £240, it now needs to be reduced by £30. The double entry is:

1 Debit Allowance for Doubtful Debts Account.
2 Credit Profit and Loss Account (i.e. add it as a gain to gross profit).

These entries are illustrated in Exhibit 25.5.

Exhibit 25.5

Allowance for Doubtful Debts

			£				£
2010			£	2010			£
Dec	31	Profit and loss	30	Jan	1	Balance b/d	240
	31	Balance c/d	210				
			240				240
				2011			
				Jan	1	Balance b/d	210

Profit and Loss

2010			£
Dec	31	Allowance for doubtful debts	30

Income Statement (extract) for the year ending 31 December 2010

	£
Gross profit	xxx
Add Reduction in allowance for doubtful debts	30

Balance Sheet (extract) as on 31 December 2010

Current assets	£	£
Accounts receivable	10,500	
Less Allowance for doubtful debts	(210)	
		10,290

You will have noticed that increases in the allowance for doubtful debts increases the total for expenses and so reduce net profit. On the other hand, a reduction in the allowance for doubtful debts will increase the gross profit.

Without looking back in your textbook, write down the double entries for (*a*) an increase and (*b*) a decrease in the allowance for doubtful debts.

Let us now look at a comprehensive example in Exhibit 25.6:

Exhibit 25.6

A business starts on 1 January 2002 and its financial year end is 31 December annually. A table of the accounts receivable, the bad debts written off and the estimated bad debts at the rate of 2 per cent of accounts receivable at the end of each year is now given. The double entry accounts and the extracts from the financial statements follow.

Year to 31 December	*Bad debts written off during year*	*Accounts receivable at end of year (after bad debts written off)*	*Debts thought at end of year to be impossible to collect: 2% of accounts receivable*
	£	£	£
2007	423	6,000	120 (2% of £6,000)
2008	510	7,000	140 (2% of £7,000)
2009	604	7,750	155 (2% of £7,750)
2010	610	6,500	130 (2% of £6,500)

Bad Debts

			£				£
2007				2007			
Dec	31	Various accounts receivable	423	Dec	31	Profit and loss	423
2008				2008			
Dec	31	Various accounts receivable	510	Dec	31	Profit and loss	510
2009				2009			
Dec	31	Various accounts receivable	604	Dec	31	Profit and loss	604
2010				2010			
Dec	31	Various accounts receivable	610	Dec	31	Profit and loss	610

Allowance for Doubtful Debts

			£				£
2007				2007			
Dec	31	Balance c/d	120	Dec	31	Profit and loss	120
2008				2008			
Dec	31	Balance c/d	140	Jan	1	Balance b/d	120
				Dec	31	Profit and loss	20
			140				140
2009				2009			
Dec	31	Balance c/d	155	Jan	1	Balance b/d	140
				Dec	31	Profit and loss	15
			155				155
2010				2010			
Dec	31	Profit and loss	25	Jan	1	Balance b/d	155
		Balance c/d	130				
			155				155
				2011			
				Jan	1	Balance b/d	130

→

Income Statements (extracts) for the years ending 31 December

		£	£
Gross profit for 2007, 2008, 2009, 2010			xxx
2007	*Less* Expenses:		
	Bad debts	423	
	Allowance for doubtful debts (increase)	120	
			(543)
2008	*Less* Expenses:		
	Bad debts	510	
	Allowance for doubtful debts (increase)	20	
			(530)
2009	*Less* Expenses:		
	Bad debts	604	
	Allowance for doubtful debts (increase)	15	
			(619)
2010	*Add* Reduction in allowance for doubtful debts	25	
	Less Expenses:		
	Bad debts	(610)	
			(585)

Balance Sheets (extracts) as at 31 December

		£	£
2007	Accounts receivable	6,000	
	Less Allowance for doubtful debts	(120)	
			5,880
2008	Accounts receivable	7,000	
	Less Allowance for doubtful debts	(140)	
			6,860
2009	Accounts receivable	7,750	
	Less Allowance for doubtful debts	(155)	
			7,595
2010	Accounts receivable	6,500	
	Less Allowance for doubtful debts	(130)	
			6,370

25.5 Bad debts recovered

Sometimes, a debt written-off in previous years is recovered. When this happens, you:

1 Reinstate the debt by making the following entries:

Dr Debtor's account
  Cr Bad debts recovered account

2 When payment is received from the debtor in settlement of all or part of the debt:

Dr Cash/bank
  Cr Debtor's account

with the amount received.

At the end of the financial year, the credit balance in the bad debts recovered account is transferred either to the bad debts account or direct to the credit side of the profit and loss account. The effect is the same, since the bad debts account will, in itself, be transferred to the profit and loss account at the end of the financial year.

Why do you think we reinstate the debt just to cancel it out again? Why don't we simply debit the bank account and credit the bad debts recovered account?

25.6 Provisions for cash discounts on accounts receivable

Some businesses create provisions for cash discounts to be allowed on the accounts receivable outstanding at the balance sheet date. This, they maintain, is quite legitimate, as the amount of accounts receivable less any allowance for doubtful debts is not the best estimate of collectable debts, owing to cash discounts which will be given to debtors if they pay within a given time. The cost of discounts, it is argued, should be charged in the period when the sales were made. While this practice is of dubious merit (as cash discount is treated as a finance charge, not as an adjustment to sales revenue), it is one used in practice by some businesses.

The procedure for dealing with this is similar to the allowance for doubtful debts. It must be borne in mind that the estimate of discounts to be allowed should be based on the net figure of accounts receivable less the allowance for doubtful debts, as it is obvious that cash discounts are not allowed on bad debts! Let's look at an example in Exhibit 25.7:

Exhibit 25.7

Year ended 31 December	*Accounts receivable*	*Allowance for doubtful debts*	*Provision for cash discounts allowed*
	£	£	%
2007	4,000	200	2
2008	5,000	350	2
2009	4,750	250	2

Provision for Cash Discounts on Accounts Receivable

			£				£
2007			£	2007			£
Dec	31	Balance c/d	76	Dec	31	Profit and loss	76
2008				2008			
Dec	31	Balance c/d	93	Jan	1	Balance b/d	76
				Dec	31	Profit and loss	17
			93				93
2009				2009			
Dec	31	Profit and loss	3	Jan	1	Balance b/d	93
		Balance c/d	90				
			93				93
				2010			
				Jan	1	Balance b/d	90

→

Income Statements (extracts) for the years ending 31 December

	£
Gross profits (2007, 2008 and 2009)	xxx
Less Expenses:	
(2007) Provision for cash discounts on accounts receivable	(76)
(2008) Increase in provision for cash discounts on accounts receivable	(17)
Add (2009) Reduction in provision for cash discounts on accounts receivable	3

Balance Sheets (extracts) as at 31 December

		£	£	£
2007	Accounts receivable		4,000	
	Less Allowance for doubtful debts	200		
	Provision for cash discounts on accounts receivable	76		
			(276)	
				3,724
2008	Accounts receivable		5,000	
	Less Allowance for doubtful debts	350		
	Provision for cash discounts on accounts receivable	93		
			(443)	
				4,557
2009	Accounts receivable		4,750	
	Less Allowance for doubtful debts	250		
	Provision for cash discounts on accounts receivable	90		
			(340)	
				4,410

Activity 25.6

Which one of the following would result from a decrease in the allowance for doubtful debts?

(a) An increase in gross profit
(b) A reduction in gross profit
(c) An increase in net profit
(d) A reduction in net profit

25.7 Finally

As with distinguishing between capital expenditure and revenue expenditure, students generally find this topic very difficult to grasp. It seems to be too difficult for some students to remember the difference between the treatment of bad debts and the treatment of allowances for doubtful debts. They also often struggle to make the correct adjustments when the allowance changes, with the most common error being that they charge all the allowance, instead of only the change, to profit and loss.

There is no shortcut to getting this right. You need to keep the difference between bad debts and allowances for doubtful debts very clearly in your mind. Learning them as two separate topics seems to help. So far as the treatment of the change in the allowance is concerned, don't try calling it 'change in the allowance for doubtful debts', you'll only get confused when you make the entry in the balance sheet. And there is where the difficulty lies. *In the balance sheet, the entire allowance is deducted from the figure for accounts receivable but, in the income statement, you only include the change*. Try to memorise this last sentence. It may make all the difference.

Learning outcomes

You should now have learnt:

1. That debts we are unable to collect are called bad debts.
2. That bad debts are credited to the customer's account (to cancel them) and debited to a bad debts account.
3. That allowances for doubtful debts are needed, otherwise the value of the accounts receivable in the balance sheet will show too high a value, and could mislead anyone looking at the balance sheet. Also, making a provision of this type allows for more accurate calculation of profits and losses.
4. That the allowance for doubtful debts is calculated *after* bad debts have been deducted from the debtor balances.
5. That the amount of the allowance for doubtful debts is based on the best estimate that can be made taking all the facts into account.
6. That an increase in the allowance for doubtful debts will create a debit entry in the profit and loss account.
7. That a reduction in the allowance for doubtful debts will create a credit entry in the profit and loss account.
8. That the allowance for doubtful debts is shown as a deduction from accounts receivable in the balance sheet.
9. That provisions for cash discount are made in the same way as provisions for doubtful debts.
10. How to record bad debts, allowances for doubtful debts, and provisions for cash discounts in the accounting books and in the income statement and balance sheet.

Answers to activities

25.1 Sometimes a debtor will contest an invoice and refuse to pay it while continuing to pay all other invoices. This may happen, for example, when the debtor claims that the goods were delivered damaged and you have refused to issue a credit note because you believe the goods were delivered intact. Another example occurs when the debtor is refusing to pay part of an invoice. This may happen, for example, when the customer claims not to have received all the items on the invoice. In both those circumstances, many businesses will eventually write off the debt on the disputed invoice and continue to trade with the customer.

25.2 The prudence concept which you learnt about in Chapter 10 requires it.

25.3 During the year, some debts will have been written off as bad. They will include debts from the previous year which last year's allowance for doubtful debts was intended to cover. If last year's estimate was correct, you could add this year's bad debts to the change in the allowance and the total would be the same as the total allowance you want to make this year, not just the difference between the two years' provisions. So, in effect, you've converted last year's allowance into this year's bad debts. All you need do now is adjust the balance on the allowance for doubtful debts account to make it equal to the provision you want to make against this year's closing accounts receivable balance.

25.4 (*a*) *Dr* Profit and loss account — *Cr* Allowance for doubtful debts account
(*b*) *Dr* Allowance for doubtful debts account — *Cr* Profit and loss account

Note how they are the opposite of each other.

25.5 The reason for reinstating the debt in the ledger account of the debtor is to have a detailed history of the debtor's account as a guide for granting credit in future. When a debt is written-off as bad, it is recorded in the debtor's ledger account. Therefore, when a bad debt is recovered, it should also be shown in the debtor's ledger account, so as to provide the full picture.

25.6 (*c*) An increase in net profit.

Review questions

25.1 In a new business during the year ended 31 December 2007 the following debts are found to be bad, and are written-off on the dates shown:

31 May	S Gill & Son	£340
30 September	H Black Ltd	£463
30 November	A Thom	£156

On 31 December 2008 the schedule of remaining accounts receivable totalling £14,420 is examined and it is decided to make an allowance for doubtful debts of £410.

You are required to show:

(*a*) The Bad Debts Account, and the Allowance for Doubtful Debts Account.
(*b*) The charge to the Income Statement.
(*c*) The relevant extracts from the Balance Sheet as at 31 December 2007.

25.2 A business had always made an allowance for doubtful debts at the rate of 4% of debtors. On 1 January 2008 the amount for this, brought forward from the previous year, was £320.

During the year to 31 December 2008 the bad debts written-off amounted to £680.

On 31 December 2008 the accounts receivable balance was £16,800 and the usual allowance for doubtful debts is to be made.

You are to show:

(*a*) The Bad Debts Account for the year ended 31 December 2008.
(*b*) The Allowance for Doubtful Debts Account for the year.
(*c*) Extract from the Income Statement for the year.
(*d*) The relevant extract from the Balance Sheet as at 31 December 2008.

25.3 A business started trading on 1 January 2007. During the two years ended 31 December 2007 and 2008 the following debts were written off to the Bad Debts Account on the dates stated:

31 May 2007	F Lamb	£175
31 October 2007	A Clover	£230
31 January 2008	D Ray	£190
30 June 2008	P Clark	£75
31 October 2008	J Will	£339

On 31 December 2007 the total accounts receivable was £52,400. It was decided to make an allowance for doubtful debts of £640.

On 31 December 2008 the total accounts receivable was £58,600. It was decided to make an allowance for doubtful debts of £710.

You are required to show:

(*i*) The Bad Debts Account and the Allowance for Doubtful Debts Account for each of the two years.
(*ii*) The relevant extracts from the Balance Sheets as at 31 December 2007 and 2008.

25.4A A business, which started trading on 1 January 2007, adjusted its allowance for doubtful debt at the end of each year on a percentage basis, but each year the percentage rate is adjusted in accordance with the current 'economic climate'. The following details are available for the three years ended 31 December 2007, 2008 and 2009.

	Bad debts written off year to 31 December	*Accounts receivable at 31 December after bad debts written-off*	*Percentage allowance for doubtful debts*
	£	£	
2007	1,240	41,000	4
2008	2,608	76,000	6
2009	5,424	88,000	5

You are required to show:

(*a*) Bad Debts Accounts for each of the three years.
(*b*) Allowance for Doubtful Debts Accounts for each of the three years.
(*c*) Balance Sheet extracts as at 31 December 2007, 2008 and 2009.

25.5 A business which prepares its financial statements annually to 31 December suffered bad debts which were written-off:

2007 £420
2008 £310
2009 £580

The business had a balance of £400 on the Allowance for Doubtful Debts Account on 1 January 2007.

At the end of each year, the business considered which of its debtors appeared doubtful and carried forward an allowance of:

2007 £500
2008 £600
2009 £400

Show each of the entries in the income statements and prepare the Allowance for Doubtful Debts Account for each of the three years.

25.6A

(*a*) Businesses often create an allowance for doubtful debts.

(*i*) Of which concept (or convention) is this an example? Explain your answer.
(*ii*) What is the purpose of creating an allowance for doubtful debts?
(*iii*) How might the amount of an allowance for doubtful debts be calculated?

(*b*) On 1 January 2008 there was a balance of £500 in the an Allowance for Doubtful Debts Account, and it was decided to maintain the provision at 5% of the accounts receivable at each year end. The debtors on 31 December each year were:

	£
2008	12,000
2009	8,000
2010	8,000

Show the necessary entries for the **three** years ended 31 December 2008 to 31 December 2010 inclusive in the following:

(*i*) the Allowance for Doubtful Debts Account;
(*ii*) the Income Statements.

(*c*) What is the difference between bad debts and allowance for doubtful debts?
(*d*) On 1 January 2010 Warren Mair owed Jason Dalgleish £130. On 25 August 2010 Mair was declared bankrupt. A payment of 30p in the £ was received in full settlement. The remaining balance was written off as a bad debt. Write up the account of Warren Mair in Jason Dalgleish's ledger.

(*Northern Examinations and Assessment Board: GCSE*)

→

25.7 The balance sheet as at 31 May 2007 of Forest Traders Limited included an allowance for doubtful debts of £2,300. The company's accounts for the year ended 31 May 2008 are now being prepared. The company's policy now is to relate the allowance for doubtful debts to the age of debts outstanding. The debts outstanding at 31 May 2008 and the required allowances for doubtful debts are as follows:

Debts outstanding	*Amount*	*Allowance for doubtful debts*
	£	%
Up to 1 month	24,000	1
More than 1 month and up to 2 months	10,000	2
More than 2 months and up to 3 months	8,000	4
More than 3 months	3,000	5

Customers are allowed a cash discount of $2^1/_2$% for settlement of debts within one month. It is now proposed to make a provision for discounts to be allowed in the company's accounts for the year ended 31 May 2008.

Required:
Prepare the following accounts for the year ended 31 May 2008 in the books of Forest Traders Limited to record the above transactions:

(*a*) Allowance for doubtful debts;
(*b*) Provision for discounts to be allowed on debtors.

(*Association of Accounting Technicians*)

25.8A A business makes an allowance for doubtful debts of 3% of accounts receivable, also a provision of 1% for discount on accounts receivable.

On 1 January 2008 the balances brought forward on the relevant accounts were allowance for doubtful debts £930 and provision for discounts on accounts receivable £301.

(*a*) Enter the balances in the appropriate accounts, using a separate Allowance for Doubtful Debts Account.

During 2008 the business incurred bad debts of £1,110 and allowed discounts of £362. On 31 December 2008 accounts receivable amounted to £42,800.

(*b*) Show the entries in the appropriate accounts for the year 2008, assuming that the business's accounting year ends on 31 December 2008, also income statement extracts at 31 December 2008.

25.9 J Blane commenced business on 1 January 2006 and prepares her financial statements to 31 December every year. For the year ended 31 December 2006, bad debts written off amounted to £1,400. It was also found necessary to create an allowance for doubtful debts of £2,600.

In 2007, debts amounting to £2,200 proved bad and were written-off. J Sweeny, whose debt of £210 was written off as bad in 2006, settled her account in full on 30 November 2007. As at 31 December 2007 total debts outstanding were £92,000. It was decided to bring the provision up to 4% of this figure on that date.

In 2008, £3,800 of debts were written-off during the year, and another recovery of £320 was made in respect of debts written-off in 2006. As at 31 December 2008, total debts outstanding were £72,000. The allowance for doubtful debts is to be changed to 5% of this figure.

You are required to show for the years 2006, 2007 and 2008, the
(*a*) Bad Debts Account.
(*b*) Bad Debts Recovered Account.
(*c*) Allowance for Doubtful Debts Account.
(*d*) Extract from the Income Statement.

25.10

(A) Explain why a provision may be made for doubtful debts.

(B) Explain the procedure to be followed when a customer whose debt has been written-off as bad subsequently pays the amount originally owing.

(C) On 1 January 2007 D Watson had debtors of £25,000 on which he had made an allowance for doubtful debts of 3%.

During 2007,

(*i*) A Stewart, who owed D Watson £1,200, was declared bankrupt and a settlement of 25p in the £ was made, the balance being treated as a bad debt.

(*ii*) Other bad debts written-off during the year amounted to £2,300.

On 31 December 2007 total accounts receivable amounted to £24,300 but this requires to be adjusted as follows:

(*a*) J Smith, a debtor owing £600, was known to be unable to pay and this amount was to be written off.

(*b*) A cheque for £200 from S McIntosh was returned from the bank unpaid.

D Watson maintained his allowance for doubtful debts at 3% of accounts receivable.

Required:

(1) For the financial year ended 31 December 2007, show the entries in the following accounts:
 (*i*) Allowance for doubtful debts
 (*ii*) Bad debts

(2) What is the effect on net profit of the change in the allowance for doubtful debts?

(*Scottish Qualifications Authority*)

25.11A D Faculti started in business buying and selling law textbooks, on 1 January 2003. At the end of each of the next three years, his figures for accounts receivable, before writing-off any bad debts, were as follows:

31 December 2003	£30,000
31 December 2004	£38,100
31 December 2005	£4,750

Bad debts to be written-off are as follows:

31 December 2004	£2,100
31 December 2005	£750

The allowance for doubtful debts in each year is 5% of accounts receivable.

Required:

(*a*) Prepare Faculti's bad debts expense account and allowance for doubtful debts account for 2003, 2004 and 2005.

(*b*) The amounts due from B Roke (£70) and H A Ditt (£42) became irrecoverable in 2006 and were written-off. Show the entries in the ledger accounts to record these write-offs.

You can find a range of additional self-test questions, as well as material to help you with your studies, on the website that accompanies this book at www.pearsoned.co.uk/wood.

chapter
26 Depreciation of non-current assets: nature and calculations

Learning objectives

After you have studied this chapter, you should be able to:

- define depreciation
- explain why depreciation is provided
- calculate depreciation using both the straight line and the reducing balance methods
- explain how to calculated depreciation using five other methods
- calculate depreciation on assets bought or sold within an accounting period

Introduction

In this chapter, you'll learn why depreciation must be provided and how to calculate it using the two most widely used methods, in the year of acquisition, year of disposal, and all the years in between. You will also learn how to use five other depreciation methods.

26.1 Nature of non-current assets

Before going any further, you need to be sure that you know what a non-current asset is.

Activity 26.1

Write down the three characteristics that distinguish non-current assets from current assets.

If you don't or didn't know how to define non-current assets, be sure that you do before going on to look at the topic of depreciation.

26.2 Depreciation of tangible non-current assets

Tangible non-current assets (i.e. long-term assets which can be touched, such as machinery, motor vehicles, fixtures and even buildings) do not last for ever. If the amount received (if any) on the disposal of a non-current asset is deducted from the cost of buying it, the value of the non-current asset can be said to have 'depreciated in value' by that amount over its period of usefulness to the business. For example, if a van was bought for £10,000 and sold five years later for £2,000 then its value has depreciated over the period of its use by £8,000.

This is the only time that depreciation can be calculated accurately. That is, you can only *estimate* what it should be each year while the non-current asset continues to be used.

26.3 Depreciation is an expense

Depreciation is that part of the original cost of a non-current asset that is consumed during its period of use by the business. It needs to be charged to the profit and loss account every year. The amount charged in a year for depreciation is based upon an estimate of how much of the overall economic usefulness of non-current assets has been used up in that accounting period. It is an expense for services consumed in the same way as expenses are incurred for items such as wages, rent or electricity. Because it is charged as an expense to the profit and loss account, depreciation reduces net profit.

For example, if a PC cost £1,200 and was expected to be used for three years, it might be estimated at the end of the first year that a third of its overall usefulness had been consumed. Depreciation would then be charged at an amount equal to one-third of the cost of the PC, i.e. £400. Profit would be reduced by £400 and the value of the PC in the balance sheet would be reduced from £1,200 to £800.

Using an example of a van and the petrol it consumes, you can see that the only real difference between the expense of depreciation for the van and the expense of petrol incurred in order to use the van is that the petrol expense is used up in a short time, whereas the expense for use of the van is spread over several years. Both the petrol and the cost of the van are expenses of the business.

Activity 26.2

If depreciation reduces profits and reduces the value of assets and so reduces the capital account of the owner, why do businesses bother providing for depreciation?

26.4 Causes of depreciation

Physical deterioration, economic factors, time and depletion all give rise to a reduction in the value of a tangible non-current asset. Let's look at these in more detail.

Physical deterioration

1 **Wear and tear.** When a motor vehicle or machinery or fixtures and fittings are used they eventually wear out. Some last many years, others last only a few years. This is also true of buildings, although some may last for a long time.
2 **Erosion, rust, rot and decay.** Land may be eroded or wasted away by the action of wind, rain, sun and other elements of nature. Similarly, the metals in motor vehicles or machinery will rust away. Wood will rot eventually. Decay is a process which will also be present due to the elements of nature and the lack of proper attention.

Economic factors

These may be said to be the reasons for an asset being put out of use even though it is in good physical condition. The two main factors are usually **obsolescence** and **inadequacy**.

1 **Obsolescence.** This is the process of becoming out-of-date. For instance, over the years there has been great progress in the development of synthesisers and electronic devices used by leading commercial musicians. The old equipment will therefore have become obsolete, and much of it will have been taken out of use by such musicians.

   This does not mean that the equipment is worn out. Other people may well buy the old equipment and use it, possibly because they cannot afford to buy new up-to-date equipment.

2 **Inadequacy.** This arises when an asset is no longer used because of the growth and changes in the size of the business. For instance, a small ferryboat that is operated by a business at a coastal resort will become entirely inadequate when the resort becomes more popular. Then it will be found that it would be more efficient and economical to operate a large ferryboat, and so the smaller boat will be put out of use by the business.

In this case also it does not mean that the ferryboat is no longer in good working order, nor that it is obsolete. It may be sold to a business at a smaller resort.

Time

Obviously time is needed for wear and tear, erosion, etc., and for obsolescence and inadequacy to take place. However, there are non-current assets to which the time factor is connected in a different way. These are assets which have a legal life fixed in terms of years.

For instance, you may agree to rent some buildings for ten years. This is normally called a lease. When the years have passed, the lease is worth nothing to you, as it has finished. Whatever you paid for the lease is now of no value.

A similar case arises when you buy a patent so that only you are able to produce something. When the patent's time has finished it then has no value. The usual length of life of a patent is sixteen years.

Instead of using the term depreciation, the term **amortisation** is often used for these assets.

Depletion

Other assets are of wasting character, perhaps due to the extraction of raw materials from them. These materials are then either used by the business to make something else, or are sold in their raw state to other businesses. Natural resources such as mines, quarries and oil wells come under this heading. To provide for the consumption of an asset of a wasting character is called provision for **depletion**.

26.5 Land and buildings

Prior to the issue in 1977 of a UK accounting standard (SSAP 12) which focused on this topic, freehold and long leasehold properties were very rarely subject to a charge for depreciation. It was contended that, as property values tended to rise rather than fall, it was inappropriate to charge depreciation.

The accounting standard changed all that by requiring that depreciation be written off over the property's useful life, with the exception that freehold land does not normally require a provision for depreciation. This is because land normally has an unlimited useful life. Buildings do, however, eventually fall into disrepair or become obsolete and must be subject to a charge for depreciation each year.

When FRS 15 replaced SSAP 12 in 1999, it repeated these requirements. It also dealt with the problem of the distinction between the cost of freehold land and the cost of the buildings upon it, by insisting that the two elements of the cost be separated.

IASs 16 (*Property, plant and equipment*), 23 (*Borrowing costs*) and 36 (*Impairment of assets*) are the relevant international standards and they have the same requirements on these issues as FRS 15.

26.6 Appreciation

At this stage, you may be wondering what happens when non-current assets increase (appreciate) in value. The answer is that normal accounting procedure would be to ignore any such appreciation, as to bring appreciation into account would be to contravene both the historical cost concept and the prudence concept you learnt about in Chapter 10.

Go back to Chapter 10 to refresh your understanding of the historical cost concept and the prudence concept.

However, one of the problems when SSAP 12 was introduced was that the UK was in the middle of a boom in property prices which had been going on for some time and didn't really end until the early 1990s. Businesses could see that the market value of their properties was rising. At the same time, they were being instructed (by the accounting standard) to charge their profit and loss account with depreciation that represented a fall in the value of the property over the period. Not surprisingly, this didn't seem to make any sense. To address this, IAS 16 allows non-current assets to be revalued at fair value (which is determined from market-based evidence) for land and buildings or market value (= open market value, i.e. the amount for which it could currently be sold) for plant and equipment. Depreciation is then calculated on the basis of the new value.

26.7 Provision for depreciation as an allocation of cost

Depreciation in total over the life of a non-current asset can be calculated quite simply as cost less the amount receivable when the non-current asset is put out of use by the business. This amount receivable is normally referred to as the **residual value** (or 'scrap value') of an asset. IAS 16 states that residual value should be based on prices current at the balance sheet date, not at the date of original purchase. If the item is bought and sold for a lower amount within the same accounting period, then the difference in value is charged as depreciation in arriving at that period's net profit.

The difficulties start when the asset is used for more than one accounting period: an attempt has to be made to charge each period with an appropriate amount of depreciation.

Although depreciation provisions are intended to allocate the cost of a non-current asset to each accounting period in which it is in use, it does not follow that there is any truly accurate method of performing this task. All that can be said is that the cost should be allocated over the life of the non-current asset in such a way as to charge it as equitably as possible to the periods in which it is used. The difficulties involved are considerable and include:

1 Apart from a few assets, such as leases, how accurately can a business assess an asset's useful life? Even a lease may be put out of use if the leased asset has become inadequate or inappropriate (e.g. after a change in the product being sold or unexpected growth in the size of the business).
2 How is 'use' measured? A car owned by a business for two years may have been driven one year by a very careful driver and another year by a reckless driver. The standard of driving will affect the condition of the car and also the amount of cash receivable on its disposal. How should a business apportion the car's depreciation costs?
3 There are other expenses besides depreciation, such as repairs and maintenance of the non-current asset. As both of these affect the rate and amount of depreciation, should they not also affect the depreciation provision calculations?
4 How can a business possibly know the amount receivable in x years' time when an asset is put out of use?

These are only some of the difficulties. Accounting has developed some methods that can be used to calculate depreciation. However, you will see that none of them really manages to address all these issues. Nevertheless, just as with doubtful debts, making some allowance for depreciation is better than making none at all.

26.8 Non-current assets held for sale

When non-current assets are reclassified as being held for sale, they must not be depreciated.

26.9 Methods of calculating depreciation charges

The two main methods in use are the **straight line method** and the **reducing balance method**. Other methods may be used in certain cases, and some are discussed briefly in Section 26.12. Most accountants think that the straight line method is the one that is generally most suitable.

Straight line method

In this method, the number of years of use is estimated. The cost is then divided by the number of years. This gives the depreciation charge for each year.

For instance, if a van was bought for £22,000 and we thought we would keep it for four years and then sell it for £2,000 the depreciation to be charged each year would be:

$$\frac{\text{Cost (£22,000)} - \text{Estimated disposal value (£2,000)}}{\text{Number of expected years of use (4)}} = \frac{\text{£20,000}}{4}$$

$$= \text{£5,000 depreciation each year for four years.}$$

On the other hand, if we thought that after four years the van would have no disposal value, the charge for depreciation would be:

$$\frac{\text{Cost (£22,000)}}{\text{Number of expected years of use (4)}} = \frac{\text{£22,000}}{4}$$

$$= \text{£5,500 depreciation each year for four years.}$$

Reducing balance method

In this method, a fixed percentage for depreciation is deducted from the cost in the first year. In the second and later years the same percentage is taken of the reduced balance (i.e. cost *less* depreciation already charged). This method is also known as the *diminishing balance method* or the *diminishing debit balance method*.

If a machine is bought for £10,000 and depreciation is to be charged at 20 per cent, the calculations for the first three years would be as follows:

	£
Cost	10,000
First year: depreciation (20%)	(2,000)
	8,000
Second year: depreciation (20% of £8,000)	(1,600)
	6,400
Third year: depreciation (20% of £6,400)	(1,280)
Cost not yet apportioned, end of Year 3	5,120

The basic formula used to find the percentage to apply with this method is:

$$r = 1 - \sqrt[n]{\frac{s}{c}}$$

where n = the number of years
s = the net residual value (this must be a significant amount or the answers will be absurd, since the depreciation rate would amount to nearly one)
c = the cost of the asset
r = the rate of depreciation to be applied.

Using as an example the figures

n = 4 years
s = residual value £256
c = cost £10,000

the calculations would appear as:

$$r = 1 - \sqrt[4]{\frac{256}{£10{,}000}} = 1 - \frac{4}{10} = 0.6 \text{ or } 60 \text{ per cent}$$

The depreciation calculation applied to each of the four years of use would be:

	£
Cost	10,000
Year 1: Depreciation provision 60% of £10,000	(6,000)
Cost not yet apportioned, end of Year 1	4,000
Year 2: Depreciation provision 60% of £4,000	(2,400)
Cost not yet apportioned, end of Year 2	1,600
Year 3: Depreciation provision 60% of £1,600	(960)
Cost not yet apportioned, end of Year 3	640
Year 4: Depreciation provision 60% of £640	(384)
Cost not yet apportioned, end of Year 4	256

In this case, the percentage to be applied worked out conveniently to a round figure of 60 per cent. However, the answer will often come out to several decimal places, e.g. 59.846512. When it does, normal practice is to take the nearest whole figure as a percentage to be applied. However, nowadays, this calculation is usually performed using a spreadsheet. Doing so means you don't need to worry any more about the difficulties of performing calculations using numbers with lots of decimal places. You simply build the formula into the calculation and don't need to worry about how many decimal places the depreciation rate may have. The spreadsheet will then produce the depreciation amount for each year.

What do you think you do when the *amount* of depreciation to be charged in a period is not a whole number?

The depreciation rate percentage to be applied under this method, assuming a significant amount for residual value, is usually between two and three times greater than under the straight line method.

The advocates of the reducing balance method usually argue that it helps to even out the total amount charged as expenses for the use of the asset each year. Provisions for depreciation are not the only costs charged. There are also the running costs. The repairs and maintenance element of running costs usually increases with age. Therefore, in order to equate total usage costs for each year of use, the depreciation provisions should fall over time, while the repairs and maintenance element increases. However, as can be seen from the figures in the example already given, the repairs and maintenance element would have to be comparatively large after the first year to bring about an equal total charge for each year of use.

To summarise, the people who favour this method say that:

In the early years A higher charge for depreciation + A lower charge for repairs and upkeep	will tend to be close to the sum of	*In the later years* A lower charge for depreciation + A higher charge for repairs and upkeep

26.10 Choice of method

The purpose of depreciation is to spread the total cost of a non-current asset over the periods in which it is to be used. The method chosen should be that which allocates cost to each period in accordance with the proportion of the overall economic benefit from using the non-current asset that was expended during that period.

If, therefore, the main value is to be obtained from the asset in its earliest years, it may be appropriate to use the reducing balance method, which charges more in the early years. If, on the other hand, the benefits are to be gained evenly over the years, then the straight line method would be more appropriate.

The repairs and maintenance factor also has to be taken into account. One argument supporting this was mentioned in the last section.

Exhibit 26.1 gives a comparison of the calculations using the two methods.

Exhibit 26.1

A business has just bought a machine for £8,000. It will be kept in use for four years, when it will be disposed of for an estimated amount of £500. The accountant has asked you to prepare a comparison of the amounts charged as depreciation using both methods.

For the straight line method, a figure of (£8,000 – £500) ÷ 4 = £7,500 ÷ 4 = £1,875 per annum is to be used. For the reducing balance method, a percentage figure of 50 per cent will be used.

	Method 1 *Straight Line* £		*Method 2* *Reducing Balance* £
Cost	8,000		8,000
Depreciation: year 1	(1,875)	(50% of £8,000)	(4,000)
	6,125		4,000
Depreciation: year 2	(1,875)	(50% of £4,000)	(2,000)
	4,250		2,000
Depreciation: year 3	(1,875)	(50% of £2,000)	(1,000)
	2,375		1,000
Depreciation: year 4	(1,875)	(50% of £1,000)	(500)
Disposal value	500		500

This example illustrates the fact that using the reducing balance method has a much higher charge for depreciation in the early years, and lower charges in the later years.

26.11 Depreciation provisions and assets bought or sold

There are two main methods of calculating depreciation provisions for assets bought or sold during an accounting period.

1 Ignore the dates during the accounting period that the assets were bought or sold, and simply calculate a full period's depreciation on the assets in use at the end of the period. Thus, assets sold during the accounting period will have had no provision for depreciation made for that last period irrespective of how many months they were in use. Conversely, assets bought during the period will have a full period of depreciation provision calculated even though they may not have been owned throughout the whole of the period.
2 Provide for depreciation on the basis of 'one month's ownership = one month's provision for depreciation'. Fractions of months are usually ignored. This is obviously a more precise method than Method 1.

The first method is the one normally used in practice. However, for examination purposes, where the dates on which assets are bought and sold are shown, you should use Method 2. If no such dates are given then, obviously, Method 1 is the one to use, but you should indicate that you are assuming this is the method to be adopted.

26.12 Other methods of calculating depreciation

There are many more methods of calculating depreciation, some of which are used in particular industries, such as the hotel and catering industry. We'll now look briefly at five of these other methods so that you are aware of how and why they may be used.

There is no information easily available to show how many organisations are using each method. It is possible to devise one's own special method. If it brings about an equitable charge for depreciation for the organisation, then the method will be suitable.

The revaluation method

When there are a few expensive non-current assets, it is not difficult to draw up the necessary accounts for depreciation. For each item we:

(*a*) Find its cost.
(*b*) Estimate its years of use to the business.
(*c*) Calculate and provide depreciation.
(*d*) Make the adjustments when the asset is disposed of.
(*e*) Calculate profit or loss on disposal.

This is worth doing for expensive items. There are, however, many examples of non-current assets for which the calculation would not be worth doing and, in fact, may be impossible. Some businesses will have many low-cost non-current assets. Garages or engineering works will have a lot of spanners, screwdrivers and other small tools; brewers will have crates; laboratories will have many small, low-cost glass instruments.

It would be impossible to follow procedures (*a*) to (*e*) above for every screwdriver or crate. Instead the revaluation method is used.

The method is not difficult to use. An example is shown in Exhibit 26.2:

Exhibit 26.2

A business has a lot of steel containers. These are not sold but are used by the business.

	£
On 1 January 2006 the containers were valued at	3,500
During the year to 31 December containers were purchased costing	1,300
On 31 December 2006 the containers were valued at	3,800

The depreciation is calculated:

	£
Value at start of period	3,500
Add Cost of items bought during period	1,300
	4,800
Less Value at close of period	(3,800)
Depreciation for year to 31 December 2006	1,000

The depreciation figure of £1,000 will be charged as an expense. Using this approach, we can look at Exhibit 26.3, where depreciation is entered in the books for the first three years of a business starting trading.

Exhibit 26.3

The business starts in business on 1 January 2006.

	£
In its first year it buys crates costing	800
Their estimated value at 31 December 2006	540
Crates bought in the year ended 31 December 2007	320
Estimated value of all crates in hand on 31 December 2007	530
Crates bought in the year ended 31 December 2008	590
Estimated value of all crates in hand on 31 December 2008	700

Crates

			£				£
2006				2006			
Dec	31	Cash (during the year)	800	Dec	31	Profit and loss	260
					31	Inventory c/d	540
			800				800
2007				2007			
Jan	1	Inventory b/d	540	Dec	31	Profit and loss	330
Dec	31	Cash (during the year)	320		31	Inventory c/d	530
			860				860
2008				2008			
Jan	1	Inventory b/d	530	Dec	31	Profit and loss	420
Dec	31	Cash (during the year)	590		31	Inventory c/d	700
			1,120				1,120
2009							
Jan	1	Inventory b/d	700				

Profit and Loss Account for the year ended 31 December

		£	
2006	Use of crates	260	
2007	Use of crates	330	
2008	Use of crates	420	

The balance of the crates account at the end of each year is shown as a non-current asset in the balance sheet.

Sometimes the business may make its own items such as tools or crates. In these instances the tools account or crates account should be debited with labour costs and material costs.

Revaluation is also used, for instance, by farmers for their cattle. As with other non-current assets depreciation should be provided for, but during the early life of an animal it will be appreciating in value, only to depreciate later. The task of calculating the cost of an animal becomes virtually impossible if it has been born on the farm, and reared on the farm by grazing on the pasture land and being fed on other foodstuffs, some grown on the farm and others bought by the farmer.

To get over this problem the revaluation method is used. Because of the difficulty of calculating the cost of the animals, they are valued at the price which they would fetch if sold at market. This is an exception to the general rule of assets being shown at cost price.

Depletion unit method

With non-current assets such as a quarry from which raw materials are dug out to be sold to the building industry, a different method is needed: the depletion unit method.

If a quarry was bought for £5,000 and it was expected to contain 1,000 tonnes of saleable materials, then for each tonne taken out we would depreciate it by £5, since £5,000 ÷ 1,000 = £5.

This can be shown as:

$$\frac{\text{Cost of asset}}{\text{Expected total contents in units}} \times \text{Number of units taken in period}$$

$$= \text{Depreciation for that period.}$$

Machine hour method

With a machine the depreciation provision may be based on the number of hours that the machine was operated during the period compared with the total expected running hours during the machine's life with the business. A business which bought a machine costing £2,000 having an expected running life of 1,000 hours, and no scrap value, could provide for depreciation of the machine at the rate of £2 for every hour it was operated during a particular accounting period.

Sum of the years' digits method

This method is popular in the USA but not common in the UK. It provides for higher depreciation to be charged early in the life of an asset with lower depreciation in later years.

Given an asset costing £3,000 which will be in use for five years, the calculations will be:

From purchase the asset will last for	5 years
From the second year the asset will last for	4 years
From the third year the asset will last for	3 years
From the fourth year the asset will last for	2 years
From the fifth year the asset will last for	1 year
Sum of these digits	15

	£
1st year 5/15 of £3,000 is charged =	1,000
2nd year 4/15 of £3,000 is charged =	800
3rd year 3/15 of £3,000 is charged =	600
4th year 2/15 of £3,000 is charged =	400
5th year 1/15 of £3,000 is charged =	200
	3,000

Units of output method

This method establishes the total expected units of output expected from the asset. Depreciation, based on cost less salvage value, is then calculated for the period by taking that period's units of output as a proportion of the total expected output over the life of the asset.

An instance of this could be a machine which is expected to be able to produce 10,000 widgets over its useful life. It has cost £6,000 and has an expected salvage value of £1,000. In year 1 a total of 1,500 widgets are produced, and in year 2 the production is 2,500 widgets.

The depreciation per period is calculated:

$$(\text{Cost} - \text{salvage value}) \times \left(\frac{\text{period's production}}{\text{total expected production}}\right)$$

$$\text{Year 1:} \quad £5{,}000 \times \frac{1{,}500}{10{,}000} = £750 \text{ depreciation}$$

$$\text{Year 2:} \quad £5{,}000 \times \frac{2{,}500}{10{,}000} = £1{,}250 \text{ depreciation}$$

Learning outcomes

You should now have learnt:

1. That depreciation is an expense of the business and has to be charged against any period during which a non-current asset has been in use.
2. That the main causes of depreciation are: physical deterioration, economic factors, the time factor and depletion.
3. How to calculate depreciation using the straight line method.
4. How to calculate depreciation using the reducing balance method.
5. How to calculate depreciation on assets bought or sold within an accounting period.
6. That there are other methods of calculating depreciation in addition to the straight line and reducing balance methods.

Answers to activities

26.1 Non-current assets are those assets of material value which are:

- of long life, and
- to be used in the business, and
- not bought with the main purpose of resale.

26.2 Firstly, financial statements must show a true and fair view of the financial performance and position of the business. If depreciation was not provided for, both non-current assets and profits would be stated in the financial statements at inflated amounts. This would only mislead the users of those financial statements and so depreciation must be charged. Secondly, IAS 16 requires that non-current assets are depreciated.

26.3 Just as with the depreciation percentage, you round it to the nearest whole number.

Review questions

26.1 A Gill purchased a notebook PC for £2,600. It has an estimated life of four years and a scrap value of £200.

She is not certain whether she should use the straight line or the reducing balance basis for the purpose of calculating depreciation on the computer.

You are required to calculate the depreciation (to the nearest £) using both methods, showing clearly the balance remaining in the computer account at the end of each of the four years under each method. (Assume that 45 per cent per annum is to be used for the reducing balance method.)

26.2 A machine costs £8,000. It will be kept for five years, and then sold for an estimated figure of £2,400. Show the calculations of the figures for depreciation (to nearest £) for each of the five years using (*a*) the straight line method, (*b*) the reducing balance method, for this method using a depreciation rate of 20 per cent.

26.3 A car costs £9,600. It will be kept for three years, and then sold for £2,600. Calculate the depreciation for each year using (*a*) the reducing balance method, using a depreciation rate of 35 per cent, (*b*) the straight line method.

26.4A A photocopier costs £23,000. It will be kept for four years, and then traded in for £4,000. Show the calculations of the figures for depreciation for each year using (*a*) the straight line method, (*b*) the reducing balance method, for this method using a depreciation rate of 35 per cent.

26.5A A printer costs £800. It will be kept for five years and then scrapped. Show your calculations of the amount of depreciation each year if (a) the reducing balance method at a rate of 60 per cent was used, (b) the straight line method was used.

26.6A A bus is bought for £56,000. It will be used for four years, and then sold back to the supplier for £18,000. Show the depreciation calculations for each year using (a) the reducing balance method with a rate of 25 per cent, (b) the straight line method.

26.7 A company, which makes up its financial statements annually to 31 December, provides for depreciation of its machinery at the rate of 15 per cent per annum using the reducing balance method.

On 31 December 2008, the machinery consisted of three items purchased as shown:

	£
On 1 January 2006 Machine A	Cost 2,000
On 1 September 2007 Machine B	Cost 4,000
On 1 May 2008 Machine C	Cost 3,000

Required:
Your calculations showing the depreciation provision for the year 2008.

26.8 A motor vehicle which cost £12,000 was bought on credit from Trucks Ltd on 1 January 2006. Financial statements are prepared annually to 31 December and depreciation of vehicles is provided at 25 per cent per annum under the reducing balance method.

Required:
Prepare the motor vehicle account and the accumulated provision for depreciation on motor vehicles account for the first two years of the motor vehicle's working life.

26.9 Ivor Innes has supplied you with the following information:

	1 April 2007	31 March 2008
	£	£
Cash	840	700
Fixtures	7,600	7,600
Balance at bank	5,500	8,320
Inventory	17,800	19,000
Accounts receivable	8,360	4,640
Accounts payable	5,200	8,800

→

During the year to 31 March 2008, Ivor withdrew £11,400 from the business for private purposes. In November 2007, Ivor received a legacy of £18,000 which he paid into the business bank account.

Ivor agrees that £600 should be provided for depreciation of fixtures and £200 for doubtful debts.

Required:
Prepare a balance sheet as at 31 March 2008 which clearly indicates the net profit or loss for the year.

26.10A On 10 August 2003 Joblot, a computer software retailer, bought a non-current asset which cost £100,000. It had an anticipated life of four years and an estimated residual value of £20,000. Due to unforeseen events in the computer industry, the asset was suddenly sold on 10 March 2006 for £45,000.

The policy of the company is to provide depreciation in full in the year of purchase and none in the year of sale.

Required:
- (*a*) Calculate the charge for depreciation for each of the years using both the straight line method and the reducing balance method, showing clearly the net book values as at the end of each of the years.
- (*b*) Calculate the profit or loss on the disposal of the asset under both of the above methods.
- (*c*) Explain why assets are depreciated and provide an example where it would be more appropriate to use the straight line method and another example where it would be more appropriate to use the reducing balance method.
- (*d*) Explain what the figures for net book value that are shown in the balance sheet represent.

26.11A Black and Blue Ltd depreciates its forklift trucks using a reducing balance rate of 30 per cent. Its accounting year end is 30 September. On 30 September 2006, it owned four forklift trucks:

- (A) Purchased on 1 January 2003 for £2,400
- (B) Purchased on 1 May 2004 for £2,500
- (C) Purchased on 1 October 2004 for £3,200
- (D) Purchased on 1 April 2006 for £3,600

Required:
Calculate the depreciation provision for the year ending 30 September 2006.

26.12 State which depreciation method will be the most appropriate in the case of each of the following assets and why. Also, indicate to what extent obsolescence will affect each of the assets.

- (*a*) A delivery van used by a baker.
- (*b*) A filing cabinet.
- (*c*) A shop held on a 20-year lease.
- (*d*) A plastic moulding machine to manufacture a new novelty – plastic fireguards. It is expected that these will be very popular next Christmas and that sales will continue for a year or two thereafter but at a very much lower level.
- (*e*) Machine X. This machine is used as a standby when the normal machines are being maintained. Occasionally it is used to increase capacity when there is a glut of orders. Machine X is of an old type and is inefficient compared with new machines. When used on a full-time basis, the machine should last for approximately four years.

You can find a range of additional self-test questions, as well as material to help you with your studies, on the website that accompanies this book at www.pearsoned.co.uk/wood.

hapter 27

Double entry records for depreciation

Learning objectives

After you have studied this chapter, you should be able to:

- incorporate depreciation calculations into the accounting records
- record the entries relating to disposal of non-current assets
- make depreciation entries using either a one-stage or a two-stage approach to recording depreciation

Introduction

Now that you know what depreciation is and how it may be calculated, in this chapter you'll learn how to make the appropriate entries for depreciation in the accounting books. You'll also learn how to make the appropriate period-end entries in the financial statements.

27.1 Recording depreciation

Previously, the charge for depreciation on a non-current asset was recorded in the account for that fixed asset. This is no longer done.

Why do you think this is no longer done?

Recording depreciation now involves maintaining each non-current asset at its cost in the ledger account while operating another ledger account where the depreciation to date is recorded. This account is known as the '**accumulated provision for depreciation account**', often shortened to the **accumulated depreciation account** (or sometimes, confusingly, known as the 'provision for depreciation account').

Why do you think it would be confusing to call the accumulated provision for depreciation account the 'provision for depreciation account'?

Let's look at how this is done by first looking at the double entry required and then looking at how it is used in an example, shown in Exhibit 27.1.

The depreciation is posted directly into the cumulative provision for depreciation account. The double entry is:

Debit the profit and loss account
Credit the accumulated provision for depreciation account

Exhibit 27.1

A business has a financial year end of 31 December. A computer is bought for £2,000 on 1 January 2005. It is to be depreciated at the rate of 20 per cent using the reducing balance method. The records for the first three years are:

Computer

			£				
2005							
Jan	1	Cash	2,000				

Accumulated Provision for Depreciation – Computer

			£				£
2005				2005			
Dec	31	Balance c/d	400	Dec	31	Profit and loss	400
2006				2006			
Dec	31	Balance c/d	720	Jan	1	Balance b/d	400
				Dec	31	Profit and loss	320
			720				720
2007				2007			
Dec	31	Balance c/d	976	Jan	1	Balance b/d	720
				Dec	31	Profit and loss	256
			976				976
				2008			
				Jan	1	Balance b/d	976

Profit and Loss

			£		
2005					
Dec	31	Acc Provn for Depn: Computer	400		
2006					
Dec	31	Acc Provn for Depn: Computer	320		
2007					
Dec	31	Acc Provn for Depn: Computer	256		

Income Statement (extracts) for the years ending 31 December

		£
2005	Depreciation	400
2006	Depreciation	320
2007	Depreciation	256

***Note*: In this case, the depreciation for the period being entered in the income statement is being described as 'depreciation' and *not* by the name of the account it originated from (the accumulated provision for depreciation account).**

What advantages are there in making this exception to the rule by using 'depreciation' rather than 'accumulated provision for depreciation' in the entry in the income statement?

Now the balance on the Computer Account is shown on the balance sheet at the end of each year less the balance on the Accumulated Provision for Depreciation Account.

Balance Sheets (extracts)

	£	£
As at 31 December 2005		
Computer at cost	2,000	
Less Accumulated depreciation	(400)	
		1,600
As at 31 December 2006		
Computer at cost	2,000	
Less Accumulated depreciation	(720)	
		1,280
As at 31 December 2007		
Computer at cost	2,000	
Less Accumulated depreciation	(976)	
		1,024

27.2 The disposal of a non-current asset

Reason for accounting entries

Upon the sale of a non-current asset, we will want to remove it from our ledger accounts. This means that the cost of that asset needs to be taken out of the asset account. In addition, the accumulated depreciation on the asset which has been sold will have to be taken out of the accumulated provision. Finally, the profit and loss on sale, if any, will have to be calculated and posted to the profit and loss account.

When we charge depreciation on a non-current asset we are having to make an informed guess. We will not often guess correctly. This means that, when we dispose of an asset, the amount received for it is usually different from our estimate.

List as many things as you can think of in one minute that could cause the amount charged for depreciation to have been incorrect.

Accounting entries needed

On the sale of a non-current asset, in this example a computer, the following entries are needed:

(A) Transfer the cost price of the asset sold to an assets disposal account (in this case a computer disposals account):

Debit computer disposals account
Credit computer account

(B) Transfer the depreciation already charged to the assets disposal account:

Debit accumulated provision for depreciation: computer
Credit computer disposals account

(C) For the amount received on disposal:

Debit cash book
Credit computer disposals account

(D) Transfer the difference (i.e. the amount needed to balance the computer disposals account) to the profit and loss account.

(i) If the computer disposals account shows a difference on the debit side (i.e. if more has been credited to the account than has been debited to it), there is a profit on the sale:

Debit computer disposals account
Credit profit and loss account

(ii) If the computer disposals account shows a difference on the credit side, there is a loss on sale:

Debit profit and loss account
Credit computer disposals account

These entries can be illustrated by looking at those needed if the computer in Exhibit 27.1 was sold on 2 January 2008. At 31 December 2007, the cost was £2,000 and a total of £976 had been written off as depreciation leaving a net book value of £2,000 – £976 = £1,024. If the computer is sold in 2008 for *more* than £1,024 a profit on sale will be made. If, on the other hand, the computer is sold for *less* than £1,024 then a loss will be incurred.

Exhibit 27.2 shows the entries needed when the computer has been sold for £1,070 and a profit of £46 on sale has, therefore, been made. Exhibit 27.3 shows the entries where the computer has been sold for £950, thus incurring a loss on sale of £74. In both cases, the sale is on 2 January 2008 and no depreciation is to be charged for the two days' ownership in 2008. (The letters in brackets refer to the accounting double entries, A–D, above.)

Exhibit 27.2 Non-current asset sold at a profit

Computer

				£					£
2005					2008				
Jan	1	Cash		2,000	Jan	2	Machinery disposals	(A)	2,000

Accumulated Provision for Depreciation: Computer

				£					£
2008					2008				
Jan	2	Machinery disposals	(B)	976	Jan	1	Balance b/d		976

Computer Disposals

				£					£
2008					2008				
Jan	2	Computer	(A)	2,000	Jan	2	Accumulated provision for depreciation	(B)	976
Dec	31	Profit and loss	(D)	46		2	Cash	(C)	1,070
				2,046					2,046

Profit and Loss

				£					£
					2008				
					Dec	31	Computer disposals (gain)	(D)	46

Income Statement (extract) for the year ending 31 December 2008

	£
Gross profit	xxx
Add Gain on sale of computer	46

Exhibit 27.3 Non-current asset sold at a loss

Computer

2005			£	2008					£
Jan	1	Cash	2,000	Jan	2	Computer disposals		(A)	2,000

Accumulated Provision for Depreciation: Computer

2008				£	2008			£
Jan	2	Computer disposals	(B)	976	Jan	1	Balance b/d	976

Computer Disposals

2008				£	2008				£
Jan	2	Computer	(A)	2,000	Jan	2	Accumulated provision for depreciation	(B)	976
						2	Cash	(C)	950
					Dec	31	Profit and loss	(D)	74
				2,000					2,000

Profit and Loss

2008			£	
Dec	31	Computer disposal (loss) (D)	74	

Income Statement (extract) for the year ending 31 December 2008

	£
Gross profit	xxx
Less Loss on sale of computer	(74)

In many cases, the disposal of an asset will mean that we have sold it. This will not always be the case. For example, a car may be given up in part payment for a new car. Here the disposal value is the exchange value. If a new car costing £10,000 was to be paid for with £6,000 in cash and an allowance of £4,000 for the old car, then the disposal value of the old car is £4,000.

Similarly a car may have been in an accident and now be worthless. If a payment is received from an insurance company, the amount of that payment will be the disposal value. If an asset is scrapped, the disposal value is that received from the sale of the scrap, which may be nil.

27.3 Change of depreciation method

It is possible to make a change in the method of calculating depreciation. This should not be done frequently, and it should only be undertaken after a thorough review. Where a change is made, if material (see Chapter 10 on materiality), the effect of the change on the figures reported should be shown as a note to the financial statements in the year of change.

Further examples

So far, the examples have deliberately been kept simple. Only one non-current asset has been shown in each case. Exhibits 27.4 and 27.5 give examples of more complicated cases.

Exhibit 27.4

A machine is bought on 1 January 2005 for £1,000 and another one on 1 October 2006 for £1,200. The first machine is sold on 30 June 2007 for £720. The business's financial year ends on 31 December. The machinery is to be depreciated at 10 per cent, using the straight line method. Machinery in existence at the end of each year is to be depreciated for a full year. No depreciation is to be charged on any machinery disposed of during the year.

Machinery

			£				£
2005				2005			
Jan	1	Cash	1,000	Dec	31	Balance c/d	1,000
2006				2006			
Jan	1	Balance b/d	1,000	Dec	31	Balance c/d	2,200
Oct	1	Cash	1,200				
			2,200				2,200
2007				2007			
Jan	1	Balance b/d	2,200	Jun	30	Machinery disposals	1,000
				Dec	31	Balance c/d	1,200
			2,200				2,200
2008							
Jan	1	Balance b/d	1,200				

Accumulated Provision for Depreciation: Machinery

			£				£
2005				2005			
Dec	31	Balance c/d	100	Dec	31	Profit and loss	100
2006				2006			
Dec	31	Balance c/d	320	Jan	1	Balance b/d	100
				Dec	31	Profit and loss	220
			320				320
2007				2007			
Jun	30	Disposals of machinery (2 years × 10 per cent × £1,000)	200	Jan	1	Balance b/d	320
Dec	31	Balance c/d	240	Dec	31	Profit and loss	120
			440				440
				2008			
				Jan	1	Balance b/d	240

Machinery Disposals

			£				£
2007				2007			
Jun	30	Machinery	1,000	Jun	30	Cash	720
					30	Accumulated provision for depreciation	200
				Dec	31	Profit and loss	80
			1,000				1,000

Profit and Loss (extracts)

			£	
2005				
Dec	31	Acc Provn for Depn: Machinery	100	
2006				
Dec	31	Acc Provn for Depn: Machinery	220	
2007				
Dec	31	Acc Provn for Depn: Machinery	120	
	31	Machinery disposals (loss)	80	

Income Statement (extracts) for the years ending 31 December

		£
Gross profit		xxx
	Less Expenses:	
2005	Provision for depreciation: Machinery	(100)
2006	Provision for depreciation: Machinery	(220)
2007	Provision for depreciation: Machinery	(120)
	Loss on machinery sold	(80)

Balance Sheet (extracts) as at 31 December

		£	£
2005	Machinery at cost	1,000	
	Less Accumulated depreciation	(100)	
			900
2006	Machinery at cost	2,200	
	Less Accumulated depreciation	(320)	
			1,880
2007	Machinery at cost	1,200	
	Less Accumulated depreciation	(240)	
			960

Another example can now be given. This is somewhat more complicated. Firstly, it involves a greater number of items. Secondly, the depreciation provisions are calculated on a proportionate basis, i.e. one month's depreciation for one month's ownership.

Exhibit 27.5

A business with its financial year end on 31 December buys two vans on 1 January 2001, No 1 for £8,000 and No 2 for £5,000. It also buys another van, No 3, on 1 July 2003 for £9,000 and another, No 4, on 1 October 2003 for £7,200. The first two vans are sold, No 1 for £2,290 on 30 September 2004, and No 2 for scrap for £50 on 30 June 2005.

Depreciation is on the straight line basis, 20 per cent per annum, ignoring scrap value in this particular case when calculating depreciation per annum. Shown below are extracts from the assets account, provision for depreciation account, disposal account, profit and loss account and income statements for the years ended 31 December 2001, 2002, 2003, 2004 and 2005, and the balance sheets as at those dates.

Vans

			£				£
2001				2001			
Jan	1	Cash	13,000	Dec	31	Balance c/d	13,000
2002				2002			
Jan	1	Balance b/d	13,000	Dec	31	Balance c/d	13,000
2003				2003			
Jan	1	Balance b/d	13,000				
July	1	Cash	9,000				
Oct	1	Cash	7,200	Dec	31	Balance c/d	29,200
			29,200				29,200
2004				2004			
Jan	1	Balance b/d	29,200	Sept	30	Disposals	8,000
				Dec	31	Balance c/d	21,200
			29,200				29,200
2005				2005			
Jan	1	Balance b/d	21,200	June	30	Disposals	5,000
				Dec	31	Balance c/d	16,200
			21,200				21,200
2006							
Jan	1	Balance b/d	16,200				

Accumulated Provision for Depreciation: Vans

			£				£
2001				2001			
Dec	31	Balance c/d	2,600	Dec	31	Profit and loss	2,600
2002				2002			
				Jan	1	Balance b/d	2,600
Dec	31	Balance c/d	5,200	Dec	31	Profit and loss	2,600
			5,200				5,200
2003				2003			
				Jan	1	Balance b/d	5,200
Dec	31	Balance c/d	9,060	Dec	31	Profit and loss	3,860
			9,060				9,060
2004				2004			
Sept	30	Disposals	6,000	Jan	1	Balance b/d	9,060
Dec	31	Balance c/d	8,500	Dec	31	Profit and loss	5,440
			14,500				14,500
2005				2005			
June	30	Disposals	4,500	Jan	1	Balance b/d	8,500
Dec	31	Balance c/d	7,740	Dec	31	Profit and loss	3,740
			12,240				12,240
				2006			
				Jan	1	Balance b/d	7,740

Workings – depreciation provisions		£	£
2001	20% of £13,000		2,600
2002	20% of £13,000		2,600
2003	20% of £13,000 × 12 months	2,600	
	20% of £9,000 × 6 months	900	
	20% of £7,200 × 3 months	360	
			3,860
2004	20% of £21,200 × 12 months	4,240	
	20% of £8,000 × 9 months	1,200	
			5,440
2005	20% of £16,200 × 12 months	3,240	
	20% of £5,000 × 6 months	500	
			3,740

Workings – transfers of depreciation provisions to disposal accounts

Van 1 Bought Jan 1 2001 Cost £8,000
Sold Sept 30 2004
Period of ownership $3\frac{3}{4}$ years
Depreciation provisions $3\frac{3}{4} \times 20\% \times £8{,}000 = £6{,}000$

Van 2 Bought Jan 1 2001 Cost £5,000
Sold June 30 2005
Period of ownership $4\frac{1}{2}$ years
Depreciation provisions $4\frac{1}{2} \times 20\% \times £5{,}000 = £4{,}500$

Disposals of Vans

			£				£
2004				2004			
Sept	30	Van	8,000	Sept	30	Accumulated provision for depreciation	6,000
Dec	31	Profit and loss	290			Cash	2,290
			8,290				8,290
2005				2005			
Jun	30	Van	5,000	Jun	30	Accumulated provision for depreciation	4,500
						Cash	50
				Dec	31	Profit and loss	450
			5,000				5,000

Profit and Loss (extracts)

			£				£
2001							
Dec	31	Acc Provn for Depn: Vans	2,600				
2002							
Dec	31	Acc Provn for Depn: Vans	2,600				
2003							
Dec	31	Acc Provn for Depn: Vans	3,860				
2004				2004			
Dec	31	Acc Provn for Depn: Vans	5,440	Dec	31	Disposal of Vans (Gain)	290
2005							
Dec	31	Acc Provn for Depn: Vans	3,740				
		Disposal of Vans (loss)	450				

Income Statement (extracts) for the years ending 31 December

		£	£
Gross profit (each year 2001, 2002, 2003)			xxx
	Less Expenses:		
2001	Provision for depreciation: vans		(2,600)
2002	Provision for depreciation: vans		(2,600)
2003	Provision for depreciation: vans		(3,860)
2004	Gross profit		x,xxx
	Add Profit on van sold		290
			x,xxx
	Less Expenses:		
	Provision for depreciation: vans		(5,440)
			x,xxx
2005	Gross profit		x,xxx
	Less Expenses:		
	Provision for depreciation: vans	3,740	
	Loss on van sold	450	
			(4,190)

Balance Sheets (extracts) as at 31 December

		£	£
2001	Vans at cost	13,000	
	Less Accumulated depreciation	(2,600)	
			10,400
2002	Vans at cost	13,000	
	Less Accumulated depreciation	(5,200)	
			7,800
2003	Vans at cost	29,200	
	Less Accumulated depreciation	(9,060)	
			20,140
2004	Vans at cost	21,200	
	Less Accumulated depreciation	(8,500)	
			12,700
2005	Vans at cost	16,200	
	Less Accumulated depreciation	(7,740)	
			8,460

27.4 Depreciation provisions and the replacement of assets

Making a provision for depreciation does not mean that money is invested somewhere to finance the replacement of the asset when it is put out of use. It is simply a bookkeeping entry, and the end result is that lower net profits are shown because the provisions have been charged to the profit and loss account.

It is not surprising to find that many people – especially students – who have not studied accounting misunderstand the situation. They often think that a provision is the same as money kept somewhere with which to replace the asset eventually. Never make that mistake. It may cost you a lot of marks in an exam!

A cautious owner may take out less drawings if the net profit is lower, but that is no justification for arguing that depreciation results in funds being available to replace the fixed asset later!

27.5 Another approach

In this chapter, you've learnt how to perform the double entries necessary to record the periodic charge for depreciation. The approach you learnt about is known as the 'one-stage approach'. It was based upon the use of one double entry, a credit to the accumulated provision for depreciation account and a debit to the profit and loss account.

There is another approach which is widely used in practice. It involves using a '**provision for depreciation account**', often shortened to '**depreciation account**', as well as the 'accumulated provision for depreciation account'. At the end of the period, you calculate the depreciation for the period and make the following double entries:

1 **Debit the depreciation account**
   Credit the accumulated provision for depreciation account
2 Debit the profit and loss account
   Credit the depreciation account

Compare this two-stage approach to the one-stage approach you learnt earlier:

Debit the profit and loss account
   Credit the accumulated provision for depreciation account

Note how the double entry you learnt earlier combines the two entries used in the two-stage approach by cancelling out the debit and credit to the depreciation account. This makes it much simpler to record the entries required, but adopting the two-stage approach has the advantage that it actually shows what has happened rather than compressing the two double entries that theory says should be used into one.

However, some accountants still prefer to keep recording the entries as simple as possible and so use only the 'accumulated provision for depreciation account' (i.e. the 'one-stage approach').

Nevertheless, you need to be aware of and able to use the two-stage approach described above, just in case you should be asked to do so by an examiner. If you are *not* asked for two accounts (a depreciation account *plus* an accumulated provision for depreciation account) you should assume that the one-stage approach is the one you are expected to use.

***Note*: As in Review Questions 27.7A, 27.8 and 27.9A, examiners sometimes ask for a 'depreciation' account to be shown in an answer and they do not mention an 'accumulated provision for depreciation' account. When this happens, it is usually the 'accumulated provision for depreciation' account they are looking for. That is, they expect the balance on it to be carried forward to the next period, as in the case of the one-stage method. It is the one-stage method they want you to use but they have given the account the 'wrong' name. Use the name they used ('depreciation') but treat it as if it were an 'accumulated provision for depreciation' account. When examiners want you to prepare both a 'depreciation' account and an 'accumulated provision for depreciation' account, it will be obvious from the wording of the question.**

27.6 Finally

This chapter has covered all the principles involved. Obviously examiners can present their questions in their own way. In fact, in order to better test your understanding, examiners do tend to vary the way questions involving depreciation are presented. Practise all the questions in this book, including those in the exhibits, and compare them with the answers shown in full. Doing so will demonstrate the truth of this statement and prepare you better for your examination when you can be virtually guaranteed that you will need to be able to calculate and make appropriate entries for depreciation.

Learning outcomes

You should now have learnt:

1. That the method of showing depreciation in the asset account is now used only by some small organisations, and should be avoided.
2. That non-current asset accounts should show only the cost. Depreciation is credited to an accumulated provision for depreciation account.
3. That when we sell a non-current asset, we must transfer both the cost and the accumulated depreciation to a separate disposal account.
4. That it is very rare for the depreciation provided to have been accurate.
5. That a profit on the disposal of a non-current asset is transferred to the credit of the profit and loss account.
6. That a loss on the disposal of a non-current asset is transferred to the debit of the profit and loss account.
7. That there are two approaches which may be adopted when entering depreciation into the accounting books.
8. That the approach you have learnt does so in one double entry and uses one ledger account for the accumulated provision for depreciation.
9. That the other, 'two-stage', approach uses two journal entries and two ledger accounts, one for the depreciation expense and the other to record the accumulated provision for depreciation.
10. That there are a number of alternatives for the names of the depreciation accounts involved under these two approaches.
11. That the name 'provision for depreciation' is often used in place of 'accumulated provision for depreciation' in the balance sheet account that shows the depreciation accumulated to date.

Answers to activities

27.1 It has the effect of reducing the balance shown in the ledger for the non-current asset so that, over time, it may be very much less than the original cost. This makes it difficult to identify the original cost of non-current assets and means that, in the balance sheet, the only information that can be given is the value to which each non-current asset has been written down. Anyone looking at this information will have no way of assessing whether a non-current asset was originally very expensive (which may be relevant, for example, if it is a building) and so cannot arrive at a realistic view of what the non-current assets really comprise. Nor, especially in the case of smaller businesses, is it immediately obvious how long a non-current asset is likely to continue to be used or, in fact, whether there is actually an asset in current use – if the value has been written down to zero, it wouldn't have a balance, may have been written out of the ledger, and certainly wouldn't be included in the balance sheet.

27.2 Use of the term 'provision for depreciation account' can be very confusing as the name of the account used to record provisions for doubtful debts is the 'allowance for doubtful debts account' and, as you know, that account is closed off at the end of the accounting period and the balance transferred to the debit side of the profit and loss account. In contrast, the balance on the 'accumulated provision for depreciation account' is shown in the balance sheet at the year end and carried forward to the next accounting period. The two treatments could hardly be more different. It is, therefore, asking for mistakes to be made if you use the same stem, 'provision for . . .', for them both. It must be said, however, that many people do, including some examiners. So, you need to be aware that when you see an account called the 'provision for depreciation account', it is referring to the account we shall call in this book the 'accumulated provision for depreciation account'. To help you get used to this, some of the multiple choice questions and review questions at the end of this chapter use the term 'provision for depreciation account'.

27.3 Doing so makes it clear that just one period's depreciation is involved and *not* the entire accumulated depreciation to date.

27.4 We cannot be absolutely certain how long we will keep the asset in use, nor can we be certain how much the asset will be sold for when we dispose of it, or even that it will be possible to sell it at that time. We may also have chosen the wrong depreciation method causing the net book value of the asset (i.e. cost less accumulated depreciation) to have been reduced too quickly (reducing balance) or too slowly (straight line) in the event that it is disposed of earlier than expected.

Multiple choice questions: Set 3

Now attempt Set 3 of multiple choice questions. (Answers to all the multiple choice questions are given in Appendix 2 at the end of this book.)

Each of these multiple choice questions has four suggested answers, (A), (B), (C) and (D). You should read each question and then decide which choice is best, either (A) or (B) or (C) or (D). ***Write down your answers on a separate piece of paper.*** **You will then be able to redo the set of questions later without having to try to ignore your answers.**

MC41 A cash discount is best described as a reduction in the sum to be paid

(A) If payment is made within a previously agreed period
(B) If payment is made by cash, not cheque
(C) If payment is made either by cash or cheque
(D) If purchases are made for cash, not on credit

MC42 Discounts received are

(A) Deducted when we receive cash
(B) Given by us when we sell goods on credit
(C) Deducted by us when we pay our accounts
(D) None of these

MC43 The total of the 'Discounts Allowed' column in the Cash Book is posted to

(A) The debit of the Discounts Allowed account
(B) The debit of the Discounts Received account
(C) The credit of the Discounts Allowed account
(D) The credit of the Discounts Received account

MC44 Sales invoices are first entered in

(A) The Cash Book
(B) The Purchases Journal
(C) The Sales Account
(D) The Sales Journal

MC45 The total of the Sales Journal is entered on

(A) The credit side of the Sales Account in the General Ledger
(B) The credit side of the General Account in the Sales Ledger
(C) The debit side of the Sales Account in the General Ledger
(D) The debit side of the Sales Day Book

MC46 Given a purchases invoice showing five items of £80 each, less trade discount of 25 per cent and cash discount of 5 per cent, if paid within the credit period, your cheque would be made out for

(A) £285
(B) £280
(C) £260
(D) None of these

MC47 An alternative name for a Sales Journal is

(A) Sales Invoice
(B) Sales Day Book
(C) Daily Sales
(D) Sales Ledger

MC48 Entered in the Purchases Journal are

(A) Payments to suppliers
(B) Trade discounts
(C) Purchases invoices
(D) Discounts received

MC49 The total of the Purchases Journal is transferred to the

(A) Credit side of the Purchases Account
(B) Debit side of the Purchases Day Book
(C) Credit side of the Purchases Book
(D) Debit side of the Purchases Account

MC50 Credit notes issued by us will be entered in our

(A) Sales Account
(B) Returns Inwards Account
(C) Returns Inwards Journal
(D) Returns Outwards Journal

MC51 The total of the Returns Outwards Journal is transferred to

(A) The credit side of the Returns Outwards Account
(B) The debit side of the Returns Outwards Account
(C) The credit side of the Returns Outwards Book
(D) The debit side of the Purchases Returns Book

→

→ **MC52** We originally sold 25 items at £12 each, less $33\frac{1}{3}$ per cent trade discount. Our customer now returns 4 of them to us. What is the amount of credit note to be issued?

(A) £48
(B) £36
(C) £30
(D) £32

MC53 Depreciation is

(A) The amount spent to buy a non-current asset
(B) The salvage value of a non-current asset
(C) The part of the cost of the non-current asset consumed during its period of use by the firm
(D) The amount of money spent replacing non-current assets

MC54 A firm bought a machine for £3,200. It is to be depreciated at a rate of 25 per cent using the reducing balance method. What would be the remaining book value after two years?

(A) £1,600
(B) £2,400
(C) £1,800
(D) Some other figure

MC55 A firm bought a machine for £16,000. It is expected to be used for five years then sold for £1,000. What is the annual amount of depreciation if the straight line method is used?

(A) £3,200
(B) £3,100
(C) £3,750
(D) £3,000

MC56 At the balance sheet date the balance on the Accumulated Provision for Depreciation Account is

(A) Transferred to Depreciation Account
(B) Transferred to Profit and Loss Account
(C) Simply deducted from the asset in the Balance Sheet
(D) Transferred to the Asset Account

MC57 In the trial balance the balance on the Provision for Depreciation Account is

(A) Shown as a credit item
(B) Not shown, as it is part of depreciation
(C) Shown as a debit item
(D) Sometimes shown as a credit, sometimes as a debit

MC58 If an accumulated provision for depreciation account is in use then the entries for the year's depreciation would be

(A) Credit Provision for Depreciation Account, debit Profit and Loss Account
(B) Debit Asset Account, credit Profit and Loss Account
(C) Credit Asset Account, debit Provision for Depreciation Account
(D) Credit Profit and Loss Account, debit Provision for Depreciation Account

MC59 When the financial statements are prepared, the Bad Debts Account is closed by a transfer to the

(A) Balance Sheet
(B) Profit and Loss Account

(C) Trading Account
(D) Allowance for Doubtful Debts Account

MC60 An Allowance for Doubtful Debts is created

(A) When debtors become bankrupt
(B) When debtors cease to be in business
(C) To provide for possible bad debts
(D) To write-off bad debts

Review questions

27.1 A company starts in business on 1 January 2005. You are to write up the vans account and the provision for depreciation account for the year ended 31 December 2005 from the information given below. Depreciation is at the rate of 25 per cent per annum, using the basis that one complete month's ownership needs one month's depreciation.

2005	Bought two vans for £6,900 each on 1 January
	Bought one van for £7,200 on 1 August

27.2 A company starts in business on 1 January 2003, the financial year end being 31 December. You are to show:

(*a*) The machinery account.
(*b*) The provision for depreciation account.
(*c*) The balance sheet extracts for each of the years 2003, 2004, 2005, 2006.

The machinery bought was:

2003	1 January	1 machine costing £1,400
2004	1 July	2 machines costing £600 each
	1 October	1 machine costing £1,000
2006	1 April	1 machine costing £400

Depreciation is over ten years, using the straight line method, machines being depreciated for the proportion of the year that they are owned.

27.3A A company maintains its non-current assets at cost. Depreciation provision accounts, one for each type of asset, are in use. Machinery is to be depreciated at the rate of 15% per annum, and fixtures at the rate of 5% per annum, using the reducing balance method. Depreciation is to be calculated on assets in existence at the end of each year, giving a full year's depreciation even though the asset was bought part of the way through the year. The following transactions in assets have taken place:

2005	1 January	Bought machinery £2,800, fixtures £290
	1 July	Bought fixtures £620
2006	1 October	Bought machinery £3,500
	1 December	Bought fixtures £130

The financial year end of the business is 31 December.

You are to show:
(*a*) The machinery account.
(*b*) The fixtures account.
(*c*) The two separate provision for depreciation accounts.
(*d*) The non-current assets section of the balance sheet at the end of each year, for the years ended 31 December 2005 and 2006.

→

27.4 A company depreciates its plant at the rate of 25 per cent per annum, straight line method, for each month of ownership. From the following details draw up the plant account and the provision for depreciation account for each of the years 2004, 2005, 2006 and 2007.

2004	Bought plant costing £2,600 on 1 January.
	Bought plant costing £2,100 on 1 October.
2006	Bought plant costing £2,800 on 1 September.
2007	Sold plant which had been bought for £2,600 on 1 January 2004 for the sum of £810 on 31 August 2007.

You are also required to draw up the plant disposal account and the extracts from the balance sheet as at the end of each year.

27.5 A company maintains its non-current assets at cost. Depreciation provision accounts for each asset are kept.

At 31 December 2008 the position was as follows:

	Total cost to date	*Total depreciation to date*
	£	£
Machinery	94,500	28,350
Office furniture	3,200	1,280

The following additions were made during the financial year ended 31 December 2009:

Machinery £16,000, office furniture £460.

A machine bought in 2005 for £1,600 was sold for £360 during the year.

The rates of depreciation are:

Machinery 20 per cent, office furniture 10 per cent, using the straight line basis, calculated on the assets in existence at the end of each financial year irrespective of the date of purchase.

You are required to show the asset and depreciation accounts for the year ended 31 December 2009 and the balance sheet entries at that date.

27.6 A vehicle bought on 1 January 2010 cost £16,000. Its useful economic life is estimated at four years and its trade-in value at that point is estimated as being £4,000.

During 2012 a review of the vehicle's probable useful economic life suggested that it should be retained until 1 January 2015 and its residual value should be £2,500.

Required:
What is the amount of straight line depreciation charged in the income statement in the year ending 31 December 2012 and the amount included in the balance sheet for accumulated depreciation at that date?

27.7A

(*a*) What is the meaning of depreciation?

(*b*) Give **three** reasons why depreciation may occur.

(*c*) Name **two** methods of depreciation.

(*d*) In what way do you think the concept of consistency applies to depreciation?

(*e*) 'Since the calculation of depreciation is based on estimates, not facts, why bother to make the calculation?'

Explain briefly why you think that the calculation of depreciation is based on estimates.

(*f*) If depreciation was omitted, what effects would this have on the final accounts?

(*g*) 'Some assets increase (appreciate) in value, but normal accounting procedure would be to ignore any such appreciation.'

Explain why bringing appreciation into account would go against the prudence concept.

(*h*) A business whose financial year ends at 31 December purchased on 1 January 2007 a machine for £5,000. The machine was to be depreciated by ten equal instalments. On 4 January 2009 the machine was sold for £3,760.

Ignoring any depreciation in the year of sale, show the relevant entries for each of the following accounts for the years ended 31 December 2007, 2008 and 2009:

(*i*) Machinery
(*ii*) Provision for depreciation of machinery[Authors' Note]
(*iii*) Machinery disposals
(*iv*) Profit and loss

(*Northern Examinations and Assessment Board: GCSE*)
Authors' Note: this is the accumulated provision for depreciation of machinery account.

27.8

(*a*) Identify the four factors which cause non-current assets to depreciate.
(*b*) Which one of these factors is the most important for each of the following assets?
  (*i*) a gold mine,
  (*ii*) a van,
  (*iii*) a 50 year lease on a building,
  (*iv*) land,
  (*v*) a ship used to ferry passengers and vehicles across a river following the building of a bridge across the river,
  (*vi*) a franchise to market a new computer software package in a certain country.
(*c*) The financial year of Ochre Ltd will end on 31 December 2006. At 1 January 2006 the company had in use equipment with a total accumulated cost of £135,620 which had been depreciated by a total of £81,374. During the year ended 31 December 2006 Ochre Ltd purchased new equipment costing £47,800 and sold off equipment which had originally cost £36,000, and which had been depreciated by £28,224, for £5,700. No further purchases or sales of equipment are planned for December. The policy of the company is to depreciate equipment at 40% using the diminishing balance method. A full year's depreciation is provided for on all equipment in use by the company at the end of each year.

Required:
Show the following ledger accounts for the year ended 31 December 2006:
  (*i*) the Equipment Account;
  (*ii*) the Provision for Depreciation on Equipment Account;[Authors' Note]
  (*iii*) the Assets Disposals Account.

(*Association of Accounting Technicians*)
Authors' Note: this is the accumulated provision for depreciation account.

27.9A Mavron plc owned the following motor vehicles as at 1 April 2006:

Motor Vehicle	*Date Acquired*	*Cost* £	*Estimated Residual Value* £	*Estimated Life (years)*
AAT 101	1 October 2003	8,500	2,500	5
DJH 202	1 April 2004	12,000	2,000	8

Mavron plc's policy is to provide at the end of each financial year depreciation using the straight line method applied on a month-by-month basis on all motor vehicles used during the year.

During the financial year ended 31 March 2007 the following occurred:

(*i*) On 30 June 2006 AAT 101 was traded in and replaced by KGC 303. The trade-in allowance was £5,000. KGC 303 cost £15,000 and the balance due (after deducting the trade-in allowance) was paid partly in cash and partly by a loan of £6,000 from Pinot Finance. KGC 303 is expected to have a residual value of £4,000 after an estimated economic life of 5 years.
(*ii*) The estimated remaining economic life of DJH 202 was reduced from 6 years to 4 years with no change in the estimated residual value.

→ **Required:**

(a) Show any Journal entries necessary to give effect to the above.

(b) Show the Journal entry necessary to record depreciation on Motor Vehicles for the year ended 31 March 2007.

(c) Reconstruct the Motor Vehicles Account and the Provision for Depreciation Account for the year ended 31 March 2007.[Authors' Note]

Show the necessary calculations clearly.

(Association of Accounting Technicians)

Authors' Note: this is the accumulated provision for depreciation account.

27.10 A business buys a non-current asset for £10,000. The business estimates that the asset will be used for 5 years. After exactly 2½ years, however, the asset is suddenly sold for £5,000. The business always provides a full year's depreciation in the year of purchase and no depreciation in the year of disposal.

Required:

(*a*) Write up the relevant accounts (including disposal account but not profit and loss account) for each of Years 1, 2 and 3:
- (*i*) Using the straight line depreciation method (assume 20% pa);
- (*ii*) Using the reducing balance depreciation method (assume 40% pa).

(*b*) (*i*) What is the purpose of depreciation? In what circumstances would each of the two methods you have used be preferable?
- (*ii*) What is the meaning of the net figure for the non-current asset in the balance sheet at the end of Year 2?

(c) If the asset was bought at the beginning of Year 1, but was not used at all until Year 2 (and it is confidently anticipated to last until Year 6), state under each method the appropriate depreciation charge in Year 1, and briefly justify your answer.

(Association of Chartered Certified Accountants)

27.11A Contractors Ltd was formed on 1 January 2006 and the following purchases and sales of machinery were made during the first 3 years of operations.

Date	*Asset*	*Transaction*	*Price*
1 January 2006	Machines 1 and 2	purchase	£40,000 each
1 October 2006	Machines 3 and 4	purchase	£15,200 each
30 June 2008	Machine 3	sale	£12,640
1 July 2008	Machine 5	purchase	£20,000

Each machine was estimated to last 10 years and to have a residual value of 5% of its cost price. Depreciation was by equal instalments, and it is company policy to charge depreciation for every month an asset is owned.

Required:

(*a*) Calculate
- (*i*) the total depreciation on Machinery for each of the years 2006, 2007 and 2008;
- (*ii*) the profit or loss on the sale of Machine 3 in 2008.

(*b*) Contractors Ltd depreciates its vehicles by 30% per annum using the diminishing balance method. What difference would it have made to annual reported profits over the life of a vehicle if it had decided instead to depreciate this asset by 20% straight line?

(Scottish Qualifications Authority)

27.12 A friend of the family believes that depreciation provides him with a reserve to purchase new assets. His secretary has blown up his computer, but he knows he has the funds to replace it in the accumulated depreciation account. You know he is wrong and have grown tired of listening to him going on about it, but he won't listen to what you have to say. You decide to put him out of his misery by writing a letter to him about it that he may actually read before he realises that it is telling him things he does not want to hear.

Write him a letter, using fictitious names and addresses, which defines depreciation and explains why his view is incorrect.

27.13A A machine cost £40,000 on 1 January 2007. The reducing balance depreciation method is used at 25% per annum. Year end is 31 December. During 2009, it was decided that a straight line method would be more appropriate. At that time, the remaining useful economic life of the machine was seven years with a residual value of £1,500.

Required:
The accumulated provision for depreciation account for the years 2007 to 2009 inclusive together with the relevant balance sheet extract on 31 December in each of those years.

27.14 (a) A machine was bought on credit for £15,000 from the XY Manufacturing Co Ltd, on 1 October 2001. The estimated useful economic life of the machine was seven years and the estimated scrap value £1,000. The machine account is to be maintained at cost. Financial statements are prepared annually to 30 September and the straight line depreciation method is used on machines.

Required:
(*a*) Prepare the journal entries and ledger accounts to record the machine and its depreciation for the first two years of its working life.
(*b*) Illustrate how the machine would appear in the balance sheet at 30 September 2003.

(b) The machine was sold for £7,500 cash to another manufacturer on 1 October 2004. A new replacement machine was bought on credit for £18,000 from the XY Manufacturing Co Ltd. It also has an estimated useful economic life of seven years but its estimated scrap value is £1,200.

Required:
(*a*) Prepare the machine account, the accumulated provision for depreciation account and the machine disposal account for the year to 30 September 2005.
(*b*) Repeat (*a*) but this time assume that the selling price of the old machine was £12,000.

27.15A Distance Limited owned three lorries at 1 April 2006:

A Purchased 21 May 2002 Cost £31,200
B Purchased 20 June 2004 Cost £19,600
C Purchased 1 January 2006 Cost £48,800

Depreciation is charged annually at 20% on cost on all vehicles in use at the end of the year.

During the year ended 31 March 2007, the following transactions occurred:

(*i*) 1 June 2006 lorry B was involved in an accident and considered to be a write-off by the insurance company which paid £10,500 in settlement.
(*ii*) 7 June 2006 lorry D was purchased for £32,800
(*iii*) 21 August 2006 lorry A was sold for £7,000
(*iv*) 30 October 2006 lorry E was purchased for £39,000
(*v*) 6 March 2007 lorry E was considered not to be suitable for carrying the type of goods required and was exchanged for lorry F. The value of lorry F was deemed to be £37,600.

Required:
Prepare the ledger T-accounts recording these transactions for the year ending 31 March 2007 and bring down the balances at 1 April.

27.16 XY Ltd provides for depreciation of its machinery at 20% per annum on cost; it charges for a full year in the year of purchase but no provision is made in the year of sale/disposal.

Financial statements are prepared annually to 31 December.

2005
January 1 Bought machine 'A' £10,000
July 1 Bought machine 'B' £6,000.

→

2006
March 31 Bought machine 'C' £8,000

2007
October 7 Sold machine 'A' – proceeds £5,500
November 5 Bought machine 'D' £12,000

2008
February 4 Sold machine 'B' – proceeds £3,000
February 6 Bought machine 'B' £9,000
October 11 Exchanged machine 'D' for machinery valued at £7,000

Prepare

(*a*) The machinery account for the period 1 January 2005 to 31 December 2008.
(*b*) The accumulated provision for depreciation on machinery account, for the period 1 January 2005 to 31 December 2008.
(*c*) The disposal of machinery accounts showing the profit/loss on sale for each year.
(*d*) The balance sheet extract for machinery at (i) 31 December 2007 and (ii) 31 December 2008.

27.17A A company maintains its non-current assets at cost. Accumulated provision for depreciation accounts are kept for each asset.

At 31 December 2008 the position was as follows:

	Total cost to date	*Total depreciation to date*
	£	£
Machinery	52,950	25,670
Office furniture	2,860	1,490

The following transactions were made in the year ended 31 December 2009:

(*a*) Purchased – machinery £2,480 and office furniture £320
(*b*) Sold machinery which had cost £2,800 in 2005 for £800

Depreciation is charged, on a straight line basis, at 10% on machinery and at 5% on office furniture on the basis of assets in use at the end of the year irrespective of the date of purchase.

Required:
Show the asset and accumulated provision for depreciation accounts for the year 31 December 2009 and the relevant balance sheet entries at that date.

27.18 Alice Burke prepares her financial statements on 31 December each year and maintains a Plant and Equipment register at cost. She provides depreciation for the full year on non-current assets which are in use at the end of the year, and none in the year of disposal.

At 31 December 2003 the plant account balance was £180,000 and the balance on the accumulated provision for depreciation account was £70,000. Depreciation was provided on the reducing balance method at 20%.

Early in 2006, an item of plant which had cost £20,000 on 1 March 2004 was sold for £14,000.

At the end of 2006, it was decided that for that and all succeeding years the straight line method of calculating depreciation should be used. It was assumed that all the plant would be sold at the end of 2009 for approximately £30,000.

Required:
Prepare the ledger accounts recording all of the above. You are not required to prepare the profit and loss account.

27.19A

(*a*) The following trial balance was extracted from the books of M Jackson on 30 April 2007. From it, and the note below it, prepare his income statement for the year ending 30 April 2007, and a balance sheet as at that date.

	Dr	Cr
	£	£
Sales		18,614
Purchases	11,570	
Inventory 1 May 2006	3,776	
Carriage outwards	326	
Carriage inwards	234	
Returns inwards	440	
Returns outwards		355
Salaries and wages	2,447	
Motor expenses	664	
Rent	576	
Sundry expenses	1,202	
Motor vehicles	3,400	
Fixtures and fittings	600	
Accounts receivable	4,577	
Accounts payable		3,045
Cash at bank	3,876	
Cash in hand	120	
Drawings	2,050	
Capital		13,844
	35,858	35,858

Note:
Closing inventory amounted to £4,000. Depreciation is to be charged at rates of 10% on cost for fixtures and fittings and 25% on cost for motor vehicles. Bad debts of £800 are to be written off.

(*b*) Michael has indicated that he thinks that the accounts receivable amounts that have been written off will be paid eventually. He is also querying why adjustments are made in the financial statements for bad debts and depreciation. Write a short note to him, making appropriate references to accounting concepts, outlining why these adjustments are made.

27.20 On 1 April 2006 a business purchased a machine costing £112,000. The machine can be used for a total of 20,000 hours over an estimated life of 48 months. At the end of that time the machine is expected to have a trade-in value of £12,000.

The financial year of the business ends on 31 December each year. It is expected that the machine will be used for:

4,000 hours during the financial year ending 31 December 2006
5,000 hours during the financial year ending 31 December 2007
5,000 hours during the financial year ending 31 December 2008
5,000 hours during the financial year ending 31 December 2009
1,000 hours during the financial year ending 31 December 2010

Required:

(*a*) Calculate the annual depreciation charges on the machine on each of the following bases for each of the financial years ending on 31 December 2006, 2007, 2008, 2009 and 2010:
 (*i*) the straight line method applied on a month for month basis,
 (*ii*) the diminishing balance method at 40% per annum applied on a full year basis, and
 (*iii*) the units of output method.

(*b*) Suppose that during the financial year ended 31 December 2007 the machine was used for only 1,500 hours before being sold for £80,000 on 30 June.

Assuming that the business has chosen to apply the straight line method on a month for month basis, show the following accounts for 2007 only:
 (*i*) the Machine account,
 (*ii*) the Provision for Depreciation – Machine account, and
 (*iii*) the Assets Disposals account.

(*Association of Accounting Technicians*)

27.21A On 1 January 2001 a business purchased a laser printer costing £1,800. The printer has an estimated life of 4 years after which it will have no residual value.

It is expected that the output from the printer will be:

Year	*Sheets printed*
2001	35,000
2002	45,000
2003	45,000
2004	55,000
	180,000

Required:

(*a*) Calculate the annual depreciation charges for 2001, 2002, 2003 and 2004 on the laser printer on the following bases:

(*i*) the straight line basis,

(*ii*) the diminishing balance method at 60% per annum, and

(*iii*) the units of output method.

Note: Your workings should be to the nearest £.

(*b*) Suppose that in 2004 the laser printer were to be sold on 1 July for £200 and that the business had chosen to depreciate it at 60% per annum using the diminishing balance method applied on a month for month basis.

Reconstruct the following accounts for 2004 only:

(*i*) the Laser Printer account,

(*ii*) the Provision for Depreciation – Laser Printer account, and

(*iii*) the Assets Disposals account.

(*Association of Accounting Technicians*)

You can find a range of additional self-test questions, as well as material to help you with your studies, on the website that accompanies this book at www.pearsoned.co.uk/wood.

hapter 28

Accruals and prepayments and other adjustments for financial statements

Learning objectives

After you have studied this chapter, you should be able to:

- adjust expense accounts for accruals and prepayments
- adjust revenue accounts for amounts owing
- show accruals, prepayments and revenue accounts receivable in the balance sheet
- ascertain the amounts of expense and revenue items to be shown in the income statement after making adjustments for accruals and prepayments
- make the necessary end-of-period adjustments relating to drawings that have not yet been entered in the books
- explain what an extended trial balance is and describe what it looks like
- prepare accrual and prepayment entries to the accounts using two different methods

Introduction

In this chapter, you'll continue to learn about adjustments made to the ledger accounts at the end of a period. You'll learn how to make the appropriate entries in the accounts for outstanding balances on expense and income accounts and make the appropriate entries in the income statement and the balance sheet.

28.1 Financial statements so far

The income statements you have looked at so far have taken the sales for a period and deducted all the expenses for that period, the result being a net profit or a net loss.

Up to this part of the book it has always been assumed that the expenses belonged to the period of the income statement. If the income statement for the year ending 31 December 2005 was being prepared, then the rent paid as shown in the trial balance was all for 2005. There was no rent owing at the beginning of 2005 nor any owing at the end of 2005, nor had any rent been paid in advance relating to 2006.

This was done to make your first meeting with financial statements as straight forward as possible.

28.2 Adjustments needed

Let's look at two businesses which pay rent for buildings in Oxford. The rent for each building is £6,000 a year.

1 Business A pays £5,000 in the year. At the year end it owes £1,000 for rent.

Rent expense used up	=	£6,000
Rent paid for	=	£5,000

2 Business B pays £6,500 in the year. This figure includes £500 paid in advance for the following year.

Rent expense used up	=	£6,000
Rent paid for	=	£6,500

An income statement for 12 months needs 12 months' rent as an expense = £6,000. This means that in both 1 and 2 the double entry accounts will have to be adjusted.

Activity 28.1

From your knowledge of double entry, you should be able to work out what the double entry required is in these two cases. What do you think it is? If you don't know what names to give the accounts, have a guess. (Hint: in the first case, there will be a credit balance in the balance sheet and in the other, it will be a debit balance.)

In all the examples in this chapter the income statements are for the year ending 31 December 2008. Unless otherwise indicated, all entries in the income statement are in the profit and loss section of the statement. All mentions of 'profit and loss' refer to the ledger account of that name which is summarised in the income statement.

28.3 Accrued expenses

Assume that rent of £4,000 per year is payable at the end of every three months. The rent was paid on time in March, but this is not always the case.

Amount	Rent due	Rent paid
£1,000	31 March 2008	31 March 2008
£1,000	30 June 2008	2 July 2008
£1,000	30 September 2008	4 October 2008
£1,000	31 December 2008	5 January 2008

Rent

2008			£	
Mar	31	Cash	1,000	
Jul	2	Cash	1,000	
Oct	4	Cash	1,000	

The rent for the last quarter was paid on 5 January 2009 and so will appear in the books of the year 2009 as the result of a double entry made on that date.

The expense for 2008 is obviously £4,000 as that is the year's rent, and this is the amount needed to be transferred to the profit and loss account. But, if £4,000 was put on the credit side of the rent account (the debit being in the profit and loss account) the account would be out of balance by £1,000 because the payment due on 31 December 2008 was not made until 5 January 2009. That is, if we posted £4,000 to profit and loss on 31 December, we would have £4,000 on the credit side of the account and only £3,000 on the debit side:

Rent

2008			£	2008			£
Mar	31	Cash	1,000	Dec	31	Profit and loss	4,000
Jul	2	Cash	1,000				
Oct	4	Cash	1,000				

This cannot be right.

To make the account balance the £1,000 rent owing for 2008, but paid in 2009, must be carried down to 2009 as a credit balance because it is a liability on 31 December 2008. Instead of rent owing it could be called rent accrued or just simply an 'accrual'.

The completed account can now be shown:

Rent

2008			£	2008			£
Mar	31	Cash	1,000	Dec	31	Profit and loss	4,000
Jul	2	Cash	1,000				
Oct	4	Cash	1,000				
Dec	**31**	**Accrued c/d**	1,000				
			4,000				4,000
				2009			
				Jan	1	Accrued b/d	1,000

The balance c/d has been described as 'accrued c/d', rather than as 'balance c/d'. This is to explain what the balance is for. It is for an **accrued expense**.

28.4 Prepaid expenses

Insurance for a business is at the rate of £840 a year, starting from 1 January 2008. The business has agreed to pay this at the rate of £210 every three months. However, payments were not made at the correct times. Details were:

Amount	Insurance due	Insurance paid
£210	31 March 2008	£210 28 February 2008
£210 £210	30 June 2008 30 September 2008	£420 31 August 2008
£210	31 December 2008	£420 18 November 2008

The insurance account in the ledger for the year ended 31 December 2008 is:

Insurance

2008			£	2008			£
Feb	28	Bank	210	Dec	31	Profit and loss	840
Aug	31	Bank	420				
Nov	18	Bank	420				

The last payment of £420 is not just for 2008. It can be split as £210 for the three months to 31 December 2008 and £210 for the three months ended 31 March 2009. For a period of 12 months the cost of insurance is £840 and this is, therefore, the figure needing to be transferred to the income statement.

If £840 is posted to the debit of profit and loss at 31 December 2008, the insurance account will still have a debit balance of £210. This is a benefit paid for but not used up at the end of the period. It is an asset and needs carrying forward as such to 2009, i.e. as a debit balance. Items like this are called **prepaid expenses**, 'prepayments' or 'amounts paid in advance'.

The account can now be completed:

Insurance

2008			£	2008			£
Feb	28	Bank	210	Dec	31	Profit and loss	840
Aug	31	Bank	420				
Nov	18	Bank	420		31	**Prepaid c/d**	210
			1,050				1,050
2009							
Jan	1	Prepaid b/d	210				

Prepayment happens when items other than purchases are bought for use in the business, but are not fully used up in the period.

For instance, packing materials are normally not entirely used up over the period in which they are bought. There is usually an inventory of packing materials in hand at the end of the period. This is a form of prepayment and needs carrying down to the period in which it will be used.

This can be seen in the following example:

Year ended 31 December 2008:
Packing materials bought in the year = £2,200.
Inventory of packing materials in hand as at 31 December 2008 = £400.

Looking at the example, it can be seen that in 2008 the packing materials used up will have been £2,200 – £400 = £1,800. (We are assuming that there was no inventory of packing materials at the start of 2008.) We have an inventory of £400 packing materials at 31 December 2008 to be carried forward to 2009. The £400 inventory of packing materials will be carried forward as an asset balance (i.e. a debit balance) to 2009:

Packing Materials

2008			£	2008			£
Dec	31	Bank	2,200	Dec	31	Profit and loss	1,800
					31	**Inventory c/d**	400
			2,200				2,200
2009							
Jan	1	Inventory b/d	400				

The inventory of packing materials is *not* added to the inventory of unsold goods in hand in the balance sheet, but is added to the other prepaid expenses in the balance sheet.

28.5 Revenue owing at the end of period

The revenue owing for sales is already shown in the books as the debit balances on customers' accounts, i.e. accounts receivable. There may be other kinds of revenue, all of which has not been received by the end of the period, e.g. rent receivable. An example now follows.

Example

Our warehouse is larger than we need. We rent part of it to another business for £1,800 per annum. Details for the year ended 31 December were as follows:

Amount	Rent due	Rent received
£450	31 March 2008	4 April 2008
£450	30 June 2008	6 July 2008
£450	30 September 2008	9 October 2008
£450	31 December 2008	7 January 2009

The Rent Receivable Account entries for 2008 will appear as:

Rent Receivable

				2008			£
				Apr	4	Bank	450
				Jul	6	Bank	450
				Oct	9	Bank	450

The rent received of £450 on 7 January 2009 will be entered in the accounting records in 2009.

Any rent paid by the business would be charged as a debit to the profit and loss account. Any rent received, being the opposite, is transferred to the credit of the profit and loss account, as it is a revenue.

The amount to be transferred for 2008 is that earned for the 12 months, i.e. £1,800. The rent received account is completed by carrying down the balance owing as a debit balance to 2009. The £450 owing is an asset on 31 December 2008.

The rent receivable account can now be completed:

Rent Receivable

2008			£	2008			£
Dec	31	Profit and loss	1,800	Apr	4	Bank	450
				Jul	6	Bank	450
				Oct	9	Bank	450
				Dec	31	Accrued c/d	450
			1,800				1,800
2009							
Jan	1	Accrued b/d	450				

28.6 Expenses and revenue account balances and the balance sheet

In all cases dealing with adjustments in the financial statements, there will still be a balance on each account after the preparation of the income statement. All such balances remaining should appear in the balance sheet. The only question left is where and how they should be shown.

The amounts owing for expenses could be called expenses payable, expenses owing or accrued expenses. However, we'll use the term 'accruals'. They represent *very* current liabilities – they will have to be paid in the very near future.

The items prepaid could be called prepaid expenses or payments in advance, but we'll call them 'prepayments'. Similarly to accruals, they represent *very* current assets as they should be received very soon.

Activity 28.2

From your knowledge of accounting, how should all the expense account debit and credit balances appear in the balance sheet – as one debit entry and one credit entry or as a separate entry for each item? Why?

Activity 28.3

(*a*) Where in the current asset sequence do you place prepayments?
(*b*) Where in the current liability sequence do you place accruals?
(*c*) Why?

Amounts owing for rents receivable or other revenue owing are a special case. If you look back at the T-account in Section 28.5, you'll see that they are described as 'accrued'. However, they are not accrued expenses, as they represent amounts receivable. They are, therefore, **accrued income**.

Activity 28.4

Where do you think these items of accrued income go in the balance sheet?

The part of the balance sheet in respect of the accounts so far seen in this chapter is therefore:

Balance Sheet as at 31 December 2008 (extract)

	£	£
Current assets		
Inventory	xxx	
Accounts receivable	450	
Prepayments (400 + 210)	610	
Bank	xxx	
Cash	xxx	
⋮		x,xxx
Current liabilities		
Trade accounts payable	xxx	
Accrued expenses	1,000	
		(x,xxx)

28.7 Expenses and revenue accounts covering more than one period

So far we've only looked at accounts where there were closing accruals or prepayments. In real life, you will also expect to see some opening accruals and prepayments, such as that shown in the final version of the Rent Receivable Account in Section 28.5. This is something that students are often asked to deal with in examinations as it tests their knowledge and ability to distinguish the treatment of these items at the beginning and end of a period. Typically, they may be asked to draw up an expense or revenue account for a full year which has amounts owing or prepaid at both the beginning and end of the year. We can now see how this is done.

Example A

The following details are available:

(A) On 31 December 2007, three months' rent amounting to a total of £3,000 was owing.
(B) The rent chargeable per year was £12,000.
(C) The following rent payments were made in the year 2008:
6 January £3,000; 4 April £3,000; 7 July £3,000; 18 October £3,000.
(D) The final three months' rent for 2008 is still owing.

Now we can look at the completed rent account. The letters (A) to (D) give reference to the details above.

Rent

2008				£	2008				£
Jan	6	Bank	(C)	3,000	Jan	1	Accrued b/d	(A)	3,000
Apr	4	Bank	(C)	3,000	Dec	31	Profit and loss	(B)	12,000
Jul	7	Bank	(C)	3,000					
Oct	18	Bank	(C)	3,000					
Dec	**31**	**Accrued c/d**	**(D)**	**3,000**					
				15,000					15,000
					2009				
					Jan	1	Accrued b/d		3,000

Example B

The following details are available:

(A) On 31 December 2007, packing materials in hand amounted to £1,850.
(B) During the year to 31 December 2008, we paid £27,480 for packing materials.
(C) There was no inventory of packing materials on 31 December 2008.
(D) On 31 December 2008, we still owed £2,750 for packing materials already received and used.

The packing materials account will appear as:

Packing Materials

2008				£	2008			£
Jan	1	Inventory b/d	(A)	1,850	**Dec**	**31**	**Profit and loss**	**32,080**
Dec	31	Bank	(B)	27,480				
	31	Owing c/d	(D)	2,750				
				32,080				32,080
					2009			
					Jan	1	Owing b/d	2,750

The figure of £32,080 is the difference on the account, and is transferred to the profit and loss account.

We can prove it is correct:

	£	£
Inventory at start of year		1,850
Add Bought and used:		
Paid for	27,480	
Still owed for	2,750	
Cost of packing materials bought and used in the year		30,230
Cost of packing materials used in the year		32,080

Example C

Where different expenses are put together in one account, it can get even more confusing. Let us look at where rent and rates are joined together. Here are the details for the year ended 31 December 2008:

(A) Rent is payable of £6,000 per annum.
(B) Rates of £4,000 per annum are payable by instalments.
(C) At 1 January 2008, rent of £1,000 had been prepaid in 2004.
(D) On 1 January 2008, rates of £400 were owed.
(E) During 2008, rent of £4,500 was paid.
(F) During 2008, rates of £5,000 were paid.
(G) On 31 December 2008, rent of £500 was owing.
(H) On 31 December 2008, rates of £600 had been prepaid.

A combined rent and rates account is to be drawn up for the year 2008 showing the transfer to profit and loss, and the balances to be carried down to 2009.

Rent and Rates

				£					£
2008					2008				
Jan	1	Rent prepaid b/d	(C)	1,000	Jan 1	Rates owing b/d		(D)	400
Dec	31	Bank: rent	(E)	4,500	Dec 31	Profit and loss		(A) + (B)	10,000
	31	Bank: rates	(F)	5,000					
	31	**Rent accrued c/d**	**(G)**	**500**	31	**Rates prepaid c/d**		**(H)**	**600**
				11,000					11,000
2009					2009				
Jan	1	Rates prepaid b/d	(H)	600	Jan 1	Rent accrued b/d		(G)	500

To enter the correct figures, you need to keep the two items separate in your own mind. This is easiest if you produce a schedule like the one we produced above for packing materials inventory. The one for rent would look like this:

	£	£
Rent due during the year		6,000
Less:		
Rent prepaid at start of year	1,000	
Rent paid during the year	4,500	
		(5,500)
Rent accrued at the end of the year		500

Activity 28.5 Prepare a similar schedule for rates.

28.8 Goods for own use

Traders will often take inventory out of their business for their own use without paying for them. There is nothing wrong about their doing this, but an entry should be made to record that this has happened. This is done by:

1 Debit drawings account, to show that the owner has taken the goods for private use.
2 Credit purchases account, to reduce cost of goods available for sale.

In the United Kingdom, an adjustment may be needed for Value Added Tax. If goods supplied to a trader's customers have VAT added to their price, then any such goods taken for own use will need such an adjustment. This is because the VAT regulations state that VAT should be added to the cost of goods taken. The double entry for the VAT content would be:

1 Debit drawings account.
2 Credit VAT account.

Adjustments may also be needed for other private items. For instance, if a trader's private insurance (e.g. insurance premiums for the contents of the trader's home) had been incorrectly charged to the business insurance account, then the correction would be:

1 Debit drawings account.
2 Credit insurance account.

28.9 Distinctions between various kinds of capital

The capital account represents the claim the owner has against the assets of the business at a point in time. That is, the amount of the business that belongs to the owner. The word **capital** is, however, often used in a specific sense. The main meanings are listed below.

Capital invested

This means the total monetary value of everything brought into the business by the owners from their outside interests. The amount of capital invested is not disturbed by the amount of profits made by the business or losses incurred.

Capital employed

Students at an early stage in their studies are often asked to define this term. In fact, for those who progress to a more advanced stage, it will be seen in *Business Accounting 2* that capital employed could have several meanings as the term is often used quite loosely. At its simplest, it is taken to mean the monetary value of the resources that are being used in the business. Thus, if all the assets were added together and the liabilities of the business deducted, the answer would be that the difference is the amount of money employed in the business. You will by now realise that this is the same as the closing balance of the capital account. It is also sometimes called 'net assets' or 'net worth'.

Working capital

This is a term for the excess of the current assets over the current liabilities of a business and is the same as '**net current assets**'.

28.10 Financial statements in the services sector

So far we have only looked at financial statements for businesses trading in some sort of goods. We drew up a trading account for some of these businesses because we wanted to identify the gross profit on goods sold.

There are, however, many businesses which do not deal in 'goods' but instead supply 'services'. This will include professional businesses such as accountants, solicitors, doctors, dentists, vets, management consultants, advertising agencies, estate agents and Internet service providers. Other examples include businesses specialising in computer repairs, window cleaning, gardening, hairdressing, chimney sweeping, piano tuning, and banks, football clubs, health clubs, gyms and leisure centres.

As they do not deal in 'goods' there is no point in their attempting to draw up trading accounts. While it is quite possible for, say, a dentist to treat depreciation on equipment, the costs of materials consumed, and the dental assistant's salary as deductions from income in order to arrive at a figure for gross profit, such information is likely to be of little benefit in terms of decision-making. They will, however, prepare an income statement (containing only the profit and loss items) and a balance sheet.

The first item in the income statement will be the revenue which might be called 'work done', 'fees', 'charges', 'accounts rendered', 'takings', etc., depending on the nature of the organisation. Any other items of income will be added, e.g. rent receivable, and then the expenses will be listed and deducted to arrive at a net profit or net loss.

An example of the income statement of a solicitor might be as per Exhibit 28.1:

Exhibit 28.1

J Plunkett, Solicitor
Income Statement for the year ending 31 December 2008

	£	£
Revenue:		
Fees charged		87,500
Insurance commissions		1,300
		88,800
Less Expenses:		
Wages and salaries	29,470	
Rent and rates	11,290	
Office expenses	3,140	
Motor expenses	2,115	
General expenses	1,975	
Depreciation	2,720	
		(50,710)
Net profit		38,090

Other than for the descriptions given in the revenue section, it doesn't look very different from the ones you've prepared for traders. In effect, if you can prepare an income statement for a trader, you can do so for a service organisation. You just need to remember that it will contain no trading account items and that the income will need to be appropriately described.

28.11 Extended trial balances

Instead of drafting a set of financial statements in the way shown so far in this textbook, you could prepare them using an 'extended trial balance', or 'worksheet'. It can be very useful when there are a large number of adjustments to be made. Professional accountants use them a lot for that very reason.

Extended trial balances are usually drawn up on specially preprinted types of stationery with suitable vertical columns printed across the page. You start with the trial balance extracted from the ledgers and then enter adjustments in the columns to the right. Columns for the trading account, the profit and loss account and the balance sheet then follow.

Exhibit 28.2 shows an example of the extended trial balance that could have been drawn up as an answer to Review Question 28.11. Once you have attempted the question yourself, compare your answer to the one shown in Exhibit 28.2. The gross profits and net profits are the same in each case; it is simply the method of displaying the information that is different.

Exhibit 28.2

JOHN BROWN WORKSHEET	Trial Balance		Adjustments		Trading Account		Profit and Loss Account		Balance Sheet	
See Review Question 28.11	1 Dr	2 Cr	3 Dr	4 Cr	5 Dr	6 Cr	7 Dr	8 Cr	9 Dr	10 Cr
Sales		400,000				400,000				
Purchases	350,000				350,000					
Sales returns	5,000				5,000					
Purchases returns		6,200				6,200				
Inventory 1.1.2007	100,000				100,000					
Allowance for doubtful debts		800		180 (*iv*)						980
Wages and salaries	30,000		5,000 (*ii*)				35,000			
Rates	6,000			500 (*iii*)			5,500			
Telephone	1,000		220 (*v*)				1,220			
Shop fittings	40,000			4,000 (*vi*)					36,000	
Van	30,000			6,000 (*vi*)					24,000	
Accounts receivable	9,800								9,800	
Accounts payable		7,000								7,000
Bad debts	200						200			
Capital		179,000								179,000
Bank	3,000								3,000	
Drawings	18,000								18,000	
	593,000	593,000								
Inventory 31.12.2007 – Asset			120,000 (*i*)						120,000	
Inventory 31.12.2007 – Cost of goods sold				120,000 (*i*)		120,000				
Accrued expenses				5,000 (*ii*)						5,000
				220 (*v*)						220
Allowance for doubtful debts			180 (*iv*)				180			
Prepaid expenses			500 (*iii*)						500	
Depreciation shop fittings			4,000 (*vi*)				4,000			
Depreciation van			6,000 (*vi*)				6,000			
			135,900	135,900						
Gross profit (balancing figure)					71,200			71,200		
					526,200	526,200				
Net profit (balancing figure)							19,100			19,100
							71,200	71,200	211,300	211,300

If you were an accountant, the financial statements you prepare and give to the owner and to anyone else who was an interested party, such as the Inspector of Taxes or the bank, would not be in the style of an extended trial balance. Instead, having completed the extended trial balance, the figures for the income statement and balance sheet would be transferred to the financial statements prepared using the conventional style of presentation.

To provide such special stationery in an examination is unusual, though it has been known to happen. In addition, for students to draw up an extended trial balance from scratch could be very time-consuming. Therefore, it is very rare for examiners to ask for one to be prepared from scratch. However, the examiner may ask you something about extended trial balances (or worksheets) or provide a partially completed one to work on, if this topic is included in the syllabus. You should note, however, that nowadays spreadsheets are often used to produce financial statements in this way. If your course includes use of spreadsheets to prepare financial statements, you are more likely to be asked to prepare an extended trial balance in your examination or as part of your assessed coursework.

28.12 Definition of accounting

In Chapter 1, you were given a definition of bookkeeping as being concerned with the work of entering information into accounting records and afterwards maintaining such records properly. This definition does not need to be amended.

However, **accounting** was not fully defined in Chapter 1. It would probably not have meant much to you at that stage in your studies. The following is a commonly used definition: '*The process of identifying, measuring, and communicating economic information to permit informed judgements and decisions by users of the information.*'

28.13 An alternative way to record accruals and prepayments

After learning in Chapter 27 that there was a second commonly used way to record provisions for depreciation, it will come as no surprise to you to learn that there is a second commonly used way to record accruals and prepayments. Just as with the two-stage method of recording depreciation provisions, the alternative way to record accruals and prepayments requires that you create additional ledger accounts. You open an accruals account and a prepayments account and post any balances on expense accounts at the period end to the appropriate one of the two new accounts.

The balance carried down in an expense account under the method you learnt earlier in this chapter is described as either 'accrued c/d' or 'prepaid c/d'. Under the alternative method, there would be no balance in the expense account after the double entry to the accruals account or prepayments account. Instead, there will be a balance on these two accounts which is then entered in the balance sheet in exactly the same way as you did under the other method.

At the start of the next period, you reverse the entry by crediting the prepayments account and debiting each of the expense accounts that had debit balances. Similarly, the accruals account is debited and the expense accounts that had credit balances are credited with the appropriate amounts.

For example, in the insurance account from Section 28.4, the entries in the insurance account were:

Insurance

2008			£	2008			£
Feb	28	Bank	210	Dec	31	Profit and loss	840
Aug	31	Bank	420				
Nov	18	Bank	420		31	Prepaid c/d	210
			1,050				1,050
2009							
Jan	1	Prepaid b/d	210				

The same information if a prepayments account were used would be entered:

Insurance

2008			£	2008			£
Feb	28	Bank	210	Dec	31	Profit and loss	840
Aug	31	Bank	420				
Nov	18	Bank	420		**31**	**Prepayments**	210
			1,050				1,050
2009							
Jan	**1**	**Prepayments**	**210**				

Prepayments

2008			£	2008			£
Dec	**31**	**Insurance**	**210**	**Dec**	**31**	**Balance c/d**	**210**
2009				2009			
Jan	**1**	**Balance b/d**	**210**	**Jan**	**1**	**Insurance**	**210**

In reality, it doesn't matter which of these two methods you use. Examiners will accept them both unless they specifically ask for one of them to be used. Your teacher or lecturer will know whether this is likely to happen. Follow the guidance of your teacher or lecturer and use whichever method he or she indicates is more appropriate.

In order not to confuse things by switching back and forth between the two methods, all examples of accruals and prepayments and all questions involving accruals and prepayments in the rest of this textbook will use the first method that has been covered in detail in this chapter. Should you be using the second method, as you will have seen above, it is very obvious what the equivalent entries would be when you look at examples prepared using the method adopted in this textbook.

Learning outcomes

You should now have learnt:

1. That adjustments are needed so that the expenses and income shown in the financial statements equal the expenses incurred in the period and the revenue that has arisen in the period.
2. That the balances relating to the adjustments will be shown on the balance sheet at the end of the period as current assets and current liabilities.
3. That goods taken for the owner's own use without anything being recorded in the books will necessitate a transfer from purchases to the drawings account, plus an adjustment for VAT if appropriate.

→

4 How to record appropriate entries in the accounts and financial statements at the end of a period for accrued expenses, prepaid expenses, accrued income, and drawings.

5 That private expenses should not be charged as an expense in the income statement, but should be charged to the drawings account.

6 That an extended trial balance is an alternative way of arriving at the figures to be included in the financial statements.

7 That there are two common ways to prepare accruals and prepayments.

Answers to activities

28.1 Don't worry if you didn't know what names to give the accounts other than the rent account. What is important is that you thought about it and that you knew which side the entries should be in the rent account.

(*a*) *Dr* Rent account £1,000   *Cr* Accruals account £1,000
(*b*) *Dr* Prepayments account £500   *Cr* Rent account £500

Note how the two entries in the rent account are on opposite sides. The £200 rent owing at the end of the year is an expense that has not yet been entered in the books, but it must be as it relates to the current year. The £100 paid in advance for next year is not an expense of the current year, so you need to reduce the amount you have currently in the rent account so that the correct expense will be included in the income statement. The accruals account is similar to a creditor's account, but it is used for expenses unpaid at the year end. Similarly, the prepayments account is like a debtor's account, but it is used to record amounts paid for expenses in advance of the accounting period in which the benefit (i.e. what was paid for) is received.

28.2 All the debit entries should be added together and shown as one entry called 'prepayments' within current assets. Similarly, all the credit entries should be added together and shown as one entry called 'accruals' under current liabilities. This is done so as to minimise the clutter in the balance sheet while providing enough information for anyone looking at the financial statement to be able to identify the figure for accruals and the figure for prepayments.

28.3 (*a*) Between accounts receivable and bank.
(*b*) Between accounts payable and bank overdraft.
(*c*) Their degree of liquidity.

28.4 They are usually added to accounts receivable. This is because these represent a regular source of income and, even though the income has nothing to do with the goods or services that form the main activity of the business, they are in every other sense another form of customer account. It makes sense, therefore, to include them in the accounts receivable balance shown in the balance sheet.

28.5

	£
Rates due during the year	4,000
Add: Rates accrued at the start of the year	400
	4,400
Less: Rates paid during the year	(5,000)
Rates prepaid at the end of the year	(600)

Review questions

28.1 The financial year of T Guiness ended on 31 December 2006. Show the ledger accounts for the following items including the balance transferred to the necessary part of the financial statements, also the balances carried down to 2007:

(*a*) Motor expenses: Paid in 2006 £819; Owing at 31 December 2006 £94.
(*b*) Insurance: Paid in 2006 £840; Prepaid as at 31 December 2006 £68.
(*c*) Stationery: Paid during 2006 £370; Owing as at 31 December 2005 £110; Owing as at 31 December 2006 £245.
(*d*) Business rates: Paid during 2006 £1,654; Prepaid as at 31 December 2005 £140; Prepaid as at 31 December 2006 £120.
(*e*) Guiness sublets part of the premises. He receives £1,400 during the year ended 31 December 2006. Harte, the tenant, owed Guiness £175 on 31 December 2005 and £185 on 31 December 2006.

28.2A W Hope's year ended on 30 June 2008. Write up the ledger accounts, showing the transfers to the financial statements and the balances carried down to the next year for the following:

(*a*) Stationery: Paid for the year to 30 June 2008 £240; Inventory of stationery at 30 June 2007 £60; at 30 June 2008 £95.
(*b*) General expenses: Paid for the year to 30 June 2008 £470; Owing at 30 June 2007 £32; Owing at 30 June 2008 £60.
(*c*) Rent and business rates (combined account): Paid in the year to 30 June 2008 £5,410; Rent owing at 30 June 2007 £220; Rent paid in advance at 30 June 2008 £370; Business rates owing 30 June 2007 £191; Business rates owing 30 June 2008 £393.
(*d*) Motor expenses: Paid in the year to 30 June 2008 £1,410; Owing as at 30 June 2007 £92; Owing as at 30 June 2008 £67.
(*e*) Hope earns commission from the sales of one item. Received for the year to 30 June 2008 £1,100; Owing at 30 June 2007 £50; Owing at 30 June 2008 £82.

28.3 On 1 January 2008 the following balances, among others, stood in the books of R Atkins, a sole trader:

(*a*) Business rates, £210 (Dr);
(*b*) Packing materials, £740 (Dr).

During the year ended 31 December 2008 the information related to these two accounts is as follows:

(*i*) Business rates of £1,920 were paid to cover the period 1 April 2008 to 31 March 2009;
(*ii*) £3,150 was paid for packing materials bought;
(*iii*) £242 was owing on 31 December 2008 in respect of packing materials bought on credit;
(*iv*) Old materials amounting to £63 were sold as scrap for cash;
(*v*) Closing inventory of packing materials was valued at £690.

You are required to write up the two accounts showing the appropriate amounts transferred to the income statement at 31 December 2008, the end of the financial year of the trader.

Note: Individual accounts are not opened for accounts payable for packing materials bought on credit.

28.4A On 1 January 2006 the following balances, among others, stood in the books of B Baxter:

(*a*) Lighting and heating, (Dr) £192.
(*b*) Insurance, (Dr) £1,410.

→

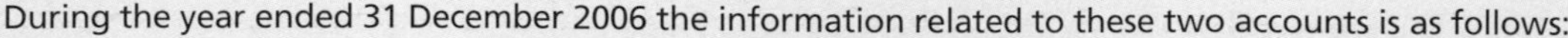

During the year ended 31 December 2006 the information related to these two accounts is as follows:

(*i*) Fire insurance, £1,164 covering the year ended 31 May 2007 was paid.
(*ii*) General insurance, £1,464 covering the year ended 31 July 2007 was paid.
(*iii*) An insurance rebate of £82 was received on 30 June 2006.
(*iv*) Electricity bills of £1,300 were paid.
(*v*) An electricity bill of £162 for December 2006 was unpaid as on 31 December 2006.
(*vi*) Oil bills of £810 were paid.
(*vii*) Inventory of oil as on 31 December 2006 was £205.

You are required to write up the accounts for lighting and heating, and for insurance, for the year to 31 December 2006. Carry forward necessary balances to 2007.

28.5 Three of the accounts in the ledger of Charlotte Williams indicated the following balances at 1 January 2010:

Insurance paid in advance £562;
Wages outstanding £306;
Rent receivable, received in advance £36.

During 2010 Charlotte:

Paid for insurance £1,019, by bank standing order;
Paid £15,000 wages, in cash;
Received £2,600 rent, by cheque, from the tenant.

At 31 December 2010, insurance prepaid was £345. On the same day rent receivable in arrears was £105 and wages accrued amounted to £419.

(*a*) Prepare the insurance, wages and rent receivable accounts for the year ended 31 December 2010, showing the year end transfers and the balances brought down.
(*b*) Prepare the income statement extract showing clearly the amounts transferred from each of the above accounts for the year ending 31 December 2010.
(*c*) Explain the effects on the financial statements of accounting for (*i*) expenses accrued and (*ii*) income received in advance at year end.
(*d*) What are the purposes of accounting for (*i*) expenses accrued and (*ii*) income received in advance at year end?

(*Edexcel Foundation, London Examinations: GCSE*)

28.6A The two accounts below were taken from the books of a retailer at the end of his financial year, 31 December 2007.

Insurance Account

Dr							Cr
2007			£	2007			£
Jan	1	Balance	80	Dec	31	Profit and loss	530
Jan–Dec		Bank	540		31	Balance c/d	90
			620				620
2008							
Jan	1	Balance b/d	90				

Rent Receivable Account

Dr							Cr
2007			£	2007			£
Dec	31	Profit and loss	885	Jan	1	Balance	60
	31	Balance c/d	75	Jan–Dec		Bank	900
			960				960
				2008			
				Jan	1	Balance b/d	75

Required:
Answers to the following questions.

1 What type of account is the insurance account?
2 What type of account is the rent receivable account?
3 In which subdivision of the ledger will these accounts be found?
4 Under which heading will the closing balance of the insurance account be found on the balance sheet?
5 Under which heading will the closing balance of the rent receivable account be found on the balance sheet?
6 In which subsidiary book (book of prime entry) will the entries transferring amounts to the profit and loss account be found?
7 Which document will be the source of information for the entry in the insurance account 'bank £540'?
8 Which document will be the source of information for the entry in the rent receivable account 'bank £900'?
9 What amount for insurance will appear in the trial balance dated 31 December 2007 prepared prior to the preparation of financial statements?
10 What amount for rent receivable will appear in the trial balance dated 31 December 2007 prepared prior to the preparation of financial statements?
11 If the adjustment in the insurance account for £90 on 31 December had been overlooked, would the net profit have been under- or overstated and by how much?
12 If the adjustment in the rent receivable account for £75 on 31 December had been overlooked, would the net profit have been under- or overstated and by how much?

(Southern Examining Group: GCSE)

28.7A The owner of a small business selling and repairing cars which you patronise has just received a copy of his accounts for the current year.

He is rather baffled by some of the items and as he regards you as a financial expert, he has asked you to explain certain points of difficulty to him. This you have readily agreed to do. His questions are as follows:

(*a*) 'What is meant by the term "assets"? My mechanical knowledge and skill is an asset to the business but it does not seem to have been included.'
(*b*) 'The house I live in cost £130,000 five years ago and is now worth £360,000, but that is not included either.'
(*c*) 'What is the difference between "non-current assets" and "current assets"?'
(*d*) 'Why do amounts for "vehicles" appear under both non-current asset and current asset headings?'
(*e*) 'Why is the "bank and cash" figure in the balance sheet different from the profit for the year shown in the income statement?'
(*f*) 'I see the income statement has been charged with depreciation on equipment etc. I bought all these things several years ago and paid for them in cash. Does this mean that I am being charged for them again?'

Required:
Answer each of his questions in terms which he will be able to understand.

(Association of Chartered Certified Accountants) →

28.8 The following trial balance was extracted from the books of R Giggs at the close of business on 28 February 2007.

	Dr	*Cr*
	£	£
Purchases and sales	92,800	157,165
Cash at bank	4,100	
Cash in hand	324	
Capital account 1 March 2006		11,400
Drawings	17,100	
Office furniture	2,900	
Rent	3,400	
Wages and salaries	31,400	
Discounts	820	160
Accounts receivable and accounts payable	12,316	5,245
Inventory 1 March 2006	4,120	
Allowance for doubtful debts 1 March 2006		405
Delivery van	3,750	
Van running costs	615	
Bad debts written off	730	
	174,375	174,375

Notes:
(*a*) Inventory 28 February 2007 £2,400.
(*b*) Wages and salaries accrued at 28 February 2007 £340.
(*c*) Rent prepaid at 28 February 2007 £230.
(*d*) Van running costs owing at 28 February 2007 £72.
(*e*) Increase the allowance for doubtful debts by £91.
(*f*) Provide for depreciation as follows: Office furniture £380; Delivery van £1,250.

Required:
Draw up the income statement for the year ending 28 February 2007 together with a balance sheet as at 28 February 2007.

28.9 The trial balance for a small business at 31 August 2008 is as follows:

	£	£
Inventory 1 September 2007	8,200	
Purchases and sales	26,000	40,900
Rent	4,400	
Business rates	1,600	
Sundry expenses	340	
Motor vehicle at cost	9,000	
Accounts receivable and accounts payable	1,160	2,100
Bank	1,500	
Provision for depreciation on motor vehicle		1,200
Capital at 1 September 2007		19,700
Drawings	11,700	
	63,900	63,900

At 31 August 2008 there was:

- Inventory valued at cost prices £9,100
- Accrued rent of £400
- Prepaid business rates of £300
- The motor vehicle is to be depreciated at 20% of cost

Required:

1 The adjustments to the ledger accounts for rent and business rates for the year to 31 August 2008.

2 An income statement for the year ending 31 August 2008, together with a balance sheet as at that date.

28.10A J Wright, a sole trader, extracted the following trial balance from his books at the close of business on 31 March 2009:

	Dr £	*Cr* £
Purchases and sales	61,420	127,245
Inventory 1 April 2008	7,940	
Capital 1 April 2008		25,200
Bank overdraft		2,490
Cash	140	
Discounts	2,480	62
Returns inwards	3,486	
Returns outwards		1,356
Carriage outwards	3,210	
Rent and insurance	8,870	
Allowance for doubtful debts		630
Fixtures and fittings	1,900	
Van	5,600	
Accounts receivable and accounts payable	12,418	11,400
Drawings	21,400	
Wages and salaries	39,200	
General office expenses	319	
	168,383	168,383

Notes:

(*a*) Inventory 31 March 2009 £6,805.
(*b*) Wages and salaries accrued at 31 March 2009 £3,500; Office expenses owing £16.
(*c*) Rent prepaid 31 March 2009 £600.
(*d*) Increase the allowance for doubtful debts by £110 to £740.
(*e*) Provide for depreciation as follows: Fixtures and fittings £190; Van £1,400.

Required:

Prepare the income statement for the year ending 31 March 2009 together with a balance sheet as at that date.

28.11 This question also relates to extended trial balances (see Exhibit 28.2).
From the following trial balance of John Brown, store owner, prepare an income statement for the year ending 31 December 2007, and a balance sheet as at that date, taking into consideration the adjustments shown below:

→

→

Trial Balance as at 31 December 2007

	Dr £	Cr £
Sales		400,000
Purchases	350,000	
Sales returns	5,000	
Purchases returns		6,200
Opening inventory at 1 January 2007	100,000	
Allowance for doubtful debts		800
Wages and salaries	30,000	
Rates	6,000	
Telephone	1,000	
Shop fittings at cost	40,000	
Van at cost	30,000	
Accounts receivable and accounts payable	9,800	7,000
Bad debts	200	
Capital		179,000
Bank balance	3,000	
Drawings	18,000	
	593,000	593,000

(*i*) Closing inventory at 31 December 2007 £120,000.
(*ii*) Accrued wages £5,000.
(*iii*) Rates prepaid £500.
(*iv*) The allowance for doubtful debts to be increased to 10 per cent of accounts receivable.
(*v*) Telephone account outstanding £220.
(*vi*) Depreciate shop fittings at 10 per cent per annum, and van at 20 per cent per annum, on cost.

28.12A The following trial balance has been extracted from the ledger of Mr Yousef, a sole trader.

Trial Balance as at 31 May 2006

	Dr £	Cr £
Sales		138,078
Purchases	82,350	
Carriage	5,144	
Drawings	7,800	
Rent, rates and insurance	6,622	
Postage and stationery	3,001	
Advertising	1,330	
Salaries and wages	26,420	
Bad debts	877	
Allowance for doubtful debts		130
Accounts receivable	12,120	
Accounts payable		6,471
Cash in hand	177	
Cash at bank	1,002	
Inventory as at 1 June 2005	11,927	
Equipment		
at cost	58,000	
accumulated depreciation		19,000
Capital		53,091
	216,770	216,770

The following additional information as at 31 May 2006 is available:

(*a*) Rent is accrued by £210.
(*b*) Rates have been prepaid by £880.
(*c*) £2,211 of carriage represents carriage inwards on purchases.
(*d*) Equipment is to be depreciated at 15% per annum using the straight line method.
(*e*) The allowance for doubtful debts to be increased by £40.
(*f*) Inventory at the close of business has been valued at £13,551.

Required:
Prepare an income statement for the year ending 31 May 2006 and a balance sheet as at that date.

(*Association of Accounting Technicians*)

28.13 Mr Chai has been trading for some years as a wine merchant. The following list of balances has been extracted from his ledger as at 30 April 2007, the end of his most recent financial year.

	£
Capital	83,887
Sales	259,870
Trade accounts payable	19,840
Returns out	13,407
Allowance for doubtful debts	512
Discounts allowed	2,306
Discounts received	1,750
Purchases	135,680
Returns inwards	5,624
Carriage outwards	4,562
Drawings	18,440
Carriage inwards	11,830
Rent, rates and insurance	25,973
Heating and lighting	11,010
Postage, stationery and telephone	2,410
Advertising	5,980
Salaries and wages	38,521
Bad debts	2,008
Cash in hand	534
Cash at bank	4,440
Inventory as at 1 May 2006	15,654
Trade accounts receivable	24,500
Fixtures and fittings – at cost	120,740
Provision for depreciation on fixtures and fittings – as at 30 April 2007	63,020
Depreciation	12,074

The following additional information as at 30 April 2007 is available:

(*a*) Inventory at the close of business was valued at £17,750.
(*b*) Insurances have been prepaid by £1,120.
(*c*) Heating and lighting is accrued by £1,360.
(*d*) Rates have been prepaid by £5,435.
(*e*) The allowance for doubtful debts is to be adjusted so that it is 3% of trade accounts receivable.

Required:
Prepare Mr Chai's income statement for the year ending 30 April 2007 and a balance sheet as at that date.

(*Association of Accounting Technicians*)

You can find a range of additional self-test questions, as well as material to help you with your studies, on the website that accompanies this book at www.pearsoned.co.uk/wood.

chapter

29 The valuation of inventory

Learning objectives

After you have studied this chapter, you should be able to:

- calculate the value of inventory using three different methods
- explain why using the most appropriate method to value inventory is important
- explain what effect changing prices has on inventory valuation under each of three different methods
- explain why net realisable value is sometimes used instead of cost for inventory valuation
- adjust inventory valuations, where necessary, by a reduction to net realisable value
- explain how subjective factors influence the choice of inventory valuation method
- explain why goods purchased on 'sale or return' are not included in the buyer's inventory

Introduction

In this chapter, you will learn how to calculate the monetary value of inventory using a variety of methods. You will learn why choosing the most appropriate method of inventory valuation is important; and that a range of subjective factors can influence the choice of method, including the need to reflect how the inventory is physically used. Finally, you'll learn how to treat goods sold on 'sale or return' and about the need to adjust inventory levels identified in a stocktake (i.e. physical count of the inventory) to the level they would have been at the balance sheet date.

29.1 Different valuations of inventory

Inventory is the name given to the goods for resale, work-in-progress and raw materials that are held at a point in time. The rules to follow in valuing inventory are contained in IAS 2 (*Inventories*). This is dealt with in detail in *Business Accounting* 2.

Most people assume that when a value is placed upon inventory, it is the only figure possible. This is not true.

Assume that a business has just completed its first financial year and is about to value inventory at cost price. It has dealt in only one item. A record of the transactions is now shown in Exhibit 29.1:

Exhibit 29.1

Bought			Sold		
2008		£	2008		£
January	10 at £30 each	300	May	8 for £50 each	400
April	10 at £34 each	340	November	24 for £60 each	1,440
October	20 at £40 each	800			
	40	1,440		32	1,840

A quick check by the storeman showed that there were still eight units in inventory at 31 December, which confirms what the records show above.

Activity 29.1 What valuation do you think should be placed on the eight units of inventory? Why?

The total figure of purchases is £1,440 and sales revenue during the year was £1,840. The trading account for the first year of trading can now be completed using the closing inventory in the calculations.

Let's now look at the three most commonly used methods of valuing inventory.

29.2 First in, first out method (FIFO)

This is usually referred to as **FIFO**, from the first letters of each word. This method says that the first items to be received are the first to be issued. Using the figures in Exhibit 29.1 we can now calculate the cost of closing inventory on a FIFO basis as follows:

Date	Received	Issued	Inventory after each transaction		
2008				£	£
January	10 at £30 each		10 at £30 each		300
April	10 at £34 each		10 at £30 each 10 at £34 each	300 340	640
May		8 at £30 each	2 at £30 each 10 at £34 each	60 340	400
October	20 at £40 each		2 at £30 each 10 at £34 each 20 at £40 each	60 340 800	1,200
November		2 at £30 each 10 at £34 each 12 at £40 each 24	8 at £40 each		320

Thus, the closing inventory at 31 December 2008 at cost is valued under FIFO at £320.

Activity 29.2 Can you see another, simpler way of arriving at the same valuation under FIFO?

29.3 Last in, first out method (LIFO)

This is usually referred to as **LIFO**. As each issue of items is made they are assumed to be from the last batch received before that date. Where there is not enough left of the last batch, then the balance needed is assumed to come from the previous batch still unsold.

From the information shown in Exhibit 29.1 the calculation can now be shown.

Date	Received	Issued	Inventory after each transaction		
				£	£
2008 January	10 at £30 each		10 at £30 each		300
April	10 at £34 each		10 at £30 each 10 at £34 each	300 340	640
May		8 at £34 each	10 at £30 each 2 at £34 each	300 68	368
October	20 at £40 each		10 at £30 each 2 at £34 each 20 at £40 each	300 68 800	1,168
November		20 at £40 each 2 at £34 each 2 at £30 each 24	8 at £30 each		240

Thus, the closing inventory at 31 December 2008 at cost is valued under LIFO at £240.

Can you see another, simpler way of arriving at the same valuation under LIFO?

29.4 Average cost method (AVCO)

Using the **AVCO** method, with each receipt of goods the average cost for each item is recalculated. Further issues of goods are then at that figure, until another receipt of goods means that another recalculation is needed. From the information in Exhibit 29.1 the calculation can be shown:

Date	Received	Issued	Average cost per unit of inventory held	Number of units in inventory	Total value of inventory
2008			£		£
January	10 at £30		30	10	300
April	10 at £34		32*	20	640
May		8 at £32	32	12	384
October	20 at £40		37**	32	1,184
November		24 at £37	37	8	296

The closing inventory at 31 December 2008 is therefore valued at £296.

* In April, this is calculated as follows: inventory 10 × £30 = £300 + inventory received (10 × £34) = £340 = total £640. You then divide the 20 units in inventory into the total cost of that inventory, i.e. £640 ÷ 20 = £32.

** In October, this is calculated as follows: inventory 12 × £32 = £384 + inventory received (20 × £40) = £800 = £1,184. There are 32 units in inventory, so the average is £1,184 ÷ 32 = £37.

Note, using this approach you recalculate the average after every receipt of a batch of new inventory and then use it as the cost of the next batch sold.

Activity 29.4

If two units had been sold in December, at what cost would they have been sold?

29.5 Inventory valuation and the calculation of profits

Using the figures from Exhibit 29.1 with inventory valuations shown by the three methods of FIFO, LIFO and AVCO, the trading account entries under each method would be:

Trading Account for the year ending 31 December 2008

	FIFO	*LIFO*	*AVCO*		*FIFO*	*LIFO*	*AVCO*
	£	£	£		£	£	£
Purchases	1,440	1,440	1,440	Sales	1,840	1,840	1,840
less Closing inventory	(320)	(240)	(296)				
Cost of goods sold	1,120	1,200	1,144				
Gross profit	720	640	696				
	1,840	1,840	1,840		1,840	1,840	1,840

Activity 29.5

Which method has produced (*a*) the highest, (*b*) the middle and (*c*) the lowest value for closing inventory? Why do you think this has occurred?

As you can see, different methods of inventory valuation result in different profits. It is, therefore, important that the method chosen is the one that is closest in its assumptions to the nature of the business.

29.6 Reduction to net realisable value

Having selected the most appropriate method to apply when determining the cost of closing inventory, you next need to consider whether that value is realistic – that is, whether it is what the inventory is *actually* worth at the end of the period. This is an example of application of the prudence concept that you learnt about in Chapter 10. Following the prudence concept, inventory should never be undervalued or overvalued.

Activity 29.6

(*a*) What happens to gross profit if closing inventory is undervalued? Why?
(*b*) What happens to gross profit if closing inventory is overvalued? Why?

To check that inventory is not overvalued, accountants calculate its **net realisable value**. This is done according to the formula:

$$\frac{\text{Saleable value}}{\text{(i.e. what it can be sold for)}} - \frac{\text{Expenses needed before completion of sale}}{\text{(such as costs of delivery to the seller's shops)}} = \text{Net realisable value.}$$

If the net realisable value of inventory is less than the cost of the inventory, then the figure to be used in the financial statements is net realisable value *not* cost.

A somewhat exaggerated example will illustrate why this is done. Assume that an art dealer has bought only two paintings during the financial year ended 31 December 2008. She starts off the year without any inventory, and then buys a genuine masterpiece for £6,000 and sells it later in the year for £11,500. The other is a fake, but she does not realise this when she buys it for £5,100. During the year she discovers that she made a terrible mistake and that its net realisable value is only £100. The fake remains unsold at the end of the year. The trading account part of the income statement, shown in Exhibit 29.2, would appear as (*a*) if inventory is valued at cost, and as (*b*) if inventory is valued at net realisable value.

Exhibit 29.2

Trading Account section of the Income Statement for the year ending 31 December 2008

		(*a*) £		(*b*) £
Sales		11,500		11,500
Purchases	11,100		11,100	
Less: Closing inventory	(5,100)		(100)	
		(6,000)		(11,000)
Gross profit		5,500		500

Method (*a*) ignores the fact that the dealer had a bad trading year owing to her mistake. If this method was used, then the loss on the fake would reveal itself in the following year's trading account. Method (*b*) recognises that the loss really occurred at the date of purchase rather than at the date of sale. Following the concept of prudence, accounting practice is to use method (*b*).

29.7 Inventory groups and valuation

If there is only one sort of item in stock, calculating the lower of cost or net realisable value is easy. If we have several or many types of item in stock, we can use one of two ways of making the calculation – by category and by item.

Exhibit 29.3

Inventory at 31 December 2008

Item	*Different categories*	*Cost*	*Net realisable value*
		£	£
1	A	100	80
2	A	120	150
3	A	300	400
4	B	180	170
5	B	150	130
6	B	260	210
7	C	410	540
8	C	360	410
9	C	420	310
		2,300	2,400

In Exhibit 29.3, Items 1, 2 and 3 are televisions; 4, 5 and 6 are DVD recorders; and 7, 8 and 9 are games consoles. From the information given in the exhibit, we will calculate the value of the inventory using both these approaches.

(1) The category method

The same sorts of items are put together in categories. Thus, televisions are in Category A, DVDs are in Category B, and Category C is games consoles.

A calculation showing a comparison of cost valuation and net realisable value for each category is now shown.

Category	*Cost*	*Net realisable value*
A	£100 + £120 + £300 = £520	£80 + £150 + £400 = £630
B	£180 + £150 + £260 = £590	£170 + £130 + £210 = £510
C	£410 + £360 + £420 = £1,190	£540 + £410 + £310 = £1,260

The lower of cost and net realisable value is, therefore:

		£
Category A: lower of £520 or £630	=	520
Category B: lower of £590 or £510	=	510
Category C: lower of £1,190 or £1,260	=	1,190
Inventory is valued for financial statements at		2,220

(2) The item method

By this method, the lower of cost or net realisable value for each item is compared and the lowest figure taken. From Exhibit 29.3 this gives us the following valuation:

Item	*Valuation*
	£
1	80
2	120
3	300
4	170
5	130
6	210
7	410
8	360
9	310
	£2,090

Of these two methods, it is Method 2, the item method, that should be used. It provides a more realistic overall value for the inventory.

29.8 Some other inventory valuation bases in use

Retail businesses often estimate the cost of inventory by calculating it in the first place at selling price, and then deducting the normal margin of gross profit on such inventory. Adjustment is made for items which are to be sold at other than normal selling prices.

Where standard costing is in use, the figure of **standard cost** is frequently used. You'll learn about standard costing in *Business Accounting 2*. Standard cost is, effectively, what you would expect something to cost. When standard costing is in use, a standard cost will have been determined for purchases and it is that standard cost that would be used to value closing inventory.

'Base inventory' (often referred to as 'base stock') is a method used in industries where a minimum level of inventory is always maintained. Power station fuel supplies, for example, may fall within this classification. The base inventory is assumed to never deteriorate or be replaced and is valued at its original cost. Any other inventory is valued using a 'normal' method, such as FIFO, LIFO or AVCO.

29.9 Periodic inventory valuation

Some businesses do not keep detailed inventory records like those shown in Exhibit 29.1. Instead, they wait until the end of a period before calculating the value of their closing inventory. In this case, AVCO is based upon the total cost of inventory available for sale in the period divided by the number of units of inventory available for sale in the period. You then multiply the closing inventory by the overall average cost of the inventory to get the value of that inventory.

If you did this for the data in Exhibit 29.1 the closing inventory value at cost would be (£1,440 ÷ 40 =) £36 × 8 = £288 (rather than £296, as calculated in Section 29.4). This method is also known as the 'weighted average cost method'.

If you used FIFO or LIFO in these circumstances, FIFO gives the same answer as under the method presented earlier. LIFO, on the other hand, would become the opposite of FIFO, with all closing inventory assumed to have come from the earliest batches of purchases.

Activity 29.7

If you have no detailed inventory records, how could you use AVCO, FIFO or LIFO?

Unless **an examiner asks you to calculate them using a periodic inventory valuation basis, you should assume that you are to calculate AVCO, FIFO and LIFO in the way they were presented earlier in this chapter (i.e. on a perpetual valuation basis).**

29.10 Factors affecting the inventory valuation decision

The overriding consideration applicable in all circumstances when valuing inventory is the need to give a 'true and fair view' of the state of affairs of the undertaking as at the balance sheet date and of the trend of the business's trading results. There is, however, no precise definition of what constitutes a 'true and fair view' and it rests on the judgement of the persons concerned. Unfortunately, the judgement of any two persons will not always be the same in the differing circumstances of various businesses.

In fact, the only certain thing about inventory valuation is that the concept of consistency (which you learnt about in Chapter 10) should be applied, i.e. once adopted, the same basis should be used in the financial statements until some good reason occurs to change it. A reference should then be made in the notes that accompany the financial statements as to the effect of the change on the reported profits, if the amount involved is material.

Let's look briefly at some of the factors which cause a particular basis to be chosen. The list is intended to be indicative rather than comprehensive, and is merely intended as a first brief look at matters which will have to be studied in depth by those intending to make a career in accountancy.

1 **Ignorance.** The people involved may not appreciate the fact that there is more than one possible way of valuing inventory.
2 **Convenience.** The basis chosen may not be the best for the purposes of profit calculation but it may be the easiest to calculate. It must always be borne in mind that the benefits which flow from possessing information should be greater than the costs of obtaining it. The only

difficulty with this is actually establishing when the benefits do exceed the cost but, in some circumstances, the decision not to adopt a given basis will be obvious.

3 **Custom.** It may be the particular method used in a certain trade or industry.
4 **Taxation.** The whole idea may be to defer the payment of tax for as long as possible. Because the inventory figures affect the calculation of profits on which the tax is based the lowest possible inventory figures may be taken to show the lowest profits up to the balance sheet date. (But doing this will result in a higher profit in the following period when the inventory is sold!)
5 **The capacity to borrow money or to sell the business at the highest possible price.** The higher the inventory value, the higher will be the profits calculated and, therefore, at first sight the business looks more attractive to a buyer or lender. Either of these considerations may be more important to the owners than anything else. It may be thought that those in business are not so gullible, but all business people are not necessarily well acquainted with accounting customs. In fact, many small businesses are bought, or money is lent to them, without the expert advice of someone well versed in accounting.
6 **Remuneration purposes.** Where someone managing a business is paid in whole or in part by reference to the profits earned, then one basis may suit them better than others. They may therefore strive to have that basis used to suit their own ends. The owner, however, may try to follow another course to minimise the remuneration that he/she will have to pay out.
7 **Lack of information.** If proper inventory records have not been kept, then such bases as the average cost method or the LIFO method may not be calculable using the approaches you learnt at the start of this chapter. Of course, a lack of proper inventory records makes it very difficult to detect theft or losses of inventory. If for no other reason than to enable these factors to be controlled, proper inventory records should be kept by all trading businesses. As a result, this barrier to adopting AVCO and LIFO should not arise very often.
8 **Advice of the auditors.** Auditors are accountants who review the accounting records and the financial statements in order to report whether or not the financial statements present a true and fair view of the financial performance and financial position of a business. Many businesses use a particular basis because the auditors advised its use in the first instance. A different auditor may well advise that a different basis be used.

29.11 The conflict of aims

The list given in the previous section of some of the factors which affect decisions concerning the valuation of inventory is certainly not exhaustive, but it does illustrate the fact that valuation is usually a compromise. There is not usually only one figure which is true and fair; there may be a variety of possibilities. The desire to borrow money and, in so doing, to paint a good picture by being reasonably optimistic in valuing inventory will be tempered by the fact that this may increase the tax bill. Inventory valuation is, therefore, a compromise between the various ends which it serves.

29.12 Work-in-progress

The valuation of work-in-progress is subject to all the various criteria and methods used in valuing inventory of finished goods. Probably the cost element is more strongly pronounced than in inventory valuation, as it is very often impossible or irrelevant to say what net realisable value or replacement price would be applicable to partly finished goods. Businesses operating in industries such as those which have contracts covering several years have evolved their own methods.

The valuation of long-term contract work-in-progress is regulated by IAS 11 (*Construction contracts*) and is dealt with in *Business Accounting 2*.

29.13 Goods on sale or return

Goods received on sale or return

Sometimes goods may be received from a supplier on a **sale or return** basis. This is, for example, typically what happens when newsagents purchase newspapers. What this means is that the goods do not have to be paid for if they are not sold. If they cannot be sold, they are returned to the supplier. This means that until the goods are sold they belong to the seller, *not* the buyer.

The effect of an arrangement of this type is that there isn't a liability to pay the seller until the goods have been sold on to a customer of the buyer. If there is no liability, the buyer cannot recognise the existence of the goods held on this basis when the buyer's financial statements are being prepared at the end of the accounting period. As a result, if goods on sale or return are held by the buyer at the stocktaking date (i.e. the date when inventory is counted), they should not be included in the buyer's inventory valuation, nor in the figure for purchases.

Goods sent to customers on sale or return

If a seller sends goods to a customer on a sale or return basis, the goods will continue to belong to the seller until they are sold on by the buyer. At the end of the supplier's accounting period, any goods held on this basis by its customers should be included in the seller's inventory valuation, not in the figure for sales.

29.14 Stocktaking and the balance sheet date

All but the very smallest of trading businesses need to physically check that the inventory their records tell them are held in stock actually exist. The process of doing so is called **stocktaking**. Students often think that all the counting and valuing of inventory is done on the last day of the accounting period. This might be true in a small business, but it is often impossible in larger businesses. There may be too many items of inventory to do it so quickly.

This means that stocktaking may take place over a period of days. To convert the physical stocktake inventory levels to their actual levels at the balance sheet date, adjustments must be made to those stocktake levels of inventory. Exhibit 29.4 gives an example of such adjustments.

Exhibit 29.4 Adjustments to stocktake inventory

Lee Ltd has a financial year which ends on 31 December 2007. The stocktaking is not done until 8 January 2008. When the items in the inventory on that date are priced out at cost, it is found that the inventory value amounts to £28,850. The following information is available about transactions between 31 December 2007 and 8 January 2008:

1 Purchases since 31 December 2007 amounted to £2,370 at cost.
2 Returns inwards since 31 December 2007 were £350 at selling price.
3 Sales since 31 December 2007 amounted to £3,800 at selling price.
4 The selling price is always cost price + 25 per cent.

Lee Ltd
Computation of inventory on 31 December 2007

			£
Inventory (at cost)			28,850
Add Items now sold which were in inventory on 31 December 2007 (at cost)			
		£	
Sales		3,800	
Less Profit content (20 per cent of selling price)(Note)		(760)	
			3,040
			31,890
Less Items which were not in inventory on 31 December 2007 (at cost)			
	£		
Returns inwards	350		
Less Profit content (20 per cent of selling price)(Note)	(70)		
		280	
Purchases (at cost)		2,370	
			(2,650)
Inventory in hand as on 31 December 2007			29,240

Note: Inventory is valued at cost (or net realisable value), and not at selling price. As this calculation has a sales figure in it which includes profit, we must deduct the profit part to get to the cost price. This is true also for returns inwards.

The professional accounting bodies encourage the auditors of companies to be present as observers at stocktaking in order to verify that procedures were correctly followed.

29.15 Inventory levels

One of the most common mistakes found in the running of a business is that too high a level of inventory is maintained.

A considerable number of businesses that have problems with a shortage of funds will find that they can help matters by having a look at the amount of inventory they hold. It would be a very rare business indeed which, if it had not investigated the matter previously, could not manage to let parts of its inventory run down. This would stop the investment of funds in items – the unneeded inventory – that are not required.

Learning outcomes

You should now have learnt:

1. That methods of valuing inventory, such as FIFO, LIFO and AVCO, are only that – methods of *valuing* inventory. It does not mean that goods are actually sold on a FIFO or LIFO basis.
2. That because different methods of valuing inventory result in different closing inventory valuations, the amount of profit reported for a particular accounting period is affected by the method of inventory valuation adopted.
3. That using net realisable when this is lower than cost, so that profits are not overstated, is an example of the application of the prudence concept in accounting.

→

4 That many subjective factors may affect the choice of inventory valuation method adopted.
5 That without inventory records of quantities of items, it would be very difficult to track down theft or losses or to detect wastage of goods.
6 That without proper inventory records, it is unlikely that AVCO and LIFO can be applied in the way described at the start of this chapter.
7 That goods sold on sale or return should be included in the inventory of the seller until the buyer has sold them.
8 That stocktaking is usually done over a period of time around the end of the accounting period.
9 That the inventory levels identified at a stocktake need to be adjusted to the level they would have been at had the stocktake taken place on the balance sheet date.

Answers to activities

29.1 This is not as easy a question to answer as it first appears, especially if you have never studied this topic before. Firstly, applying the historic cost convention you learnt about in Chapter 10, we should value the inventory at the cost of having it available for sale. That is, it should be valued at cost. If all purchases during the year cost the same per unit, arriving at the value to place on inventory would be trivially easy. For example, if all of the units cost £30 each, the closing value would be 8 × £30 = £240.

However, the goods in this example have been purchased at different prices. To cope with this, we look at it from the perspective of which of the goods purchased have been sold. Knowing which of them has been sold allows us to know which ones remain unsold, which will make valuing the inventory very straightforward. In this case, purchases were made at £30, £34 and £40. If all the £34 and £40 purchases have been sold, we know to use £30 as the unit cost of the stock.

Unfortunately, many businesses do not know whether they have sold all the older units before they sell the newer units. For instance, a business selling spanners may not know if the older spanners had been sold before the newer ones were sold. A petrol station doesn't know whether all the fuel it has in stock was from one delivery or whether it is a mixture of all the deliveries received from the supplier. Accounting deals with this by selecting the method of valuation that is most likely to fairly represent the cost of the goods sold and, hence, the value of the remaining stock.

To answer the question, you don't have enough information to decide what value to place on the eight units of inventory, but it should be based upon the best estimate you can make of the cost of those eight units.

29.2 As at least eight units were received in the last batch purchased, you can simply take the unit cost of that batch and multiply it by the units in inventory. If you are asked to show your workings for calculation of closing inventory under FIFO, this is a perfectly acceptable approach to adopt.

29.3 It's not so simple under LIFO. If you receive three batches of purchases of ten, four and six units respectively and you have ten left in inventory, there is no guarantee that they will all be from the first batch. You may have sold all ten of the first batch before the second batch was received. Alternatively, you may have sold three before the second batch of four was delivered and then sold six before the last batch of six was received and then sold one before the year end. You do have ten in inventory, but five are from the first batch received and five from the last one. There is no shortcut available for ascertaining in which batch the remaining inventory was received.

29.4 There have been no further deliveries of new inventory received so the average value of inventory is still £37.

29.5 The AVCO inventory valuation is between the values of FIFO and LIFO. FIFO has the highest value because the cost of purchases has been rising. Had they been falling, it would have been LIFO that had the greatest closing inventory value. AVCO will lie between the other two whichever way prices are moving.

29.6 (*a*) Gross profit will be understated if closing inventory is undervalued because the lower the value of closing inventory, the higher the cost of goods sold.
(*b*) Gross profit will be overstated if closing inventory is overvalued because the higher the value of closing inventory, the lower the cost of goods sold.

29.7 It may be impossible. However, whatever the quality of your inventory records, all businesses must retain evidence of their transactions. As a result, you could have a record of what was purchased, when, from whom and for how much, but you may well have no record at all of what was sold, when, to whom or for how much – if all sales are for cash, your only record may be the till receipt for each transaction, and that frequently shows no more than the date and value of the sale.

Review questions

29.1 From the following figures calculate the closing inventory-in-trade that would be shown using (*i*) FIFO, (*ii*) LIFO, (*iii*) AVCO methods.

	Bought		*Sold*
March	100 at £16 each	December	130 for £24 each
September	220 at £19 each		

29.2 For Question 29.1 draw up the trading account part of the income statement for the year showing the gross profits that would have been reported using (*i*) FIFO, (*ii*) LIFO, (*iii*) AVCO methods.

29.3A From the following figures calculate the closing inventory-in-trade that would be shown using (*i*) FIFO, (*ii*) LIFO, (*iii*) AVCO methods on a perpetual inventory basis.

	Bought		*Sold*
January	120 at £16 each	June	125 at £22 each
April	80 at £18 each	November	210 at £25 each
October	150 at £19 each		

29.4A Draw up trading account parts of the income statement using each of the three methods from the details in Question 29.3A.

29.5 The sixth formers at the Broadway School run a tuck shop business. They began trading on 1 December 2009 and sell two types of chocolate bar, 'Break' and 'Brunch'.

Their starting capital was a £200 loan from the School Fund.
Transactions are for cash only.
Each Break costs the sixth form 16p and each Brunch costs 12p.
25% is added to the cost to determine the selling price.
Transactions during December are summarised as follows:

December 6	Bought 5 boxes, each containing 48 bars, of Break; and 3 boxes, each containing 36 bars of Brunch.
December 20	The month's sales amounted to 200 Breaks and 90 Brunches.

(*a*) Record the above transactions in the cash, purchases and sales accounts. All calculations must be shown.
(*b*) On 20 December (the final day of term) a physical stocktaking showed 34 Break and 15 Brunch in inventory. Using these figures calculate the value of the closing inventory, and enter the amount in the inventory account.

→

(c) Prepare a trading account for the tuck shop, calculating the gross profit/loss for the month of December 2009.[Authors' Note]

(d) Calculate the number of each item that should have been in inventory. Explain why this information should be a cause for concern.

(Edexcel, London Examinations: GCSE)

Authors' Note: Examiners typically only ask for 'a trading account' in questions rather than 'the trading account section of the income statement'. If you get a question asking for 'a trading account', assume you are being asked to prepare the trading account section of the income statement unless it is obvious that the examiner wants the trading account in the ledger rather than the financial statement.

29.6 Thomas Brown and Partners, a business of practising accountants, have several clients who are retail distributors of the Allgush Paint Spray guns.

The current price list of Gushing Sprayers Limited, manufacturers, quotes the following wholesale prices for the Allgush Paint Spray guns:

Grade A distributors	£500 each
Grade B distributors	£560 each
Grade C distributors	£600 each

The current normal retail price of the Allgush Paint Spray gun is £750.

Thomas Brown and Partners are currently advising some of their clients concerning the valuation of stock in trade of Allgush Paint Spray guns.

1 Charles Gray – Grade B distributor
On 30 April 2009, 15 Allgush Paint Spray guns were in inventory, including one gun which was slightly damaged and expected to sell at half the normal retail price. Charles Gray considers that this gun should remain in inventory at cost price until it is sold.

K. Peacock, a customer of Charles Gray, was expected to purchase a spray gun on 30 April 2009, but no agreement was reached owing to the customer being involved in a road accident and expected to remain in hospital until late May 2009.

Charles Gray argues that he is entitled to regard this as a sale during the year ended 30 April 2009.

2 Jean Kim – Grade C distributor
On 31 May 2009, 22 Allgush Paint Spray guns were in inventory. Unfortunately Jean Kim's business is suffering a serious cash flow crisis. It is very doubtful that the business will survive and therefore a public auction of the inventory-in-trade is likely. Reliable sources suggest that the spray guns may be auctioned for £510 each; auction fees and expenses are expected to total £300.

Jean Kim has requested advice as to the basis upon which her inventory should be valued at 31 May 2009.

3 Peter Fox – Grade A distributor
Peter Fox now considers that inventory valuations should be related to selling prices because of the growing uncertainties of the market for spray guns.

Alternatively, Peter Fox has suggested that he uses the cost prices applicable to Grade C distributors as the basis for inventory valuations – 'after all this will establish consistency with Grade C distributors'.

Required:
A brief report to each of Charles Gray, Jean Kim and Peter Fox concerning the valuation of their inventories-in-trade.

Note: Answers should include references to appropriate accounting concepts.

(Association of Accounting Technicians)

29.7A Mary Smith commenced trading on 1 September 2009 as a distributor of the Straight Cut garden lawn mower, a relatively new product which is now becoming increasingly popular.

Upon commencing trading, Mary Smith transferred £7,000 from her personal savings to open a business bank account.

Mary Smith's purchases and sales of the Straight Cut garden lawn mower during the three months ended 30 November 2009 are as follows:

2009	*Bought*	*Sold*
September	12 machines at £384 each	–
October	8 machines at £450 each	4 machines at £560 each
November	16 machines at £489 each	20 machines at £680 each

Assume all purchases are made in the first half of the month and all sales are in the second half of the month.

At the end of October 2009, Mary Smith decided to take one Straight Cut garden lawn mower out of inventory for cutting the lawn outside her showroom. It is estimated that this lawn mower will be used in Mary Smith's business for eight years and have a nil estimated residual value. Mary Smith wishes to use the straight line basis of depreciation.

Additional information:

1 Overhead expenses paid during the three months ended 30 November 2009 amounted to £1,520.
2 There were no amounts prepaid on 30 November 2009, but sales commissions payable of $2^1/_2$% of the gross profit on sales were accrued due on 30 November 2009.
3 Upon commencing trading, Mary Smith resigned a business appointment with a salary of £15,000 per annum.
4 Mary Smith is able to obtain interest of 10% per annum on her personal savings.
5 One of the lawn mowers not sold on 30 November 2009 has been damaged in the showroom and is to be repaired in December 2009 at a cost of £50 before being sold for an expected £400.

Note: Ignore taxation.

Required:

(*a*) Prepare, in as much detail as possible, Mary Smith's income statement for the quarter ending 30 November 2009 using:
(*i*) the first in first out basis of inventory valuation, and
(*ii*) the last in first out basis of inventory valuation.

(*b*) Using the results in (*a*) (*i*) above, prepare a statement comparing Mary Smith's income for the quarter ended 30 November 2009 with that for the quarter ended 31 August 2009.

(*c*) Give one advantage and one disadvantage of each of the bases of inventory valuations used in (*a*) above.

(*Association of Accounting Technicians*)

29.8 'The idea that inventory should be included in accounts at the lower of historical cost and net realisable value follows the prudence convention but not the consistency convention.'

Required:

(*a*) Do you agree with the quotation?

(*b*) Explain, with reasons, whether you think this idea (that inventory should be included in accounts at the lower of historical cost and net realisable value) is a useful one. Refer to at least two classes of user of financial accounting reports in your answer.

(*Association of Chartered Certified Accountants*)

29.9 After stocktaking for the year ended 31 May 2009 had taken place, the closing inventory of Cobden Ltd was aggregated to a figure of £87,612.

During the course of the audit which followed, the undernoted facts were discovered:

(*a*) Some goods stored outside had been included at their normal cost price of £570. They had, however, deteriorated and would require an estimated £120 to be spent to restore them to their original condition, after which they could be sold for £800.

(*b*) Some goods had been damaged and were now unsaleable. They could, however, be sold for £110 as spares after repairs estimated at £40 had been carried out. They had originally cost £200.

(*c*) One inventory sheet had been over-added by £126 and another under-added by £72.

(*d*) Cobden Ltd had received goods costing £2,010 during the last week of May 2009 but, because the invoices did not arrive until June 2009, they have not been included in inventory.

(*e*) An inventory sheet total of £1,234 had been transferred to the summary sheet as £1,243.

(*f*) Invoices totalling £638 arrived during the last week of May 2009 (and were included in purchases and in accounts payable) but, because of transport delays, the goods did not arrive until late June 2009 and were not included in closing inventory.

(*g*) Portable generators on hire from another company at a charge of £347 were included, at this figure, in inventory.

(*h*) Free samples sent to Cobden Ltd by various suppliers had been included in inventory at the catalogue price of £63.

(*i*) Goods costing £418 sent to customers on a sale or return basis had been included in inventory by Cobden Ltd at their selling price, £602.

(*j*) Goods sent on a sale or return basis to Cobden Ltd had been included in inventory at the amount payable (£267) if retained. No decision to retain had been made.

Required:

Using such of the above information as is relevant, prepare a schedule amending the inventory figure as at 31 May 2009. State your reason for each amendment or for not making an amendment.

(*Association of Chartered Certified Accountants*)

29.10A Yuan Ltd has an accounting year ended 29 February 2008. Due to staff shortages, the stocktaking had not been undertaken until 9 March 2008 and the inventory valued at this date is £100,600. This value was also used in the company draft accounts for the year ended 29 February 2008 which showed a net profit of £249,600 and a current asset total of £300,000. The selling price of goods is based on cost plus 25%.

During the auditing period, the following errors were discovered:

1 Sales invoices for goods dispatched to customers during the period 1–9 March 2008 amounted to £43,838 which include carriage on sales of 5%.
2 Goods costing £14,000 were delivered to the company during the period 1–9 March 2008.
3 During the period 1–9 March 2008, returns from customers at selling price were £4,170, and returns to suppliers amounted to £850.
4 The inventory valuation of 9 March 2008 included the inventory of the company's office cleaning materials. These materials had all been bought during February 2000 at a cost of £600.
5 Inventory with selling price of £1,650 had been borrowed by the marketing department on 27 February 2008 to be displayed at an exhibition from 28 February to 16 March. This had helped to attract orders of £27,400 for delivery in April 2008.
6 Stocks with a selling price of £800 were sent to a customer on sale or return basis on 14 February 2008. On 23 February 2008, the customer sold half of the consignment. This credit sale had not yet been recorded in Yuan Ltd's accounts for the year ended 29 February 2008. On 9 March 2008, the remaining half of the consignment had not been returned to Yuan Ltd, and the customer had not signified its acceptance.
7 On 3 March 2008, Yuan Ltd. received a batch of free samples which had been included in the stock valuation at the list price of £20.

Required:

(*a*) Prepare a schedule amending the inventory figure as at 29 February 2008.

(*b*) Calculate the revised net profit for the year ending 29 February 2008 and the correct value of current assets at that date.

You can find a range of additional self-test questions, as well as material to help you with your studies, on the website that accompanies this book at www.pearsoned.co.uk/wood.

hapter 30

Bank reconciliation statements

Learning objectives

After you have studied this chapter, you should be able to:

- explain why bank reconciliations are prepared
- reconcile cash book balances with bank statement balances
- reconcile ledger accounts to suppliers' statements
- make the necessary entries in the accounts for dishonoured cheques

Introduction

In this chapter, you'll learn how to prepare a bank reconciliation statement and why you need to do this when a bank statement is received from the bank. You will also learn how to deal with dishonoured cheques in the ledger accounts.

30.1 Completing entries in the cash book

In the books of a business, funds paid into and out of the bank are entered into the bank columns of the cash book. At the same time, the bank will also be recording the flows of funds into and out of the business bank account.

If all the items entered in the cash book were the same as those entered in the records held by the bank, the balance on the business bank account as shown in the cash book and the balance on the account as shown by the bank's records would be the same.

Unfortunately, it isn't usually that simple, particularly in the case of a current account. There may be items paid into or out of the business bank account which have not been recorded in the cash book. And there may be items entered in the cash book that have not yet been entered in the bank's records of the account. To see if any of these things have happened, the cash book entries need to be compared to the record of the account held by the bank. Banks usually send a copy of that record, called a **bank statement**, to their customers on a regular basis, but a bank statement can be requested by a customer of the bank at any time.

Bank statements should *always* be checked against the cash book entries! (And you would be wise to do so yourself with your own bank account.)

Activity 30.1

What might cause the two balances to be different? Spend two minutes making a list.

Let's look at an example of a cash book and a bank statement in Exhibit 30.1:

Exhibit 30.1

Cash Book (bank columns only: *before* balancing on 31.12.2008)

2008				£	2008				£
Dec	1	Balance b/d	✔	250	Dec	5	J Gordon	✔	65
	20	P Thomas	✔	100		27	K Hughes	✔	175
	28	D Jones	✔	190					

Bank Statement

				Withdrawals	Deposits	Balance
2008				£	£	£
Dec	1	Balance b/d	✔			250
	8	10625(Note)	✔	65		185
	21	Deposit	✔		100	285
	28	Deposit	✔		190	475
	29	10626(Note)	✔	175		300
	30	Bank Giro credit: P Smith			70	370
	31	Bank charges		50		320

Note: 10625 and 10626 refer to the serial numbers on the cheques paid out.

It is now clear that the two items not shown in our cash book are:

Bank Giro credit: P Smith	£70
Bank charges	£50

P Smith had paid £70 but, instead of sending a cheque, he paid the money by bank giro credit transfer direct into the business bank account. The business did not know of this until it received the bank statement.

The other item was in respect of bank charges. The bank has charged £50 for keeping the bank account and all the work connected with it. Instead of sending an invoice, the bank has simply taken the money out of the bank account.

Activity 30.2 What sensible rule does this give you relating to when you should balance-off the bank account in the cash book at the end of the accounting period?

As we have now identified the items missing from the cash book, we can now complete writing it up by entering the two items we have identified:

Cash Book (bank columns only: *after* balancing on 31.12.2008)

2008			£	2008			£
Dec	1	Balance b/d	250	Dec	5	J Gordon	65
	20	P Thomas	100		27	K Hughes	175
	28	D Jones	190		**31**	**Bank charges**	**50**
	30	**P Smith**	**70**		31	Balance c/d	320
			610				610
2009							
Jan	1	Balance b/d	320				

Both the bank statement and cash book closing balances are now shown as being £320.

30.2 Where closing balances differ

Although a cash book may be kept up to date by a business, it obviously cannot alter the bank's own records. Even after writing up entries in the cash book, there may still be a difference between the cash book balance and the balance on the bank statement. Exhibit 30.2 shows such a case.

Exhibit 30.2

Cash Book (after being completed to date)

2009			£	2009			£
Jan	1	Balance b/d	320	Jan	10	C Morgan	110
	16	R Lomas	160		20	M McCarthy	90
	24	V Verity	140		28	Cheshire CC rates	180
	31	J Soames	470		30	M Peck	200
	31	R Johnson	90		31	Balance c/d	600
			1,180				1,180
Feb	1	Balance b/d	600				

Bank Statement

2009			*Withdrawals* £	*Deposits* £	*Balance* £
Jan	1	Balance b/d			320
	12	10627	110		210
	16	Deposit		160	370
	23	10628	90		280
	24	Deposit		140	420
	28	Direct debit: Cheshire CC	180		240
	31	Bank Giro credit: R Johnson		90	330

Activity 30.3 Try to identify which items are causing the two balances to be different even after the bank statement has been checked against the cash book and the necessary additional entries have been made in the cash book. (*Hint*: there are two items involved.)

You can see that two items are in the cash book but are not shown on the bank statement. These are:

(i) A cheque had been paid to M Peck on January 30. He deposited it in his bank on January 31 but his bank didn't collect the money from the business's bank until February 2. This is known as an **unpresented cheque**.

(ii) Although a cheque for £470 was received from J Soames on January 31 and the business deposited it with the bank on that date, the bank did not receive the funds from Soames' bank until February. This is known as a 'bank lodgement not yet credited' to the business bank account.

The cash book balance on January 31 was £600, whereas the bank statement shows a balance of £330. To prove that although the balances are different they can be 'reconciled' (i.e. made to agree) with each other, a **bank reconciliation statement** is prepared. It will either start with the bank statement balance and then reconcile it to the cash book balance, or it will start with the cash book balance and then reconcile it to the bank statement balance. If the second approach is adopted, it would appear as:

Bank Reconciliation Statement as at 31 December 2008

		£
Balance as per cash book		600
Add Unpresented cheque	(i)	200
		800
Less Bank lodgement not on statement	(ii)	(470)
Balance per bank statement		330

If the two balances cannot be reconciled then there will be an error somewhere. This will have to be located and then corrected.

This reconciliation technique is also used when dealing with other statements drawn up outside the firm: for example, when reconciling purchase ledger accounts to suppliers' statements.

30.3 The bank balance in the balance sheet

The balance to be shown in the balance sheet is that per the cash book after it has been written up to date. In Exhibit 30.2, the balance sheet figure would be £600.

This is an important point, and one that students often get wrong! The bank reconciliation shown in the last section is simply verifying that you know why there is a difference between the two balances. It is *not* calculating what the bank account figure in the balance sheet should be because it starts with the balance in the cash book *after* adjusting it for items revealed in the bank statement.

30.4 An alternative approach to bank reconciliations

In order to avoid the confusion that may arise concerning what figure to include in the balance sheet, many accountants use a slightly different form of bank reconciliation. In this approach, you take the balance as shown on the bank statement and the balance in the cash book *before* making any adjustments that are identified when it is compared to the bank statement. You then reconcile each of them in turn to arrive at the balance that should appear in the balance sheet.

Having completed the reconciliation, you then update the cash book **so that it balances at the correct amount, i.e. the amount that will be shown in the balance sheet.** An example is shown in Exhibit 30.3.

Exhibit 30.3

Cash Book (bank columns only: *before* balancing on 31.12.2008)

2008				£	2008				£
Dec	1	Balance b/d	✔	160	Dec	8	V O'Connor	✔	115
	12	D Tyrrall	✔	80		21	G Francis	✔	35
	23	P McCarthy	✔	130		**31**	**D Barnes**		**25**
	31	**S Aisbitt**		**72**					

Bank Statement

				Withdrawals	Deposits	Balance
2008				£	£	£
Dec	1	Balance b/d	✔			160
	11	24621	✔	115		45
	14	Deposit	✔		80	125
	23	24622	✔	35		90
	29	Deposit	✔		130	220
	30	**Bank Giro credit: A Parkinson**			**24**	**244**
	31	**Bank charges**		**40**		**204**

You can see that the following are missing from the cash book:

(*a*) A bank giro credit of £24 made on December 30 by A Parkinson.
(*b*) Bank charges of £40.

And you can see that the following are missing from the bank statement:

(*c*) A cheque paid to D Barnes for £25 on December 31 has not yet been presented.
(*d*) A bank lodgement has not yet been credited – the cheque for £72 received from S Aisbitt on 31 December.

The bank reconciliation statement would be:

Bank Reconciliation Statement as at 31 December 2008

		£
Balance as per cash book		267
Add Bank giro credit not yet entered	(*a*)	24
		291
Less Bank lodgement not on balance sheet	(*b*)	(40)
Balance in balance sheet		251
Add Cheque not yet presented	(*c*)	25
		276
Less Bank lodgement not on statement	(*d*)	(72)
Balance per bank statement		204

When you have adjustments to make to both the cash book and the bank account balances in order to reconcile them, this form of bank reconciliation statement is more useful than one that simply shows that you know why their balances are different (which is all the bank reconciliation statement in Section 30.2 shows).

An alternative approach that is often used in practice is to start with the balance as per the cash book and adjust it to arrive at the balance per the balance sheet (i.e. the same as in the first half of the bank reconciliation statement shown above). You then have a second section that starts with the balance as per the bank statement and adjust it to once again arrive at the balance per the balance sheet. Either of these two approaches is perfectly acceptable and both provide the same information.

30.5 Other terms used in banking

1 **Standing Orders.** A firm can instruct its bank to pay regular amounts of money at stated dates to persons or firms. For instance, you may ask your bank to pay £200 a month to a building society to repay a mortgage.

2 **Direct Debits.** These are payments which have to be made, such as gas bills, electricity bills, telephone bills, rates and insurance premiums. Instead of asking the bank to pay the money, as with standing orders, you give permission to the creditor to obtain the money directly from your bank account. This is particularly useful if the amounts payable may vary from time to time, as it is the creditor who changes the payments, not you. With standing orders, if the amount is ever to be changed, *you* have to inform the bank. With direct debits it is *the creditor* who informs the bank.

Just as with anything else omitted from the cash book, items of these types need to be included in the reconciliation and entered in the cash book before balancing it off at the end of the period.

30.6 Bank overdrafts

The adjustment needed to reconcile a bank overdraft according to the firm's books (shown by a credit balance in the cash book) with that shown in the bank's records are the same as those needed when the account is not overdrawn.

Exhibit 30.4 is of a cash book and a bank statement both showing an overdraft. Only the cheque for G Cumberbatch (A) £106 and the cheque paid to J Kelly (B) £63 need adjusting. Work through the reconciliation statement and then read the note after it. Because the balance shown by the cash book is correct (and, therefore, the balance that will appear in the balance sheet), you can use the form of bank reconciliation statement shown in Section 30.2.

Exhibit 30.4

Cash Book

2008				£	2008				£
Dec	5	I Howe		308	Dec	1	Balance b/d		709
	24	L Mason		120		9	P Davies		140
	29	K King		124		**27**	**J Kelly**	**(B)**	**63**
	31	**G Cumberbatch**	**(A)**	**106**		29	United Trust		77
	31	Balance c/d		380		31	Bank charges		49
				1,038					1,038

Bank Statement

			Dr	*Cr*	*Balance*
2008			£	£	£
Dec	1	Balance b/d			709 O/D
	5	Cheque		308	401 O/D
	14	P Davies	140		541 O/D
	24	Cheque		120	421 O/D
	29	K King: Credit transfer		124	297 O/D
	29	United Trust: Standing order	77		374 O/D
	31	Bank charges	49		423 O/D

***Note*: An overdraft is often shown with the letters 'O/D' following the amount. Alternatively, some banks use 'Dr' and 'Cr' after every balance entry to indicate whether the account is overdrawn.**

Activity 30.4 Will the bank statement show 'Dr' or 'Cr' if an account is overdrawn?

Bank Reconciliation Statement as at 31 December 2008

	£
Overdraft as per cash book	(380)
Add Unpresented cheque	63
	(317)
Less Bank lodgement not on bank statement	(106)
Overdraft per bank statement	(423)

***Note*: You may find it confusing looking at this bank reconciliation statement because the opening entry is an overdraft, i.e. a negative number. However, the adjusting entries are the same as those you make when it is positive:**

	£
Balance/overdraft per cash book	**xxxx**
Adjustments	
Unpresented cheque	**Plus**
Bank lodgement not on bank statement	**Less**
Balance/overdraft per bank statement	**xxxx**

30.7 Dishonoured cheques

When a cheque is received from a customer and paid into the bank, it is recorded on the debit side of the cash book. It is also shown on the bank statement as a deposit increasing the balance on the account. However, at a later date it may be found that the customer's bank will not pay the amount due on the cheque. The customer's bank has failed to 'honour' the cheque. The cheque is described as a **dishonoured cheque**.

There are several possible reasons for this. Imagine that K King paid a business with a cheque for £5,000 on 20 May 2009. The business deposits it at the bank but, a few days later, the bank contacts the business and informs it that the cheque has been dishonoured. Typical reasons are:

1 King had put £5,000 in figures on the cheque, but had written it in words as 'five thousand *five hundred* pounds'. A new cheque correctly completed will need to be provided by King.
2 Normally cheques are considered *stale* six months after the date on the cheque. In other words, banks will not honour cheques that are more than six months old. If King had put the year 2008 on the cheque instead of 2009, then King's bank would dishonour the cheque and King would need to be asked for a correctly dated replacement.
3 King simply did not have sufficient funds in her bank account. Suppose she had previously a balance of only £2,000 and yet she has made out a cheque for £5,000. Her bank has not allowed her an overdraft in order to honour the cheque. As a result, the cheque has been dishonoured. The bank inform the business that this has happened and the business would have to contact King, explain what has happened and ask for valid payment of the account.

In all of these cases, the bank would record the original entry in its records as being reversed. This is shown on the bank statement, for example, by the entry 'dishonoured cheque £5,000'. The business then makes the equivalent credit entry in the cash book while, at the same time, debiting King's account by the same amount.

When King originally paid the £5,000 the accounts in the ledger and cash book would have appeared as:

K King

2009			£	2009			£
May	1	Balance b/d	5,000	May	20	Bank	5,000

Bank Account

2009			£				
May	20	K King	5,000				

After recording the dishonoured cheque, the accounts would be:

K King

2009			£	2009			£
May	1	Balance b/d	5,000	May	20	Bank	5,000
May	**25**	**Bank: cheque dishonoured**	**5,000**				

Bank Account

2009			£	2009			£
May	20	K King	5,000	**May**	**25**	**K King: cheque dishonoured**	**5,000**

In other words, King is once again shown as owing the business £5,000.

Learning outcomes

You should now have learnt:

1 Why it is important to perform a bank reconciliation when a bank statement is received.

2 That a bank reconciliation statement should show whether or not errors have been made either in the bank columns of the cash book or on the bank statement.

3 That a bank reconciliation statement can be prepared either before or after updating the cash book with items omitted from it that are shown on the bank statement.

4 That a bank reconciliation statement prepared after updating the cash book with items omitted from it that are shown on the bank statement shows that you know why the bank statement balance is different from that shown in the cash book and balance sheet.

5 That a bank reconciliation statement prepared before updating the cash book with items omitted from it that are shown on the bank statement is reconciled from cash book to balance sheet amount and then to the bank statement. It shows the amount to be entered in the balance sheet and also shows that you know why the bank statement balance is different from the balances shown in the cash book and in the balance sheet.

6 That in the case of bank overdrafts, the reconciliation statement adjustments are the same as those shown when there is a positive bank balance, but the opening and closing balances are negative.

7 How to prepare a bank reconciliation statement *after* updating the cash book with items omitted from it that are shown on the bank statement.

8 How to prepare a bank reconciliation statement *before* updating the cash book with items omitted from it that are shown on the bank statement.

9 Why cheques may be dishonoured and what the effect is upon the bank balance.

10 How to make the appropriate entries to the accounts when a cheque is dishonoured.

Answers to activities

30.1 There is quite a long list of possible causes, including:

- a business may take a day or two to deposit some cheques that it has already entered in the cash book
- a cheque may take a few days to be entered in the account of the business held at the bank after it is deposited (because the bank won't recognise the amount received until a few days later, in case there is a problem with it)
- bank interest paid and bank charges often aren't known by a business until a bank statement is received
- bank interest received won't be known by a business until it receives a bank statement
- standing orders may not be written up in the cash book of the business until they are identified on the bank statement
- the amount of a direct debit is sometimes not known and so should not be entered in the cash book until it is confirmed how much was paid out of the bank account
- customers may pay their accounts by direct transfer from their bank account or by paying cash directly into the business bank account and the business may only learn of their having done so some time later
- there may have been an error made in the cash book entries
- the bank may have made an error in operating the account, such as adding funds to it instead of to the account of the person depositing the funds
- a cheque paid into the bank may have 'bounced' (i.e. there were insufficient funds in the writer of the cheque's bank account to make the payment).

30.2 It is wise to wait until receiving the bank statement before balancing-off the bank account in the cash book at the end of the accounting period. In a manual accounting system, if a cash book is balanced on a regular basis, balancing-off is usually done at the end of the time period selected and any additional entries are recorded along with the other entries made in the following day, week, month or quarter. However, at the end of the accounting year, the balancing-off is often done in pencil (so that financial statements can be drafted) and then done in ink after any missing entries and corrections of errors have been entered following receipt of the bank statement.

30.3 M Peck £200 and J Soames £470.

30.4 'Dr' indicates an overdraft. The customer is a debtor of the bank. In the customer's balance sheet, the overdraft is included in the current liabilities, indicating that the bank is a creditor. Always remember that a bank is looking at the relationship from the opposite side to the view seen by the customer.

Review questions

30.1 From the following, draw up a bank reconciliation statement from details as on 31 December 2006:

	£
Cash at bank as per bank column of the cash book	2,910
Unpresented cheques	730
Cheques received and paid into the bank, but not yet entered on the bank statement	560
Credit transfers entered as banked on the bank statement but not entered in the cash book	340
Cash at bank as per bank statement	3,420

30.2A Draw up a bank reconciliation statement, after writing the cash book up to date, ascertaining the balance on the bank statement, from the following as on 31 March 2009:

→

	£
Cash at bank as per bank column of the cash book (Dr)	2,740
Bankings made but not yet entered on bank statement	410
Bank charges on bank statement but not yet in cash book	32
Unpresented cheques W Shute	131
Standing order to Giffy Ltd entered on bank statement, but not in cash book	93
Credit transfer from B Barnes entered on bank statement, but not yet in cash book	201

30.3 The following are extracts from the cash book and the bank statement of F Perry.

You are required to:

(*a*) Write the cash book up to date, and state the new balance as on 31 December 2009, and

(*b*) Draw up a bank reconciliation statement as on 31 December 2009.

Cash Book

2009		*Dr*	£	2009		*Cr*	£
Dec	1	Balance b/d	3,419	Dec	8	B Young	462
	7	F Lamb	101		15	F Gray	21
	22	G Brock	44		28	T Errant	209
	31	W Terry	319		31	Balance c/d	3,437
	31	S Miller	246				
			4,129				4,129

Bank Statement

2009			*Dr*	*Cr*	*Balance*
			£	£	£
Dec	1	Balance b/d			3,419
	7	Cheque		101	3,520
	11	B Young	462		3,058
	20	F Gray	21		3,037
	22	Cheque		44	3,081
	31	Credit transfer: T Morris		93	3,174
	31	Bank charges	47		3,127

30.4A The bank columns in the cash book for June 2007 and the bank statement for that month for D Hogan are as follows:

Cash Book

2007		*Dr*	£	2007		*Cr*	£
Jun	1	Balance b/d	1,410	Jun	5	L Holmes	180
	7	J May	62		12	J Rebus	519
	16	T Wilson	75		16	T Silver	41
	28	F Slack	224		29	Blister Disco	22
	30	G Baker	582		30	Balance c/d	1,591
			2,353				2,353

Bank Statement

2007			*Dr*	*Cr*	*Balance*
			£	£	£
Jun	1	Balance b/d			1,410
	7	Cheque		62	1,472
	8	F Lane	180		1,292
	16	Cheque		75	1,367
	17	J Rebus	519		848
	18	T Silver	41		807
	28	Cheque		224	1,031
	29	SLM standing order	52		979
	30	Flynn: trader's credit		64	1,043
	30	Bank charges	43		1,000

You are required to:
(*a*) Write the cash book up to date to take the above into account, and then
(*b*) Draw up a bank reconciliation statement as on 30 June 2007.

30.5 Read the following and answer the questions below.

On 31 December 2008 the bank column of C Tench's cash book showed a debit balance of £1,500.

The monthly bank statement written up to 31 December 2008 showed a credit balance of £2,950.

On checking the cash book with the bank statement it was discovered that the following transactions had not been entered in the cash book:

Dividends of £240 had been paid directly to the bank.
A credit transfer – HM Revenue & Customs VAT refund of £260 – had been collected by the bank.
Bank charges £30.
A direct debit of £70 for the RAC subscription had been paid by the bank.
A standing order of £200 for C Tench's loan repayment had been paid by the bank.
C Tench's deposit account balance of £1,400 was transferred into his bank current account.

A further check revealed the following items:

Two cheques drawn in favour of T Cod £250 and F Haddock £290 had been entered in the cash book but had not been presented for payment.
Cash and cheques amounting to £690 had been paid into the bank on 31 December 2008 but were not credited by the bank until 2 January 2009.

(*a*) Starting with the debit balance of £1,500, bring the cash book (bank columns) up to date and then balance the bank account.
(*b*) Prepare a bank reconciliation statement as at 31 December 2008.

(*Midland Examining Group: GCSE*)

30.6A In the draft accounts for the year ended 31 October 2009 of Thomas P Lee, garage proprietor, the balance at bank according to the cash book was £894.68 in hand.

Subsequently the following discoveries were made:

(1) Cheque number 176276 dated 3 September 2009 for £310.84 in favour of G Lowe Limited has been correctly recorded in the bank statement, but included in the cash book payments as £301.84.
(2) Bank commission charged of £169.56 and bank interest charged of £109.10 have been entered in the bank statement on 23 October 2009, but not included in the cash book.
(3) The recently received bank statement shows that a cheque for £29.31 received from T Andrews and credited in the bank statements on 9 October 2009 has now been dishonoured and debited in the bank statement on 26 October 2009. The only entry in the cash book for this cheque records its receipt on 8 October 2009.
(4) Cheque number 177145 for £15.10 has been recorded twice as a credit in the cash book.
(5) Amounts received in the last few days of October 2009 totalling £1,895.60 and recorded in the cash book have not been included in the bank statements until 2 November 2009.
(6) Cheques paid according to the cash book during October 2009 and totalling £395.80 were not presented for payment to the bank until November 2009.
(7) Traders' credits totalling £210.10 have been credited in the bank statement on 26 October 2009, but not yet recorded in the cash book.
(8) A standing order payment of £15.00 on 17 October 2009 to Countryside Publications has been recorded in the bank statement but is not mentioned in the cash book.

Required:
(*a*) Prepare a computation of the balance at bank to be included in Thomas P Lee's balance sheet as at 31 October 2009.

→

(*b*) Prepare a bank reconciliation statement as at 31 October 2009 for Thomas P Lee.
(*c*) Briefly explain why it is necessary to prepare bank reconciliation statements at accounting year ends.

(*Association of Accounting Technicians*)

30.7 The bank statement for R Hood for the month of March 2006 is:

2006			*Dr*	*Cr*	*Balance*
			£	£	£
Mar	1	Balance			4,200 O/D
	8	T MacLeod	184		4,384 O/D
	16	Cheque		292	4,092 O/D
	20	W Milne	160		4,252 O/D
	21	Cheque		369	3,883 O/D
	31	G Frank: trader's credit		88	3,795 O/D
	31	TYF: standing order	32		3,827 O/D
	31	Bank charges	19		3,846 O/D

The cash book for March 2006 is:

2006		*Dr*	£	2006		*Cr*	£
Mar	16	G Philip	292	Mar	1	Balance b/d	4,200
	21	J Forker	369		6	T MacLeod	184
	31	S O'Hare	192		30	W Milne	160
	31	Balance c/d	4,195		30	S Porter	504
			5,048				5,048

You are required to:
(*a*) Write the cash book up to date, and
(*b*) Draw up a bank reconciliation statement as on 31 March 2006.

30.8A The following is the cash book (bank columns) of F King for December 2007:

2007		*Dr*	£	2007		*Cr*	£
Dec	6	P Pan	230	Dec	1	Balance b/d	1,900
	20	C Hook	265		10	J Lamb	304
	31	W Britten	325		19	P Wilson	261
	31	Balance c/d	1,682		29	K Coull	37
			2,502				2,502

The bank statement for the month is:

2007			*Dr*	*Cr*	*Balance*
			£	£	£
Dec	1	Balance			1,900 O/D
	6	Cheque		230	1,670 O/D
	13	J Lamb	304		1,974 O/D
	20	Cheque		265	1,709 O/D
	22	P Wilson	261		1,970 O/D
	30	Tox: standing order	94		2,064 O/D
	31	F Ray: trader's credit		102	1,962 O/D
	31	Bank charges	72		2,034 O/D

You are required to:
(*a*) Write the cash book up to date to take the necessary items into account, and
(*b*) Draw up a bank reconciliation statement as on 31 December 2007.

30.9 The following is a summary of a cash book as presented by George Ltd for the month of October:

	£		£
Receipts	1,469	Balance b/d	761
Balance c/d	554	Payments	1,262
	2,023		2,023

All receipts are banked and all payments are made by cheque.

On investigation you discover:

(1) Bank charges of £136 entered on the bank statement have not been entered in the cash book.
(2) Cheques drawn amounting to £267 had not been presented to the bank for payment.
(3) Cheques received totalling £762 had been entered in the cash book and paid into the bank, but had not been credited by the bank until 3 November.
(4) A cheque for £22 for sundries had been entered in the cash book as a receipt instead of as a payment.
(5) A cheque received from K Jones for £80 had been returned by the bank and marked 'No funds available'. No adjustment has been made in the cash book.
(6) A standing order for a business rates instalment of £150 on 30 October had not been entered in the cash book.
(7) All dividends received are credited directly to the bank account. During October amounts totalling £62 were credited by the bank but no entries were made in the cash book.
(8) A cheque drawn for £66 for stationery had been incorrectly entered in the cash book as £60.
(9) The balance brought forward in the cash book should have been £711, not £761.

Required:
(*a*) Show the adjustments required in the cash book.
(*b*) Prepare a bank reconciliation statement as at 31 October.

You can find a range of additional self-test questions, as well as material to help you with your studies, on the website that accompanies this book at www.pearsoned.co.uk/wood.

chapter

31 Control accounts

Learning objectives

After you have studied this chapter, you should be able to:

- explain why control accounts can be useful
- draw up sales ledger control accounts
- draw up purchases ledger control accounts
- reconcile the purchases ledger and the sales ledger with their respective control accounts

Introduction

In this chapter, you'll learn about the benefits of using control accounts in manual accounting systems and the process involved in both preparing control accounts and reconciling them to the ledgers.

31.1 The benefits of accounting controls

In any but the smallest business, the accounting information system (which you read about in Chapter 23) is set up so as to include controls that help ensure that errors are minimised and that nothing occurs that shouldn't, such as the cashier embezzling funds. One of the tasks undertaken by auditors is to check the various controls that are in place to ensure they are working satisfactorily and one of the things they will look out for is segregation of duties. So, for example, the same person will not both invoice customers and act as cashier when payment is received and, if someone claims reimbursement of an expense, it will be authorised for payment by someone else. Another form of control you've already learnt about involves whether or not customers are allowed to purchase goods on credit.

All these controls are 'organisational'. That is, they do not directly impose controls over the accounting data, nor do they ensure that accounting entries are correct. One control measure that does these things was covered in Chapter 30 – the process of bank reconciliation. In this chapter, we'll look at another type of accounting control which is used mainly in manual accounting systems, **control accounts**.

When all the accounts were kept in one ledger a trial balance could be drawn up as a test of the arithmetical accuracy of the accounts. If the trial balance totals disagree, the books of a small business could easily and quickly be checked so as to find the errors. Of course, as you know, even when the totals do agree, certain types of error may still have occurred, the nature of which makes it impossible for them to be detected in this way. Nevertheless, using a trial balance ensures that all the double entries appear, at least, to have been recorded correctly.

Activity 31.1 How do you find errors of the types that a trial balance cannot detect?

When a business has grown and the accounting work has been so divided up that there are several ledgers, any errors could be very difficult to find if a trial balance was the only device used to try to detect errors. Every item in every ledger may need to be checked just to find one error that caused the trial balance not to balance. What is required is a type of trial balance for each ledger, and this requirement is met by control accounts. A control account is a summary account that enables you to see at a glance whether the general ledger balance for the ledger to which that control account belongs agrees with the total of all the individual accounts held within that ledger.

If you use control accounts, only the ledgers where the control accounts do not balance need detailed checking to find errors.

31.2 Principle of control accounts

The principle on which the control account is based is simple and is as follows: if the opening balance of an account is known, together with information of the additions and deductions entered in the account, the closing balance can be calculated.

Applying this to a complete ledger, the total of opening balances together with the additions and deductions during the period should give the total of closing balances. This can be illustrated by reference to a sales ledger for entries for a month.

	£
Total of opening balances, 1 January 2006	3,000
Add Total of entries which have increased the balances	9,500
	12,500
Less Total of entries which have reduced the balances	(8,000)
Total of closing balances should be	4,500

Because totals are used, control accounts are sometimes known as 'total accounts'. Thus, a control account for a sales ledger could be known as either a **'sales ledger control account'** or as a **'total accounts receivable account'**.

Similarly, a control account for a purchases ledger could be known either as a **'purchases ledger control account'** or as a **'total accounts payable account'**.

A control account is a memorandum account. It is not part of the double entry system. It will be prepared either in the general ledger or in the ledger to which it relates, i.e. the purchases ledger or the sales ledger.

A control account looks like any other T-account:

Sales Ledger Control

2006			£	2006			£
Jan	1	Balances b/d	x,xxx	Jan	31	Returns Inwards Day Book (total of all goods returned from debtors in the period)	xxx
	31	Sales day book (total of sales invoiced in the period)	xx,xxx		31	Cash book (total of all cash received from debtors in the period)	x,xxx
					31	Cash book (total of all cheques received from debtors in the period)	xx,xxx
					31	Balances c/d	x,xxx
			xx,xxx				xx,xxx

31.3 Information for control accounts

Exhibits 31.1 and 31.2 list the sources of information used to draw up control accounts.

Exhibit 31.1

Sales Ledger Control	Source
1 Opening accounts receivable	List of debtor balances drawn up at the end of the previous period
2 Credit sales	Total from the Sales Day Book
3 Returns inwards	Total of the Returns Inwards Day Book
4 Cheques received	Cash Book: bank column on received side. List extracted or the total of a special column for cheques which has been included in the Cash Book
5 Cash received	Cash Book: cash column on received side. List extracted or the total of a special column for cash which has been included in the Cash Book
6 Discounts allowed	Total of discounts allowed column in the Cash Book
7 Closing accounts receivable	List of debtor balances drawn up at the end of the period

Exhibit 31.2

Purchases Ledger Control	Source
1 Opening accounts payable	List of creditor balances drawn up at the end of the previous period
2 Credit purchases	Total from Purchases Day Book
3 Returns outwards	Total of Returns Outwards Day Book
4 Cheques paid	Cash Book: bank column on payments side. List extracted or total of a special column for cheques which has been included in the Cash Book
5 Cash paid	Cash Book: cash column on payments side. List extracted or total of a special column for cash which has been included in the Cash Book
6 Discounts received	Total of discounts received column in the Cash Book
7 Closing accounts payable	List of creditor balances drawn up at the end of the period

31.4 Form of control accounts

As shown in Section 31.2, control accounts kept in the general ledger are normally prepared in the same form as an account, with the totals of the debit entries in the ledger on the left-hand side of the control account, and the totals of the various credit entries in the ledger on the right-hand side.

The process is very straightforward. Take the sales ledger as an example. The first two steps are identical to those you learnt in Chapters 13 and 14.

1 Individual amounts received from debtors are transferred from the cash book into the personal accounts in the sales ledger. (The double entry is completed automatically in the normal way, because the cash book is, in itself, a ledger account.)
2 Individual invoice amounts are transferred from the sales day book into the personal accounts in the sales ledger. (You would complete the double entry in the normal way, by crediting the sales account.)
3 The sales ledger control account would open each period with the total of the accounts receivable balances at the start of the period.
4 Then, post the total of the returns inwards day book to the credit side of the sales ledger control account. **(This is new.)**
5 At the end of the period, you post the totals of all the payments from debtors received during the period from the cash book to the credit side of the sales ledger control account. **(This is new.)**
6 This is followed by posting to the debit side of the sales ledger control account the totals of all new sales during the period shown in the sales day book. **(This is new.)**
7 Balance-off the control account.
8 Check whether the balance on the control account is equal to the total of all the accounts receivable balances in the sales ledger.

If the balance is not the same as the total of all the balances in the sales ledger, there is an error either in the totals entered in the control account from the books of original entry or, more likely, somewhere in the sales ledger.

***Note*: You do *not* enter the total of the balances from the sales ledger in the control account. Instead, you balance-off the control account and check whether the balance c/d is the same as the total of all the individual balances in the sales ledger.**

If you look at these eight steps, you can see that the first three are those you learnt to do earlier in the book, so you know that the other part of the double entry has been completed in the normal way. However, what about the double entries for (4), (5) and (6)? What is the other side of the double entry in each case?

Exhibit 31.3 shows an example of a sales ledger control account for a sales ledger in which all the entries are arithmetically correct and the totals transferred from the books of original entry are correct.

Exhibit 31.3

Sales Ledger Control Account data:	£
Accounts receivable balances on 1 January 2006	1,894
Total credit sales for the month	10,290
Cheques received from customers in the month	7,284
Cash received from customers in the month	1,236
Returns inwards from customers during the month	296
Accounts receivable balances on 31 January as extracted from the Sales Ledger	3,368

Sales Ledger Control

2006			£	2006			£
Jan	1	Balances b/d	1,894	Jan	31	Bank	7,284
	31	Sales	10,290		31	Cash	1,236
					31	Returns inwards	296
					31	Balances c/d	3,368
			12,184				12,184

We have proved the ledger to be arithmetically correct, because the control account balances with the amount equalling the total of the balances extracted from the sales ledger.

Like a trial balance, if the totals of a control account are not equal and the entries made to it were correct (i.e. the amounts transferred to it from the books of original entry have been corrrectly summed), this shows that there is an error somewhere in the ledger.

Exhibit 31.4 shows an example where an error is found to exist in a purchases ledger. The ledger will have to be checked in detail, the error found, and the control account then corrected.

Exhibit 31.4

Purchases Ledger Control Account data:	£
Accounts payable balances on 1 January 2006	3,890
Cheques paid to suppliers during the month	3,620
Returns outwards to suppliers in the month	95
Bought from suppliers in the month	4,936
Accounts payable balances on 31 January as extracted from the Purchases Ledger	5,151

Purchases Ledger Control

2006			£	2006			£
Jan	31	Bank	3,620	Jan	1	Balances b/d	3,890
	31	Returns outwards	95		31	Purchases	4,936
	31	Balances c/d	5,151				
			8,866 (Note)				8,826 (Note)

Note: Providing all the totals transferred into the Purchases Ledger Control Account from the books of original entry were correct, there is a £40 difference between the debit and credit entries in the Purchases Ledger.

We will have to check the purchases ledger in detail to find the error. A double line has not yet been drawn under the totals. We will do this (known as 'ruling off the account') when the error has been found and the totals corrected.

***Note*: You need to be sure that the totals transferred from the books of original entry were correct before assuming that an out-of-balance control account means that the ledger is incorrect.**

31.5 Other advantages of control accounts in a manual accounting system

Control accounts are usually only maintained in a manual accounting system. They are not normally maintained in a computerised accounting system.

Control accounts have merits other than that of locating errors. When used, control accounts are normally under the charge of a responsible official, and fraud is made more difficult because transfers made (in an effort) to disguise frauds will have to pass the scrutiny of this person.

The balances on the control account can always be taken to equal accounts receivable and accounts payable without waiting for an extraction of individual balances. Management control is thereby aided, for the speed at which information is obtained is one of the prerequisites of efficient control.

31.6 Other sources of information for control accounts

With a large organisation there may well be more than one sales ledger or purchases ledger. The accounts in the sales ledgers may be divided up in ways such as:

- alphabetically: thus we may have three sales sub-ledgers split A–F, G–O and P–Z.
- geographically: this could be split: Europe, Far East, Africa, Asia, Australia, North America and South America.

For each of these sub-ledgers we must have a separate control account. An example of a columnar sales day book is shown as Exhibit 31.5:

Exhibit 31.5

Columnar Sales Day Book

Date		*Details*	*Total*		*Ledgers*	
				A–F	G–O	P–Z
2006			£	£	£	£
Feb	1	J Archer	58	58		
	3	G Gaunt	103		103	
	4	T Brown	116	116		
	8	C Dunn	205	205		
	10	A Smith	16			16
	12	P Smith	114			114
	15	D Owen	88		88	
	18	B Blake	17	17		
	22	T Green	1,396		1,396	
	27	C Males	48		48	
			2,161	396	1,635	130

The total of the A–F column will be the total sales figures for the Sales Ledger A–F control account, the total of the G–O column for the G–O control account, and so on.

A similar form of analysis can be used in the purchases day book, the returns inwards day book, the returns outwards day book and the cash book. The *totals* necessary for each of the control accounts can be obtained from the appropriate columns in these books.

Other items, such as bad debts written off or transfers from one ledger to another, will be recorded in the Journal.

31.7 Other transfers

Transfers to bad debt accounts will have to be recorded in the sales ledger control account as they involve entries in the sales ledger.

Similarly, a contra account, whereby the same entity is both a supplier and a customer, and inter-indebtedness is set off, will also need to be entered in the control accounts. An example of this follows:

(A) The business has sold A Hughes £600 goods.
(B) Hughes has supplied the business with £880 goods.
(C) The £600 owing by Hughes is set off against £880 owing to him.
(D) This leaves £280 owing to Hughes.

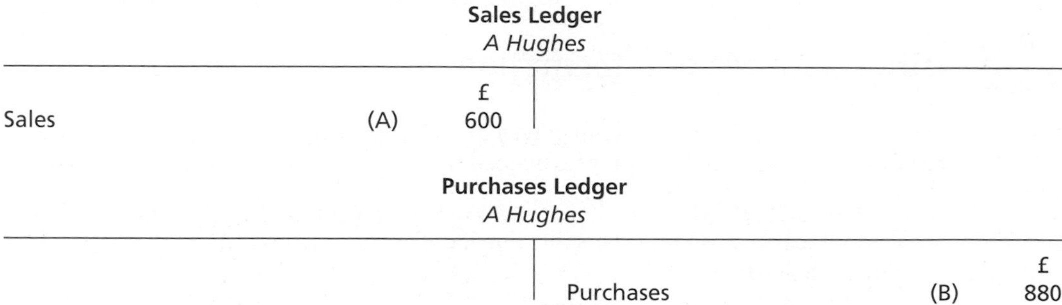

Sales Ledger
A Hughes

		£			£
Sales	(A)	600			

Purchases Ledger
A Hughes

		£			£
			Purchases	(B)	880

The set-off now takes place following the preparation of a journal entry in the Journal:

Sales Ledger
A Hughes

		£			£
Sales	(A)	600	**Set-off: Purchases ledger**	(C)	600

Purchases Ledger
A Hughes

		£			£
Set-off: Sales ledger	(C)	600	Purchases	(B)	880
Balance c/d	(D)	280			
		880			880
			Balance b/d	(D)	280

The set-off will be posted from the Journal to the credit side of the sales ledger control account and to the debit side of the purchases ledger control account.

31.8 A more complicated example

Exhibit 31.6 shows a worked example of a more complicated control account.

You will see that there are sometimes credit balances in the sales ledger as well as debit balances. Suppose for instance we sold £500 goods to W Young, he then paid in full for them, and then afterwards he returned £40 goods to us. This would leave a credit balance of £40 on the account, whereas usually the balances in the sales ledger are debit balances.

Exhibit 31.6

2006			£
Aug	1	Sales ledger – debit balances	3,816
	1	Sales ledger – credit balances	22
	31	Transactions for the month:	
		Cash received	104
		Cheques received	6,239
		Sales	7,090
		Bad debts written off	306
		Discounts allowed	298
		Returns inwards	664
		Cash refunded to a customer who had overpaid his account	37
		Dishonoured cheques	29
		Interest charged by us on overdue debt	50
		At the end of the month:	
		Sales ledger – debit balances	3,429
		Sales ledger – credit balances	40

Sales Ledger Control Account

2006			£	2006			£
Aug	1	Balances b/d	3,816	Aug	1	Balances b/d	22
	31	Sales	7,090		31	Cash	104
		Cash refunded	37			Bank	6,239
		Bank: dishonoured cheques	29			Bad debts	306
		Interest on debt	50			Discounts allowed	298
		Balances c/d	40			Returns inwards	664
						Balances c/d	3,429
			11,062				11,062

Note that you do *not* set off the debit and credit balances in the Sales Ledger.

31.9 Control accounts as part of double entry in larger organisations

In larger organisations, control accounts may be part of the double entry system, the balances of the control accounts being taken for the purpose of extracting a trial balance. In this case, the control accounts are always kept in the general ledger. When control accounts are part of the double entry system, the personal accounts are being used as subsidiary records and the sales and purchases ledgers are memorandum books lying outside the double entry system. The same entries are made to the control accounts at the end of the period as are made if they are not part of the double entry system.

31.10 Self-balancing ledgers and adjustment accounts

Because ledgers which have a control account system are proved to be correct as far as the double entry is concerned they used to be called **'self-balancing ledgers'**. The control accounts were often called **'adjustment accounts'**. These terms are very rarely used nowadays, but you should remember them in case an examiner uses them.

31.11 Reconciliation of control accounts

Errors and omissions can occur when entering information into the accounting records. We have seen in Chapter 30 how these are identified and used to reconcile differences between the bank account and the bank statement balances. When a ledger control account is not in balance, it indicates that something has gone wrong with the entries made to the accounting records. This leads to an investigation which (hopefully) reveals the cause(s). Then, in order to verify whether the identified item(s) caused the failure to balance the control account, a reconciliation is carried out.

Exhibit 31.7 shows an example of a **purchases ledger control account reconciliation**. It takes the original control account balance and adjusts it to arrive at an amended balance which should equal the revised total of the source amounts that, together, equal the control account balance.

It can be seen that the general approach is similar to that adopted for bank reconciliation statements. However, as each control account may be constructed using information from a number of sources (see Section 31.3) the extent of the investigation to identify the cause of the control account imbalance is likely to be far greater than that undertaken when performing a bank reconciliation.

Exhibit 31.7

An example of a Purchases Ledger Control Account Reconciliation

		£
Original purchases ledger control account balance		xxx
Add	Invoice omitted from control account, but entered in Purchases Ledger	xxx
	Supplier balance excluded from Purchases Ledger total because the account had been included in the Sales Ledger by mistake	xxx
	Credit sale posted in error to the debit of a Purchases Ledger account instead of the debit of an account in the Sales Ledger	xxx
	Undercasting error in calculation of total end of period creditors' balances	xxx
		xxx
Less	Customer account with a credit balance included in the Purchases Ledger that should have been included in the Sales Ledger	(xxx)
	Return inwards posted in error to the credit of a Purchases Ledger account instead of the credit of an account in the Sales Ledger	(xxx)
	Credit note entered in error in the Returns Outwards Day Book as £223 instead of £332	(xxx)
Revised purchases ledger control account balance obtained from revised source amounts		xxx

31.12 A cautionary note

Students often get the following wrong: only credit purchases are recorded in a Purchases Ledger control account. Also, in Sales Ledger control accounts, do not include cash sales or allowances for doubtful debts.

31.13 Finally

Control accounts are used in manual accounting systems. Most computerised accounting systems automatically provide all the benefits of using control accounts without the necessity of actually maintaining them. This is because computerised accounting systems automatically ensure that all double entries are completed, so ensuring that all the ledgers balance. Of course, errors can still arise, such as a posting made to the wrong ledger account, but not of the type that control accounts can detect.

Learning outcomes

You should now have learnt:

1. How to prepare control accounts.
2. How to prepare a control account reconciliation.
3. That control accounts enable errors to be traced down to the ledger that does not balance. Thus there will be no need to check all the books in full to find an error.
4. That transfers between sales and purchases ledgers should be prepared in the journal and shown in the control accounts.
5. That control accounts for most businesses are outside the double entry system and are kept as memorandum accounts in the general ledger or in the individual ledgers.
6. That control accounts of large organisations may be part of the double entry system, which means that the sales ledger and purchases ledger are treated as memorandum books outside the double entry system. The entries to such control accounts are the same as for control accounts that lie outside the double entry system.
7. That control accounts are normally only used in manual accounting systems.

Answers to activities

31.1 These errors tend to be detected either as the result of someone drawing attention to an entry that appears to be incorrect or as the result of sample checking of the entries that have been made in the accounting books. A debtor may, for example, question whether the amount on an invoice is correctly summed or suggest that one of the invoices listed in the debtor's monthly statement had nothing to do with the debtor. One of the tasks that auditors carry out involves checking a sample of the transactions during a period so as to determine the level of errors within the entries made relating to them. If the level of error detected is considered material, a more extensive check will be carried out.

31.2 (4) The other side of this double entry was to the debit of the returns inwards account.

(5) The other side of the double entry was done earlier at the time when the individual amounts received from debtors were posted as credits to the individual debtor accounts in the sales ledger. That is, *the other side of this double entry was all the debit entries to the cash book* (see Chapter 13). The posting of each receipt as a credit to the individual debtor accounts done in step (1) is actually a memorandum entry and does not form part of the double entry system. So, in effect, the sales ledger has been taken out of the double entry system and is now a memorandum book. *To summarise, step (5) is actually the credit side of the double entry whose debit side is all the debit entries in the cash book.*

(6) The other side of the double entry was done earlier at the time when each sale was posted from the sales day book to the individual accounts receivable accounts in the sales ledger. That is, *the other side of this double entry was the credit entry made when the total of the sales shown in the sales day book was posted to the sales account in the general ledger* (see Chapter 14). The posting of each sale as a debit to the individual accounts receivable accounts done in step (2) is actually a memorandum entry and does not form part of the double entry system. *To summarise, step (6) is actually the debit side of the double entry whose credit side is all the credit entries in the sales account.*

Review questions

31.1 You are required to prepare a sales ledger control account from the following information for the month of November:

2007			£
Nov	1	Sales ledger balances	23,220
		Totals for November:	
		Sales journal	14,194
		Returns inwards journal	826
		Cheques and cash received from customers	17,918
		Discounts allowed	312
	30	Sales ledger balances	18,358

31.2A You are required to prepare a purchases ledger control account from the following information for the month of April. The balance of the account is to be taken as the amount of accounts payable as on 30 April.

2005			£
April	1	Purchases ledger balances	11,241
		Totals for April:	
		Purchases journal	6,100
		Returns outwards journal	246
		Cheques paid to suppliers	8,300
		Discounts received from suppliers	749
	30	Purchases ledger balances	?

31.3 Prepare a sales ledger control account from the following information:

2009			£
March	1	Debit balances	12,271
		Totals for March:	
		Sales journal	9,334
		Cash and cheques received from debtors	11,487
		Discounts allowed	629
		Debit balances in the sales ledger set off against credit balances in the purchases ledger	82
	31	Debit balances	?
		Credit balances	47

31.4A Prepare a sales ledger control account from the following information for October 2006, carrying down the balance at 31 October:

2006			£
Oct	1	Sales ledger balances	28,409
	31	Sales journal	26,617
		Bad debts written off	342
		Cheques received from debtors	24,293
		Discounts allowed	416
		Cheques dishonoured	120
		Returns inwards	924
		Set-offs against balances in purchases ledger	319

31.5 The trial balance of Outsize Books Ltd revealed a difference in the books. In order that the error(s) could be located it was decided to prepare purchases and sales ledger control accounts.

From the following information prepare the control accounts and show where an error may have been made:

			£
2008			
Jan	1	Purchases ledger balances	19,420
		Sales ledger balances	28,227
		Totals for the year 2008	
		Purchases journal	210,416
		Sales journal	305,824
		Returns outwards journal	1,452
		Returns inwards journal	3,618
		Cheques paid to suppliers	205,419
		Petty cash paid to suppliers	62
		Cheques and cash received from customers	287,317
		Discounts allowed	4,102
		Discounts received	1,721
		Balances on the sales ledger set off against balances in the purchases ledger	640
Dec	31	The list of balances from the purchases ledger shows a total of £20,210 and that from the sales ledger a total of £38,374	

31.6 From the following figures, compile accounts receivable ledger and accounts payable ledger control accounts for the month, and ascertain what the net balances of the respective ledgers should be on 31 January 2010.

Balances on 1 January 2010	£
Accounts receivable ledger – Dr	46,462
Cr	245
Accounts payable ledger – Dr	1,472
Cr	25,465

Total for the month to 31 January 2010	£
Purchases	76,474
Sales	126,024
Purchase returns	2,154
Accounts receivable settled by contra accounts with accounts payable	455
Bad debt written off	1,253
Discounts and allowances to customers	746
Cash received from customers	120,464
Cash discount received	1,942
Cash paid to creditors	70,476
Cash paid to customers	52

31.7A

	£
Sales ledger balances, 1 July 2009 – Debit	20,040
– Credit	56
Purchases ledger balances, 1 July 2009 – Debit	12
– Credit	14,860
Activities during the half-year to 31 December 2009:	
Payments to trade accounts payable	93,685
Cheques from credit customers	119,930
Purchases on credit	95,580
Sales on credit	124,600
Bad debts written off	204
Discounts allowed	3,480
Discounts received	2,850
Returns inwards	1,063
Returns outwards	240
Sales ledger credit balances at 31 December 2009	37
Purchases ledger debit balances at 31 December 2009	26

→

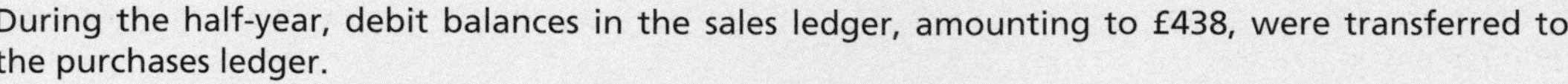

During the half-year, debit balances in the sales ledger, amounting to £438, were transferred to the purchases ledger.

Required:
Prepare the sales ledger control account and the purchases ledger control account for the half-year to 31 December 2009.

31.8A The following extracts have been taken from the subsidiary books of the business owned by D Jenkinson for the month of April 2010.

Purchases Day Book

			£
Apr	3	W Allen	480
	7	J Morris	270
	17	T Sage	410
	24	F Wilding	650

Returns Outwards Day Book

			£
Apr	14	W Allen	50
	29	T Sage	80

Cash Book (Credit side)

			Discounts received	Bank
			£	£
Apr	9	T Sage	30	690
	18	F Wilding	5	195
	24	J Morris	31	389
	27	W Allen	18	322

Journal

			£	£
Apr	30	Creditor W Allen	180	
		Debtor W Allen		180
		being transfer from sales ledger to purchases ledger		

It should be noted that the balances in the accounts of D Jenkinson's suppliers on 1 April 2010 were as follows:

	£
W Allen	360
J Morris	140
T Sage	720
F Wilding	310

Required:

(*a*) The name of the source document which will have been used for making entries in the
   (*i*) purchases day book
   (*ii*) returns outwards day book.

(*b*) The name of **two** subsidiary books (other than those shown in the extracts above) which could form part of D Jenkinson's accounting system. In the case of **one** of the subsidiary books chosen, explain its purpose.

(*c*) The account of T Sage in D Jenkinson's purchases ledger for the month of April 2010. (The account should be balanced at the end of the month.)

(*d*) D Jenkinson's purchases ledger control account for the month of April 2010. (The account should be balanced at the end of the month.)

(*e*) Advice for D Jenkinson on **two** ways in which he might find the purchases ledger control account useful.

(*Southern Examining Group: GCSE*)

31.9 The financial year of The Better Trading Company ended on 30 November 2007. You have been asked to prepare a Total Accounts Receivable Account and a Total Accounts Payable Account in order to produce end-of-year figures for Accounts Receivable and Accounts Payable for the draft final accounts.

You are able to obtain the following information for the financial year from the books of original entry:

		£
Sales	– cash	344,890
	– credit	268,187
Purchases	– cash	14,440
	– credit	496,600
Total receipts from customers		600,570
Total payments to suppliers		503,970
Discounts allowed (all to credit customers)		5,520
Discounts received (all from credit suppliers)		3,510
Refunds given to cash customers		5,070
Balance in the sales ledger set off against balance in the purchases ledger		70
Bad debts written-off		780
Increase in the allowance for doubtful debts		90
Credit notes issued to credit customers		4,140
Credit notes received from credit suppliers		1,480

According to the audited financial statements for the previous year accounts receivable and accounts payable as at 1 December 2006 were £26,555 and £43,450 respectively.

Required:
Draw up the relevant Total Accounts entering end-of-year totals for accounts receivable and accounts payable.

(*Association of Accounting Technicians*)

31.10

(*a*) Why are many accounting systems designed with a purchases ledger (accounts payable ledger) control account, as well as with a purchases ledger (accounts payable ledger)?

(*b*) The following errors have been discovered:
- (*i*) An invoice for £654 has been entered in the purchases day book as £456;
- (*ii*) A prompt payment discount of £100 from a creditor had been completely omitted from the accounting records;
- (*iii*) Purchases of £250 had been entered on the wrong side of a supplier's account in the purchases ledger;
- (*iv*) No entry had been made to record an agreement to contra an amount owed to X of £600 against an amount owed by X of £400;
- (*v*) A credit note for £60 had been entered as if it was an invoice.

State the numerical effect on the purchases ledger control account balance of correcting each of these items (treating each item separately).

(*c*) Information technology and computerised systems are rapidly increasing in importance in data recording. Do you consider that this trend will eventually remove the need for control accounts to be incorporated in the design of accounting systems? Explain your answer briefly.

(*Association of Chartered Certified Accountants*)

31.11 Control Accounts are used mainly for accounts receivable and accounts payable. Explain:

(*a*) why it may be appropriate to use control accounts;
(*b*) the advantages of using them.

You can find a range of additional self-test questions, as well as material to help you with your studies, on the website that accompanies this book at www.pearsoned.co.uk/wood.

chapter 32

Errors not affecting the balancing of the trial balance

Learning objectives

After you have studied this chapter, you should be able to:

- correct errors which are not revealed by a trial balance
- distinguish between the different kinds of errors that may arise

Introduction

In this chapter, you'll learn how to identify and correct a range of errors that can arise when financial transactions are entered in the ledger accounts.

32.1 Types of error

In Chapter 6 it was seen that if we followed the rules

- every debit entry needs a corresponding credit entry
- every credit entry needs a corresponding debit entry

and entered transactions in our ledgers using these rules then, when we extracted the trial balance, the totals of the two columns would be the same, i.e. it would 'balance'.

Suppose we correctly entered cash sales £70 to the debit of the Cash Book, but did not enter the £70 to the credit of the sales account. If this were the only error in the books, the trial balance totals would differ by £70. However, there are certain kinds of error which would not affect the agreement of the trial balance totals, and we will now consider these:

1 **Errors of omission** – where a transaction is completely omitted from the books. If we sold £90 goods to J Brewer, but did not enter it in either the sales account or Brewer's personal account, the trial balance would still 'balance'.
2 **Errors of commission** – this type of error occurs when the correct amount is entered but in the wrong account, e.g. where a sale of £11 to C Green is entered in the account of K Green.
3 **Errors of principle** – where an item is entered in the wrong class of account, e.g. if purchase of a fixed asset, such as a van, is debited to an expenses account, such as motor expenses account.
4 **Compensating errors** – where errors cancel each other out. If the sales account was added up to be £10 too much and the purchases account was also added up to be £10 too much, then these two errors would cancel out in the trial balance. This is because the totals of both the debit side and the credit side of the trial balance will be overstated by £10.

5 **Errors of original entry** – where the original figure is incorrect, yet double entry is correctly done using the incorrect figure. For example, where a sale should have totalled £150 but an error is made in calculating the total on the sales invoice. If it were calculated as £130, and £130 were credited as sales and £130 were debited to the personal account of the customer, the trial balance would still balance.
6 **Complete reversal of entries** – where the correct accounts are used but each item is shown on the wrong side of the account. Suppose we had paid a cheque to D Williams for £200, the double entry of which should be debit D Williams £200, credit Bank £200. In error it is entered as debit Bank £200, credit D Williams £200. The trial balance totals will still agree.
7 **Transposition errors** – where the wrong sequence of the individual characters within a number was entered (for example, £142 entered instead of £124). This is a common type of error and is very difficult to spot when the error has occurred in both the debit and the credit entries, as the trial balance would still balance. It is, however, more common for this error to occur on one side of the double entry only. When it does, it is easier to find.

32.2 Correction of errors

Most errors are found after the date on which they are made. When we correct errors, we should not do so by crossing out items, tearing out accounts and throwing them away, or using chemicals to make the writing disappear.

Activity 32.1 In which book should all the correcting double entries first be entered?

We make corrections to double entry accounts by preparing journal entries. We should:

1 Prepare the corrections by means of journal entries, then
2 Post the journal entries to the appropriate ledger accounts.

1 Error of omission

A sale of £59 worth of goods to E George has been completely omitted from the books. We must correct this by entering the sale in the books. The journal entry for the correction is:*

The Journal

	Dr	*Cr*
	£	£
E George	59	
Sales		59
Correction of omission of Sales Invoice Number . . . from sales journal		

***Note*: in all these examples, the folio column has been omitted so as to make the example clearer.**

2 Error of commission

A purchase £44 worth of goods from C Simons on 4 September was entered in error in C Simpson's account. The error was found on 30 September. To correct this, it must be cancelled out of C Simpson's account and entered where it should be (in C Simons' account). The journal entry will be:

The Journal

	Dr	Cr
	£	£
C Simpson	44	
C Simons		44
Purchase Invoice Number . . . entered in wrong personal account, now corrected		

The entries in the ledger accounts would be:

C Simpson

			£				£
Sept	**30**	**C Simons: Error corrected**	**44**	Sept	4	Purchases	44

C Simons

			£
Sept	**30**	**Purchases: Entered originally in C Simpson's account**	**44**

3 Error of principle

The purchase of a machine for £200 is debited to the purchases account instead of being debited to a machinery account. We therefore cancel the item out of the purchases account by crediting that account. It is then entered where it should be by debiting the machinery account.

The Journal

	Dr	Cr
	£	£
Machinery	200	
Purchases		200
Correction of error: purchase of fixed asset debited to purchases account		

4 Compensating error

In the cash book, the amount of cash sales transferred to the sales account was overstated by £20 and the amount transferred to the wages account was also overstated by £20. The trial balance therefore still balances.

The Journal

	Dr	Cr
	£	£
Sales	20	
Wages		20
Correction of two overcasts of £20 posted from the cash book to the sales account and the wages account which compensated for each other		

5 Error of original entry

A sale of £38 to A Smailes was entered in the books as £28. The other £10 must be entered:

The Journal

	Dr	Cr
	£	£
A Smailes	10	
Sales		10
Correction of error whereby sales were understated by £10		

6 Complete reversal of entries

A payment of cash of £16 to M Dickson was entered on the receipts side of the Cash Book in error and credited to M Dickson's account. This is somewhat more difficult to adjust. First must come the amount needed to cancel the error, then comes the actual entry itself. Because of this, the correcting entry is double the actual amount first recorded. We can now look at why this is so.

We should have had:

Cash

			£
		M Dickson	16

M Dickson

	£		
Cash	16		

This was entered wrongly as:

Cash

	£		
M Dickson	16		

M Dickson

			£
		Cash	16

We can now see that we have to enter double the original amount to correct the error.

Cash

	£		£
M Dickson	16	**M Dickson (error corrected)**	**32**

M Dickson

	£		£
Cash (error corrected)	**32**	M Dickson	16

Overall, when corrected, the £16 debit and £32 credit in the cash account means there is a net credit of £16. Similarly, Dickson's account shows £32 debit and £16 credit, a net debit of £16. As the final (net) answer is the same as what should have been entered originally, the error is now corrected.

The Journal entry appears:

The Journal

	Dr	*Cr*
	£	£
M Dickson	32	
Cash		32
Payment of cash £16 debited to cash and credited to **M Dickson in error on . . . Error now corrected**		

7 Transposition error

A credit purchase from P Maclaran costing £56 was entered in the books as £65. The £9 error needs to be removed.

The Journal

	Dr	*Cr*
	£	£
P Maclaran	9	
Purchases		9
Correction of error whereby purchases were overstated by £9		

32.3 Casting

You will sometimes notice the use of the term **casting**, which means adding up. **Overcasting** means incorrectly adding up a column of figures to give an answer which is greater than it should be. **Undercasting** means incorrectly adding up a column of figures to give an answer which is less than it should be.

Learning outcomes

You should now have learnt:

1. How to describe each of a range of possible errors that can be made when recording financial transactions in the accounts that will not be detected by producing a trial balance.
2. How to identify and correct each of these types of errors.
3. That when errors are found, they should be amended by using proper double entry procedures.
4. That all corrections of errors should take place via the Journal, where entries are first recorded before being posted to the appropriate ledger accounts.

Answer to activity

32.1 The Journal.

Review questions

32.1 Give an example of each of the different types of error which are ***not*** revealed by a trial balance.

32.2 Show the journal entries necessary to correct the following errors:

(*a*) A sale of goods for £412 to T More had been entered in T Mone's account.
(*b*) The purchase of a machine on credit from J Frank for £619 had been completely omitted from our books.
(*c*) The purchase of a computer for £550 had been entered in error in the Office Expenses account.
(*d*) A sale of £120 to B Wood had been entered in the books, both debit and credit, as £102.
(*e*) Commission received £164 had been entered in error in the Sales account.
(*f*) A receipt of cash from T Blair £68 had been entered on the credit side of the cash book and the debit side of T Blair's account.
(*g*) A purchase of goods for £372 had been entered in error on the debit side of the Drawings account.
(*h*) Discounts Allowed £48 had been entered in error on the debit side of the Discounts Received account.

32.3A Show the journal entries needed to correct the following errors:

(*a*) Purchases £1,410 on credit from A Ray had been entered in B Roy's account.
(*b*) A cheque of £94 paid for printing had been entered in the cash column of the cash book instead of in the bank column.
(*c*) Sale of goods £734 on credit to D Rolls had been entered in error in D Rollo's account.
(*d*) Purchase of goods on credit L Hand £819 entered in the correct accounts in error as £891.
(*e*) Cash paid to G Boyd £64 entered on the debit side of the cash book and the credit side of G Boyd's account.
(*f*) A sale of fittings £320 had been entered in the Sales account.
(*g*) Cash withdrawn from bank £200 had been entered in the cash column on the credit side of the cash book, and in the bank column on the debit side.
(*h*) Purchase of goods £1,182 has been entered in error in the Furnishings account.

32.4 After preparing its draft final accounts for the year ended 31 March 2006 and its draft balance sheet as at 31 March 2006 a business discovered that the inventory lists used to compute the value of inventory as at 31 March 2006 contained the following entry:

Inventory item	*Number*	*Cost per unit*	*Total cost*
Y 4003	100	£1.39	£1,390

Required:
(*a*) What is wrong with this particular entry?
(*b*) What would the effect of the error have been on
 (*i*) the value of inventory as at 31 March 2006?
 (*ii*) the cost of goods sold for the year ended 31 March 2006?
 (*iii*) the net profit for the year ended 31 March 2006?
 (*iv*) the total for Current Assets as at 31 March 2006?
 (*v*) the Owner's Capital as at 31 March 2006?

(*Association of Accounting Technicians*)

32.5 Give the journal entries needed to record the corrections of the following. Narratives are not required.

→

(a) Extra capital of £5,000 paid into the bank had been credited to Sales account.
(b) Goods taken for own use £72 had been debited to Sundry Expenses.
(c) Private rent £191 had been debited to the Rent account.
(d) A purchase of goods from D Pine £246 had been entered in the books as £426.
(e) Cash banked £410 had been credited to the bank column and debited to the cash column in the cash book.
(f) Cash drawings of £120 had been credited to the bank column of the cash book.
(g) Returns inwards £195 from G Will had been entered in error in T Young's account.
(h) A sale of a printer for £100 had been credited to Office Expenses.

32.6A Journal entries to correct the following are required, but the narratives can be omitted.

(a) Rent Received £430 have been credited to the Commissions Received account.
(b) Bank charges £34 have been debited to the Business Rates account.
(c) Completely omitted from the books is a payment of Motor Expenses by cheque £37.
(d) A purchase of a fax machine £242 has been entered in the Purchases account.
(e) Returns inwards £216 have been entered on the debit side of the Returns Outwards account.
(f) A loan from G Bain £2,000 has been entered on the credit side of the Capital account.
(g) Loan interest of £400 has been debited to the Van account.
(h) Goods taken for own use £84 have been debited to the Purchases account and credited to Drawings.

32.7A Thomas Smith, a retail trader, has very limited accounting knowledge. In the absence of his accounting technician, he extracted the following trial balance as at 31 March 2008 from his business's accounting records:

	£	£
Inventory-in-trade at 1 April 2007		10,700
Inventory-in-trade at 31 March 2008	7,800	
Discounts allowed		310
Discounts received	450	
Allowance for doubtful debts	960	
Purchases	94,000	
Purchases returns	1,400	
Sales		132,100
Sales returns	1,100	
Freehold property: at cost	70,000	
Provision for depreciation	3,500	
Motor vehicles: at cost	15,000	
Provision for depreciation	4,500	
Capital – Thomas Smith		84,600
Balance at bank	7,100	
Trade accounts receivable		11,300
Trade accounts payable	7,600	
Establishment and administrative expenditure	16,600	
Drawings	9,000	
	£239,010	£239,010

Required:

(a) Prepare a corrected trial balance as at 31 March 2008.

After the preparation of the above trial balance, but before the completion of the final accounts for the year ended 31 March 2008, the following discoveries were made:

(i) The correct valuation of the inventory-in-trade at 1 April 2007 is £12,000; apparently some inventory lists had been mislaid.

(ii) A credit note for £210 has now been received from J Hardwell Limited; this relates to goods returned in December 2007 by Thomas Smith. However, up to now J Hardwell

Limited had not accepted that the goods were not of merchantable quality and Thomas Smith's accounting records did not record the return of the goods.

(*iii*) Trade sample goods were sent to John Grey in February 2008. These were free samples, but were charged wrongly at £1,000 to John Grey. A credit note is now being prepared to rectify the error.

(*iv*) In March 2008, Thomas Smith painted the inside walls of his stockroom using materials costing £150 which were included in the purchases figure in the above trial balance. Thomas Smith estimates that he saved £800 by doing all the painting himself.

(*b*) Prepare the journal entries necessary to amend the accounts for the above discoveries. *Note*: narratives are required.

(*Association of Accounting Technicians*)

You can find a range of additional self-test questions, as well as material to help you with your studies, on the website that accompanies this book at www.pearsoned.co.uk/wood.

chapter 33

Suspense accounts and errors

Learning objectives

After you have studied this chapter, you should be able to:

- explain why a suspense account may be used
- create a suspense account in order to balance the trial balance
- correct errors using a suspense account
- recalculate profits after errors have been corrected
- explain why using a suspense account is generally inappropriate

Introduction

In this chapter, you'll learn how to use suspense accounts to temporarily balance an out-of-balance trial balance. You'll also learn that it is usually not a wise thing to do, even temporarily.

33.1 Errors and the trial balance

In the previous chapter, we looked at errors that do not affect the trial balance. However, many errors will mean that trial balance totals will not be equal. These include:

- incorrect additions in any account;
- making an entry on only one side of the accounts, e.g. a debit but no credit; a credit but no debit;
- entering a different amount on the debit side from the amount on the credit side.

33.2 Suspense account

We should try very hard to find errors when the trial balance totals are not equal. When such errors cannot be found, the trial balance totals can be made to agree with each other by inserting the amount of the difference between the two totals in a **suspense account**. This is shown in Exhibit 33.1 where there is a £40 difference.

Exhibit 33.1

Trial Balance as at 31 December 2008

	Dr	*Cr*
	£	£
Totals after all the accounts have been listed	100,000	99,960
Suspense		40
	100,000	100,000

To make the two totals the same, a figure of £40 for the suspense account has been shown on the credit side of the trial balance. A suspense account is opened and the £40 difference is also shown there on the credit side:

Suspense

	2008		£
	Dec 31	Difference per trial balance	40

Activity 33.1 Where is the debit side of this entry made?

33.3 Suspense accounts and the balance sheet

If the errors are not found before the financial statements are prepared, the suspense account balance will be included in the balance sheet. The balance should be included shown after the figure for net current assets, either as a negative amount (credit balance) or a positive amount (debit balance) (see Exhibit 33.5).

Activity 33.2 Does the use of a suspense account in financial statements affect the true and fair view that they are meant to portray?

33.4 Correction of errors

When errors are found they must be corrected using double entry. Each correction must first have an entry in the journal describing it, and then be posted to the accounts concerned.

One error only

We will look at two examples:

Example 1

Assume that the cause of the error of £40 in Exhibit 33.1 is found on 31 March 2009. The error was that the sales account was undercast by £40. The action taken to correct this is:

Debit suspense account to close it: £40.
Credit sales account to show item where it should have been: £40.

The accounts now appear as Exhibit 33.2:

Exhibit 33.2

Suspense

2009			£	2009			£
Mar	**31**	**Sales**	**40**	Jan	1	Balance b/d	40

Sales

				2009			£
				Mar	**31**	**Suspense**	**40**

This can be shown in journal form as:

The Journal

			Dr	*Cr*
2009			£	£
Mar	31	Suspense	40	
		Sales		40
		Correction of undercasting of sales by £40 last year		

Here's another example.

Example 2

The trial balance on 31 December 2009 had a difference of £168. It was a shortage on the debit side.

A suspense account is opened, and the difference of £168 is entered on the debit side in the account. On 31 May 2010 the error was found. We had made a payment of £168 to K Leek to close his account. It was correctly entered in the cash book, but was not entered in K Leek's account.

First of all, the account of K Leek is debited with £168, as it should have been in 2009. Second, the suspense account is credited with £168 so that the account can be closed.

Exhibit 33.3

K Leek

2010			£	2010			£
May	**31**	**Bank**	**168**	Jan	1	Balance b/d	168

The account of K Leek is now correct.

Suspense

2010			£	2010			£
Jan	1	Balance b/d	168	**May**	**31**	**K Leek**	**168**

The Journal entry is:

The Journal

			Dr	*Cr*
2010			£	£
May	31	K Leek	168	
		Suspense		168
		Correction of non-entry of payment last year in K Leek's account		

More than one error

Let's now look at Example 3 where the suspense account difference was caused by more than one error.

Example 3

The trial balance at 31 December 2007 showed a difference of £77, being a shortage on the debit side. A suspense account is opened, and the difference of £77 is entered on the debit side of the account.

On 28 February 2008 all the errors from the previous year were found.

(A) A cheque of £150 paid to L Kent had been correctly entered in the cash book, but had not been entered in Kent's account.
(B) The purchases account had been undercast by £20.
(C) A cheque of £93 received from K Sand had been correctly entered in the cash book, but had not been entered in Sand's account.

These three errors resulted in a net error of £77, shown by a debit of £77 on the debit side of the suspense account. These are corrected as follows:

(*a*) Make correcting entries in accounts for (A), (B) and (C).
(*b*) Record double entry for these items in the suspense account.

Exhibit 33.4

L Kent

				£					
2008				£					
Feb	28	Suspense	(A)	150					

Purchases

2008				£					
Feb	28	Suspense	(B)	20					

K Sand

					2008				£
					Feb	28	Suspense	(C)	93

Suspense

2008				£	2008				£
Jan	1	Balance b/d		77	Feb	28	L Kent	(A)	150
Feb	28	K Sand	(C)	93		28	Purchases	(B)	20
				170					170

The Journal

			Dr	Cr
2008			£	£
Feb	28	L Kent	150	
		Suspense		150
		Cheque paid omitted from Kent's account		
	28	Purchases	20	
		Suspense		20
		Undercasting of purchases by £20 in last year's accounts		
	28	Suspense	93	
		K Sand		93
		Cheque received omitted from Sand's account		

***Note*: Only errors which make the trial balance totals different from each other can be corrected using a suspense account.**

33.5 The effect of errors on profits

Some of the errors will have meant that original profits calculated will be wrong. Other errors will have no effect upon profits. We will use Exhibit 33.5 to illustrate the different kinds of errors.

Exhibit 33.5 shows a set of financial statements in which errors have been made.

Exhibit 33.5

K Davis
Income Statement for the year ending 31 December 2005

		£	£
Sales			180,000
Less	Cost of goods sold:		
	Opening inventory	15,000	
	Add Purchases	92,000	
		107,000	
	Less Closing inventory	(18,000)	
			(89,000)
Gross profit			91,000
Add Discounts received			1,400
			92,400
Less	Expenses:		
	Rent	8,400	
	Insurance	1,850	
	Lighting	1,920	
	Depreciation	28,200	
			(40,370)
Net profit			52,030

Balance Sheet as at 31 December 2005

	£	£
Non-current assets		
Equipment at cost		62,000
Less Depreciation to date		(41,500)
		20,500
Current assets		
Inventory	18,000	
Accounts receivable	23,000	
Bank	19,000	
	60,000	
Less Current liabilities		
Accounts payable	(14,000)	
		46,000
Suspense account		**80**
		66,580
Capital		
Balance as at 1.1.2005		46,250
Add Net profit		52,030
		98,280
Less Drawings		(31,700)
		66,580

The errors that have been made may be of three types.

1 Errors which do not affect profit calculations

If an error affects items only in the balance sheet, then the original calculated profit will not need to be changed. Example 4 shows this.

Example 4

Assume that in Exhibit 33.5 the £80 debit balance on the suspense account was because of the following error:

On 1 November 2005 we paid £80 to a creditor T Monk. It was correctly entered in the cash book. It was not entered anywhere else. The error was identified on 1 June 2006.

The journal entries to correct it will be:

The Journal

			Dr	Cr
2006			£	£
June	1	T Monk	80	
		Suspense		80
		Payment to T Monk on 1 November 2005 not entered in his account. Correction now made.		

Both of these accounts appeared in the balance sheet only with T Monk as part of accounts payable. The net profit of £52,030 does not have to be changed.

2 Errors which do affect profit calculations

If the error is in one of the figures shown in the income statement, then the original profit will need to be amended. Example 5 shows this.

Example 5

Assume that in Exhibit 33.5 the £80 debit balance was because the rent account was added up incorrectly. It should be shown as £8,480 instead of £8,400. The error was identified on 1 June 2006. The journal entries to correct it are:

The Journal

			Dr	Cr
2006			£	£
Jun	1	Rent	80	
		Suspense		80
		Correction of rent undercast last year		

Rent last year should have been increased by £80. This would have reduced net profit by £80. A statement of corrected profit for the year is now shown.

K Davis
Statement of Corrected Net Profit for the year ended 31 December 2005

	£
Net profit per the financial statements	52,030
Less Rent understated	(80)
Corrected net profit for the year	51,950

3 Where there have been several errors

Let's assume that in Exhibit 33.5 there had been four errors in the ledger accounts of K Davis that were all identified on 31 March 2006:

(A) Sales overcast by	£90
(B) Insurance undercast by	£40
(C) Cash received from a debtor, E Silva, entered in the Cash Book only	£50
(D) A purchase of £59 is entered in the books, debit and credit entries as	£95

***Note*: Error (D) is known as an 'error of transposition', as the correct numbers have been included but in the wrong order, i.e. they have been 'transposed'. It did not affect the trial balance, so it is not included in the £80 adjustment made by opening the suspense account.**

The entries in the suspense account and the journal entries will be as follows:

Suspense Account

2006				£	2006				£
Jan	1	Balance b/d		80	Mar	31	Sales	(A)	90
Mar	31	E Silva	(C)	50		31	Insurance	(B)	40
				130					130

The Journal

				Dr	Cr
2006				£	£
1	Mar	31	Sales	90	
			Suspense		90
			Sales overcast of £90 in 2005		
2	Mar	31	Insurance	40	
			Suspense		40
			Insurance expense undercast by £40 in 2005		
3	Mar	31	Suspense	50	
			E Silva		50
			Cash received omitted from accounts receivable account in 2005		
4	Mar	31	Creditor's account	36	
			Purchases		36
			Credit purchase of £59 entered both as debit and credit as £95 in 2005		

***Note*: Remember that in (D), the correction of the overstatement of purchases does *not* pass through the suspense account because it did not affect the balancing of the trial balance.**

Now we can calculate the corrected net profit for the year 2005. Only items (A), (B) and (D) affect figures in the income statement. These are the only adjustments to be made to profit.

K Davis
Statement of Corrected Net Profit for the year ended 31 December 2005

			£
Net profit per the financial statements			52,030
Add Purchases overstated	(D)		36
			52,066
Less Sales overcast	(A)	90	
Insurance undercast	(B)	40	
			(130)
Corrected net profit for the year			51,936

Error (C), the cash not posted to an accounts receivable account, did not affect profit calculations.

33.6 Suspense accounts: businesses and examinations

Businesses

Every attempt should be made to find errors. A suspense account should be opened only if all other efforts have failed, and they *never* should!

Examinations

Unless it is part of a question, *do not* make your balance sheet totals agree by using a suspense account. The same applies to trial balances. Examiners are very likely to penalise you for showing a suspense account when it should not be required.

Overall

Suspense accounts have probably been used ever since people first started keeping accounts and using them to produce financial statements. However, just because suspense accounts have been used for a very long time does not mean that they should still be used today.

Long ago, accounting records were very poorly maintained. The people maintaining them were frequently untrained. Errors were fairly common, and no one was very concerned when it proved difficult to find out what had caused a trial balance not to balance, if they even went to the extent of preparing one.

Businesses were largely owned by one person who would often also prepare the financial statements, more out of interest than in order to make much use of what they showed which, before there was some regulation concerning what they presented, was frequently little more than the excess or shortfall of revenue over expenditure.

Nowadays, accounting is far more sophisticated and the people maintaining the accounting records are much better trained. Many organisations use computerised accounting systems and very few organisations of any complexity continue to do everything manually. When they do, their records will be good enough to make tracing an error reasonably straightforward.

Errors of the types that cause trial balances not to balance are, therefore, much less common and much easier to detect. As a result, it is inconceivable that a suspense account will ever be needed in practice when an accountant is involved in preparing or auditing the financial statements.

Nevertheless, circumstances may make it impossible for a sole trader's financial statements to be ready in time, for example, to show the bank manager when asking for a loan. It is probably only in circumstances of this type that you may find suspense accounts still in use, albeit rarely. An example may be when money is received by post or credited in to the business's bank account with no explanation and no information. It needs to be put somewhere in the ledger accounts, so a suspense account is used while the reason it was sent to the business is identified.

Learning outcomes

You should now have learnt:

1 How to make the appropriate entries in setting up a suspense account.

2 How to make the correcting entries involving the suspense account when the cause of an error is identified.

3 That some errors may cause the profits originally calculated to have been incorrect.

4 That errors that do not affect profit calculations will have an effect only on items in the balance sheet.

5 That nowadays suspense accounts very rarely need to be used, if at all.

Answers to activities

33.1 This is a major problem in the use of suspense accounts. There is no double entry and, therefore, no debit to match the credit of £40! The justification for this is that there is either a £40 hidden credit somewhere in the accounts that has been omitted when the balances were extracted for the trial balance, or that an extra £40 has been added by mistake to the debit entries in the trial balance. As a result, making this single entry is only completing the existing double entry, the other side being the mistake. Many accountants believe that it is bad practice to open a suspense account as it contravenes the basic principles of double entry. You would be wise to follow that advice and only open a suspense account if an examiner requires you to do so.

33.2 If it is material, definitely. If it is not material, it could be argued that no one will be concerned. However, the appearance of a suspense account in the balance sheet is, by definition, material – you don't include anything in the financial statements as a separate entry that is not of interest to the users of the financial statements. There has been *at least* one error made in the accounting entries and the fact that it cannot be found may indicate a much more serious problem with the accounting system. This is of concern to anyone with a knowledge of accounting for, nowadays, when all complex accounting systems are computerised, *no* error should be that difficult to find, no matter how large or complicated the financial system or the organisation.

Multiple choice questions: Set 4

Now attempt Set 4 of multiple choice questions. (Answers to all the multiple choice questions are given in Appendix 2 at the end of this book.)

Each of these multiple choice questions has four suggested answers, (A), (B), (C) and (D). You should read each question and then decide which choice is best, either (A) or (B) or (C) or (D). *Write down your answers on a separate piece of paper*. You will then be able to redo the set of questions later without having to try to ignore your answers.

MC61 Working Capital is a term meaning

(A) The amount of capital invested by the proprietor
(B) The excess of the current assets over the current liabilities
(C) The capital less drawings
(D) The total of Non-current Assets – Current Assets

MC62 A credit balance brought down on a Rent Account means

(A) We owe that rent at that date
(B) We have paid that rent in advance at that date
(C) We have paid too much rent
(D) We have paid too little in rent

MC63 A debit balance brought down on a Packing Materials Account means

(A) We owe for packing materials
(B) We are owed for packing materials
(C) We have lost money on packing materials
(D) We have an inventory of packing materials unused

MC64 If we take goods for own use we should

(A) Debit Drawings Account: Credit Purchases Account
(B) Debit Purchases Account: Credit Drawings Account
(C) Debit Drawings Account: Credit Inventory Account
(D) Debit Sales Account: Credit Inventory Account

MC65 Capital Expenditure is

(A) The extra capital paid in by the proprietor
(B) The costs of running the business on a day-to-day basis
(C) Money spent on buying non-current assets or adding value to them
(D) Money spent on selling non-current assets

MC66 In the business of C Sangster, who owns a clothing store, which of the following are Capital Expenditure?

(*i*) Shop fixtures bought
(*ii*) Wages of assistants
(*iii*) New van bought
(*iv*) Petrol for van

(A) (*i*) and (*iii*)
(B) (*i*) and (*ii*)
(C) (*ii*) and (*iii*)
(D) (*ii*) and (*iv*)

MC67 If £500 was shown added to Purchases instead of being added to a non-current asset

(A) Net profit only would be understated
(B) Net profit only would be overstated
(C) It would not affect net profit
(D) Both gross profit and net profit would be understated

MC68 A cheque paid by you, but not yet passed through the banking system, is

(A) A standing order
(B) A dishonoured cheque
(C) A credit transfer
(D) An unpresented cheque

MC69 A Bank Reconciliation Statement is a statement

(A) Sent by the bank when the account is overdrawn
(B) Drawn up by us to verify our cash book balance with the bank statement balance
(C) Drawn up by the bank to verify the cash book
(D) Sent by the bank when we have made an error

MC70 Which of the following are not true? A Bank Reconciliation Statement is

(*i*) Part of the double entry system
(*ii*) Not part of the double entry system
(*iii*) Sent by the firm to the bank
(*iv*) Posted to the ledger accounts

(A) (*i*), (*iii*) and (*iv*)
(B) (*i*) and (*ii*)
(C) (*i*), (*ii*) and (*iv*)
(D) (*ii*), (*iii*) and (*iv*)

MC71 Which of the following should be entered in the Journal?

(*i*) Payment for cash purchases
(*ii*) Fixtures bought on credit
(*iii*) Credit sale of goods
(*iv*) Sale of surplus machinery

→

➔ (A) (*i*) and (*iv*)
(B) (*ii*) and (*iii*)
(C) (*iii*) and (*iv*)
(D) (*ii*) and (*iv*)

MC72 The Journal is

(A) Part of the double entry system
(B) A supplement to the Cash Book
(C) Not part of the double entry system
(D) Used when other journals have been mislaid

MC73 Given a desired cash float of £200, if £146 is spent in the period, how much will be reimbursed at the end of the period?

(A) £200
(B) £54
(C) £254
(D) £146

MC74 When a petty cash book is kept there will be

(A) More entries made in the general ledger
(B) Fewer entries made in the general ledger
(C) The same number of entries in the general ledger
(D) No entries made at all in the general ledger for items paid by petty cash

MC75 Which of the following do *not* affect trial balance agreement?

(*i*) Sales £105 to A Henry entered in P Henry's account
(*ii*) Cheque payment of £134 for Motor expenses entered only in Cash Book
(*iii*) Purchases £440 from C Browne entered in both accounts as £404
(*iv*) Wages account added up incorrectly, being totalled £10 too much

(A) (*i*) and (*iv*)
(B) (*i*) and (*iii*)
(C) (*ii*) and (*iii*)
(D) (*iii*) and (*iv*)

MC76 Which of the following are *not* errors of principle?

(*i*) Motor expenses entered in Motor Vehicles account
(*ii*) Purchases of machinery entered in Purchases account
(*iii*) Sale of £250 to C Phillips completely omitted from books
(*iv*) Sale to A Henriques entered in A Henry's account

(A) (*ii*) and (*iii*)
(B) (*i*) and (*ii*)
(C) (*iii*) and (*iv*)
(D) (*i*) and (*iv*)

MC77 Errors are corrected via the Journal because

(A) It saves the bookkeeper's time
(B) It saves entering them in the ledger
(C) It is much easier to do
(D) It provides a good record explaining the double entry records

MC78 Which of these errors would be disclosed by the trial balance?

(A) Cheque £95 from C Smith entered in Smith's account as £59
(B) Selling expenses had been debited to Sales Account
(C) Credit sales of £300 entered in both double entry accounts as £30
(D) A purchase of £250 was omitted entirely from the books.

MC79 If the two totals of a trial balance do *not* agree, the difference must be entered in

(A) The Income Statement
(B) A Suspense Account
(C) A Nominal Account
(D) The Capital Account

MC80 What should happen if the balance on a Suspense Account is of a material amount?

(A) Should be written off to the balance sheet
(B) Carry forward the balance to the next period
(C) Find the error(s) before publishing the final accounts
(D) Write it off in the Income Statement.

Review questions

33.1 A trial balance was extracted from the books of V Baker, and it was found that the debit side exceeded the credit side by £40. This amount was entered in the suspense account. The following errors were later discovered and corrected:

(*i*) Purchases were over-summed by £20.
(*ii*) An amount paid to B Simpkins was debited to the control account as £98 instead of £89.
(*iii*) Sales were under-summed by £11.

Required:
Write up and rule off the suspense account as it would appear in Baker's ledger.

33.2 Your bookkeeper extracted a trial balance on 31 December 2005 which failed to agree by £210, a shortage on the credit side of the trial balance. A suspense account was opened for the difference.

In January 2006 the following errors made in 2005 were found:

(*i*) Sales day book had been undercast by £200.
(*ii*) Sales of £610 to T Vantuira had been debited in error to T Ventura's account.
(*iii*) Rent account had been undercast by £90.
(*iv*) Discounts allowed account had been overcast by £100.
(*v*) The sale of a computer at net book value had been credited in error to the Sales account £230.

You are required to:
(*a*) Show the journal entries necessary to correct the errors.
(*b*) Draw up the suspense account after the errors described have been corrected.
(*c*) If the net profit had previously been calculated at £31,400 for the year ending 31 December 2005, show the calculations of the corrected net profit.

33.3A You have extracted a trial balance and drawn up accounts for the year ended 31 December 2007. There was a shortage of £78 on the credit side of the trial balance, a suspense account being opened for that amount.

During 2008 the following errors made in 2007 were found:

(*i*) £125 received from sales of old office equipment has been entered in the sales account.
(*ii*) Purchases day book had been overcast by £10.

→

(*iii*) A private purchase of £140 had been included in the business purchases.
(*iv*) Bank charges £22 entered in the cash book have not been posted to the bank charges account.
(*v*) A sale of goods to K Lamb £230 was correctly entered in the sales book but entered in the personal account as £320.

Required:
(*a*) Show the requisite journal entries to correct the errors.
(*b*) Write up the suspense account showing the correction of the errors.
(*c*) The net profit originally calculated for 2007 was £28,400. Show your calculation of the correct figure.

33.4 Show how each of the following errors would affect trial balance agreement:

(*i*) Computer repairs £184 was debited to the computer account.
(*ii*) £819 discounts received credited to discounts allowed account.
(*iii*) Inventory at close undervalued by £1,100.
(*iv*) £145 commission received was debited to the sales account.
(*v*) Drawings £94 credited to the capital account.
(*vi*) Cheque paying £317 to T Burnett entered in the cash book but not in the personal account.
(*vii*) Cheque £212 from J Hare credited to J Hare.

Use the following format for your answer:

Item	*If no effect state 'No'*	*Debit side exceeds credit side by amount shown*	*Credit side exceeds debit side by amount shown*
(*i*)			
(*ii*)			
(*iii*)			
(*iv*)			
(*v*)			
(*vi*)			
(*vii*)			

33.5 The following is a trial balance which has been incorrectly drawn up:

Trial Balance at 31 January 2003

	£	£
Capital 1 February 2002	7,845	
Drawings	19,500	
Inventory 1 February 2002		8,410
Trade accounts receivable		34,517
Furniture and fittings	2,400	
Cash in hand	836	
Trade accounts payable		6,890
Sales		127,510
Returns inwards		2,438
Discount received	1,419	
Business expenses	3,204	
Purchases	72,100	
	107,304	179,765

In addition to the mistakes evident above, the following errors were also discovered:

1 A payment of £315 made to a creditor had not been posted from the cash book into the purchases ledger.
2 A cheque for £188 received from a customer had been correctly entered in the cash book but posted to the customer's account as £180.
3 A purchase of fittings £407 had been included in the purchases account.

4 The total of the discounts allowed column in the cash book of £42 had not been posted into the general ledger.
5 A page of the sales day book was correctly totalled as £765 but carried forward as £675.

Show the trial balance as it would appear after all the errors had been corrected. Show all your workings.

33.6 Study the following and answer the questions below.

The trial balance of Mary Harris (Gowns) as at 31 December 2008 showed a difference which was posted to a suspense account. Draft final accounts for the year ended 31 December 2008 were prepared showing a net profit of £47,240. The following errors were subsequently discovered:

- Sales of £450 to C Thomas had been debited to Thomasson Manufacturing Ltd.
- A payment of £275 for telephone charges had been entered on the debit side of the Telephone account as £375.
- The sales journal had been undercast by £2,000.
- Repairs to a machine, amounting to £390, had been charged to Machinery account.
- A cheque for £1,500, being rent received from Atlas Ltd, had only been entered in the cash book.
- Purchases from P Brooks, amounting to £765, had been received on 31 December 2008 and included in the closing inventory at that date, but the invoice had not been entered in the purchases journal.

Questions:

(*a*) (*i*) Give the journal entries, without narratives, necessary to correct the above errors.
(*ii*) Show the effect of each of these adjustments on the net profit in the draft financial statements and the correct profit for the year ended 31 December 2008.

(*b*) (*i*) State briefly the purpose of the journal, giving a suitable example of its use.
(*ii*) State why it is necessary to distinguish between capital and revenue expenditure.

(*Midland Examining Group: GCSE*)

33.7A Gail Dawson is the owner of a retail business. She has employed an inexperienced bookkeeper to maintain her accounting records.

(*a*) On 31 March 2009, the end of the business's accounting year, the bookkeeper extracted the following trial balance from the business's records:

Trial Balance at 31 March 2009

	Dr	*Cr*
	£	£
Non-current assets at cost	18,300	
Provision for depreciation of non-current assets, 1 April 2008	2,800	
Inventory		
1 April 2008	3,700	
31 March 2009		2,960
Trade accounts receivable		1,825
Trade accounts payable	864	
Balance at bank (overdrawn)	382	
Capital		26,860
Drawings	7,740	
Sales	26,080	
Purchases		18,327
Running expenses	6,904	
Allowance for doubtful debts	90	
Suspense		16,888
	£66,860	£66,860

Required:

1 A corrected version of Gail Dawson's trial balance dated 31 March 2009 based on the above information, but with an amended figure for the suspense account.

(*b*) The following errors were found in the accounting system after a corrected version of the trial balance above was prepared.

(*i*) The total of the sales day book for December 2008 had been overstated by £120.
(*ii*) In January 2009 some new office equipment had been purchased for £360; this had been debited to the purchases account.
(*iii*) A payment by cheque to a creditor, £216, had been entered in the books as £261.
(*iv*) A credit note for £37 sent to a customer had been overlooked.
(*v*) The owner had withdrawn a cheque for £80 for private use in October 2008; both the bank and drawings account had been credited with this amount.

Required:

In the books of Gail Dawson

2 Journal entries to correct each of these errors.
(**Note:** narratives are NOT required.)
3 The suspense account. (Start with the amount in the corrected trial balance given in answer to Required 1 above, and include any entries arising from the correction of the errors.)
4 An explanation of the term 'error of commission'. (Give an example of such an error to illustrate your answer.)

(*Southern Examining Group: GCSE*)

33.8 The trial balance as at 30 April 2007 of Timber Products Limited was balanced by the inclusion of the following debit balance:

Difference on trial balance suspense account £2,513.

Subsequent investigations revealed the following errors:

(*i*) Discounts received of £324 in January 2007 have been posted to the debit of the discounts allowed account.
(*ii*) Wages of £2,963 paid in February 2007 have not been posted from the cash book.
(*iii*) A remittance of £940 received from K Mitcham in November 2006 has been posted to the credit of B Mansell Limited.
(*iv*) In December 2006, the company took advantage of an opportunity to purchase a large quantity of stationery at a bargain price of £2,000. No adjustments have been made in the accounts for the fact that three-quarters, in value, of this stationery was in the inventory on 30 April 2007.
(*v*) A payment of £341 to J Winters in January 2007 has been posted in the personal account as £143.
(*vi*) A remittance of £3,000 received from D North, a credit customer, in April 2007 has been credited to sales.

The draft accounts for the year ended 30 April 2007 of Timber Products Limited show a net profit of £24,760.

Timber Products Limited has very few personal accounts and therefore does not maintain either a purchases ledger control account or a sales ledger control account.

Required:

(*a*) Prepare the difference on trial balance suspense account showing, where appropriate, the entries necessary to correct the accounting errors.
(*b*) Prepare a computation of the corrected net profit for the year ended 30 April 2007 following corrections for the above accounting errors.
(*c*) Outline the principal uses of trial balances.

(*Association of Accounting Technicians*)

33.9A Chi Knitwear Ltd is an old-fashioned business with a handwritten set of books. A trial balance is extracted at the end of each month, and an income statement and a balance sheet are computed. This month, however, the trial balance will not balance, the credits exceeding debits by £1,536.

You are asked to help and after inspection of the ledgers discover the following errors.

(*i*) A balance of £87 on a debtor's account has been omitted from the schedule of debtors, the total of which was entered as accounts receivable in the trial balance.
(*ii*) A small piece of machinery purchased for £1,200 had been written off to repairs.
(*iii*) The receipts side of the cash book had been undercast by £720.
(*iv*) The total of one page of the sales day book had been carried forward as £8,154, whereas the correct amount was £8,514.
(*v*) A credit note for £179 received from a supplier had been posted to the wrong side of his account.
(*vi*) An electricity bill in the sum of £152, not yet accrued for, is discovered in a filing tray.
(*vii*) Mr Smith, whose past debts to the company had been the subject of a provision, at last paid £731 to clear his account. His personal account has been credited but the cheque has not yet passed through the cash book.

Required:
(*a*) Write up the suspense account to clear the difference, and
(*b*) State the effect on the accounts of correcting each error.

(*Association of Chartered Certified Accountants*)

33.10A The trial balance of Happy Bookkeeper Ltd, as produced by its bookkeeper, includes the following items:

Sales ledger control account	£110,172
Purchases ledger control account	£78,266
Suspense account (debit balance)	£2,315

You have been given the following information:

(*i*) The sales ledger debit balances total £111,111 and the credit balances total £1,234.
(*ii*) The purchases ledger credit balances total £77,777 and the debit balances total £1,111.
(*iii*) The sales ledger includes a debit balance of £700 for business X, and the purchases ledger includes a credit balance of £800 relating to the same business X. Only the net amount will eventually be paid.
(*iv*) Included in the credit balance on the sales ledger is a balance of £600 in the name of H Smith. This arose because a sales invoice for £600 had earlier been posted in error from the sales day book to the debit of the account of M Smith in the purchases ledger.
(*v*) An allowance of £300 against some damaged goods had been omitted from the appropriate account in the sales ledger. This allowance had been included in the control account.
(*vi*) An invoice for £456 had been entered in the purchases day book as £654.
(*vii*) A cash receipt from a credit customer for £345 had been entered in the cash book as £245.
(*viii*) The purchases day book had been overcast by £1,000.
(*ix*) The bank balance of £1,200 had been included in the trial balance, in error, as an overdraft.
(*x*) The bookkeeper had been instructed to write off £500 from customer Y's account as a bad debt, and to reduce the provision for doubtful debts by £700. By mistake, however, he had written off £700 from customer Y's account and *increased* the allowance for doubtful debts by £500.
(*xi*) The debit balance on the insurance account in the nominal ledger of £3,456 had been included in the trial balance as £3,546.

Required:
Record corrections in the control and suspense accounts. Attempt to reconcile the sales ledger control account with the sales ledger balances, and the purchases ledger control account with the purchases ledger balances. What further action do you recommend?

(*Association of Chartered Certified Accountants*)

→

→ **33.11** The following points were discovered in the books of a small building business before the closing entries had been made. Draft financial statements had already been prepared and showed a net profit of £23,120.

(*i*) The purchase of a new van for £6,000 was included in the motor vehicle expenses account.
(*ii*) The drawings account included £250 for the purchase of fuel which was used to heat the business offices.
(*iii*) £300 paid by a customer, B Burton Ltd, had been credited to B Struton's account in error.
(*iv*) The water rates on the proprietor's home of £750 has been paid by the business and debited to the business rates account.
(*v*) £720 included in the wages account was paid to workmen for building a greenhouse in the proprietor's garden.
(*vi*) Building materials bought on credit from K Jarman for £500, has been delivered to the business on the balance sheet date and had been included in the inventory figure at that date, but the invoice for these goods had not been entered in the purchases day book.

Required:
(*a*) The journal entries to record the necessary adjustments arising from the above.
(*b*) A statement showing the effect of these adjustments on the profit shown in the draft financial statements.

33.12 At the end of a financial year, the trial balance of a small company failed to agree and the difference was entered in a suspense account. Subsequently, the following errors were discovered:

(*i*) The sales day book had been undercast by £10.
(*ii*) A customer's personal account has been correctly credited with £2 discount, but no corresponding entry was made in the discount column of the cash book.
(*iii*) Discounts allowed for July amounting to £70 were credited instead of being debited to the discount account.
(*iv*) A debit balance on the account of D Bird, a customer, was carried forward £10 short.
(*v*) An old credit balance of £3 on a customer's account (J Flyn) had been entirely overlooked when extracting the balances.

Required:
(*a*) Prepare, where necessary, the journal entries to correct the errors.
(*b*) Draw up a statement showing the impact of these errors upon the trial balance.

33.13A Journalise the matters arising from the following items in the books of B Danby, including the narrative in each case. Note that for this purpose cash and bank items may be journalised.

In the case of those items which gave rise to a difference in the trial balance you are to assume that the difference was previously recorded in a suspense account.

(*a*) Discounts allowed during March amounting to £62 were posted to the credit of the discounts received account.
(*b*) The sales day book was overcast by £100.
(*c*) The motor van standing in the ledger at £1,800 was exchanged for fittings valued at £1,400 plus a cheque for £700.
(*d*) £470 has been included in the wages account and £340 in the purchases account. These amounts represent expenditure on an extension to the business premises.
(*e*) A cheque for £86 received from C Blimp and discount of £4 allowed to him were correctly recorded but, when the cheque was subsequently dishonoured, no further entries were recorded.
(*f*) A cheque for £76 paid to D Hood was correctly recorded in the cash book but was posted in error to D I Hoade's account as £67.

33.14 The bookkeeper of a firm failed to agree the trial balance at 30 June, the end of the financial year. She opened a suspense account into which she entered the amount she was out of balance and carried this amount to a draft balance sheet which she prepared.

The following errors were subsequently discovered in the books:

(*i*) The purchase day book had been undercast by £10.
(*ii*) Goods bought on credit from A Supplier for £5 had been posted to his account as £50.
(*iii*) A new machine costing £70 had been posted to the debit of the repairs to machinery account.
(*iv*) S Kane, a customer, returned goods valued at £10. This had been entered in the sales returns day book and posted to the debit of the customer's account.
(*v*) The sale on credit of various items of plant and machinery at their book value of £300 had been recorded in the sales day book.
(*vi*) £60 owed by D Clarke, a customer, had been overlooked when drawing up a schedule of accounts receivable from the ledger.
(*vii*) An item of cash discount allowed £2 had been correctly entered in the cash book but had not been posted to the account of B Luckwood, the customer.
(*viii*) Business rates, treated as having been paid in advance in the previous accounting period, amounting to £45 had not been brought down as a balance on the business rates account at the start of the accounting period. Instead it was included in the prepayments account.

As a result of posting these errors to the suspense account, the balance on the suspense account was reduced to zero.

Required:
(*a*) Prepare the suspense account, including the initial opening entry made by the bookkeeper, along with all the necessary adjusting entries identified above.
(*b*) Explain clearly the effect of correcting the above errors:
  (*i*) on the net profit shown in the draft income statement
  (*ii*) on any of the items in the draft balance sheet

Note: You will find this question easier if you prepare journal entries for each item before answering (*a*) and (*b*).

You can find a range of additional self-test questions, as well as material to help you with your studies, on the website that accompanies this book at www.pearsoned.co.uk/wood.

Scenario questions

The following questions are designed to reinforce learning of the adjustments covered in Part 4 through their application in the preparation of financial statements previously learnt in Parts 1–3.

The answers to these questions are to be found on pages 701–3.

SQ1

Michael Angelo owns Picta Simpla, a company specialising in selling painting by numbers packs by mail order. The packs are purchased from a wholesaler and then resold. The public have no access to the wholesaler and so there is no competition.

During the year ended 30 June 2007 Michael sold 2,900 units at £89 each, having started the year with £19,250 of inventory (600 units). During the year, he purchased a total of 3,150 packs from the wholesaler at £59 each. Michael wants to value his inventory using the FIFO basis.

Staff have been paid wages totalling £14,500, which is only slightly less than the advertising bills paid of £15,000. Michael is upset since the advertising agency has yet to send a final bill, estimated to be £500. Postage per unit sent out was £2. The packing costs were £0.50 per unit.

Rent was £1,000 per month. Insurance of £3,500 has been paid but £650 of this relates to the year ending 30 June 2008. Electricity bills amounted to £2,900, but the bill for the final quarter is still outstanding and is expected to be approximately £500.

The business has a computer which was purchased about two years ago and which Michael reckons has about another three years of useful life left, at which point it will be worthless. It cost £4,000 and Michael uses the straight line method when calculating the depreciation charge. He also has a fax machine which he uses to communicate with his suppliers.

Stationery charges have amounted to £1,350 and he has had telephone bills of £3,500, of which £200 relates to July and August 2007. In the year ending 30 June 2006, he paid £150 for July and August 2006.

Michael has also paid £5,000 from the business bank account for a month-long holiday in Florida. He has asked you whether he can class this as business expenses since it has enabled him to recover from the stresses and strain of running his own business.

Required:

(*a*) Prepare an income statement for the year ending 30 June 2007.

(*b*) Write a brief letter to Michael explaining what drawings are in relation to a small business and answering his query concerning his holiday.

SQ2

The following balance sheet has been prepared by your client, Mr Conman, proprietor of the Sleasy Cars second-hand car dealership:

Balance Sheet as at 31 December 2006

	£	£
Non-current Assets		
Freehold land, at valuation		10,000
Offices		1,000
Breakdown truck		5,000
		16,000
Current Assets		
Inventory	23,000	
Accounts receivable and prepayments	3,500	
Cash in hand	100	
		26,600
Total assets		42,600
Current Liabilities		
Account payable and accruals	8,200	
Bank Overdraft	6,400	
Total liabilities		(14,600)
Net assets		28,000
Capital		
Capital Introduced		15,500
Add Profit for the year		23,500
		39,000
Less Drawings		(11,000)
Total capital		28,000

This was the first year of trading for Sleasy Cars. Mr Conman acquired a field in Hull (which had previously been used for a rubbish tip and then filled in) for £5,000 on 1 January 2006 and erected a portacabin on the site to be used as an office at a cost of £500. He then bought ten second-hand cars from a national dealership for £10,000. He has some accountancy training and has taken a lot of care in producing the balance sheet but confesses that he did not produce an income statement. Instead, as it must be the correct figure, the amount shown for profit in the balance sheet was the amount required to make it balance.

The following points have come to light in your discussion:

(*i*) The office was bought at a discount from a friend who had acquired it from a builder's yard and Conman has included it in the balance sheet at the proper price as he knows that accountants like original costs to be shown. The office should last for five years and Conman agrees that maybe that thing called depreciation should be included at straight line. The office will be worthless at the end of the five years.

(*ii*) The land was a bargain. Conman heard on the grapevine that the council were going to take the previous owners to court as it was an environmental hazard. The owners put it up for sale at £10,000 so he made an offer to the owners of £5,000 which was accepted. He is ignoring the court order to clean up the site since this would cost approximately £3,000. His reason for ignoring it is that although the order was made in December 2005 (i.e. before he bought the land), he did not receive the notice until January 2007 (i.e. after he had bought the land).

(*iii*) The breakdown truck is very old and was bought at the start of the year. It has been shown at cost although it is probably only going to last another year and will have no residual value.

(*iv*) Inventory has all been valued at cost although on one car there is a good chance that it will sell at a loss of £500. Another one was sold in January 2007 for £3,000 but the new owner has not picked it up yet – the profit was £1,500 so this has been included in the valuation of the car. As he has included the car, Conman has not included the debtor in the balance sheet.

(*v*) A customer has owed £2,000 for six months and Mr Conman is becoming slightly bothered. The customer has moved away from the address she gave Mr Conman and he thinks that this debt might not be recoverable.

(*vi*) After hearing the above, you have decided to check the figures and have found that the cash, overdraft and drawings figures are correct and also that there has been no adjustment for the fact that he has not paid his electricity bill of £250 nor his telephone bill of £150. The reason for this is that he is subletting part of the field and is owed £400 in rent and therefore, the two cancel each other out.

Required

(*a*) A revised balance sheet after taking into account all of the above.

(*b*) A description of each of the adjustments that have been made and why each of them is necessary.

SQ3

The following represents the trial balance extracted from the books of Mr Jones, a small businessman based in Aboyne. The books are well-maintained and there is no reason to doubt the accuracy of the entries.

	£	£
Sales		430,000
Purchases	293,500	
Carriage in	2,100	
Drawings	31,000	
Rent	5,200	
Business rates	2,600	
Insurance	550	
Postage	250	
Stationery	986	
Advertising	250	
Wages	10,500	
Bad debts	400	
Allowance for doubtful debts		400
Accounts receivable	5,120	
Accounts payable		3,600
Cash in hand	120	
Cash at bank	3,257	
Inventory	6,520	
Equipment at cost	150,000	
Accumulated depreciation – equipment		35,000
Capital		43,353
	512,353	512,353

Following a discussion with Mr Jones, the following points have come to light:

(*a*) Accruals are necessary for rent (£150), business rates (£200), and stationery (£16).

(*b*) Insurance has been prepaid by £150, advertising by £50.

(*c*) Inventory at the year end is £7,000.

(*d*) Depreciation is to be charged on the equipment at a rate of 10% on cost.

(*e*) The allowance for doubtful debts is to be increased to 10% of the year-end balance.

(*f*) Purchase invoices to the value of £12,000 were found in a desk drawer the day before the meeting with Mr Jones. Half of them have been paid by cheque (but no record made in the cash book) and the rest are outstanding.

Required

(*a*) Prepare an income statement for the year ending on the date of extraction of the trial balance together with a balance sheet as at that date.

(*b*) Mr Jones has kept accurate records (with the exception of point (f)) and yet the accountant must still adjust the figures in the trial balance before preparing the financial statements. As the accountant, write a letter to Mr Jones outlining why the accountant must adjust the figures to convey meaningful information.

SQ4

The following balances were extracted from the books of Mr Try, a window cleaner. He has no knowledge of double entry bookkeeping but records everything correctly. His year end is 30 June and the following balances relate to the year ended 30 June 2007:

	£
Accounts to be paid	100
Cleaning income	17,644
Cash balance	35
Own wages	10,600
Ladders and equipment	750
Repairs to customers' houses due to damage	230
Miscellaneous expenses	110
Owed by customers	220
Insurances	350
Accountancy fees (relating to 2006 – paid in this year)	250
Postage and stationery	50
Bank	2,345
Cleaning materials and cloths	3,400

He has not included the following items as he is not sure how to record them:

(*i*) Bank charges of £45 are to be levied for the year – they are to be processed by the bank in September 2007.
(*ii*) Insurances have been prepaid by £50.
(*iii*) None of the amounts owed by customers can be realistically recovered but Mr Try wants to keep on trying and therefore wants a provision to be made of 50% of the balances.
(*iv*) Accountancy charges for the current year ended 2007 are to be £275.
(*v*) The ladders, including the ones bought in the year, will only last until the end of 2008 and are to be depreciated using the straight line method with no residual value.

Required

(*a*) Prepare an income statement for the year ending 30 June 2007.
(*b*) Prepare a balance sheet at that date.
(*c*) Mr Try has heard about a treatment of non-current assets which he thinks is 'consumables'. He wonders if his ladders could be treated as consumables and not depreciated. Write a letter to Mr Try, using fictitious names and addresses, to answer his query.

SQ5

Michael Baldwin owns B's Casuals, a company specialising in low-quality, high-priced clothing. The material is purchased from Canada, made up into the finished garments in his own factory, and then sold in the local markets through stallholders.

During the year ended 30 June 2007 Michael had sales of £260,040.

Inventory levels have remained relatively consistent over the years, the starting inventory being £21,500 and the closing inventory £22,500.

Michael is not very generous to his staff. This is reflected in the wages paid during the year of only £24,500.

Business rates are a problem, since there is a dispute with the local council. He has paid a total of £7,500 but there is a good chance that he will have to pay a further £2,450.

Postage and advertising is another problem area. For the imports from Canada it is necessary to pay all of the flight costs. These amounted to £5,200 over the year.

He delivers all of his invoices to the stallholders in person and is paid promptly, with the exception of one debtor who owes £2,000 and who has been declared bankrupt. This amount is to be written off.

Advertising is minimal and is done in the local pub: £20 per week is paid to the landlord in return for permission to pin leaflets on the walls and an agreement that the landlord will place a leaflet every day on each table in the bar.

Insurance of £3,500 has been paid, but £650 of this relates to the year ending 30 June 2008.

Electricity bills amounted to £2,900, but the bill for the final quarter is still outstanding and is expected to be approximately £500. Purchases of cloth from Canada for the year are currently recorded as being £65,000, but there is an outstanding bill of £3,500 which is not yet included in that figure.

The factory and the machinery were bought at the same time and originally cost £400,000. Depreciation has accumulated to the sum of £100,000. The current year charge is 5% on the reducing balance basis.

The business had a computer which was purchased about three years ago and which Michael reckons has about another two years of life left. It cost £4,000 and Michael uses the straight line method of calculating the depreciation charge. The computer will be worthless at the end of that time.

Stationery charges amounted to £1,350 and he had telephone bills of £3,500, £200 of which relates to July and August 2007. In the year ending 30 June 2006, he had paid £150 which related to telephone charges in the year ending 30 June 2007.

Michael has also paid £5,000 for a top-of-the-range digital home cinema system. He has enquired as to whether he can class this as a business expense as it has enabled him to unwind after long days at the office.

His salary for the year was £50,000.

Cash in hand at 30 June 2007 was £600 which he borrowed from his wife temporarily on 30 June when he realised that there was no cash available to pay any expenses.

Required

(*a*) Prepare an income statement for the year ending 30 June 2007.

(*b*) Prepare a balance sheet as at 30 June 2007 showing clearly Mr Baldwin's opening capital, net assets and the profit for the year.

(*c*) Michael has enquired why he should include the amounts owing to both the council and the Canadians in the current year's financial statements and also why he cannot include his own wages within expenses since they have been paid out from the business. Write a letter to Michael explaining these points and answering his query concerning the home cinema system.

part

5

SPECIAL ACCOUNTING PROCEDURES

Introduction

This part is concerned with the accounting procedures that have to be followed with different forms of organisations, and commences with a chapter outlining the basic accounting ratios which may be found necessary at this stage.

Chapter 34

Introduction to accounting ratios

Learning objectives

After you have studied this chapter, you should be able to:

- calculate some basic accounting ratios
- use accounting ratios to calculate missing figures in financial statements
- offer some explanations for changes in these ratios over time

Introduction

In this chapter, you'll learn about the relationship between mark-up and margin and how to use the relationship between them and sales revenue and gross profit to find figures that are missing in the trading account. You will also learn how to calculate the inventory turnover ratio and some explanations for why these ratios change over time.

34.1 The need for accounting ratios

We will see in, Chapter 47, that accounting ratios are used to enable us to analyse and interpret accounting statements.

This chapter has been inserted at this point in the book simply so that you will be able to deal with the material in Chapter 35 which includes the drawing up of financial statements from incomplete records. The ratios described in this chapter will be sufficient for you to deduce the data needed to make the incomplete records into a complete set of records, so that you can then prepare the financial statements. Without the use of such accounting ratios, the construction of financial statements from incomplete records would often be impossible.

Activity 34.1 What do you think is meant by the term 'incomplete records'?

34.2 Mark-up and margin

The purchase cost, gross profit and selling price of goods or services may be shown as:

Cost Price + Gross Profit = Selling Price

When shown as a fraction or percentage of the *cost price*, the gross profit is known as the **mark-up**.

When shown as a fraction or percentage of the *selling price*, gross profit is known as the **margin**. We can calculate mark-up and margin using this example:

$$\text{Cost Price} + \text{Gross Profit} = \text{Selling Price}$$
$$£4 \quad + \quad £1 \quad = £5$$

$$\text{Mark-up} = \frac{\text{Gross Profit}}{\text{Cost Price}}$$ as a fraction, or if required as a percentage, multiply by 100:

$$\frac{£1}{£4} = \frac{1}{4}, \quad \text{or } \frac{1}{4} \times 100 = 25 \text{ per cent.}$$

$$\text{Margin} = \frac{\text{Gross Profit}}{\text{Selling Price}}$$ as a fraction, or if required as a percentage, multiply by 100:

$$\frac{£1}{£5} = \frac{1}{5}, \quad \text{or } \frac{1}{5} \times 100 = 20 \text{ per cent.}$$

Can you see a simple rule connecting mark-up to margin?

34.3 Calculating missing figures

Now we can use these ratios to complete trading accounts where some of the figures are missing. In all the examples in this chapter, we shall:

- assume that all the inventory in a business has the same rate of mark-up, and
- ignore wastages and theft of inventory.

Example 1

The following figures are for the year 2005:

	£
Inventory 1.1.2005	400
Inventory 31.12.2005	600
Purchases	5,200

A uniform rate of mark-up of 20% is applied.

Required: find the gross profit and the sales figures.

Firstly, you prepare the trading account section of the income statement with the various missing figures shown as blank (or highlighted with a highlight pen, or with '?' inserted where the missing number should go):

Trading Account section of the Income Statement for the year ending 31 December 2005

	£	£
Sales		?
Less Cost of goods sold:		
Inventory 1.1.2005	400	
Add Purchases	5,200	
	5,600	
Less Inventory 31.12.2005	(600)	
		(5,000)
Gross profit		?

Answer:			
It is known that:	Cost of goods sold + Gross profit		= Sales
and you know that you can use mark-up to find the profit, because:	Cost of goods sold + Percentage mark-up		= Sales
So:	£5,000	+ 20%	= Sales
and Sales =	£5,000	+ £1,000	= £6,000

The trading account section of the income statement can be completed by inserting the Gross Profit £1,000 and £6,000 for Sales.

Trading Account section of the Income Statement for the year ending 31 December 2005

	£	£
Sales		**6,000**
Less Cost of goods sold:		
Inventory 1.1.2005	400	
Add Purchases	5,200	
	5,600	
Less Inventory 31.12.2005	(600)	
		(5,000)
Gross profit		**1,000**

Example 2

Another business has the following figures for 2006:

	£
Inventory 1.1.2006	500
Inventory 31.12.2006	800
Sales	6,400

A uniform rate of margin of 25% is in use.

Required: find the gross profit and the figure for purchases.

Trading Account section of the Income Statement for the year ending 31 December 2006

	£	£
Sales		6,400
Less Cost of goods sold:		
Inventory 1.1.2006	500	
Add Purchases	?	
	?	
Less Inventory 31.12.2006	800	?
Gross profit		?

Answer:	Cost of goods sold	+ Gross profit	= Sales
Moving items about:	Sales	– Gross profit	= Cost of goods sold
	Sales	– 25% margin	= Cost of goods sold
	£6,400	– £1,600	= £4,800

Now the following figures are known:

		£	£
Sales			6,400
Less Cost of goods sold:			
Inventory 1.1.2006		500	
Add Purchases	(1)	?	
	(2)	?	
Less Inventory 31.12.2006		(800)	
			(4,800)
Gross profit			**1,600**

The two missing figures are found by normal arithmetical deduction:

	(2) less £800	= £4,800
	Therefore (2)	= £5,600
So that:	£500 opening inventory + (1)	= £5,600
	Therefore (1)	= £5,100

The completed trading account section of the income statement can now be shown:

Trading Account section of the Income Statement for the year ending 31 December 2006

	£	£
Sales		6,400
Less Cost of goods sold:		
Inventory 1.1.2006	500	
Add Purchases	5,100	
	5,600	
Less Inventory 31.12.2006	(800)	
		(4,800)
Gross profit		1,600

This technique is found very useful by retail stores when estimating the amount to be bought if a certain sales target is to be achieved. Alternatively, inventory levels or sales figures can be estimated given information as to purchases and opening inventory figures.

34.4 The relationship between mark-up and margin

As you learnt in Activity 34.2, both of these figures refer to the same gross profit, but express it as a fraction or a percentage of different figures. This connection through gross profit means that if you know one of the two (*mark-up* or *margin*) you will be able to determine the other.

You learnt a simple definition of this relationship in Activity 34.2. Now we'll take it further so that you can use the relationship in any situation.

If the mark-up is known, to find the margin take the same numerator to be numerator of the margin, then for the denominator of the margin take the total of the mark-up's denominator plus the numerator. For example:

Mark-up		*Margin*
$\frac{1}{4}$	$\frac{1}{4+1} =$	$\frac{1}{5}$
$\frac{2}{11}$	$\frac{2}{11+2} =$	$\frac{2}{13}$

If the margin is known, to find the mark-up take the same numerator to be the numerator of the mark-up, then for the denominator of the mark-up take the figure of the margin's denominator less the numerator:

Margin		*Mark-up*
$\frac{1}{6}$	$\frac{1}{6-1} =$	$\frac{1}{5}$
$\frac{3}{13}$	$\frac{3}{13-3} =$	$\frac{3}{10}$

Be sure that you learn this relationship. It is very often required in examinations.

34.5 Manager's commission

Managers of businesses are very often remunerated by a basic salary plus a percentage of profits. It is quite common to find the percentage expressed not as a percentage of profits before such commission has been deducted, but as a percentage of the amount remaining after deduction of the commission.

For example, assume that profits before the manager's commission was deducted amounted to £8,400 and that the manager was entitled to 5% of the profits remaining after the commission was deducted. If 5% of £8,400 was taken, this amounts to £420, and the profits remaining would amount to £7,980. However, 5% of £7,980 amounts to £399 so that the answer of £420 is wrong.

The formula to be used to arrive at the correct answer is:

$$\frac{\text{Percentage commission}}{100 + \text{Percentage commission}} \times \text{Profit before commission}$$

In the above problem this would be used as follows:

$$\frac{5}{100 + 5} \times £8{,}400 = £400 \text{ manager's commission.}$$

The profits remaining are £8,000 and as £400 represents 5% of it the answer is verified.

Activity 34.3

The same approach is taken when you want to know the VAT included in a bill you've paid. Assuming a VAT rate of 17.5%, what is the VAT when the total bill is £235?

34.6 Commonly used accounting ratios

There are some ratios that are in common use for the purpose of comparing one period's results with those of a previous period. Two of those most in use are the ratio of gross profit to sales, and the rate of **inventory turnover** (also known as 'stockturn').

Gross profit as percentage of sales

The basic formula is:

$$\frac{\text{Gross profit}}{\text{Sales}} \times \frac{100}{1} = \text{Gross profit as percentage of sales}$$

This represents the amount of gross profit for every £100 of sales revenue. If the answer turned out to be 15%, this would mean that for every £100 of sales revenue £15 gross profit was made before any expenses were paid.

This ratio is used as a test of the profitability of the sales. Just because sales revenue has increased does not, of itself, mean that gross profit will increase.

Spend a minute thinking about this and then write down why you think gross profit won't always increase if sales revenue increases.

Exhibit 34.1 illustrates this.

Exhibit 34.1

Trading account sections of the income statements for the years ending 31 December 2006 and 2007

		2006		2007
	£	£	£	£
Sales		7,000		8,000
Less Cost of goods sold:				
Opening inventory	500		900	
Add Purchases	6,000		7,200	
	6,500		8,100	
Less Closing inventory	(900)		(1,100)	
		(5,600)		(7,000)
Gross profit		1,400		1,000

In the year 2006 the gross profit as a percentage of sales was

$$\frac{1,400}{7,000} \times \frac{100}{1} = 20 \text{ per cent.}$$

In the year 2007 it became

$$\frac{1,000}{8,000} \times \frac{100}{1} = 12^1/_2 \text{ per cent.}$$

Sales had increased but, as the gross profit percentage had fallen by a relatively greater amount, the gross profit has fallen. There can be many reasons for such a fall in the gross profit percentage, including:

1 Perhaps the goods being sold have cost more, but the selling price of the goods has not risen to the same extent.
2 There may have been a greater wastage or theft of goods.
3 There could be a difference in how much has been sold of each sort of goods, called the sales mix, between the two years, with different kinds of goods carrying different rates of gross profit per £100 of sales.
4 Perhaps in order to increase sales, reductions have been made in the selling price of goods.

(The last reason was used in the answer to Activity 34.4, but any of these possible causes could have been used instead.) These are only some of the possible reasons for the decrease. The idea of calculating the ratio is to show that the profitability per £100 of sales has changed. The business would then try to find out why and how such a change has taken place.

As the figure of sales revenue less returns inwards is also known as 'turnover', the ratio is sometimes referred to as 'gross profit percentage on turnover'. However, the most frequently used names for it are 'gross profit on sales' and 'gross margin'.

Inventory turnover

If we always kept just £100 of inventory at cost which, when we sold it, would always sell for £125, and we sold this amount eight times in a year, we would make 8 × £25 = £200 gross profit. The quicker we sell our inventory (we could say the quicker we turn over our inventory) the more the profit we will make, if our gross profit percentage stays the same.

To check on how quickly we are turning over our inventory we can use the formula:

$$\frac{\text{Cost of goods sold}}{\text{Average inventory}} = \text{Number of times inventory is turned over within a period}$$

Spend a minute thinking about this and then write down why you think it might be useful to know how many times we turn over our inventory in a period.

It would be best if the average inventory held could be calculated by valuing the inventory quite a few times each year, then dividing the totals of the figures obtained by the number of valuations. For instance, monthly inventory figures could be added up and then divided by twelve. This would provide a far more meaningful figure for 'average' inventory. However, it is quite common, especially in examinations or in cases where no other information is available, to calculate the average inventory by using the figures for the opening inventory plus the closing inventory divided by two. Using the figures in Exhibit 34.1 we can calculate the inventory turnover for 2006 and 2007:

$$2006 \quad \frac{5{,}600}{(500 + 900) \div 2} = 8 \text{ times per year}$$

$$2007 \quad \frac{7{,}000}{(900 + 1{,}100) \div 2} = 7 \text{ times per year}$$

Instead of saying that the inventory turnover is so many times per year, we could say on average how long we keep inventory before we sell it. We do this by the formula:

To express it in months: $12 \div \text{Inventory turnover} = x$ months
To express it in days: $365 \div \text{Inventory turnover} = x$ days

From Exhibit 34.1:

	2006	*2007*
In months	$\frac{12}{8} = 1.5$ months	$\frac{12}{7} = 1.7$ months
In days	$\frac{365}{8} = 45.6$ days	$\frac{365}{7} = 52.1$ days

All the above figures are rounded to one decimal place.

When the rate of inventory turnover is falling it can be due to such causes as a slowing down of sales activity, or to keeping a higher amount of inventory than is really necessary. The ratio does not prove anything by itself, it merely prompts enquiries as to why it should be changing.

Current ratio

This ratio is current assets:current liabilities and indicates whether there are sufficient relatively liquid (i.e. convertible cash) assets to meet short-term debts when due. It is discussed in greater detail in Chapter 47.

This chapter has introduced ratios so as to help you understand the material in the next chapter.

In Chapter 47, we will return again to ratios, and cover the topic with a more advanced and detailed survey of what a range of ratios can be used for.

Learning outcomes

You should now have learnt:

1. That accounting ratios can be used to deduce missing figures, given certain assumptions.
2. That if the mark-up is known, the margin can easily be calculated.
3. That if the margin is known, the mark-up can easily be calculated.
4. How to calculate the gross profit on sales and inventory turnover ratios.
5. What may cause these ratios to change over time.

Answers to activities

34.1 Incomplete records exist where a business does not keep detailed accounting records. Perhaps it only operates a cash book, maybe not even that. In these circumstances, accountants have to construct the records that would have existed had a proper set of books been maintained, so that they can then prepare the financial statements. This involves working through invoices, receipts and bank records, plus any records the business has actually kept, and trying to identify and record what actually occurred during the period. Because of the logical relationships that exist between many of the items in financial statements, and because of the unambiguous rule of double entry, ratios defining the relationship between various items can be used to assist in this investigation. So, for example, if you know what inventory was held at the start, what was purchased and what inventory is left at the end, you can easily work out what was sold.

34.2 If you take mark-up and add one to the denominator (the bottom part of the fraction), you get the margin. This is *always* the case when the numerator (the top line) is 1.

34.3 As you will remember from Chapter 19 (p. 213), you use the same formula but replace both the '5s' in the example with '17.5' and 'Profit before commission' with the total amount of the bill:

$$\frac{17.5}{100 + 17.5} \times £235 = £35$$

This is a *very* useful formula to know. You would be wise to remember it.

34.4 Gross profit may increase at the same rate as sales revenue because demand absorbed more units at the original price. This is normally the case if you make relatively small increases in the volume offered for sale when demand is currently exceeding supply. However, when sales volume increases, it is often partly because selling price has been reduced. Even though total sales volume has increased, sales revenue per unit is less than previously and so gross profit as a percentage of sales revenue will be lower than previously. Unless enough additional units are sold to recover the profit lost as a result of cutting the selling price, total gross profit will fall, not increase.

When a business is in trouble and cutting selling prices to try to make more profits by selling more units, it can often look as if it is doing much better if you only look at the sales revenue and gross profit figures. However, when you calculate the gross profit as a percentage of sales (i.e. the gross margin) and compare it with the previous gross margin, you can see that the business is possibly doing less well than before in terms of overall profitability.

34.5 It is useful to know as you can compare how quickly inventory is turning over now compared to the past. If it is turning over more slowly now (i.e. less times in a period than before), inventory levels may have grown higher, which may mean that the costs of holding inventory have risen. This rise in inventory levels may be due to our now buying more inventory every time we place an order – perhaps suppliers are offering discounts for larger orders. This may be good, or it may be bad. You need to investigate the situation and find out. Hence, checking the trend in inventory turnover alerts you to the possibility that costs may be rising and that they may exceed any savings being made. You can also check your rate of inventory turnover with those of your competitors, enabling you to detect whether your ordering and storing practices are significantly different from theirs. If they are, you would then investigate what is happening so as to ensure that you are not wasting resources unnecessarily.

Review questions

34.1 G Flynn is a trader who sells all of his goods at 20% above cost. His books give the following information at 31 December 2007:

	£
Inventory 1 January 2007	19,400
Inventory 31 December 2007	26,660
Sales for year	155,880

You are required to:

(*a*) Ascertain cost of goods sold.
(*b*) Show the value of purchases during the year.
(*c*) Calculate the profit made by Flynn.

Show your answer in the form of the trading account section of an income statement.

34.2A R Jack gives you the following information as at 31 March 2005:

	£
Inventory 1 April 2004	14,000
Purchases	82,000

Jack's mark-up is 40% on 'cost of goods sold'. His average inventory during the year was £17,000. Draw up an income statement for the year ending 31 March 2005.

(*a*) Calculate the closing inventory as at 31 March 2005.
(*b*) State the total amount of profit and loss expenditure Jack must not exceed if he is to maintain a *net* profit on sales of 8%.

34.3 L Hope's business has a rate of inventory turnover of 8 times per year. Average inventory is £16,240. Mark-up is 60%. Expenses are 70% of gross profit.

You are to calculate:

(*a*) Cost of goods sold.
(*b*) Gross profit.
(*c*) Turnover.
(*d*) Total expenses.
(*e*) Net profit.

34.4A The following figures relate to the retail business of A Bell for the month of July 2003. Goods which are on sale fall into two categories, X and Y.

	Category X	*Category Y*
Sales to the public at manufacturer's recommended list price	£9,000	£24,000
Trade discount allowed to retailers	15%	18%
Total expenses as a percentage of sales	14%	14%
Annual rate of inventory turnover	10	16

You are to calculate for each category of goods:

(*a*) Cost of goods sold.
(*b*) Gross profit.
(*c*) Total expenses.
(*d*) Net profit.
(*e*) Average inventory at cost, assuming that sales are distributed evenly over the year, and that each month is of the same length.

→

34.5 The following trading account is extracted from the income statement for the year ending 31 December 2008 and is given to you by the owner of the business, M Pole:

	£	£
Sales		271,400
Less Cost of goods sold:		
Opening inventory	34,000	
Add Purchases	237,000	
	271,000	
Less Closing inventory	(41,000)	
		(230,000)
Gross profit		41,400

Pole says that normally he adds 20% to the cost of goods to fix the sales price. However, this year there were some arithmetical errors in these calculations.

(*a*) Calculate what his sales would have been if he had not made any errors.
(*b*) Given that his expenses remain constant at 9% of his sales, calculate his net profit for the year 2008.
(*c*) Work out the rate of inventory turnover for 2008.
(*d*) He thinks that next year he can increase his mark-up to 25%, selling goods which will cost him £260,000. If he does not make any more errors in calculating selling prices, you are to calculate the expected gross and net profits for 2009.

34.6A **Trading Account for the year ending 31 December 2009**

	£		£
Inventory 1 January 2009	3,000	Sales	60,000
Purchases	47,000		
	50,000		
Inventory 31 December 2009	(4,500)		
Cost of sales	45,500		
Gross profit	14,500		
	60,000		60,000

R Sheldon presents you with the trading account set out above.(Authors' note) He always calculates his selling price by adding $33\frac{1}{3}$% of cost on to the cost price.

(*a*) If he has adhered strictly to the statement above, what should be the percentage of gross profit to sales?
(*b*) Calculate his actual percentage of gross profit to sales.
(*c*) Give two reasons for the difference between the figures you have calculated above.
(*d*) His suppliers are proposing to increase their prices by 5%, but R Sheldon considers that he would be unwise to increase his selling price. To obtain some impression of the effect on gross profit if his costs should be increased by 5% he asks you to reconstruct his trading account to show the gross profit if the increase had applied from 1 January 2009.
(*e*) Using the figures given in the trading account at the beginning of the question, calculate R Sheldon's rate of inventory turnover.
(*f*) R Sheldon's expenses amount to 10% of his sales. Calculate his net profit for the year ending 31 December 2009.
(*g*) If all expenses remained unchanged, but suppliers of inventory increased their prices by 5% as in (*d*) above, calculate the percentage reduction in the amount of net profit which R Sheldon's accounts would have shown.

(*Edexcel, London Examinations: GCSE*)

***Authors' note*: The trading account shown in the question has been prepared in an unconventional way. It is, in effect, a different form of presentation of the trading account section of the income statement. Do not, yourself, ever use this format when preparing an income statement.**

34.7 L Mann started business with £5,000 in the bank on 1 April. The business transactions during the month were as follows:

(*i*) Took £300 out of the bank for petty cash
(*ii*) Bought a second-hand van and paid by cheque £3,500
(*iii*) Bought goods on credit from A Supplier for £2,500
(*iv*) Sold goods for cash for £300
(*v*) Sold goods on credit for £1,000 to B Safe
(*vi*) Returned faulty goods to A Supplier £500
(*vii*) Paid sundry expenses of £50 in cash
(*viii*) Paid the rent of £500 by cheque
(*ix*) Withdrew cash drawings of £500

Inventory at cost at 30 April was £1,250.

Required:
(*a*) Prepare the ledger accounts recording the transactions.
(*b*) Prepare the trial balance at 30 April.
(*c*) Prepare an income statement for the month ending 30 April.
(*d*) Prepare a balance sheet as at 30 April.
(*e*) Calculate the percentages of:
  (*i*) gross profit to sales
  (*ii*) net profit to opening capital.
(*f*) Comment on:
  (*i*) the relationship between drawings and net profit and why it is important that Mann keeps an eye on it
  (*ii*) working capital.

34.8A Arthur deals in bicycles. His business position at 1 October was as follows:

Capital £3,369
Inventory £306 (3 x Model A bicycles @ £54 and 3 x Model B @ £48)
Balance at bank £3,063

Having established good relations with his supplier he is able to obtain bicycles on one month's credit. He kept notes of all transactions during October which he then summarised as follows:

(*i*) Purchased on credit from Mr Raleigh: 12 Model A at £54 and 10 Model B at £48. Total purchase £1,128.
(*ii*) Sales for cash were: 11 Model A at £81 and 8 Model B at £72.
(*iii*) Paid rent by cheque £60, advertising £66 and miscellaneous expenses £12.
(*iv*) Drawings were £150.

Arthur's valuation of the closing inventory was £456 as at 31 October.

Required:
(*a*) Prepare a statement showing the bank transactions during October.
(*b*) Check the closing inventory valuation.
(*c*) Prepare a statement showing the gross profit and net profit for October and calculate the percentages of gross profit to sales and net profit to sales.
(*d*) Prepare an income statement for the month of October together with a balance sheet as at 31 October.
(*e*) Prepare a statement to show where the profit for the month has gone.

→

34.9 The following information is available for the years 2007, 2008 and 2009:

	2007	2008	2009
	£	£	£
Opening inventory	10,000	20,000	28,000
Purchases	70,000	86,000	77,000
	80,000	106,000	105,000
Less Closing inventory	(20,000)	(28,000)	(23,000)
Cost of sales	60,000	78,000	82,000
Sales	90,000	125,000	120,000
Gross profit	30,000	47,000	38,000

The inventory valuations used above at the end of 2007 and at the end of 2008 were inaccurate. The inventory at 31 December 2007 had been under-valued by £1,000, whilst that at 31 December 2008 had been over-valued by £3,000.

Required:

(*a*) Give the corrected figures of gross profit for each of the years affected by the errors in inventory valuation.

(*b*) Using the figures in the revised trading accounts, calculate for each year:

(*i*) the percentage of gross profit to sales, and

(*ii*) the rate of turnover of inventory.

You can find a range of additional self-test questions, as well as material to help you with your studies, on the website that accompanies this book at www.pearsoned.co.uk/wood.

chapter 35

Single entry and incomplete records

Learning objectives

After you have studied this chapter, you should be able to:

- deduce the figure of profits where only the increase in capital and details of drawings are known
- draw up an income statement and balance sheet from records not kept on a double entry system
- deduce the figure for cash drawings when all other cash receipts and cash payments are known
- deduce the figures of sales and purchases from incomplete records

Introduction

In this chapter, you'll learn about single entry and incomplete records. You will learn how to use the accounting equation to identify the profit for a period when only the opening and closing capital figures and drawings are known. You will also learn how to find the figure for cash drawings or the figure for cash expenses when all other cash receipts and payments are known. And you will learn how to find the figures for purchases and sales from incomplete records.

35.1 Why double entry is not used

For every small shopkeeper, market stall, Internet cafe or other small business to keep its books using a full double entry system would be ridiculous. Apart from anything else, a large number of the owners of such businesses would not know how to write up double entry records, even if they wanted to.

It is more likely that they would enter details of a transaction once only, using a single entry system. Many of them would fail to record every transaction, resulting in incomplete records.

It is, perhaps, only fair to remember that accounting is supposed to be an aid to management – accounting *is not* something to be done as an end in itself. Therefore, many small firms, especially retail shops, can have all the information they want by merely keeping a cash book and having some form of record, not necessarily in double entry form, of their debtors and creditors.

However, despite many small businesses not having any need for accounting records, most do have to prepare financial statements or, at least, calculate their sales or profits once a year. How can these be calculated if the bookkeeping records are inadequate or incomplete?

Activity 35.1

What may cause these accounting statements and figures to need to be calculated?

(*i*) profits
(*ii*) sales
(*iii*) financial statements

35.2 Profit as an increase in capital

From your knowledge of the accounting equation, you know that unless there has been an introduction of extra cash or resources into a business, the only way that capital can be increased is by making profits.

Identifying profits when opening and closing capital are known

If you know the capital at the start of a period and the capital at the end of the period, profit is the figure found by subtracting capital at the start of the period from that at the end of the period.

Let's look at a business where capital at the end of 2004 was £20,000. During 2005 there have been no drawings, and no extra capital has been brought in by the owner. At the end of 2005 the capital was £30,000.

	This year's capital		Last year's capital	
Net profit =	£30,000	–	£20,000	= £10,000

If drawings had been £7,000, the profits must have been £17,000:

Last year's Capital	+	Profits	–	Drawings	=	This year's Capital
£20,000	+	?	–	£7,000	=	£30,000

We can see that £17,000 profits is the figure needed to complete the formula:

$$£20,000 + £17,000 - £7,000 = £30,000$$

Identifying profits when you only have a list of the opening and closing assets and liabilities

In this case, you use the accounting equation.

Activity 35.2

What is the formula for the accounting equation? Write down both (a) the normal form and (b) the alternate form.

Exhibit 35.1 shows the calculation of profit where insufficient information is available to draft an income statement. The only information available is about the assets and liabilities.

Exhibit 35.1

H Taylor has not kept proper bookkeeping records, but she has kept notes in diary form of the transactions of her business. She is able to give you details of her assets and liabilities as at 31 December 2005 and 31 December 2006:

At 31 December 2005

Assets: Van £6,000; Fixtures £1,800; Inventory £3,000; Accounts receivable £4,100; Bank £4,800; Cash £200.

Liabilities: Accounts payable £1,200; Loan from J Ogden £3,500.

At 31 December 2006

Assets: Van (after depreciation) £5,000; Fixtures (after depreciation) £1,600; Inventory £3,800; Accounts receivable £6,200; Bank £7,500; Cash £300.

Liabilities: Accounts payable £1,800; Loan from J Ogden £2,000.

Drawings during 2006 were £5,200.

You need to put all these figures into a format that will enable you to identify the profit. Firstly, you need to draw up a **statement of affairs** as at 31 December 2005. This is really just a balance sheet, but is the name normally used when you are dealing with incomplete records.

From the accounting equation, you know that capital is the difference between the assets and liabilities.

H Taylor
Statement of Affairs as at 31 December 2005

	£	£
Non-current assets		
Van		6,000
Fixtures		1,800
		7,800
Current assets		
Inventory	3,000	
Accounts receivable	4,100	
Bank	4,800	
Cash	200	
		12,100
Total assets		19,900
Current liabilities		
Accounts payable	1,200	
Non-current liability		
Loan from J Ogden	3,500	
Total liabilities		(4,700)
Net assets		15,200
Capital[Note]		15,200

Note: the accounting equation tells you that this must be the figure to use.

You now draw up a second statement of affairs, this time as at the end of 2006. The formula of *Opening Capital + Profit – Drawings = Closing Capital* is then used to deduce the figure of profit. →

H Taylor
Statement of Affairs as at 31 December 2006

		£	£
Non-current assets			
Van			5,000
Fixtures			1,600
			6,600
Current assets			
Inventory		3,800	
Accounts receivable		6,200	
Bank		7,500	
Cash		300	
			17,800
Total assets			24,400
Current liabilities			
Accounts payable		1,800	
Non-current liability			
Loan from J Ogden		2,000	
Total liabilities			(3,800)
Net assets			20,600
Capital			
Balance at 1.1.2006			15,200
Add **Net profit**	(C)		?
	(B)		?
Less Drawings			(5,200)
	(A)		

Deduction of net profit:
Opening Capital + Net Profit − Drawings = Closing Capital. Finding the missing figures (A), (B) and (C) by deduction:

(A) is the same as the total of the top half of the statement of affairs, i.e. £20,600;
(B) is therefore £20,600 + £5,200 = £25,800;
(C) is therefore £25,800 − £15,200 = £10,600.

To check:

		£
Capital		
Balance at 1.1.2006		15,200
Add **Net profit**	(C)	10,600
	(B)	25,800
Less Drawings		(5,200)
	(A)	20,600

Obviously, this method of calculating profit is very unsatisfactory. It is much more informative when an income statement can be drawn up. Therefore, whenever possible, this 'comparisons of capital method' of ascertaining profit should be avoided and a full set of financial statements should be drawn up from the available records.

It is important to realise that businesses should have exactly the same income statements and balance sheets whether they keep their books by single entry or double entry. However, as you will see, whereas the double entry system uses the trial balance in preparing the financial statements, the single entry system will have to arrive at the same answer by different means.

35.3 Drawing up the financial statements

The following example shows the various stages of drawing up financial statements from a single entry set of records.

The accountant has found the following details of transactions for J Frank's shop for the year ended 31 December 2005.

(*a*) The sales are mostly on credit. No record of sales has been kept, but £61,500 has been received from persons to whom goods have been sold – £48,000 by cheque and £13,500 in cash.
(*b*) Amount paid by cheque to suppliers during the year = £31,600.
(*c*) Expenses paid during the year: by cheque: Rent £3,800; General Expenses £310; by cash: Rent £400.
(*d*) J Frank took £250 cash per week (for 52 weeks) as drawings.
(*e*) Other information is available:

	At 31.12.2004	*At 31.12.2005*
	£	£
Accounts receivable	5,500	6,600
Accounts payable for goods	1,600	2,600
Rent owing	–	350
Bank balance	5,650	17,940
Cash balance	320	420
Inventory	6,360	6,800

(*f*) The only non-current asset consists of fixtures which were valued at 31 December 2004 at £3,300. These are to be depreciated at 10 per cent per annum.

We'll now prepare the financial statements in five stages.

Stage 1

Draw up a Statement of Affairs on the closing day of the earlier accounting period:

J Frank
Statement of Affairs as at 31 December 2004

	£	£
Non-current assets		
Fixtures		3,300
Current assets		
Inventory	6,360	
Accounts receivable	5,500	
Bank	5,650	
Cash	320	
		17,830
Total assets		21,130
Current liabilities		
Accounts payable		(1,600)
Net assets		19,530
Financed by:		
Capital (difference)		**19,530**

All of these opening figures are then taken into account when drawing up the financial statements for 2005.

Stage 2

Prepare a cash and bank summary, showing the totals of each separate item, plus opening and closing balances.

	Cash	Bank		Cash	Bank
	£	£		£	£
Balances 31.12.2004	320	5,650	Suppliers		31,600
Receipts from debtors	13,500	48,000	Rent	400	3,800
			General expenses		310
			Drawings	13,000	
			Balances 31.12.2005	420	17,940
	13,820	53,650		13,820	53,650

Stage 3

Calculate the figures for purchases and sales to be shown in the trading account. Remember that the figures needed are the same as those which would have been found if double entry records had been kept.

Purchases: In double entry, 'purchases' are the goods that have been bought in the period irrespective of whether they have been paid for or not during the period. The figure of payments to suppliers must, therefore, be adjusted to find the figure for purchases.

	£
Paid during the year	31,600
Less Payments made, but which were for goods purchased in a previous year (accounts payable at 31.12.2004)	(1,600)
	30,000
Add Purchases made in the current year for which payment has not yet been made (accounts payable at 31.12.2005)	2,600
Goods bought in this year, i.e. purchases	32,600

The same answer could have been obtained if the information had been shown in the form of a total accounts payable account, the figure for purchases being the amount required to make the account totals agree.

Total Accounts Payable

	£		£
Cash paid to suppliers	31,600	Balances b/d	1,600
Balances c/d	2,600	**Purchases (missing figure)**	**32,600**
	34,200		34,200

Sales: The sales figure will only equal receipts where all the sales are for cash. Therefore, the receipts figures need adjusting to find sales. This can only be done by constructing a total accounts receivable account, the sales figure being the one needed to make the totals agree.

Total Accounts Receivable

	£		£
Balances b/d	5,500	Receipts: Cash	13,500
Sales (missing figure)	**62,600**	Cheque	48,000
		Balances c/d	6,600
	68,100		68,100

Stage 4

Expenses. Where there are no accruals or prepayments either at the beginning or end of the accounting period, then expenses paid will equal expenses used up during the period. These figures will be charged to the income statement.

On the other hand, where such prepayments or accruals exist, an expense account should be drawn up for that particular item. When all known items are entered, the missing figure will be the expenses to be charged for the accounting period. In this case, only the rent account needs to be drawn up.

Rent

	£		£
Bank	3,800	**Profit and loss (missing figure)**	**4,550**
Cash	400		
Accrued c/d	350		
	4,550		4,550

Stage 5

Now draw up the financial statements.

J Frank
Income Statement for the year ending 31 December 2005

	£	£
Sales (stage 3)		**62,600**
Less Cost of goods sold:		
Inventory at 1.1.2005	6,360	
***Add* Purchases (stage 3)**	**32,600**	
	38,960	
Less Inventory at 31.12.2005	(6,800)	
		(32,160)
Gross profit		30,440
Less Expenses:		
Rent (stage 4)	**4,550**	
General expenses	310	
Depreciation: Fixtures	330	
		(5,190)
Net profit		25,250

Balance Sheet as at 31 December 2005

	£	£
Non-current assets		
Fixtures at 1.1.2005		3,300
Less Depreciation		(330)
		2,970
Current assets		
Inventory	6,800	
Accounts receivable	6,600	
Bank	17,940	
Cash	420	
		31,760
Total assets		34,730
Current liabilities		
Accounts payable	2,600	
Rent owing	350	
Total liabilities		(2,950)
Net assets		31,780
Financed by:		
Capital		
Balance 1.1.2005 (per Opening Statement of Affairs)		19,530
Add Net profit		25,250
		44,780
Less Drawings		(13,000)
Total capital		31,780

35.4 Incomplete records and missing figures

In practice, part of the information relating to *cash* receipts or payments is often missing. If the missing information is in respect of one type of payment, then it is normal to assume that the missing figure is the amount required to make both totals agree in the *cash* column of the cash and bank summary. (This does not happen with bank items owing to the fact that another copy of the bank statement can always be obtained from the bank.)

Exhibit 35.2 shows an example where the figure for Drawings is unknown. The exhibit also shows the contra entry made in the cash book when cash receipts are banked.

Exhibit 35.2

The following information on cash and bank receipts and payments is available:

	Cash	*Bank*
	£	£
Cash paid into the bank during the year	35,500	
Receipts from debtors	47,250	46,800
Paid to suppliers	1,320	44,930
Drawings during the year	?	–
Expenses paid	150	3,900
Balances at 1.1.2004	235	11,200
Balances at 31.12.2004	250	44,670

Now, you need to enter this information in a cash book:

	Cash	*Bank*		*Cash*	*Bank*
	£	£		£	£
Balances 1.1.2004	235	11,200	Bank ¢	35,500	
Received from debtors	47,250	46,800	Suppliers	1,320	44,930
Cash ¢		35,500	Expenses	150	3,900
			Drawings	?	
			Balances 31.12.2004	250	44,670
	47,485	93,500		47,485	93,500

The amount needed to make the two sides of the cash columns agree is £10,265, i.e. £47,485 minus £(35,500 + 1,320 + 150 + 250). This is the figure for drawings.

Exhibit 35.3 shows an example where the amount of cash received from debtors is unknown.

Exhibit 35.3

Information on cash and bank transactions is available as follows:

	Cash	*Bank*
	£	£
Receipts from debtors	?	78,080
Cash withdrawn from the bank for business use (this is the amount which is used besides cash receipts from debtors to pay drawings and expenses)		10,920
Paid to suppliers	–	65,800
Expenses paid	640	2,230
Drawings	21,180	315
Balances at 1.1.2007	40	1,560
Balances at 31.12.2007	70	375

	Cash	Bank		Cash	Bank
	£	£		£	£
Balances 1.1.2007	40	1,560	Suppliers		65,800
Received from debtors	?	78,080	Expenses	640	2,230
Withdrawn from Bank ¢	10,920		Withdrawn from Bank ¢		10,920
			Drawings	21,180	315
			Balances 31.12.2007	70	375
	21,890	79,640		21,890	79,640

As it is the only missing item, receipts from debtors is, therefore, the amount needed to make each side of the cash column agree, £10,930, i.e. £21,890 minus £(10,920 + 40).

It must be emphasised that the use of balancing figures is acceptable *only* when all the other figures have been verified. Should, for instance, a cash expense be omitted when cash received from debtors is being calculated, this would result in an understatement not only of expenses but also, ultimately, of sales.

35.5 Where there are two missing pieces of information

Quite often, the only cash expense item for which there is some doubt is drawings. Receipts will normally have been retained for all the others.

If both cash drawings and cash receipts from debtors (or from cash sales) were not known, it would not be possible to deduce both of these figures separately. The only course available would be to estimate whichever figure was more capable of being accurately assessed, use this as if it were a 'known' figure, then deduce the other figure. However, this is a most unsatisfactory position as both of the figures are estimates, the accuracy of each one relying entirely upon the accuracy of the other.

Activity 35.3

Why is arriving at a figure for drawings that is as accurate as possible *very* important for the owner of a business?

35.6 Cash sales and purchases for cash

Where there are cash sales as well as sales on credit terms, then the cash sales must be added to sales on credit to give the total sales for the year. This total figure of sales will be the one shown in the trading account part of the income statement.

Similarly, purchases for cash will need to be added to credit purchases in order to produce the figure of total purchases for the trading account.

35.7 Inventory stolen, lost or destroyed

When inventory is stolen, lost or destroyed, its value will have to be calculated. This could be needed to justify an insurance claim or to settle problems concerning taxation, etc.

If the inventory had been valued immediately before the fire, burglary, etc., then the value of the inventory lost would obviously be known. Also, if a full and detailed system of inventory records were kept, then the value would also be known. However, as the occurrence of fires or burglaries cannot be foreseen, and many small businesses do not keep full and proper inventory records, the value of the inventory lost has to be calculated in some other way.

The methods described in this chapter and in Chapter 34 are used. Bear in mind that you are going to be calculating figures as at the time of the fire or theft, not at the end of the accounting period.

Let's now look at Exhibits 35.4 and 35.5. The first exhibit involves a very simple case, where figures of purchases and sales are known and all goods are sold at the same gross profit margin. The second exhibit is rather more complicated.

Exhibit 35.4

J Collins lost the whole of his inventory in a fire on 17 March 2009. The last time that stocktaking had been done was on 31 December 2008, the last balance sheet date, when the inventory was valued at cost at £19,500. Purchases from then until 17 March 2009 amounted to £68,700 and sales in that period were £96,000. All sales were made at a uniform gross profit margin of 20 per cent.

First, the trading account section of the income statement can be drawn up with the known figures included. Then the missing figures can be deduced.

J Collins
Trading Account section of the income statement for the period
1 January 2009 to 17 March 2009

		£		£
Sales				96,000
Less Cost of goods sold:				
Opening inventory		19,500		
Add Purchases		68,700		
		88,200		
***Less* Closing inventory**	(C)	(?)		
			(B)	(?)
Gross profit			(A)	?

Now the missing figures can be deduced:

It is known that the gross profit margin is 20 per cent, therefore gross profit (A) is 20% of £96,000 = £19,200.

Now (B) + (A) £19,200 = £96,000, so that (B) is the difference, i.e. £76,800.

Now that (B) is known, (C) can be deduced: £88,200 – (C) = £76,800, so (C) is the difference, i.e. £11,400.

The figure for inventory destroyed by fire, at cost, is therefore £11,400.

Note: you should always do this calculation in the sequence shown (i.e. A then B then C).

Exhibit 35.5

T Scott had the whole of his inventory stolen from his warehouse on the night of 20 August 2006 along with many of his accounting records including his sales and purchases day books. The sales and purchases ledgers were found in the car park. The following facts are known:

(*a*) Inventory at the last balance sheet date, 31 March 2006, was £12,480 at cost.

(*b*) Receipts from debtors during the period 1 April to 20 August 2006 amounted to £31,745. Accounts receivable were: at 31 March 2006 £14,278, at 20 August 2006 £12,333.

(*c*) Payments to creditors during the period 1 April to 20 August 2006 amounted to £17,270. Accounts payable were: at 31 March 2006 £7,633, at 20 August 2006 £6,289.

(*d*) The gross profit margin on all sales has been constant at 25 per cent.

Before we can start to construct a trading account for the period, we need to find out the figures for sales and purchases. These can be found by drawing up total accounts receivable and total accounts payable accounts, sales and purchases figures being the difference on the accounts.

Total Accounts Receivable

	£		£
Balances b/d	14,278	Cash and bank	31,745
Sales (difference)	**29,800**	Balances c/d	12,333
	44,078		44,078

Total Accounts Payable

	£		£
Cash and bank	17,270	Balances b/d	7,633
Balances c/d	6,289	**Purchases (difference)**	**15,926**
	23,559		23,559

Activity 35.4 You already did this for another example earlier in this chapter. Where?

The trading account section of the income statement can now show the figures so far known:

Trading Account section of the income statement for the period 1 April to 20 August 2006

		£		£
Sales				29,800
Less Cost of goods sold:				
Opening inventory		12,480		
Add Purchases		15,926		
		28,406		
***Less* Closing inventory**	(C)	(?)		
			(B)	(?)
Gross profit			(A)	?

Gross profit can be found, as the margin on sales is known to be 25%, therefore (A) = 25% of £29,800 = £7,450.

Cost of goods sold (B) + Gross profit £7,450 = £29,800, therefore (B) is £22,350.

£28,406 – (C) = (B) £22,350, therefore (C) is £6,056.

The figure for cost of goods stolen is therefore £6,056.

The completed trading account is, therefore:

Trading Account section of the income statement for the period 1 April to 20 August 2006

		£		£
Sales				29,800
Less Cost of goods sold:				
Opening inventory		12,480		
Add Purchases		15,926		
		28,406		
***Less* Closing inventory**	(C)	(6,056)		
			(B)	(22,350)
Gross profit			(A)	7,450

Learning outcomes

You should now have learnt:

1. The difference between a single entry system and a double entry system.
2. How to calculate net profit for a small trader when you know the change in capital over a period and the amount of drawings during the period.
3. How to prepare an income statement and balance sheet from records not kept on a double entry system.
4. How to deduce the figures for purchases and sales from a total accounts payable account and a total accounts receivable account.

Answers to activities

35.1 There are a range of possible reasons. Of the three examples shown here, the first must be done once a year, the second must be done from time to time, and the third is done on demand:

(*i*) Profits need to be calculated for the purpose of determining the income tax payable.
(*ii*) Turnover (i.e. sales) needs to be calculated in order to know whether or not the business needs to register for VAT.
(*iii*) Financial statements may be required by the bank.

35.2 (*a*) Capital = Assets − Liabilities
(*b*) Assets = Capital + Liabilities

35.3 Normal practice would be to try to get the owner to list all the cash withdrawn as accurately as possible and then use that figure for drawings. However, care needs to be taken to make this as accurate as possible because the Revenue and Customs (the UK tax authority) has very sophisticated data on the relationship between business income and expenditure and profitability, and also on level of income and standard of living enjoyed by a taxpayer. If the drawings are underestimated, this could have very serious repercussions for the owner.

35.4 This is exactly the same as what you did in Section 35.3 Stage 3.

Review questions

35.1 F Lee started in business on 1 January 2002 with £35,000 in a bank account. Unfortunately he did not keep proper books of account.

He must submit a calculation of profit for the year ending 31 December 2002 to the Inspector of Taxes. At 31 December 2002 he had inventory valued at cost £6,200, a van which had cost £6,400 during the year and which had depreciated during the year by £1,600, accounts receivable of £15,200, expenses prepaid of £310, a bank balance of £33,490, a cash balance £270, trade accounts payable £7,100, and expenses owing £640.

His drawings were: cash £400 per week for 50 weeks, cheque payments £870.

Draw up statements to show the profit or loss for the year.

35.2 Ivor Clue is a magician. He has conjured up the following results from his non-existent accounting records.

Fees are equal to five times his direct costs. (This term is explained in Section 37.3.)
At any given time his inventory equals one week's direct costs.
He defines a month as four weeks.
His inventory at both 31 May and 30 June was valued at £500.

Required:
Calculate his fees and profit for the month of June.

35.3A B Barnes is a dealer who has not kept proper books of account. At 31 October 2003 his state of affairs was as follows:

	£
Cash	210
Bank balance	4,700
Fixtures	2,800
Inventory	18,200
Accounts receivable	26,600
Accounts payable	12,700
Van (at valuation)	6,800

During the year to 31 October 2004 his drawings amounted to £32,200. Winnings from the Lottery of £7,600 were put into the business. Extra fixtures were bought for £900.

At 31 October 2004 his assets and liabilities were: Cash £190; Bank overdraft £1,810; Inventory £23,900; Accounts payable for goods £9,100; Accounts payable for expenses £320; Fixtures to be depreciated £370; Van to be valued at £5,440; Accounts receivable £29,400; Prepaid expenses £460.

Draw up a statement showing the profit or loss made by Barnes for the year ending 31 October 2004.

35.4 The following is a summary of Jane's bank account for the year ended 31 December 2002:

	£		£
Balance 1.1.2002	4,100	Payments to creditors for goods	67,360
Receipts from debtors	91,190	Rent	3,950
Balance 31.12.2002	6,300	Insurance	1,470
		Sundry expenses	610
		Drawings	28,200
	101,590		101,590

All of the business takings have been paid into the bank with the exception of £17,400. Out of this, Jane has paid wages of £11,260, drawings of £1,200 and purchase of goods £4,940.

The following additional information is available:

	31.12.2001	*31.12.2002*
Inventory	10,800	12,200
Accounts payable for goods	12,700	14,100
Accounts receivable for goods	21,200	19,800
Insurance prepaid	420	440
Rent owing	390	–
Fixtures at valuation	1,800	1,600

You are to draw up a set of financial statements for the year ended 31 December 2002. Show all of your workings.

35.5A A Bell has kept records of his business transactions in a single entry form, but he did not realise that he had to record cash drawings. His bank account for the year 2008 is as follows:

	£		£
Balance 1.1.2008	920	Cash withdrawn from bank	12,600
Receipts from debtors	94,200	Trade accounts payable	63,400
Loan from F Tung	2,500	Rent	3,200
		Insurance	1,900
		Drawings	11,400
		Sundry expenses	820
		Balance 31.12.2008	4,300
	97,620		97,620

→

Records of cash paid were: Sundry expenses £180; Trade accounts payable £1,310. Cash sales amounted to £1,540.

The following information is also available:

	31.12.2007	*31.12.2008*
	£	£
Cash in hand	194	272
Trade accounts payable	7,300	8,100
Accounts receivable	9,200	11,400
Rent owing	–	360
Insurance paid in advance	340	400
Van (at valuation)	5,500	4,600
Inventory	24,200	27,100

You are to draw up an income statement for the year ending 31 December 2008, and a balance sheet as at that date. Show all of your workings.

35.6 On 1 May 2008 Jenny Barnes, who is a retailer, had the following balances in her books: Premises £70,000; Equipment £8,200; Vehicles £5,100; Inventory £9,500; Trade accounts receivable £150. Jenny does not keep proper books of account, but bank statements covering the 12 months from 1 May 2008 to 30 April 2009 were obtained from the bank and summarised as follows:

	£
Money paid into bank:	
Extra capital	8,000
Shop takings	96,500
Received from debtors	1,400
Payments made by cheque:	
Paid for inventory purchased	70,500
Purchase of delivery van	6,200
Vehicle running expenses	1,020
Lighting and heating	940
Sales assistants' wages	5,260
Miscellaneous expenses	962

It has been discovered that, in the year ending 30 April 2009, the owner had paid into the bank all shop takings apart from cash used to pay (*i*) £408 miscellaneous expenses and (*ii*) £500 per month drawings.

At 30 April 2009:

£7,600 was owing to suppliers for inventory bought on credit.

The amount owed by trade accounts receivable is to be treated as a bad debt. Assume that there had been no sales on credit during the year.

Inventory was valued at £13,620.

Depreciation for the year was calculated at £720 (equipment) and £1,000 (vehicles).

You are asked to prepare an income statement for the year ending 30 April 2009. (Show all necessary workings separately.)

(Edexcel Foundation, London Examinations: GCSE)

35.7A Bill Smithson runs a second-hand furniture business from a shop which he rents. He does not keep complete accounting records, but is able to provide you with the following information about his financial position at 1 April 2008: Inventory of furniture £3,210; Trade accounts receivable £2,643; Trade accounts payable £1,598; Motor vehicle £5,100; Shop fittings £4,200; Motor vehicle expenses owing £432.

He has also provided the following summary of his bank account for the year ended 31 March 2009:

	£		£
Balance at 1 Apr 2008	2,420	Payments of trade accounts payable	22,177
Cheques received from trade debtors	44,846	Electricity	1,090
Cash sales	3,921	Telephone	360
		Rent	2,000
		Advertising	1,430
		Shop fittings	2,550
		Insurance	946
		Motor vehicle expenses	2,116
		Drawings	16,743
		Balance at 31 Mar 2009	1,775
	£51,187		£51,187

All cash and cheques received were paid into the bank account immediately.

You find that the following must also be taken into account:

- Depreciation is to be written-off the motor vehicle at 20% and off the shop fittings at 10%, calculated on the book values at 1 April 2008 plus additions during the year.
- At 31 March 2009 motor vehicle expenses owing were £291 and insurance paid in advance was £177.
- Included in the amount paid for shop fittings were:
  a table bought for £300, which Smithson resold during the year at cost,
  some wooden shelving (cost £250), which Smithson used in building an extension to his house.
  Other balances at 31 March 2009 were:

	£
Trade accounts receivable	4,012
Trade accounts payable	2,445
Inventory of furniture	4,063

Required:

(*a*) For the year ended 31 March 2009
  (*i*) calculate Smithson's sales and purchases,
  (*ii*) prepare his income statement.

(*b*) Prepare Smithson's balance sheet as at 31 March 2009.

(Midland Examining Group: GCSE)

35.8 Although Janet Lambert has run a small business for many years, she has never kept adequate accounting records. However, a need to obtain a bank loan for the expansion of the business has necessitated the preparation of 'final' accounts for the year ended 31 August 2009. As a result, the following information has been obtained after much careful research:

1 Janet Lambert's business assets and liabilities are as follows:

As at	*1 September 2008*	*31 August 2009*
	£	£
Inventory	8,600	16,800
Accounts receivable for sales	3,900	4,300
Accounts payable for purchases	7,400	8,900
Rent prepaid	300	420
Electricity accrued due	210	160
Balance at bank	2,300	1,650
Cash in hand	360	330

→

2 All takings have been banked after deducting the following payments:

Cash drawings – Janet Lambert has not kept a record of cash drawings, but suggests these will be in the region of	£8,000
Casual labour	£1,200
Purchase of goods for resale	£1,800

Note: Takings have been the source of all amounts banked.

3 Bank payments during the year ended 31 August 2009 have been summarised as follows:

	£
Purchases	101,500
Rent	5,040
Electricity	1,390
Delivery costs (to customers)	3,000
Casual labour	6,620

4 It has been established that a gross profit of $33^1/_3$% on cost has been obtained on all goods sold.

5 Despite her apparent lack of precise accounting records, Janet Lambert is able to confirm that she has taken out of the business during the year under review goods for her own use costing £600.

Required:

(*a*) Prepare a computation of total purchases for the year ending 31 August 2009.

(*b*) Prepare an income statement for the year ending 31 August 2009 and a balance sheet as at that date, both in as much detail as possible.

(*c*) Explain why it is necessary to introduce accruals and prepayments into accounting.

(*Association of Accounting Technicians*)

35.9A Jean Smith, who retails wooden ornaments, has been so busy since she commenced business on 1 April 2005 that she has neglected to keep adequate accounting records. Jean's opening capital consisted of her life savings of £15,000 which she used to open a business bank account. The transactions in this bank account during the year ended 31 March 2006 have been summarised from the bank account as follows:

	£
Receipts:	
Loan from John Peacock, uncle	10,000
Takings	42,000
Payments:	
Purchases of goods for resale	26,400
Electricity for period to 31 December 2005	760
Rent of premises for 15 months to 30 June 2006	3,500
Rates of premises for the year ended 31 March 2006	1,200
Wages of assistants	14,700
Purchase of van, 1 October 2005	7,600
Purchase of holiday caravan for Jean Smith's private use	8,500
Van licence and insurance, payments covering a year	250

According to the bank account, the balance in hand on 31 March 2006 was £4,090 in Jean Smith's favour.

While the intention was to bank all takings intact, it now transpires that, in addition to cash drawings, the following payments were made out of takings before bankings:

	£
Van running expenses	890
Postages, stationery and other sundry expenses	355

On 31 March 2006, takings of £640 awaited banking; this was done on 1 April 2006. It has been discovered that amounts paid into the bank of £340 on 29 March 2006 were not credited to Jean's bank account until 2 April 2006 and a cheque of £120, drawn on 28 March 2006 for purchases, was not paid until 10 April 2006. The normal rate of gross profit on the goods sold by Jean Smith is 50% on sales. However, during the year a purchase of ornamental goldfish costing £600 proved to be unpopular with customers and therefore the entire inventory had to be sold at cost price.

Interest at the rate of 5% per annum is payable on each anniversary of the loan from John Peacock on 1 January 2006.

Depreciation is to be provided on the van on the straight line basis; it is estimated that the van will be disposed of after five years' use for £100.

The inventory of goods for resale at 31 March 2006 has been valued at cost at £1,900.

Accounts payable for purchases at 31 March 2006 amounted to £880 and electricity charges accrued due at that date were £180.

Trade accounts receivable at 31 March 2006 totalled £2,300.

Required:
Prepare an income statement for the year ending 31 March 2006 and a balance sheet as at that date.

(*Association of Accounting Technicians*)

35.10 David Denton set up in business as a plumber a year ago, and he has asked you to act as his accountant. His instructions to you are in the form of the following letter.

Dear Henry,

I was pleased when you agreed to act as my accountant and look forward to your first visit to check my records. The proposed fee of £250 p.a. is acceptable. I regret that the paperwork for the work done during the year is incomplete. I started my business on 1 January last, and put £6,500 into a business bank account on that date. I brought my van into the firm at that time, and reckon that it was worth £3,600 then. I think it will last another three years after the end of the first year of business use.

I have drawn £90 per week from the business bank account during the year. In my trade it is difficult to take a holiday, but my wife managed to get away for a while. The travel agent's bill for £280 was paid out of the business account. I bought the lease of the yard and office for £6,500. The lease has ten years to run, and the rent is only £300 a year payable in advance on the anniversary of the date of purchase, which was 1 April. I borrowed £4,000 on that day from Aunt Jane to help pay for the lease. I have agreed to pay her 10 per cent interest per annum, but have been too busy to do anything about this yet.

I was lucky enough to meet Miss Prism shortly before I set up on my own, and she has worked for me as an office organiser right from the start. She is paid a salary of £3,000 p.a. All the bills for the year have been carefully preserved in a tool box, and we analysed them last week. The materials I have bought cost me £9,600, but I reckon there was £580 worth left in the yard on 31 December. I have not yet paid for them all yet, I think we owed £714 to the suppliers on 31 December. I was surprised to see that I had spent £4,800 on plumbing equipment, but it should last me five years or so. Electricity bills received up to 30 September came to £1,122; but motor expenses were £912, and general expenses £1,349 for the year. The insurance premium for the year to 31 March next was £800. All these have been paid by cheque but Miss Prism has lost the rate demand. I expect the Local Authority will send a reminder soon since I have not yet paid. I seem to remember that rates came to £180 for the year to 31 March next.

Miss Prism sent out bills to my customers for work done, but some of them are very slow to pay. Altogether the charges made were £29,863, but only £25,613 had been received by 31 December. Miss Prism thinks that 10 per cent of the remaining bills are not likely to be paid. Other customers for jobs too small to bill have paid £3,418 in cash for work done, but I only managed to bank £2,600 of this money. I used £400 of the difference to pay the family's grocery bills, and Miss Prism used the rest for general expenses, except for £123 which was left over in a drawer in the office on 31 December.

Kind regards,
Yours sincerely,
David.

→

You are required to draw up an income statement for the year ending 31 December 2010, and a balance sheet as at that date.

(*Association of Chartered Certified Accountants*)

35.11 The following are summaries of the cash book and bank accounts of J Duncan who does not keep his books using the double entry system.

Bank Summary	£	£
Balance on 1 January 2008		8,000
Receipts		
Accounts receivable	26,000	
Cash banked	4,100	30,100
		38,100
Payments		
Trade accounts payable	18,500	
Rent	1,400	
Machinery	7,500	
Wages	6,100	
Insurance	1,450	
Accounts receivable (dishonoured cheque)	250	
Loan interest	300	35,500
Balance on 31 December 2008		2,600

Cash Summary	£	£
Balance on 1 January 2008		300
Receipts		
Cash sales	14,000	
Accounts receivable	400	14,400
		14,700
Payments		
Drawings	9,500	
Repairs	300	
Electricity	750	
Cash banked	4,100	14,650
Balance on 31 December 2008		50

The following referred to 2008	£
Bad debts written-off	400
Discount received	350
Goods withdrawn by J Duncan for own use	300
Credit note issued	1,200

The following additional information is available.	*1 January 2008*	*31 December 2008*
	£	£
Inventory	4,100	3,200
Machinery	12,600	15,900
Rent prepaid	200	
Rent owing		250
Accounts receivable	6,300	5,000
Accounts payable	2,400	2,500
Loan from bank at 8%	5,000	5,000
Loan interest owing		100

You are required to:

(*a*) Calculate the value of J Duncan's capital on 1 January 2008.

(*b*) Prepare the Income Statement for the year ending 31 December 2008.

(*Scottish Qualifications Authority*)

35.12 Using the information in Review Question 35.11, prepare J Duncan's Balance Sheet as at 31 December 2008.

35.13A The following are summaries of the cash book and bank accounts of P Maclaran who does not keep her books using the double entry system.

Bank Summary	£	£
Balance on 1 January 2008		6,000
Receipts		
Accounts receivable	35,000	
Cash banked	2,200	37,200
		43,200
Payments		
Trade accounts payable	31,000	
Rent	1,100	
Machinery	3,400	
Wages	9,200	
Insurance	850	
Accounts receivable (dishonoured cheque)	80	
Loan interest	500	(46,130)
Balance on 31 December 2008		(2,930)

Cash Summary	£	£
Balance on 1 January 2008		60
Receipts		
Cash sales	9,700	
Accounts receivable	1,100	10,800
		10,860
Payments		
Drawings	6,600	
Repairs	1,400	
Electricity	570	
Cash banked	2,200	(10,770)
Balance on 31 December 2008		90

The following referred to 2008	£
Bad debts written-off	240
Discount received	600
Goods withdrawn by P Maclaran for own use	1,200
Credit note issued	640

The following additional information is available.	*1 January 2008*	*31 December 2008*
	£	£
Inventory	2,300	5,400
Machinery	9,800	10,400
Rent prepaid		100
Rent owing	150	
Accounts receivable	8,100	9,200
Accounts payable	5,700	4,800
Loan from bank at 10%	7,000	7,000
Loan interest owing		200

You are required to:

(*a*) Calculate the value of P Maclaran's capital on 1 January 2008.

(*b*) Prepare the Income Statement for the year ending 31 December 2008.

35.14A Using the information in Review Question 35.13, prepare P Maclaran's Balance Sheet as at 31 December 2008.

35.15 A business prepares its financial statements annually to 30 April and stocktaking is carried out on the next following weekend. In 2008, 30 April was a Wednesday. Inventory was taken on 3 May and the inventory actually on the premises on that date had a value at cost of £124,620.

The following additional information is ascertained:

(*i*) The cash and credit sales totalled £2,300 during the period 1–3 May.
(*ii*) Purchases recorded during the period 1–3 May amounted to £1,510 but, of this amount, goods to the value of £530 were not received until after 3 May.
(*iii*) Sales returns during 1–3 May amounted to £220.
(*iv*) The average ratio of gross profit to sales is 20%.
(*v*) Goods in the inventory at 30 April and included in stocktaking on 3 May at £300 were obsolete and valueless.

Required:
Ascertain the value of the inventory on 30 April 2008 for inclusion in the financial statements.

You can find a range of additional self-test questions, as well as material to help you with your studies, on the website that accompanies this book at www.pearsoned.co.uk/wood.

chapter 36

Receipts and payments accounts and income and expenditure accounts

Learning objectives

After you have studied this chapter, you should be able to:

- explain the main differences between the financial statements of non-profit-oriented organisations and those of profit-oriented organisations
- prepare receipts and payments accounts
- prepare income and expenditure accounts and balance sheets for non-profit-oriented organisations
- calculate profits and losses from special activities and incorporate them into the financial statements
- make appropriate entries relating to subscriptions, life membership, and donations

Introduction

In this chapter, you'll learn about the financial statements prepared by non-profit-oriented organisations, and about how they differ from those prepared for profit-oriented organisations.

36.1 Non-profit-oriented organisations

As their main purpose is not trading or profit-making, charities, clubs, associations and other non-profit-oriented organisations do not prepare income statements. They are run so that their members can do things such as play tennis, bridge, football, chess, role playing games, etc. Rather than producing income statements, they prepare either 'receipts and payments accounts' or 'income and expenditure accounts'.

36.2 Receipts and payments accounts

Receipts and payments accounts are a summary of the cash book for the period. For an organisation with no assets (other than cash) and no liabilities, a summary of the cash book reveals everything about what has happened financially during a period.

Exhibit 36.1 is an example:

Exhibit 36.1

The Haven Running Club
Receipts and Payments Account for the year ended 31 December 2005

Receipts	£	*Payments*	£
Bank balance at 1.1.2005	2,360	Groundsman's wages	7,280
Subscriptions received in 2005	11,480	Sports ground rental	2,960
Rent received	1,160	Committee expenses	580
		Printing and stationery	330
		Bank balance at 31.12.2005	3,850
	15,000		15,000

Why do you think non-profit-oriented organisations prepare receipts and payments accounts when they have all this information in the cash book already?

36.3 Income and expenditure accounts

When assets are owned and/or there are liabilities, the receipts and payments account is not sufficient. Other than the cash received and paid out, it shows only the cash balances. The other assets and liabilities are not shown at all. What is required is:

1 a balance sheet, and
2 a statement showing whether the association's capital has increased.

In a profit-oriented organisation, 2 would be an income statement. In a non-profit-oriented organisation, 2 would be an **income and expenditure account**.

An income and expenditure account follows the same rules as an income statement. The only differences are the terms used.

A comparison between the terminology of financial statements produced by profit-oriented and non-profit-oriented organisations now follows.

Terms used

Profit-oriented organisation	Non-profit-oriented organisation
1 Income Statement	1 Income and Expenditure Account
2 Net Profit	2 Surplus of Income over Expenditure
3 Net Loss	3 Deficit of Income over Expenditure

36.4 Profit or loss for a special purpose

Sometimes there are reasons why a non-profit-oriented organisation would want to prepare either a trading account or a full income statement.

This is where something is done by it in order to make a profit. The profit is not to be kept, but is used to pay for the main purpose of the organisation.

For instance, a football club may organise and run dances which people pay to go to. Any profit from these helps to pay football expenses. For these dances, either a trading account or a full income statement would be drawn up. Any profit (or loss) would be transferred to the income and expenditure account.

36.5 Accumulated fund

A sole trader has a capital account. A non-profit-oriented organisation has an **accumulated fund**. In effect, it is the same as a capital account, as it is the difference between the assets and liabilities.

For a sole trader

Capital = Assets – Liabilities

For a non-profit-oriented organisation

Accumulated Fund = Assets – Liabilities

36.6 Drawing up income and expenditure accounts

We can now look at the preparation of an income and expenditure account and a balance sheet of a club in Exhibit 36.2. A separate trading account is to be prepared for a bar, where refreshments are sold to make a profit.

The majority of clubs and associations keep their accounts using single entry methods. This example will therefore be from single entry records, using the principles described in the previous chapter.

Exhibit 36.2

The treasurer of the Long Lane Football Club has prepared a receipts and payments account, but members have complained about the inadequacy of such an account. She therefore asks an accountant to prepare a trading account for the bar, and an income and expenditure account and a balance sheet. The treasurer gives the accountant a copy of the receipts and payments account together with information on assets and liabilities at the beginning and end of the year:

Long Lane Football Club
Receipts and Payments Account for the year ended 31 December 2006

Receipts	£	*Payments*	£
Bank balance at 1.1.2006	524	Payment for bar supplies	38,620
Subscriptions received for		Wages:	
2005 (arrears)	1,400	Groundsman and assistant	19,939
2006	14,350	Barman	8,624
2007 (in advance)	1,200	Bar expenses	234
Bar sales	61,280	Repairs to stands	740
Donations received	800	Ground upkeep	1,829
		Secretary's expenses	938
		Transport costs	2,420
		Bank balance at 31.12.2006	6,210
	79,554		79,554

→

Additional information:	*31.12.2005*	*31.12.2006*
1	£	£
Inventory in the bar – at cost	4,496	5,558
Owing for bar supplies	3,294	4,340
Bar expenses owing	225	336
Transport costs	–	265

2 The land and football stands were valued at 31 December 2005 at: land £40,000; football stands £20,000; the stands are to be depreciated by 10 per cent per annum.
3 The equipment at 31 December 2005 was valued at £2,500, and is to be depreciated at 20 per cent per annum.
4 Subscriptions owing by members amounted to £1,400 on 31 December 2005, and £1,750 on 31 December 2006.

From this information, in the following three stages, the accountant drew up the appropriate accounts and statements:

Stage 1

Draw up a Statement of Affairs at the end of the previous period in order to identify the balance on the Accumulated Fund brought forward to 2006.

Statement of Affairs as at 31 December 2005

	£	£
Non-current assets		
Land		40,000
Stands		20,000
Equipment		2,500
		62,500
Current assets		
Inventory in bar	4,496	
Accounts receivable for subscriptions	1,400	
Cash at bank	524	
		6,420
Total assets		71,920
Current liabilities		
Accounts payable	3,294	
Bar expenses owing	225	
Total liabilities		(3,519)
Net assets		65,401
Accumulated fund (difference)		**65,401**

Activity 36.2

Why do you think this statement was described as being a 'statement of affairs' rather than a 'balance sheet'?

Stage 2

Draw up a Bar Trading Account.

Long Lane Football Club
Bar Trading Account for the year ending 31 December 2006

	£	£
Sales		
Less Cost of goods sold:		61,280
Inventory 1.1.2006	4,496	
Add **Purchases**(Note 1)	**39,666**	
	44,162	
Less Inventory 31.12.2006	(5,558)	
		(38,604)
Gross profit		22,676
Less **Bar expenses**(Note 2)	**345**	
Barman's wages	8,624	
		(8,969)
Net profit to income and expenditure account		13,707

Notes:

1 **Purchases Control**

	£		£
Cash	38,620	Balances (creditors) b/d	3,294
Balances c/d	4,340	**Trading account (difference)**	**39,666**
	42,960		42,960

2 **Bar Expenses**

	£		£
Cash	234	Balance b/d	225
Balance c/d	336	**Trading account (difference)**	**345**
	570		570

Stage 3

Draw up the financial statements.

Long Lane Football Club
Income and Expenditure Account for the year ending 31 December 2006

Income	£	£	£
Subscriptions for 2006(Note 1)			**16,100**
Profit from the bar			13,707
Donations received			800
			30,607
Less Expenditure			
Wages – Groundsman and assistant		19,939	
Repairs to stands		740	
Ground upkeep		1,829	
Secretary's expenses		938	
Transport costs(Note 2)		**2,685**	
Depreciation			
Stands	2,000		
Equipment	500		
		2,500	
			(28,631)
Surplus of income over expenditure			1,976

Notes:

1 **Subscriptions Received**

	£		£
Balance (accounts receivable) b/d	1,400	Cash 2005	1,400
Income and expenditure (difference)	**16,100**	2006	14,350
		2007	1,200
Balance (in advance) c/d	1,200	Balance (accounts receivable) c/d	1,750
	18,700		18,700

2 **Transport Costs**

	£		£
Cash	2,420	**Income and expenditure (difference)**	**2,685**
Accrued c/d	265		
	2,685		2,685

Note that subscriptions received in advance are carried down as a credit balance to the following period.

The Long Lane Football Club
Balance Sheet as at 31 December 2006

	£	£
Non-current assets		
Land at valuation		40,000
Football stands at valuation	20,000	
Less Depreciation	(2,000)	
		18,000
Equipment at valuation	2,500	
Less Depreciation	(500)	
		2,000
		60,000
Current assets		
Inventory of bar supplies	5,558	
Accounts receivable for subscriptions	1,750	
Cash at bank	6,210	
		13,518
Total assets		73,518
Current liabilities		
Accounts payable for bar supplies	4,340	
Bar expenses owing	336	
Transport costs owing	265	
Subscriptions received in advance	1,200	
Total liabilities		(6,141)
Net assets		67,377
Accumulated fund		
Balance as at 1.1.2006		65,401
Add Surplus of income over expenditure		1,976
		67,377

36.7 Outstanding subscriptions and the prudence concept

So far we have treated subscriptions owing as being an asset. However, as any treasurer of a club would tell you, most subscriptions that have been owing for a long time are never paid – members lose interest or simply go somewhere else. As a result, many clubs do not include unpaid subscriptions as an asset in the balance sheet.

Does this policy of ignoring subscriptions due when preparing the financial statements comply with the prudence concept? Why/Why not?

In an examination, you should assume that subscriptions owing are to be brought into the financial statements, unless instructions to the contrary are given.

Exhibit 36.3 shows an instance where subscriptions in arrears and in advance occur at the beginning and end of a period.

Exhibit 36.3

An amateur theatrical group charges its members an annual subscription of £20 per member. It accrues for subscriptions owing at the end of each year and also adjusts for subscriptions received in advance.

(A) On 1 January 2002, 18 members had not yet paid their subscriptions for the year 2001.
(B) In December 2001, 4 members paid £80 for the year 2002.
(C) During the year 2002 it received £7,420 in cash for subscriptions:

	£
For 2001	360
For 2002	6,920
For 2003	140
	7,420

(D) At 31 December 2002, 11 members had not paid their 2002 subscriptions.

Subscriptions

				£					£
2002					2002				
Jan	1	Owing b/d	(A)	360	Jan	1	Prepaid b/d	(B)	80
Dec	**31**	**Income and expenditure***		**7,220**	Dec	31	Bank	(C)	7,420
	31	Prepaid c/d	(C)	140		31	Owing c/d	(D)	220
				7,720					7,720
2003					2003				
Jan	1	Owing b/d	(D)	220	Jan	1	Prepaid b/d	(C)	140

***This is the difference between the two sides of the account.**

36.8 Life membership

In some clubs and societies, members can make a payment for life membership. This means that by paying a fairly large amount once, members can enjoy the facilities of the club for the rest of their lives.

Such a receipt should not be treated as income in the income and expenditure account solely in the year in which the member paid the money. It should be credited to a life membership account, and transfers should be made from that account to the credit of the income and expenditure account of an appropriate amount annually.

Exactly what is meant by 'an appropriate amount' to transfer each year is decided by the committee of the club or society. The usual basis is to establish, on average, how long members will continue to use the benefits of the club. To take an extreme case, if a club was in existence which could not be joined below the age of 70, then the expected number of years' use of the club on average per member would be relatively few. Another club, such as a golf club, where a fair proportion of the members joined when reasonably young, and where the game is capable of being played by members until and during old age, would expect a much higher average of years of use per member. In the end, the club has to decide for itself.

As a club has to provide amenities for life members without any further payment, the credit balance remaining on the account, after the transfer of the agreed amount has been made to the credit of the income and expenditure account, should be shown on the balance sheet as a liability.

In an examination, be sure to follow the instructions set by the examiner.

36.9 Donations

Any donations received are usually shown as income in the year that they are received.

36.10 Entrance fees

When they first join a club, in addition to the membership fee for that year, new members often have to pay an entrance fee. Entrance fees are normally included as income in the year that they are received. A club could, however, decide to treat them differently, perhaps by spreading the income over a number of years. It all depends on the circumstances.

Learning outcomes

You should now have learnt:

1. That a receipts and payments account does not show the full financial position of an organisation, except for one where the only asset is cash and there are no liabilities.
2. That an income and expenditure account is drawn up to show either the surplus of income over expenditure or the excess of expenditure over income. These are the same as 'profit' or 'loss' in a profit-oriented organisation.
3. That the accumulated fund is basically the same as a capital account.
4. That although the main object of the organisation is non-profit-oriented, certain activities may be run at a profit (or may lose money) in order to help finance the main objectives of the organisation.
5. That in an examination you should treat subscriptions owing at the end of a period in the same way as accounts receivable, unless told otherwise.
6. That donations are usually treated as income in the period in which they are received.
7. That entrance fees are usually treated as income in the year in which they are received.
8. That the treatment of life membership fees is purely at the discretion of the organisation, but that they are usually amortised over an appropriate period.

Answers to activities

36.1 Just as you would prepare a balance sheet for a profit-oriented organisation in order to summarise its financial position at a specific point in time, so non-profit-oriented organisations that deal only in cash, own no assets and have no liabilities, may prepare a receipts and payments account in order to show what happened over a period and the amount of funds left at the end. Non-profit-oriented organisations with assets and liabilities may also prepare them, but only normally in order to help prepare their main financial statements.

36.2 You could just as easily draw up a balance sheet but you're trying to summarise the financial statement even more than in a balance sheet. You would not, for example, show provision for doubtful debts being subtracted from debtors in a statement of affairs, but you might in the balance sheet of a sole trader. To avoid confusion, the title 'statement of affairs' is used when performing any preparatory work prior to preparing the balance sheet. (It must be said, however, that you would not be wrong if you called the statement of affairs a balance sheet.)

36.3 It does not comply with the prudence concept. You will remember from your coverage of the prudence concept in Chapter 10 that you should not overstate *or* understate income and expenditure. While this practice ensures the figure for subscriptions due is not overstated, it does understate them.

Review questions

36.1 A summary of the Downline Rugby Club's cash book is shown below. From it, and the additional information, you are to construct an income and expenditure account for the year ending 31 December 2006, and a balance sheet as at that date.

Cash Book Summary

	£		£
Balance at 1.1.2006	1,440	Purchase of equipment	380
Collections at matches	4,218	Rent for pitch	1,600
Profit on sale of refreshments	5,520	Printing and stationery	104
		Secretary's expenses	220
		Repairs to equipment	210
		Groundsman's wages	6,400
		Miscellaneous expenses	96
		Balance at 31.12.2006	2,168
	11,178		11,178

Further information:

(*i*) At 1.1.2006 equipment was valued at £2,000.
(*ii*) Depreciate all equipment 20 per cent for the year 2006.
(*iii*) At 31.12.2006 rent paid in advance was £400.
(*iv*) At 31.12.2006 there was £25 owing for printing.

36.2A The following trial balance of The Shire Golf Club was extracted from the books as on 31 December 2003:

	Dr £	*Cr* £
Clubhouse	142,000	
Equipment	18,600	
Profits from raffles		6,508
Subscriptions received		183,400
Wages of bar staff	29,200	
Bar inventory 1 January 2003	9,400	
Bar purchases and sales	41,300	84,600
Greenkeepers' wages	21,500	
Golf professional's salary	37,000	
General expenses	910	
Cash at bank	3,924	
Accumulated fund at 1 January 2003		29,326
	303,834	303,834

→

Notes:
(*i*) Bar purchases and sales were on a cash basis. Bar inventory at 31 December 2003 was valued at £6,410.
(*ii*) Subscriptions paid in advance by members at 31 December 2003 amounted to £1,870.
(*iii*) Provide for depreciation of equipment £2,400.

You are required to:
(*a*) Draw up the bar trading account for the year ending 31 December 2003.
(*b*) Draw up the income and expenditure account for the year ending 31 December 2003, and a balance sheet as at 31 December 2003.

36.3 Read the following and answer the questions below.

On 1 January 2008 The Happy Haddock Angling Club had the following assets:

	£
Cash at bank	200
Snack bar inventory	800
Club house buildings	12,500

During the year to 31 December 2008 the Club received and paid the following amounts:

Receipts	£	*Payments*	£
Subscriptions 2008	3,500	Rent and rates	1,500
Subscriptions 2009	380	Extension to club house	8,000
Snack bar income	6,000	Snack bar purchases	3,750
Visitors' fees	650	Secretarial expenses	240
Loan from bank	5,500	Interest on loan	260
Competition fees	820	Snack bar expenses	600
		Games equipment	2,000

Notes: The snack bar inventory on 31 December 2008 was £900.
The games equipment should be depreciated by 20%.

(*a*) Prepare an income and expenditure account for the year ending 31 December 2008. Show, either in this account or separately, the snack bar profit or loss.
(*b*) Prepare a balance sheet as at 31 December 2008.

(*Midland Examining Group: GCSE*)

36.4A The treasurer of the Plumpton Leisure Centre has produced the following receipts and payments account for the year ended 31 December 2004:

Receipts	£	*Payments*	£
Balance at bank 1 January 2004	3,900	Refreshment supplies bought	4,320
Subscriptions received	45,060	Wages of attendants and cleaners	31,400
Profits from dances	4,116	Rent of building	8,700
Profit on exhibition	890	New equipment bought	18,200
Refreshment takings	16,290	Travelling expenses of teams	1,900
Sale of equipment	340	Balance at bank 31 December 2004	6,076
	70,596		70,596

Notes:
(*i*) Refreshment inventory was valued: 31 December 2003 £680; 31 December 2004 £920. There was nothing owing for refreshment inventory on either of these dates.
(*ii*) On 1 January 2004 the club's equipment was valued at £32,400. Included in this figure, valued at £420, was the equipment sold during the year for £340.
(*iii*) The amount to be charged for depreciation of equipment for the year is £5,200. This is in addition to the loss on equipment sold during the year.
(*iv*) Subscriptions owing by members at 31 December 2003 nil; at 31 December 2004 £860.

You are required to:

(*a*) Draw up the refreshment trading account for the year ending 31 December 2004. For this purpose £4,680 of the wages is to be charged to this account; the remainder is to be charged in the income and expenditure account.

(*b*) Calculate the accumulated fund as at 1 January 2004.

(*c*) Draw up the income and expenditure account for the year ending 31 December 2004, and a balance sheet as at 31 December 2004.

36.5 The following is a summary of the receipts and payments of the Miniville Rotary Club during the year ended 31 July 2009.

Miniville Rotary Club
Receipts and Payments Account for the year ended 31 July 2009

	£		£
Cash and bank balances b/d	210	Secretarial expenses	163
Sales of competition tickets	437	Rent	1,402
Members' subscriptions	1,987	Visiting speakers' expenses	1,275
Donations	177	Donations to charities	35
Refund of rent	500	Prizes for competitions	270
Balance c/d	13	Stationery and printing	179
	£3,324		£3,324

The following valuations are also available:

as at 31 July	*2008*	*2009*
	£	£
Equipment (original cost £1,420)	975	780
Subscriptions in arrears	65	85
Subscriptions in advance	10	37
Owing to suppliers of competition prizes	58	68
Inventory of competition prizes	38	46

Required:

(*a*) Calculate the value of the accumulated fund of the Miniville Rotary Club as at 1 August 2008.

(*b*) Reconstruct the following accounts for the year ended 31 July 2009:
  (*i*) the subscriptions account,
  (*ii*) the competition prizes account.

(*c*) Prepare an income and expenditure account for the Miniville Rotary Club for the year ending 31 July 2009 and a balance sheet as at that date.

(*Association of Accounting Technicians*)

36.6A The Milham Theatre Club has been in existence for a number of years. Members pay an annual subscription of £15 which entitles them to join trips to professional productions at a reduced rate.

On 1 February 2007 the Club's assets and liabilities were as follows:

Cash in hand £80, Bank balance (overdrawn) £180, Subscriptions in arrears £150, Savings account £1,950, Amount owing for coach hire £60.

Required:

(*a*) A *detailed* calculation of the Milham Theatre Club's accumulated fund at 1 February 2007.

The Club's treasurer was able to present the following information at 31 January 2008:

Receipts and Payments Accounts for year ended 31 January 2008

	£	£
Opening balances		
Cash in hand	80	
Cash at bank (overdrawn)*	(180)	
		(100)
Receipts		
Subscriptions		
For year ended 31 January 2007	120	
For year ended 31 January 2008	1,620	
For year ended 31 January 2009	165	
Gift from member	1,000	
Interest on savings account	140	
Theatre outings		
Receipts from members for theatre tickets	2,720	
Receipts from members for coach travel	1,240	
		7,005
		6,905
Payments		
Transfer to savings account	1,210	
Theatre trips		
Tickets	3,120	
Coach hire	1,540	
Secretarial and administrative expenses	55	
		(5,925)
		980
Closing balances		
Cash in hand	35	
Cash at bank	945	
		980

- On 31 January 2008 the club committee decided to write off any arrears of subscriptions for the year ended 31 January 2007; the membership secretary reported that £75 is due for subscriptions for the year ended 31 January 2008.
- The treasurer has calculated that the full amount of interest receivable on the savings account for the year ended 31 January 2008 is £155.
- The club committee has decided that the gift should be capitalised.

Required:

(*b*) An account showing the surplus or deficit made by the Milham Theatre Club on theatre trips.

(*c*) An income and expenditure account for the Milham Theatre Club for the year ending 31 January 2008.

(*d*) An extract from the Milham Theatre Club's balance sheet as at 31 January 2008, showing the accumulated fund and current liability sections only.

The club committee have been concerned by the fact that the club's income has been steadily declining over recent years.

Required:

(*e*) Advice for the committee on *four* ways in which they could improve the club's income.

(*Southern Examining Group: GCSE*)

******Note*: Figures in brackets represent negative amounts.**

36.7 The accounting records of the Happy Tickers Sports and Social Club are in a mess. You manage to find the following information to help you prepare the accounts for the year to 31 December 2008.

Summarised Balance Sheet as at 31 December 2007

	£
Half-share in motorised roller	600
New sports equipment unsold	1,000
Used sports equipment at valuation	700
Rent prepaid (2 months)	200
Subscriptions 2007	60
Café inventory	800
Cash and bank	1,210
	4,570
Life subscriptions	1,400
Subscriptions 2008	120
Insurance accrued (3 months)	150
Accumulated fund	2,900
	4,570

Receipts in the year to 31 December 2008:	£
Subscriptions – 2007	40
– 2008	1,100
– 2009	80
– Life	200
From sales of new sports equipment	900
From sales of used sports equipment	14
Café takings	4,660
	6,994

Payments in the year to 31 December 2008:	
Rent (for 12 months)	1,200
Insurance (for 18 months)	900
To suppliers of sports equipment	1,000
To café suppliers	1,900
Wages of café manager	2,000
Total cost of repairing motorised roller	450
	7,450

Notes:

(*i*) Ownership and all expenses of the motorised roller are agreed to be shared equally with the Carefree Conveyancers Sports and Social Club which occupies a nearby site. The roller cost a total of £2,000 on 1 January 2006 and had an estimated life of 10 years.

(*ii*) Life subscriptions are brought into income equally over 10 years, in a scheme begun 5 years ago in 2003. Since the scheme began the cost of £200 per person has been constant. Prior to 31 December 2007 10 life subscriptions had been received.

(*iii*) Four more annual subscriptions of £20 each had been promised relating to 2008, but not yet received. Annual subscriptions promised but unpaid are carried forward for a maximum of 12 months.

(*iv*) New sports equipment is sold to members at cost plus 50%. Used equipment is sold off to members at book valuation. Half the sports equipment bought in the year (all from a cash and carry supplier) has been used within the club, and half made available for sale, new, to members. The 'used equipment at valuation' figure in the 31 December 2008 balance sheet is to remain at £700.

(*v*) Closing café inventory is £850, and £80 is owed to suppliers at 31 December 2008.

→

Required:

(*a*) Calculate the profit on café operations and the profit on sale of sports equipment.
(*b*) Prepare a statement of subscription income for 2008.
(*c*) Prepare an income and expenditure statement for the year ending 31 December 2008, and balance sheet as at 31 December 2008.
(*d*) Why do life subscriptions appear as a liability?

(*Association of Chartered Certified Accountants*)

You can find a range of additional self-test questions, as well as material to help you with your studies, on the website that accompanies this book at www.pearsoned.co.uk/wood.

hapter 37

Manufacturing accounts

Learning objectives

After you have studied this chapter, you should be able to:

- calculate prime cost and production cost of goods manufactured
- draw up a manufacturing account and income statement
- adjust the manufacturing account in respect of work-in-progress

Introduction

In this chapter, you'll learn how to prepare manufacturing accounts and the reasons for doing so.

37.1 Manufacturing: not retailing

We now have to deal with businesses which are manufacturers. For these businesses, a **manufacturing account** is prepared in addition to the income statement. **It is produced for internal use only**. People other than the owners and managers of the organisation concerned rarely see a manufacturing account.

If a business is using manufacturing accounts, instead of a figure for purchases (of finished goods) the trading account will contain the cost of manufacturing the goods that were manufactured during the period. The manufacturing account is used to calculate and show the cost of manufacturing those goods. The figure it produces that is used in the trading account is known as the **production cost**.

37.2 Divisions of costs

In a manufacturing business the costs are divided into different types. These may be summarised in chart form as in Exhibit 37.1:

Exhibit 37.1

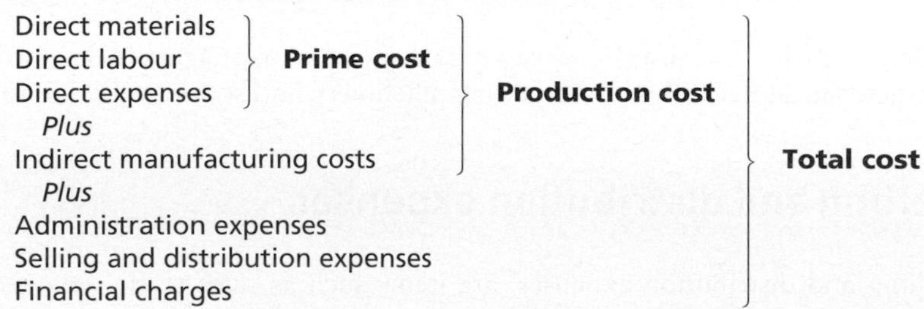

The prime cost items and the other production cost items are shown in the manufacturing account. The administration expenses, selling and distribution expenses and the financial charges appear in the income statement.

37.3 Direct and indirect costs

With reference to Exhibit 37.1, when you see the word *direct* followed by a type of cost, you know that it has been possible to trace the costs to an item being manufactured.

As shown in the chart, the sum of all the **direct costs** is known as the **prime cost**. If a manufacturing-related cost cannot easily be traced to the item being manufactured, then it is an indirect cost and will be included under **indirect manufacturing costs** (which are also sometimes known as 'factory overhead expenses'). 'Production cost' is the sum of prime cost plus the indirect manufacturing costs.

For example, the wages of a machine operator making a particular item will be direct labour. The wages of a foreman in charge of many men on different jobs will be indirect labour, and will be part of the indirect manufacturing costs. Other examples of costs being direct costs would be:

1 Cost of raw materials including carriage inwards on those raw materials.
2 Hire of special machinery for a job.

Activity 37.1 Think about it for a minute and then list five costs you think are direct and five that you think are indirect.

37.4 Indirect manufacturing costs

'Indirect manufacturing costs' are all those costs which occur in the factory or other place where production is being done, but which cannot easily be traced to the items being manufactured. Examples are:

- wages of cleaners
- wages of crane drivers
- rent of a factory
- depreciation of plant and machinery
- costs of operating forklift trucks
- factory power
- factory lighting.

37.5 Administration expenses

'Administration expenses' consist of such items as managers' salaries, legal and accountancy charges, the depreciation of accounting machinery and secretarial salaries.

37.6 Selling and distribution expenses

'Selling and distribution expenses' are items such as sales staff's salaries and commission, carriage outwards, depreciation of delivery vans, advertising and display expenses.

37.7 Financial charges

'Financial charges' are expense items such as bank charges and discounts allowed.

Activity 37.2 Place a tick in the appropriate column for each of the following cost items:

	Direct materials	*Direct labour*	*Direct expenses*	*Indirect manufacturing costs*	*Administration expenses*	*Selling and distribution expenses*	*Financial charges*
(*a*) Purchases of raw materials							
(*b*) Direct wages							
(*c*) General factory expenses							
(*d*) Depreciation of machinery							
(*e*) Commission on sales							
(*f*) Factory rent							
(*g*) Carriage inwards of raw materials							
(*h*) Royalties paid							
(*i*) Inventory of raw materials							
(*j*) Administration salaries							
(*k*) Indirect labour							
(*l*) Bank charges							
(*m*) Carriage outwards							
(*n*) Discounts allowed							
(*o*) Factory lighting							

37.8 Format of financial statements

Manufacturing account section

This is debited with the production cost of goods completed during the accounting period. It contains costs of:

- direct materials,
- direct labour,
- direct expenses, and
- indirect manufacturing costs.

The manufacturing account includes all purchases of raw materials, including the inventory adjustments for raw materials. It also includes inventory adjustments for **work-in-progress** (goods that are partly completed at the end of a period). Let's put this into a series of steps:

1 Add opening inventory of raw materials to purchases and subtract the closing inventory of raw materials.
2 Add in all the direct costs to get the prime cost.
3 Add in all the indirect manufacturing costs.
4 Add the opening inventory of work-in-progress and subtract the closing inventory of work-in-progress to get the production cost of all goods completed in the period.

Thus, when completed, the manufacturing account shows the total of production cost that relates to those manufactured goods that have been available for sale during the period. This figure will then be transferred down to the income statement where it will replace the entry for purchases.

Trading account section of the income statement

This account includes:

- production cost brought down from the manufacturing account
- opening and closing inventory of finished goods
- sales.

When completed, this account shows the gross profit. This is then carried down to the profit and loss account part.

The manufacturing account and the trading account can be shown as in Exhibit 37.2.

Exhibit 37.2

Manufacturing Account

	£
Production costs for the period:	
Direct materials	xxx
Direct labour	xxx
Direct expenses	xxx
Prime cost	xxx
Indirect manufacturing costs	xxx
Production cost of goods completed c/d to trading account	xxx

Trading Account

		£	£
Sales			xxx
Less Production cost of goods sold:			
Opening inventory of finished goods	**(A)**	xxx	
Add Production costs of goods completed b/d		xxx	
		xxx	
Less Closing inventory of finished goods	**(B)**	(xxx)	
			(xxx)
Gross profit			xxx

(A) is production costs of goods unsold in previous period.
(B) is production costs of goods unsold at end of the current period.

Profit and loss section of the income statement

This is prepared in the way you learnt in earlier chapters in this book. You know, therefore, that it includes:

- gross profit brought down from the trading account
- all administration expenses
- all selling and distribution expenses
- all financial charges.

However, some of the items you would normally put in the profit and loss account part are already included in the manufacturing account, e.g. depreciation on machines, and canteen wages. When completed, this account will show the net profit.

Why do you think some expenses have been moved to the manufacturing account?

37.9 A worked example of a manufacturing account

Exhibit 37.3 shows the necessary details for a manufacturing account. It has been assumed that there were no partly completed units (work-in-progress) either at the beginning or end of the period.

Exhibit 37.3

Details of production costs for the year ended 31 December 2007:

	£
1 January 2007, inventory of raw materials	5,000
31 December 2007, inventory of raw materials	7,000
Raw materials purchased	80,000
Manufacturing (direct) wages	210,000
Royalties	1,500
Indirect wages	90,000
Rent of factory – excluding administration and selling and distribution blocks	4,400
Depreciation of plant and machinery in factory	4,000
General indirect expenses	3,100

Manufacturing Account for the year ending 31 December 2007

	£	£
Inventory of raw materials 1.1.2007		5,000
Add Purchases		80,000
		85,000
Less Inventory of raw materials 31.12.2007		(7,000)
Cost of raw materials consumed		78,000
Manufacturing wages		210,000
Royalties		1,500
Prime cost		289,500
Indirect manufacturing costs		
Rent	4,400	
Indirect wages	90,000	
General expenses	3,100	
Depreciation of plant and machinery	4,000	
		101,500
Production cost of goods completed c/d		391,000

Sometimes, if a business has produced less than the customers have demanded, it may buy in some finished goods. In this case, the trading account will have both a figure for purchases of finished goods and a figure for production cost of goods completed.

37.10 Work-in-progress

The production cost to be carried down to the trading account is that of production cost of goods completed during the period. If items have not been completed, they cannot be sold. Therefore, they should not appear in the trading account.

For instance, if we have the following information, we can calculate the transfer to the trading account:

	£
Total production costs expended during the year	50,000
Production costs last year on goods not completed last year, but completed in this year (work-in-progress)	3,000
Production costs this year on goods which were not completed by the year end (work-in-progress)	4,400

The calculation is:

Total production costs expended this year	50,000
Add Costs from last year, in respect of goods completed in this year (work-in-progress)	3,000
	53,000
Less Costs in this year, for goods to be completed next year (work-in-progress)	(4,400)
Production costs expended on goods completed this year	48,600

37.11 Another worked example

Exhibit 37.4

	£
1 January 2007, Inventory of raw materials	8,000
31 December 2007, Inventory of raw materials	10,500
1 January 2007, Work-in-progress	3,500
31 December 2007, Work-in-progress	4,200
Year to 31 December 2007:	
Wages: Direct	39,600
Indirect	25,500
Purchase of raw materials	87,000
Fuel and power	9,900
Direct expenses	1,400
Lubricants	3,000
Carriage inwards on raw materials	2,000
Rent of factory	7,200
Depreciation of factory plant and machinery	4,200
Internal transport expenses	1,800
Insurance of factory buildings and plant	1,500
General factory expenses	3,300

This information produces the following manufacturing account:

Manufacturing Account for the year ending 31 December 2007

	£	£
Inventory of raw materials 1.1.2007		8,000
Add Purchases		87,000
Carriage inwards		2,000
		97,000
Less Inventory of raw materials 31.12.2007		(10,500)
Cost of raw materials consumed		86,500
Direct wages		39,600
Direct expenses		1,400
Prime cost		127,500
Indirect manufacturing costs:		
Fuel and power	9,900	
Indirect wages	25,500	
Lubricants	3,000	
Rent	7,200	
Depreciation of plant and machinery	4,200	
Internal transport expenses	1,800	
Insurance	1,500	
General factory expenses	3,300	
		56,400
		183,900
Add Work-in-progress 1.1.2007		3,500
		187,400
Less Work-in-progress 31.12.2007		(4,200)
Production cost of goods completed c/d		183,200

The trading account is concerned with finished goods. If in the above example there had been £3,500 inventory of finished goods at 1 January 2007 and £4,400 at 31 December 2007, and the sales of finished goods amounted to £250,000 then the trading account would be:

Trading Account for the year ending 31 December 2007

	£	£
Sales		250,000
Less Cost of goods sold:		
Inventory of finished goods 1.1.2007	3,500	
Add Production cost of goods completed b/d	183,200	
	186,700	
Less Inventory of finished goods 31.12.2007	(4,400)	
		182,300
Gross profit c/d		67,700

The profit and loss section is then constructed in the normal way.

37.12 Apportionment of expenses

Quite often expenses will have to be split between

- Indirect manufacturing costs: to be charged in the manufacturing account section

and

- Administration expenses:
- Selling and distribution expenses:
- Financial charges:

} to be charged in the profit and loss section

An example of this could be the rent expense. If the rent is paid separately for each part of the organisation, then it is easy to charge the rent to each sort of expense. However, only one figure of rent may be paid, without any indication as to how much is for the factory, how much is for the selling and distribution building and how much is for the administration building.

How the rent expense will be apportioned in the latter case will depend on the circumstances, using the most equitable way of doing it. A range of methods may be used. Common ones include apportionment on the basis of:

- floor area
- property valuations of each part of the buildings and land.

37.13 Full set of financial statements

A complete worked example is now given. Note that in the profit and loss account part the expenses have been separated so as to show whether they are administration expenses, selling and distribution expenses, or financial charges.

The trial balance in Exhibit 37.5 has been extracted from the books of J Jarvis, Toy Manufacturer, as at 31 December 2007.

Exhibit 37.5

J Jarvis
Trial Balance as at 31 December 2007

	Dr	*Cr*
	£	£
Inventory of raw materials 1.1.2007	21,000	
Inventory of finished goods 1.1.2007	38,900	
Work-in-progress 1.1.2007	13,500	
Wages (direct £180,000; factory indirect £145,000)	325,000	
Royalties	7,000	
Carriage inwards (on raw materials)	3,500	
Purchases of raw materials	370,000	
Productive machinery (cost £280,000)	230,000	
Administration computers (cost £20,000)	12,000	
General factory expenses	31,000	
Lighting	7,500	
Factory power	13,700	
Administration salaries	44,000	
Sales reps' salaries	30,000	
Commission on sales	11,500	
Rent	12,000	
Insurance	4,200	
General administration expenses	13,400	
Bank charges	2,300	
Discounts allowed	4,800	
Carriage outwards	5,900	
Sales		1,000,000
Accounts receivable and accounts payable	142,300	64,000
Bank	16,800	
Cash	1,500	
Drawings	60,000	
Capital as at 1.1.2007		357,800
	1,421,800	1,421,800

Notes at 31.12.2007:

1 Inventory of raw materials £24,000; inventory of finished goods £40,000; work-in-progress £15,000.
2 Lighting, rent and insurance are to be apportioned: factory 5/6, administration 1/6.
3 Depreciation on productive machinery and administration computers at 10 per cent per annum on cost.

J Jarvis
Manufacturing Account and Income Statement for the year ending 31 December 2007

	£	£	£
Inventory of raw materials 1.1.2007			21,000
Add Purchases			370,000
Carriage inwards			3,500
			394,500
Less Inventory raw materials 31.12.2007			(24,000)
Cost of raw materials consumed			370,500
Direct labour			180,000
Royalties			7,000
Prime cost			557,500
Indirect manufacturing costs:			
General factory expenses		31,000	
Lighting 5/6		6,250	
Power		13,700	
Rent 5/6		10,000	
Insurance 5/6		3,500	
Depreciation of productive machinery		28,000	
Indirect labour		145,000	
			237,450
			794,950
Add Work-in-progress 1.1.2007			13,500
			808,450
Less Work-in-progress 31.12.2007			(15,000)
Production cost of goods completed c/d			793,450
Sales			1,000,000
Less Cost of goods sold:			
Inventory of finished goods 1.1.2007		38,900	
Add Production cost of goods completed		793,450	
		832,350	
Less Inventory of finished goods 31.12.2007		(40,000)	
			(792,350)
Gross profit			207,650
Administration expenses			
Administration salaries	44,000		
Rent 1/6	2,000		
Insurance 1/6	700		
General expenses	13,400		
Lighting 1/6	1,250		
Depreciation of administration computers	2,000		
		63,350	
Selling and distribution expenses			
Sales reps' salaries	30,000		
Commission on sales	11,500		
Carriage outwards	5,900		
		47,400	
Financial charges			
Bank charges	2,300		
Discounts allowed	4,800		
		7,100	
			(117,850)
Net profit			89,800

→

→

J Jarvis
Balance Sheet as at 31 December 2007

Non-current assets	£	£
Productive machinery at cost	280,000	
Less Depreciation to date	(78,000)	
		202,000
Administration computers at cost	20,000	
Less Depreciation to date	(10,000)	
		10,000
		212,000
Current assets		
Inventory		
Raw materials	24,000	
Finished goods	40,000	
Work-in-progress	15,000	
Accounts receivable	142,300	
Bank	16,800	
Cash	1,500	
		239,600
		451,600
Less Current liabilities		
Accounts payable		(64,000)
		387,600
Financed by		
Capital		
Balance as at 1.1.2007		357,800
Add Net profit		89,800
		447,600
Less Drawings		(60,000)
		387,600

37.14 Market value of goods manufactured

The financial statements of Jarvis, just illustrated, are subject to the limitation that the respective amounts of the gross profit which are attributable to the manufacturing side or to the selling side of the business are not known. A technique is sometimes used to bring out this additional information. This method uses the cost which would have been involved if the goods had been bought in their finished state instead of being manufactured by the business. This figure is credited to the manufacturing account and debited to the trading account so as to throw up two figures of gross profit instead of one. It should be pointed out that the net profit will remain unaffected. All that will have happened will be that the figure of £207,650 gross profit will be shown as two figures instead of one. When added together, they will total £207,650.

Assume that the cost of buying the goods instead of manufacturing them had been £950,000. The relevant parts of the Manufacturing Account and Income Statement will then be:

Manufacturing Account and Income Statement extract for the year ending 31 December 2007

	£	£
Market value of goods completed		950,000
Less Production cost of goods completed (as before)		(793,450)
Gross profit on manufacture c/d		156,550
Sales		1,000,000
Inventory of finished goods 1.1.2007	38,900	
Add Market value of goods completed b/d	950,000	
	988,900	
Less Inventory of finished goods 31.12.2007	(40,000)	
		(948,900)
Gross profit on trading c/d		51,100
Gross profit		
On manufacturing	156,550	
On trading	51,100	
		207,650

Learning outcomes

You should now have learnt:

1. Why manufacturing accounts are used.
2. How to prepare a manufacturing account and income statement.
3. That the trading account section of the income statement is used for calculating the gross profit made by selling the goods manufactured.
4. That the profit and loss account section of the income statement shows as net profit what is left of gross profit after all administration, selling and distribution and finance costs incurred have been deducted.
5. That work-in-progress, both at the start and the close of a period, must be adjusted so as to identify the production costs of goods completed in the period.

Answers to activities

37.1 You may have included some of the following:

	Direct costs	*Indirect costs*
(1)	raw materials	canteen wages
(2)	machine operator's wages	business rates
(3)	packer's wages	rent
(4)	machine set-up costs	insurance
(5)	crane hire for building contract	storage of finished goods costs

However, you can only really do a split like this if you have a specific job or product in mind. You must first identify the 'cost object', that is, the item you are making or providing. Taking the example of a construction company building a hotel (it is engaged in other similar projects at the same time). The direct and indirect costs may include:

	Direct costs	*Indirect costs*
(1)	concrete	site canteen wages
(2)	forklift truck operator's wages	company lawyer's salary
(3)	bricklayer's wages	company architect's salary
(4)	steel girders	company headquarters insurance
(5)	windows	company warehousing costs

Now you should see that the indirect costs are not solely incurred in order to build the hotel. This is the key. Direct costs are those costs you can specifically link to a specific job. All the other costs of a job are indirect.

37.2 Direct materials (a) (g) (i)
Direct labour (b)
Direct expenses (h)
Indirect manufacturing costs (c) (d) (f) (k) (o)
Administration expenses (j)
Selling and distribution expenses (e) (m)
Financial charges (l) (n)

37.3 Because only administration expenses, selling and distribution expenses, and financial charges appear in the profit and loss account part when a manufacturing account is being used. The rest all arose because manufacturing was taking place and can be directly or indirectly attributed to the products being produced, so they appear in the manufacturing account.

Review questions

37.1 A business both buys loose tools and also makes some itself. The following data is available concerning the years ended 31 December 2007, 2008 and 2009.

		£
2007		
Jan 1	Inventory of loose tools	2,400
	During the year:	
	Bought loose tools from suppliers	3,800
	Made own loose tools: the cost of wages of employees being £490 and the materials cost £340	
Dec 31	Loose tools valued at	5,100
2008		
	During the year:	
	Loose tools bought from suppliers	1,820
	Made own loose tools: the cost of wages of employees being £610 and the materials cost £420	
Dec 31	Loose tools valued at	5,940
2009		
	During the year:	
	Loose tools bought from suppliers	2,760
	Made own loose tools: the cost of wages of employees being £230 and the materials cost £370. Received refund from a supplier for faulty tools returned to him	142
Dec 31	Loose tools valued at	5,990

You are to draw up the Loose Tools Account for the three years, showing the amount transferred as an expense in each year to the Manufacturing Account.

37.2 Using whichever of the following figures are required, prepare a manufacturing account and trading account for 2003. The manufacturing account should show clearly the prime cost of manufacture and the production cost of finished goods produced.

	£
Inventory, 1 January 2003:	
Raw materials	13,500
Partly finished goods	11,800
Finished goods	13,400
Inventory, 31 December 2003:	
Raw materials	14,100
Partly finished goods	11,450
Finished goods	14,160
Purchases of raw materials	82,700
Carriage on raw materials	4,430
Salaries and wages: factory (including £22,700 for management and supervision)	75,674
Salaries and wages: general office	14,200
Rent and business rates (three-quarters works, one-quarter office)	1,600
Lighting and heating (seven-eighths works, one-eighth office)	2,960
Repairs to machinery	1,527
Depreciation of machinery	2,700
Factory direct expenses	365
Insurance of plant and machinery	440
Sales	202,283

Note: partly finished goods are valued at their production cost.

37.3A From the following information, prepare a manufacturing account and income statement for the year ending 31 December 2006 and a balance sheet as at 31 December 2006 for the firm of J Jones Limited.

	£	£
Purchase of raw materials	258,000	
Fuel and light	21,000	
Administration salaries	17,000	
Factory wages	59,000	
Carriage outwards	4,000	
Rent and business rates	21,000	
Sales		482,000
Returns inward	7,000	
General office expenses	9,000	
Repairs to plant and machinery	9,000	
Inventory at 1 January 2006:		
Raw materials	21,000	
Work-in-progress	14,000	
Finished goods	23,000	
Sundry accounts payable		37,000
Capital account		457,000
Freehold premises	410,000	
Plant and machinery	80,000	
Accounts receivable	20,000	
Accumulated provision for depreciation on plant and machinery		8,000
Cost in hand	11,000	
	984,000	984,000

Make provision for the following:

(*i*) Inventory in hand at 31 December 2006:
Raw materials £25,000
Work-in-progress £11,000
Finished goods £26,000.

(*ii*) Depreciation of 10% on plant and machinery using the straight line method.
(*iii*) 80% of fuel and light and 75% of rent and rates to be charged to manufacturing.
(*iv*) Allowance for doubtful debts: 5% of sundry accounts receivable.
(*v*) £4,000 outstanding for fuel and light.
(*vi*) Rent and business rates paid in advance: £5,000.
(*vii*) Market value of finished goods: £382,000.

37.4 Prepare a manufacturing account and income statement from the following balances of W Miller for the year ending 31 December 2003.

	£
Inventory at 1 January 2003:	
Raw materials	25,400
Work-in-progress	31,100
Finished goods	23,260
Purchases: Raw materials	91,535
Carriage on raw materials	1,960
Direct labour	84,208
Office salaries	33,419
Rent	5,200
Office lighting and heating	4,420
Depreciation: Works machinery	10,200
Office equipment	2,300
Sales	318,622
Factory fuel and power	8,120

Rent is to be apportioned: Factory $^3/_4$; Office $^1/_4$. Inventory at 31 December 2003 was: Raw materials £28,900; Work-in-progress £24,600; Finished goods £28,840.

37.5 From the following information, draw up a manufacturing account and the trading account section of the income statement for the six months ending 30 September 2005. You should show clearly:

(*a*) Cost of raw materials consumed.
(*b*) Prime cost of production.
(*c*) Production cost of finished goods.
(*d*) Gross profit on sales.

	£
Inventory, 1 April 2005:	
Raw materials	2,990
Work-in-progress	3,900
Finished goods	15,300
Inventory, 30 September 2005:	
Raw materials	4,200
Work-in-progress	3,600
Finished goods	17,700
Purchases of raw materials	15,630
Carriage on raw materials	126
Direct wages	48,648
Factory general expenses	7,048
Office salaries	22,200
Depreciation of office furniture	420
Carriage outwards	191
Advertising	1,472
Bad debts	200
Sales less returns	112,410
Sales of scrap	1,317
Discounts received	188
Depreciation of factory equipment	4,200
Rent and business rates (factory three-quarters, office one-quarter)	2,800

37.6A From the following figures prepare a manufacturing account and the trading account section of the income statement so as to show:

(*a*) Cost of raw materials used in production.
(*b*) Prime cost.
(*c*) Production cost of finished goods produced.
(*d*) Cost of goods sold.
(*e*) Gross profit.

	£
Inventory at 1 January 2002	
Raw materials	10,500
Goods in course of manufacture (at factory cost)	2,400
Finished goods	14,300
Inventory at 31 March 2002	
Raw materials	10,200
Goods in course of manufacture (at factory cost)	2,900
Finished goods	13,200
Expenditure during the quarter:	
Purchases of raw materials	27,200
Factory wages: direct	72,600
indirect	13,900
Carriage on purchases of raw materials	700
Rent and business rates of the factory	1,200
Power	2,000
Depreciation of machinery	3,900
Repairs to factory buildings	1,300
Sundry factory expenses	900
Sales during the quarter	160,400

37.7 E Wilson is a manufacturer. His trial balance at 31 December 2002 is as follows:

	£	£
Delivery van expenses	1,760	
Lighting and heating: Factory	7,220	
Office	1,490	
Manufacturing wages	72,100	
General expenses: Factory	8,100	
Office	1,940	
Sales reps: commission	11,688	
Purchase of raw materials	57,210	
Rent: Factory	6,100	
Office	2,700	
Machinery (cost £40,000)	28,600	
Office equipment (cost £9,000)	8,200	
Office salaries	17,740	
Accounts receivable	34,200	
Accounts payable		9,400
Bank	16,142	
Sales		194,800
Van (cost £6,800)	6,200	
Inventory at 31 December 2001:		
Raw materials	13,260	
Finished goods	41,300	
Drawings	24,200	
Capital		155,950
	360,150	360,150

→

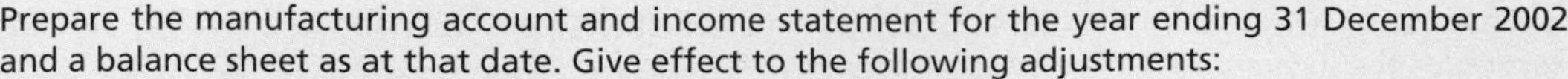

Prepare the manufacturing account and income statement for the year ending 31 December 2002 and a balance sheet as at that date. Give effect to the following adjustments:

1 Inventory at 31 December 2002: raw materials £14,510; finished goods £44,490. There is no work-in-progress.
2 Depreciate machinery £3,000; office equipment £600; van £1,200.
3 Manufacturing wages due but unpaid at 31 December 2002 £550; office rent prepaid £140.

37.8 The financial year end of Mendip Limited is 30 June. At 30 June 2002, the following balances are available:

	£
Freehold land and buildings at cost	143,000
Plant and machinery at cost	105,000
Accumulated depreciation on plant and machinery	23,000
Purchase of raw materials	130,100
Sales	317,500
Factory rates	3,000
Factory heat and light	6,500
Accounts receivable	37,200
Accounts payable	30,900
Wages (including £15,700 for supervision)	63,000
Direct factory expenses	9,100
Selling expenses	11,000
Office salaries and general expenses	43,000
Bank	24,500
General reserve	30,000
Retained profits	18,000
Inventory 1 July 2001: Raw materials	20,000
Finished goods	38,000
Dividends paid: Preference shares	840
Ordinary shares	20,000

(*i*) The inventory at 30 June 2002 was: raw materials £22,000; finished goods £35,600.
(*ii*) Salaries include £6,700 for directors' fees.
(*iii*) Depreciation is to be charged at 10% on cost of plant and machinery.

Required
Prepare a manufacturing account and income statement for the year ending 30 June 2002.

37.9A Jean Marsh owns a small business making and selling children's toys. The following trial balance was extracted from her books on 31 December 2009.

	Dr £	*Cr* £
Capital		15,000
Drawings	2,000	
Sales		90,000
Inventory at 1 January 2009:		
Raw materials	3,400	
Finished goods	6,100	
Purchases of raw materials	18,000	
Carriage inwards	800	
Factory wages	18,500	
Office salaries	16,900	
J Marsh: salary and expenses	10,400	
General expenses:		
Factory	1,200	
Office	750	
Lighting	2,500	
Rent	3,750	
Insurance	950	
Advertising	1,400	
Bad debts	650	
Discount received		1,600
Carriage outwards	375	
Plant and machinery, at cost less depreciation	9,100	
Car, at cost less depreciation	4,200	
Bank	3,600	
Cash in hand	325	
Accounts receivable and accounts payable	7,700	6,000
	112,600	112,600

You are given the following additional information.

1 Inventory at 31 December 2009

Raw materials	£2,900
Finished goods	£8,200

There was no work-in-progress.

2 Depreciation for the year is to be charged as follows:

Plant and machinery	£1,500
Car	£500

3 At 31 December 2009 insurance paid in advance was £150 and office general expenses unpaid were £75.

4 Lighting and rent are to be apportioned: $\frac{4}{5}$ Factory, $\frac{1}{5}$ Office
Insurance is to be apportioned: $\frac{3}{4}$ Factory, $\frac{1}{4}$ Office

5 Jean is the business's salesperson and her salary and expenses are to be treated as a selling expense. She has sole use of the business's car.

→

Questions:

For the year ended 31 December 2009 prepare

(*a*) the manufacturing account showing prime cost and factory cost of production.

(*b*) the trading account section of the income statement.

(*c*) the profit and loss account section of the income statement, distinguishing between administrative and selling costs.

(*d*) a balance sheet as at 31 December 2009.*

(*Midland Examining Group: GCSE*)

***Part (*d*) of the question was not in the original examination question. It has been added to give you further practice.**

37.10 The following list of balances as at 31 July 2006 has been extracted from the books of Jane Seymour who commenced business on 1 August 2005 as a designer and manufacturer of kitchen furniture:

	£
Plant and machinery, at cost on 1 August 2005	60,000
Motor vehicles, at cost on 1 August 2005	30,000
Loose tools, at cost	9,000
Sales	170,000
Raw materials purchased	43,000
Direct factory wages	39,000
Light and power	5,000
Indirect factory wages	8,000
Machinery repairs	1,600
Motor vehicle running expenses	12,000
Rent and insurances	11,600
Administrative staff salaries	31,000
Administrative expenses	9,000
Sales and distribution staff salaries	13,000
Capital at 1 August 2005	122,000
Sundry accounts receivable	16,500
Sundry accounts payable	11,200
Balance at bank	8,500
Drawings	6,000

Additional information for the year ended 31 July 2006:

(*i*) It is estimated that the plant and machinery will be used in the business for ten years and the motor vehicles used for four years: in both cases it is estimated that the residual value will be nil. The straight line method of providing for depreciation is to be used.

(*ii*) Light and power charges accrued due at 31 July 2006 amounted to £1,000 and insurances prepaid at 31 July 2006 totalled £800.

(*iii*) Inventory was valued at cost at 31 July 2006 as follows:

Raw materials	£7,000
Finished goods	£10,000

(*iv*) The valuation of work-in-progress at 31 July 2006 included variable and fixed factory overheads and amounted to £12,300.

(*v*) Two-thirds of the light and power and rent and insurances costs are to be allocated to the factory costs and one-third to general administration costs.

(*vi*) Motor vehicle costs are to be allocated equally to factory costs and general administration costs.

(*vii*) Goods manufactured during the year are to be transferred to the trading account at £95,000.

(*viii*) Loose tools in hand on 31 July 2006 were valued at £5,000.

Required:

(*a*) Prepare a manufacturing account and income statement for the year ending 31 July 2006 of Jane Seymour.

(*b*) An explanation of how each of the following accounting concepts have affected the preparation of the above accounts:

- conservatism,
- matching,
- going concern.

(*Association of Accounting Technicians*)

You can find a range of additional self-test questions, as well as material to help you with your studies, on the website that accompanies this book at www.pearsoned.co.uk/wood.

chapter 38

Departmental accounts

Learning objectives

After you have studied this chapter, you should be able to:

- draw up departmental income statements on the gross profit basis
- draw up departmental income statements on the contribution basis
- calculate the contribution made by each section of a business
- explain why departmental accounts can be more meaningful to management than a single income statement
- apportion expenses between departments on an appropriate basis

Introduction

In this chapter, you'll learn how to prepare departmental income statements and about how they can be used in order to inform decision-makers considering the closure of a department. You'll learn how to apportion indirect costs and, finally, you'll learn that basing departmental income statements on contribution is both more helpful and informative and less misleading than when they are prepared on the gross profit basis.

38.1 Use of departmental accounts

Some items of accounting information are more useful than others. For a retail store with five departments, it is better to know that the store has made £100,000 gross profit than not to know what the gross profit was. However, it would obviously be better if we knew how much gross profit was made in each department.

Assume that the gross profits and losses of a business's departments were as follows:

Department	*Gross profit*	*Gross loss*
	£	£
A	40,000	
B	30,000	
C	50,000	
D		80,000
E	60,000	
	180,000	80,000

Gross profit of the business, £100,000.

If we knew the above information, we could see how well, or how badly, each part of the business was doing. If we closed down Department D we could make a greater total gross profit of £180,000. Perhaps we could replace Department D with a department which would make a gross profit instead of a gross loss.

Why do you think we have only mentioned gross profit and haven't referred to net profit?

You would have to know more about the business before you could be certain what the figures in the account mean. For example, some stores deliberately allow parts of their business to lose money, so that customers come to the store to buy the cheap goods and then spend money in the other departments.

Accounting information seldom tells all the story. It serves as one measure, but there are other non-accounting factors to be considered before a relevant decision for action can be made.

The various pros and cons of the actions to be taken to increase the overall profitability of a business cannot therefore be properly considered until the departmental gross profits or gross losses are known. It must not be thought that departmental accounts refer only to department stores. They can be prepared for the various departments or sections of any business.

The reputation of many a successful business person has been built up on an ability to utilise the departmental account principle to guide decision-making and so increase the profitability of a business. The lesson still has to be learnt by many medium-sized and small businesses. It is one of accounting's greatest and simplest aids to business efficiency.

To find out how profitable each part of the business is, we have to prepare departmental accounts to give us the facts for each department.

38.2 Allocation of expenses

The expenses of a business can be split between the various departments, and then the net profit for each department calculated. Each expense is divided between the departments on what is considered to be the most logical basis. This will differ considerably between businesses. An example of a departmental income statement drawn up in such a manner is shown in Exhibit 38.1:

Exhibit 38.1

Northern Stores has three departments:

	(a) *Jewellery* £	*(b)* *Hairdressing* £	*(c)* *Clothing* £
Inventory of goods or materials at 1 January 2008	20,000	15,000	30,000
Purchases	110,000	30,000	150,000
Inventory of goods or materials at 31 December 2008	30,000	25,000	40,000
Sales and work done	180,000	90,000	270,000
Wages of assistants in each department	28,000	50,000	60,000

The following expenses cannot be traced to any particular department:

	£
Rent	8,200
Administration expenses	48,000
Air conditioning and lighting	6,000
General expenses	2,400

→

It is decided to apportion (i.e. spread) the cost of rent together with air conditioning and lighting in accordance with the floor space occupied by each department. These were taken up in the ratios of (*a*) one-fifth, (*b*) half, (*c*) three-tenths. Administration expenses and general expenses are to be split in the ratio of sales and work done.

Northern Stores
Departmental Income Statement for the year ending 31 December 2008[Note]

	(*a*) *Jewellery* £	£	(*b*) *Hairdressing* £	£	(*c*) *Clothing* £	£
Sales and work done		180,000		90,000		270,000
Less: Cost of goods or materials:						
Inventory 1.1.2008	20,000		15,000		30,000	
Add Purchases	110,000		30,000		150,000	
	130,000		45,000		180,000	
Less Inventory 31.12.2008	(30,000)		(25,000)		(40,000)	
		(100,000)		(20,000)		(140,000)
Gross profit		80,000		70,000		130,000
Less Expenses:						
Wages	28,000		55,000		60,000	
Rent	1,640		4,100		2,460	
Administration expenses	16,000		8,000		24,000	
Air conditioning and lighting	1,200		3,000		1,800	
General expenses	800		400		1,200	
		(47,640)		(70,500)		(89,460)
Net profit/(loss)		32,360		(500)		40,540

The overall net profit is, therefore, £32,360 – £500 + £40,540 = £72,400.

Note: This has been prepared on the gross profit basis.

This way of calculating net profits and losses seems to imply a precision that is, in fact, lacking. This can lead to the mistaken interpretation that the loss of £500 by the Hairdressing Department would be saved if the department were closed down. This is not what the loss of £500 implies. It has already been stated that different departments are very often dependent on one another, and the answer to Activity 38.1 explained why. Therefore, you should realise that this amount of loss would not necessarily be saved by closing the Hairdressing Department.

To explain this further, the calculation of departmental net profits and losses is dependent on the arbitrary division of indirect costs. It is by no means certain that the indirect costs of the Hairdressing Department would be avoided if it were closed down. Assuming that the sales staff of the department could be discharged without compensation, then £55,000 would be saved in wages. The other expenses shown under the Hairdressing Department would not, however, necessarily disappear.

The rent may still be payable in full even if the department were closed down. The administration expenses may turn out to be only slightly down, say from £48,000 to £46,100 – a saving of £1,900; air conditioning and lighting may fall by £300 to £5,700; general expenses may be reduced by £100 to £2,300. None of these reductions are obvious from the Departmental Income Statement.

Taking these cost reductions as what would actually happen were the Hairdressing Department to be closed, indicates that there would be a saving of £57,300:

	£
Administration expenses	1,900
Air conditioning and lighting	300
General expenses	100
Wages	55,000
	57,300

But when open, assuming this year is typical, the Hairdressing Department makes £70,000 gross profit. The business is therefore £12,700 a year better off (i.e. £70,000 minus £57,300) when the department is open than when it is closed, subject to certain assumptions, such as:

(*a*) That the remaining departments would not be profitably expanded into the space vacated to give greater proportionate benefits than the Hairdressing Department.
(*b*) That a new type of department which would be more profitable than hairdressing could not be set up.
(*c*) That the floor space could not be leased to another business at a more profitable figure than that shown by hairdressing – you can see examples of this in many large stores where a part of the store has been leased to a coffee house like Starbucks or Costa Coffee.

What other possible events that can only occur if the department is closed could make it profitable to close the Hairdressing Department?

There are also other factors which, though not easily seen in an accounting context, are still extremely pertinent. They are concerned with the possible loss of confidence in the business by customers generally – what appears to be an ailing business does not usually attract large numbers of customers.

Also, the effect on the remaining staff should not be ignored. The fear that the dismissal of the hairdressing staff may also happen to them may result in the loss of other staff, especially the most competent members who could easily find work elsewhere, and so the general quality of the staff may decline with serious consequences for the business.

38.3 Allocation of expenses: a better method

It is less misleading to show costs split as follows:

First section of income statement	**Direct costs** allocated entirely to the department (i.e. costs which would *not* be paid if the department closed down)
Second section of income statement	Costs not directly traceable to the department or which would still be payable even if the department closed down (i.e. **indirect costs** and **fixed costs**)

The *surpluses* brought down from the first of these two sections represent the **contribution** that each department has made to cover the remaining costs, the remainder being the net profit for the whole of the business. If direct costs of a department were greater than the sales figure then the result would be a **negative contribution**.

From the figures given in Exhibit 38.1 the departmental income statement prepared on the basis of contribution rather than gross profit would appear as in Exhibit 38.2:

Exhibit 38.2

Northern Stores
Departmental Income Statement for the year ending 31 December 2008 (Contribution basis)

	(a) *Jewellery* £	£	(b) *Hairdressing* £	£	(c) *Clothing* £	£
Sales and work done		180,000		90,000		270,000
Less Cost of goods or materials:						
Inventory 1.1.2008	20,000		15,000		30,000	
Add Purchases	110,000		30,000		150,000	
	130,000		45,000		180,000	
Less Inventory 31.12.2008	(30,000)		(25,000)		(40,000)	
	100,000		20,000		140,000	
Wages	28,000		55,000		60,000	
		(128,000)		(75,000)		(200,000)
Contribution c/d		52,000		15,000		70,000

All Departments

	£	£
Contribution b/d:		
Jewellery	52,000	
Hairdressing	15,000	
Clothing	70,000	
		137,000
Less		
Rent	8,200	
Administration expenses	48,000	
Air conditioning and lighting	6,000	
General expenses	2,400	
		(64,600)
Net profit		72,400

As you can see, this is the same overall net profit as found in Exhibit 38.1, and now no department is seen as making a loss.

The contribution of a department is the result of activities which are under the control of a departmental manager. The efficiency of their control will affect the amount of the contribution. If a department's contribution is negative, it would be a strong candidate for closure, or for a change in its management. Similarly, if a department has a far lower contribution to revenue ratio than the others, it may be a candidate for closure if its closure would allow other departments to expand.

The costs in the second section, such as rent, insurance or lighting, cannot be affected by the departmental manager. It is therefore only fair if the departmental manager is judged by the *contribution* of his or her department rather than the net profit of the department.

In examinations, students must answer the questions as set, and not give their own interpretations of what the question should be. Therefore, if examiners give details of the methods of apportionment of expenses, then they are really looking for an answer in the same style as Exhibit 38.1. However, if you are then asked to comment on the performance of individual departments, it would be wise to indicate that, had a contribution approach been adopted, a different view of their performance may have been obtained which would have been more meaningful and useful than the one produced using the approach taken in Exhibit 38.1.

38.4 The balance sheet

The balance sheet does not usually show assets and liabilities split between different departments.

38.5 Inter-departmental transfers

Purchases made for one department may be subsequently sold in another department. In such a case, the items should be deducted from the figure for purchases of the original purchasing department, and added to the figure for purchases for the subsequent selling department.

Learning outcomes

You should now have learnt:

1 How to prepare departmental income statements on the gross profit basis.

2 How to prepare departmental income statements on the contribution basis.

3 That it is desirable for the contribution of each section of a business to be calculated to aid management decisions and that the contribution-based income statement is more appropriate for departmental closure decisions than the gross-profit-based statement.

4 That costs should be divided between those which can logically be allocated to departments and those which cannot.

5 That a negative contribution is only one guide as to whether a section of a business should be closed. There may be other factors which would go against such a closure, and others that would suggest that even departments with positive contributions should be closed.

Answers to activities

38.1 Indirect costs and fixed costs. Net profit includes them. Unlike a manufacturing company, in a trading company, the only costs that are included in the calculation of gross profit are the purchase costs of the items that were sold.

Indirect costs and direct wages and direct expenses appear in the income statement as deductions from gross profit. So far as the direct costs are concerned, it would be appropriate to include them in any comparison between departments because they were definitely incurred for and by the department to which their cost is charged. However, it is not appropriate to include the indirect costs because they have to be spread across all the departments on a basis that is subjective rather than objective. That is, you cannot be certain that they were incurred in respect of the department to which they are charged.

Fixed costs can be direct expenses (e.g. lease of a cash register) or indirect expenses (e.g. rates). They are period costs of the business. They cannot be changed in the timescale you are looking at. If you wanted to know the net profit of a department, you would need to spread the indirect fixed costs across all the departments. This results in charges that are, at best, a close approximation to the extent to which each department merits that level of indirect fixed cost.

Often it has very little to do with appropriateness of the charge made on each department. If you tried to use net profit to make comparisons, you would be basing any conclusion on figures that could easily have been very different had another, possibly, more appropriate method of spreading the indirect fixed costs been used. In addition to all this, there is also the question of what happens to the fixed costs, both direct and indirect, that you have charged to a department that you have decided to close because it is making a net loss. Perhaps the other departments are only profitable because the loss-making department is absorbing some of the fixed costs.

38.2 There is a large range of possibilities. You may have suggested some of the following:

- a restaurant could be opened by the store, attracting more shoppers and, therefore, boosting the sales of the remaining departments;
- the floor space could be used for a children's play area, thereby making the store more attractive to shoppers with young children;
- the floor space could be converted to contain chairs, tables, plants and sculptures so that shoppers can relax and chat to each other during the time they are in the store – you can see examples of this in many modern shopping centres.

Review questions

38.1 From the following you are to draw up a departmental trading account for Fine's Department Store for the year ending 30 June 2006.

Inventory:	*1.7.2005*		*30.6.2006*
	£		£
Carpet Department	16,100		18,410
White Goods Department	37,916		35,119
Music Department	31,222		40,216
Sales for the year:		£	
Carpet Department		62,400	
White Goods Department		151,300	
Music Department		94,820	
Purchases for the year:			
Carpet Department		43,600	
White Goods Department		118,260	
Music Department		55,924	

38.2 J Horner is the proprietor of a shop selling paintings and ornaments. For the purposes of his financial statements he wishes the business to be divided into two departments:

Department A Paintings
Department B Ornaments

The following balances have been extracted from his nominal ledger at 31 August 2007:

	Dr	*Cr*
	£	£
Sales Department A		75,000
Sales Department B		50,000
Inventory Department A, 1 September 2006	1,250	
Inventory Department B, 1 September 2006	1,000	
Purchases Department A	51,000	
Purchases Department B	38,020	
Wages of sales assistants Department A	7,200	
Wages of sales assistants Department B	6,800	
Picture framing costs	300	
General office salaries	13,200	
Fire insurance – buildings	360	
Lighting and heating	620	
Repairs to premises	175	
Internal telephone	30	
Cleaning	180	
Accountancy charges	1,490	
General office expenses	510	

Inventory at 31 August 2007 was valued at:
Department A £1,410
Department B £912

The proportion of the total floor area occupied by each department was:
Department A two-fifths
Department B three-fifths

Prepare J Horner's departmental income statement for the year ending 31 August 2007, apportioning the costs, where necessary, to show the net profit or loss of each department. The apportionment should be made by using the methods as shown:

Area – Fire insurance, Lighting and heating, Repairs, Telephone, Cleaning; Turnover – General office salaries, Accountancy, General office expenses.

38.3A From the following list of balances you are required to prepare a departmental income statement for the year ending 31 March 2005, in respect of the business carried on under the name of Jack's Superstores:

			£	£
Rent and business rates				9,300
Delivery expenses				3,600
Commission				10,000
Insurance				1,800
Purchases:	Dept.	A	101,300	
		B	81,200	
		C	62,900	
				245,400
Discounts received				2,454
Salaries and wages				91,200
Advertising				2,307
Sales:	Dept.	A	180,000	
		B	138,000	
		C	82,000	
				400,000
Depreciation				4,200
Opening inventory:	Dept.	A	27,100	
		B	21,410	
		C	17,060	
				65,570
Administration and general expenses				19,800
Closing inventory:	Dept.	A	23,590	
		B	15,360	
		C	18,200	
				57,150

Except as follows, expenses are to be apportioned equally between the departments.

Delivery expenses – proportionate to sales.
Commission – $2^1/_2$ per cent of sales.
Salaries and wages; Insurance – in the proportion of 3:2:1.
Discounts received – 1 per cent of purchases.

You can find a range of additional self-test questions, as well as material to help you with your studies, on the website that accompanies this book at www.pearsoned.co.uk/wood.

chapter 39

Statements of cash flows

Learning objectives

After you have studied this chapter, you should be able to:

- draw up a statement of cash flows for any type of organisation
- explain how statements of cash flows can give a different view of a business to that simply concerned with profits
- describe the contents of International Accounting Standard 7 (IAS 7) and the format to be used when preparing cash flow statements using IAS 7
- describe some of the uses that can be made of statements of cash flows

Introduction

In this chapter, you'll learn about statements of cash flows, how to prepare them, and the requirements of IAS 7, the accounting standard that regulates their preparation.

39.1 Need for cash flow statements

For any business it is important to ensure that

- sufficient profits are made to finance the business activities, and that
- sufficient cash funds are available as and when needed.

Activity 39.1 What do you think is meant by 'cash' in this context? (*Hint*: which are the truly liquid assets?)

We ascertain the amount of profits in an income statement. We also show what the assets, capital and liabilities are at a given date by drawing up a balance sheet. Although the balance sheet shows the cash balance (see the definition in the solution to Activity 39.1) at a given date, it does not show us how we have used our cash funds during the accounting period.

What we really need, to help throw some light on to the cash situation, is some form of statement which shows us exactly where the cash has come from during the year, and exactly what we have done with it. The statement that fulfils these needs is called a **statement of cash flow**.

It is also sometimes called a 'cash flow statement' but IAS1 recommends use of 'statement of cash flows' so this is the term we will use in this book. You need to be aware of the alternative title in case your examiner uses it.

39.2 International Accounting Standard 7: Cash Flow Statements

This standard, as its title suggests, concerns the preparation of statements of cash flows.

The International Accounting Standards Board requires all companies to include a statement of cash flows with their published financial statements.

39.3 Businesses other than companies

Although partnerships and sole traders do not have to prepare them, statements of cash flows can be of considerable use to all organisations.

IAS 7 prescribes a format for statements of cash flows. An example is shown later in Exhibit 39.7. This is suitable for a company but, obviously, there are factors concerning partnerships and sole traders which do not occur in companies. It will be of help to students if the statements of cash flows for sole traders and partnerships are fashioned to be as similar to those for companies as is possible. Consequently, the layouts for statements of cash flows of sole traders and partnerships in this book will follow the style of layout presented in IAS 7.

39.4 Profit and liquidity are *not* directly related

Many people think that if we are making profits then there should be no shortage of cash. As you have learnt earlier in this book, this is not necessarily so. Let's look at a few instances where, although reasonable profits are being made by each of the following businesses, they could find themselves short of cash, maybe not now, but at some time in the future.

- A sole trader is making £40,000 a year profits. However, his drawings have been over £60,000 a year for some time.
- A company has been over-generous with credit terms to debtors, and last year extended the time in which debtors could pay from one month to three months. In addition it has taken on quite a few extra customers who are not creditworthy and such sales may result in bad debts in the future.
- A partnership whose products will not be on the market for quite a long time has invested in some very expensive machinery. A lot of money has been spent now, but no income will result in the near future.

In all of these cases, each of the businesses could easily run out of cash. In fact many businesses fail and are wound up because of cash shortages, despite adequate profits being made. Statements of cash flows can help to signal the development of such problems.

Activity 39.2

Can you think of any more examples? Spend a minute thinking about this and then write down any you come up with.

39.5 Where from: where to

Basically a statement of cash flows shows where the cash resources came from, and where they have gone to. Exhibit 39.1 shows details of such cash flows.

Exhibit 39.1

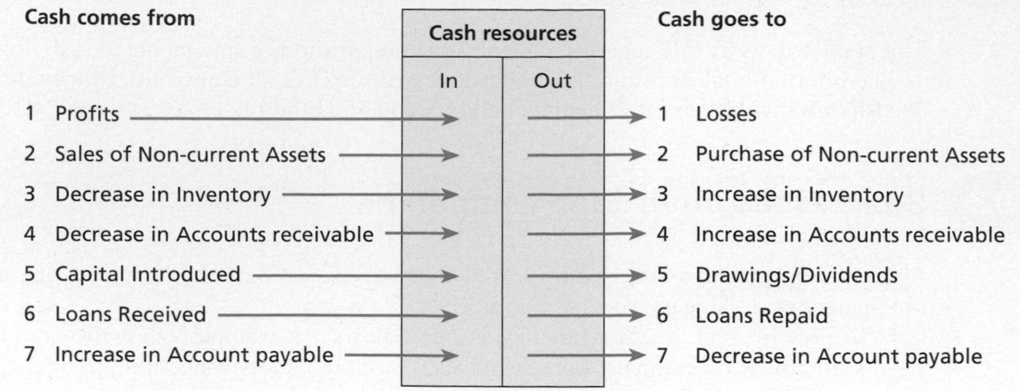

These can be explained as follow:

1 Profits bring a flow of cash into the business. Losses take cash out of it.
2 The cash received from sales of non-current assets comes into the business. A purchase of non-current assets takes it out.
3 Reducing inventory in the normal course of business means turning it into cash. An increase in inventory ties up cash funds.
4 A reduction in accounts receivable means that the extra amount paid comes into the business as cash. Letting accounts receivable increase stops that extra amount of cash coming in.
5 An increase in a sole proprietor's capital, or issues of shares in a company, brings cash in. Drawings or dividends take it out.
6 Loans received bring in cash, while their repayment reduces cash.
7 An increase in accounts payable keeps the extra cash in the business. A decrease in accounts payable means that the extra payments take cash out.

If, therefore, we take the cash (and bank) balances at the start of a financial period, and adjust it for cash flows in and out during the financial period, then we should arrive at the cash (and bank) balances at the end of the period. This can be shown as:

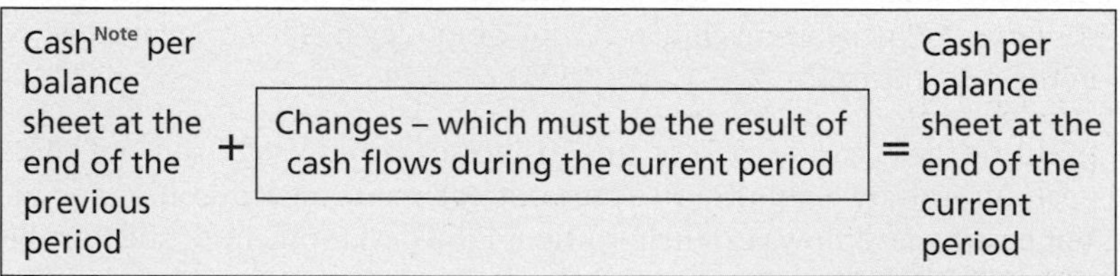

***Note*: 'Cash' in this context includes amounts held in bank accounts. We don't usually refer to 'cash and bank', but simply to 'cash'.**

39.6 Construction of a statement of cash flows

We will first of all look at a couple of examples of statements of cash flows drawn up for sole trader businesses, as this will make it easier to understand the process of preparing one before we go on to look at a more complicated example of a limited company's statement of cash flows in Exhibit 39.7.

First, we will start with Exhibit 39.2 and use it to construct Exhibit 39.3, a statement of cash flows using the (indirect method) format prescribed by IAS 7. (We'll explain what is meant by 'indirect method' in Section 39.11.)

Exhibit 39.2

The following are the balance sheets of T Holmes as at 31 December 2006 and 31 December 2007:

	31.12.2006		*31.12.2007*	
Non-current assets	£	£	£	£
Premises at cost		25,000		28,800
Current assets				
Inventory	12,500		12,850	
Accounts receivable	21,650		23,140	
Cash and bank balances	4,300		5,620	
		38,450		41,610
Total assets		63,450		70,410
Current liabilities				
Accounts payable		(11,350)		(11,120)
		52,100		59,290
Net assets				
Capital				
Opening balances b/d		52,660		52,100
Add Net profit for year		16,550		25,440
		69,210		77,540
Less Drawings		(17,110)		(18,250)
Total capital		52,100		59,290

***Note*: For simplicity, no depreciation has been charged.**

Exhibit 39.3

T Holmes
Statement of Cash Flows for the year ending 31 December 2007

		£
Net cash flow from operating activities (see Note 1)		23,370
Investing activities		
Payment to acquire extra premises		(3,800)
Financing activities		
Drawings		(18,250)
Increase in cash		1,320

Notes:

	£	£
1 Reconciliation of net profit to net cash inflow:		
Net profit		25,440
Less cash used for:		
Increase in inventory	350	
Increase in accounts receivable	1,490	
Decrease in accounts payable	230	
		(2,070)
Net cash flow from operating activities		23,370

2 Analysis of changes in cash during the year:	£
Balance at 1 January 2007	4,300
Net cash inflow	1,320
Balance at 31 December 2007	5,620

39.7 Note on the use of brackets

As you know, in accounting it is customary to show a figure in brackets if it is a minus figure. This would be deducted from the other figures to arrive at the total of the column. These are seen very frequently in statements of cash flows. For example, instead of bringing out a sub-total of the deductions, Note 1 accompanying Exhibit 39.3 would normally be shown as:

	£
Net profit	25,440
Increase in inventory	(350)
Increase in accounts receivable	(1,490)
Decrease in accounts payable	(230)
Net cash flow from operating activities	23,370

39.8 Adjustments needed to net profit

You saw in the statement of cash flows in Exhibit 39.3 that when net profit is included as a source of cash funds, the net profit figure has to be adjusted to take account of items included which do not involve a movement of cash *in the period covered by the statement of cash flows*. The most common examples are depreciation, allowances for doubtful debts, and book profits and losses on the sale or disposal of non-current assets.

Depreciation

For example, suppose we bought equipment costing £3,000 in the year ended 31 December 2006. It is depreciated at £1,000 per annum for three years and then scrapped, disposal value being nil. This would result in the following:

	Years to 31 December		
	2006	*2007*	*2008*
(*i*) Item involving flow of cash:	£	£	£
Cost of equipment **(as this is purchase of an asset this is not part of the net profit calculation)**	3,000		
(*ii*) Net profit before depreciation	12,000	13,000	15,000
(*iii*) Items not involving flow of cash:			
Depreciation	1,000	1,000	1,000
(*iv*) Net profit after depreciation	13,000	14,000	15,000

Now the question arises as to which of figures (*i*) to (*iv*) are the ones to be used in statements of cash flows. Let's consider items (*i*) to (*iv*):

(*i*) **A payment of £3,000 is made to buy equipment. This *does* involve a flow of cash and should therefore be included in the statement of cash flows for 2006.**

(*ii*) **Net profit before depreciation. This brings cash flowing into the business and therefore *should* be shown in statements of cash flows.**

(*iii*) **Depreciation does not involve a flow of cash. It is represented by a bookkeeping entry:**
Debit profit and loss: Credit provision for depreciation.
As this does not involve any outflow of cash, it *should not* be shown in a statement of cash flows.

(*iv*) **Net profit after depreciation. Depreciation does not involve cash flow, and therefore (*ii*) is the net profit we need.**

In most examination questions (*ii*) will not be shown. As we will show you, the figure for net profit before depreciation is calculated in the statement of cash flows itself.

Allowances for doubtful debts

An allowance for doubtful debts is similar to a provision for depreciation. The cash flow occurs when a debt is paid, *not* when provisions are made in case there may be bad debts in the future. As a result, **when preparing the statement of cash flows, you need to add back to net profit any increase in the allowance for doubtful debts or deduct from net profit any decrease in the allowance for doubtful debts.**

If an examination question gives you the net profits *after* an allowance for doubtful debts, then the allowance has to be added back to exclude it from the profit calculations.

What about bad debts? Should you make similar adjustments in the cash flow statement for them? Why/why not?

Book profit/loss on sales of non-current assets

If a non-current asset with a book value (after depreciation) of £5,000 is sold for £6,400 cash, the flow of cash is £6,400. The fact that there has been a book profit of £1,400 does not provide any more cash above the figure of £6,400. Similarly, the sale of an asset with a book value of £3,000 for £2,200 cash produces a flow of cash of £2,200. **Book profits and losses of this type need to be eliminated by adjusting the net profit when preparing the statement of cash flows.**

39.9 Example of adjustments

As the net profit figure in accounts is

(*i*) *after* adjustments for depreciation,
(*ii*) *after* adjustment to allowances for doubtful debts, and
(*iii*) *after* book profits/losses on sales of non-current assets,

net profit needs to be adjusted in statements of cash flows for these three events. However, the adjustments are only for depreciation in *that period*, and for non-current asset book profits/losses for *that period*. No adjustments are needed with reference to previous periods. Exhibit 39.4 shows examples of three businesses.

Exhibit 39.4

	Business A	*Business B*	*Business C*
	£	£	£
Depreciation for the year	2,690	4,120	6,640
Increase in allowance for doubtful debts	540	360	
Decrease in allowance for doubtful debts			200
Book loss on sale of non-current assets	1,200		490
Book profit on sale of non-current assets		750	
Net profit after the above items are included	16,270	21,390	32,410
Reconciliation of net profit to net cash inflow	£	£	£
Net profit	16,270	21,390	32,410
Adjustment for items not involving the movement of cash:			
Depreciation	2,690	4,120	6,640
Book profit on sale of non-current assets		(750)	
Book loss on sale of non-current assets	1,200		490
Increase in allowance for doubtful debts	540	360	
Decrease in allowance for doubtful debts			(200)
Net cash flow from operating activities	20,700	25,120	39,340

You will notice that the items in brackets, i.e. (750) and (200), had been credits in the income statements and need to be deducted, while the other items were debits and need to be added back.

39.10 A comprehensive example

Exhibit 39.5

The balance sheets of R Lester are as follows:

	31.12.2007			31.12.2008		
	£	£	£	£	£	£
Non-current assets						
Equipment at cost			28,500			26,100
Less Depreciation to date			(11,450)			(13,010)
			17,050			13,090
Current assets						
Inventory		18,570			16,250	
Accounts receivable	8,470			14,190		
Less Allowance for doubtful debts	(420)			(800)		
		8,050			13,390	
Cash and bank balances		4,060			3,700	
			30,680			33,340
Total assets			48,730			46,430
Current liabilities						
Accounts payable		4,140			5,730	
Non-current liability						
Loan from J Gorsey		10,000			4,000	
			(14,140)			(9,730)
Total liabilities			33,590			36,700
Net assets						
Capital						
Opening balances b/d			35,760			33,590
Add Net profit			10,240			11,070
Add Cash introduced			–			600
			46,000			45,260
Less Drawings			(12,410)			(8,560)
Total capital			33,590			36,700

***Note*: Equipment with a book value of £1,350 was sold for £900. Depreciation of equipment during the year was £2,610.**

The (indirect method) cash flow statement will be as follows:

Exhibit 39.6

R Lester
Statement of Cash Flows for the year ending 31 December 2008

	£	£
Net cash flow from operating activities (*see* Note 1)		12,700
Investing activities		
Receipts from sale of non-current assets		900
Financing activities		
Capital introduced	600	
Loan repaid to J Gorsey	(6,000)	
Drawings	(8,560)	
		(13,960)
Decrease in cash		(360)

Notes:
1 Reconciliation of net profit to net cash inflow:

	£
Net profit	11,070
Depreciation	2,610
Loss on sale of non-current assets	450
Increase in allowance for doubtful debts	380
Decrease in inventory	2,320
Increase in accounts payable	1,590
Increase in accounts receivable	(5,720)
Net cash flow from operating activities	12,700

2 Analysis of changes in cash during the year:

	£
Balance at 1 January 2008	4,060
Net cash inflow	(360)
Balance at 31 December 2008	3,700

39.11 Companies and statements of cash flows

We have already stated that companies must publish a statement of cash flows for each accounting period. Students whose level of studies terminates with the conclusion of *Business Accounting 1* will not normally need to know more than has already been explained in this chapter. However, some will need to know the basic layout given in IAS 7.

There are two approaches available under the standard: the 'direct' method, which shows the operating cash receipts and payments summing to the net cash flow from operating activities – in effect, it summarises the cash book; and the 'indirect' method, which (as you've seen already) identifies the net cash flow via a reconciliation to operating profit. As the reconciliation has also to be shown when the direct method is used, it is hardly surprising that the indirect method is the more commonly adopted one. Although the IASB recommend use of the direct method, the indirect method is permitted because the cost of producing the data required for the direct method is likely to be greater than the benefit of doing so, in most cases. The direct method is too advanced for this book and is dealt with in Business Accounting Volume 2.

As you've already seen, IAS 7 requires that cash flows be shown under only three categories of activity: operating; investing; and financing. (This is how it was presented in Exhibits 39.3 and 39.6.)

IAS 7 defines cash flows to include cash equivalents: 'short-term, highly liquid investments that are readily convertible to known amounts of cash and which are subject to an insignificant risk of changes in values'.

You have already been introduced to the basic layout of the indirect method in Exhibits 39.3 and 39.6. Exhibit 39.7 shows another example using the indirect method, this time for a company.

Exhibit 39.7 Format for an IAS 7 Statement of Cash Flows (indirect method)

X Limited
Statement of Cash Flows for the year ending 31 December 2007

	£000	£000
Cash flows from operating activities		
Operating profit before taxation	XXX	
Adjustments for:		
Depreciation	XXX	
(Profit)/Loss on sale of tangible non-current assets	XXX	
Operating cash flows before movements in working capital		XXX
(Increase)/Decrease in inventory	XXX	
(Increase)/Decrease in accounts receivable	XXX	
Increase/(Decrease) in accounts payable	XXX	
		XXX
Cash generated by operations		XXX
Tax paid	(XXX)	
Interest paid	(XXX)	
		(XXX)
Net cash from/(used in) operating activities		XXX
Cash flows from investing activities		
Dividends from joint ventures	XXX	
Dividends from associates	XXX	
Interest received	XXX	
Payments to acquire intangible non-current assets	(XXX)	
Payments to acquire tangible non-current assets	(XXX)	
Receipts from sales of tangible non-current assets	XXX	
Purchase of subsidiary undertaking	(XXX)	
Sale of business	XXX	
Net cash from/(used in) investing activities		(XXX)
Cash flows from financing activities		
Ordinary dividends paid	(XXX)	
Preference dividends paid	(XXX)	
Issue of ordinary share capital	XXX	
Repurchase of loan note	(XXX)	
Expenses paid in connection with share issues	(XXX)	
Net cash from/(used in) financing activities		XXX
Net Increase/(decrease) in cash and cash equivalents		XXX
Cash and cash equivalents at beginning of year		XXX
Cash and cash equivalents at end of year		XXX

***Note*: The inclusion of the reconciliation of operating profit to net cash from/(used in) operating activities at the start of the statement of cash flows in Exhibit 39.7 rather than as a note follows the approach given in the Appendix to IAS 7.**

39.12 Uses of statements of cash flows

Statements of cash flows have many uses other than the legal need for some companies to prepare them.

Cases where a business might find them useful in helping to answer their queries include:

(*a*) A small businessman wants to know why he now has an overdraft. He started off the year with money in the bank, he has made profits, and yet he now has a bank overdraft.
(*b*) Another businessman wants to know why the bank balance has risen even though the business is losing money.
(*c*) The partners in a business have put in additional capital during the year. Even so, the bank balance has fallen dramatically. They want an explanation as to how this has happened.

A study of the other financial statements themselves would not provide the information they needed. However, a study of the statement of cash flows in each case will reveal the answers to their questions.

Besides the answers to such specific queries, statements of cash flows should also help businesses to assess the following:

- the cash flows which the business may be able to generate in the future;
- how far the business will be able to meet future commitments, e.g. tax due, loan repayments, interest payments, contracts that could possibly lose quite a lot of money;
- how far future share issues may be needed, or additional capital in the case of sole traders or partnerships;
- a valuation of the business.

Learning outcomes

You should now have learnt:

1 Why statements of cash flows provide useful information for decision-making.
2 A range of sources and applications of cash.
3 How to adjust net profit for non-cash items to find the net cash flow from operating activities.
4 How to prepare a statement of cash flows as defined by IAS 7.
5 How to present the net cash flow from operating activities using the indirect method.
6 Some of the uses that can be made of statements of cash flows.

Answers to activities

39.1 Liquidity is the key. Nowadays, something is generally considered as sufficiently liquid to be described as 'cash' in this context if it can definitely be turned into cash within three months. Not only does **cash** in this sense include the obvious – cash balances and bank balances – it also includes funds invested in **cash equivalents**. These cash equivalents consist of the temporary investments of cash not required at present by the business, such as funds put on short-term deposit with a bank. Such investments must be readily convertible into cash, or available as cash.

This is an important definition and is one you should memorise if cash flow statements are examinable under the syllabus of your course.

39.2 Other examples include:

- The bank overdraft has been growing steadily and is now greater than the amount owed by debtors.
- A major supplier is experiencing cash flow problems and is threatening not to provide any further goods unless all bills are paid within 5 working days. Your business has no other sources of supply for these goods and the bank has indicated that it will not advance any further loans or increase the overdraft facility.
- A seriously dangerous defect has been identified in the sole product manufactured by the business. This could lead to all items sold in the last year having to be replaced with newly produced replacements. The faulty items cannot be repaired. The business has already borrowed as much as it is allowed by the bank.

39.3 A bad debt that is written-off represents an expense that *does not* involve a flow of cash during the period. A debt becomes cash when paid, and only does so at the time payment is received. In writing-off the debt, you are saying that cash will not be received and have written off the debt to the profit and loss account. In theory, you need to adjust both the profit (by adding it back) and the change in the debtor balance. *However, these adjustments cancel each other out, so you need do nothing when preparing the statement of cash flows.*

Review questions

39.1 The balance sheets of F Black, a sole trader, for two successive years are shown below. You are required to draw up a statement of cash flows for the year ending 31 December 2004 using the IAS 7 layout.

Balance Sheets as at 31 December

	2005		*2006*	
	£	£	£	£
Non-current assets				
Land and premises (cost £52,000)		44,000		40,000
Plant and machinery				
(cost £19,000)		14,250		–
(cost £25,000)		–		19,600
		58,250		59,600
Current Assets				
Inventory	6,600		6,300	
Trade accounts receivable	17,800		12,600	
Bank	–		7,100	
		24,400		26,000
Total assets		82,650		85,600
Current Liabilities				
Trade accounts payable	22,000		11,600	
Bank overdraft	13,650		–	
	35,650		11,600	
Non-current liabilities				
Loan (repayable December 2008)	–	–	20,000	
Total liabilities		(35,650)		(31,600)
Net assets		47,000		54,000
Capital account:				
Balance at 1 January		42,000		47,000
Add Net profit for the year		18,000		22,000
		60,000		69,000
Less Drawings		(13,000)		(15,000)
		47,000		54,000

39.2A

Gerry Peace
Balance Sheets as at 31 December

	2002		2003	
	£	£	£	£
Non-current assets				
Buildings		50,000		50,000
Fixtures *less* Depreciation		1,800		2,000
Van *less* Depreciation		3,920		7,400
		55,720		59,400
Current assets				
Inventory	5,600		12,400	
Trade accounts receivable	6,400		8,200	
Bank	900		–	
Cash	220		200	
		13,120		20,800
Total assets		68,840		80,200
Current liabilities				
Accounts payable	6,300		3,006	
Bank overdraft	–		94	
	6,300		3,100	
Non-current liabilities				
Loan (repayable in 10 years' time)	10,000		15,000	
Total liabilities		(16,300)		(18,100)
Net assets		52,540		62,100
Capital account:				
Balance at 1 January		37,040		52,540
Add Net profit for the year		35,200		21,160
Cash introduced		–		10,000
		72,240		83,700
Less Drawings		(19,700)		(21,600)
Total capital		52,540		62,100

Draw up a statement of cash flows for Gerry Peace for the year ending 31 December 2003 using the IAS 7 layout. You are told that fixtures bought in 2003 cost £400, whilst a van was bought for £5,500.

→

39.3 Malcolm Phillips is a sole trader who prepares his financial statements annually to 30 April. His summarised balance sheets for the last two years are shown below.

Balance Sheets as at 30 April

	2008		2009	
	£	£	£	£
Non-current assets		15,500		18,500
Less Provision for depreciation		(1,500)		(1,700)
		14,000		16,800
Current assets				
Inventory	3,100		5,900	
Trade accounts receivable	3,900		3,400	
Bank	1,500		–	
		8,500		9,300
Total assets		22,500		26,100
Current liabilities				
Trade accounts payable	2,000		2,200	
Bank overdraft	–		900	
Total liabilities		(2,000)		(3,100)
Net assets		20,500		23,000
Capital account:				
Balance at 1 May		20,000		20,500
Add Net profit for the year		7,000		8,500
Additional capital introduced		–		2,000
		27,000		31,000
Less Drawings		(6,500)		(8,000)
Total capital		20,500		23,000

Malcolm is surprised to see that he now has an overdraft, in spite of making a profit and bringing in additional capital during the year.

Questions:

(*a*) Draw up a suitable financial statement which will explain to Malcolm how his overdraft has arisen.

(*b*) The following further information relates to the year ended 30 April 2009.

	£
Sales (all on credit)	30,000
Cost of sales	22,500

Calculate Malcolm's

(*i*) gross profit margin

(*ii*) rate of inventory turnover.

(*Midland Examining Group: GCSE*)

39.4 From the following details you are to draft a statement of cash flows for D Duncan for the year ending 31 December 2005, using the IAS 7 layout.

D Duncan
Income Statement for the year ending 31 December 2005

	£	£
Gross profit		44,700
Add Discounts received	410	
Profit on sale of van	620	1,030
		45,730
Less Expenses		
Motor expenses	1,940	
Wages	17,200	
General expenses	830	
Bad debts	520	
Increase in allowance for doubtful debts	200	
Depreciation: Van	1,800	22,490
		23,240

Balance Sheets as at 31 December

	2004 £	2004 £	2005 £	2005 £
Non-current assets				
Vans at cost		15,400		8,200
Less Depreciation to date		(5,300)		(3,100)
		10,100		5,100
Current assets				
Inventory	18,600		24,000	
Accounts receivable *less* allowance*	8,200		6,900	
Bank	410		720	
		27,210		31,620
Total assets		37,310		36,720
Current liabilities				
Accounts payable	5,900		7,200	
Non-current liability				
Loan from J Fry	10,000		7,500	
Total liabilities		(15,900)		(14,700)
Net assets		21,410		22,020
Capital				
Opening balance b/d		17,210		21,410
Add Net profit		21,200		23,240
		38,410		44,650
Less Drawings		(17,000)		(22,630)
Total capital		21,410		22,020

*Accounts receivable 2004 £8,800 – allowance £600.
Accounts receivable 2005 £7,700 – allowance £800.

Note: A van was sold for £3,820 during 2005. No new vans were purchased during the year.

39.5A You are required to draw up a statement of cash flows for K Rock for the year ending 30 June 2009 from the following information using the IAS 7 layout.

K Rock
Income Statement for the year ending 30 June 2009

	£	£
Gross profit		155,030
Add Reduction in allowance for doubtful debts		200
		155,230
Less Expenses:		
Wages and salaries	61,400	
General trading expenses	15,200	
Equipment running costs	8,140	
Motor vehicle expenses	6,390	
Depreciation: Motor vehicles	5,200	
Equipment	6,300	
Loss on sale of equipment	1,600	
		(104,230)
Net profit		51,000

Balance Sheets as at 30 June

	2008		*2009*	
	£	£	£	£
Non-current assets				
Equipment at cost	40,400		30,800	
Less Depreciation to date	(24,600)		(20,600)	
		15,800		10,200
Motor vehicles at cost	28,300		28,300	
Less Depreciation to date	(9,200)		(14,400)	
		19,100		13,900
		34,900		24,100
Current assets				
Inventory	41,700		44,600	
Accounts receivable *less* allowance*	21,200		19,800	
Bank	12,600		28,100	
		75,500		92,500
Total assets		110,400		116,600
Current liabilities				
Accounts payable	14,300		17,500	
Non-current liability				
Loan from T Pine	20,000		10,000	
Total liabilities		(34,300)		(27,500)
Net assets		76,100		89,100
Capital				
Opening balance		65,600		76,100
Add Net profit		42,500		51,000
		108,100		127,100
Less Drawings		(32,000)		(38,000)
Total capital		76,100		89,100

*Accounts receivable 2008 £22,100 – allowance £900.
Accounts receivable 2009 £20,500 – allowance £700.
Note: Equipment was sold for £15,800. Equipment costing £18,100 was purchased during the year.

You can find a range of additional self-test questions, as well as material to help you with your studies, on the website that accompanies this book at www.pearsoned.co.uk/wood.

chapter 40

Joint venture accounts

Learning objectives

After you have studied this chapter, you should be able to:

- explain what is meant by the term 'joint venture'
- explain why separate joint venture accounts are kept by each of the parties to a joint venture
- make the entries in the accounts for a joint venture
- calculate and enter the profits of the joint venture into the accounts of the parties to the joint venture
- identify the amount owing to or owed by each of the parties to the other parties in the joint venture and make the appropriate entries in the joint venture accounts when payment is made and received
- name two accounting standards relating to joint ventures

Introduction

Joint ventures, which were the reason why the system of bookkeeping we use today was developed in the thirteenth century, are becoming increasingly common. In this chapter, you'll learn how to record joint ventures in the books of the parties to a joint venture. You'll learn how to calculate profits and identify how much each of the parties must pay to the other parties at the end of the joint venture. Finally you'll learn that accounting standards have been issued to regulate accounting for longer-term and larger joint ventures.

40.1 Nature of joint ventures

Sometimes a particular business venture can best be done by two or more businesses joining together to do it instead of doing it separately. The joining together is for that one venture only, it is not joining together to make a continuing business.

Such projects are known as **joint ventures**. For instance, a merchant might provide the capital, the transport to the markets and the selling skills. The farmer grows the produce. The profits or losses are then shared between them in agreed ratios. It is like a partnership, but only for this one venture. There may be several joint ventures between the same businesses, but each one is a separate venture. The agreements for each venture may be different from each other.

40.2 Accounting for large joint ventures

For large-scale or long-term joint ventures, a separate bank account and separate set of books are kept. In such cases the calculation of profit is not difficult. It is similar to preparing a set of financial statements for an ordinary business.

40.3 Accounting for smaller joint ventures

No separate set of books or separate bank accounts are kept for smaller joint ventures. Each of the parties will record in their own books only those transactions with which they have been concerned. Exhibit 40.1 gives an example of such a joint venture.

Exhibit 40.1

White of London and Green of Glasgow enter into a joint venture. White is to supply the goods and pay some of the expenses. Green is to sell the goods and receive the cash, and pay the remainder of the expenses. Profits are to be shared equally.

Details of the transactions are as follows:

	£
White supplied the goods costing	1,800
White paid wages	200
White paid for storage expenses	160
Green paid transport expenses	120
Green paid selling expenses	320
Green received cash from sales of all the goods	3,200

Stage 1

White and Green will each have entered up their own part of the transactions. White will have opened an account named 'Joint Venture with Green'. Similarly, Green will have opened a 'Joint Venture with White' account. The double entry to these joint venture accounts will be:

In White's books:

Payments by White:	Debit Joint venture with Green Credit Cash Book
Goods supplied to Green:	Debit Joint venture with Green Credit purchases

In Green's books:

Payments by Green:	Debit Joint venture with White Credit Cash Book
Cash received by Green:	Debit Cash Book Credit Joint venture with White

At this point the joint venture accounts in each of their books will appear as follows:

White's books (in London):

Joint Venture with Green

	£		
Purchases	1,800		
Cash: wages	200		
Cash: storage expenses	160		

Green's books (in Glasgow):

Joint Venture with White

	£		£
Cash: transport expenses	120	Cash: sales	3,200
Cash: selling expenses	320		

Stage 2

At this stage, White and Green know only the details in their own set of books. They do not yet know what the details are in the other person's books.

This means that they cannot yet calculate profits, or find out how much cash has to be paid or received to close the venture. To do this they must each send a copy of their joint venture accounts to the other person.

Each person will then draw up a **memorandum joint venture account**, to include all the details from each joint venture account. The memorandum joint venture account is not a double entry account. It is drawn up only (*a*) to find out the shares of net profit or loss of each party to the joint venture, and (*b*) to help calculate the amounts payable and receivable to close the venture. White and Green's memorandum joint venture account is now shown:

White and Green
Memorandum Joint Venture Account

	£	£		£
Purchases		1,800	Sales	3,200
Wages		200		
Storage expenses		160		
Transport expenses		120		
Selling expenses		320		
Net profit:				
White (one-half)	300			
Green (one-half)	300			
		600		
		3,200		3,200

***Note*: The profit is the difference between the two sides of the account. You find out what the balancing figure is; in this case, it is £600. Then you split it in the profit sharing ratio. In this case, profits are shared equally. White and Green, therefore, each receive half the profit, £300 each. Now you enter the figures, £300 to White, £300 to Green, and the total of £600, which balances and closes off the account.**

Look closely at the Memorandum Joint Venture account. Where does each entry in the Memorandum Joint Venture account appear in the Joint Venture with Green and Joint Venture with White T-accounts? Are they on the same side in each case, or the opposite side? What does this tell you about making entries in the Memorandum Joint Venture account?

Stage 3

The net profit shares for White and Green need to be brought into their own books. This is done as follows:

White's books:

Debit share of profit to Joint Venture with Green account

Credit White's profit and loss account

The Joint Venture account in White's books now looks like this:

White's books (in London):

Joint Venture with Green

	£		
Purchases	1,800		
Cash: wages	200		
Cash: storage expenses	160		
Profit and loss: share of profit	**300**		

You then do the same in Green's books:

Green's books:

Debit share of profit to Joint Venture with White account
Credit Green's profit and loss account

Green's books (in Glasgow):

Joint Venture with White

	£		£
Cash: transport expenses	120	Cash: sales	3,200
Cash: selling expenses	320		
Profit and loss: share of profit	**300**		

It won't come as a surprise to see that you have now copied the profit share entries from the Memorandum Joint Venture account into the Joint Venture accounts held by White and Green. Now you need to balance-off the two Joint Venture accounts:

White's books (in London):

Joint Venture with Green

	£		£
Purchases	1,800	**Balance c/d**	**2,460**
Cash: wages	200		
Cash: storage expenses	160		
Profit and loss: share of profit	**300**		
	2,460		2,460
Balance b/d	2,460		

Green's books (in Glasgow):

Joint Venture with White

	£		£
Cash: transport expenses	120	Cash: sales	3,200
Cash: selling expenses	320		
Profit and loss: share of profit	**300**		
Balance c/d	**2,460**		
	3,200		3,200
		Balance b/d	2,460

Can you remember what is meant by a debit balance? Is it where the balance c/d is a debit or where the balance b/d is a debit?

Finally, the parties in the joint venture need to settle their debts to each other. They know whether they are to pay money or receive money when they look at the side of their copy of the joint venture account and see whether the balance is a debit or a credit:

(*a*) If the balance brought down is a credit balance, money is owing to the other party in the joint venture. In this case, Green owes White the amount shown by the credit balance, £2,460.

(*b*) If the balance brought down is a debit balance, money is due from the other party in the joint venture. In this case White is owed the amount of the balance, £2,460 by Green.

The payment is now made by Green to White and the final entry is made in each of the joint venture accounts, closing off the accounts.

White's books (in London):

Joint Venture with Green

	£		£
Purchases	1,800	Balance c/d	2,460
Cash: wages	200		
Cash: storage expenses	160		
Profit and loss: share of profit	300		
	2,460		2,460
Balance b/d	2,460	**Cash: settlement from Green**	**2,460**

Green's books (in Glasgow):

Joint Venture with White

	£		£
Cash: transport expenses	120	Cash: sales	3,200
Cash: selling expenses	320		
Profit and loss: share of profit	300		
Balance c/d	2,460		
	3,200		3,200
Cash: settlement to White	**2,460**	Balance b/d	2,460

40.4 IAS 31: Financial Reporting of Interests in Joint Ventures

The international accounting standard relating to joint ventures was issued in 1991. The treatment of short-term joint ventures illustrated in this chapter is acceptable under IAS 31. In 1997, the ASB issued FRS9 (*Associates and joint ventures*) confirming the re-emergence of joint ventures in the modern world.

Learning outcomes

You should now have learnt:

1. That when two or more businesses join together for a particular business venture, and do not form a permanent business entity, they have entered into a joint venture.
2. That larger and long-term joint ventures operate a separate bank account and books dedicated to the project.
3. That the participants in smaller joint ventures rely on their own bank accounts and books to run and record their part of the project, using a *memorandum joint venture account* to pass the details of their part of the project to the other participant(s).
4. Why separate joint venture accounts are kept by each party to smaller and short-term joint ventures.
5. How to make the appropriate entries in the books of the parties to the joint venture, calculate the profit, share that profit among the parties to the joint ventures and close off the joint venture accounts at the end of the joint venture.
6. That IAS 31 regulates accounting for joint ventures.

Answers to activities

40.1 It's quite simple really, isn't it? You take each debit entry in the first of the T-accounts (Joint Venture with Green) and copy it as a debit entry into the Memorandum Joint Venture account. You then do the same with the debits in the second T-account (Joint Venture with White). Then you do exactly the same with the credit entries. The order you do this in doesn't matter. All you need to ensure is that you have replicated all the T-account entries from the individual joint venture accounts in the Memorandum Joint Venture account. You have to do this because the Memorandum Joint Venture account lies outside the double entry system.

40.2 An account with a debit balance has more value on the debit side. That is, it is the side on which the balance b/d figure lies that tells you whether the balance is a debit or a credit. In this case, the Joint Venture account in White's books has a debit balance. The one in Green's books has a credit balance. Therefore, Green owes White £2,460.

Review questions

40.1 Stanley and Barclay enter a joint venture to share profits or losses equally resulting from dealings in second-hand digital TVs. Both parties take an active part in the business, each recording his own transactions. They have no joint banking account or separate set of books.

2003		
July	1	Stanley buys four TVs for a total of £1,100.
	3	Stanley pays for repairs £840.
	4	Barclay pays office rent £300 and advertising expenses £90.
	6	Barclay pays for packaging materials £34.
	7	Barclay buys a TV in excellent condition for £600.
	31	Stanley sells the five TVs to various customers, the sales being completed on this date, and totalling £3,100.

Show the relevant accounts in the books of both joint venturers.

40.2A Frank entered into a joint venture with Graham for the purchase and sale of robot mowers. They agreed that profits and losses should be shared equally.

The following transactions took place:

(*a*) Frank purchased mowers for £120,400 and paid carriage £320.
(*b*) Graham purchased mowers for £14,860 and paid carriage £84.
(*c*) Graham paid to Frank £70,000.
(*d*) Frank sold mowers for £104,590 and sent a cheque for £50,000 to Graham.
(*e*) Graham sold for £19,200 all the mowers he had purchased.
(*f*) The unsold mowers in the possession of Frank were taken over by him at a valuation of £40,000.
(*g*) The amount due from one venturer to the other was paid and the joint venture was dissolved.

You are required to prepare:
(*i*) a statement to show the net profit or loss of the joint venture, and
(*ii*) the accounts for the joint venture in the books of Frank and Graham.

40.3 Bull, Craig and Finch entered into a joint venture for dealing in strawberries. The transactions connected with this venture were:

2009		
May	1	Bull rented land for two months for £600.
	2	Craig supplied plants cost £510.
	3	Bull employed labour for planting £260.
	16	Craig charged motor expenses £49.
	19	Bull employed labour for fertilising £180.
	29	Bull paid the following expenses: Sundries £19, Labour £210, Fertiliser £74.
June	11	Finch employed labour for lifting strawberries £416.
	24	Sale expenses paid by Finch £318.
	26	Finch received cash from sale proceeds £2,916.

Required:
Show the joint venture accounts in the books of Bull, Craig and Finch. Also show in full the method of arriving at the profit on the venture which is to be apportioned: Bull four-sevenths; Craig two-sevenths; Finch one-seventh.

Any outstanding balances between the parties are settled by cheque on 31 July.

40.4A Rock, Hill and Pine enter into a joint venture for dealing in paintings. The following transactions took place:

2004		
May	1	Rock rented a shop paying 3 months' rent £2,100.
	3	Hill bought a van for £2,200.
	5	Hill bought paintings for £18,000.
	17	Pine received cash from sale proceeds of paintings £31,410.
	23	Rock bought paintings for £317,000.
June	9	Van broke down. Pine agreed to use his own van for the job until cessation of the joint venture at an agreed charge of £600.
	14	Van bought on May 3 was sold for £1,700. Proceeds were kept by Rock.
	17	Sales of paintings, cash being paid by Hill £4,220.
	25	Lighting bills paid for shop by Pine £86.
	29	Pine bought paintings for £1,700.
July	3	General expenses of shop paid for £1,090, Pine and Rock paying half each.
	16	Paintings sold by Pine £2,300, proceeds being kept by him.
	31	Joint venture ended. The paintings still in inventory were taken over at an agreed valuation of £6,200 by Hill.

→

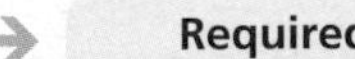

Required:
Show the joint venture accounts in the books of the three parties. Show in full the workings needed to arrive at the profit on the venture. The profit or loss was to be split: Hill one-half; Rock one-third; Pine one-sixth. Any outstanding balances between the parties were settled on 31 July 2004.

You can find a range of additional self-test questions, as well as material to help you with your studies, on the website that accompanies this book at www.pearsoned.co.uk/wood.

part

6

PARTNERSHIP ACCOUNTS AND COMPANY ACCOUNTS

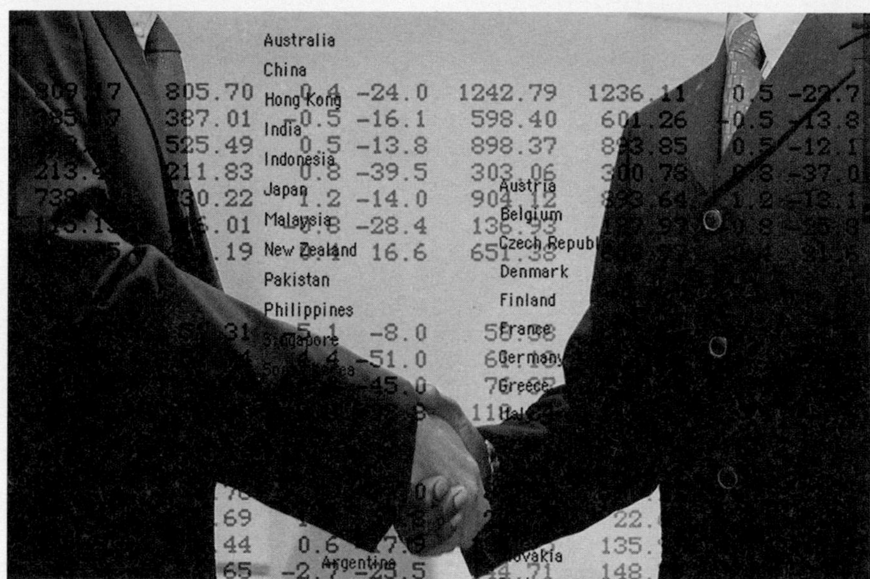

Introduction

This part is concerned with accounting procedures, particularly those affecting partnerships; it gives an introduction to goodwill in relation to partnerships and other business organisations, and introduces the accounts of limited liability companies.

chapter 41

Partnership accounts: an introduction

Learning objectives

After you have studied this chapter, you should be able to:

- explain what a partnership is and how it differs from a joint venture
- explain the rules relating to the number of partners
- distinguish between limited partners and general partners
- describe the main features of a partnership agreement
- explain what will happen if no agreement exists on how to share profits or losses
- draw up the ledger accounts and financial statements for a partnership

Introduction

In this chapter, you'll learn about the nature of partnerships and the regulations governing them. You'll learn that there are two types of partner, limited and general, and about the difference between them, and about the difference between partnerships that are limited partnerships and those that are not. Finally, you'll learn how to prepare partnership ledger accounts and how to prepare partnership financial statements.

41.1 The need for partnerships

So far we have mainly considered businesses owned by only one person. We've also looked at joint ventures, which are temporary projects involving two or more parties where they work together to make a profit and then disband the venture. When a more permanent possibility exists, two or more people may form themselves into a **partnership**. This is a long-term commitment to operate in business together. The people who own a partnership are called **partners**. They do not have to be based or work in the same place, though they do in most cases. However, they maintain one set of accounting records and share the profits and losses.

From your general knowledge, can you think of any well-known partnerships where the partners are located, not just in different cities, but in different countries? What line of business are they in?

There are various reasons for multiple ownership of a business.

Think about this for a minute and then write down as many reasons as you can for people wanting to form a partnership.

In addition to the reasons suggested in the answer, there is also the fact that many business ventures carry financial risk should they fail. When a partnership is formed, the level of risk is reduced. Firstly, any loss can be shared by all the partners and, secondly, when more than one person's expertise is involved, the chances of failure are reduced.

There are two types of multiple ownership: partnerships and limited companies. This chapter deals only with partnerships. Limited companies are the subject of Chapter 45.

41.2 Nature of a partnership

A partnership has the following characteristics:

1 It is formed to make profits.
2 It must obey the law as given in the Partnership Act 1890. If there is a **limited partner** (as described in Section 41.3 below), it must also comply with the Limited Partnership Act of 1907.
3 Normally there can be a minimum of two partners and a maximum of twenty partners. Exceptions are banks, where there cannot be more than ten partners; and there is no maximum for firms of accountants, solicitors, stock exchange members, surveyors, auctioneers, valuers, estate agents, land agents, estate managers or insurance brokers.
4 Each partner (except for limited partners, described below) must pay their share of any debts that the partnership could not pay. If necessary, they could be forced to sell all their private possessions to pay their share of the debts. This can be said to be unlimited liability.
5 Partners who are not limited partners are known as **general partners**.

41.3 Limited partnerships

Limited partnerships are partnerships containing one or more **limited partners**. Limited partnerships must be registered with the Registrar of Companies. Limited partners are not liable for the debts as in Section 41.2 (4) above. Limited partners have the following characteristics and restrictions on their role in the partnership:

1 Their liability for the debts of the partnership is limited to the capital they have put in. They can lose that capital, but they cannot be asked for any more money to pay the debts unless they contravene the regulations relating to their involvement in the partnership (see 2 and 3 below).
2 They are not allowed to take out or receive back any part of their contribution to the partnership during its lifetime.
3 They are not allowed to take part in the management of the partnership or to have the power to make the partnership take a decision. If they do, they become liable for all the debts and obligations of the partnership up to the amount taken out or received back or incurred while they were taking part in the management of the partnership.
4 All the partners cannot be limited partners, so there must be at least one general partner with unlimited liability.

What advantages do you think there might be to general partners in having a limited partner?

41.4 Limited liability partnerships

This form of partnership was first introduced in 2000. They differ from limited partnerships (Section 41.3) in that partners are liable only to the extent of their capital invested. Also, all partners are permitted to take part in the management of the partnership.

41.5 Partnership agreements

Agreements in writing are not necessary. However, it is better if a written agreement is drawn up by a lawyer or an accountant. Where there is a proper written agreement there will be fewer problems between partners. A written agreement means less confusion about what has been agreed.

41.6 Contents of partnership agreements

The written agreement can contain as much, or as little, as the partners want. The law does not say what it must contain. The usual accounting contents are:

1 the capital to be contributed by each partner;
2 the ratio in which profits (or losses) are to be shared;
3 the rate of interest, if any, to be paid on capital before the profits are shared;
4 the rate of interest, if any, to be charged on partners' drawings;
5 salaries to be paid to partners;
6 arrangements for the admission of new partners;
7 procedures to be carried out when a partner retires or dies.

Some partnerships don't bother drawing up a partnership agreement. How do you think the partners in those partnerships know what rights and responsibilities they have? (You have not been told this yet, but it should be obvious if you think about it.)

Points **1** to **5** in the list above are considered below. Points **6** and **7** will be taken up in later chapters.

1 Capital contributions

Partners need not contribute equal amounts of capital. What matters is how much capital each partner *agrees* to contribute. It is not unusual for partners to increase the amount of capital they have invested in the partnership.

2 Profit (or loss) sharing ratios

Partners can agree to share profits/losses in any ratio or any way that they may wish. However, it is often thought by students that profits should be shared in the same ratio as that in which capital is contributed. For example, suppose the capitals were Allen £40,000 and Beet £20,000. Some would assume that the partners would share the profits in the ratio of two-thirds to one-third, even though the work to be done by each partner is similar. The division of the profits of the first few years on such a basis might be:

Years	*1*	*2*	*3*	*4*	*5*	*Total*
	£	£	£	£	£	£
Net profits	36,000	48,000	60,000	60,000	72,000	276,000
Shared:						
Allen $^2/_3$	24,000	32,000	40,000	40,000	48,000	184,000
Beet $^1/_3$	12,000	16,000	20,000	20,000	24,000	92,000

Overall, Allen would receive £184,000, i.e. £92,000 more than Beet. As the duties of the partners are the same, in order to treat each partner fairly, the difference between the two shares of profit should be adequate to compensate Allen for putting extra capital into the firm. It should not be excessive. It is obvious that £92,000 extra profits is excessive, as Allen only put in an extra £20,000 as capital.

Consider too the position of capital ratio sharing of profits if one partner puts in £99,000 and the other puts in £1,000 as capital.

To overcome the difficulty of compensating fairly for the investment of extra capital, the concept of **interest on capital** was devised.

3 Interest on capital

If the work to be done by each partner is of equal value but the capital contributed is unequal, it is reasonable to pay interest on the partners' capitals out of partnership profits. This interest is treated as a deduction prior to the calculation of profits and their distribution among the partners according to the profit sharing ratio.

The rate of interest is a matter of agreement between the partners. Often it will be based upon the return which they would have received if they had invested the capital elsewhere.

Taking Allen and Beet's partnership again, but sharing the profits equally after charging 5 per cent per annum interest on capital, the division of profits would become:

Years	*1*	*2*	*3*	*4*	*5*		*Total*
	£	£	£	£	£		£
Net profit	36,000	48,000	60,000	60,000	72,000		276,000
Interest on capitals							
Allen	2,000	2,000	2,000	2,000	2,000	=	10,000
Beet	1,000	1,000	1,000	1,000	1,000	=	5,000
Remainder shared:							
Allen $^1/_2$	16,500	22,500	28,500	28,500	34,500	=	130,500
Beet $^1/_2$	16,500	22,500	28,500	28,500	34,500	=	130,500

Summary	*Allen*	*Beet*
	£	£
Interest on capital	10,000	5,000
Balance of profits	130,500	130,500
	140,500	135,500

Allen has thus received £5,000 more than Beet, this being adequate return (in the partners' estimation) for having invested an extra £20,000 in the partnership for five years.

4 Interest on drawings

It is obviously in the best interests of the partnership if cash is withdrawn from it by the partners in accordance with the two basic principles of (*a*) as little as possible, and (*b*) as late as possible. The more cash that is left in the partnership, the more expansion can be financed, the greater the economies of having ample cash to take advantage of bargains and of not missing cash discounts because cash is not available, and so on.

To deter the partners from taking out cash unnecessarily the concept can be used of charging the partners interest on each withdrawal, calculated from the date of withdrawal to the end of the financial year. The amount charged to them helps to swell the profits divisible between the partners. The rate of interest should be sufficient to achieve this without being too harsh.

Suppose that Allen and Beet have decided to charge **interest on drawings** at 5 per cent per annum, and that their year end was 31 December. The following drawings are made:

Allen

Drawings		*Interest*		
	£			£
1 January	2,000	£2,000 × 5% × 12 months	=	100
1 March	4,800	£4,800 × 5% × 10 months	=	200
1 May	2,400	£2,400 × 5% × 8 months	=	80
1 July	4,800	£4,800 × 5% × 6 months	=	120
1 October	1,600	£1,600 × 5% × 3 months	=	20
		Interest charged to Allen	=	520

Beet

Drawings		*Interest*		
	£			£
1 January	1,200	£1,200 × 5% × 12 months	=	60
1 August	9,600	£9,600 × 5% × 5 months	=	200
1 December	4,800	£4,800 × 5% × 1 month	=	20
		Interest charged to Beet	=	280

5 Partnership salaries

One partner may have more responsibility or tasks than the others. As a reward for this, rather than change the profit and loss sharing ratio, the partner may have a **partnership salary** which is deducted before sharing the balance of profits.

6 Performance-related payments to partners

Partners may agree that commission or performance-related bonuses be payable to some or all of the partners linked to their individual performance. As with salaries, these would be deducted before sharing the balance of profits.

41.7 An example of the distribution of profits

Taylor and Clarke have been in partnership for one year sharing profits and losses in the ratio of Taylor $^3/_5$, Clarke $^2/_5$. They are entitled to 5 per cent per annum interest on capitals, Taylor having £20,000 capital and Clarke £60,000. Clarke is to have a salary of £15,000. They charge interest on drawings, Taylor being charged £500 and Clarke £1,000. The net profit, before any distributions to the partners, amounted to £50,000 for the year ended 31 December 2007.

The way in which the net profit is distributed among the partners can be shown as:

	£	£	£
Net profit			50,000
Add Charged for interest on drawings:			
Taylor		500	
Clarke		1,000	
			1,500
			51,500
Less Salary: Clarke		15,000	
Interest on capital:			
Taylor	1,000		
Clarke	3,000		
		4,000	
			(19,000)
Balance of profits			32,500
Shared:			
Taylor 3/5		19,500	
Clarke 2/5		13,000	
			32,500

The £50,000 net profits have therefore been shared:

	Taylor £	*Clarke* £
Balance of profits	19,500	13,000
Interest on capital	1,000	3,000
Salary	–	15,000
	20,500	31,000
Less Interest on drawings	(500)	(1,000)
	20,000	30,000
	£50,000	

41.8 The financial statements

If the sales, inventory and expenses of a partnership were exactly the same as those of a sole trader, then the income statement would be identical with that prepared for the sole trader. However, a partnership would have an extra section at the end of the income statement. This section is called the **profit and loss appropriation account**, and it is in this account that the distribution of profits is shown. The heading to the income statement for a partnership does not normally include the words 'appropriation account'. It is purely an accounting custom not to include it in the heading. (**Sometimes examiners ask for it to be included in the heading, in which case, you need to do so!**)

The profit and loss appropriation account of Taylor and Clarke from the details given would be:

Taylor and Clarke
Income Statement for the year ending 31 December 2007

(Trading Account section – same as for sole trader)
(Profit and Loss Account section – same as for sole trader)
Profit and Loss Appropriation Account

	£	£	£
Net profit (from the Profit and Loss Account section)			50,000
Interest on drawings:			
Taylor		500	
Clarke		1,000	
			1,500
			51,500
Less: Salary: Clarke		15,000	
Interest on capitals			
Taylor	1,000		
Clarke	3,000		
		4,000	(19,000)
			32,500
Balance of profits shared:			
Taylor $^3/_5$		19,500	
Clarke $^2/_5$		13,000	
			32,500

41.9 Fixed and fluctuating capital accounts

There are two choices open to partnerships: **fixed capital accounts** plus current accounts, and **fluctuating capital accounts**.

1 Fixed capital accounts plus current accounts

The capital account for each partner remains year by year at the figure of capital put into the partnership by the partners. The profits, interest on capital and the salaries to which the partner may be entitled are then credited to a separate current account for the partner, and the drawings and the interest on drawings are debited to it. The balance of the current account at the end of each financial year will then represent the amount of undrawn (or withdrawn) profits. A credit balance will be undrawn profits, while a debit balance will be drawings in excess of the profits to which the partner was entitled.

For Taylor and Clarke, capital and current accounts, assuming drawings of £15,000 for Taylor and £26,000 for Clarke will be:

Taylor – *Capital*

	2007			£
	Jan	1	Bank	20,000

Clarke – *Capital*

	2007			£
	Jan	1	Bank	60,000

Taylor – *Current Account*

2007			£	2007			£
Dec	31	Cash: Drawings	15,000	Dec	31	Profit and loss appropriation account:	
	31	Profit and loss appropriation account:				Interest on capital	1,000
		Interest on drawings	500			Share of profits	19,500
	31	Balance c/d	5,000				
			20,500				20,500
				2008			
				Jan	1	Balance b/d	5,000

Clarke – *Current Account*

2007			£	2007			£
Dec	31	Cash: Drawings	26,000	Dec	31	Profit and loss appropriation account:	
	31	Profit and loss appropriation account:				Salary	15,000
		Interest on drawings	1,000			Interest on capital	3,000
	31	Balance c/d	4,000			Share of profits	13,000
			31,000				31,000
				2008			
				Jan	1	Balance b/d	4,000

Notice that the salary of Clarke was not paid to him, it was merely credited to his current account. If instead it was paid in addition to his drawings, the £15,000 cash paid would have been debited to the current account, changing the £4,000 credit balance into a £11,000 debit balance.

Note also that the drawings have been posted to the current accounts at the end of the year. The amounts withdrawn which add up to these amounts were initially recorded in the Cash Book. Only the totals for the year are posted to the current account, rather than each individual withdrawal.

Examiners often ask for the capital accounts and current accounts to be shown in columnar form rather than as T-accounts. For Taylor and Clarke, these would appear as follows:

Capital Accounts

			Taylor	*Clarke*				*Taylor*	*Clarke*
			£	£	2007			£	£
					Jan	1	Bank	20,000	60,000

Current Accounts

			Taylor	*Clarke*				*Taylor*	*Clarke*
2007			£	£	2007			£	£
Dec	31	Cash: Drawings	15,000	26,000	Dec	31	Salary	19,500	15,000
	31	Interest on drawings	500	1,000		31	Interest on capital	1,000	3,000
	31	Balances c/d	5,000	4,000		31	Share of profits		13,000
			20,500	31,000				20,500	31,000
					2008				
					Jan	1	Balances b/d	5,000	4,000

2 Fluctuating capital accounts

The distribution of profits would be credited to the capital account, and the drawings and interest on drawings debited. Therefore the balance on the capital account will change each year, i.e. it will fluctuate.

If fluctuating capital accounts had been kept for Taylor and Clarke they would have appeared:

Taylor – *Capital*

			£				£
2007				2007			
Dec	31	Cash: Drawings	15,000	Jan	1	Bank	20,000
	31	Profit and loss appropriation account:		Dec	31	Profit and loss appropriation account:	
		Interest on drawings	500			Interest on capital	1,000
	31	Balance c/d	25,000			Share of profits	19,500
			40,500				40,500
				2008			
				Jan	1	Balance b/d	25,000

Clarke – *Capital*

			£				£
2007				2007			
Dec	31	Cash: Drawings	26,000	Jan	1	Bank	60,000
	31	Profit and loss appropriation account:		Dec	31	Profit and loss appropriation account:	
						Salary	15,000
		Interest on drawings	1,000			Interest on capital	3,000
	31	Balance c/d	64,000			Share of profit	13,000
			91,000				91,000
				2008			
				Jan	1	Balance b/d	64,000

Fixed capital accounts preferred

The keeping of fixed capital accounts plus current accounts is considered preferable to fluctuating capital accounts. When partners are taking out greater amounts than the share of the profits that they are entitled to, this is shown up by a debit balance on the current account and so acts as a warning.

41.10 Where no partnership agreement exists

As mentioned in the answer to Activity 41.4, where no partnership agreement exists, express or implied, Section 24 of the Partnership Act 1890 governs the situation. The accounting content of this section states:

(*a*) Profits and losses are to be shared equally.
(*b*) There is to be no interest allowed on capital.
(*c*) No interest is to be charged on drawings.
(*d*) Salaries are not allowed.
(*e*) Partners who put a sum of money into a partnership in excess of the capital they have agreed to subscribe are entitled to interest at the rate of 5 per cent per annum on such an advance.

Section 24 applies where there is no agreement. There may be an agreement not by a partnership deed but in a letter, or it may be implied by conduct, for instance when a partner signs a balance sheet which shows profits shared in some other ratio than equally. Where a dispute arises as to whether an agreement exists or not, and this cannot be resolved by the partners, only the courts are competent to decide.

41.11 The balance sheet

For the partnership, the capital part of the balance sheet will appear in this form:

Taylor and Clarke
Balance Sheet as at 31 December 2007 (extract)

					£	£
Capital accounts Taylor					20,000	
Clarke					60,000	
						80,000
Current accounts		*Taylor*		*Clarke*		
	£	£	£	£		
Salary		–		15,000		
Interest on capital		1,000		3,000		
Share of profits		19,500		13,000		
		20,500		31,000		
Less Drawings	15,000		26,000			
Interest on drawings	500		1,000			
		(15,500)		(27,000)		
		5,000		4,000		
						9,000

If one of the current accounts had finished in debit, for instance if the current account of Clarke had finished up as £400 debit, the figure of £400 would appear in brackets and the balances would appear net in the totals column:

	Taylor	*Clarke*	
	£	£	£
Closing balance	5,000	(400)	4,600

If the net figure turned out to be a debit figure then this would be deducted from the total of the capital accounts.

Learning outcomes

You should now have learnt:

1 That there is no limited liability in partnerships except for 'limited partners'.

2 That limited partners cannot withdraw any of the capital they invested in the partnership or take part in the management of the partnership.

3 That apart from some professions, if more than twenty owners of an organisation are needed, a limited company would need to be formed, not a partnership.

4 That the contents of a partnership agreement will override anything written in this chapter. Partners can agree to anything they want to, in as much or as little detail as they wish.

5 That if there is no partnership agreement, then the provisions of the Partnership Act 1890 (details shown in section 41.10) will apply.

6 That partners can agree to show their capital accounts using either the fixed capital or fluctuating capital methods.

7 How to prepare the ledger accounts and financial statements of partnerships.

Answers to activities

41.1 The best example is accounting partnerships. Some of them have offices all over the world.

41.2 Your answer could have included some of the following:

- The capital required is more than one person can provide.
- The experience or ability required to manage the business cannot be found in one person alone.
- Many people want to share management instead of doing everything on their own.
- Very often the partners will be members of the same family.

41.3 Limited partners contribute capital. They may also contribute expertise. Either of these is a benefit to the general partners – they have to contribute less capital and they can rely on the additional expertise when appropriate without needing to seek assistance from people outside the partnership. Also, because limited partners cannot be involved in the management of the partnership, general partners can take decisions without consulting a limited partner, thus saving time and effort when, in many instances, the limited partner will be busy doing other things that have nothing to do with the partnership business.

41.4 The Partnership Act 1890 imposes a standard partnership agreement upon partnerships that do not draw up a partnership agreement. See Section 41.10.

Review questions

41.1 Black, Brown and Cook are partners. They share profits and losses in the ratios of $^2/_9$, $^1/_3$ and $^4/_9$ respectively.

For the year ending 31 July 2002, their capital accounts remained fixed at the following amounts:

	£
Black	60,000
Brown	40,000
Cook	20,000

They have agreed to give each other 6 per cent interest per annum on their capital accounts.

In addition to the above, partnership salaries of £30,000 for Brown and £18,000 for Cook are to be charged.

The net profit of the partnership, before taking any of the above into account was £111,000.

You are required to draw up the appropriation account of the partnership for the year ending 31 July 2002.

41.2A Gray, Wilkes and Booth are partners. They share profits and losses in the ratios of $^3/_8$, $^3/_8$ and $^1/_4$ respectively.

For the year ending 31 December 2003 their capital accounts remained fixed at the following amounts:

	£
Gray	50,000
Wilkes	40,000
Booth	30,000

They have agreed to give each other 5 per cent interest per annum on their capital accounts.

In addition to the above, partnership salaries of £32,000 for Wilkes and £14,000 for Booth are to be charged.

The net profit of the partnership before taking any of the above into account was £84,800.

Required:
Draw up the appropriation account of the partnership for the year ending 31 December 2003.

41.3 I Skip and U Jump sell toys. Their individual investments in the business on 1 January 2004 were: Skip £80,000, Jump £40,000.

For the year to 31 December 2004, the net profit was £30,000 and the partners' drawings were: Skip £8,000, Jump £9,000.

→

For 2004 (their first year), the partners agreed to share profits and losses equally, but they decided that from 1 January 2005:

(*i*) The partners should be entitled to annual salaries of: Skip £10,000; Jump £14,000.
(*ii*) Interest should be allowed on capital at 7% per annum.
(*iii*) The profit remaining should be shared equally (as should losses).

	Net trading profit before dealing with partners' items	Drawings Skip	Drawings Jump
	£	£	£
2005	38,000	13,000	17,000
2006	29,000	12,000	20,000

Required:
Prepare the profit and loss appropriation accounts and the partners' current accounts for the three years.

41.4 Draw up a profit and loss appropriation account for the year ending 31 December 2007 and balance sheet extract at that date, from the following:

(*i*) Net profits £111,100.
(*ii*) Interest to be charged on capitals: Blair £3,000; Short £2,000; Steel £1,500.
(*iii*) Interest to be charged on drawings: Blair £400; Short £300; Steel £200.
(*iv*) Salaries to be credited: Short £20,000; Steel £25,000.
(*v*) Profits to be shared: Blair 70%; Short 20%; Steel 10%.
(*vi*) Current accounts: balances b/d Blair £18,600; Short £9,460; Steel £8,200.
(*vii*) Capital accounts: balances b/d Blair £100,000; Short £50,000; Steel £25,000.
(*viii*) Drawings: Blair £39,000; Short £27,100; Steel £16,800.

41.5A Draw up a profit and loss appropriation account for Cole, Knox and Lamb for the year ending 31 December 2005, and a balance sheet extract at that date, from the following:

(*i*) Net profits £184,800.
(*ii*) Interest to be charged on capitals: Cole £3,600; Knox £2,700; Lamb £2,100.
(*iii*) Interest to be charged on drawings: Cole £1,200; Knox £900; Lamb £500.
(*iv*) Salaries to be credited: Knox £22,000; Lamb £28,000.
(*v*) Profits to be shared: Cole 55%; Knox 25%; Lamb 20%.
(*vi*) Current accounts: Cole £18,000; Knox £8,000; Lamb £6,000.
(*vii*) Capital accounts: Cole £60,000; Knox £45,000; Lamb £35,000.
(*viii*) Drawings: Cole £27,000; Knox £23,000; Lamb £17,000.

41.6A Penrose and Wilcox are in partnership, sharing profits and losses in the ratio 3:2. The following information was taken from their books for the year ending 31 December 2009, before the completion of their profit and loss appropriation account.

		£	
Current accounts (1 January 2009)			
	Penrose	640	(*Dr*)
	Wilcox	330	(*Cr*)
Drawings	Penrose	3,000	
	Wilcox	2,000	
Net trading profit		6,810	
Interest on capital	Penrose	540	
	Wilcox	720	
Salary	Penrose	2,000	
Interest on drawings	Penrose	270	
	Wilcox	180	

(*a*) Prepare, for the year ending 31 December 2009:
   (*i*) the profit and loss appropriation account of Penrose and Wilcox;
   (*ii*) the current accounts in the ledger for Penrose and Wilcox.
(*b*) Why in many partnerships are current accounts prepared as well as capital accounts?
(*c*) At 1 January 2009 Penrose had a debit balance in his current account. What does this mean?
(*d*) In partnership accounts what is the purpose of preparing:
   (*i*) an income statement?
   (*ii*) a profit and loss appropriation account?
(e) In partnership accounts why is:
   (*i*) interest allowed on capital?
   (*ii*) interest charged on drawings?

(*Northern Examinations and Assessment Board: GCSE*)

41.7A A and B are in partnership sharing profits and losses 3:2. Under the terms of the partnership agreement, the partners are entitled to interest on capital at 5 per cent per annum and B is entitled to a salary of £4,500. Interest is charged on drawings at 5 per cent per annum and the amounts of interest are given below. No interest is charged or allowed on current accounts.

The partners' capitals at 1 July 2006 were: A £30,000 and B £10,000.

The net trading profit of the firm before dealing with partners' interest or B's salary for the year ended 30 June 2007 was £25,800. Interest on drawings for the year amounted to A £400, B £300.

At 1 July 2006, there was a credit balance of £1,280 on B's current account, while A's current account balance was a debit of £500. Drawings for the year to 30 June 2007 amounted to £12,000 for A and £15,000 for B.

Required:
Prepare, for the year to 30 June 2007:

(*a*) The profit and loss appropriation account.
(*b*) The partners' current accounts.

41.8 Bee, Cee and Dee have been holding preliminary discussions with a view to forming a partnership to buy and sell antiques.

The position has now been reached where the prospective partners have agreed the basic arrangements under which the partnership will operate.

Bee will contribute £40,000 as capital, and up to £10,000 as a long-term loan to the partnership, if needed. He has extensive other business interests and will not therefore be taking an active part in the running of the business.

Cee is unable to bring in more than £2,000 as capital initially, but, because he has an expert knowledge of the antique trade, will act as the manager of the business on a full-time basis.

Dee is willing to contribute £10,000 as capital. He will also assist in running the business as the need arises. In particular, he is prepared to attend auctions anywhere within the United Kingdom in order to acquire trading stock which he will transport back to the firm's premises in his van. On occasions he may also help Cee to restore the articles prior to sale to the public.

At the meeting, the three prospective partners intend to decide upon the financial arrangements for sharing out the profits (or losses) made by the firm, and have approached you for advice.

You are required to prepare a set of explanatory notes, under suitable headings, of the considerations which the prospective partners should take into account in arriving at their decisions at the next meeting.

(*Association of Chartered Certified Accountants*)

→

41.9 Frame and French are in partnership sharing profits and losses in the ratio 3:2. The following is their trial balance as at 30 September 2009.

	Dr	*Cr*
	£	£
Buildings (cost £210,000)	160,000	
Fixtures at cost	8,200	
Provision for depreciation: Fixtures		4,200
Accounts receivable	61,400	
Accounts payable		26,590
Cash at bank	6,130	
Inventory at 30 September 2008	62,740	
Sales		363,111
Purchases	210,000	
Carriage outwards	3,410	
Discounts allowed	620	
Loan interest: P Prince	3,900	
Office expenses	4,760	
Salaries and wages	57,809	
Bad debts	1,632	
Allowance for doubtful debts		1,400
Loan from P Prince		65,000
Capitals: Frame		100,000
French		75,000
Current accounts: Frame		4,100
French		1,200
Drawings: Frame	31,800	
French	28,200	
	640,601	640,601

Required:
Prepare an income statement and profit and loss appropriation account for the year ending 30 September 2009, and a balance sheet as at that date.

(*a*) Inventory, 30 September 2009, £74,210.
(*b*) Expenses to be accrued: Office Expenses £215; Wages £720.
(*c*) Depreciate fixtures 15 per cent on reducing balance basis, buildings £5,000.
(*d*) Reduce provision for doubtful debts to £1,250.
(*e*) Partnership salary: £30,000 to Frame. Not yet entered.
(*f*) Interest on drawings: Frame £900; French £600.
(*g*) Interest on capital account balances at 5 per cent.

41.10A Scot and Joplin are in partnership. They share profits in the ratio: Scot 70 per cent; Joplin 30 per cent. The following trial balance was extracted as at 31 December 2007.

	Dr £	*Cr* £
Office equipment at cost	9,200	
Motor vehicles at cost	21,400	
Provision for depreciation at 31.12.2006:		
Motor vehicles		12,800
Office equipment		3,600
Inventory at 31 December 2006	38,410	
Accounts receivable and accounts payable	41,940	32,216
Cash at bank	2,118	
Cash in hand	317	
Sales		180,400
Purchases	136,680	
Salaries	27,400	
Office expenses	2,130	
Discounts allowed	312	
Current accounts at 31.12.2006		
Scot		7,382
Joplin		7,009
Capital accounts: Scot		50,000
Joplin		20,000
Drawings: Scot	17,500	
Joplin	16,000	
	313,407	313,407

Required:

Draw up a set of financial statements for the year ending 31 December 2007 for the partnership. The following notes are applicable at 31 December 2007.

(*a*) Inventory, 31 December 2007 £41,312.
(*b*) Office expenses owing £240.
(*c*) Provide for depreciation: motor 25 per cent of cost, office equipment 20 per cent of cost.
(*d*) Charge interest on capitals at 5 per cent.
(*e*) Charge interest on drawings: Scot £300; Joplin £200.

→

→ **41.11** Sage and Onion are trading in partnership, sharing profits and losses equally. Interest at 5% per annum is allowed or charged on both the capital account and the current account balances at the beginning of the year. Interest is charged on drawings at 5% per annum. The partners are entitled to annual salaries of: Sage £12,000; Onion £8,000.

Required:
From the information given below, prepare the partnership income statement and profit and loss appropriation account for the year ending 31 December 2001, and the balance sheet as at that date.

Sage and Onion
Trial Balance as at 31 December 2001

	Dr £	*Cr* £
Capital accounts: Sage		100,000
Onion		50,000
Current accounts: Sage		2,000
Onion	600	
Cash drawings for the year: Sage	15,000	
Onion	10,000	
Freehold premises at cost	50,000	
Inventory at 1 January 2001	75,000	
Fixtures and fittings at cost	15,000	
Purchases and purchase returns	380,000	12,000
Bank	31,600	
Sales and sales returns	6,000	508,000
Accounts receivable and accounts payable	52,400	33,300
Carriage inwards	21,500	
Carriage outwards	3,000	
Staff salaries	42,000	
VAT		8,700
Office expenses	7,500	
Allowance for doubtful debts		2,000
Advertising	5,000	
Discounts received		1,000
Discounts allowed	1,200	
Bad debts	1,400	
Rent and business rates	2,800	
Accumulated provision for depreciation of fixtures and fittings		3,000
	720,000	720,000

At 31 December 2001:

(*a*) Inventory was valued at £68,000.
(*b*) Purchase invoices amounting to £3,000 for goods included in the inventory valuation at (*a*) above had not been recorded.
(*c*) Staff salaries owing £900.
(*d*) Business rates paid in advance £200.
(*e*) Allowance for doubtful debts to be increased to £2,400.
(*f*) Goods withdrawn by partners for private use had not been recorded and were valued at: Sage £500, Onion £630. No interest is to be charged on these amounts.
(*g*) Provision is to be made for depreciation of fixtures and fittings at 10% on cost.
(*h*) Interest on drawings for the year is to be charged: Sage £360, Onion £280.

41.12A Bush, Home and Wilson share profits and losses in the ratios 4:1:3 respectively. Their trial balance as at 30 April 2004 was as follows:

	Dr	Cr
	£	£
Sales		334,618
Returns inwards	10,200	
Purchases	196,239	
Carriage inwards	3,100	
Inventory 30 April 2003	68,127	
Discounts allowed	190	
Salaries and wages	54,117	
Bad debts	1,620	
Allowance for doubtful debts 30 April 2003		950
General expenses	1,017	
Business rates	2,900	
Postage	845	
Computers at cost	8,400	
Office equipment at cost	5,700	
Provisions for depreciation at 30 April 2003:		
Computers		3,600
Office equipment		2,900
Accounts payable		36,480
Accounts receivable	51,320	
Cash at bank	5,214	
Drawings: Bush	39,000	
Home	16,000	
Wilson	28,000	
Current accounts: Bush		5,940
Home	2,117	
Wilson		9,618
Capital accounts: Bush		60,000
Home		10,000
Wilson		30,000
	494,106	494,106

Draw up a set of financial statements for the year ending 30 April 2004. The following notes are relevant at 30 April 2004:

(*i*) Inventory 30 April 2004, £74,223.
(*ii*) Business rates in advance £200; Inventory of postage stamps £68.
(*iii*) Increase Allowance for doubtful debts to £1,400.
(*iv*) Salaries: Home £18,000; Wilson £14,000. Not yet recorded.
(*v*) Interest on Drawings: Bush £300; Home £200; Wilson £240.
(*vi*) Interest on Capitals at 8 per cent.
(*vii*) Depreciate Computers £2,800; Office equipment £1,100.

→

41.13 Reid and Benson are in partnership as lecturers and tutors. Interest is to be allowed on capital and on the opening balances on the current accounts at a rate of 5% per annum and Reid is to be given a salary of £18,000 per annum. Interest is to be charged on drawings at 5% per annum (see notes below) and the profits and losses are to be shared Reid 60% and Benson 40%.

The following trial balance was extracted from the books of the partnership at 31 December 2003.

	£	£
Capital account – Benson		50,000
Capital account – Reid		75,000
Current account – Benson		4,000
Current account – Reid		5,000
Drawings – Reid	17,000	
Drawings – Benson	20,000	
Sales – goods and services		541,750
Purchases of textbooks for distribution	291,830	
Returns inwards and outwards	800	330
Carriage inwards	3,150	
Staff salaries	141,150	
Rent	2,500	
Insurance – general	1,000	
Insurance – public indemnity	1,500	
Compensation paid due to Benson error	10,000	
General expenses	9,500	
Bad debts written-off	1,150	
Fixtures and fittings – cost	74,000	
Fixtures and fittings – depreciation		12,000
Accounts receivable and accounts payable	137,500	23,400
Cash	400	
Total	711,480	711,480

- An allowance for doubtful debts is to be created of £1,500.
- Insurances paid in advance at 31 December 2002 were General £50; Professional Indemnity £100.
- Fixtures and fittings are to be depreciated at 10% on cost.
- Interest on drawings: Benson £550, Reid £1,050.
- Inventory of books at 31 December 2003 was £1,500.

Required:
Prepare an income statement together with an appropriation account at 31 December 2003 together with a balance sheet as at that date.

You can find a range of additional self-test questions, as well as material to help you with your studies, on the website that accompanies this book at www.pearsoned.co.uk/wood.

chapter 42

Goodwill for sole traders and partnerships

Learning objectives

After you have studied this chapter, you should be able to:

- describe a range of methods for arriving at the selling price of a business
- explain and calculate super profits
- explain why goodwill exists
- explain why goodwill has a monetary value
- distinguish between purchased and non-purchased goodwill
- calculate purchased goodwill
- calculate the adjustments needed when there is some form of change in a partnership

Introduction

In this chapter, you'll learn about purchased goodwill and its treatment in the books and financial statements of sole traders and partnerships. You will also learn how to make adjustments to the partnership capital accounts when circumstances change.

42.1 Nature of goodwill

Suppose you have been running a business for some years and you want to sell it. How much would you ask as the total sale price of the business? You decide to list how much you could get for each asset if sold separately. This list might be as follows:

	£
Buildings	225,000
Machinery	75,000
Accounts receivable	60,000
Inventory	40,000
	400,000

Note: if there are any liabilities, you would deduct them from the total value of the assets to arrive at the value of the net assets, which is the net amount you would have left if you sold all the assets and paid off all the creditors.

So, if you sold off everything separately, you would expect to receive £400,000.

If you were running a successful business, would you be willing to sell it for the value of its net assets? Why/why not?

As the business is successful, a prospective buyer has been found who is willing to pay more than the £400,000 net asset value. As a result, you sell the whole of the business as a going concern to Mr Lee for £450,000. He has, therefore, paid £50,000 more than the total value of all the assets. This extra payment of £50,000 is called **goodwill**. He has paid this because he wanted to take over the business as a going concern, and so benefit from the product and customer base that already exists. Thus:

Purchased Goodwill = Total Price *less* value of net identifiable assets

Goodwill is an intangible asset. It can only exist if the business was purchased and the amount paid was greater than the value of the net assets. In many cases, goodwill represents the value of the reputation of the business at the time it was purchased.

42.2 Reasons for payment of goodwill

In buying an existing business which has been established for some time there may be quite a few possible advantages. Some of them are listed here:

- The business has a large number of regular customers who will continue to deal with the new owner.
- The business has a good reputation.
- It has experienced, efficient and reliable employees.
- The business is situated in a good location.
- It has good contacts with suppliers.
- It has well-known brand names that have not been valued and included as assets.

None of these advantages is available to completely new businesses. For this reason, many people are willing to pay an additional amount for goodwill when they buy an existing business.

42.3 Existence of goodwill

Goodwill does not necessarily exist in a business. If a business has a bad reputation, an inefficient labour force or other negative factors, it is unlikely that the owner would be paid for goodwill on selling the business.

Activity 42.2

In the earlier example, goodwill was a positive figure of £50,000. If, instead, it had been a negative figure of £100,000 (being the estimated cost of a marketing campaign that would be necessary to restore customers' faith in the business) at what price would the business be most likely to be sold? Why?

42.4 Methods of calculating goodwill

There is no single way of calculating goodwill on which everyone can agree. The seller will probably want more for the goodwill than the buyer will want to pay. All that is certain is that when agreement is reached between buyer and seller concerning how much is to be paid for a business, the amount by which the agreed price exceeds the value of the net assets represents the goodwill. Various methods are used to help buyer and seller come to an agreed figure for a business. The calculations give the buyer and the seller a figure with which to begin discussions of the value.

Very often an industry or occupation has its own customary way of calculating goodwill:

(*a*) In more than one type of retail business it has been the custom to value goodwill at the average weekly sales for the past year multiplied by a given figure. The given figure will, of course, differ between different types of businesses, and often changes gradually in the same type of business in the long term.
(*b*) With many professional firms, such as accountants in public practice, it is the custom to value goodwill as being the gross annual fees times a given number. For instance, what is termed a two years' purchase of a firm with gross fees of £300,000 means goodwill = 2 × £300,000 = £600,000.
(*c*) The average net annual profit for a specified past number of years multiplied by an agreed number. This is often said to be *x* years' purchase of the net profits.
(*d*) The super-profits method.

Let's consider the last of these, the super-profits method. It may be argued, as in the case of a sole trader for example, that the net profits are not 'true profits'. This is because the sole trader has not charged for the following expenses:

(*a*) Services of the proprietor. He has worked in the business, but he has not charged for such services. Any drawings he makes are charged to a capital account, not to the profit and loss account.
(*b*) The use of the money he has invested in the business. If he had invested his money elsewhere he would have earned interest or dividends on such investments.

Super profits are what an accountant would call what is left of the net profits after allowances have been made for (*a*) services of the proprietor and (*b*) the use of the capital.

They are usually calculated as:

	£	£
Annual net profits		80,000
Less (*i*) Remuneration proprietor would have earned for similar work elsewhere	36,000	
(*ii*) Interest that would have been earned if capital had been invested elsewhere	7,000	
		(43,000)
Annual super profits		37,000

The annual super profits are then multiplied by a number agreed by seller and purchaser of the business in order to arrive at the selling price.

42.5 Sole traders' books

Goodwill is only entered in a sole trader's accounts when it has been purchased. The existence of goodwill in the financial statements usually means that the business was purchased as a going concern by the owner. That is, the owner did not start the business from scratch.

There is another possible explanation for purchased goodwill appearing in a sole trader's balance sheet. What do you think it might be?

42.6 Partnership books

Although goodwill is not *normally* entered in the financial statements unless it has been purchased, sometimes it is necessary where partnerships are concerned.

Unless it has been agreed differently, partners own a share in the goodwill in the same ratio in which they share profits. For instance, if A takes one-quarter of the profits, A will be the owner of one-quarter of the goodwill. This is true even if there is no goodwill account.

This means that when something happens such as

(*a*) existing partners deciding to change profit and loss sharing ratios, or
(*b*) a new partner being introduced, or
(*c*) a partner retiring or dying,

then the ownership of goodwill by partners changes in some way.

The change may involve cash passing from one partner to another, or an adjustment in the books, so that the changes in ownership do not lead to a partner (or partners) giving away their share of ownership for nothing.

42.7 Change in profit sharing ratios of existing partners

Sometimes the profit and loss sharing ratios have to be changed. Typical reasons are:

- A partner may now not work as much as in the past, possibly because of old age or ill-health.
- A partner's skills and ability may have changed, perhaps after attending a course or following an illness.
- A partner may now be doing much more for the business than in the past.

If the partners decide to change their profit sharing ratios, an adjustment will be needed.

To illustrate why this is so, let's look at the following example of a partnership in which goodwill is not already shown in a goodwill account at its correct value.

(*a*) A, B and C are in partnership, sharing profits and losses equally.
(*b*) On 31 December 2005 they decide to change this to A one-half, B one-quarter and C one-quarter.
(*c*) On 31 December 2005 the goodwill, which had never been shown in the books, was valued at £60,000. If, just before the change in the profit sharing ratio, the business had been sold and £60,000 received for goodwill, then each partner would have received £20,000 as they shared profits equally.
(*d*) At any time after 31 December 2005, once the profit sharing ratio has changed, their ownership of goodwill is worth A £30,000, B £15,000 and C £15,000. If goodwill is sold for that amount then those figures will be received by the partners for goodwill.
(*e*) If, when (*b*) above happened, there had been no change in activity or commitment to the business by A, B, or C, or no other form of adjustment, then B and C would each have given away a £5,000 share of the goodwill for nothing. This would not be sensible.

We can now look at how the adjustments can be made when a goodwill account with the correct valuation does not already exist.

Exhibit 42.1

E, F and G have been in business for ten years. They have always shared profits equally. No goodwill account has ever existed in the books. On 31 December 2006 they agree that G will take only a one-fifth share of the profits as from 1 January 2007, because he will be devoting less of his time to the business in the future. E and F will each take two-fifths of the profits. The summarised balance sheet of the business on 31 December 2006 appears as follows:

Balance Sheet as at 31 December 2006

	£
Net Assets	70,000
Capital: E	30,000
F	18,000
G	22,000
	70,000

The partners agree that the goodwill should be valued at £30,000. Answer (1) shows the solution when a goodwill account is opened. Answer (2) is the solution when a goodwill account is not opened.

1 Goodwill account opened

Open a goodwill account. Then make the following entries: Debit goodwill account: total value of goodwill.

Credit partners' capital accounts: each one with his share of goodwill in old profit sharing ratio.

The goodwill account will appear as:

Goodwill

	£		£
Capitals: valuation shared		Balance c/d	30,000
E	10,000		
F	10,000		
G	10,000		
	30,000		30,000

The capital accounts may be shown in columnar fashion as:

Capital Accounts

	E	F	G		E	F	G
	£	£	£		£	£	£
Balances c/d	40,000	28,000	32,000	Balances b/d	30,000	18,000	22,000
				Goodwill: old ratios	10,000	10,000	10,000
	40,000	28,000	32,000		40,000	28,000	32,000

The balance sheet items before and after the adjustments will appear as:

	Before	*After*		*Before*	*After*
	£	£		£	£
Goodwill	–	30,000	Capitals: E	30,000	40,000
Other assets	70,000	70,000	F	18,000	28,000
			G	22,000	32,000
	70,000	100,000		70,000	100,000

2 Goodwill account not opened

The effect of the change of ownership of goodwill may be shown in the following form:

Before		*After*		*Loss or Gain*		*Action Required*
	£		£			
E One-third	10,000	Two-fifths	12,000	Gain	£2,000	Debit E's capital account £2,000
F One-third	10,000	Two-fifths	12,000	Gain	£2,000	Debit F's capital account £2,000
G One-third	10,000	One-fifth	6,000	Loss	£4,000	Credit G's capital account £4,000
	30,000		30,000			

The column headed '*Action Required*' shows that a partner who has gained goodwill because of the change must be charged for it by having his capital account debited with the value of the gain. A partner who has lost goodwill must be compensated for it by having his capital account credited.

The capital accounts will appear as:

Capital Accounts

	E	F	G		E	F	G
	£	£	£		£	£	£
Goodwill adjustments	2,000	2,000		Balances b/d	30,000	18,000	22,000
Balances c/d	28,000	16,000	26,000	Goodwill adjustments			4,000
	30,000	18,000	26,000		30,000	18,000	26,000

As there is no goodwill account the balance sheet items before and after the adjustments will therefore appear as:

	Before	*After*		*Before*	*After*
	£	£		£	£
Net assets	70,000	70,000	Capitals: E	30,000	28,000
			F	18,000	16,000
			G	22,000	26,000
	70,000	70,000		70,000	70,000

Comparison of methods 1 and 2

Let's compare the methods. Assume that shortly afterwards the assets in 1 and 2 are sold for £70,000 and the goodwill for £30,000. The total of £100,000 would be distributed as follows, using each of the methods:

Method 1. The £100,000 is exactly the amount needed to pay the partners according to the balances on their capital accounts. The payments are therefore made of

		£
Capitals paid to	E	40,000
	F	28,000
	G	32,000
Total cash paid		100,000

Method 2. First of all the balances on capital accounts, totalling £70,000, are to be paid. Then the £30,000 received for goodwill will be split between the partners in their profit and loss ratios. This will result in payments as follows:

	Capitals	*Goodwill Shared*		*Total Paid*
	£		£	£
E	28,000	($^2/_5$)	12,000	40,000
F	16,000	($^2/_5$)	12,000	28,000
G	26,000	($^1/_5$)	6,000	32,000
	70,000		30,000	100,000

You can see that the final amounts paid to the partners are the same whether a goodwill account is opened or not.

42.8 Admission of new partners

New partners may be admitted, usually for one of two reasons:

1 As an extra partner, either because the firm has grown or because someone is needed with different skills.
2 To replace partners who are leaving the firm. This might be because of retirement or death of a partner.

42.9 Goodwill on admission of new partners

The new partner will be entitled to a share in the profits, and, normally, also to the same share of the value of goodwill. It is correct to charge the new partner for taking over that share of the goodwill.

42.10 Goodwill adjustments when new partners are admitted

This calculation is done in four stages:

1 Show value of goodwill divided between old partners in old profit and loss sharing ratios.
2 Then show value of goodwill divided between partners (including new partner) in the new profit and loss sharing ratio.
3 Goodwill gain shown: charge these partners for the gain.
4 Goodwill loss shown: give these partners an allowance for their losses.

This is illustrated in Exhibits 42.2 and 42.3.

Exhibit 42.2

A and B are in partnership, sharing profits and losses equally. C is admitted as a new partner. The three partners will share profits and losses one-third each.

Total goodwill is valued at £60,000.

Stage 1			Stage 2		Stage 3	
Partners	*Old profit shares*	*Share of goodwill* £	*New profit shares*	*Share of goodwill* £	*Gain or loss* £	*Adjustment needed*
A	1/2	30,000	1/3	20,000	10,000 Loss	Cr A Capital
B	1/2	30,000	1/3	20,000	10,000 Loss	Cr B Capital
C		–	1/3	20,000	20,000 Gain	Dr C Capital
		60,000		60,000		

This means that A and B need to have their capitals increased by £10,000 each. C's capital needs to be reduced by £20,000.

Note that A and B have kept their profits in the same ratio to each other. While they used to have one-half each, now they have one-third each.

We will now see in Exhibit 42.3 that the method shown is the same even when existing partners take a different share of the profit to that before the change.

Exhibit 42.3

D and E are in partnership sharing profits one-half each. A new partner F is admitted. Profits will now be shared D one-fifth, and E and F two-fifths each. D and E have therefore not kept their shares equal to each other. Goodwill is valued at £60,000.

Stage 1			**Stage 2**		**Stage 3**	
Partners	*Old profit shares*	*Share of goodwill*	*New profit shares*	*Share of goodwill*	*Gain or loss*	*Adjustment needed*
		£		£	£	
D	1/2	30,000	1/5	12,000	18,000 Loss	Cr D Capital
E	1/2	30,000	2/5	24,000	6,000 Loss	Cr E Capital
F		–	2/5	24,000	24,000 Gain	Dr F Capital
		60,000		60,000		

D needs his capital increased by £18,000. E's capital is to be increased by £6,000. F's capital needs to be reduced by £24,000.

42.11 Accounting entries for goodwill adjustments

These depend on how the partners wish to arrange the adjustment. Three methods are usually used:

1 Cash is paid by the new partner privately to the old partners for his/her share of the goodwill. No goodwill account is to be opened.

In Exhibit 42.3, F would therefore give £24,000 in cash, being £18,000 to D and £6,000 to E. They would bank these amounts in their private bank accounts. No entry is made for this in the accounts of the partnership.

2 Cash is paid by the new partner into the business bank account for his/her share of the goodwill. No goodwill account is to be opened. Assume that the capital balances before F was admitted were D £50,000, E £50,000, and F was to pay in £50,000 as capital plus £24,000 for goodwill.

The £24,000 payment is made in order to secure a share of the £60,000 existing goodwill. The £24,000 is shared between the two existing partners by increasing their capital accounts by the amounts shown in Stage 3 of Exhibit 42.3. The debit entry is to the bank account. The entries in the capital accounts are:

Capital Accounts

	D	E	F		D	E	F
	£	£	£		£	£	£
Adjustments for goodwill			24,000	Balances b/d	50,000	50,000	
				Cash for capital			50,000
				Cash for goodwill			24,000
Balances c/d	68,000	56,000	50,000	Loss of goodwill	18,000	6,000	
	68,000	56,000	74,000		68,000	56,000	74,000

3 Goodwill account to be opened. No extra cash to be paid in by the new partner for goodwill.

In Exhibit 42.3, the opening capitals were D £50,000, E £50,000. F paid in £50,000 as capital.

Here, the situation is different from under the second method. The new partner is not paying anything in order to secure a share of the £60,000 of existing goodwill. As a result, it is shared now among the two original partners in their original profit sharing ratio (half each) and the new partner's capital account is credited only with the £50,000 he/she is investing. This is done because the new partner is not entitled to any of the previously established goodwill and the only way to prevent that permanently is to recognise all the goodwill now and credit it to the existing partners' capital accounts.

The action required is:

- Debit goodwill account: with total value of goodwill.
- Credit capitals of old partners: with their shares of goodwill in old profit sharing ratios.

No adjustments for goodwill gains and losses are required as the capital accounts of D and E have been increased by the full value of the goodwill at the time of F's admission to partnership.

For Exhibit 42.3, the entries would appear as:

Goodwill

	£		£
Value divided: D Capital	30,000	Balance c/d	60,000
E Capital	30,000		
	60,000		60,000

Capital Accounts

	D	E	F		D	E	F
	£	£	£		£	£	£
				Balances b/d	50,000	50,000	
				Cash for capital			50,000
Balances c/d	80,000	80,000	50,000	Goodwill	30,000	30,000	
	80,000	80,000	50,000		80,000	80,000	50,000

As shown in Section 42.7, if the partnership was dissolved and realised the £210,000 it was valued at when F was admitted, this would first be used to repay the capital account balances. D and F would, therefore, be fully compensated for the value of the goodwill at the time of F's admission to partnership, and F would receive exactly the amount of his/her investment.

42.12 Where new partners pay for share of goodwill

The last section looked at how the partners' capital accounts are adjusted to account for goodwill when a new partner is admitted. In the second case, £24,000 was paid for goodwill by the new partner. Total goodwill at that time was £60,000. The profit share of the new partner is 2/5. If you divide £24,000 by 2/5 you get £60,000. Therefore, if you didn't know that the total goodwill was £60,000 you can calculate it by dividing the amount a new partner pays for goodwill by that new partner's profit sharing ratio.

Unless otherwise agreed, the assumption is that the total value of goodwill is directly proportionate to the amount paid by the new partner for the share of profit the new partner will receive in future. If a new partner pays £12,000 for a one-fifth share of future profits, goodwill is taken to be £60,000. A sum of £18,000 for a one-quarter share of future profits would, therefore, be taken to imply a total value of £72,000 for goodwill.

42.13 Goodwill on withdrawal or death of partners

This depends on whether or not a goodwill account exists.

If there was no goodwill account

If no goodwill account already existed the partnership goodwill should be valued because the outgoing partner is entitled to his/her share of its value. This value is entered in double entry accounts:

- Debit goodwill account with valuation.
- Credit each old partner's capital account in profit sharing ratios.

Exhibit 42.4

H, I and J have been in partnership for many years sharing profit and losses equally. No goodwill account has ever existed.

J is leaving the partnership. The other two partners are to take over his share of profits equally. Each partner's capital before entering goodwill was £50,000. The goodwill is valued at £45,000.

Goodwill

		£		£
Valuation:	Capital H	15,000	Balance c/d	45,000
	Capital I	15,000		
	Capital J	15,000		
		45,000		45,000
Balance b/d		45,000		

Capital Accounts

	H	I	J		H	I	J
	£	£	£		£	£	£
Balances c/d	65,000	65,000	65,000	Balances b/d	50,000	50,000	50,000
				Goodwill shares	15,000	15,000	15,000
	65,000	65,000	65,000		65,000	65,000	65,000
				Balances b/d	65,000	65,000	65,000

When J leaves the partnership, his capital balance of £65,000 will be paid to him.

If a goodwill account exists

1 If a goodwill account exists with the correct valuation of goodwill entered in it, no further action is needed.
2 If the valuation in the goodwill account needs to be changed, the following will apply:

Goodwill undervalued: Debit increase needed to goodwill account.
Credit increase to old partners' capital accounts in their old profit sharing ratios.

Goodwill overvalued: Debit reduction to old partners' capital accounts in their old profit sharing ratios.
Credit reduction needed to goodwill account.

Learning outcomes

You should now have learnt:

1 What is meant by the term 'goodwill'.
2 What is meant by the term 'purchased goodwill', and how to calculate it.
3 How to calculate super profits.
4 How to record goodwill in the accounts of a partnership.
5 That the true value of goodwill can be established only when the business is sold, but for various reasons of fairness between partners it is valued the best way possible when there is no imminent sale of a business.
6 That if the old partners agree, a new partner can be admitted without paying anything in as capital.
7 That goodwill is usually owned by the partners in the ratio in which they share profits.
8 That if there is a change in partnership without adjustments for goodwill, then some partners will make an unfair gain while others will quite unfairly lose money.
9 That if a new partner pays a specific amount for his or her share of the goodwill, then that payment is said to be a 'premium'.

Answers to activities

42.1 What if someone wanted to buy the business so that they could run it for themselves? Would they not be willing to pay a bit extra so as to benefit from the customer and product base you've built up? When a business is sold as a 'going concern', the owners can usually receive more than simply the value of the assets or, to be more accurate, the value of its net assets (i.e. all assets less all liabilities). This difference is known as 'goodwill'.

42.2 It is unlikely that a potential buyer would be willing to pay more than £300,000 for the business and so it would most likely be sold, asset by asset, for £400,000.

42.3 The business may have been founded by the present owner who, at some time after starting the business, bought another business and combined the two businesses into one. For example, a newsagent may take over another newsagent and run both shops as one business. The purchased goodwill included in the amount paid for the second business would appear in the balance sheet of the combined business.

Review questions

42.1 The partners have always shared their profits in the ratios of Vantuira 3: Aparecida 2: Fraga 5. They are to alter their profit ratios to Vantuira 4: Aparecida 1: Fraga 3. The last balance sheet before the change was:

Balance Sheet as at 31 March 2003

	£
Net Assets (not including goodwill)	100,000
	100,000
Capitals:	
Vantuira	30,000
Aparecida	20,000
Fraga	50,000
	100,000

The partners agree to bring in goodwill, being valued at £24,000 on the change.

Show the balance sheets on 1 April 2003 after goodwill has been taken into account if:

(*a*) Goodwill account was opened.
(*b*) Goodwill account was not opened.

42.2A The partners are to change their profit ratios as shown:

	Old ratio	*New ratio*
Mack	1	2
Burns	4	3
Flint	2	4
Tonks	3	1

They decide to bring in a goodwill amount of £72,000 on the change. The last balance sheet before any element of goodwill has been introduced was:

Balance Sheet as at 30 September 2002

	£
Net assets (not including goodwill)	180,000
	180,000
Capitals:	
Mack	30,000
Burns	70,000
Flint	35,000
Tonks	45,000
	180,000

Show the balance sheets on 1 October 2002 after necessary adjustments have been made if:

(*a*) Goodwill account was opened.
(*b*) Goodwill account was not opened.

42.3 Black and Smart are in partnership, sharing profits and losses equally. They decide to admit King. By agreement, goodwill valued at £40,000 is to be introduced into the business books. King is required to provide capital equal to that of Smart after she has been credited with her share of goodwill. The new profit sharing ratio is to be 8:3:5 respectively for Black, Smart and King.

The balance sheet before admission of King showed:

	£
Non-current and current assets (other than cash)	160,000
Cash	1,000
Total assets	161,000
Current liabilities	(41,000)
Net assets	120,000
Capital: Black	70,000
Capital: Smart	50,000
	120,000

Show:

(*a*) Journal entries for admission of Smart.

(*b*) Opening balance sheet of new business.

(*c*) Journal entries for writing off the goodwill which the new partners decided to do soon after the start of the new business.

42.4A Blunt, Dodds and Fuller are in partnership. They shared profits in the ratio 1:3:2. It is decided to admit Baxter. It is agreed that goodwill is worth £60,000, but that this is not to be brought into the business records. Baxter will bring £24,000 cash into the business for capital. The new profit sharing ratio is to be Blunt 4: Dodds 5: Fuller 2: Baxter 1.

The balance sheet before Baxter was introduced was as follows:

	£
Assets (other than in cash)	66,000
Cash	1,200
Total assets	67,200
Accounts payable	(8,400)
Net assets	58,800
Capitals: Blunt	14,000
Dodds	24,400
Fuller	20,400
	58,800

Show:

(*a*) The entries in the capital accounts of Blunt, Dodds, Fuller and Baxter, the accounts to be in columnar form.

(*b*) The balance sheet after Baxter has been introduced.

42.5 Wilson, Player and Sharp are in partnership. They shared profits in the ratio 2:4:3. It is decided to admit Titmus. It is agreed that goodwill is worth £72,000 and that it is to be brought into the business records. Titmus will bring £30,000 cash into the business for capital. The new profit sharing ratio is to be Wilson 5: Player 8: Sharp 4: Titmus 3.

The balance sheet before Titmus was introduced was as follows:

	£
Assets (other than in cash)	200,000
Cash	2,000
Total assets	202,000
Liabilities	(31,000)
Net assets	171,000
Capitals: Wilson	57,000
Player	76,000
Sharp	38,000
	171,000

→

Show:

(*a*) The entries in the capital accounts of Wilson, Player, Sharp and Titmus, the accounts to be in columnar form.

(*b*) The balance sheet after Titmus has been introduced.

42.6 A new partner has joined the business during the year and has paid in £10,000 for 'goodwill'. This £10,000 has been credited by the bookkeeper to the account of the new partner. The senior partner had objected to this, but the bookkeeper had replied: 'Why not credit the £10,000 to the account of the new partner? It is his money after all.'

Required:

Give your advice as to the proper treatment of this £10,000. Explain your reasons fully.

(*Association of Chartered Certified Accountants*)

42.7 Owing to staff illnesses, the draft final accounts for the year ended 31 March 2009 of Messrs Stone, Pebble and Brick, trading in partnership as the Bigtime Building Supply Company, have been prepared by an inexperienced, but keen, clerk. The draft summarised balance sheet as at 31 March 2009 is as follows:

				£
Tangible non-current assets: At cost less depreciation to date				45,400
Current assets				32,290
Total assets				77,690
Trade accounts payable				(6,390)
Net assets				71,300
Represented by:	*Stone*	*Pebble*	*Brick*	*Total*
	£	£	£	£
Capital accounts: at 1 April 2008	26,000	18,000	16,000	60,000
Current accounts:				
Share of net profit for the year ended 31 March 2009	12,100	12,100	12,100	
Drawings year ended 31 March 2009	(8,200)	(9,600)	(7,200)	
At 31 March 2009	3,900	2,500	4,900	11,300
				71,300

The partnership commenced on 1 April 2008 when each of the partners introduced, as their partnership capital, the net tangible non-current and current assets of their previously separate businesses. However, it has now been discovered that, contrary to what was agreed, no adjustments were made in the partnership books for the goodwill of the partners' former businesses now incorporated in the partnership. The agreed valuations of goodwill at 1 April 2008 are as follows:

	£
Stone's business	30,000
Pebble's business	20,000
Brick's business	16,000

It is agreed that a goodwill account should not be opened in the partnership's books.

It has now been discovered that effect has not been given in the accounts to the following provisions in the partnership agreement effective from 1 January 2009:

1 Stone's capital to be reduced to £20,000, the balance being transferred to a loan account upon which interest at the rate of 11% per annum will be paid on 31 December each year.
2 Partners to be credited with interest on their capital account balances at the rate of 5% per annum.
3 Brick to be credited with a partner's salary at the rate of £8,500 per annum.
4 The balance of the net profit or loss to be shared between Stone, Pebble and Brick in the ratio 5:3:2 respectively.

Notes:

1 It can be assumed that the net profit indicated in the draft accounts accrued uniformly throughout the year.

2 It has been agreed between the partners that no adjustments should be made for any partnership goodwill as at 1 January 2009.

Required:

(*a*) Prepare the profit and loss appropriation account for the year ended 31 March 2009.

(*b*) Prepare a corrected statement of the partners' capital and current accounts for inclusion in the partnership balance sheet as at 31 March 2009.

(*Association of Accounting Technicians*)

You can find a range of additional self-test questions, as well as material to help you with your studies, on the website that accompanies this book at www.pearsoned.co.uk/wood.

chapter 43

Revaluation of partnership assets

Learning objectives

After you have studied this chapter, you should be able to:

- explain why there may be a need for revaluation of assets in a partnership
- calculate the amount of asset revaluation gain or loss attributable to each partner
- make the necessary entries to the ledger accounts when assets are revalued

Introduction

In this chapter, you'll learn about the events that make it necessary to revalue the assets of a partnership. You'll learn the journal entries required to record asset revaluations in the ledger accounts of the partnership and how to apportion gains and losses on revaluation between the partners.

43.1 Need for revaluation

When a business is sold and the sale price of the assets differs from their book values, there will be a profit or loss on the sale. This profit or loss will be shared between the partners in their profit and loss sharing ratios.

This sharing of profits and losses that result from changing asset values doesn't just need to be done when a partnership is sold. It should also be done whenever any of the following happens:

- a new partner is admitted;
- a partner leaves the firm;
- the partners change profit and loss sharing ratios.

As no sale has taken place in any of these circumstances, the assets will have to be revalued to reflect what they are worth at the date when the change occurs. Once they are revalued, the gains and losses can be identified.

Why do the assets need to be revalued in these cases? The business has not been sold. (*Hint*: there is no legal requirement to do so; and consider this question in the light of what you learnt in the previous chapter about goodwill when new partners are admitted.)

Once the assets have been revalued, you need to record the changes and gains and losses in the ledger accounts of the partnership.

43.2 Profit or loss on revaluation

If the revaluation shows no difference in asset values, no further action is needed. This will not happen very often, especially if assets include buildings. These are normally shown at cost less accumulated depreciation, but this is very rarely the actual value of buildings after they have been owned for a few years.

		£
If:	New total valuation of assets	90,000
Is *more* than:	Old total valuation of assets	(60,000)
The result is:	Gain on revaluation	30,000

		£
If:	New total valuation of assets	40,000
Is *less* than:	Old total valuation of assets	(50,000)
The result is:	Loss on revaluation	(10,000)

43.3 Accounting for revaluation

The first thing you do upon revaluing partnership assets is to open a **revaluation account** and make the appropriate entries:

1 *For each asset showing a gain on revaluation:*
Debit asset account with gain.
Credit revaluation account.

2 *For each asset showing a loss on revaluation:*
Debit revaluation account.
Credit asset account with loss.

3 *If there is an increase in total valuation of assets:*
Debit profit to revaluation account.
Credit **old** partners' capital accounts in **old** profit and loss sharing ratios.[Note]

4 *If there is a fall in total valuations of assets:*
Debit **old** partners' capital accounts in **old** profit and loss sharing ratios.[Note]
Credit loss to revaluation account.

Note: If current accounts are kept for the partners, the entries should be made in their current accounts.

When you were looking at goodwill in the previous chapter, you were interested in the difference between the amount received and the value of *net* assets. Why do we consider *only the assets* when there is a change in partners or a change in the profit sharing ratio?

Exhibit 43.1

Following is the balance sheet as at 31 December 2005 of W and Y, who shared profits and losses in the ratios: W two-thirds; Y one-third. From 1 January 2006 the profit and loss sharing ratio is to be altered to W one-half; Y one-half.

Balance Sheet as at 31 December 2005

	£	£
Premises (at cost)		65,000
Equipment (at cost less depreciation)		15,000
		80,000
Inventory	20,000	
Accounts receivable	12,000	
Bank	8,000	
		40,000
Total assets		120,000
Capitals: W		70,000
Y		50,000
		120,000

The assets were revalued on 1 January 2006 to be: Premises £90,000; Equipment £11,000. Other asset values were unchanged.

Accounts to show the assets at revalued amounts show:

Revaluation

	£	£		£
Assets reduced in value:			Assets increased in value:	
Equipment		4,000	Premises	25,000
Gain on revaluation carried to Capital accounts:				
W two-thirds	14,000			
Y one-third	7,000			
		21,000		
		25,000		25,000

Premises

	£		£
Balance b/d	65,000	Balance c/d	90,000
Revaluation: Increase	25,000		
	90,000		90,000
Balance b/d	90,000		

Equipment

	£		£
Balance b/d	15,000	Revaluation: Reduction	4,000
		Balance c/d	11,000
	15,000		15,000
Balance b/d	11,000		

Capital: W

	£		£
Balance c/d	84,000	Balance b/d	70,000
		Revaluation: Share of gain	14,000
	84,000		84,000
		Balance b/d	84,000

Capital: Y

	£		£
Balance c/d	57,000	Balance b/d	50,000
		Revaluation: Share of gain	7,000
	57,000		57,000
		Balance b/d	57,000

43.4 Revaluation of goodwill

This chapter deals with the revaluation of all assets other than goodwill. The revaluation of goodwill has already been dealt with in Chapter 42.

Learning outcomes

You should now have learnt:

1. How to make the entries arising from revaluations of partnership assets.
2. That when a new partner joins a firm, or a partner retires or dies, the partnership assets should be revalued.
3. That revaluation of assets should also occur when there is a change in the profit and loss sharing ratios of partners.
4. That profits on revaluation of assets are credited to the old partners' capital accounts in the old profit and loss sharing ratios.
5. That losses on revaluation of assets are debited to the old partners' capital accounts in the old profit and loss sharing ratios.
6. That the asset accounts also show the revalued amounts. Losses will have been credited to them and profits debited.

Answers to activities

43.1 When partners join or partners leave a partnership, there is, in effect, a new partnership. You learnt in the previous chapter about goodwill that, when a new partner is admitted, the existing partners generally seek to ensure that they retain their share of the goodwill that has built up to that date. It should be fairly obvious, therefore, that the existing partners will also want to maintain the true value of their share of the business at that date in their capital accounts, rather than some historically-based figure.

If this were not done, new partners admitted would benefit from increases in value before they joined the business, without having to pay anything for them. Similarly, if the value of assets had fallen before they had joined the business, and no revaluation took place, they would share that loss of value without any adjustment being made for it. Partners who leave or change their profit and loss sharing ratios would also be affected if there were no payments or allowances for such gains or losses.

43.2 In this case, you are only concerned about whether the assets are stated at their true values. You assume that the liabilities are correctly stated and ignore them because they are already included in the calculation of capital. In other words, when considering goodwill, you are comparing the amount received with the total of the partners' account balances, i.e. the net worth of the business (assets less liabilities). In this case, you are only concerned in the first instance with what the true value is of *part* of the other side of the accounting equation, assets, and not with the true value of the net worth. When you make the entries in the ledger accounts, you effectively bring in the liabilities and calculate a new net worth, which is reflected in the new balances on the partners' account balances. The overall effect is the same, only you don't need to calculate net worth to know whether there has been a gain or loss on revaluation of the assets. You do need to do that in order to calculate goodwill.

Review questions

43.1

Pitt, Lamb and Soul
Balance Sheet as at 31 December 2005

	£	£
Buildings (at cost)		80,000
Motor vehicles (at cost *less* depreciation)		16,500
Office fittings (at cost *less* depreciation)		1,800
		98,300
Inventory	6,100	
Accounts receivable	7,400	
Bank	800	
		14,300
Net assets		112,600
		£
Capitals:		
Pitt		60,000
Lamb		30,000
Soul		22,600
Total capital		112,600

The above partners have always shared profits and losses in the ratio: Pitt 4: Lamb 2: Soul 1.

From 1 January the assets were to be revalued as the profit sharing ratios are to be altered soon. The following assets are to be revalued to the figures shown: Buildings £106,000; Motor vehicles £13,000; Inventory £4,894; Office fittings £1,450.

Required:

(*a*) You are required to show all the ledger accounts necessary to record the revaluation.
(*b*) Draw up a balance sheet as at 1 January 2006.

43.2A Fitch and Wall have been in partnership for many years sharing profits and losses in the ratio 5:3 respectively. The following was their balance sheet as at 31 December 2002:

	£	£
Goodwill		12,400
Plant and machinery		16,320
		28,720
Inventory	6,420	
Accounts receivable	4,100	
Cash at bank	626	
		11,146
Total assets		39,866
Sundry accounts payable		(5,928)
		33,938
Capital: Fitch		19,461
Wall		14,477
Total capital		33,938

On 1 January 2003, they decided to admit Home as a partner on the condition that she contributed £12,000 as her capital but that the plant and machinery and inventory should be revalued at £16,800 and £6,100 respectively, with the other assets, excepting goodwill, remaining at their book values. The goodwill was agreed to be valueless.

You are required to show:

(*a*) The ledger entries dealing with the above in the following accounts:
- (*i*) Goodwill account,
- (*ii*) Revaluation accounts,
- (*iii*) Capital accounts;

(*b*) The balance sheet of the partnership immediately after the admission of Home.

43.3 Alan, Bob and Charles are in partnership sharing profits and losses in the ratio 3:2:1 respectively. The balance sheet for the partnership as at 30 June 2006 is as follows:

	£	£
Non-current assets		
Premises		90,000
Plant		37,000
Vehicles		15,000
Fixtures		2,000
		144,000
Current assets		
Inventory	62,379	
Accounts receivable	34,980	
Cash	760	
		98,119
Total assets		242,119
Current liabilities		
Accounts payable	19,036	
Bank overdraft	4,200	
	23,236	
Loan – Charles	28,000	
Total liabilities		(51,236)
Net assets		190,883
Capital		
Alan		85,000
Bob		65,000
Charles		35,000
		185,000
Current account		
Alan	3,714	
Bob	(2,509)	
Charles	4,678	
		5,883
Total capital		190,883

→

Charles decides to retire from the business on 30 June 2006, and Don is admitted as a partner on that date. The following matters are agreed:

(*a*) Certain assets were revalued: Premises £120,000; Plant £35,000; Inventory £54,179.
(*b*) Provision is to be made for doubtful debts in the sum of £3,000.
(*c*) Goodwill is to be recorded in the books on the day Charles retires in the sum of £42,000. The partners in the new firm do not wish to maintain a goodwill account so that amount is to be written back against the new partners' capital accounts.
(*d*) Alan and Bob are to share profits in the same ratio as before, and Don is to have the same share of profits as Bob.
(*e*) Charles is to take his car at its book value of £3,900 in part payment, and the balance of all he is owed by the firm in cash except £20,000 which he is willing to leave as a loan account.
(*f*) The partners in the new firm are to start on an equal footing so far as capital and current accounts are concerned. Don is to contribute cash to bring his capital and current accounts to the same amount as the original partner from the old firm who has the lower investment in the business.

The original partner in the old firm who has the higher investment will draw out cash so that his capital and current account balances equal those of his new partners.

Required:
(*a*) Account for the above transactions, including goodwill and retiring partners' accounts.
(*b*) Draft a balance sheet for the partnership of Alan, Bob and Don as at 30 June 2006.

(*Association of Accounting Technicians*)

43.4A The balance sheet of A Barnes and C Darwin at 31 March 2008 is as follows:

	£	£
Non-current assets		
Building		51,000
Fittings		29,000
		80,000
Current assets		
Inventory	16,000	
Accounts receivable	5,000	
		21,000
Total assets		101,000
Current liabilities		
Bank	3,000	
Accounts payable	8,000	
Total liabilities		(11,000)
Net assets		90,000
Capital accounts		
Barnes		60,000
Darwin		30,000
Total capital		90,000

The partners share profits and losses: Barnes three-fifths and Darwin two-fifths. At the date of the above balance sheet, it was agreed to admit E Fox who was to bring cash of £25,000 into the firm as capital. The new profit and loss ratio would be Barnes, one-half; Darwin, one-third; and Fox, one-sixth.

Barnes and Darwin agreed the following revaluation amounts prior to the admission of Fox. Any goodwill arising is to remain in the ledger.

	£
Buildings	55,000
Fittings	27,000
Inventory	15,500
Accounts receivable	4,800
Goodwill	12,000
Accrued expenses (previously omitted)	300

Required:

(*a*) Prepare the journal entries to record the above.

(*b*) Prepare the balance sheet of the new business.

(*c*) Show by journal entry how the necessary adjustment would be made if the partners agreed that goodwill should *not* remain in the ledger.

43.5 At 31 December 2007, the balance sheet of A, B and C, who are equal partners, was as follows:

	£	£
Non-current assets		
Freehold premises		16,000
Machinery and tools		15,100
Investment, at cost		4,000
		35,100
Current assets		
Inventory	16,000	
Accounts receivable	12,800	
Bank	12,100	
		40,900
Total assets		76,000
Current liabilities		
Accounts payable		(14,000)
Net assets		62,000
Capital accounts		
A		20,000
B		17,000
C		25,000
Total capital		62,000

A retired at that date. In order to determine the amount due to him the following revaluations were made: Freehold premises £18,000; machinery and tools £16,000; investments £5,100.

The value of the goodwill was agreed at £8,000. It was arranged that A should take over the investments in part payment of the amount due to him, the balance to be settled in cash. B and C would increase their capitals by paying in £10,000 and £6,000 respectively. These changes were all carried out.

Required:

(*a*) Prepare the revaluation account, bank account and capital accounts.

(*b*) Prepare the opening balance sheet of B and C.

You can find a range of additional self-test questions, as well as material to help you with your studies, on the website that accompanies this book at www.pearsoned.co.uk/wood.

chapter 44

Partnership dissolution

Learning objectives

After you have studied this chapter, you should be able to:

- explain what happens upon dissolution of a partnership
- record the entries relating to the dissolution of a partnership
- explain the differences between recording a partnership dissolution and making the entries when one partner leaves a partnership
- explain the Partnership Act 1890 rules relating to partnership dissolution
- explain the *Garner* v *Murray* rule

Introduction

In this chapter, you'll learn how to calculate and record the necessary entries when a partnership is dissolved. You'll learn that the process is laid down in the Partnership Act 1890 and what to do under the *Garner* v *Murray* rule when partners are unable to pay the amount they owe the partnership. Finally, you'll learn how to deal with a situation where the partnership assets are being disposed of over a long period of time.

44.1 Need for dissolution

You will recall from Chapter 40 that joint ventures are often short-term and that when the project they were formed to do has ended, the joint venture is terminated. You learnt in Chapter 41 that partnerships are long-term ventures that are formed with a long-term commitment on the part of the partners to operate in business together. In Chapter 42, you learnt that new partners are admitted from time to time; and, in Chapter 43, you learnt that partners can also leave partnerships. So, you'll have realised by now that partnerships really are not as permanent as they may at first appear.

Can you think of any partnership you know of where a partner left? How do you think the change in the partnership was treated in the ledgers?

In fact, as far as the UK tax authorities are concerned, every time a partner joins or leaves a partnership, a new partnership is brought into existence. Intuitively, this does make sense. Partnerships exist because of the desire to merge the skills, resources and expertise of the partners. Imagine a band whose lead singer leaves. The replacement is never quite the same. As another example, if two people are in a partnership running a restaurant and the one that does the cooking leaves, the replacement isn't going to want to prepare exactly the same meals.

Partnerships do change when a partner leaves. And they do change when a new partner joins. However, for accounting purposes, we only consider partnerships as changing sufficiently to merit treating them as ceasing to exist when the partners go their separate ways. When they do, this is known as partnership **dissolution** – the partnership has been dissolved.

Reasons for dissolution include:

(*a*) The partnership is no longer profitable, and there is no longer any reason to carry on trading.
(*b*) The partners cannot agree between themselves how to operate the partnership. They therefore decide to finish the partnership.
(*c*) Factors such as ill-health or old age may bring about the close of the partnership.

What is the difference between these events and partners simply leaving a partnership? For example, if there are three partners in a dental practice and two leave, why can't the third continue the business with new partners?

44.2 What happens upon dissolution

Upon **dissolution** the partnership firm stops trading or operating. Then, in accordance with the Partnership Act 1890:

(*a*) the assets are disposed of;
(*b*) the liabilities of the business to everyone other than partners are paid;
(*c*) the partners are repaid their advances and current balances – advances are the amounts they have put in above and beyond the capital;
(*d*) the partners are paid the final amounts due to them on their capital accounts.

Any profit or loss on dissolution would be shared by all the partners in their profit and loss sharing ratios. Profits would increase capitals repayable to partners. Losses would reduce the capitals repayable.

If a partner's final balance on his/her capital and current accounts is in deficit, he/she will have to pay that amount into the partnership bank account.

44.3 Disposal of assets

The assets do not have to be sold to external parties. Quite often one or more existing partners will take assets at values agreed by all the partners. In such a case the partner may not pay in cash for such assets; instead they will be charged to that partner's capital account.

44.4 Accounting for partnership dissolution

The main account around which the dissolution entries are made is known as the **realisation account**. It is this account in which the profit or loss on the realisation of the assets is calculated.

Exhibit 44.1 shows the simplest of partnership dissolutions. We will then look at a more difficult example in Exhibit 44.2.

Exhibit 44.1

The last balance sheet of X and Y, who share profits X two-thirds: Y one-third is shown below. On this date they are to dissolve the partnership.

Balance Sheet at 31 December 2009

	£	£
Non-current assets		
Buildings		100,000
Motor vehicle		12,000
		112,000
Current assets		
Inventory	6,000	
Accounts receivable	8,000	
Bank	2,000	
		16,000
Total assets		128,000
Current liabilities		
Accounts payable		(5,000)
Net assets		123,000
Capitals: X		82,000
Y		41,000
Total capital		123,000

The buildings were sold for £105,000 and the inventory for £4,600. £6,800 was collected from debtors. The motor vehicle was taken over by X at an agreed value of £9,400, but he did not pay any cash for it. £5,000 was paid to settle the accounts payable. The £400 cost of the dissolution was paid.

The accounting entries needed are:

(A) Transfer book values of all assets to the realisation account:
Debit realisation account
Credit asset accounts

(B) Amounts received from disposal of assets:
Debit bank
Credit realisation account

(C) Values of assets taken over by partner without payment:
Debit partner's capital account
Credit realisation account

(D) Creditors paid:
Debit accounts payable
Credit bank

(E) Costs of dissolution:
Debit realisation account
Credit bank

(F) Profit or loss on realisation to be shared between partners in profit and loss sharing ratios:
If a profit: Debit realisation account
Credit partners' capital accounts

If a loss: Debit partners' capital accounts
Credit realisation account

(G) Pay to the partners their final balances on their capital accounts:
Debit capital accounts
Credit bank

The entries are now shown. The letters (A) to (G) as above are shown against each entry:

Buildings

		£			£
Balance b/d		100,000	Realisation	(A)	100,000

Motor Vehicle

		£			£
Balance b/d		12,000	Realisation	(A)	12,000

Inventory

		£			£
Balance b/d		6,000	Realisation	(A)	6,000

Accounts Receivable

		£			£
Balance b/d		8,000	Realisation	(A)	8,000

Realisation

		£			£	£
Assets to be realised:			Bank: Assets sold			
Buildings	(A)	100,000	Buildings	(B)		105,000
Motor vehicle	(A)	12,000	Inventory	(B)		4,600
Inventory	(A)	6,000	Accounts receivable	(B)		6,800
Accounts receivable	(A)	8,000	Taken over by partner A:			
Bank:			Motor vehicle	(C)		9,400
Dissolution costs	(E)	400	Loss on realisation		£	
			X ⅔	(F)	400	
			Y ⅓	(F)	200	
						600
		126,400				126,400

Accounts Payable

		£			£
Bank	(D)	5,000	Balance b/d		5,000

X: Capital

		£		£
Realisation: Motor	(C)	9,400	Balance b/d	82,000
Realisation: Share of loss	(F)	400		
Bank: to close	(G)	72,200		
		82,000		82,000

Y: Capital

		£			£
Realisation: Share of loss	(F)	200	Balance b/d		41,000
Bank: to close	(G)	40,800			
		41,000			41,000

Bank

		£			£
Balance b/d		2,000	Accounts payable	(D)	5,000
Realisation: Assets sold			Realisation: Costs	(E)	400
Buildings	(B)	105,000	Capitals: to close		
Inventory	(B)	4,600	X	(G)	72,200
Accounts receivable	(B)	6,800	Y	(G)	40,800
		118,400			118,400

The final balances on the partners' capital accounts should always equal the amount in the bank account from which they are to be paid. For instance, in the above exhibit there was £113,000 in the bank from which to pay X £72,200 and Y £40,800. **You should always complete the capital account entries before you can complete the bank account entries. If the final bank balance does not pay out the partners' capital accounts exactly, you will have made a mistake somewhere.**

44.5 A more detailed example

Exhibit 44.1 did not show the more difficult accounting entries. A more difficult example appears in Exhibit 44.2.

The extra complexities are:

(*a*) Any allowance such as doubtful debts or depreciation is to be transferred to the credit of the asset account: see entries (A) in Exhibit 44.2.

(*b*) Discounts on accounts payable – to balance the accounts payable, transfer the discounts on accounts payable to the credit of the realisation account: see entries (F) in the exhibit.

(*c*) Transfer the balances on the partners' current accounts to their capital accounts: see entries (I) of the exhibit.

(*d*) A partner who owes the partnership money because his capital account is in deficit must now pay the money owing: see entries (J) of the exhibit.

As a result, you will see that the list of accounting entries to be made is extended to run from A to K, compared with A to G.

Exhibit 44.2

On 31 December 2008, *P*, *Q* and *R* decided to dissolve their partnership. They had always shared profits in the ratio of *P*3 : *Q*2 : *R*1.

Their goodwill was sold for £30,000, the machinery for £24,000 and the inventory for £12,000. There were three cars, all taken over by the partners at agreed values, *P* taking one for £4,000, *Q* one for £6,000 and *R* one for £3,000. The premises were taken over by *R* at an agreed value of £162,000. The amounts collected from debtors amounted to £7,400 after bad debts and discounts had been deducted. The creditors were discharged for £6,280, the difference being due to discounts received. The costs of dissolution amounted to £700.

Their last balance sheet prior to dissolution of the partnership is summarised as:

Balance Sheet as at 31 December 2008

	£	£	£
Non-current assets			
Premises			150,000
Machinery			36,000
Motor vehicles			14,000
			200,000
Current assets			
Inventory		11,000	
Accounts receivable	8,000		
Less Allowance for doubtful debts	(400)		
		7,600	
Bank		1,200	
			19,800
Total assets			219,800
Current liabilities			
Accounts payable			(6,400)
Net assets			213,400
Capital accounts: *P*			70,000
Q			60,000
R			50,000
			180,000
Current accounts: *P*		9,700	
Q		7,500	
R		16,200	
			33,400
Total capital			213,400

Description of transactions:

(A) The provision accounts are transferred to the relevant asset accounts so that the net balance on the asset accounts may be transferred to the realisation account. Debit provision accounts. Credit asset accounts.
(B) The net book values of the assets are transferred to the realisation account. Debit realisation account. Credit asset accounts.
(C) Assets sold. Debit bank account. Credit realisation account.
(D) Assets taken over by partners. Debit partners' capital accounts. Credit realisation account.
(E) Liabilities discharged. Credit bank account. Debit liability accounts.
(F) Discounts on accounts payable. Debit accounts payable account. Credit realisation account.
(G) Costs of dissolution. Credit bank account. Debit realisation account.
(H) Profit or loss split in profit/loss sharing ratio. Profit – debit realisation account. Credit partners' capital accounts. The opposite if a loss.
(I) Transfer the balances on the partners' current accounts to their capital accounts.
(J) Any partner with a capital account in deficit, i.e. debits exceeding credits, must now pay in the amount needed to cancel his/her indebtedness to the partnership. Credit capital account. Debit bank account.
(K) The credit balances on the partners' capital accounts can now be paid to them. Debit partners' capital accounts. Credit bank account.

The payments made under (K) should complete the payment of all the balances in the partnership books.

The accounts recording the dissolution are shown below. The letters (A) to (K) against each entry indicate the relevant descriptions. →

→

Premises

		£			£
Balance b/d		150,000	Realisation	(B)	150,000

Machinery

		£			£
Balance b/d		36,000	Realisation	(B)	36,000

Motor Vehicles

		£			£
Balance b/d		14,000	Realisation	(B)	14,000

Inventory

		£			£
Balance b/d		11,000	Realisation	(B)	11,000

Accounts Receivable

		£			£
Balance b/d		8,000	Allowance for doubtful debts	(A)	400
			Realisation	(B)	7,600
		8,000			8,000

Realisation

			£			£
Assets to be realised:				Bank: Assets sold		
Premises	(B)		150,000	Goodwill	(C)	30,000
Machinery	(B)		36,000	Machinery	(C)	24,000
Motor vehicles	(B)		14,000	Inventory	(C)	12,000
Inventory	(B)		11,000	Accounts receivable	(C)	7,400
Accounts receivable	(B)		7,600	Taken over by partners:		
Bank: Dissolution costs	(G)		700	*P*: Car	(D)	4,000
Profit on realisation:	(H)			*Q*: Car	(D)	6,000
		£		*R*: Car	(D)	3,000
P		14,610		*R*: Premises	(D)	162,000
Q		9,740		Accounts payable: Discounts	(F)	120
R		4,870				
			29,220			
			248,520			248,520

Accounts Payable

		£			£
Bank	(E)	6,280	Balance b/d		6,400
Realisation: Discounts	(F)	120			
		6,400			6,400

Allowance for Doubtful Debts

		£			£
Accounts receivable	(A)	400	Balance b/d		400

P Capital

		£			£
Realisation: Car	(D)	4,000	Balance b/d		70,000
Bank	(K)	90,310	Current account transferred (I)		9,700
			Realisation: Share of profit (H)		14,610
		94,310			94,310

P Current

		£		£
P: Capital	(I)	9,700	Balance b/d	9,700

Q Capital

		£		£
Realisation: Car	(D)	6,000	Balance b/d	60,000
Bank	(K)	71,240	Current account transferred (I)	7,500
			Realisation: Share of profit (H)	9,740
		77,240		77,240

Q Current

		£		£
Q: Capital	(I)	7,500	Balance b/d	7,500

R Capital

		£			£
Realisation: Car	(D)	3,000	Balance b/d		50,000
Realisation: Premises	(D)	162,000	Current account transferred (I)		16,200
			Realisation: Share of profit (H)		4,870
			Bank	(J)	93,930
		165,000			165,000

R Current

		£		£
R: Capital	(I)	16,200	Balance b/d	16,200

Bank

		£			£
Balance b/d		1,200	Accounts payable	(E)	6,280
Realisation: Assets sold			Realisation: Costs	(G)	700
Goodwill	(C)	30,000	*P*: Capital	(K)	90,310
Machinery	(C)	24,000	*Q*: Capital	(K)	71,240
Inventory	(C)	12,000			
Accounts receivable	(C)	7,400			
R: Capital	(J)	93,930			
		168,530			168,530

44.6 The *Garner* v *Murray* rule

It sometimes happens that a partner's capital account finishes up with a debit balance. Normally the partner will pay in an amount to clear his/her indebtedness to the firm. However, sometimes the partner will be unable to pay all, or part, of such a balance. In the case of ***Garner* v *Murray*** in 1904 (a case in England) the court ruled that, subject to any agreement to the contrary, such a deficiency was to be shared by the other partners *not* in their profit and loss sharing ratios but in the ratio of their 'last agreed capitals'. By 'their last agreed capitals' is meant the credit balances on their capital accounts in the normal balance sheet drawn up at the end of their last accounting period.

It must be borne in mind that the balances on their capital accounts after the assets have been realised may be far different from those on the last balance sheet. Where a partnership deed is drawn up it is commonly found that agreement is made to use normal profit and loss sharing ratios instead, thus rendering the *Garner* v *Murray* rule inoperative. **The *Garner* v *Murray* rule does not apply to partnerships in Scotland.**

Before reading further you should check whether or not this topic is in the requirements for your examinations.

Exhibit 44.3

After completing the realisation of all the assets, in respect of which a loss of £14,000 was incurred, but before making the final payments to the partners, the balance sheet appears:

Balance Sheet

	£	£
Cash at bank		91,000
Capitals: *R*	66,000	
S	18,000	
T	8,000	
	92,000	
Less Q (debit balance)	(1,000)	
		91,000

According to the last balance sheet drawn up before the dissolution, the partners' capital account credit balances were: *Q* £5,000; *R* £70,000; *S* £20,000; *T* £10,000; while the profits and losses were shared *Q*3 : *R*2 : *S*1 : *T*1.

Q is unable to meet any part of his deficiency. Under the *Garner* v *Murray* rule, each of the other partners suffers the deficiency as follows:

$$\frac{\text{Own capital per balance sheet before dissolution}}{\text{Total of all solvent partners' capitals per same balance sheet}} \times \text{Deficiency}$$

This can now be calculated.

$$R \quad \frac{£70{,}000}{£70{,}000 + £20{,}000 + £10{,}000} \times 1{,}000 = \quad £700$$

$$S \quad \frac{£20{,}000}{£70{,}000 + £20{,}000 + £10{,}000} \times 1{,}000 = \quad £200$$

$$T \quad \frac{£10{,}000}{£70{,}000 + £20{,}000 + £10{,}000} \times 1{,}000 = \quad £100$$

$$£1{,}000$$

When these amounts have been charged to the capital accounts, then the balances remaining on them will equal the amount of the bank balance. Payments may therefore be made to clear their capital accounts.

	Credit balance b/d		*Share of deficiency now debited*		*Final credit balances*
	£		£		£
R	66,000	–	700	=	65,300
S	18,000	–	200	=	17,800
T	8,000	–	100	=	7,900
Equals the bank balance					91,000

44.7 Piecemeal realisation of assets

Frequently the assets may take a long time to be turned into cash (i.e. 'realised'). The partners will naturally want payments made to them on account as cash is received. They will not want to wait for payments until the dissolution is completed just for the convenience of the accountant. There is, however, a danger that if too much is paid to a partner, and he is unable to repay it, then the person handling the dissolution could be placed in a very awkward position.

To counteract this, the concept of prudence is brought into play. This is done as follows:

(*a*) Each receipt of sale money is treated as being the final receipt, even though more could be received.
(*b*) Any loss then calculated so far to be shared between partners in profit and loss sharing ratios.
(*c*) Should any partner's capital account after each receipt show a debit balance, then he is assumed to be unable to pay in the deficiency. This deficit will be shared (failing any other agreement) between the partners using the *Garner* v *Murray* rule.
(*d*) After payments of liabilities and the costs of dissolution the remainder of the cash is then paid to the partners.
(*e*) In this manner, even if no further money were received, or should a partner become insolvent, the division of the available cash would be strictly in accordance with the legal requirements. Exhibit 44.4 shows such a series of calculations.

Exhibit 44.4

The following is the summarised balance sheet of *H*, *I*, *J* and *K* as at 31 December 2008. The partners had shared profits in the ratios *H*6 : *I*4 : *J*1 : *K*1.

Balance Sheet as at 31 December 2008

	£
Assets	84,000
Accounts payable	(18,000)
	66,000
Capitals:	
H	6,000
I	30,000
J	20,000
K	10,000
	66,000

On 1 March 2009 some of the assets were sold for cash £50,000. Out of this the creditors' £18,000 and the cost of dissolution £800 are paid, leaving £31,200 distributable to the partners.

On 1 July 2009 some more assets are sold for £21,000. As all of the liabilities and the costs of dissolution have already been paid, the whole of the £21,000 is available for distribution between the partners.

→

On 1 October 2009 the final sale of the assets realised £12,000.

First distribution: 1 March 2009	*H*	*I*	*J*	*K*	Total
	£	£	£	£	£
Capital balances before dissolution	6,000	30,000	20,000	10,000	66,000
Loss if no further assets realised: Assets £84,000 – Sales £50,000 = £34,000 + Costs £800 = £34,800 loss					
Loss shared in profit/loss ratios	(17,400)	(11,600)	(2,900)	(2,900)	(34,800)
	11,400Dr	18,400Cr	17,100Cr	7,100Cr	31,200
H's deficiency shared in *Garner* v *Murray* ratios		3/6 (5,700)	2/6 (3,800)	1/6 (1,900)	
Cash paid to partners		12,700	13,300	5,200	31,200

Second distribution: 1 July 2009	*H*	*I*	*J*	*K*	Total
	£	£	£	£	£
Capital balances before dissolution	6,000	30,000	20,000	10,000	66,000
Loss if no further assets realised: Assets £84,000 – Sales (£50,000 + £21,000) = £13,000 + Costs £800 = £13,800 loss					
Loss shared in profit/loss ratios	(6,900)	(4,600)	(1,150)	(1,150)	(13,800)
	900Dr	25,400Cr	18,850Cr	8,850Cr	52,200
H's deficiency shared in *Garner* v *Murray* ratios		3/6 (450)	2/6 (300)	1/6 (150)	
		24,950	18,550	8,700	
Less First distribution already paid		(12,700)	(13,300)	(5,200)	31,200
Cash now paid to partners		12,250	5,250	3,500	21,000
					52,200

Third and final distribution: 1 October 2009	*H*	*I*	*J*	*K*	Total
	£	£	£	£	£
Capital balances before dissolution	6,000	30,000	20,000	10,000	66,000
Loss finally ascertained: Assets £84,000 – Sales (£50,000 + £21,000 + £12,000) = £1,000 + Costs £800 = £1,800 loss					
Loss shared in profit/loss ratios	(900)	(600)	(150)	(150)	(1,800)
	5,100Cr	29,400Cr	19,850Cr	9,850Cr	64,200
(No deficiency now exists on any capital account)					
Less First and second distributions	–	(24,950)	(18,550)	(8,700)	52,200
Cash now paid to partners	5,100	4,450	1,300	1,150	12,000
					64,200

In any subsequent distribution following that in which all the partners have shared (i.e. no partners could then have had a deficiency left on their capital accounts) all receipts of cash are divided between the partners in their profit and loss sharing ratios. Following the above method would give the same answer for these subsequent distributions but obviously an immediate division in the profit and loss sharing ratios would be quicker. Try it for yourself and you'll see that the same answer would result.

44.8 A final word

The partnership income statement and profit and loss appropriation account which you have headed-up using that rather long-winded heading is often simply referred to and headed-up as 'Income Statement'. You will see an example of this shorter heading when you look at the solution to Review Question 44.7.

Learning outcomes

You should now have learnt:

1. How to calculate the amounts due to and from each partner when a partnership is dissolved.
2. How to record partnership dissolution in the ledger accounts.
3. That upon dissolution, a partnership stops trading or operating, any profit or loss on dissolution being shared by the partners in their profit sharing ratio.
4. That the *Garner* v *Murray* rule does not apply to partnerships in Scotland.

Answers to activities

44.1 There is obviously no 'right' answer to this question. You may have noticed partnership changes at your local doctor's or dental practice. They can have quite an impact upon some of the patients. Similarly, there have been famous partnerships in ice skating, the theatre, music, and in sport, especially tennis, where switching partners creates a very different visual effect and level of satisfaction for the audience.

Many of these examples are really short-term joint ventures rather than partnerships. The doctors and dentists are most definitely partnerships. In many cases where one of *these* examples of joint ventures or partnerships change, a new one tends to develop in its place. In the case of partnerships where the business is continuing with new partners, you can apply the techniques you've already learnt to apply when a partner leaves a partnership and when a partner joins and make the necessary entries in the partnership ledger accounts.

44.2 That may happen, in which case it could be argued that it should be treated as simply a change of membership of the partnership. There's nothing wrong with doing so if the business is continuing as before but, even in those cases, you will probably find it easier to treat it as a partnership dissolution, close off all the books and start afresh with the new partnership. This is because if only one partner is left in the business, you would need to remove each of the partners who have left from the accounts anyway before adding in the new one(s).

Review questions

44.1 Poole and Burns, who share profits and losses equally, decide to dissolve their partnership as at 30 June 2001. Their balance sheet on that date was as follows:

		£	£
Buildings			80,000
Tools and fixtures			2,900
			82,900
Accounts receivable		8,400	
Cash		600	
			9,000
			91,900
Sundry accounts payable			4,100
			87,800
Capital account:	Poole		52,680
	Burns		35,120
			87,800

The accounts receivable realised £8,200, the buildings £66,000 and the tools and fixtures £1,800. The expenses of dissolution were £400 and discounts totalling £300 were received from creditors.

Required:
Prepare the accounts necessary to show the results of the realisation and of the disposal of the cash.

44.2 X, Y and Z have been in partnership for several years, sharing profits and losses in the ratio 3 : 2 : 1. Their last balance sheet which was prepared on 31 October 2009 is as follows:

Balance Sheet of X, Y and Z as at 31 October 2009

	£	£
Non-current assets		
At cost		20,000
Less Depreciation		(6,000)
		14,000
Current assets		
Inventory	5,000	
Accounts receivable	21,000	
		26,000
Total assets		40,000
Current liabilities		
Bank	13,000	
Accounts payable	17,000	
Total liabilities		(30,000)
Net assets		10,000
Capital		
X		4,000
Y		4,000
Z		2,000
Total capital		10,000

Despite making good profits during recent years they had become increasingly dependent on one credit customer, Smithson, and in order to retain his custom they had gradually increased his credit limit until he owed the partnership £18,000. It has now been discovered that Smithson is insolvent and that he is unlikely to repay any of the money owed by him to the partnership. Reluctantly X, Y and Z have agreed to dissolve the partnership on the following terms:

(*i*) The inventory is to be sold to Nelson Ltd for £4,000.
(*ii*) The non-current assets will be sold for £8,000 except for certain items with a book value of £5,000 which will be taken over by X at an agreed valuation of £7,000.
(*iii*) The debtors, except for Smithson, are expected to pay their accounts in full.
(*iv*) The costs of dissolution will be £800 and discounts received from creditors will be £500. Z is unable to meet his liability to the partnership out of his personal funds.

Required:
(*a*) the realisation account;
(*b*) the capital accounts to the partners recording the dissolution of the partnership.

(*Associated Examining Board*)

44.3A The following trial balance has been extracted from the books of Gain and Main as at 31 March 2008; Gain and Main are in partnership sharing profits and losses in the ratio 3 to 2:

	£	£
Capital accounts:		
Gain		10,000
Main		5,000
Cash at bank	1,550	
Accounts payable		500
Current accounts:		
Gain		1,000
Main	2,000	
Accounts receivable	2,000	
Depreciation: Fixtures and fittings		1,000
Motor vehicles		1,300
Fixtures and fittings	2,000	
Land and buildings	30,000	
Motor vehicles	4,500	
Net profit (for the year to 31 March 2008)		26,250
Inventory, at cost	3,000	
	£45,050	£45,050

In appropriating the net profit for the year, it has been agreed that Main should be entitled to a salary of £9,750. Each partner is also entitled to interest on his opening capital account balance at the rate of 10 per cent per annum.

Gain and Main have decided to convert the partnership into a limited company, Plain Limited, as from 1 April 2008. The company is to take over all the assets and liabilities of the partnership, except that Gain is to retain for his personal use one of the motor vehicles at an agreed transfer price of £1,000.

The purchase consideration will consist of 40,000 ordinary shares of £1 each in Plain Limited, to be divided between the partners in profit-sharing ratio. Any balance on the partners' current accounts is to be settled in cash.

You are required to:
Prepare the main ledger accounts of the partnership in order to close off the books as at 31 March 2008.

(Association of Accounting Technicians)

44.4A A, B and C are partners sharing profits and losses in the ratio 2 : 2 : 1. The balance sheet of the partnership as at 30 September 2007 was as follows:

	£	£
Freehold premises		18,000
Equipment and machinery		12,000
Cars		3,000
		33,000
Inventory	11,000	
Accounts receivable	14,000	
Bank	9,000	
		34,000
		67,000
Accounts payable	10,000	
Loan account – A	7,000	
Total liabilities		(17,000)
Net assets		50,000
Capital accounts		
A		22,000
B		18,000
C		10,000
		50,000

→

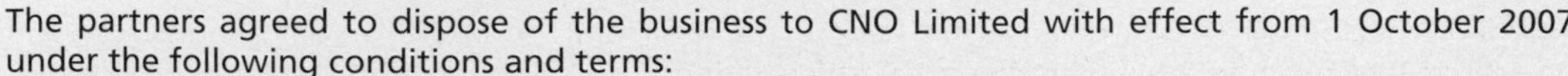

The partners agreed to dispose of the business to CNO Limited with effect from 1 October 2007 under the following conditions and terms:

(*i*) CNO Limited will acquire the goodwill, all non-current assets and the inventory for the purchase consideration of £58,000. This consideration will include a payment of £10,000 in cash and the issue of 12,000 10 per cent preference shares of £1 each at par, and the balance by the issue of £1 ordinary shares at £1.25 per share.
(*ii*) The partnership business will settle amounts owing to creditors.
(*iii*) CNO Limited will collect the debts on behalf of the vendors.

Purchase consideration payments and allotments of shares were made on 1 October 2007.

The partnership accounts payable were paid off by 31 October 2007 after the taking of cash discounts of £190.

CNO Limited collected and paid over all partnership debts by 30 November 2007 except for bad debts amounting to £800. Discounts allowed to debtors amounted to £400.

Required:
(*a*) Journal entries (including those relating to cash) necessary to close the books of the partnership, and
(*b*) Set out the basis on which the shares in CNO Limited are allotted to partners. Ignore interest.

(*Institute of Chartered Secretaries and Administrators*)

44.5 Amis, Lodge and Pym were in partnership sharing profits and losses in the ratio 5 : 3 : 2. The following trial balance has been extracted from their books of account as at 31 March 2008:

	£	£
Bank interest received		750
Capital accounts (as at 1 April 2007):		
Amis		80,000
Lodge		15,000
Pym		5,000
Carriage inwards	4,000	
Carriage outwards	12,000	
Cash at bank	4,900	
Current accounts:		
Amis	1,000	
Lodge	500	
Pym	400	
Discounts allowed	10,000	
Discounts received		4,530
Drawings:		
Amis	25,000	
Lodge	22,000	
Pym	15,000	
Motor vehicles:		
at cost	80,000	
accumulated depreciation (at 1 April 2007)		20,000
Office expenses	30,400	
Plant and machinery:		
at cost	100,000	
accumulated depreciation (at 1 April 2007)		36,600
Allowance for doubtful debts (at 1 April 2007)		420
Purchases	225,000	
Rent, rates, heat and light	8,800	
Sales		404,500
Inventory (at 1 April 2007)	30,000	
Trade accounts payable		16,500
Trade accounts receivable	14,300	
	£583,300	£583,300

Additional information:

(*a*) Inventory at 31 March 2008 was valued at £35,000.

(*b*) Depreciation on the non-current assets is to be charged as follows:
Motor vehicles – 25 per cent on the reduced balance.
Plant and machinery – 20 per cent on the original cost.
There were no purchases or sales of non-current assets during the year to 31 March 2008.

(*c*) The allowance for doubtful debts is to be maintained at a level equivalent to 5 per cent of the total trade accounts receivable as at 31 March 2008.

(*d*) An office expense of £405 was owing at 31 March 2008, and some rent amounting to £1,500 had been paid in advance as at that date. These items had not been included in the list of balances shown in the trial balance.

(*e*) Interest on drawings and on the debit balance on each partner's current account is to be charged as follows:

	£
Amis	1,000
Lodge	900
Pym	720

(*f*) According to the partnership agreement, Pym is allowed a salary of £13,000 per annum. This amount was owing to Pym for the year to 31 March 2008, and needs to be accounted for.

(*g*) The partnership agreement also allows each partner interest on his capital account at a rate of 10 per cent per annum. There were no movements on the respective partners' capital accounts during the year to 31 March 2008, and the interest had not been credited to them as at that date.

Note: The information given above is sufficient to answer part (*a*) (*i*) and (*ii*) of the question, and notes (*h*) and (*i*) below are pertinent to requirements (*b*) (*i*), (*ii*) and (*iii*) of the question.

(*h*) On 1 April 2008, Fowles Limited agreed to purchase the business on the following terms:
- (*i*) Amis to purchase one of the partnership's motor vehicles at an agreed value of £5,000, the remaining vehicles being taken over by the company at an agreed value of £30,000;
- (*ii*) the company agreed to purchase the plant and machinery at a value of £35,000 and the inventory at a value of £38,500;
- (*iii*) the partners to settle the trade accounts payable: the total amount agreed with the creditors being £16,000;
- (*iv*) the trade accounts receivable were not to be taken over by the company, the partners receiving cheques on 1 April 2008 amounting to £12,985 in total from the trade debtors in settlement of the outstanding debts;
- (*v*) the partners paid the outstanding office expense on 1 April 2008, and the landlord returned the rent paid in advance by cheque on the same day;
- (*vi*) as consideration for the sale of the partnership, the partners were to be paid £63,500 in cash by Fowles Limited, and to receive £75,000 in £1 ordinary shares in the company, the shares to be apportioned equally amongst the partners.

(*i*) Assume that all the matters relating to the dissolution of the partnership and its sales to the company took place on 1 April 2008.

Required:

(*a*) Prepare:
- (*i*) Amis, Lodge and Pym's income statement and profit and loss appropriation account for the year ending 31 March 2008;
- (*ii*) Amis, Lodge and Pym's current accounts (in columnar format) for the year to 31 March 2008 (the final balance on each account is to be then transferred to each partner's respective capital account);

and

(*b*) Compile the following accounts:
- (*i*) the partnership realisation account for the period up to and including 1 April 2008;
- (*ii*) the partners' bank account for the period up to and including 1 April 2008; and
- (*iii*) the partners' capital accounts (in columnar format) for the period up to and including 1 April 2008.

Note: Detailed workings should be submitted with your answer.

(*Association of Accounting Technicians*)

→

44.6A Proudie, Slope and Thorne were in partnership sharing profits and losses in the ratio 3 : 1 : 1. The draft balance sheet of the partnership as at 31 May 2009 is shown below:

	£000 *Cost*	£000 *Depreciation*	£000 *Net book value*
Non-current assets			
Land and buildings	200	40	160
Furniture	30	18	12
Motor vehicles	60	40	20
	290	98	192
Current assets			
Inventory		23	
Trade accounts receivable	42		
Less Allowance for doubtful debts	(1)		
		41	
Prepayments		2	
Cash		10	
			76
Total assets			268
Current liabilities			
Trade accounts payable	15		
Accruals	3		
		18	
Non-current liabilities			
Loan – Proudie		8	
Total liabilities			(26)
Net assets			242
Capital accounts			
Proudie		100	
Slope		60	
Thorne		40	
			200
Current accounts			
Proudie		24	
Slope		10	
Thorne		8	
			42
Total capital			242

Additional information:

1 Proudie decided to retire on 31 May 2009. However, Slope and Thorne agreed to form a new partnership out of the old one, as from 1 June 2009. They agreed to share profits and losses in the same ratio as in the old partnership.

2 Upon the dissolution of the old partnership, it was agreed that the following adjustments were to be made to the partnership balance sheet as at 31 May 2009.
   (*a*) Land and buildings were to be revalued at £200,000.
   (*b*) Furniture was to be revalued at £5,000.
   (*c*) Proudie agreed to take over one of the motor vehicles at a value of £4,000, the remaining motor vehicles being revalued at £10,000.
   (*d*) Inventory was to be written down by £5,000.
   (*e*) A bad debt of £2,000 was to be written off, and the allowance for doubtful debts was then to be adjusted so that it represented 5 per cent of the then outstanding trade accounts receivable as at 31 May 2009.
   (*f*) A further accrual of £3,000 for office expenses was to be made.
   (*g*) Professional charges relating to the dissolution were estimated to be £1,000.

3 It has not been the practice of the partners to carry goodwill in the books of the partnership, but on the retirement of a partner it had been agreed that goodwill should be taken into account. Goodwill was to be valued at an amount equal to the average annual profits of the three years expiring on the retirement. For the purpose of including goodwill in the dissolution arrangement when Proudie retired, the net profits for the last three years were as follows:

	£000
Year to 31 May 2007	130
Year to 31 May 2008	150
Year to 31 May 2009	181

The net profit for the year to 31 May 2009 had been calculated before any of the items listed in 2 above were taken into account. The net profit was only to be adjusted for items listed in 2(*d*), 2(*e*) and 2(*f*) above.

4 Goodwill is not to be carried in the books of the new partnership.

5 It was agreed that Proudie's old loan of £8,000 should be repaid to him on 31 May 2009, but any further amount owing to him as a result of the dissolution of the partnership should be left as a long-term loan in the books of the new partnership.

6 The partners' current accounts were to be closed and any balances on them as at 31 May 2009 were to be transferred to their respective capital accounts.

Required:

(*a*) Prepare the revaluation account as at 31 May 2009.

(*b*) Prepare the partners' capital accounts as at the date of dissolution of the partnership, and bring down any balances on them in the books of the new partnership.

(*c*) Prepare Slope and Thorne's balance sheet as at 1 June 2009.

(*Association of Accounting Technicians*)

44.7 Lock, Stock and Barrel have been in partnership as builders and contractors for many years. Owing to adverse trading conditions it has been decided to dissolve the partnership. Profits are shared Lock 40 per cent, Stock 30 per cent, Barrel 30 per cent. The partnership deed also provides that in the event of a partner being unable to pay off a debit balance the remaining partners will treat this as a trading loss.

The latest partnership balance sheet was as follows:

	Cost	*Depreciation*	
Non-current tangible assets	£	£	£
Freehold yard and buildings	20,000	3,000	17,000
Plant and equipment	150,000	82,000	68,000
Motor vehicles	36,000	23,000	13,000
	206,000	108,000	98,000
Current assets			
Land for building		75,000	
Houses in course of construction		115,000	
Inventory of materials		23,000	
Accounts receivable for completed houses		62,000	
			275,000
Total assets			373,000
Current liabilities			
Trade accounts payable		77,000	
Deposits and progress payments		82,000	
Bank overdraft		132,500	
Total liabilities			(291,500)
Net assets			81,500
Partners' capital accounts			
Lock		52,000	
Stock		26,000	
Barrel		3,500	
Total capital			81,500

During the six months from the date of the latest balance sheet to the date of dissolution the following transactions have taken place:

		£
Purchase of materials		20,250
Materials used for houses in course of construction		35,750
Payments for wages and subcontractors on building sites		78,000
Payments to trade creditors for materials		45,000
Sales of completed houses		280,000
Cash received from customers for houses		225,000
Payments for various general expenses		12,500
Payments for administration salaries		17,250
Cash withdrawn by partners:	Lock	6,000
	Stock	5,000
	Barrel	4,000

All deposits and progress payments have been used for completed transactions.

Depreciation is normally provided each year at £600 on the freehold yard and buildings, at 10 per cent on cost for plant and equipment and 25 per cent on cost for motor vehicles.

The partners decide to dissolve the partnership on 1 February 2007 and wish to take out the maximum cash possible, as items are sold. At this date there are no houses in course of construction and one-third of the land had been used for building.

It is agreed that Barrel is insolvent and cannot bring any money into the partnership. The partners take over the partnership cars at an agreed figure of £2,000 each. All other vehicles were sold on 28 February 2007 for £6,200. At the same date the inventory of materials was sold for £7,000, and the sale of the land realised £72,500. On 30 April 2007 the accounts receivable were paid in full and all the plant and equipment was sold for £50,000.

The freehold yard and buildings realised £100,000 on 1 June 2007, on which date all remaining cash was distributed.

There are no costs of realisation or distribution.

Required:

(*a*) Prepare a partnership income statement for the six months to 1 February 2007, partners' capital accounts for the same period and a balance sheet at 1 February 2007.

(*b*) Show calculations of the amounts distributable to the partners.

(*c*) Prepare a realisation account and the capital accounts of the partners to the final distribution.

(*Association of Chartered Certified Accountants*)

44.8A Grant and Herd are in partnership sharing profits and losses in the ratio 3 to 2. The following information relates to the year to 31 December 2008:

	Dr £000	*Cr* £000
Capital accounts (at 1 January 2008):		
Grant		300
Herd		100
Cash at bank	5	
Accounts payable and accruals		25
Accounts receivable and prepayments	18	
Drawings during the year: Grant (all at 30 June 2008)	40	
Herd (all at 31 March 2008)	40	
Non-current assets: at cost	300	
accumulated depreciation (at 31 December 2008)		100
Herd – salary	10	
Net profit (for the year to 31 December 2008)		60
Inventory at cost (at 31 December 2008)	90	
Trade accounts payable		141
Trade accounts receivable	223	
	726	726

Additional information:

1 The partnership agreement allows for Herd to be paid a salary of £20,000 per annum, and for interest of 5 per cent per annum to be paid on the partners' capital account balances as at 1 January in each year. Interest at a rate of 10 per cent per annum is charged on the partners' drawings.

2 The partners decide to dissolve the partnership as at 31 December 2008, and the business was then sold to Valley Limited. The purchase consideration was to be 400,000 £1 ordinary shares in Valley at a premium of 25p per share. The shares were to be issued to the partners on 31 December 2008, and they were to be shared between them in their profit-sharing ratio.

The sale agreement allowed Grant to take over one of the business cars at an agreed valuation of £10,000. Apart from the car and the cash and bank balances, the company took over all the other partnership assets and liabilities at their book values as at 31 December 2008.

3 Matters relating to the appropriation of profit for the year to 31 December 2008 are to be dealt with in the partners' capital accounts, including any arrears of salary owing to Herd.

Required:

(*a*) Write up the following accounts for the year to 31 December 2008:
 (*i*) the profit and loss appropriation account;
 (*ii*) Grant's and Herd's capital accounts; and
 (*iii*) the realisation account.

(*b*) Prepare Valley's balance sheet as at 1 January 2009 immediately after the acquisition of the partnership and assuming that no further transactions have taken place in the meantime.

(*Association of Accounting Technicians*)

You can find a range of additional self-test questions, as well as material to help you with your studies, on the website that accompanies this book at www.pearsoned.co.uk/wood.

chapter 45

An introduction to the financial statements of limited liability companies

Learning objectives

After you have studied this chapter, you should be able to:

- explain how limited companies differ from sole traders and partnerships
- explain the differences between different classes of shares
- calculate how distributable profits available for dividends are divided between the different classes of shares
- explain the differences between shares and loan notes
- prepare the income statement for a company for internal purposes
- prepare the balance sheet for a company for both internal and external purposes
- explain what is shown in a statement of changes in equity
- explain what an audit report is
- explain how to present goodwill in company financial statements

Introduction

In this chapter, you'll learn about the different types of companies that can exist and about the different types of long-term funds they can raise in order to finance their activities. You'll learn how to prepare the financial statements for companies and about the differences between the treatment of goodwill in company accounts and its treatment in the accounts of sole traders and partnerships.

45.1 Need for limited companies

Limited liability companies, more commonly referred to as **limited companies**, came into existence originally because of the growth in the size of businesses, and the need to have a lot of people investing in the business who would not be able to take part in its management.

Activity 45.1 Why do you think a partnership was not an appropriate form of business in this case?

The UK law governing companies, their formation and the duties relating to their members, directors, auditors and officials is largely contained in the Companies Act 2006. This Act consolidated the Companies Acts of 1985, 1989 and 2004. However much of the requirements concerning financial statements continue to be found in the 1985 Act.

45.2 Limited liability

The capital of a limited company is divided into **shares**. Shares can be of any nominal value – 10p, 25p, £1, £5, £10 or any other amount per share. To become a member of a limited company, or a **shareholder**, a person must buy one or more of the shares.

If shareholders have paid in full for their shares, their liability is limited to what they have already paid for those shares. If a company loses all its assets, all those shareholders can lose is their shares. They cannot be forced to pay anything more in respect of the company's losses.

Shareholders who have only partly paid for their shares can be forced to pay the balance owing on the shares, but nothing else.

Shareholders are therefore said to have 'limited liability' and this is why companies are known as 'limited liability' or, more usually, simply 'limited' companies. By addressing the need for investors to have limited risk of financial loss, the existence of limited liability encourages individuals to invest in these companies and makes it possible to have both a large number of owners and a large amount of capital invested in the company.

There are a few companies which have unlimited liability, but these are outside the scope of this book.

45.3 Public and private companies

In the UK, there are two main classes of company, the **public company** and the **private company**. Private companies far outnumber public companies. In the Companies Act, a public company is defined as one which fulfils the following conditions:

- Its memorandum (a document that describes the company) states that it is a public company, and that it has registered as such.
- It has an authorised share capital of at least £50,000.
- Minimum membership is one. There is no maximum.
- Its name must end with the words 'public limited company' or the abbreviation 'PLC'. It can have the Welsh equivalent ('CCC') if registered in Wales.

PLCs can, but don't have to, offer their shares for sale on the Stock Exchange. It is through the Stock Exchange that a large ownership base can be established.

A private company is usually, but not always, a smaller business, and may be formed by one or more persons. It is defined by the Act as a company which is not a public company. The main differences between a private company and a public company are that a private company

- can have an authorised capital of less than £50,000, and
- *cannot* offer its shares for subscription to the public at large, whereas public companies can.

This means that if you were to walk into a bank, or similar public place, and see a prospectus offering anyone the chance to take up shares in a company, then that company would be a public company, i.e. a PLC.

The shares that are dealt in on the Stock Exchange are all those of public limited companies. This does not mean that shares of all public companies are traded on the Stock Exchange. For various reasons, some public companies have either chosen not to, or have not been allowed to, have their shares traded there. The ones whose shares are traded are known as 'quoted companies' meaning that their shares have prices quoted on the Stock Exchange. They have to comply with Stock Exchange requirements in addition to those laid down by the Companies Act and accounting standards.

Apart from not having to worry about complying with the Stock Exchange requirements, what other reasons can you think of that would explain why some PLCs do not wish to offer their shares on the Stock Market?

45.4 Directors of the company

The day-to-day business of a company is *not* carried out by the shareholders. The possession of a share normally confers voting rights on the holder, who is then able to attend general meetings of the company. At one of these general meetings, normally the **Annual General Meeting** or AGM, the shareholders vote for **directors**, these being the people who will be entrusted with the running of the business. At each AGM, the directors report on their stewardship, and this report is accompanied by a set of financial statements and other documents – the 'annual report'.

45.5 Legal status of a limited company

A limited company is said to possess a 'separate legal identity' from that of its shareholders. Put simply, this means that a company is not seen as being exactly the same as its shareholders. For instance, a company can sue one or more of its shareholders, and similarly, a shareholder can sue the company. This would not be the case if the company and its shareholders were exactly the same thing, as one cannot sue oneself. This concept is often referred to as the **veil of incorporation.**

***Note*: This is an extremely important concept. The most frequently cited example of the strength of the veil of incorporation is a case that went to the House of Lords in 1897. The case is known as *Saloman* v *Saloman & Co Ltd*. It involved a company formed by a Mr Saloman. The company was run by Mr Saloman in the same way as when he was operating as a sole trader. He received all the profits and made all the decisions. However, the *veil of incorporation* meant that the company was treated as completely separate from him. When the business failed owing a large amount of money, Mr Saloman did not have to pay for the business debts personally. The debts were the responsibility of the company, not of Mr Saloman. This was held to be the case even though Mr Saloman had lent some money to the company in the form of secured debentures (now called secured loan notes). This meant that any funds left in the company when it failed were first used to repay *those* loan notes (because they were 'secured' on the assets of the company) and the rest of the creditors (who were not 'secured') received nothing.**

45.6 Share capital

Shareholders of a limited company obtain their reward in the form of a share of the profits, known as a **dividend**. The directors decide on the amount of profits which are placed in reserves (i.e. 'retained'). The directors then propose the payment of a certain amount of dividend from the remaining profits. It is important to note that the shareholders cannot propose a higher dividend for themselves than that already proposed by the directors. They can, however, propose that a lesser dividend should be paid, although this is very rare indeed. If the directors propose that no dividend be paid, then the shareholders are powerless to alter the decision.

The decision by the directors as to the amount proposed as dividends is a very complex one and cannot be fully discussed here. Such points as government directives to reduce dividends, the effect of taxation, the availability of bank balances to pay the dividends, the possibility of take-over bids and so on will all be taken into account.

The dividend is usually expressed as a percentage. A dividend of 10 per cent in Business A on 500,000 ordinary shares of £1 each will amount to £50,000. A dividend of 6 per cent in Business B on 200,000 ordinary shares of £2 each will amount to £24,000. A shareholder having 100 shares in each business would receive £10 from Business A and £12 from Business B.

There are two main types of shares:

1 **Preference shares.** Holders of these shares get an agreed percentage rate of dividend before the ordinary shareholders receive anything.
2 **Ordinary shares.** Holders of these shares receive the remainder of the total profits available for dividends. There is no upper limit to the amounts of dividends they can receive.

For example, if a company had 50,000 5 per cent preference shares of £1 each and 200,000 ordinary shares of £1 each, then the dividends could be payable as in Exhibit 45.1.

Exhibit 45.1

Year	*1*	*2*	*3*	*4*	*5*
	£	£	£	£	£
Profits appropriated for dividends	6,500	10,500	13,500	28,500	17,500
Preference dividends (5%)	2,500	2,500	2,500	2,500	2,500
Ordinary dividends	(2%)4,000	(4%)8,000	(5½%)11,000	(13%)26,000	(7½%)15,000
	6,500	10,500	13,500	28,500	17,500

The two main types of preference shares are non-cumulative preference shares and cumulative preference shares:

1 **Non-cumulative preference shares.** These can receive a dividend up to an agreed percentage each year. If the amount paid is less than the maximum agreed amount, the shortfall is lost by the shareholder. The shortfall cannot be carried forward and paid in a future year.
2 **Cumulative preference shares.** These also have an agreed maximum percentage dividend. However, any shortfall of dividend paid in a year can be carried forward. These arrears of preference dividends will have to be paid before the ordinary shareholders receive anything.

Why do you think an investor might purchase preference shares rather than ordinary shares in a company?

Exhibit 45.2

A company has 500,000 £1 ordinary shares and 100,000 5 per cent non-cumulative preference shares of £1 each. The profits available for dividends are: year 1 £145,000, year 2 £2,000, year 3 £44,000, year 4 £118,000, year 5 £264,000. Assuming all profits are paid out in dividends, the amounts paid to each class of shareholder are:

Year	*1*	*2*	*3*	*4*	*5*
	£	£	£	£	£
Profits appropriated for dividends	145,000	2,000	44,000	118,000	264,000
Preference dividend (non-cumulative) (limited in year 2)	5,000	2,000	5,000	5,000	5,000
Dividends on ordinary shares	140,000	–	39,000	113,000	259,000
	145,000	2,000	44,000	118,000	264,000

Exhibit 45.3

Assume that the preference shares in Exhibit 45.2 had been cumulative. The dividends would have been:

Year	*1*	*2*	*3*	*4*	*5*
	£	£	£	£	£
Profits appropriated for dividends	145,000	2,000	44,000	118,000	264,000
Preference dividend	5,000	2,000	8,000*	5,000	5,000
Dividends on ordinary shares	140,000	–	36,000	113,000	259,000
	145,000	2,000	44,000	118,000	264,000

***including arrears.**

***Note*: This exhibit shows how much of the profit made in each year was paid out as dividend. The dividends are shown in the financial statements in the year they were paid, which may be a year later than the year in which the profit used to pay them was earned – see Section 45.12, especially Exhibit 45.5.**

45.7 Share capital: different meanings

The term 'share capital' can have any of the following meanings:

1 **Authorised share capital.** Sometimes known as 'registered capital' or 'nominal capital'. This is the total of the share capital which the company is allowed to issue to shareholders.
2 **Issued share capital.** This is the total of the share capital actually issued to shareholders.

***Note*: Some students mix up these two terms and throw away marks in examinations as a result. In order to remember which is which, you only need to think about what the words 'authorised' and 'issued' mean.**

If all of the authorised share capital has been issued, then 1 and 2 above would be the same amount.

3 **Called-up capital.** Where only part of the amount payable on each issued share has been asked for, the total amount asked for on all the issued shares is known as the called-up capital.
4 **Uncalled capital.** This is the total amount which is to be received in future relating to issued share capital, but which has not yet been asked for.
5 **Calls in arrears.** The total amount for which payment has been asked for (i.e. 'called for'), but has not yet been paid by shareholders.
6 **Paid-up capital.** This is the total of the amount of share capital which has been paid for by shareholders.

Exhibit 45.4 illustrates these different meanings.

Exhibit 45.4

1 Better Enterprises Ltd was formed with the legal right to issue 1 million shares of £1 each.
2 The company has actually issued 750,000 shares.
3 None of the shares has yet been fully paid up. So far, the company has made calls of 80p (£0.80) per share.
4 All the calls have been paid by shareholders except for £200 owing from one shareholder.

(*a*) Authorised or nominal share capital is:	1	£1 million.
(*b*) Issued share capital is:	2	£750,000.
(*c*) Called-up share capital is:	3	750,000 × £0.80 = £600,000.
(*d*) Calls in arrears amounted to:	4	£200.
(*e*) Paid-up share capital is:	(*c*)	£600,000 less (*d*) £200 = £599,800.

45.8 Bonus shares

The issue of **bonus shares** would appear to be outside the scope of syllabuses at this level. However, some examinations have included a minor part of a question concerned with bonus shares. All that is needed here is a very brief explanation only, leaving further explanations for a later stage in your studies.

Bonus shares are 'free' shares issued to shareholders without their having to pay anything for them. The reserves (e.g. retained profits shown in the balance sheet) are utilised for the purpose. Thus, if before the bonus issue there were £20,000 of issued share capital and £12,000 reserves, and a bonus issue of 1 for 4 was then made (i.e. 1 bonus share for every 4 shares already held) the bonus issue would amount to £5,000. The share capital then becomes £25,000 and the reserves become £7,000.

A proper and fuller explanation appears in *Business Accounting 2*. An issue of bonus shares is often referred to as a **scrip issue**.

45.9 Loan notes

You will recall the note about the veil of incorporation where loan notes had been issued to the owner of company. The term **loan note** is used when a limited company receives money on loan, and a document called a loan note certificate is issued to the lender. Interest will be paid to the holder, the rate of interest being shown on the certificate. (You will sometimes see them referred to as 'debentures', 'loan stock' or 'loan capital', but the correct term is 'loan note'.)

Interest on loan notes has to be paid whether profits are made or not. They are, therefore, different from shares, where dividends depend on profits being made. A loan note may be either:

- Redeemable, i.e. repayable at or by a particular date, or
- Irredeemable, normally repayable only when the company is officially terminated by going into liquidation. (Also sometimes referred to as 'perpetual' loan notes.)

If dates are shown on a loan note, e.g. 2005/2012, it means that the company can redeem it in any of the years covered by the date(s) showing, in this case 2005 to 2012 inclusive.

People lending money to companies in the form of loan notes will be interested in how safe their investment will be. Some loan notes are assigned the legal right that on certain happenings the holders of the loan notes will be able to take control of specific assets, or of the whole of the assets. They can then sell the assets and recoup the amount due under their loan notes, or deal with the assets in ways specified in the deed under which the loan notes were issued. Such loan notes are said to be 'secured' against the assets – this was the case in the veil of incorporation note in Section 45.5. (The term 'mortgage' loan note is sometimes used instead of 'secured'.) Other loan notes have no prior right to control the assets under any circumstances. These are known as 'simple' or 'naked' loan notes.

Why do you think a loan note might be 'secured' rather than being designated as a 'simple' loan note? (*Hint*: think about Mr Saloman.)

45.10 Goodwill

Companies can recognise goodwill arising on acquisitions as an intangible non-current asset. However, each year they must consider whether the value it is carried at has been impaired (i.e. has fallen), when this happens, the reduction must be shown in the profit and loss section of the income statement. The rules relating to this are to be found in IFRS 3 (*Business combinations*), IAS 36 (*Impairment of assets*) and IAS 38 (*Intangible assets*).

45.11 Income statements of companies

The income statements of both private and public companies are drawn up in exactly the same way.

The trading account section of the income statement of a limited company is no different from that of a sole trader or a partnership. However, some differences may be found in the profit and loss account section. Two expenses that would be found only in company accounts are directors' remuneration and loan note interest.

Directors' remuneration

As directors exist only in companies, this type of expense is found only in company financial statements.

Directors are legally employees of the company, appointed by the shareholders. Their remuneration is charged to the profit and loss account.

Loan note interest

The interest payable for the use of the money borrowed is an expense of the company, and is payable whether profits are made or not. This means that interest on loan notes is charged as an expense in the profit and loss account. Contrast this with dividends which are dependent on profits having been made.

45.12 Statement of changes in equity

Unlike partnership income statements, following the profit and loss account section of company income statements there is no section called the 'profit and loss appropriation account'. Instead, companies produce a **statement of changes in equity**. This shows separately:

(a) the retained profit for the period
(b) distributions of equity (e.g. dividends) and contributions of equity (e.g. share issues)
(c) a reconciliation between the opening and closing carrying amount of each component of equity (i.e. share capital and **reserves**)

Taxation is shown as a deduction when arriving at retained profits on the face of the income statement. This differs from its treatment in partnership and role trader financial statements.

Exhibit 45.5 contains an example showing the changes in equity of a new business for its first three years of trading.

Exhibit 45.5

IDC Ltd has share capital of 400,000 ordinary shares of £1 each and 200,000 5 per cent preference shares of £1 each.

- The retained profits for the first three years of business ended 31 December are: 2004, £109,670; 2005 £148,640; and 2006 £158,220.
- Transfers to reserves are made as follows: 2004 nil; 2005, general reserve, £10,000; and 2006, non-current assets replacement reserve, £22,500.
- Dividends were paid for each year on the preference shares at 5 per cent and on the ordinary shares at: 2004, 10 per cent; 2005, 12.5 per cent; 2006, 15 per cent.

IDC Ltd
Statements of changes in equity (extracts)
(1) For the year ending 31 December 2004

			£
Retained profits			109,670
Less Dividends paid: Preference 5%			10,000
Ordinary 10%			40,000
			(50,000)
Retained profits carried forward			59,670

(2) For the year ended 31 December 2005

	£	£	£
Retained profits			148,640
Add Retained profits brought forward			59,670
			244,310
Less Transfer to general reserve		10,000	
Dividends paid:			
Preference dividend of 5%	10,000		
Ordinary dividend of 12.5%	50,000		
		60,000	
			(70,000)
Retained profits carried forward			174,310

(3) For the year ended 31 December 2006

	£	£	£
Retained profits			158,220
Add Retained profits brought forward			174,310
			332,530
Less Transfer to non-current assets replacement reserve		22,500	
Dividends paid:			
Preference dividend of 5%	10,000		
Ordinary dividend of 15%	60,000		
		70,000	
			(92,500)
Retained profits carried forward			240,030

45.13 The balance sheet

Prior to the UK Companies Act 1981, provided it disclosed the necessary information, a company could draw up its balance sheet and income statement for publication in any way that it wished. The 1981 Act, however, stopped this, and laid down the precise details to be shown. These are unchanged in the Companies Act 2006 and the current legal requirements are largely contained in the Companies Act 1985. International standards are not specific about the layout to adopt so UK companies tend to continue to use the Companies Act layouts. We will cover this topic in more detail in *Business Accounting 2*.

Exhibits 45.6 and 45.7 present two versions of a balance sheet. They both comply with International GAAP. Exhibit 45.6 shows more detail. The detail that is omitted in Exhibit 45.7 would be shown separately as a note. Both these balance sheets would be prepared by companies for their own use. Balance sheets prepared for publication (i.e. for external users) contain much less detail and will be covered in detail in *Business Accounting 2*.

Exhibit 45.6 Greater detail for internal use

Balance Sheet as at 31 December 2007

		Cost	*Depreciation to date (b)*	*Net book value*
Non-current assets	(*a*)	£000	£000	£000
Goodwill		15,000	5,000	10,000
Buildings		15,000	6,000	9,000
Machinery		8,000	2,400	5,600
Motor vehicles		4,000	1,600	2,400
		42,000	15,000	27,000
Current assets				
Inventory			6,000	
Accounts receivable			3,000	
Bank			4,000	
				13,000
Total assets				40,000
Less Current liabilities				
Accounts payable		3,000		
Corporation tax owing		2,000		
			5,000	
Net current assets				
Non-current liabilities				
Six per cent loan notes: repayable 2009			8,000	
Total liabilities				(13,000)
Net assets				27,000
Equity				
Share capital				
Authorised 30,000 shares of £1 each	(*c*)			30,000
Issued 20,000 ordinary shares of £1 each, fully paid	(*d*)			20,000
Reserves	(*e*)			
Share premium			1,200	
General reserve			3,800	
Retained profits			2,000	
				7,000
Total equity	(*f*)			27,000

Notes:

(*a*) Non-current assets should normally be shown either at cost or alternatively at some other valuation. In either case, the method chosen should be clearly stated. As you will see in Exhibit 45.7, you could show the intangible non-current asset (goodwill) separately from the other non-current assets.

(*b*) The total depreciation from date of purchase to the date of the balance sheet should be shown.

(*c*) The authorised share capital, where it is different from the issued share capital, is shown as a note.

(*d*) Where shares are only partly called-up, it is the amount actually called up that appears in the balance sheet and not the full amount.

(*e*) Reserves consist either of those unused profits remaining in the retained profits, or those transferred to a reserve account appropriately titled, e.g. general reserve or non-current assets replacement reserve. These reserves are shown in the balance sheet after share capital under the heading of 'Reserves'.

(*f*) The share capital and reserves should be totalled so as to show the book value of all the shares in the company. Either the term 'shareholders' funds' or 'members' equity' is often given to the total of share capital plus reserves.

Exhibit 45.7 Less detail for internal use

Letters in brackets (A) to (G) refer to notes following the balance sheet.

Balance Sheet as at 31 December 2007

		£000	£000	£000
Non-current assets				
Intangible assets	(A)			
Goodwill				10,000
Tangible assets	(B)			
Buildings			9,000	
Machinery			5,600	
Motor vehicles			2,400	
				17,000
				27,000
Current assets				
Inventory			6,000	
Accounts receivable			3,000	
Bank			4,000	
				13,000
Total assets				40,000
Current liabilities	(C)			
Accounts payable		3,000		
Corporation tax owing		2,000		
			5,000	
Total assets less current liabilities				
Non-current liabilities	(D)			
Loan notes			8,000	
Total liabilities				(13,000)
Net assets				27,000
Equity				
Called-up share capital	(E)			20,000
Share premium account	(F)			1,200
Other reserves				
General reserve				3,800
Retained profits				2,000
Total equity				27,000

Notes:

(A) Intangible assets are those not having a 'physical' existence; for instance, you can see and touch tangible assets under (B), i.e. buildings, machinery etc., but you cannot see and touch goodwill.

(B) Tangible non-current assets under a separate heading. Note that figures are shown net after depreciation. In a note accompanying the financial statements the cost and depreciation on these assets would be given.

(C) Only items payable within one year go under this heading.

(D) These loan notes are repayable in several years' time. If they had been payable within one year they would have been shown under current liabilities.

(E) An analysis of share capital will be given in supplementary notes to the balance sheet.

(F) One reserve that is not labelled with the word 'reserve' in its title is the share premium account. (Another is retained profits.) For various reasons (discussed fully in *Business Accounting 2*) shares can be issued for more than their face (or 'nominal') value. The excess of the price at which they are issued over the nominal value of the shares is credited to a share premium account. This is then shown with the other reserves in the balance sheet.

If you are asked in an examination to prepare a balance sheet for internal use and choose to present a balance sheet similar to Exhibit 45.7 you should include in a note the details from the layout as in Exhibit 45.6 that you have omitted from the balance sheet.

In *Business Accounting 2* you will be told more about the differences between 'revenue reserves' and 'capital reserves'. The most important reason for the distinction has to do with deciding how much can be treated as being available for paying out to shareholders as dividends. 'Revenue reserves', which include the retained profits and the general reserve, can be treated as available for such dividends. 'Capital reserves', which will include revaluation reserves on property and land, and also some reserves (which you have not yet met) which have to be created to meet some legal statutory requirement, cannot be treated as available for payment of dividends.

A term which sometimes appears in examinations is that of 'fungible assets'. Fungible assets are assets which are substantially indistinguishable one from another.

Now, let's prepare two more balance sheets and an income statement for internal use.

A fully worked example

Exhibit 45.8

The following trial balance is extracted from the books of F W Ltd as on 31 December 2005.

Trial balance as on 31 December 2005

	Dr £	*Cr* £
10% preference share capital		200,000
Ordinary share capital		700,000
10% loan notes (repayable 2009)		300,000
Goodwill at cost	255,000	
Buildings at cost	1,050,000	
Equipment at cost	120,000	
Motor vehicles at cost	172,000	
Provision for depreciation: buildings 1.1.2005		100,000
Provision for depreciation: equipment 1.1.2005		24,000
Provision for depreciation: motor vehicles 1.1.2005		51,600
Inventory 1.1.2005	84,912	
Sales		1,022,000
Purchases	439,100	
Carriage inwards	6,200	
Salaries and wages	192,400	
Directors' remuneration	123,000	
Motor expenses	3,120	
Business rates and insurances	8,690	
General expenses	5,600	
Loan note interest	15,000	
Accounts receivable	186,100	
Accounts payable		113,700
Bank	8,390	
General reserve		50,000
Share premium account		100,000
Interim ordinary dividend paid	35,000	
Retained profits 31.12.2004		43,212
	2,704,512	2,704,512

The following adjustments are needed:

(*i*) Inventory at 31.12.2005 was £91,413.
(*ii*) Depreciate buildings £10,000; motor vehicles £18,000; equipment £12,000.
(*iii*) Accrue loan note interest £15,000.
(*iv*) Provide for preference dividend £20,000 and final ordinary dividend of 10 per cent.
(*v*) Transfer £10,000 to general reserve.
(*vi*) Write-off goodwill impairment of £30,000.
(*vii*) Authorised share capital is £200,000 in preference shares and £1 million in ordinary shares.
(*viii*) Provide for corporation tax £50,000.

The financial statements are shown below. First, there's an income statement for internal use. (The income statement for publication is greatly summarised and we will cover that topic in *Business Accounting 2*.) We then show two versions of the internal balance sheet.

(a) Income statement **for internal use only,** not for publication.

F W Ltd
Income Statement for the year ending 31 December 2005

		£	£
Revenue			1,022,000
Less Cost of goods sold:			
Opening inventory		84,912	
Add Purchases		439,100	
Add Carriage inwards		6,200	
		530,212	
Less Closing inventory		(91,413)	
			(438,799)
Gross profit			583,201
Less Expenses:			
Salaries and wages		192,400	
Motor expenses		3,120	
Business rates and insurances		8,690	
General expenses		5,600	
Directors' remuneration	**(A)**	123,000	
Loan note interest	**(B)**	30,000	
Goodwill impairment		30,000	
Depreciation: Buildings		10,000	
Equipment		12,000	
Motor vehicles		18,000	
			(432,810)
Profit for the year before taxation			150,391
Less Corporation tax			(50,000)
Retained profits			100,391
Note			
Ordinary share dividends paid	**(C)**	35,000	

Notes:
(A) Directors' remuneration is shown as an expense in the income statement.
(B) Loan note interest is an expense to be shown in the income statement.
(C) The final dividend of 10 per cent is based on the issued ordinary share capital and *not* on the authorised ordinary share capital. It is, therefore, £70,000. However, both it and the preference dividend of £20,000 should only be included as notes to the income statement. They should not be treated as current liabilities and should not appear in any financial statement. As only the interim ordinary dividend was paid during the year, this is the only one of these three dividend items that will appear in the statement of changes in equity.

 **(b)** Balance sheet in greater detail for internal use.

Balance Sheet as at 31 December 2005

	Cost	*Depreciation to date*	*Net book value*
Non-current assets	£	£	£
Goodwill	255,000	30,000	225,000
Buildings	1,050,000	110,000	940,000
Equipment	120,000	36,000	84,000
Motor vehicles	172,000	69,600	102,400
	1,597,000	245,600	1,351,400
Current assets			
Inventory		91,413	
Accounts receivable		186,100	
Bank		8,390	
			285,903
Total assets			1,637,303
Current liabilities			
Accounts payable	113,700		
Loan note interest accrued	15,000		
Taxation	50,000		
		(178,700)	
Non-current liabilities			
10% loan notes		300,000	
Total liabilities			(478,700)
Net assets			1,158,603
Equity			
Share Capital		*Authorised*	*Issued*
		£	£
Preference shares		200,000	200,000
Ordinary shares		1,000,000	700,000
		1,200,000	900,000
Reserves			
Share premium		100,000	
General reserve		60,000	
Retained profits		98,603	
			258,603
Total equity			1,158,603

The proposed dividends should be shown in a note.

Note that the difference between the two balance sheets is solely that of detail. You should use whichever layout is more appropriate.

(c) Balance sheet in less detail for internal use.

F W Ltd
Balance Sheet as at 31 December 2005

Non-current assets	£	£	£
Intangible assets			
Goodwill			225,000
Tangible assets	(A)		
Buildings		940,000	
Equipment		84,000	
Motor vehicles		102,400	
			1,126,400
			1,351,400
Current assets			
Inventory		91,413	
Accounts receivable		186,100	
Bank		8,390	
			285,903
Total assets			1,637,303
Current liabilities			
Accounts payable	113,700		
Loan note interest accrued	15,000		
Taxation	50,000		
		178,700	
Non-current liabilities			
10% Loan notes		300,000	
			(478,700)
Total liabilities			1,158,603
Net assets			
Equity	(B)		
Called-up share capital	(C)		900,000
Share premium account			100,000
Other reserves			
General reserve			60,000
Retained profits			98,603
Total equity			1,158,603

The proposed dividends should be shown in a note.

(A) Notes to be given in an appendix as to cost, acquisitions and sales in the year and depreciation.

(B) Reserves consist either of those unused profits remaining in the appropriation account, or those transferred to a reserve account appropriately titled, e.g. general reserve, non-current assets replacement reserve, etc.

The closing balance of retained profits from the statement of changes in equity (not prepared for this example) is shown under reserves. These are profits not already appropriated, and therefore 'reserved' for future use.

(C) The authorised share capital, where it is different from the issued share capital, is shown as a note. Notice that the total figure of £1,200,000 for authorised capital is not included when adding up the balance sheet sides. Only the issued capital amounts are included in balance sheet totals.

45.14 True and fair view

When the financial statements of a company are published no one, neither the directors nor the auditors, ever states that 'the financial statements are correct'. This is because in preparing company financial statements many subjective estimates and judgements affect the figures. The valuation of inventory, or the estimates of depreciation, cannot be said to be 'correct', just as it is impossible to say that the allowance for doubtful debts is 'correct'. Only time will tell whether these estimates and judgements will turn out to have been 'correct'.

The expression that is used is that the financial statements give a **true and fair view** of the financial position and financial performance of the company.

45.15 IFRS 5 Non-current assets held for sale and discontinued operations

Accounting is not a static subject. Changes occur over the years as they are seen to be necessary, and also get general agreement as to their usefulness. Since the introduction of accounting standards over thirty years ago, the number of changes that practitioners and students have had to learn has increased at a very fast rate.

Suppose that you are considering the affairs of a business over the years. The business has not changed significantly, there have been no acquisitions, no discontinued operations, no fundamental reorganisation or restructuring of the business. In these circumstances, when comparing the financial statements over the years, you are comparing like with like, subject to the problem of the effects of inflation or deflation.

On the other hand, suppose that it has been decided to sell some non-current assets or to discontinue some of the operations of the business. When trying to see what the future might hold for the company, simply basing your opinions on what has happened in the past could be very misleading.

To help you to distinguish the past and the future, and to give you some idea as to what changes have occurred, IFRS 5 requires that:

- non-current assets held for sale are shown at the lower of carrying amount and fair value less selling costs
- non-current assets held for sale are presented separately on the face of the balance sheet after current assets
- non-current assets held for sale are not depreciated
- gains or losses on the remeasurement of a non-current asset held for sale should be included in profit or loss from continuing operations
- the results of discontinued operations are shown separately on the face of the income statement after the figure for profit for the period from continuing operations.

45.16 IAS 1 and financial statements

IAS 1 (*Presentation of financial statements*) was revised and reissued in 2007. In the revised standard, the balance sheet was renamed the 'statement of financial position' (though use of the term 'balance sheet' is still permitted). It also changes the title of the 'cash flow statement' to 'statement of cash flows'. It also introduced a new primary statement: the statement of comprehensive income. It states that there are four primary statements:

- a statement of financial position
- a statement of comprehensive income
- a statement of changes in equity
- a statement of cash flows.

When a separate income statement is presented as well, it is presented immediately before the statement of comprehensive income. In that case, the statement of comprehensive income starts with the profit or loss identified in the income statement. The difference in approach is cosmetic and the option to show a separate income statement simply enables continuation of use of the term 'income statement'.

As a minimum, **the statement of comprehensive income** must include line items presenting:

(a) revenue
(b) finance costs
(c) share of profits or losses of associates and joint ventures accounted for using the equity method
(d) tax
(e) the total of post-tax profit or loss on discontinued operations *plus* the post-tax gain or loss recognised on the measurement to fair value less costs to sell or on the disposal of the assets or disposal group(s) constituting the discontinued operations
(f) profit or loss
(g) each component of other comprehensive income classified by nature excluding amounts in (h)
(h) share of the other comprehensive income of associates and joint ventures accounted for using the entity method
(i) total comprehensive income.

If a separate income statement is presented, it will contain items (a) to (f). Other comprehensive income comprises items that are not recognised in profit or loss, such as:

- changes in revaluation surplus
- gains or losses arising from translating the financial statements of a foreign operation
- gains and losses on remeasuring available-for-sale financial assets.

Total comprehensive income is the change in equity during a period other than those changes resulting from transactions with owners (i.e. holders of equity) in their capacity as owners (e.g. dividend payments).

The statement of changes in equity presents:

(a) total comprehensive income
(b) the amounts of transactions with owners in their capacity as owners
(c) for each component of equity, a reconciliation between the opening and closing carrying amount.

Either in the statement of changes in equity or in a note, the amount of dividend distributed to owners during the period must be shown, along with the related amount per share.

IAS 1 is covered in greater detail in *Business Accounting 2*. In this book we are simply explaining some of its requirements. The overall effect is that financial statements prepared for publication (i.e. for external users) are very different from those produced for internal use. You will not be required to prepare either a statement of comprehensive income in this book.

45.17 The Audit Report

The Companies Act requires that all companies other than dormant companies (i.e. companies that have not traded during the year) and small private companies be audited every year. ('Small' is currently defined as having a turnover of not more than £5.6 million and a balance sheet total (of assets) of not more than £2.8 million.)

The auditors are appointed each year by the shareholders at the company annual general meeting (AGM). The auditors complete the report after examining the books and accounts and, in the report, they must say whether or not they agree that the accounts give a true and fair view. The report is presented to the shareholders at the same time as the financial statements are presented to them at the AGM.

In preparing the audit report, the auditor must consider whether

- the accounts have been prepared in accordance with the Companies Act;
- the balance sheet shows a true and fair view of the state of the company's affairs at the end of the period and the income statement shows a true and fair view of the results for the period;
- proper accounting records have been kept and proper returns received from parts of the company not visited by the auditor;
- the accounts are in agreement with the accounting records;
- the directors' report is consistent with the accounts.

While smaller companies are exempt from the requirement to have their financial statements audited, they may still do so, if they wish.

Organisations that are not required to have their financial statements audited, such as sole traders, partnerships, clubs and societies, can still have their accounts audited. In this case, the audit is described as a *non-statutory audit*.

A qualified audit report indicates that the auditor is not satisfied that the financial statements present a true and fair view. When a company receives a qualified audit report, it acts as a signal to all stakeholders that something may be amiss. As such, it is a vitally important safeguard of the interests of the shareholders.

Contrary to what most of the public think, auditors do not guarantee to discover any fraud that may have occurred. That is not what the audit is for. Following such financial scandals as Enron, the Maxwell affair, BCCI bank, Polly Peck and Barlow Clowes there has been pressure exerted upon the accounting profession to reconsider its position regarding the discovery of fraud when auditing the financial statements of a company.

Learning outcomes

You should now have learnt:

1. That limited companies exist because of the disadvantages and constraints arising from partnerships.
2. That a fully paid-up shareholder's liability is limited to the shares he or she holds in the company. Shareholders cannot then be asked to pay any other company debt from their private resources.
3. The difference between public and private companies.
4. That there are far more private companies than public companies.
5. The difference between a PLC and a company that is not a PLC.
6. That a limited company has a 'separate legal entity' from that of its members.
7. The difference between ordinary shares and preference shares.
8. How dividends are calculated.
9. The difference between shares and loan notes.

10 The contents of and purpose of a company's appropriation account.
11 That directors' remuneration is charged to the profit and loss account section of the income statement.
12 That loan note interest is charged to the profit and loss account section of the income statement.
13 That taxation is shown in the income statement.
14 That transfers to reserves and dividends are shown in the statement of changes in equity.
15 How to prepare company income statements for internal purposes.
16 How to prepare company balance sheets for internal purposes.
17 How IAS 1 governs the preparation of financial statements prepared for publication.
18 That financial statements for publication differ greatly from those prepared for internal use.

Answers to activities

45.1 Partnerships were not suitable for such businesses because:

- normally they cannot have more than twenty partners, not counting limited partners.
- if a partnership business fails, partners could lose part, or all, of their private assets to pay the debts of the business.

Limited companies do not have restrictions on the number of owners. Nor do the owners of limited companies generally run the risk of losing everything they own if the company fails.

45.2 There may be any number of explanations, including:

- they may not want a wide ownership base
- they may feel that the costs of doing so are prohibitive
- they may feel that there would not be sufficient demand for the shares to make it worthwhile
- the directors may be concerned that it would make it easier for the company to be taken over
- they may wish to wait until the Stock Market is at a higher level, i.e. they may wish to wait until they can maximise the amount they can sell the shares for when they first offer them for sale on the Stock Market
- the Stock Market may be very volatile, making choosing a price at which to sell the shares very difficult – if the company gets it wrong, they may not sell all the shares they wanted to sell or they may not receive as much for each share as they could have done had they waited for the Stock Market to stabilise.

45.3 There is less risk for the investor. The annual preference dividend is known and it will be paid before any funds left over are used to pay a dividend on the ordinary shares. Even when an ordinary dividend is paid, it is not known in advance how much this will be, as it depends on how profitable the business has been over the financial period. It could be more than the preference dividend (which is normally the case) or it could be less. Although the preference dividend will often be at a lower rate than an ordinary dividend (i.e. a preference shareholder will receive less of a dividend for the same investment as an ordinary shareholder) the reduced risk results in some people preferring to purchase preference shares.

45.4 The lender may require it or the company may offer secured loan note status in order to attract funds at a more favourable rate of interest.

Multiple choice questions: Set 5

Now attempt Set 5 of multiple choice questions. (Answers to all the multiple choice questions are given in Appendix 2 at the end of this book.)

Each of these multiple choice questions has four suggested answers, (A), (B), (C) and (D). You should read each question and then decide which choice is best, either (A) or (B) or (C) or (D). *Write down your answers on a separate piece of paper.* You will then be able to redo the set of questions later without having to try to ignore your answers.

MC81 Given opening accounts receivable of £11,500, Sales £48,000 and receipts from debtors £45,000, the closing accounts receivable total should be

(A) £8,500
(B) £14,500
(C) £83,500
(D) £18,500

MC82 In a Sales Ledger Control Account the Bad Debts written off should be shown in the account

(A) As a debit
(B) As a credit
(C) Both as a debit and as a credit
(D) As a balance carried down

MC83 If cost price is £90 and selling price is £120, then

(*i*) Mark-up is 25 per cent
(*ii*) Margin is 33⅓ per cent
(*iii*) Margin is 25 per cent
(*iv*) Mark-up is 33⅓ per cent

(A) (*i*) and (*ii*)
(B) (*i*) and (*iii*)
(C) (*iii*) and (*iv*)
(D) (*ii*) and (*iv*)

MC84 Given cost of goods sold £16,000 and margin of 20 per cent, then sales figure is

(A) £20,160
(B) £13,600
(C) £21,000
(D) £20,000

MC85 If opening inventory is £3,000, closing inventory £5,000, sales £40,000 and margin 20 per cent, then inventory turnover is

(A) 8 times
(B) 7½ times
(C) 5 times
(D) 6 times

MC86 If accounts payable at 1 January 2003 were £2,500, accounts payable at 31 December 2003 £4,200 and payments to creditors £32,000, then purchases for 2003 are

(A) £30,300
(B) £33,700
(C) £31,600
(D) £38,700

MC87 Given opening capital of £16,500; closing capital as £11,350; and drawings of £3,300, then

(A) Loss for the year was £1,850
(B) Profit for the year was £1,850
(C) Loss for the year was £8,450
(D) Profit for the year was £8,450

MC88 A Receipts and Payments Account is one

(A) Which is accompanied by a balance sheet
(B) In which the profit is calculated
(C) In which the opening and closing cash balances are shown
(D) In which the surplus of income over expenditure is calculated

MC89 Prime cost includes

(*i*) Direct labour
(*ii*) Factory overhead expenses
(*iii*) Raw materials consumed
(*iv*) Direct expenses

(A) (*i*), (*ii*) and (*iii*)
(B) (*ii*), (*iii*) and (*iv*)
(C) (*i*), (*iii*) and (*iv*)
(D) (*i*), (*ii*) and (*iv*)

MC90 Which of the following should be charged in the Income Statement?

(A) Office rent
(B) Work-in-progress
(C) Direct materials
(D) Carriage on raw materials

MC91 In the Manufacturing Account is calculated

(A) The production costs paid in the year
(B) The total cost of goods produced
(C) The production cost of goods completed in the period
(D) The gross profit on goods sold

MC92 The recommended method of departmental accounts is

(A) To allocate expenses in proportion to sales
(B) To charge against each department its controllable costs
(C) To allocate expenses in proportion to purchases
(D) To charge against each department its uncontrollable costs

MC93 Where there is no partnership agreement then profits and losses

(A) Must be shared in the same proportion as capitals
(B) Must be shared equally
(C) Must be shared equally after adjusting for interest on capital
(D) None of these

MC94 If it is required to maintain fixed capitals then the partners' shares of profits must be

(A) Debited to capital accounts
(B) Credited to capital accounts
(C) Debited to partners' current accounts
(D) Credited to partners' current accounts

→

→ **MC95** You are to buy an existing business which has assets valued at Buildings £50,000, Motor vehicles £15,000, Fixtures £5,000 and Inventory £40,000. You are to pay £140,000 for the business. This means that

(A) You are paying £40,000 for Goodwill
(B) Buildings are costing you £30,000 more than their value
(C) You are paying £30,000 for Goodwill
(D) You have made an arithmetical mistake

MC96 Assets can be revalued in a partnership change because

(A) The law insists upon it
(B) It helps prevent injustice to some partners
(C) Inflation affects all values
(D) The depreciation charged on them needs to be reversed

MC97 Any loss on revaluation is

(A) Credited to old partners in old profit-sharing ratios
(B) Credited to new partners in new profit-sharing ratios
(C) Debited to old partners in old profit-sharing ratios
(D) Debited to new partners in new profit-sharing ratios

MC98 In a limited company which of the following is shown in the statement of changes in equity?

(*i*) Loan note interest
(*ii*) Dividends paid
(*iii*) Transfers to reserves
(*iv*) Directors' remuneration

(A) (*i*) and (*ii*)
(B) (*ii*) and (*iii*)
(C) (*i*) and (*iv*)
(D) (*ii*) and (*iv*)

MC99 The Issued Capital of a company is

(A) Always the same as the Authorised Capital
(B) The same as Preference Share Capital
(C) Equal to the reserves of the company
(D) None of the above

MC100 A company wishes to pay out all available profits as dividends. Net profit is £26,600. There are 20,000 8% Preference shares of £1 each, and 50,000 Ordinary shares of £1 each. £5,000 is to be transferred to General Reserve. What Ordinary dividends are to be paid, in percentage terms?

(A) 20 per cent
(B) 40 per cent
(C) 10 per cent
(D) 60 per cent

Review questions

45.1 Flyer Ltd started in business on 1 April 2004. Its issued share capital was 200,000 ordinary shares of £1 each and 100,000 5 per cent preference shares of £1 each. The following information is available:

- Its net profits for the first two years of business were: 2004/5 £90,200; 2005/6 £84,600.
- Preference dividends were paid for each of these years, whilst ordinary dividends were proposed as 2004/5 8 per cent and 2005/6 6 per cent.
- Transfers to general reserve took place: 2004/5 £20,000; 2005/6 £15,000.

Draw up a statement of changes in equity for each of the years ending 31 March 2005 and 2006.

45.2 Trainsign Ltd has an authorised capital of £500,000, consisting of 350,000 ordinary shares of £1 each and 150,000 7 per cent preference shares of £1 each. Of these, 260,000 ordinary shares and 90,000 preference shares had been issued when the company first started trading. The following information is available:

- The company has a financial year end of 31 December. The first three years of business resulted in net profit as follows: 2002 £62,400; 2003 £81,900; 2004 £114,190.
- Dividends were paid each year on the preference shares. Dividends on the ordinary shares were proposed as follows: 2002 6 per cent; 2003 8 per cent; 2004 12 per cent.
- Transfers to reserves were: general reserve 2002 £10,000, 2003 £18,000, and foreign exchange reserve 2004 £15,000.

You are to show the statement of changes in equity for each of the years 2002, 2003 and 2004.

45.3 A balance sheet is to be drawn up from the following information as at 30 September 2002:

		£
Issued share capital: ordinary shares £1 each		200,000
Authorised share capital: ordinary shares of £1 each		500,000
6 per cent loan notes (repayable 30 September 2006)		40,000
Buildings at cost		330,000
Motor vehicles at cost		74,000
Fixtures at cost		9,200
Retained profits		32,000
Non-current assets replacement reserve		30,000
Inventory		21,400
Accounts receivable		10,300
General reserve		50,000
Accounts payable		13,700
Depreciation to date:	Buildings	40,000
	Motor vehicles	41,000
	Fixtures	5,100
Bank (balancing figure for you to ascertain)		?

45.4 The following balances remained in the ledger of OK Ltd after preparation of the income statement for the year ending 31 March 2006

	£000
Inventory	52
Accounts receivable	24
Ordinary share capital	100
8% preference share capital	50
Accounts payable	37
Balance at bank	14
General reserve	30
Retained profits 2005	27
Net profit for the year to 31 March 2006	29
Non-current assets at cost, less depreciation	167

→

The directors propose:

(*i*) a transfer to general reserve of £10,000;

(*ii*) payment of the preference dividend and a 12% dividend on the ordinary shares (Dividends relating to 2005 were paid in March 2006 at the same rates.).

Required:

(*a*) Prepare a statement of changes in equity for the year ended 31 March 2006.

(*b*) Prepare a balance sheet as at 31 March 2006, showing clearly the ordinary shareholders' equity, the total shareholders' funds and the working capital.

45.5A Developing Ltd has an authorised capital of 50,000, 10% preference shares of £1 each and 200,000 ordinary shares of 50p each. After preparation of the income statement for 2004, the following balances remained in the ledger:

	£000
Share capital: fully paid-up:	
Preference	30
Ordinary	80
Loan notes	20
Share premium account	4
General reserve	7
Retained profits 2003	3
Net profit for 2004	27
Non-current assets	140
Current assets	50
Accounts payable	19

The directors recommend:

(*i*) that £10,000 be transferred to general reserve,

(*ii*) payment of the preference dividend,

(*iii*) an ordinary dividend of 15%.

Required:

Prepare a statement of changes in equity for 2004 and a balance sheet as at 31 December 2004.

45.6 Select Ltd is registered with an authorised capital of 300,000 ordinary shares of £1. The following trial balance was extracted from the books of the company on 31 March 2000, after the preparation of the trading account:

	Dr £	*Cr* £
Ordinary share capital, fully paid		200,000
Land and buildings at cost	170,000	
Sundry accounts receivable	38,300	
Furniture and fittings at cost	80,000	
VAT	3,800	
Sundry accounts payable		25,000
Inventory at 31 March 2000	42,000	
Bank	12,000	
Trading account: gross profit		98,050
Office salaries and expenses	25,000	
Accumulated provision for depreciation on furniture and fittings		32,000
Share premium account		20,000
Advertising and selling expenses	5,000	
Bad debts	250	
Allowance for doubtful debts		600
Retained profits		12,000
Directors' fees	11,300	
	387,650	387,650

Required:
Prepare the profit and loss account section of the income statement and a statement of changes in equity for of the company for the year ending 31 March 2010, and balance sheet as at that date, after taking into account the following adjustments:

(*i*) The allowance for doubtful debtors is to be adjusted to £700.
(*ii*) Depreciation is to be provided in respect of furniture and fittings at 10% per annum on cost.
(*iii*) £25,000 is to be transferred from profit and loss to general reserve.
(*iv*) Provide for a proposed dividend on share capital at 10%.

Present the balance sheet in a form which shows the shareholders' equity and the working capital.

45.7A

	£000
Non-current assets, at cost	160
Inventory	40
Bank overdraft	30
Ordinary share capital	100
Accounts payable	45
Retained profits	22
Accumulated depreciation	50
Accounts receivable	47

Required:
(*a*) From the above information, prepare the balance sheet of Budgie Limited indicating clearly the shareholders' funds and working capital.
(*b*) Comment on the capital position disclosed by the balance sheet you have prepared.

45.8 The trial balance extracted from the books of Tailor Times Ltd at 31 December 2003 was as follows:

	£	£
Share capital		200,000
Retained profits 31 December 2002		27,500
Freehold premises at cost	271,000	
Provision for depreciation on freehold premises at 31 December 2002		54,000
Machinery at cost	84,000	
Provision for depreciation on machinery account as at 31 December 2002		21,000
Purchases	563,700	
Sales		925,300
General expenses	14,600	
Wages and salaries	179,400	
Business rates	6,100	
Electricity	4,800	
Bad debts	1,400	
Allowance for doubtful debts at 31 December 2002		1,200
Accounts receivable	74,200	
Accounts payable		68,300
Inventory at 31 December 2002	81,900	
Bank balance	16,200	
	1,297,300	1,297,300

You are given the following additional information:

(*i*) The authorised and issued share capital is divided into 400,000 ordinary shares of 50p each.
(*ii*) Inventory at 31 December 2003, £94,300.

→

(*iii*) Wages and salaries due at 31 December 2003 amounted to £1,800.
(*iv*) Business rates paid in advance at 31 December 2003 amounted to £700.
(*v*) A dividend of £20,000 is proposed for 2003.
(*vi*) The allowance for doubtful debts is to be increased to £1,500.
(*vii*) A depreciation charge is to be made on freehold premises of £25,000 and machinery at the rate of 25 per cent per annum on cost.

Required:
An income statement for 2003 and a balance sheet as at 31 December 2003.

45.9A The following is the trial balance of Tully Ltd as on 31 December 2005:

	Dr £	*Cr* £
Share capital issued: ordinary shares 20p		375,000
Accounts receivable and accounts payable	169,600	74,900
Inventory 31 December 2004	81,300	
Bank	17,900	
Premises at cost	265,000	
Machinery at cost	109,100	
Motor vehicles at cost	34,700	
Depreciation provisions at 31.12.2004:		
Premises		60,000
Machinery		41,400
Motor vehicles		18,200
Sales		975,600
Purchases	623,800	
Motor expenses	4,300	
Repairs to machinery	3,600	
Sundry expenses	2,900	
Wages and salaries	241,500	
Directors' remuneration	82,600	
Retained profits as at 31.12.2004		31,200
General reserve		60,000
	1,636,300	1,636,300

Given the following information, you are to draw up an income statement for the year ending 31 December 2005, and a balance sheet as at that date:

(*i*) Authorised share capital: £500,000 in ordinary shares of 20p.
(*ii*) Inventory at 31 December 2005 £102,400.
(*iii*) Motor expenses owing £280.
(*iv*) Ordinary dividend proposed of 5 per cent.
(*v*) Transfer £7,500 to general reserve.
(*vi*) Provide for depreciation: motor vehicles and machinery 20% on cost; premises 5% on cost.

45.10 You are to draw up an income statement for the year ending 31 December 2002, and a balance sheet as at that date from the following trial balance and details of Partido Ltd:

	Dr	Cr
	£	£
Bank	8,100	
Accounts receivable	321,219	
Accounts payable		237,516
Inventory at 31 December 2001	290,114	
Buildings at cost	800,000	
Equipment at cost	320,000	
Retained profits as at 31 December 2001		136,204
General reserve		120,000
Foreign exchange reserve		20,000
Authorised and issued share capital		800,000
Purchases	810,613	
Sales		1,606,086
Carriage inwards	2,390	
Carriage outwards	13,410	
Salaries	384,500	
Business rates	14,800	
Office expenses	9,100	
Sundry expenses	2,360	
Provisions for depreciation at 31 December 2001:		
Buildings		80,000
Equipment		96,000
Directors' remuneration	119,200	
	3,095,806	3,095,806

Notes at 31 December 2002:

(*i*) Inventory £317,426.
(*ii*) Business rates owing £1,700; Office expenses owing £245.
(*iii*) Dividend of 15 per cent proposed.
(*iv*) Transfers to reserves: General £70,000; Foreign exchange £30,000.
(*v*) Depreciation on cost: Buildings 5 per cent; Equipment 15 per cent.

45.11A Here is the trial balance of Falta Ltd as at 30 April 2005:

	Dr	Cr
	£	£
Share capital: authorised and issued		200,000
Inventory as at 30 April 2004	102,994	
Accounts receivable	227,219	
Accounts payable		54,818
8% loan notes		40,000
Non-current assets replacement reserve		30,000
General reserve		15,000
Retained profits as at 30 April 2004		12,411
Loan note interest	1,600	
Equipment at cost	225,000	
Motor vehicles at cost	57,200	
Bank	4,973	
Cash	62	
Sales		880,426
Purchases	419,211	
Returns inwards	18,400	
Carriage inwards	1,452	
Wages and salaries	123,289	
Rent, business rates and insurance	16,240	
Discounts allowed	3,415	
Directors' remuneration	82,400	
Provision for depreciation at 30 April 2004:		
Equipment		32,600
Motor vehicles		18,200
	1,283,455	1,283,455

→

Given the following information as at 30 April 2005, draw up an income statement and balance sheet for the year to that date:

(*i*) Inventory £111,317.
(*ii*) The share capital consisted of 300,000 ordinary shares of 50p each and 50,000 12 per cent preference shares of £1 each. The dividend on the preference shares was proposed to be paid as well as a dividend of 18 per cent on the ordinary shares.
(*iii*) Accrued: rent £802; Directors' remuneration £6,000.
(*iv*) Loan note interest 1/2 year's interest owing.
(*v*) Depreciation on cost: Equipment 20 per cent; Motor vehicles 25 per cent.
(*vi*) Transfers to reserves: General reserve £5,000; Non-current assets replacement reserve £10,000.

45.12 Burden PLC has an authorised capital of 500,000 ordinary shares of £0.50 each.

(*a*) At the end of its financial year, 31 May 2009, the following balances appeared in the company's books:

	£
Issued capital: 400,000 shares fully paid	200,000
Freehold land and buildings at cost	320,000
Inventory	17,800
10% loan notes	30,000
Trade accounts receivable	6,840
Trade accounts payable	28,500
Expenses prepaid	760
Share premium	25,000
General reserve	20,000
Expenses outstanding	430
Retained profits balance (1 June 2008)	16,200
Bank overdrawn	3,700
Fixtures, fittings and equipment at cost	54,000
provision for depreciation	17,500

The company's income statement had been prepared and revealed a net profit of £58,070. However, this figure and certain balances shown above needed adjustment in view of the following details which had not been recorded in the company's books.

(*i*) It appeared that a trade debtor who owed £300 would not be able to pay. It was decided to write his account off as a bad debt.
(*ii*) An examination of the company's inventory on 31 May 2009 revealed that some items shown in the accounts at a cost of £1,800 had deteriorated and had a resale value of only £1,100.
(*iii*) At the end of the financial year some equipment which had cost £3,600 and which had a net book value of £800 had been sold for £1,300. A cheque for this amount had been received on 31 May 2009.

Required:

1 A statement which shows the changes which should be made to the net profit of £58,070 in view of these unrecorded details.

(*b*) The directors proposed to pay a final dividend of 10% and to transfer £50,000 to general reserve on 31 May 2009.

Required:

For Burden PLC (taking account of *all* the available information)

2 A statement of changes in equity for the year ended 31 May 2009.
3 Two *extracts* from the company's balance sheet as at 31 May 2009, showing in detail:
(*i*) the current assets, current liabilities and working capital
(*ii*) the items which make up the shareholders' funds.

(*c*) The directors are concerned about the company's liquidity position.

Required:

4 **THREE** transactions which will increase the company's working capital. State which balance sheet items will change as a result of each transaction and whether the item will increase or decrease in value.

(*Southern Examining Group: GCSE*)

45.13A The accountant of Fiddles PLC has begun preparing financial statements but the work is not yet complete. At this stage the items included in the trial balance are as follows:

	£000
Land	100
Buildings	120
Plant and machinery	170
Depreciation provision	120
Share capital	100
Retained profits brought forward	200
Accounts receivable	200
Accounts payable	110
Inventory	190
Operating profit	80
Loan notes (16%)	180
Allowance for doubtful debts	3
Bank balance (asset)	12
Suspense	1

Notes (*i*) to (*vii*) below are to be taken into account:

(*i*) The accounts receivable control account figure, which is used in the trial balance, does not agree with the total of the accounts receivable ledger. A contra of £5,000 has been entered correctly in the individual ledger accounts but has been entered on the wrong side of both control accounts.

A batch total of sales of £12,345 had been entered in the double entry system as £13,345, although individual ledger account entries for these sales were correct. The balance of £4,000 on sales returns account has inadvertently been omitted from the trial balance, though correctly entered in the ledger records.

(*ii*) A standing order received from a regular customer for £2,000, and bank charges of £1,000, have been completely omitted from the records.

(*iii*) A debtor for £1,000 is to be written off. The allowance for doubtful debts balance is to be adjusted to 1% of accounts receivable.

(*iv*) The opening inventory figure had been overstated by £1,000 and the closing inventory figure had been understated by £2,000.

(*v*) Any remaining balance on suspense account should be treated as purchases if a debit balance and as sales if a credit balance.

(*vi*) The loan notes were issued three months before the year end. No entries have been made as regards interest.

(*vii*) A dividend of 10% of share capital is to be proposed.

Required:

(*a*) Prepare journal entries to cover items in notes (*i*) to (*v*) above. You are NOT to open any new accounts and may use only those accounts included in the trial balance as given.

(*b*) Prepare financial statements for internal use in good order within the limits of the available information. For presentation purposes all the items arising from notes (*i*) to (*vii*) above should be regarded as material.

(*Association of Chartered Certified Accountants*)

45.14 'The historical cost convention looks backwards but the going concern convention looks forwards.'

Required:

(*a*) Explain clearly what is meant by:
  (*i*) the historical cost convention;
  (*ii*) the going concern convention.

(*b*) Does traditional financial accounting, using the historical cost convention, make the going concern convention unnecessary? Explain your answer fully.

(*c*) Which do you think a shareholder is likely to find more useful – a report on the past or an estimate of the future? Why?

(*Association of Chartered Certified Accountants*)

45.15 The chairman of a public limited company has written his annual report to the shareholders, extracts of which are quoted below.

Extract 1

'In May 2006, in order to provide a basis for more efficient operations, we acquired PAG Warehousing and Transport Ltd. The agreed valuation of the net tangible assets acquired was £1.4 million. The purchase consideration, £1.7 million, was satisfied by an issue of 6.4 million equity shares, of £0.25 per share, to PAG's shareholders. These shares do not rank for dividend until 2007.'

Extract 2

'As a measure of confidence in our ability to expand operations in 2007 and 2008, and to provide the necessary financial base, we issued £0.5 million 8% Redeemable Loan Stock, 2001/2007, 20 million 6% £1 Redeemable Preference Shares and 4 million £1 equity shares. The opportunity was also taken to redeem the whole of the 5 million 11% £1 Redeemable Preference Shares.'

Required:

Answer the following questions on the above extracts.

Extract 1

(*a*) What does the difference of £0.3 million between the purchase consideration (£1.7m) and the net tangible assets value (£1.4m) represent?

(*b*) What does the difference of £0.1 million between the purchase consideration (£1.7m) and the nominal value of the equity shares (£1.6m) represent?

(*c*) What is the meaning of the term 'equity shares'?

(*d*) What is the meaning of the phrase 'do not rank for dividend'?

Extract 2

(*e*) In the description of the loan note issue, what is the significance of
  (*i*) 8%?
  (*ii*) 2001/2007?

(*f*) In the description of the preference share issue, what is the significance of
  (*i*) 6%?
  (*ii*) Redeemable?

(*g*) What is the most likely explanation for the company to have redeemed existing preference shares but at the same time to have issued others?

(*h*) What effect will these structural changes have had on the gearing of the company?[Authors' Note]

(*j*) Contrast the accounting treatment in the company's income statement of the interest due on the loan notes with dividends proposed on the equity shares.

(*k*) Explain the reasons for the different treatments you have outlined in your answer to (*j*) above.

(*Association of Chartered Certified Accountants*)

Authors' Note: Part (*h*) of the question is covered in the text in Section 47.4.

45.16 The directors of the company by which you are employed as an accountant have received the forecast income statement for 2009 which disclosed a net profit for the year of £36,000.

This is considered to be an unacceptably low figure and a working party has been set up to investigate ways and means of improving the forecast profit.

The following suggestions have been put forward by various members of the working party:

(*a*) 'Every six months we deduct income tax of £10,000 from the loan note interest and pay it over to the HM Revenue & Customs. If we withhold these payments, the company's profit will be increased considerably.'

(*b*) 'I see that in the three months August to October 2009 we have forecast a total amount of £40,000 for repainting the exterior of the company's premises. If, instead, we charge this amount as capital expenditure, the company's profit will be increased by £40,000.'

(*c*) 'In November 2009, the replacement of a machine is forecast. The proceeds from the sale of the old machinery should be credited to profit and loss account.'

(*d*) 'There is a credit balance of £86,000 on general reserve account. We can transfer some of this to the income statement to increase the 2009 profit.'

(*e*) 'The company's £1 ordinary shares, which were originally issued at £1 per share, currently have a market value of £1.60 per share and this price is likely to be maintained. We can credit the surplus £0.60 per share to the 2009 profit and loss account.'

(*f*) 'The company's premises were bought many years ago for £68,000, but following the rise in property values, they are now worth at least £300,000. This enhancement in value can be utilised to increase the 2009 profit.'

You are required, as the accounting member of the working party, to comment on the feasibility of each of the above suggestions for increasing the 2009 forecast profit.

(*Association of Chartered Certified Accountants*)

45.17 Explain what you understand by the accounting term 'loan notes' and indicate the circumstances under which a loan note issue would or would not be an appropriate form of financing.

(*Scottish Qualifications Authority*)

You can find a range of additional self-test questions, as well as material to help you with your studies, on the website that accompanies this book at www.pearsoned.co.uk/wood.

chapter 46

Purchase of existing partnership and sole traders' businesses

Learning objectives

After you have studied this chapter, you should be able to:

- enter up the purchase of a business in the purchaser's books
- draw up the balance sheet of the purchaser after taking over the assets and liabilities of the vendor

Introduction

In this chapter, you'll learn how to record the entries in the accounting books when a sole trader or a partnership is taken over by individuals, sole trader businesses, partnerships and companies.

46.1 Types of purchase

You learnt in Chapter 42 that a sole trader's business may be sold as a going concern, rather than being broken up and its assets sold off one by one. The seller normally prefers to sell the business as a going concern, as more money is usually generated arising from the goodwill of the business. Buyers often prefer to purchase a going concern as it saves them all the problems of building markets and reputation.

In that chapter we also looked at the calculation of partnership goodwill when there was a change in the partners. We didn't consider what happens when a partnership is sold as a going concern. This happens relatively frequently. Now that you've learnt how to maintain partnership accounts, we're going to look further at the accounting treatment of sole traders being taken over as going concerns. **While we will focus on sole traders, everything you will learn in this chapter applies also to partnerships when they are taken over as going concerns.**

There are many ways in which a sole trader or a partnership may be taken over as a going concern. For example, an individual may purchase the business of a sole trader (this was the example used at the start of Chapter 42) or a sole trader may take over a partnership.

Think about this for a minute and then write down as many different entities (i.e. a person or persons, or a type of business) as you can think of that might purchase a sole trader or a partnership as a going concern.

46.2 Value of assets bought in purchaser's books

It must not be thought that because the assets bought are shown in the selling firm's books at one value, that the purchaser must record the assets taken over in its own books at the same value – you learnt about recording changes in asset values in Chapter 43 when you looked at revaluation of partnership assets but, in that case, you were looking at what you do when you revalue the assets of a partnership that is continuing in business, not when it is sold.

When a business is sold, the seller has no need to revalue the assets and adjust the values shown in the balance sheet. However, the buyer really ought to show the assets (and liabilities) of the business it has taken over at their current values.

Activity 46.2 Why does the seller not need to revalue the assets of the business and change the values shown in the balance sheet?

The values shown in the books of the purchaser are, therefore, those values at which it is buying the assets, such values being frequently quite different from those shown in the selling firm's books. As an instance of this, the selling firm may have bought premises many years ago for £10,000 which are now worth £50,000. The purchaser buying the premises will obviously have to pay £50,000 for them. It is, therefore, this value that is recorded in the books of the purchaser.

Activity 46.3 Why would an accounting firm want to purchase another accounting firm?

46.3 Goodwill on purchase

As you might have guessed, when the total purchase price is *greater* than the new valuation made by the purchaser of the assets taken over, the difference is goodwill in the eyes of the purchaser. (The seller may have a very different view concerning the value of the assets.) This can be shown as:

	£
Total purchase consideration	90,000
Less New valuation of assets taken over (not usually the same values as per the old balance sheet)	(75,000)
Goodwill	15,000

The revised balance sheet of the purchaser will include goodwill as an intangible asset at the calculated figure. It will also include the assets bought at their new valuations.

46.4 Capital reserve on purchase

Where the total purchase price is *less* than the new valuations of the assets taken over, the difference can either be treated in the purchaser's sole trader or partnership books as **negative goodwill** or as a **capital reserve**. **(Companies *must* reassess the values placed on the assets and liabilities and adjust them so as to eliminate the negative goodwill.)** When treated as a capital reserve, it can be shown as:

	£
Total purchase consideration	55,000
Less New valuation of assets taken over (not usually the same values as per the old balance sheet)	(75,000)
Capital reserve	(20,000)

The new valuations of the assets will appear in the revised balance sheet of the purchaser. Any capital reserve arising will be shown in the capital section of the balance sheet.

46.5 Taking over a sole trader's business

It is easier to start with the takeover of the simplest sort of business unit, that of a sole trader. Some of the balance sheets shown will be deliberately simplified so that the principles involved are not hidden behind a mass of complicated calculations.

To illustrate the takeover of a business, given varying circumstances, the same business will be assumed to be taken over in different ways. The balance sheet of this business is that of A Brown, as shown in Exhibit 46.1.

Exhibit 46.1

A Brown
Balance Sheet as at 31 December 2006

	£	£
Non-current assets		
Fixtures		30,000
Current assets		
Inventory	8,000	
Accounts receivable	7,000	
Bank	1,000	
		16,000
Total assets		46,000
Current liabilities		
Accounts payable		(3,000)
Net assets		43,000
Capital		43,000

1 An individual purchases the business of a sole trader

(a) Assume that the assets and liabilities of A Brown, with the exception of the bank balance, are taken over by D Towers. He is to take over the assets and liabilities at the valuations as shown in Brown's balance sheet. The price to be paid is £52,000.

The opening balance sheet of Towers will be as shown in Exhibit 46.2.

Exhibit 46.2

D Towers
Balance Sheet as at 1 January 2007

	£	£
Non-current assets		
Goodwill		10,000
Fixtures		30,000
		40,000
Current assets		
Inventory	8,000	
Accounts receivable	7,000	
		15,000
Total assets		55,000
Current liabilities		
Accounts payable		(3,000)
Net assets		52,000
Capital		52,000

As £52,000 has been paid for the net assets (assets less liabilities) valued at £30,000 + £8,000 + £7,000 – £3,000 = £42,000, the excess £10,000 represents the amount paid for goodwill.

(**b**) Suppose that, instead of the information just given, the same amount (£52,000) has been paid by Towers, but the assets were taken over at a value of Fixtures £37,000; Inventory £7,500; Accounts receivable £6,500.

The opening balance sheet of D Towers would be as shown in Exhibit 46.3.

Exhibit 46.3

D Towers
Balance Sheet as at 1 January 2007

	£	£
Non-current assets		
Goodwill		4,000
Fixtures		37,000
		41,000
Current assets		
Inventory	7,500	
Accounts receivable	6,500	
		14,000
Total assets		55,000
Current liabilities		
Accounts payable		(3,000)
Net assets		52,000
Capital		52,000

As £52,000 had been paid for net assets valued at £37,000 + £7,500 + £6,500 – £3,000 = £48,000, the excess £4,000 represents the amount paid for goodwill. The other assets are shown at their value to the purchaser, Towers.

2 A partnership acquires the business of a sole trader

Assume instead that the business of Brown had been taken over by M Ukridge and D Allen. The partners are to introduce £30,000 each as capital. The price to be paid for the net assets, other than the bank balance, is £52,000. The purchasers placed the following values on the assets taken over: Fixtures £40,000; Inventory £7,000; Accounts receivable £6,000.

The opening balance sheet of Ukridge and Allen will be as in Exhibit 46.4.

Exhibit 46.4

M Ukridge and D Allen
Balance Sheet as at 1 January 2007

	£	£
Non-current assets		
Goodwill		2,000
Fixtures		40,000
		42,000
Current assets		
Inventory	7,000	
Accounts receivable	6,000	
Bank*	8,000	
		21,000
Total assets		63,000
Current liabilities		
Accounts payable		(3,000)
Net assets		60,000
Capitals		
M Ukridge		30,000
D Allen		30,000
		60,000

***The bank balance is made up of £30,000 + £30,000 introduced by the partners, less £52,000 paid to Brown = £8,000.**

The sum of £52,000 has been paid for net assets of £40,000 + £7,000 + £6,000 − £3,000 = £50,000. This makes goodwill to be the excess of £2,000.

3 Amalgamation of existing sole traders

Now assume that Brown was to enter into partnership with T Owens whose last balance sheet is shown in Exhibit 46.5.

Exhibit 46.5

T Owens
Balance Sheet as at 31 December 2006

	£	£
Non-current assets		
Premises		20,000
Fixtures		5,000
		25,000
Current assets		
Inventory	6,000	
Accounts receivable	9,000	
Bank	2,000	
		17,000
Total assets		42,000
Current liabilities		
Accounts payable		(5,000)
Net assets		37,000
Capital		37,000

(a) If the two traders were to amalgamate all their business assets and liabilities, at the values as shown, the opening balance sheet of the partnership would be as in Exhibit 46.6 (remember that Brown's balance sheet is shown above in Exhibit 46.1).

Exhibit 46.6

A Brown & T Owens
Balance Sheet as at 1 January 2007

	£	£
Non-current assets		
Premises		20,000
Fixtures		35,000
		55,000
Current assets		
Inventory	14,000	
Accounts receivable	16,000	
Bank	3,000	
		33,000
Total assets		88,000
Current liabilities		
Accounts payable		(8,000)
Net assets		80,000
Capitals		
Brown		43,000
Owens		37,000
		80,000

(b) Suppose that instead of both parties agreeing to amalgamation at the asset values as shown, the following values had been agreed to:

Owens' premises to be valued at £25,000 and his inventory at £5,500; other items as per the balance sheet in Exhibit 46.6. Brown's fixtures to be valued at £33,000; his inventory at £7,200 and accounts receivable at £6,400. It is also to be taken that Brown has goodwill of £7,000 whereas Owens' goodwill was considered non-existent. Other items are as per the balance sheet in Exhibit 46.6.

The opening balance sheet will be at the revised figures, and is shown as Exhibit 46.7.

Exhibit 46.7

A Brown & T Owens
Balance Sheet as at 1 January 2007

	£	£
Non-current assets		
Goodwill		7,000
Premises		25,000
Fixtures		38,000
		70,000
Current assets		
Inventory	12,700	
Accounts receivable	15,400	
Bank	3,000	
		31,100
Total assets		101,000
Current liabilities		
Accounts payable		(8,000)
Net assets		93,100
Capitals		
Brown		51,600
Owen		41,500
		93,100

Brown's capital can be seen to be £43,000 + £3,000 (fixtures) – £800 (inventory) – £600 (accounts receivable) + £7,000 (goodwill) = £51,600.

Owens' capital is £37,000 + £5,000 (premises) – £500 (inventory) = £41,500.

4 A limited company acquires the business of a sole trader

In this book, only an elementary treatment of this topic will be considered. More complicated examples will be covered in *Business Accounting 2*.

This time, D Lucas Ltd is taking over Brown's business. For Brown, you need to use the balance sheet shown in Exhibit 46.1. Before the acquisition, the balance sheet of D Lucas Ltd was as shown in Exhibit 46.8.

Exhibit 46.8

D Lucas Ltd
Balance Sheet as at 1 January 2007

	£	£
Non-current assets		
Fixtures		36,000
Current assets		
Inventory	23,000	
Accounts receivable	14,000	
Bank	6,000	
		43,000
Total assets		79,000
Current liabilities		
Accounts payable		(11,000)
Net assets		68,000
Equity		
Preference shares		20,000
Ordinary shares		40,000
Retained profits		8,000
		68,000

(a) Assume that Brown's business had been acquired, except for the bank balance, goodwill being valued at £8,000 and the other assets and liabilities at balance sheet values. D Lucas Ltd is to issue an extra 32,000 £1 ordinary shares at par and 18,000 £1 preference shares at par to Brown, in full settlement of the £50,000 net assets taken over.

Exhibit 46.9 presents the summarised balance sheet of the company before and after the acquisition. (Note that the increase in the accounts payable amount is shown as a negative adjustment as it increases the amount to be deducted from the assets.)

Exhibit 46.9

D Lucas Ltd
Summarised Balance Sheet

	Before	*+ or −*	*After*
	£	£	£
Goodwill	–	+8,000	8,000
Fixtures	36,000	+30,000	66,000
Inventory	23,000	+8,000	31,000
Accounts receivable	14,000	+7,000	21,000
Bank	6,000		6,000
	79,000		132,000
Accounts payable	(11,000)	−3,000	(14,000)
	68,000		118,000
	Before	*+ or −*	*After*
	£	£	£
Capital and reserves			
Preference shares	20,000	+18,000	38,000
Ordinary shares	40,000	+32,000	72,000
Retained profits	8,000		8,000
	68,000		118,000

(**b**) If instead we assume that the business of Brown was acquired as follows:
The purchase price to be satisfied by Brown being given £5,000 cash and issue an extra 50,000 ordinary shares at par and £10,000 loan notes at par. The assets taken over to be valued at Fixtures £28,000; Inventory £7,500; Accounts receivable £6,500. The bank balance is not taken over.

Exhibit 46.10 shows the summarised balance sheet of the company after the acquisition. (Note that both the increase in the accounts payable amount and the loan notes are shown as minus adjustments as they increase the amount to be deducted from the assets.)

Exhibit 46.10

D Lucas Ltd
Summarised Balance Sheet

	Before	*+ or −*	*After*
	£	£	£
Goodwill		+26,000	26,000
Fixtures	36,000	+28,000	64,000
Inventory	23,000	+7,500	30,500
Accounts receivable	14,000	+6,500	20,500
Bank	6,000	−5,000	1,000
	79,000		142,000
Accounts payable	(11,000)	−3,000	(14,000)
	68,000		128,000
Loan notes	–	−10,000	(10,000)
	68,000		118,000
	Before	*+ or −*	*After*
	£	£	£
Capital and reserves			
Preference shares	20,000		20,000
Ordinary shares	40,000	+50,000	90,000
Retained profits	8,000		8,000
	68,000		118,000

Goodwill is calculated: Purchase consideration is made up of ordinary shares £50,000 + loan notes £10,000 + bank £5,000 = £65,000.

Net assets bought are: Fixtures £28,000 + Inventory £7,500 + Accounts receivable £6,500 – Accounts payable £3,000 = £39,000.

Therefore, Goodwill is £65,000 – £39,000 = £26,000.

46.6 Business purchase account

In this chapter, to economise on space and descriptions, only the balance sheets have been shown. However, in the books of the purchaser the purchase of a business should pass through a Business Purchase Account.

This would be as follows:

Business Purchase Account

Debit		*Credit*	
Each liability taken over	(B)	Each asset taken over	
Vendor: net amount of		at values placed on it,	
purchase price	(C)	including goodwill	(A)

Vendor's Account (Name of seller/s)

Debit		*Credit*	
Bank (or share capital)		Amount to be paid	
Amount paid	(D)	for business	(C)

Various Asset Accounts

Debit			
Business purchase (value placed			
on asset taken over)	(A)		

Various Liability Accounts

		Credit	
		Amount of liability	
		taken over	(B)

Bank (or Share Capital)

		Credit	
		Amount paid to vendor	(D)

Learning outcomes

You should now have learnt:

1. That assets purchased when a business is taken over are shown in the purchaser's balance sheet at their valuation, not at the value shown in the closing balance sheet of the seller.
2. That where a greater price is paid than the total valuation of identifiable net assets then the difference is shown as goodwill.
3. That where the purchase price is less than the total valuation of identifiable net assets then the difference is shown as a capital reserve or as negative goodwill (except for limited companies, which *must* remove it by amending the values of its assets and liabilities).
4. That a limited company may use shares or loan notes, as well as cash, to pay for the acquisition of another business.
5. How to enter up the purchase of a business in the purchaser's books.
6. How to draw up the balance sheet of the purchaser after taking over the assets and liabilities of the vendor.

Answers to activities

46.1 These include:

- an individual purchases the business of a sole trader
- an existing sole trader buys the business of another sole trader
- a partnership acquires the business of a sole trader
- a partnership acquires the business of another partnership (this happens quite a lot in accounting partnerships)
- existing businesses of sole traders join together to form a partnership
- a limited company takes over the business of a sole trader
- a limited company takes over the business of a partnership.

46.2 Goodwill. The total amount received less the value of net assets shown in the balance sheet represents the goodwill paid by the purchaser. Adjusting the asset values first simply increases the accounting work to be done by the seller. (In a partnership, the change in value of the assets would need to be shared among the partners, and then followed by a similar series of entries to account for the goodwill.)

46.3 There could be many reasons, including:

- to gain the specialist expertise of the other firm – one may specialise in small business accounts and the other in tax. Combining them removes the need to pay a specialist when they need the expertise the other firm specialises in.
- to save money by relocating the staff of one firm into the offices of the other, enabling the existing offices of the other firm to be sold.

However, the most common reason is to achieve growth. The number of times over the last fifteen years or so that the list by size of the largest accounting firms in the UK has changed is testimony to this drive for market dominance through growth.

Review questions

46.1

V A Fraga
Balance Sheet as at 31 March 2006

	£	£
Non-current assets		
Premises		190,000
Current assets		
Inventory	39,200	
Accounts receivable	18,417	
Bank	828	
		58,445
Total assets		248,445
Current liabilities		
Accounts payable		(23,216)
Net assets		225,229
Capital		225,229

Required:

(*a*) The business of V A Fraga is taken over by T Malloy in its entirety. The assets are deemed to be worth the balance sheet values as shown. The price paid by Malloy is £260,000. Show the opening balance sheet of Malloy.

(*b*) Suppose instead that F Templar had taken over Fraga's business. He does not take over the bank balance, and values premises at £205,000 and inventory at £36,100. The price paid by him is also £260,000. Show the opening balance sheet of Templar.

46.2A I Dodgem's balance sheet as at 31 December 2008 was as follows:

	£	£
Non-current assets		
Premises		55,000
Plant and machinery at cost *less* depreciation		21,000
Fixtures and fittings at cost *less* depreciation		4,000
		80,000
Current assets		
Inventory	17,000	
Trade accounts receivable	9,500	
Cash	4,500	
		31,000
Total assets		111,000
Less Current liabilities		
Trade accounts payable	8,000	
Bank overdraft	15,800	
Expenses owing	200	
		(24,000)
Net assets		87,000
Capital		87,000

An opportunity had arisen for Dodgem to acquire the business of A Swing who is retiring.

A Swing
Balance Sheet as at 31 December 2008

	£	£
Non-current assets		
Premises		25,000
Plant		9,000
Motor vehicle		3,500
		37,500
Current assets		
Inventory	11,000	
Trade accounts receivable	6,000	
Bank	8,000	
Cash	500	
		25,500
Total assets		63,000
Less Current liabilities		
Trade accounts payable		(9,000)
Net assets		54,000
Capital		54,000

Dodgem agreed to take over Swing's premises, plant, inventory, trade accounts receivable and trade accounts payable.

For the purpose of his own records Dodgem valued the premises at £35,000, plant at £6,000 and inventory at £8,000.

The agreed purchase price was £50,000 and in order to finance the purchase Dodgem had obtained a fixed loan for 5 years from his bank, for one half of the purchase price on the condition that he contributed the same amount from his own private resources in cash. The purchase price was paid on 1 January 2009.

Dodgem also decided to scrap some of his oldest plant and machinery which cost £9,000 with depreciation to date £8,000. This was sold for scrap for £300 cash on 1 January 2009. On the same date he bought one new plant for £4,000, paying in cash.

Required:

(*a*) The purchase of business account in I Dodgem's books.

(*b*) I Dodgem's balance sheet as at 1 January 2009 after all the above transactions have been completed.

(*Associated Examining Board*)

46.3 Spectrum Ltd is a private company with an authorised capital of £700,000 divided into shares of £1 each. 500,000 shares have been issued and are fully paid. The company has been formed to acquire small retail shops and establish a chain of outlets.

The company made offers to three sole traders and purchased the businesses run by Red, Yellow and Blue.

The assets acquired, liabilities taken over, and prices paid are listed below:

	Red	*Yellow*	*Blue*
	£	£	£
Premises	75,000	80,000	90,000
Delivery vans	7,000	–	10,000
Furniture and fittings	12,000	13,000	13,000
Inventory	8,000	7,000	12,000
Accounts payable	6,000	8,000	7,000
Purchase price	120,000	130,000	150,000

The company also purchased a warehouse to be used as a central distribution store for £60,000. This has been paid.

Preliminary expenses (formation expenses) of £15,000 have also been paid.

The company took over the three shops outlined above and started trading on 1 January 2002.

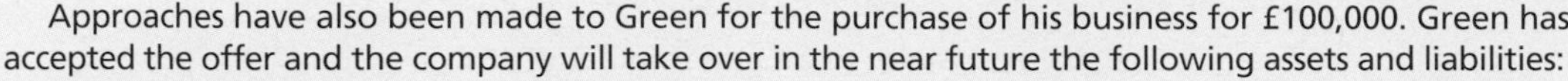

Approaches have also been made to Green for the purchase of his business for £100,000. Green has accepted the offer and the company will take over in the near future the following assets and liabilities:

	£
Premises	70,000
Inventory	18,000
Accounts payable	3,000

The transaction had not been completed on 1 January 2002 and Green was still running his own business.

(*a*) Prepare the opening balance sheet of Spectrum Ltd as at 1 January 2002.
(*b*) How would you advise Spectrum Ltd to finance the purchase of Green's business when the deal is completed?

(Edexcel Foundation, London Examinations (University of London))

46.4 Dinho and Manueli are in partnership sharing profits and losses equally after interest of 10% on each partner's capital account in excess of £100,000. At 31 December 2008, the partnership trial balance was:

	Dr £	*Cr* £
Bank		56,700
Capital accounts: Dinho		194,000
Manueli		123,000
Accounts payable		85,800
Accounts receivable	121,000	
Equipment, at cost	85,000	
Long-term loan		160,000
Freehold property	290,000	
Provision for depreciation on equipment		20,000
Inventory	143,500	
	639,500	639,500

On 31 December 2008, the partnership was converted to a limited company, Bin Ltd. All the partnership assets and liabilities were taken over by the company in exchange for shares in Bin Ltd valued at £304,000. The share capital was allocated so as to preserve the rights previously enjoyed by the partners under their partnership agreement.

The assets and liabilities and shares issued were all entered in the books of Bin Ltd at 31 December. In the company's books, the accounts receivable were recorded at £116,000 and the freehold property was valued at £260,000.

On 1 January 2009, Pa invested £120,000 in the company and was issued shares on the same basis as had been applied when deciding the share allocations to Dinho and Manueli – i.e. as if he had been an equal partner in the partnership.

Pa had previously been an employee of the partnership earning £40,000 per annum. The £120,000 he invested in the company had been earning interest of 6% per annum from the bank. His salary will continue to be paid.

Assume that all profits will be paid as dividends. Ignore taxation.

Required:

(*a*) Prepare the partnership realisation account after the sale of the business to Bin Ltd had been completed and recorded in the partnership books.
(*b*) Prepare Bin Ltd's balance sheet as at 1 January 2009 after the purchase of shares by Pa.
(*c*) Calculate the annual profit that Bin Ltd needs to make before it pays any dividends if Pa is to receive the same amount of income as he was receiving before buying shares in Bin Ltd.

You can find a range of additional self-test questions, as well as material to help you with your studies, on the website that accompanies this book at www.pearsoned.co.uk/wood.

part

7

AN INTRODUCTION TO FINANCIAL ANALYSIS

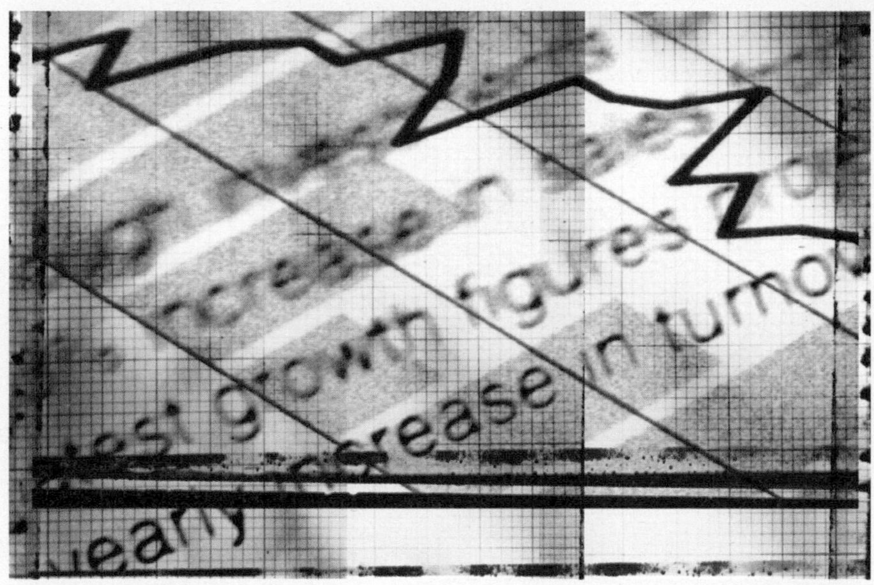

Introduction

This part deals with the interpretation of figures contained in financial statements using ratio analysis.

Chapter 47

An introduction to the analysis and interpretation of accounting statements

Learning objectives

After you have studied this chapter, you should be able to:

- explain how the use of ratios can help in analysing the profitability, liquidity, efficiency and capital structure of businesses
- calculate the main accounting ratios
- interpret the results of calculating accounting ratios
- explain the advantages and disadvantages of the gearing of an organisation being high or low
- explain how the proportion of costs that are fixed and variable impacts profit at different levels of activity
- explain the relevance of IAS 1 and IAS 8, and accounting standards in general, to the preparation of financial statements

Introduction

In this chapter, you'll learn how to calculate and interpret the most commonly used accounting ratios. You'll learn how to assess an organisation's profitability, liquidity, efficiency, and capital structure using ratio analysis. In addition, you'll learn more about IAS 1 (*Presentation of financial statements*) and IAS 8 (*Accounting policies, changes in accounting estimates and errors*), their importance, and the importance of accounting standards in general to the preparation of financial statements.

47.1 The need for ratios

Without ratios, financial statements would be largely uninformative to all but the very skilled. With ratios, financial statements can be interpreted and usefully applied to satisfy the needs of the reader.

For example, let's take the performance of four companies, all dealing in the same type of goods:

	Gross profit	*Sales*
	£	£
Company *A*	200,000	848,000
Company *B*	300,000	1,252,000
Company *C*	500,000	1,927,500
Company *D*	350,000	1,468,400

Suppose you want to know which company gets the 'best' profit. Simply inspecting these figures and trying to decide which performance was the best, and which was the worst, is virtually impossible. To bring the same basis of comparison to each company we need some form of common measure. As you have already seen in Chapter 34, one measure commonly used is a ratio – the gross margin, i.e. the amount of gross profit on sales as a percentage. Applying this to these four companies, we find that their margins are:

	%
Company *A*	23.58
Company *B*	23.96
Company *C*	25.94
Company *D*	23.84

On this basis, Company C with a gross margin of 25.94% or, in other words, £25.94 gross profit per £100 sales, has performed better than the other companies.

47.2 How to use ratios

You can only sensibly compare like with like. There is not much point, for example, in comparing the gross profit percentage of a wholesale chemist with that of a restaurant.

Similarly, figures are only comparable if they have been built up on a similar basis. The sales figures of Company X, which treats items as sales *only when cash is received*, **cannot** be properly compared with those of Company Z, which treats items as sales *as soon as they are invoiced*.

Another instance of this could be that of inventory turnover, which you learnt about in Chapter 34. Let's compare two companies, Company *K* and Company *L*. They are both toy shops so would seem to be comparable. Both companies have annual sales revenue of £400,000. However, the average inventory of *K* is £50,000 whilst that of *L* is £20,000. Cost of sales for both companies is £200,000, so their inventory turnover ratios are:

$$\frac{\text{Cost of sales}}{\text{Average inventory}} \qquad \overset{K}{\frac{200{,}000}{50{,}000} = 4} \qquad \overset{L}{\frac{200{,}000}{20{,}000} = 10}$$

It looks as though *L* has managed to turn its inventory over ten times during the year compared with *K*, four times. Is this true? Well, it depends. Let's imagine that *K* had a financial year end of 30 November, just before Christmas, so toy inventory would be extremely high; that *L* had a year end of 31 January when, following the Christmas sales, its inventory had dropped to the year's lowest level; and that at 30 November both this year and last year *L* also had inventory valued at £50,000. Can you see how the difference in the timing of the year end can affect this ratio significantly?

Ratios therefore need *very* careful handling. They are extremely useful if used and interpreted appropriately, and very misleading otherwise.

47.3 Users of ratios

As you know, there are a great many parties interested in analysing financial statements, including shareholders, lenders, customers, suppliers, employees, government agencies and competitors. Yet, in many respects, they will be interested in different things. There is not, therefore, any definitive, all-encompassing list of points for analysis that would be useful to all these stakeholder groups.

Nevertheless, it is possible to construct a series of ratios that together will provide all of them with something that they will find relevant and from which they can investigate further if necessary.

Ratio analysis is a first step in financially assessing an entity. It removes some of the mystique surrounding the financial statements and makes it easier to pinpoint items which it would be interesting to investigate further.

Exhibit 47.1 shows some categories of ratios and indicates some of the stakeholder groups that would be interested in them.

Exhibit 47.1

Ratio category	*Examples of interested groups*
Profitability	Shareholders, management, employees, creditors, competitors, potential investors
Liquidity	Shareholders, suppliers, creditors, competitors
Efficiency	Shareholders, potential purchasers, competitors
Shareholder	Shareholders, potential investors
Capital structure	Shareholders, lenders, creditors, potential investors

As you will see, **some ratios belong in more than one of these categories.**

47.4 Categories of ratio

Profitability ratios

1 Return on capital employed (ROCE)

This is one of the most important profitability ratios, as it encompasses all the other ratios, and because an adequate return on capital employed is why people invest their money in a business in the first place.

(a) Sole traders

In this chapter, we will use the average of the capital account as the figure for capital employed, i.e. (opening balance + closing balance) ÷ 2.

In Businesses *C* and *D* in Exhibit 47.2, both businesses have made the same amount of net profit, but the capitals employed are different.

Exhibit 47.2

Balance Sheets

	C	*D*
	£	£
Non-current assets + Current assets – Current liabilities	100,000	160,000
Capital accounts		
Opening balance	80,000	140,000
Add Net profit	36,000	36,000
	116,000	176,000
Less Drawings	(16,000)	(16,000)
	100,000	160,000

$$\textbf{Return on capital employed (ROCE)} = \frac{\text{Net profit}}{\text{Capital employed}} \times 100$$

therefore,

C	*D*
$\frac{36,000}{(80,000 + 100,000) \div 2} \times \frac{100}{1} = 40\%$	$\frac{36,000}{(140,000 + 160,000) \div 2} \times \frac{100}{1} = 24\%$

The ratio illustrates that what is important is not simply how much profit has been made but how well the capital has been employed. Business *C* has made far better use of its capital, achieving a return of £40 net profit for every £100 invested, whereas *D* has received only a net profit of £24 per £100.

(b) Limited companies

There is no universally agreed definition of return on capital employed for companies. The main ones used are:

(*i*) return on capital employed sourced from ordinary shareholders
(*ii*) return on capital employed sourced from all long-term suppliers of capital.

Let's now look at each of these:

(*i*) In a limited company this is known as **Return on Owners' Equity (ROOE)** or, more commonly, **Return on Shareholders' Funds (ROSF). From now on, we shall use the second of these terms, 'Return on Shareholders' Funds', but you will need to remember that when you see 'Return on Owners' Equity', it is the same as ROSF.**

The 'Return' is the net profit for the period. The term 'Shareholders' Funds' means the book value of all things in the balance sheet that describe the owners' capital and reserves. 'Owners' are the holders of the **ordinary** share capital. This is calculated: Ordinary Share Capital + all Reserves including Retained Profits.

(*ii*) This is often known simply as 'Return on Capital Employed' (ROCE). The word 'Return' in this case means net profit + any preference share dividends + loan notes and long-term loan interest. The word 'Capital' means Ordinary Share Capital + Reserves including Retained Profits + Preference Shares + Loan notes and Long-term Loans.

Given the following balance sheets and income statements of two companies, *P* Ltd and *Q* Ltd, the calculations of ROSF and ROCE can be attempted:

Balance Sheets as at 31 December

	P Ltd		*Q Ltd*	
	£	£	£	£
	2008	*2009*	*2008*	*2009*
Non-current assets	520,000	560,000	840,000	930,000
Net current assets	280,000	340,000	160,000	270,000
	800,000	900,000	1,000,000	1,200,000
10% loan notes	–	–	(120,000)	(120,000)
	800,000	900,000	880,000	1,080,000
Share capital (ordinary)	300,000	300,000	500,000	500,000
Reserves	500,000	600,000	380,000	580,000
	800,000	900,000	880,000	1,080,000

Income Statements for the year ending 31 December 2009 (extracts)

	P Ltd	*Q Ltd*
	£	£
Net profit	220,000	380,000
Dividends	(120,000)	(180,000)
	100,000	200,000

Return on Shareholders' Funds (ROSF)

P Ltd

$$\frac{220{,}000}{(800{,}000 + 900{,}000) \div 2} \times \frac{100}{1} = 25.9\%$$

Q Ltd

$$\frac{380{,}000}{(880{,}000 + 1{,}080{,}000) \div 2} \times \frac{100}{1} = 38.8\%$$

Return on Capital Employed (ROCE)

P Ltd

Same as ROSF[Note 1] **= 25.9%**

Q Ltd

$$\frac{380{,}000 + 12{,}000^{\text{(Note 2)}}}{(1{,}000{,}000 + 1{,}200{,}000) \div 2} \times \frac{100}{1} = 35.6\%$$

***Note 1*: The return on capital employed by all long-term sources of capital (in *Q Ltd's* case, the shareholders' funds and the debentures) is the same as the ROSF in the case of *P Ltd*, as it has no debentures.**
***Note 2*: The loan note interest (i.e. 10% of £120,000 = £12,000) must be added back, as it was an expense in calculating the £380,000 net profit.**

2 Gross profit as percentage of sales

The formula is:

$$\frac{\text{Gross profit}}{\text{Sales}} \times 100$$

Go back to Chapter 34 to refresh your understanding of gross profit as a percentage of sales.

3 Net profit as a percentage of sales

The formula is:

$$\frac{\text{Net profit}}{\text{Sales}} \times 100$$

Liquidity ratios

You saw earlier in this section that the ratio called 'return on capital employed' is used to provide an overall picture of profitability. It cannot always be assumed, however, that profitability is everything that is desirable. It must be stressed that **accounting is used, not just to calculate profitability, but also to provide information that indicates whether or not the business will be able to pay its creditors, expenses, loans falling due, etc. at the correct times.** Failure to ensure that these payments are covered effectively could mean that the business would have to be closed down. Being able to pay one's debts as they fall due is known as being 'liquid'.

It is also essential that a business is aware if a customer or borrower is at risk of not repaying the amount due. New customers are usually vetted prior to being allowed to trade on credit rather than by cash. For private individuals, there are credit rating agencies with extensive records of the credit histories of many individuals. For a small fee, a company can receive a report indicating whether a new customer might be a credit risk. Similarly, information can be purchased concerning companies that indicates their solvency, i.e. whether they are liable to be bad credit risks.

The difference between these two sources of information is that, while the information on private individuals is based on their previous credit record, that of the companies is generally based on a ratio analysis of their financial statements.

When it comes to the liquidity of a business, both its own ability to pay its debts when due and the ability of its debtors to pay the amount they owe to the business are of great importance. Ratio analysis that focuses upon liquidity (or solvency) of the business generally starts with a look at two ratios (**liquidity ratios**) that are affected most by these two aspects of liquidity, the **current ratio** and the **acid test ratio**.

1 Current ratio

This compares assets which will become liquid within approximately twelve months (i.e. total current assets) with liabilities which will be due for payment in the same period (i.e. total current liabilities) and is intended to indicate whether there are sufficient short-term assets to meet the short-term liabilities.

$$\text{Current ratio} = \frac{\text{Current assets}}{\text{Current liabilities}}$$

When calculated, the ratio may be expressed as either a ratio to 1, with current liabilities being set to 1, or as a 'number of times', representing the relative size of the amount of total current assets compared with total current liabilities.

With *all* ratios, once you have performed the calculation, you need to decide what it tells you. To do so, there is no point in using a universal guide, such as *'the ratio should always lie between 1 : 1 and 2 : 1'*. Any such guidance is at best useless and at worst misleading. Instead, you need to consider the result in its context.

For example:

- What is the norm in this industrial sector? (For example, retailers are often below 1 : 1.)
- Is this company significantly above or below that norm?
- If so, can this be justified after an analysis of the nature of these assets and liabilities, and of the reasons for the amounts of each held?

You need to contextualise *every* ratio you calculate when you are trying to understand what the result means, not just this one.

2 Acid test ratio

This shows that, provided creditors and debtors are paid at approximately the same time, a view might be made as to whether the business has sufficient liquid resources to meet its current liabilities.

$$\text{Acid test ratio} = \frac{\text{Current assets} - \text{inventory}}{\text{Current liabilities}}$$

What is the difference between the formulae for the current ratio and the acid test ratio?

Exhibit 47.3 shows how two businesses may have similar profitability, yet their liquidity positions may be quite different.

Exhibit 47.3

	E		*F*	
	£	£	£	£
Non-current assets		40,000		70,000
Current assets				
Inventory	30,000		50,000	
Accounts receivable	45,000		9,000	
Bank	15,000		1,000	
		90,000		60,000
Total assets		130,000		130,000
Current liabilities: accounts payable		(30,000)		(30,000)
Net assets		100,000		100,000
Capital				
Opening capital		80,000		80,000
Add Net profit		36,000		36,000
		116,000		116,000
Less Drawings		(16,000)		(16,000)
		100,000		100,000

Note: Sales for both *E* and *F* amounted to £144,000. Gross profits for *E* and *F* were identical at £48,000.

Profitability is the same for both businesses. However, there is a vast difference in the liquidity of the two businesses.

Current ratios

$$E = \frac{90,000}{30,000} = 3$$

$$F = \frac{60,000}{30,000} = 2$$

This looks adequate on the face of it, but let's look at the acid test ratio:

Acid test ratios

$$E = \frac{60,000}{30,000} = 2$$

$$F = \frac{10,000}{30,000} = 0.33$$

This reveals that *F* may be in trouble, as it will probably find it difficult to pay its current liabilities on time. **No matter how profitable a business is, unless it is adequately liquid it may fail.**

However, although a business should be adequately liquid, it is possible for it to have too high a current ratio or acid test ratio. If too many resources are being held as current assets, it would make these two ratios appear healthy, but those resources could have been used more profitably – you don't get any interest on inventory! Too high a balance in a current account at the bank also means that resources are being wasted.

Activity 47.2 Why is inventory omitted from the acid test ratio?

Efficiency ratios

1 Inventory turnover

Inventory turnover measures how efficient a business is at maintaining an appropriate level of inventory. When it is not being as efficient as it used to be, or is being less efficient than its competitors, this may indicate that control over inventory levels is being undermined.

A reduction in inventory turnover can mean that the business is slowing down. Inventory may be piling up and not being sold. This could lead to a liquidity crisis, as money may be being taken out of the bank simply to increase inventory which is not then sold quickly enough.

***Note*: In this chapter, we are classifying inventory turnover as an efficiency ratio. It is often also classified as a liquidity ratio.**

For Exhibit 47.3 the cost of sales for each company was £144,000 – £48,000 = £96,000. If opening inventory had been *E* £34,000 and *F* £46,000 then, using the average of the opening and closing inventory, the inventory turnovers would have been:

	E	*F*
$\dfrac{\text{Cost of sales}}{\text{Average inventory}}$	$\dfrac{96{,}000}{(34{,}000 + 30{,}000) \div 2}$	$\dfrac{96{,}000}{(46{,}000 + 50{,}000) \div 2}$
	$= \dfrac{96{,}000}{32{,}000} = 3 \text{ times}$	$= \dfrac{96{,}000}{48{,}000} = 2 \text{ times}$

It appears that *F*'s inventory may be too high, perhaps because it is having difficulty selling it compared with *E*. Or perhaps it is *E* that has a problem obtaining enough inventory. Either way, further investigation is needed.

2 Accounts receivable/sales ratio

The resources tied up in accounts receivable is an important ratio subject. Money tied up unnecessarily in accounts receivable is unproductive money. In the example in Exhibit 47.3 the **accounts receivable/sales ratio** can be calculated for the two companies as:

	E	*F*
Accounts receivable/sales	45,000/144,000 = 1 : 3.2	9,000/144,000 = 1 : 16

This relationship is often translated into the length of time a debtor takes to pay:

E	*F*
$365 \times \dfrac{1}{3.2} = 114 \text{ days}$	$365 \times \dfrac{1}{16} = 22.8 \text{ days}$

Why Company *E* should have allowed so much time for its debtors to pay is a matter for investigation. Possibly the company was finding it harder to sell goods, and to sell at all was eventually forced to sell to customers on long credit terms. It could well be that *E* has no proper credit control system, whereas *F* has an extremely efficient one.

When the ratio is deteriorating (i.e. it is rising) this may signal liquidity problems.

***Note*: In this chapter, we are classifying accounts receivable/sales as an efficiency ratio. Like inventory turnover, it is often also classified as a '*liquidity ratio*', as it can reveal both efficiency and liquidity issues. The next ratio, accounts payable/purchases, also provides this double aspect view.**

3 Accounts payable/purchases ratio

Assuming that purchases for *E* amounted to £92,000 and for *F* £100,000 then the **accounts payable/purchases ratio** can be calculated for each as:

	E	F
Accounts payable/purchases	30,000/92,000 = 1 : 3.07	30,000/100,000 = 1 : 3.3

This also is often translated into the length of time we take to pay our creditors. This turns out to be:

E	F
$365 \times \frac{1}{3.07} = 119$ days	$365 \times \frac{1}{3.3} = 110$ days

Shareholder ratios

These will include the following ratios. **Note that 'price' means the price of the shares on the Stock Exchange.**

1 Earnings per share (EPS)

The formula is:

$$\text{Earnings per share} = \frac{\text{Net profit after interest and tax and preference dividends}}{\text{Number of ordinary shares issued}}$$

This gives the shareholder (or prospective shareholder) a chance to compare one year's earnings with another in terms easily understood. Many people consider EPS to be *the* most important ratio that can be calculated from the financial statements.

2 Price/earnings ratio (P/E)

The formula is:

$$\text{Price/earnings ratio} = \frac{\text{Market price per share}}{\text{Earnings per share}}$$

This puts the price into context as a multiple of the earnings. The greater the P/E ratio, the greater the demand for the shares.

3 Dividend yield

This is found by the formula:

$$\text{Dividend yield} = \frac{\text{Gross dividend per share}}{\text{Market price per share}}$$

This measures the real rate of return by comparing the dividend paid to the market price of a share.

4 Dividend cover

This is found by the formula:

$$\text{Dividend cover} = \frac{\text{Net profit after tax and preference dividends}}{\text{Ordinary dividends paid and proposed}}$$

This gives the shareholder some idea as to the proportion that the ordinary dividends bear to the amount available for distribution to ordinary shareholders. Usually, the dividend is described as being so many times covered by profits made. If, therefore, the dividend is said to be *three times covered*, it means that one-third of the available profits is being distributed as dividends.

Capital structure ratios

Gearing

The relationship of equity shares (ordinary shares) to other forms of long-term financing (long-term loans plus preference shares) can be extremely important. Analysts are, therefore, keen to ascertain a ratio to express this relationship.

There is more than one way of calculating **gearing**. The most widely used method is as follows:

$$\frac{\text{Long-term loans} + \text{Preference shares}}{\text{Ordinary share capital} + \text{Reserves} + \text{Preference shares} + \text{Long-term liabilities}} \times 100$$

This formula is sometimes abbreviated to:

$$\frac{\text{Prior charge capital}}{\text{Total capital}} \times 100$$

which is exactly the same.

Long-term loans include loan notes. Total capital includes preference shares and ordinary shares, all the reserves and long-term loans.

Let's look at the calculations of the gearing of two small companies, *A Ltd* and *B Ltd* in Exhibit 47.4. Both have been trading for five years.

Exhibit 47.4

Year 5: items per balance sheet	*A Ltd*	*B Ltd*
	£	£
10% loan notes	20,000	200,000
10% preference shares	40,000	100,000
Ordinary shares	200,000	40,000
Reserves	140,000	60,000
	400,000	400,000

Gearing ratios:

$$\textit{A Ltd}: \quad \frac{20{,}000 + 40{,}000}{20{,}000 + 40{,}000 + 200{,}000 + 140{,}000} \times \frac{100}{1} = 15\% \text{ (low gearing)}$$

$$\textit{B Ltd}: \quad \frac{200{,}000 + 100{,}000}{200{,}000 + 100{,}000 + 40{,}000 + 60{,}000} \times \frac{100}{1} = 75\% \text{ (high gearing)}$$

Now let us look at how dividends are affected, given the same level of profits made before payment of loan note interest and preference dividends. All the profits made in these years are to be distributed.

A Ltd: Low gearing		*Year 6*	*Year 7*	*Year 8*	*Year 9*
		£	£	£	£
Profits before deducting the following:		40,000	30,000	60,000	80,000
Loan note interest	2,000				
Preference dividend	4,000				
		(6,000)	(6,000)	(6,000)	(6,000)
Profits left for ordinary dividend		34,000	24,000	54,000	74,000
Rate of ordinary dividend		17%	12%	27%	37%

B Ltd: High gearing		*Year 6*	*Year 7*	*Year 8*	*Year 9*
		£	£	£	£
Profits before deducting the following:		40,000	30,000	60,000	80,000
Loan note interest	20,000				
Preference dividend	10,000				
		(30,000)	(30,000)	(30,000)	(30,000)
Profits left for ordinary dividend		10,000	–	30,000	50,000
Rate of ordinary dividend		25%	–	75%	125%

A company with a high percentage gearing ratio is said to be *high geared*, whereas one with a low percentage gearing is said to be *low geared*. As you can see from the above example, the proportionate effect gearing has upon ordinary shareholders is far greater in a high geared company, ranging from 0 to 125 per cent dividend for B Ltd, whilst the range of ordinary dividends for A Ltd varied far less and lay between 17 and 37 per cent.

A high rate of debt (i.e. long-term loans and preference shares) means that in bad times very little might be left over for ordinary shareholders after payment of interest on the debt items and also preference dividends. In good times, however, the ordinary shareholders will enjoy a far higher return than in a low geared company.

This means that people investing in ordinary shares in a high geared company are taking a far greater risk with their money than if they had invested instead in a low geared company. It would have only required a drop of profits of £5,000 in Year 6 for B Ltd to find that there would be no ordinary dividends at all for Years 6 and 7. Such a drop in Year 6 for A Ltd would still have allowed a dividend of 12 per cent for both of Years 6 and 7. Investors therefore who are prepared to risk their money in the hope of large dividends would have chosen B Ltd, whilst those who wanted to cut down on their risk and be more certain about receiving dividends would choose A Ltd.

Changing the gearing of a company

The management might decide that for various reasons it would like to change the gearing of the company. It can do this as follows:

To reduce gearing
1 By issuing new ordinary shares
2 By redeeming loan notes
3 By retaining profits

To increase gearing
1 By issuing loan notes
2 By buying back ordinary shares in issue
3 By issuing new preference shares

Such changes will be influenced by what kinds of investors the company wishes to attract. A highly geared company will attract risk-taking buyers of ordinary shares, whilst a low geared company will be more attractive to potential ordinary shareholders who wish to minimise risk.

Other ratios

There are a large number of other ratios which could be used, far more than can be mentioned in a textbook such as this. It will depend on the type of company exactly which ratios are the most important and it is difficult to generalise too much.

Different users of the financial statements will want to use the ratio analysis which is of vital concern to them. If we can take as an example a bank which lends money to a company, it will want to ensure two things:

(*a*) that the company will be able to pay interest on the loan as it falls due; *and*
(*b*) that it will be able to repay the loan on the agreed date.

The bank is therefore interested in:

(*a*) short-term liquidity, concerning payment of loan interest; and
(*b*) long-term solvency for eventual repayment of the loan.

Possible ratios for each of these could be:

(*a*) ***Short-term liquidity ratios***, mainly the *acid test ratio* and the *current ratio*, already described.
(*b*) ***Long-term solvency ratios***, which might include:
   (i) ***Operating profit/loan interest.*** This indicates how much of the profits are taken up by paying loan interest. Too great a proportion would mean that the company was borrowing more than was sensible, as a small fall in profits could mean the company operating at a loss with the consequent effect upon long-term solvency.
   (ii) ***Total external liabilities/shareholders' funds.*** This ratio measures how much financing is done via share capital and retained profits, and how much is from external sources. Too high a proportion of external liabilities could bring about long-term solvency problems if the company's profit-making capacity falls by a relatively small amount, as outside liabilities still have to be met.
   (iii) ***Shareholders' funds/total assets (excluding intangibles).*** This highlights the proportion of assets financed by the company's own funds. Large falls in this ratio will tend to show a difficulty with long-term solvency. Similarly, investors will want to see ratios suitable for their purposes, which are not the same as those for the bank. These will not only be used on a single company comparison, but probably with the average of the same type of ratios for other companies in the same industry.

47.5 The investor: choosing between shares and loan notes

The choice of an investor will always be related to the amount of acceptable risk. We can list the possible investments under the headings of risk.

Lowest risk

Loan note holders have their interest paid to them whether or not profits are made. This contrasts with shares, both preference and ordinary, where there have to be profits available for distribution as dividends.

In addition, should there be insufficient cash funds available to pay loan note interest, many loan notes give their holders the right to sell off some or all of the assets of the company, and to recoup the amount of their loan notes before anyone else has a claim. Such an investment does not have as much security as, say, government stocks, but it certainly ranks above the shares of that same company.

Medium risk

Preference shareholders have their dividends paid after the loan note interest has been paid, but before the ordinary shareholders. They still are dependent upon profits being available for distribution. If they are of the cumulative variety then any shortfall can be carried forward to future years and paid before any ordinary dividends are taken.

Highest risk

Ordinary shareholders have the highest risk. They must give way to both loan note holders and to preference shareholders for interest and dividends. However, should the remaining profits for distribution be very high then they may get a high return on their money.

47.6 Trend figures

In examinations, a student is often given just one year's accounting figures and asked to comment on them. Obviously, lack of space on an examination paper may preclude several years' figures being given; also, the student lacks the time to prepare a comprehensive survey of several years' financial statements.

In real life, however, it would be extremely stupid for anyone to base decisions on just one year's financial statements, if more information was available. What is important for a business is not just what, say, accounting ratios are for one year, but what the trend has been.

Given two similar types of businesses *G* and *H*, both having existed for five years, if both of them had exactly the same ratios in Year 5, are they both equally desirable as investments? Given one year's accounts it may appear so, but if one had all the five years' figures it may not give the same picture, as Exhibit 47.5 illustrates.

Exhibit 47.5

	Years	1	2	3	4	5 (current)
Gross profit as % of sales	*G*	**40**	**38**	**36**	**35**	**34**
	H	30	32	33	33	34
Net profit as % of sales	*G*	**15**	**13**	**12**	**12**	**11**
	H	10	10	10	11	11
Net profit as % of capital employed	*G*	**13**	**12**	**11**	**11**	**10**
	H	8	8	9	9	10
Current ratio	*G*	**3**	**2.8**	**2.6**	**2.3**	**2.0**
	H	1.5	1.7	1.9	1.0	2.0

From these figures *G* appears to be the worse investment for the future, as the trend appears to be downwards. If the trend for *G* is continued it could be in a very dangerous financial situation in a year or two. Business *H*, on the other hand, is strengthening its position all the time.

Of course, it would be ridiculous to assert that *H* will continue on an upward trend. One would have to know more about the business to be able to judge whether or not that could be true.

However, given all other desirable information, trend figures would be an extra important indicator.

47.7 Fixed and variable costs

Some costs will remain constant whether activity increases or falls, at least within a given range of change of activity. These costs are called **fixed costs**. An example of this would be the rent of a shop which would remain at the same figure whether sales increased 10 per cent or fell 10 per cent. The same would remain true of such things as rates, fire insurance and so on.

Wages of shop assistants could also remain constant in such a case. If, for instance, the shop employed two assistants, then it would probably keep the same two assistants, on the same wages, whether sales increased or fell by 10 per cent.

Of course, such fixed costs can only be viewed as fixed in the short term. If sales doubled, then the business might well need a larger shop or more assistants. A larger shop would also certainly mean higher rates, higher fire insurance and so on, and with more assistants the total wage bill would be larger.

Variable costs, on the other hand, will change with swings in activity. Suppose that wrapping materials are used in the shop, then an increase in sales of 10 per cent should see 10 per cent more wrapping materials used. Similarly an increase of 10 per cent of sales, if all sales are despatched by parcel post, should see delivery charges increase by 10 per cent.

Some costs could be part fixed and part variable. Suppose that because of an increase in sales of 10 per cent, telephone calls made increased by 10 per cent. With telephone bills the cost is often in two parts, one for the rent of the phone line and the second part corresponding to the actual number of calls made. The rental charge would not change in such a case, and therefore this part of telephone expense would be 'fixed' whereas the calls part of the cost could increase by 10 per cent.

This means that the effect of a percentage change in activity could result in a greater or lesser percentage change in net profit, because the fixed costs (within that range of activity) may not alter.

Exhibit 47.6 shows the change in net profit in Business *A*, which has a low proportion of its expenses as 'fixed' costs, and in Business *B*, in which the 'fixed' costs are a relatively high proportion of its expenses.

Exhibit 47.6

Business A

			(a) If sales fell 10%		*(b)* If sales rose 10%	
	£	£	£	£	£	£
Sales		500,000		450,000		550,000
Less Cost of goods sold		(300,000)		(270,000)		(330,000)
Gross profit		200,000		180,000		220,000
Less Expenses:						
Fixed	30,000		30,000		30,000	
Variable	130,000		117,000		143,000	
		(160,000)		(147,000)		(173,000)
Net profit		40,000		33,000		47,000

Business B

			(a) If sales fell 10%		*(b)* If sales rose 10%	
	£	£	£	£	£	£
Sales		500,000		450,000		550,000
Less Cost of goods sold		(300,000)		(270,000)		(330,000)
Gross profit		200,000		180,000		220,000
Less Expenses:						
Fixed	120,000		120,000		120,000	
Variable	40,000		36,000		44,000	
		(160,000)		(156,000)		(164,000)
Net profit		40,000		24,000		56,000

The comparison of percentage changes in net profit therefore works out as follows:

	Business *A*	Business *B*
Decrease of 10% sales:		
$\frac{\textbf{Reduction in profit}}{\textbf{Original profit}} \times \frac{100}{1}$	$\frac{7{,}000}{40{,}000} \times \frac{100}{1} = 17.5\%$	$\frac{16{,}000}{40{,}000} \times \frac{100}{1} = 40\%$
Increase of 10% sales:		
$\frac{\textbf{Increase in profit}}{\textbf{Original profit}} \times \frac{100}{1}$	$\frac{7{,}000}{40{,}000} \times \frac{100}{1} = 17.5\%$	$\frac{16{,}000}{40{,}000} \times \frac{100}{1} = 40\%$

You can see that a change in activity in Business *B*, which has a higher fixed expense content, results in greater percentage changes in profit: 40% in *B* compared with 17.5% in *A*.

47.8 Limitations of accounting statements

Financial statements are only partial information. They show the reader of them, in financial terms, what has happened *in the past*. This is better than having no information at all, but much more information is needed to fully understand the present situation.

First, it is impossible to sensibly compare two businesses which are completely unlike one another. To compare a supermarket's figures with those of a chemical factory would be rather pointless. It would be like comparing a lion with a lizard.

Second, there are a whole lot of factors that the past-focused financial statements do not disclose. The desire to keep to the money measurement concept, and the desire to be objective, both dealt with in Chapter 10, exclude a great deal of desirable information.

Go back to Chapter 10 to refresh your understanding of the money measurement concept and objectivity.

Some typical desirable information can be listed but, beware, the list is indicative rather than exhaustive.

(*a*) What are the future plans of the business? Without knowing this, making an investment in a business would be sheer guesswork.
(*b*) Has the firm got good quality staff?
(*c*) Is the business situated in a location desirable for such a business? A shipbuilding business situated a long way up a river which was becoming unnavigable, to use an extreme example, could soon be in trouble.
(*d*) What is its position as compared with its competitors? A business manufacturing a single product, which has a foreign competitor which has just invented a much improved product which will capture the whole market, is obviously in for a bad time.
(*e*) Will future government regulations affect it? Suppose that a business which is an importer of goods from Country X, which is outside the EU, finds that the EU is to ban all imports from Country *X*?
(*f*) Is its plant and machinery obsolete? If so, the business may not have sufficient funds to be able to replace it.
(*g*) Is the business of a high-risk type or in a relatively stable industry?
(*h*) Has the business got good customers? A business selling largely to Country *Y*, which is getting into trouble because of shortage of foreign exchange, could soon lose most of its trade. Also if one customer was responsible for, say, 60 per cent of sales, then the loss of that one customer would be calamitous.
(*i*) Has the business got good suppliers of its needs? A business in wholesaling could, for example, be forced to close down if manufacturers decided to sell direct to the general public.
(*j*) Problems concerned with the effects of distortion of accounting figures caused by inflation (or deflation).

You can see that the list would have to be an extremely long one if it was intended to cover all possibilities.

47.9 IAS 1: *Presentation of financial statements*

The way in which accounting information is presented in financial statement is governed by IAS 1. It lays down the statements that must be produced and what they contain. It will be covered in detail in *Business Accounting 2*. Some aspects were covered briefly in Section 45.16.

47.10 IAS 8: *Accounting policies, changes in accounting estimates and errors*

Users of financial statements issued by organisations want to analyse and evaluate the figures contained within them. They cannot do this effectively unless they know which accounting policies have been used when preparing such statements.

Accounting policies

Accounting policies are defined in IAS 8 as:

> *the specific principles, bases, conventions, rules and practices applied by an entity in preparing and presenting financial statements.*

Accounting policies, therefore, define the processes whereby transactions and other events are reflected in the financial statements. The accounting policies selected should enable the financial statements to give a true and fair view and should be consistent with accounting standards and with relevant legislation.

When selecting an accounting policy, its appropriateness should be considered in the context of four characteristics that financial information must possess:

- **Relevance** – Does it produce information that is useful for assessing stewardship and for making economic decisions?
- **Reliability** – Does it reflect the substance of the transaction and other events that have occurred? Is it free of bias, i.e. neutral? Is it free of material error? If produced under uncertainty, has prudence been exercised?
- **Comparability** – Can it be compared with similar information about the entity for some other period or point in time?
- **Understandability** – Is it capable of being understood by users who have a reasonable knowledge of business and economic activities and accounting?

The financial information must also reflect economic reality and be neutral, prudent and complete. In addition, accounting policies must be applied consistently to 'similar transactions, events and conditions'.

Changes to accounting policies

Changes can only be made if required by a standard or if they result in reliable and more relevant information. Where the change is voluntary, it must be applied retrospectively and items restated.

Estimation techniques

Estimation techniques are the methods adopted in order to arrive at estimated monetary amounts for items that appear in the financial statements. Changes in accounting estimates relate to the carrying amount of an asset or liability or the amount of the periodic consumption of an asset. Where a change in an accounting estimate gives rise to changes in assets or liabilities, or relates to an item of equity, it is recognised by adjusting the carrying amount of the asset, liability or equity item in the period in which the change of estimate occurred.

From your knowledge of accounting, what do you think these methods may include? Think about this for a minute and then write down as many examples of estimation techniques as you can think of.

Examples of accounting policies

- The treatment of gains and losses on disposals of non-current assets – they could be applied to adjust the depreciation charge for the period, or they may appear as separate items in the financial statements.
- The classification of overheads in the financial statements – for example, some indirect costs may be included in the trading account section of the income statement, or they may be included in administration costs in the profit and loss account section of the income statement.
- The treatment of interest costs incurred in connection with the construction of non-current assets – these could be charged to profit and loss as a finance cost, or they could be capitalised and added to the other costs of creating the fixed assets (this is permitted by the relevant accounting standard).

Identifying whether an accounting policy has changed

This is done by considering whether any of three aspects have changed:

- **Recognition** – some items may be recognised in more than one way. For example, expenditure on developing new products may be recognised either as a profit and loss expense or as an asset in the balance sheet.
- **Presentation** – how something is presented in the financial statements. For example, where certain indirect costs appear in the profit and loss account.
- **Measurement basis** – the monetary aspects of the items in the financial statements, such as the basis of valuation of inventory, say FIFO or LIFO.

If any of these three aspects have changed, this represents a change in accounting policy. If they haven't, something else has occurred, for example, the estimation technique in use. If depreciation was changed from straight line to reducing balance this would be **a change in estimation technique**, not a change in accounting policy. On the other hand, a decision to switch from valuing stock using FIFO to LIFO would constitute **a change in accounting policy** as the measurement basis would have changed.

47.11 Further thoughts on concepts and conventions

In Chapter 10, you were introduced to the concepts and conventions used in accounting. Since then, further chapters have consolidated your knowledge on specific points.

In recent years there has been a considerable change in the style of examinations in accounting at all levels. At one time nearly every examination question was purely computational, requiring you to prepare financial statements, draft journal entries, extract a trial balance and so on. Now, *in addition* to all that (which is still important) there are quite a lot of questions asking such things as:

- **Why do we do it?**
- **What does it mean?**
- **How does it relate to the concepts and conventions of accounting?**

Such questions depend very much on the interests and ingenuity of examiners. They like to set questions worded to find out those who can understand and interpret financial information, and eliminate those who cannot and simply try to repeat information learned by rote.

The examiners will often draw on knowledge from any part of the syllabus. It is therefore impossible for a student (or an author) to guess exactly how examiners will select questions and how they will word them.

An example of this is where the examiner could ask you to show how different concepts contradict one another. Someone who has just read about the concepts, and memorised them, could not answer this unless they had thought further about it. **Think about whether or not you could have answered that question before you read further.**

One instance is the use of the concept of consistency. Basically it says that one should keep to the same method of entering an item each year. Yet if the net realisable value of stock is less than cost, then the normal method of showing it at cost should be abandoned and the net realisable value used instead. Thus, at the end of one period, inventory may be shown at cost and at the end of the next period it will be shown at net realisable value. In this case the concept of prudence has overridden the concept of consistency.

Another instance of this is the practice of calculating profit based on sales whether they have been paid for or not. If the prudence concept were taken to extremes, then profit would only be calculated on a sale when the sale had been paid for. Instead, the realisation concept has overridden the prudence concept so you recognise a sale when it is reasonably certain that it will be paid for.

Review questions 47.11 to 47.20 are typical examination questions which obviously relate to concepts and conventions, and to general understanding of the subject.

47.12 Some other accounting standards

As well as the accounting standards that you have read about in this book, there are some other standards which may appear in your examinations. We will cover them briefly here.

IAS 38: *Intangible assets*

Money spent on research and development presents a problem for accountants. You could argue that:

- Such costs are incurred so that profits can be earned in the future, and should therefore be carried forward to those future periods.
- Just because you have incurred such costs, you cannot be certain about future profitability occurring. It should therefore be written off as an expense in the period when the costs are incurred.

The costs can be divided between:

- **Research.** This is carried out to advance knowledge or application of knowledge.

Examples include:

- searching for new knowledge
- search for revaluation of and final selection of applications of research findings or other knowledge
- search for alternative materials, devices, products, processes, systems or services
- formulation, design, evaluation and final selection of possible alternatives for new and improved materials, devices, products, processes, systems or services.

- **Development.** Work undertaken to develop research that creates an asset that will generate probable future economic benefits.

IAS 38 requires that all research expenditure must be recognised as an expense when it is incurred. However, development costs, subject to satisfying technical and commercial feasibility being confirmed, may be capitalised as an intangible asset and carried forward to future periods.

IAS 10: *Events after the balance sheet date*

The balance sheet is supposed to reflect the financial position of an organisation at the balance sheet date. However, between the balance sheet date and the date when the financial statements are authorised for issue, events may occur which mean that the financial statements will need to be amended.

The events can be divided between:

- **Adjusting events.** When these exist, the financial statements must be amended. Examples would include settlement of a court case, information indicating that an asset was impaired at the balance sheet date, and the discovery of fraud or errors which show that the financial statements are incorrect.
- **Non-adjusting events.** These do not lead to amendments to the financial statements, but they may be shown as notes accompanying the financial statements. Examples would include changes in the market value of investments and dividends proposed.

IAS 37: *Provisions, contingent liabilities and contingent assets*

A provision may be defined as:

a liability of uncertain timing or amount.

A provision should only be recognised when an entity has a present obligation as a result of a past event *and* it is probable that an outflow of resources embodying economic benefits will have to occur *and* a reasonable estimate can be made of the amount involved.

A contingent liability may be defined as:

either a possible obligation arising from past events whose existence will be confirmed only by the occurrence of one or more uncertain future events not wholly within the entity's control; or a present obligation that arises from past events but is not recognised because it is not probable that an outflow of resources embodying economic benefits will be required to settle the obligation or the amount of the obligation cannot be measured with sufficient reliability.

An example of this could be where a legal action is being carried on, but the case has not yet been decided. For instance, a company may have been sued for £10 million damages, but the case is not yet over. The company may or may not have to pay the damages, but the case is so complex that it has no way of knowing.

A contingent asset may be defined as:

a possible asset arising from past events whose existence will be confirmed only by the occurrence or non-occurrence of one or more uncertain events not wholly within the entity's control.

Neither contingent liabilities nor contingent assets should be recognised. This is consistent with the prudence concept. A contingent liability should be disclosed.

Small and medium-sized entities and accounting standards

The UK has had an FRSSE (Financial Reporting Standard for Smaller Entities) for many years. It provides a simplified version of the body of UK accounting standards and is for use by 'smaller entities', i.e. small companies and other organisations that would be classified as 'small' if they were companies. However, no such standard exists under International GAAP. In February 2007, the IASB issued an exposure draft, IFRS for Small and Medium Sized Entities. It reduces disclosure requirements and simplifies recognition and measurement requirements and is only 15 per cent of the length of the extant body of international standards. It is likely that an IFRS will be issued sooner rather than later.

Learning outcomes

You should now have learnt:

1. That comparing the trends to see if the ratios are getting better or worse as each period passes is essential for proper control. Prompt action needs to be taken where the trend in a ratio is deteriorating.
2. The importance of interpreting ratios in their context: that is, against those of other similar businesses or against the same ratios calculated for the same organisation using data from other time periods.
3. That a business must be both profitable *and* sufficiently liquid to be successful. One factor without the other can lead to serious trouble.
4. That careful credit control to ensure that the accounts receivable/sales ratio is not too high is usually essential to the well-being of any business.
5. That gearing affects the risk factor for ordinary share investors. High gearing means greater risk whilst low gearing means lower risks.
6. How to calculate and interpret the most commonly used ratios.
7. The relevance of ratio analysis to an assessment of liquidity, efficiency, profitability and capital structure.
8. That the relative amounts of fixed and variable costs can affect profit significantly when there are swings in business activity.
9. The importance of IAS 1 and IAS 8, and accounting standards in general, to the preparation of financial statements.

Answers to activities

47.1 The only difference in the items involved between the two ratios is that the acid test (or 'quick') ratio does not include inventory. Otherwise, it is identical to the current ratio, comparing current assets *other than inventory* to current liabilities.

47.2 Inventory is omitted as it is considered to be relatively illiquid, because, depending on prevailing and future market forces, it may be impossible to convert to cash in a relatively short time.

47.3 All depreciation methods and methods used to estimate doubtful debts are the main ones we have encountered so far in this book. However, we've also looked at asset revaluation, another aspect of accounting for which the methods adopted in arriving at the valuation would be considered estimation techniques. Basically, any method used to arrive at an *estimated* figure shown in the financial statements is an estimation technique. So, to answer the question fully, you need to make a list of all those items that appear in financial statements that are estimates. The methods used to arrive at the value used for those figures are all estimation techniques. This would include, for example, the method used in order to arrive at the proportion of an electricity bill spanning the period end that belongs in the period for which the financial statements are being prepared. More obviously estimates may be required for bad debts, inventory obsolescence, and the useful lives or consumption pattern of non-current assets.

Review questions

47.1 You are to study the following financial statements for two furniture stores and then answer the questions which follow.

Financial Statements

	X		Y	
	£	£	£	£
Income Statements				
Sales		555,000		750,000
Less Cost of goods sold				
Opening inventory	100,000		80,000	
Add Purchases	200,000		320,000	
	300,000		400,000	
Less Closing inventory	(60,000)	(240,000)	(70,000)	(330,000)
Gross profit		315,000		420,000
Less Depreciation	5,000		15,000	
Wages, salaries and commission	165,000		220,000	
Other expenses	45,000	(215,000)	35,000	(270,000)
Net profit		100,000		150,000
Balance sheets				
Non-current assets				
Equipment at cost	50,000		100,000	
Less Depreciation to date	(40,000)	10,000	(30,000)	70,000
Current assets				
Inventory	60,000		70,000	
Accounts receivable	125,000		100,000	
Bank	25,000	210,000	12,500	182,500
Total assets		220,000		252,500
Current liabilities				
Accounts payable		(104,000)		(100,500)
Net assets		116,000		152,000
Financed by:				
Capitals				
Balance at start of year		76,000		72,000
Add Net profit		100,000		150,000
		176,000		222,000
Less Drawings		(60,000)		(70,000)
Total capital		116,000		152,000

Required:

(*a*) Calculate the following ratios for each business:

(*i*) gross profit as percentage of sales;
(*ii*) net profit as percentage of sales;
(*iii*) expenses as percentage of sales;
(*iv*) inventory turnover;
(*v*) rate of return of net profit on capital employed (use the average of the capital account for this purpose);
(*vi*) current ratio;
(*vii*) acid test ratio;
(*viii*) accounts receivable/sales ratio;
(*ix*) accounts payable/purchases ratio.

(*b*) Drawing upon all your knowledge of accounting, comment upon the differences and similarities of the accounting ratios for *A* and *B*. Which business seems to be the most efficient? Give possible reasons.

→

47.2A Study the following financial statements of two companies and then answer the questions which follow. Both companies are stores selling carpets and other floorcoverings. The values shown are in £000s.

	Spreadlight Ltd		*Easylawn Ltd*	
	£000	£000	£000	£000
Income Statements				
Sales		2,500		1,600
Less Cost of goods sold				
Opening inventory	190		110	
Add Purchases	2,100		1,220	
	2,290		1,330	
Less Closing inventory	(220)		(160)	
		(2,070)		(1,170)
Gross profit		430		430
Less Expenses				
Wages and salaries	180		130	
Directors' remuneration	70		120	
Other expenses	14		10	
		(264)		(260)
Net profit		166		170
Balance sheets				
Non-current assets				
Equipment at cost	200		50	
Less Depreciation to date	(80)		(20)	
		120		30
Vans	64		48	
Less Depreciation to date	(26)		(16)	
		38		32
		158		62
Current assets				
Inventory	220		160	
Accounts receivable	104		29	
Bank	75		10	
		399		199
Total assets		557		261
Less Current liabilities				
Accounts payable		(189)		(38)
Net assets		368		223
Equity				
Issued share capital		200		100
Reserves				
General reserve	68		35	
Retained profits	100		88	
		168		123
Total equity		368		223

Notes:
Spreadlight paid a dividend of £140,000 during the year and transferred £30,000 to a general reserve of the year end. Easylawn paid a dividend of £112,000 during the year and transferred £30,000 to a general reserve of the year end. The retained profits brought forward at the start of the year were: Spreadlight £104,000; Easylawn £60,000.

Required:

(*a*) Calculate the following ratios for both Spreadlight Ltd and Easylawn Ltd:

(*i*) gross profit as percentage of sales;
(*ii*) net profit as percentage of sales;
(*iii*) expenses as percentage of sales;
(*iv*) inventory turnover;
(*v*) rate of return of net profit on capital employed (for the purpose of this question only, take capital as being total of share capitals + reserves at the balance sheet date);
(*vi*) current ratio;
(*vii*) acid test ratio;
(*viii*) accounts receivable/sales ratio;
(*ix*) accounts payable/purchases ratio.

(*b*) Comment briefly on the comparison of each ratio as between the two companies. State which company appears to be the most efficient, giving what you consider to be possible reasons.

47.3 Durham Limited had an authorised capital of £200,000 divided into 100,000 ordinary shares of £1 each and 200,000 8% preference shares of 50p each. The following balances remained in the accounts of the company after the income statement had been prepared for the year ending 30 April 2009.

	Debit £	*Credit* £
Premises at cost	86,000	
General reserve		4,000
Ordinary shares: fully paid		100,000
8% Preference shares: fully paid		50,000
Electricity		100
Cash at bank	13,100	
Retained profits 1 May 2008		14,500
Accounts receivable and accounts payable	20,000	12,900
Net profit (year ending 30 April 2009)		16,500
Machinery and plant at cost	60,000	
Provision for depreciation on machinery and plant		40,000
Inventory	60,000	
Allowance for doubtful debts		4,000
Insurance	900	
Preference share dividend paid	2,000	
	242,000	242,000

The Directors have recommended:
a transfer of £5,000 to general reserve;
an ordinary dividend of £0.15p per share; and that the unpaid preference share dividend be paid.

(*a*) Prepare an appropriate extract from the statement of changes in equity for year ending 30 April 2009.

(*b*) Prepare the balance sheet as at 30 April 2009, in a form which shows clearly the **working capital** and the **shareholders' funds**.

(*c*) Identify and calculate:

(*i*) one ratio indicating the firm's profitability;
(*ii*) two ratios indicating the firm's liquidity position.

(*d*) Make use of your calculations in (*c*) above to comment on the firm's financial position.

(*e*) Name two points of comparison which are not available from the information above in this question but which could make your comments in (*d*) above more meaningful.

(*Edexcel Foundation, London Examinations: GCSE*)

→

47.4 The summarised accounts of Hope (Eternal Springs) Ltd for the years 2008 and 2009 are given below.

Income Statements for the years ending 31 December

	2008		2009	
	£000	£000	£000	£000
Sales		200		280
Less Cost of sales		(150)		(210)
Gross profit		50		70
Less				
Administration expenses	38		46	
Loan note interest	–		4	
		(38)		(50)
Net profit		12		20

Balance Sheets as at 31 December

	2008		2009	
	£000	£000	£000	£000
Non-current assets at cost *less* depreciation		110		140
Current assets				
Inventory	20		30	
Accounts receivable	25		28	
Bank	–		5	
		45		63
Total assets		155		203
Current liabilities				
Accounts payable	15		12	
Bank	10		–	
	25		12	
Non-current liabilities				
8% loan notes	–		50	
Total liabilities		(25)		(62)
Net assets		130		141
Equity				
Ordinary share capital		100		100
Retained profits		30		41
Total equity		130		141

Inventory at 1 January 2008 was £50,000.

Required:

(*a*) Calculate the following ratios for 2008 and 2009:

- (*i*) Gross profit: Sales
- (*ii*) Inventory turnover
- (*iii*) Net profit: Sales
- (*iv*) Quick ('acid test')
- (*v*) Working capital
- (*vi*) Net profit: Capital employed

(*b*) State the possible reasons for and significance of any changes in the ratios shown by your calculations.

(*Midland Examining Group: GCSE*)

47.5A The following figures are for AB Engineering Supplies Ltd at 31 December 2009:

	£000	*£000*
Turnover		160
Gross profit		40
Average inventory at cost price		10
Expenses		8
Non-current assets		108
Current assets		
Inventory	10	
Accounts receivable	8	
Bank	2	
		20
		128
Current liabilities		(10)
		118
Capital		118

(*a*) Calculate:
- (*i*) gross profit as a percentage of the sales;
- (*ii*) rate of inventory turnover;
- (*iii*) net profit as a percentage of sales;
- (*iv*) net profit as a percentage of total capital employed (non-current assets plus current assets);
- (*v*) current ratio;
- (*vi*) quick asset (acid test) ratio.

(*b*) The following figures are for another firm in the same line of business, CD Engineering Services Ltd, for the year ending 31 December 2009.

	CD Engineering Services Ltd
Gross profit as a percentage of the sales	25%
Rate of inventory turnover	9
Net profit as a percentage of sales	10%
Net profit as a percentage of total capital employed	12½%
Current ratio	1 : 1
Quick asset (acid test) ratio	0.5 : 1

Compare your results in (*a*) with those given for CD Engineering Services Ltd.

As a result of your comparison, say which you think was the more successful business during 2009, giving your reasons.

(*Northern Examinations and Assessment Board: GCSE*)

47.6A Galloway Ltd has an authorised capital of 250,000 ordinary shares of £1 each.

(*a*) At the end of its financial year, 30 April 2008, the following balances remained in the company's books after preparation of the income statement.

	£
Motor vehicles:	
at cost	38,400
provision for depreciation	16,300
Net profit for year	36,600
Freehold premises at cost	190,000
Inventory in trade	32,124
Share capital: 200,000 ordinary shares of £1 each, fully paid	200,000
Insurance prepaid	280
Retained profits brought forward	3,950
Wages and salaries due	774
General reserve	24,000
Trade accounts payable	3,847
Trade accounts receivable	4,782
8% loan notes	15,000
Rent receivable outstanding	175
Bank overdraft	1,830
Furniture and equipment:	
at cost	44,000
provision for depreciation	7,460

The directors have proposed

(*i*) the transfer of £5,000 to the general reserve
(*ii*) a final dividend on the ordinary shares of 12.5%.

(*b*) Galloway Ltd's directors are making an assessment of the company's performance for the year. They are concerned by a decline in both profitability and liquidity despite an increase in turnover.

Required:

1 THREE significant differences between ordinary shares and debentures.
2 For Galloway Ltd
  (*i*) a profit and loss appropriation account for the year ending 30 April 2008
  (*ii*) a balance sheet as at 30 April 2008 in a form which shows clearly:
  total shareholders' funds
  working capital.
3 Concerning the company's performance
  (*i*) Name ONE ratio which could be used to assess profitability.
  (*ii*) State TWO possible reasons why the profitability ratio may have declined despite increased turnover.
  (*iii*) Name ONE ratio, other than working capital ratio, which could be used to assess liquidity.
  (*iv*) Give FOUR suggestions as to how working capital could be increased during the year ahead.

(*Southern Examining Group: GCSE*)

47.7 The trading inventory of Joan Street, retailer, has been reduced during the year ending 31 March 2008 by £6,000 from its commencing figure of £21,000.

A number of financial ratios and related statistics have been compiled relating to the business of Joan Street for the year ending 31 March 2008. These are shown below alongside comparative figures for a number of retailers who are members of the trade association to which Joan Street belongs:

	Joan Street	*Trade association*
	%	%
Net profit as % net capital employed (Authors' Note)	15	16
$\frac{\text{Net profit}}{\text{Sales}}$	9	8
$\frac{\text{Sales}}{\text{Net capital employed}}$	166⅔	200
$\frac{\text{Non-current assets}}{\text{Sales}}$	45	35
Working capital ratio:		
$\frac{\text{Current assets}}{\text{Current liabilities}}$	400	287½
Acid test ratio:		
$\frac{\text{Bank + Accounts receivable}}{\text{Current liabilities}}$	275	187½
$\frac{\text{Gross profit}}{\text{Sales}}$	25	26
Accounts receivable collection period:		
$\frac{\text{Accounts receivable} \times 365}{\text{Sales}}$	36½ days	$32\frac{17}{20}$ days
Inventory turnover (based on average inventory for the year)	10 times	8 times

Joan Street has supplied all the capital for her business and has had no drawings from the business during the year ending 31 March 2008.

Required:

(*a*) Prepare the income statement for the year ending 31 March 2008 and balance sheet as at that date of Joan Street in as much detail as possible.

(*b*) Identify two aspects of Joan Street's results for the year ending 31 March 2008 which compare favourably with the trade association's figures and identify two aspects which compare unfavourably.

(*c*) Outline two drawbacks of the type of comparison used in this question.

(*Association of Accounting Technicians*)

***Authors' Note*: take the closing figure at 31 March 2008.**

47.8A Harold Smart, who is a small manufacturer trading as Space Age Projects, is very pleased with his recently completed financial results which show that a planned 20% increase in turnover has been achieved in the last accounting year.

The summarised results relating to the last three financial years are as follows:

Year ended 30 September		*2007*	*2008*	*2009*
		£	£	£
Sales		90,000	100,000	120,000
Cost of sales		(74,000)	(75,000)	(92,000)
Gross profit		16,000	25,000	28,000
Administrative overheads		(3,000)	(5,000)	(6,000)
Net profit		13,000	20,000	22,000
As at 30 September	*2006*	*2007*	*2008*	*2009*
	£	£	£	£
Non-current assets:				
At cost	155,000	165,000	190,000	206,000
Provision for depreciation	(42,000)	(45,000)	(49,000)	(53,000)
	113,000	120,000	141,000	153,000
Current assets:				
Inventory	3,000	4,000	7,000	30,000
Accounts receivable	14,000	19,000	15,000	10,000
Balance at bank	2,000	1,000	3,000	–
	19,000	24,000	25,000	40,000
Current liabilities:				
Accounts payable	5,000	4,000	6,000	9,000
Bank overdraft	–	–	–	2,000
	5,000	4,000	6,000	11,000

Since 30 September 2006, Harold Smart has not taken any drawings from the business.

Harold Smart has been invited recently to invest £150,000 for a 5-year fixed term in government loan stock earning interest at 12½% per annum.

Note: Taxation is to be ignored.

Notwithstanding his response to these financial results, Harold Smart is a very cautious person and therefore has asked a financial consultant for a report.

Required:

(*a*) A schedule of six accounting ratios or measures of resource utilisation covering each of the three years ended 30 September 2009 of Space Age Projects.

(*b*) As financial consultant prepare a report to Harold Smart on the financial results of Space Age Projects given above including comments on the alternative future actions that he might take.

Note: Reports should utilise the information given in answers to part (a) of this question.

(*Association of Accounting Technicians*)

47.9 Business A and Business B are both engaged in retailing, but seem to take a different approach to this trade according to the information available. This information consists of a table of ratios, shown below:

Ratio	*Business A*	*Business B*
Current ratio	2 : 1	1.5 : 1
Quick assets (acid test) ratio	1.7 : 1	0.7 : 1
Return on capital employed (ROCE)	20%	17%
Return on shareholders' funds (ROSF)	30%	18%
Accounts receivable turnover	63 days	21 days
Accounts payable turnover	50 days	45 days
Gross profit percentage	40%	15%
Net profit percentage	10%	10%
Inventory turnover	52 days	25 days

Required:
(*a*) Explain briefly how each ratio is calculated.
(*b*) Describe what this information indicates about the differences in approach between the two businesses. If one of them prides itself on personal service and one of them on competitive prices, which do you think is which and why?

(*Association of Chartered Certified Accountants*)

47.10A You are given summarised information about two firms in the same line of business, A and B, as follows.

Balance sheets at 30 June	*A*		*B*	
	£000	£000	£000	£000
Land		80		260
Buildings	120		200	
Less: Depreciation	(40)		–	
		80		200
Plant	90		150	
Less: Depreciation	(70)		(40)	
		20		110
		180		570
Inventory	80		100	
Accounts receivable	100		90	
Bank	–		10	
		180		200
		360		770
Accounts payable	110		120	
Bank	50		–	
Loan (10% p.a.)	160	(260)	120	(250)
	100	100	130	520
Capital at start of year		100		300
Add: Profit for year		30		100
		130		400
Less: Drawings		(30)		(40)
		100		360
Land revaluation		–		160
		100		520
Sales		1,000		3,000
Cost of sales		400		2,000

Required:
(*a*) Produce a table of eight ratios calculated for both businesses.
(*b*) Write a report briefly outlining the strengths and weaknesses of the two businesses. Include comment on any major areas where the simple use of the figures could be misleading.

(*Association of Chartered Certified Accountants*)

47.11 The following letter has been received from a client. 'I gave my bank manager those audited accounts you prepared for last year. But he says he needs more information before he will agree to increase my overdraft. What could he possibly want to know that he can't get from those accounts? If they are not good enough why bother to prepare them?'

Required:
Outline the major points which should be included in a reply to this letter.

(*Association of Chartered Certified Accountants*)

47.12 An acquaintance of yours, H Gee, has recently set up in business for the first time as a general dealer.

The majority of his sales will be on credit to trade buyers but he will sell some goods to the public for cash.

He is not sure at which point of the business cycle he can regard his cash and credit sales to have taken place.

After seeking guidance on this matter from his friends, he is thoroughly confused by the conflicting advice he has received. Samples of the advice he has been given include:

The sale takes place when:

(*i*) 'you have bought goods which you know you should be able to sell easily';
(*ii*) 'the customer places the order';
(*iii*) 'you deliver the goods to the customer';
(*iv*) 'you invoice the goods to the customer';
(*v*) 'the customer pays for the goods';
(*vi*) 'the customer's cheque has been cleared by the bank'.

He now asks you to clarify the position for him.

Required:
(*a*) Write notes for Gee, setting out, in as easily understood a manner as possible, the accounting conventions and principles which should generally be followed when recognising sales revenue.
(*b*) Examine each of the statements (*i*) to (*vi*) above and advise Gee (stating your reasons) whether the method advocated is appropriate to the particular circumstances of his business.

(*Association of Chartered Certified Accountants*)

47.13 The annual final accounts of businesses are normally prepared on the assumption that the business is a going concern.

Required:
Explain and give a simple illustration of:

(*a*) the effect of this convention on the figures which appear in those final accounts.
(*b*) the implications for the final accounts figures if this convention were deemed to be inoperative.

(*Association of Chartered Certified Accountants*)

47.14 One of the well known accounting concepts is that of materiality.

Required:
(*a*) Explain what is meant by this concept.
(*b*) State and explain three types of situation to which this concept might be applicable.
(*c*) State and explain two specific difficulties in applying this concept.

(*Association of Chartered Certified Accountants*)

47.15 State three classes of people, other than managers and owners, who are likely to need to use financial accounting information. Discuss whether you think their requirements are compatible.

(*Association of Chartered Certified Accountants*)

47.16 A business produces a standard manufactured product. The stages of the production and sale of the product may be summarised as follows:

Stage	*A*	*B*	*C*	*D*
Activity	*Raw material*	*WIP-I*	*WIP-II*	*Finished product*
	£	£	£	£
Costs to date	100	120	150	170
Net realisable value	80	130	190	300
Stage	*E*	*F*	*G*	*H*
Activity	*For sale*	*Sale agreed*	*Delivered*	*Paid for*
	£	£	£	£
Costs to date	170	170	180	180
Net realisable value	300	300	300	300

Required:

(*a*) What general rule do accountants apply when deciding when to recognise revenue on any particular transaction?

(*b*) Apply this rule to the above situation. State and explain the stage at which you think revenue will be recognised by accountants.

(*c*) How much would the gross profit on a unit of this product be? Why?

(*d*) Suggest arguments in favour of delaying the recognition of revenue until Stage H.

(e) Suggest arguments in favour of recognising revenue in appropriate successive amounts at Stages B, C and D.

(*Association of Chartered Certified Accountants*)

47.17

(*a*) In accounting practice a distinction is drawn between the terms 'reserves' and 'provisions' and between 'accrued expenses' and 'accounts payable'.

Required:
Briefly define each of the four terms quoted and explain the effect of each on the preparation of accounts.

(*b*) While preparing the final accounts for year ending 30 September 2007, the accountant of Lanep Lighting Ltd had to deal with the following matters:

(*i*) the exterior of the company's premises was being repaired. The contractors had started work in August but were unlikely to finish before the end of November 2007. The total cost would not be known until after completion. Cost of work carried out to 30 September 2007 was estimated at £21,000;

(*ii*) the company rented a sales showroom from Commercial Properties plc at a rental of £6,000 per annum payable half yearly in arrears on 1 August and 1 February;

(*iii*) on 3 October 2007 an invoice was received for £2,500 less a trade discount of 30 per cent, from Lucifer Ltd for goods for resale supplied during September 2007;

(*iv*) the directors of Lanep Lighting Ltd have decided that an annual amount of £5,000 should be set aside, starting with year ending 30 September 2007, for the purpose of plant replacement.

Required:
State the accounting treatment which should be accorded to each of the above matters in the Lanep Lighting Ltd income statement for year ending 30 September 2007 and balance sheet at that date.

(*Association of Chartered Certified Accountants*)

47.18 Bradwich plc is a medium-sized engineering company whose shares are listed on a major Stock Exchange.

It has recently applied to its bankers for a 7-year loan of £500,000 to finance a modernisation and expansion programme.

→

Mr Whitehall, a recently retired civil servant, is contemplating investing £10,000 of his lump sum pension in the company's ordinary shares in order to provide both an income during his retirement and a legacy to his grandchildren after his death.

The bank and Mr Whitehall have each acquired copies of the company's most recent annual report and accounts.

Required:

(*a*) State, separately for each of the two parties, those aspects of the company's performance and financial position which would be of particular interest and relevance to their respective interests.

(*b*) State, separately for each of the two parties, the formula of four ratios which would assist in measuring or assessing the matters raised in your answer to (*a*).

(*Association of Chartered Certified Accountants*)

47.19 Explain what you understand by the accounting term 'capital gearing', showing clearly the benefits of, and the potential problems associated with high gearing.

(*Scottish Qualifications Authority*)

47.20A What benefits can result through the use of ratios and what limitations should be imposed on any conclusions drawn from their use?

You can find a range of additional self-test questions, as well as material to help you with your studies, on the website that accompanies this book at www.pearsoned.co.uk/wood.

part

8

AN INTRODUCTION TO MANAGEMENT ACCOUNTING

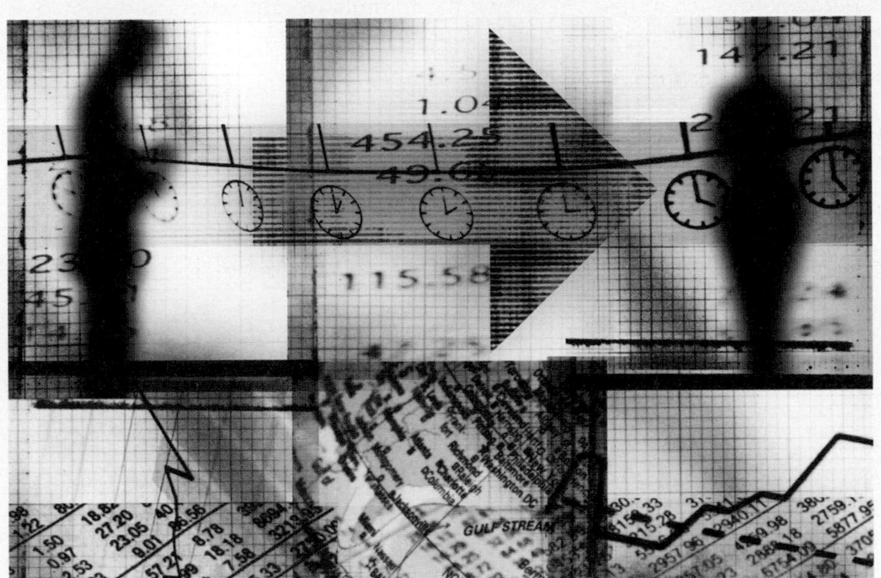

Introduction

This part introduces the management accounting side of accounting and looks at how costs can be gathered and utilised in decision-making within an organisation.

chapter 48

An introduction to management accounting

Learning objectives

After you have studied this chapter, you should be able to:

- explain why cost accounting is needed for there to be an effective management accounting system
- explain why the benefits of operating a costing system should always outweigh the costs of operating it
- explain what characteristic must exist before anything can be described as information
- explain why different costs are often needed when making decisions about the future compared to those that are used to calculate profit in the past
- explain which costing approach is the relevant one to use when considering a change in what and/or how much is produced
- explain what is meant by marginal cost and why selling prices should always exceed it
- explain why budgets are prepared
- describe the role of management accountants in the budgetary process
- describe the relationship between financial accounting data and management accounting data

Introduction

In this chapter, you'll learn about the importance of data being suitable for the purpose for which it is to be used and of the need for information to be useful. You'll learn how costs are recorded and of two of the most used approaches to costing. You'll also learn about systems of costing and of the importance of budgeting, not just to business but also to the role of the management accountant. Finally, you will learn about how management accounting data often forms the basis of data used in financial accounting.

48.1 Background

So far, you have learnt about bookkeeping and the preparation of financial statements. In accounting, these are the two components of what is known as financial accounting. The information that is produced by financial accounting is usually historical, backwards-looking and, mainly, for the use of decision-makers external to the organisation to which the data relates. You learnt about the sort of things that are done with this information in Chapter 47.

Activity 48.1 What sort of things are done with this information?

There is a second side to accounting. This one looks forwards and the output from it is used by decision-makers within the organisation. It also consists of two components: one where costs are recorded and one where the data is processed and converted into reports for managers and other decision-makers. The cost recording component is called **cost accounting** and the processing and reporting component is called **management accounting**, which is also the name used to refer to this side of accounting. It is also sometimes referred to as 'managerial accounting'.

48.2 Cost accounting

Cost accounting is needed so that there can be an effective management accounting system. Without a study of costs such a system could not exist. Before entering into any detailed description of costs it is better if we first ask what use we are going to make of information about costs in the business.

This can best be done by referring to something which is not accounting, and then relating it to accounting. Suppose that your employer asked you to 'measure the distance between Manchester and London', but walked away from you without giving any further information. As you thought about the request the following thoughts might go through your head:

1 *How* is the distance to be measured? – e.g. by road, rail, plane or train.
2 The *costs* and *benefits* of obtaining the information – how much can you spend finding out the information without making it cost more to find out than will be saved by knowing the information we seek?
3 What is the *purpose* for which the measurement will be used? – e.g. to travel there by car, to walk there, to have goods shipped there by train or by road.

The lesson to be learnt from this is that measurement depends entirely on the use that is to be made of the data. Too often businesses make measurements of financial and other data without looking first at the use that is going to be made of it. In fact, it could be said that 'information' is useful data that is provided for someone.

Data given to someone which is not relevant to the purpose required is just not information. Data which is provided for a particular purpose, and which is completely wrong for the purpose, is worse than no data at all. At least when there is no data, the manager knows that the best that can be done is to guess.

When useless data is collected it has cost money to collect, in itself a waste of money. Second, it is often assumed to be useful and so misleads a manager into taking decisions that are completely inappropriate. Third, it clogs up the communication system within a business, so that other data is not acted on properly because of the general confusion that has been caused.

When looking at costs, you need to consider the following:

1 What is the data on costs wanted for?
2 How are the costs to be measured? and
3 The cost of obtaining costing data should not exceed the benefits to be gained from having it.

When it is known what the costs are for, and how much is to be spent on studying them, the appropriate method for measuring them can be decided.

48.3 Costs

There are many classifications of cost. Let's briefly summarise those that you already know about.

Historical costs

These are the foundation of financial accounting. Exhibit 48.1 shows costs flowing through the financial accounting system.

Exhibit 48.1

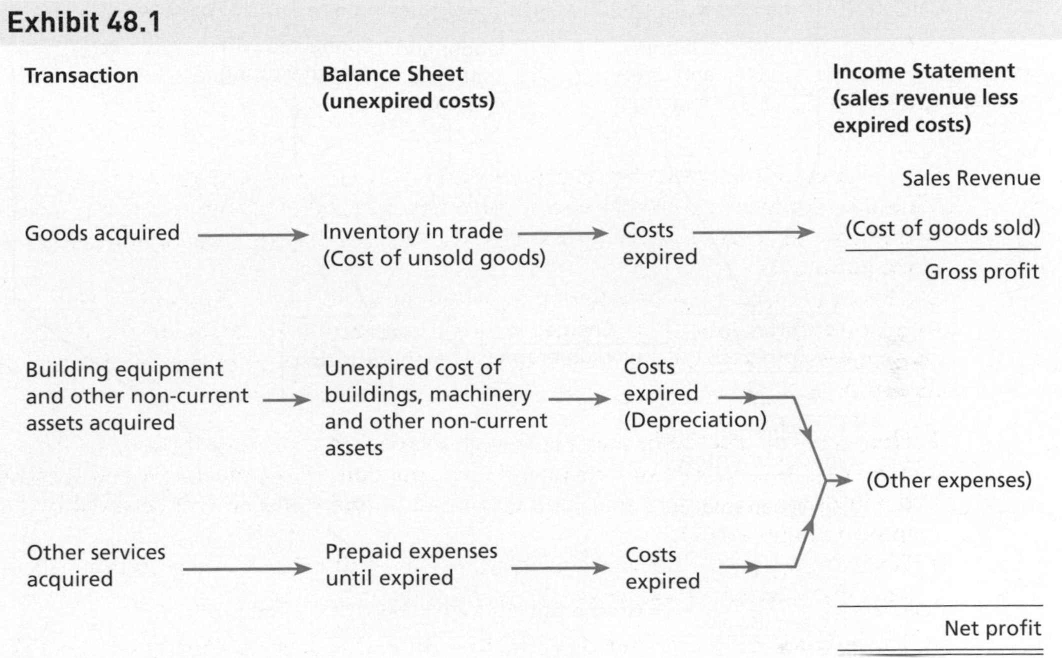

Product costs

These are the costs attributed to the units of goods manufactured. They are charged up to the cost of goods manufactured in the trading account, and would normally be part of the valuation of unsold goods if the goods to which they refer had not been sold by the end of the period. Product costs are therefore matched up against revenue as and when the goods are sold and not before.

Period costs

Period costs are those of a non-manufacturing nature and represent the selling and distribution, administration and financial expenses. They are treated as expenses of the period in which they were incurred irrespective of the volume of goods sold.

Combining all this, you arrive at the manufacturing accounts you covered in Chapter 37. Exhibit 48.2 shows the flow of costs through to finished products.

Exhibit 48.2

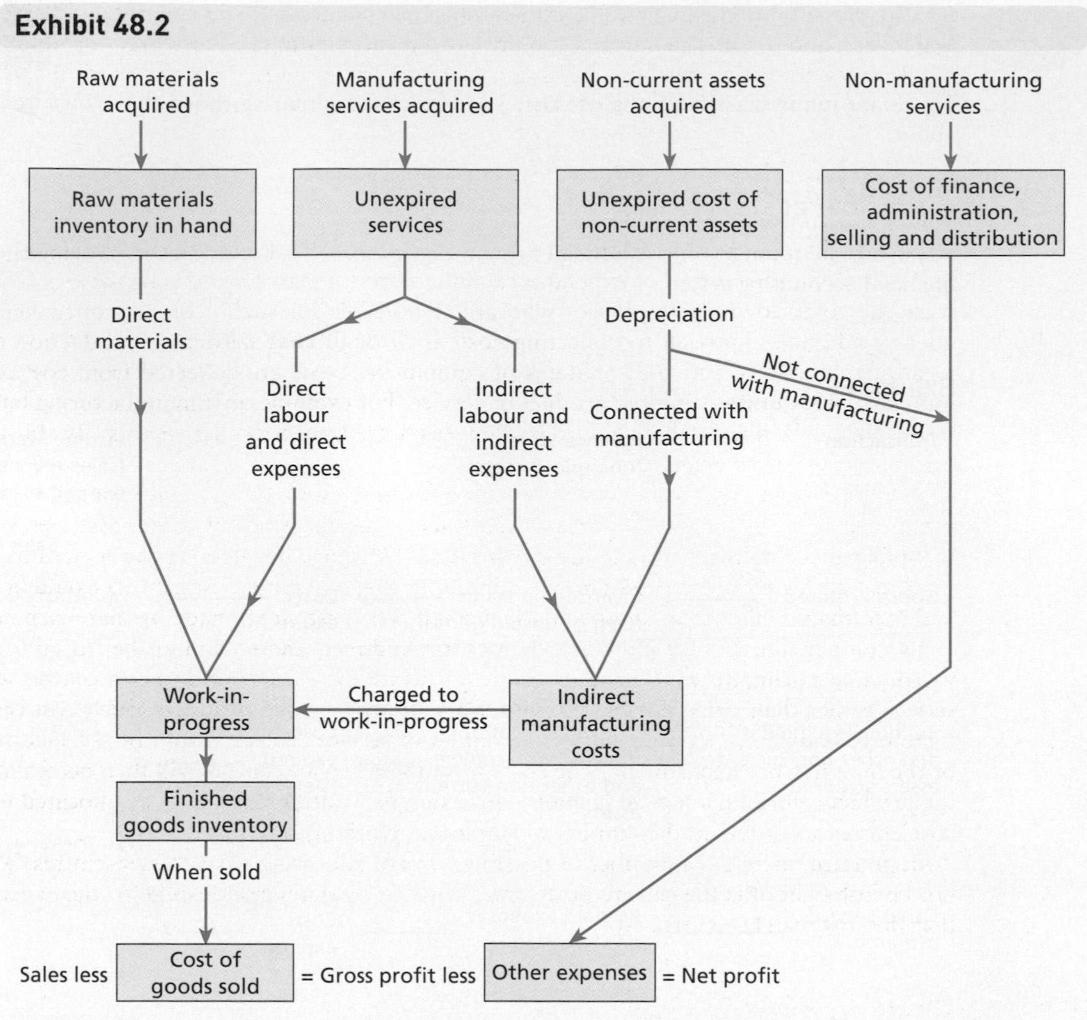

This, therefore, is what you use costs information for in financial accounting – to produce the information you need in order to prepare the financial statements. In management accounting, there is a different emphasis, some of which overlaps with the needs of financial accounting but some of which is for something quite different.

For example, most businesses want to know how much each item has cost to make. This means that the total costs for the whole business are not sufficient, and so these costs must be analysed further. They also want to know what costs are likely to be in the future. Again, more analysis is needed. Cost accounting is the process of measuring and recording all these costs.

Many advantages are gained by having a cost accounting system that provides this detail of cost information. When armed with the cost information that management accounting techniques can provide, managers and other internal decision-makers are far more able to make sensible decisions about what should be done to aid the progress of the business towards its objectives.

For example, imagine trying to decide which item to stop producing out of twelve items made by a business if you have little information as to the amount each item contributes towards the profitability of the business. Very often the solution will be that a new layout in the factory is needed; special training given to certain employees; changes made in the system of remunerating employees; and so on. The information provided by accounting is, therefore, only one part of the whole story for any problem requiring a decision to be made. Sometimes *it will be the least important information* available, as far as the decision-maker is concerned.

48.4 Cost control

One of the most important features of cost accounting is its use for control purposes, meaning, in this context, the control of expenditure. But control of expenditure is possible only if you can trace the costs down to employees who are responsible for such costs. A convenient and frequently adopted approach to collecting costs is through **cost centres** – production or service locations, functions, activities or items of equipment. Costs are collected from cost centres for individual **cost units** – units of product or service. For example, in a manufacturing business, all direct materials, direct labour and direct expenses are traced to cost centres. (In this case, they may be known as 'product centres'.)

A cost centre may be a single machine used for jobbing work, i.e. quite a lot of separate jobs performed specially to conform with the customer's specifications. It could, however, be a group of similar machines or a production department. Thus, if a business makes metal boxes on one machine, all the costs incurred directly relating to that machine (cost centre) would be gathered and then shared (allocated) among all the metal boxes (cost units) made by that machine.

By comparison, factory indirect expenses are 'indirect' and so cannot be traced (or it is not worthwhile tracing them) to product centres. Instead, these are traced to cost centres which give service rather than being concerned with work directly on the products. Such cost centres are, therefore, known as 'service centres'. Examples of service centres would be the factory canteen or the maintenance department. The costs from these service centres will then need allocating to the product centres in a logical fashion – for example, canteen costs may be allocated to product cost centres according to the number of employees working at each of them.

In practice, there are a number of possible ways of allocating costs to cost centres. What must not be lost sight of is the endeavour to trace costs to a person responsible for the expenditure so that the costs can be controlled.

48.5 Costing approaches

There are a number of ways costs can be gathered and collated. The two most commonly used are **absorption costing** and **marginal costing**.

Absorption costing

This involves allocating all direct costs and factory indirect expenses to products. The factory indirect expenses are seen as adding to the value of work-in-progress and, therefore, to finished goods. The production cost of any article is thus comprised of direct materials, direct labour, any direct expenses and a share of factory indirect expense.

After the financial year end, it is possible to look back and calculate exactly what the factory indirect expenses were. This means that this figure is used when calculating the valuation of the closing inventory. For a business which had produced 1,000 units, of which 200 units have not yet been sold, with a total production cost of £100,000, the closing inventory valuation becomes:

$$\frac{\text{Unsold units}}{\text{Total units produced}} \times \text{Production cost of goods completed} = \frac{200}{1{,}000} \times \pounds 100{,}000$$

$$= \pounds 20{,}000 \text{ closing inventory valuation}$$

Cost data is, however, used for purposes other than that of valuing inventory. The question is, therefore, often asked as to whether or not this method is suitable for all costing purposes. The short answer is that it is not. A fuller consideration of this question is beyond the scope of this book and is covered in *Business Accounting 2*.

Marginal costing

Where costing is used which takes account of only the variable cost of products rather than the full production cost, this is known as marginal costing. By ignoring the fixed costs, it is possible to see how much something contributes towards the profitability of a business. So, for example, if an order was received to buy 100 tables from a business for £65 each and the absorption cost of a table, £70, was considered, the order might be rejected, but if marginal costing was used and the marginal cost was £60, the order might be accepted as every table sold would contribute £5 towards the overall profitability of the business. Whether it is or not will depend upon whether there is any spare production capacity.

When using marginal costing for decisions like this, care needs to be taken that over all the decisions taken, sufficient additional income is generated to pay for all the fixed costs that are ignored by marginal costing.

48.6 Costing systems

Having decided which costing approach to adopt, you then need to decide which costing system to adopt. The one you choose will depend upon how your products or services are produced. There are two main types of costing system, **job costing** and **process costing**.

Job costing

This is used when production consists of separate jobs. For instance, where a Rolls-Royce is made to each customer's specifications, each car can be regarded as a separate job. When a job is long-term, the term 'project costing' is often used.

Job costing also applies where batches of items are made. For example, a jam bottling company may make jam in batches of 10,000 bottles and then switch over to making a different type of jam for the next batch. A printer may print a batch of 2,000 copies of a book. The 'job' can thus be one item or a batch of similar items. When a batch is involved, it is usually referred to as 'batch costing'.

Process costing

Process costing is used where production is regarded as a continuous flow. It is applicable to industries such as oil, paint manufacturing, steel, textiles, and food processing, where production is repetitive and continuous. For example, an oil refinery where crude oil is processed continually, emerging as different grades of petrol, paraffin, motor oil, etc., would use process costing, as would a salt works where sea water is pumped into the works and the resulting product is slabs or packets of salt. Another example would be a car manufacturer that produced one model of car for an extended period.

Overall

Job costing treats production as a number of separate jobs being performed, each of which needs to have costs allocated to it. Process costing, on the other hand, sees production as a continuous flow and no attempt is made to allocate costs to specific units being produced because the same thing is being produced continuously. As a result, costs per unit produced can always be calculated by dividing the costs for the period by the number of units produced.

Activity 48.2

For which of the following would you use job costing and for which would you use process costing? Split the job costing ones between job, batch and project costing.

Newspaper printing
School meals
A film in a cinema
Making a film
Manufacturing computer memory chips
A play in a theatre
Egg production
Building a space satellite

48.7 Budgeting and budgetary control

Management accounting is concerned with providing information for planning and control so that organisations can achieve their objectives. One of the central supporting devices of both of these aims is budgeting.

When a plan is expressed quantitatively it is known as a **budget** and the process of converting plans into budgets is known as **budgeting**.

The budgeting process may be quite formal in a large organisation with committees set up to perform the task. On the other hand in a very small business the owner may jot down the budget on a piece of scrap paper or even on the back of a used envelope. Some even manage without writing anything down at all – they have done the budgets in their heads and can easily remember them.

The methodology of budgetary control is probably accountancy's major contribution to management. Budgets are drawn up by management and recorded by management accountants. Actual results are compared against the budgets by the management accountants who pass reports to management concerning the extent to which budgets are being met. This enables managers to control activities and to step in and stop situations where the budget is being ignored or overlooked.

When budgets are being drawn up, two main objectives must be uppermost in the minds of management and management accountants – that budgets are for planning and for control. Management accountants must, therefore, operate a system of budgeting that enables these two aims to be achieved. They do so mainly through a system called variance analysis, which compares actual data to budgeted data and endeavours to identify what has given rise to any differences that are found. For example, if the gross profit on an item is lower than was budgeted, this could be because costs have risen or because the selling price has fallen. The management accountant uses special formulae to pinpoint the cause and passes the information to management so that they can exercise control if required.

48.8 Other aspects of management accounting

Management accounting is, therefore, all about gathering costs appropriately so that businesses can take appropriate decisions relating to manufacturing and selling their goods and services. Management accountants are primarily involved in establishing the costs incurred in producing the output of a business and in maintaining a budgeting system that provides managers with the capability to plan and control activity and so meet the objectives of the organisation.

Apart from the activities mentioned already in this chapter, management accountants are also involved in preparing any information of a financial nature that managers and other decision-makers require and which is not considered part of the role of the financial accountant. This can range from identifying the cost of a component part to the expected returns on a twenty-year project to build a chain of hotels. Their work can be very much more varied than that of a financial accountant, and they are not tied by any rules and regulations concerning either how they perform calculations or how they present information.

However, as much of the cost information they produce is also used in the financial accounting system, they do need to ensure that their cost data are capable of being used in that medium. As it is easier to simply have one set of costs for an entire business, rather than one calculated for the management accountants and one calculated for the financial accountants, most management accountants follow the rules relating to cost determination that financial accountants are obliged to follow.

This chapter has been very much an introduction to management accounting. The topic is covered in detail in *Business Accounting 2*.

Learning outcomes

You should now have learnt that:

1. Cost accounting is needed for there to be an effective management accounting system.
2. The benefits of operating a costing system should always outweigh the costs of operating it.
3. Information is data prepared for a purpose. To qualify as 'information', the 'information' must be useful.
4. Different costs will often be needed when making decisions about the future than were used when calculating profit in the past.
5. Marginal cost, not absorption cost, is the relevant cost when considering a change in what and/or how much is produced.
6. Selling prices should exceed marginal costs. (Almost the only exception to this would be where a product was being promoted as a 'loss leader'.)
7. In the long term, the total of all the differences between revenue and marginal cost must exceed the fixed costs of the business.
8. Budgets are prepared in order to guide the business towards its objectives.
9. Budgets should be drawn up within the context of *planning* and *control*.

Answers to activities

48.1 It is used for ratio analysis, particularly for trend analysis and benchmarking against appropriate comparators such as the previous year's figures or the equivalent figures relating to competitors.

48.2

Job costing	*Process costing*
Newspaper printing (batch)	Manufacturing computer memory chips
School meals (batch)	Egg production
A film in a cinema (job)	
Making a film (project)	
A play in a theatre (job)	
Building a space satellite (project)	

Review questions

48.1 What makes information useful?

48.2 What is the difference between absorption costing and marginal costing?

48.3 What is the difference between job costing, batch costing, project costing and process costing?

48.4 What are the two main objectives of budgeting?

48.5 What role do management accountants play in the budgetary process?

You can find a range of additional self-test questions, as well as material to help you with your studies, on the website that accompanies this book at www.pearsoned.co.uk/wood.

Answers to review questions

***Note*: All the answers are the work of the author. None has been supplied by an examining body. The examining bodies accept no responsibility whatsoever for the accuracy or method of working in the answers given.**

***Note*: In order to save space, in most cases brackets have not been entered to indicate negative numbers. Also, £ signs have been omitted from columns of figures, except where the figures refer to £000, or where the denomination needs to be specified.**

1.1

(*a*) 10,700	(*b*) 23,100	(*c*) 4,300	(*d*) 3,150
(*e*) 25,500	(*f*) 51,400		

1.3

(*a*) Asset	(*b*) Liability	(*c*) Asset
(*d*) Asset	(*e*) Liability	(*f*) Asset

1.5

Wrong: Assets: Loan from C Smith, Accounts payable; Liabilities: Inventory, Accounts receivable.

1.7

Assets: Van 4,500; Market stall 2,000; Inventory 1,500; Bank 1,100; Cash 400 = total 9,500.
Liabilities: Loan 5,000; Accounts payable 1,000 = total 6,000.
Capital: 9,500 – 6,000 = 3,500.

1.9

G Putty
Balance sheet as at 31 December 2008

Non-current assets		
Fixtures	1,800	
Van	3,800	5,600
Current assets		
Inventory	4,200	
Accounts receivable	1,200	
Cash at bank	300	5,700
		11,300
Current liabilities		
Accounts payable		(1,600)
		9,700
Capital		9,700

1.11

	Assets	*Liabilities*	*Capital*
(*a*)	– Cash	– Accounts payable	
(*b*)	– Bank		
	+ Fixtures		
(*c*)	+ Inventory	+ Accounts payable	
(*d*)	+ Cash		+ Capital
(*e*)	+ Cash	+ Loan from J Walker	
(*f*)	+ Bank		
	– Accounts receivable		
(*g*)	– Inventory	– Accounts payable	
(*h*)	+ Premises		
	– Bank		

1.13

G Brown
Balance sheet as at 7 May 2008

Non-current assets		
Fixtures	2,800	
Car	3,900	
Computer	850	7,550
Current assets		
Inventory	4,950	
Accounts receivable	1,860	
Bank	6,320	
Cash	220	13,350
		20,900
Current liabilities		
Accounts payable		(2,500)
		18,400
Capital		18,400

2.1

	Debited	Credited		Debited	Credited
(*a*)	Office machinery	D Isaacs Ltd	(*b*)	C Jones	Capital
(*c*)	Cash	N Fox	(*d*)	Loan: P Exeter	Bank
(*e*)	D Isaacs Ltd	Office machinery	(*f*)	Bank	N Lyn
(*g*)	Van	Cash			

2.3

Bank

(1) Capital	15,000	(2) Office furn.	1,200
		(5) Van	6,010
		(15) Trees	1,400
		(31) Machinery	650

Capital

		(1) Bank	15,000

Office furniture

(2) Bank	1,200	(8) D Twig	150

Machinery

(3) Trees Ltd	1,400		
(31) Bank	650		

Cash

(23) D Twig	150		

Trees Ltd

(15) Bank	1,400	(3) Machinery	1,400

Van

(5) Bank	6,010		

D Twig & Sons

(8) Off. furn.	150	(23) Cash	150

2.4

Cash

(1) Capital	12,000	(2) Bank	11,700
(25) Equipment	200		
(28) Bank	130		

Capital

		(1) Cash	12,000

Office furniture

(5) Dream	1,900	(18) Dream	120

Van

(8) Bank	5,250		

Equipment

(12) Pearce & Sons	2,300	(25) Cash	200

Bank

(2) Cash	11,700	(8) Van	5,250
(30) F Brown	4,000	(26) Dream	1,780
		(28) Cash	130

Dream Ltd

(18) Office furn.	120	(5) Office furn.	1,900
(26) Bank	1,780		

Pearce & Sons

		(12) Equipment	2,300

F Brown (Loan)

		(30) Bank	4,000

3.1

	Debited	Credited		Debited	Credited
(*a*)	Purchases	J Reid	(*b*)	B Perkins	Sales
(*c*)	Van	H Thomas	(*d*)	Bank	Sales
(*e*)	Cash	Sales	(*f*)	H Hardy	Returns outwards
(*g*)	Cash	Machinery	(*h*)	Returns inwards	J Nelson
(*i*)	Purchases	D Simpson	(*j*)	H Forbes	Returns outwards

3.3

Cash

(1) Capital	750	(3) Purchases	110
(10) Sales	64	(25) F Herd	274
(31) B Squire	82		

Purchases

(3) Cash	110		
(7) F Herd	320		
(18) D Exodus	414		

Sales

		(10) Cash	64
		(24) B Squire	82

Returns outwards

		(14) F Herd	46
		(21) D Exodus	31

B Squire

(24) Sales	82	(31) Cash	82

F Herd

(14) Returns	46	(7) Purchases	320
(25) Cash	274		

D Exodus

(21) Returns	31	(18) Purchases	414

Capital

		(1) Cash	750

3.5

Bank

(1) Capital	20,000	(25) B Brown	1,924
(6) Cash	200	(29) Aberdeen Cars	4,370

Sales

		(4) Cash	1,910
		(8) H Rise	1,374
		(10) P Taylor	341
		(14) G Pate	535
		(14) R Sim	262
		(24) Cash	110

Returns inwards

(12) H Rise	65		
(26) G Pate	34		

Van

(17) Aberdeen Cars	4,370		

Office furniture

(18) J Winter	1,800	(27) J Winter	180
(31) Cash	365		

Capital

		(1) Bank	20,000
		(28) Cash	2,500

P Taylor

(10) Sales	341		

G Pate

(14) Sales	535	(26) Returns	34

H Rise

(8) Sales	1,374	(12) Returns	65

R Sim

(14) Sales	262		

Cash

(2) R Hughes (Loan)	5,000	(6) Bank	200
(4) Sales	1,910	(20) Purchases	390
(24) Sales	110	(31) Office furn.	365
(28) Capital	2,500		

Purchases

(3) B Brown	1,530		
(3) I Jess	4,162		
(11) B Brown	488		
(20) Cash	390		

Returns outwards

		(15) B Brown	94
		(19) I Jess	130

Aberdeen Cars

(29) Bank	4,370	(17) Van	4,370

J Winter Ltd

(27) Office furn.	180	(18) Office furn.	1,800

B Brown

(15) Returns	94	(3) Purchases	1,530
(25) Bank	1,924	(11) Purchases	488

I Jess

(19) Returns	130	(3) Purchases	4,162

R Hughes (Loan)

		(2) Cash	5,000

4.1

Bank

(1) Capital	9,000	(3) Fixtures	1,150
(21) Rent received	25	(24) Van	4,100

Cash

(1) Capital	1,000		
(5) Sales	140	(10) Rent	200
		(12) Stationery	45
		(30) Wages	360
		(31) Drawings	80

Purchases

(2) D James	290		
(6) C Monty	325		

Sales

		(5) Cash	140
		(23) G Cross	845

Fixtures

(3) Bank	1,150		

Rent

(10) Cash	200		

Capital

		(1) Bank	9,000
		(1) Cash	1,000

D James

(18) Returns out	41	(2) Purchases	290

C Monty

		(6) Purchases	325

G Cross

(23) Sales	845		

Rent received

		(21) Bank	25

Stationery

(12) Cash	45		

Returns out

		(18) D James	41

Van

(24) Bank	4,100		

Wages

(30) Cash	360		

Drawings

(31) Cash	80		

4.2

Cash

(1) Capital	8,500	(3) Rent	210
(11) Sales	81	(4) Bank	6,000
		(20) B repairs	78
		(28) Purchases	470
		(30) Motor exps	62

Bank

(4) Cash	6,000	(7) Stationery	25
		(27) W Young	366
		(29) Van	3,850

Purchases

(2) W Young	420		
(28) Cash	470		

Sales

		(5) D Unbar	192
		(11) Cash	81
		(17) J Harper	212

Stationery

(7) Bank	25		

Returns outwards

		(14) W Young	54

Fixtures

(31) B Coal	840		

Capital

		(1) Cash	8,500

Rent

(3) Cash	210		

Building repairs

(20) Cash	78		

Motor expenses

(30) Cash	62		

Van

(29) Bank	3,850		

W Young

(14) Returns out	54	(2) Purchases	420
(27) Bank	366		

D Unbar

(5) Sales	192	(22) Returns in	22

J Harper

(17) Sales	212		

Returns inwards

(22) D Unbar	22		

B Coal

		(31) Fixtures	840

4.5

(*A*) Bought motor vehicle £5,000, paying by bank.
(*B*) Paid off £4,000 creditors in cash.
(*C*) Lee lent us £150,000, this being paid into the bank.
(*D*) Bought land and buildings £125,000, paying by bank.
(*E*) Debtors paid cheques £80,000, being paid into bank.
(*F*) Land and buildings sold for £300,000, the proceeds being paid into the bank.
(*G*) Loan from Lee repaid out of the bank.
(*H*) Creditors £8,000 paid in cash.
(*I*) Stock costing £17,000 sold for £12,000 on credit. Loss of £5,000 shown deducted from Capital.

5.1

B Flyn

(1) Sales	810	(10) Returns	93
(4) Sales	134	(24) Cash	500
		(31) Balance c/d	351
	944		944
(1) Balance b/d	351		

F Start

(4) Sales	480	(31) Balance c/d	720
(31) Sales	240		
	720		720
(1) Balance b/d	720		

G Goh

(1) Sales	763	(18) Bank	763

T Fey

(1) Sales	392	(10) Returns	41
		(20) Bank	351
	392		392

5.2

J Saville

(10) Returns	65	(1) Purchases	240
(28) Cash	300	(15) Purchases	210
(30) Balance c/d	85		
	450		450
		(1) Balance b/d	85

J Fry

(10) Returns	82	(1) Purchases	810
(30) Balance c/d	728		
	810		810
		(1) Balance b/d	728

P Todd

(30) Returns	39	(1) Purchases	390
(30) Balance c/d	821	(3) Purchases	470
	860		860
		(1) Balance b/d	821

J Mehan

(19) Bank	1,450	(3) Purchases	1,450

5.3

B Flyn

2008		Dr	Cr	Balance	
May 1	Sales	810		810	Dr
4	Sales	134		944	Dr
10	Returns		93	851	Dr
24	Cash		500	351	Dr

G Goh

2008		Dr	Cr	Balance	
May 1	Sales	763		763	Dr
18	Bank		763	0	

T Fey

2008		Dr	Cr	Balance	
May 1	Sales	392		392	Dr
10	Returns		41	351	Dr
20	Bank		351	0	

F Start

2008		Dr	Cr	Balance	
May 4	Sales	480		480	Dr
31	Sales	240		720	Dr

5.4

J Saville

2008		Dr	Cr	Balance	
Jun 1	Purchases		240	240	Cr
10	Returns	65		175	Cr
15	Purchases		210	385	Cr
28	Cash	300		85	Cr

P Todd

2008		Dr	Cr	Balance	
Jun 1	Purchases		390	390	Cr
3	Purchases		470	860	Cr
30	Returns	39		821	Cr

J Fry

2008		Dr	Cr	Balance	
Jun 1	Purchases		810	810	Cr
10	Returns	82		728	Cr

J Mehan

2008		Dr	Cr	Balance	
Jun 3	Purchases		1,450	1,450	Cr
19	Bank	1,450		0	

5.5

J Bee

(1)	Sales	520	(24)	Bank	400
			(28)	Cash	80
			(30)	Balance c/d	40
		520			520
(1)	Balance b/d	40			

T Day

(1)	Sales	630	(12)	Returns	190
(8)	Sales	640	(30)	Bal c/d	1,080
		1,270			1,270
(1)	Bal b/d	1,080			

J Soul

(1)	Sales	240	(12)	Returns	25
			(30)	Balance c/d	215
		240			240
(1)	Balance b/d	215			

L Hope

(8)	Sales	418	(30)	Bank	418

D Blue

(20)	Bank	390	(2)	Purchases	390

F Rise

(17)	Returns	12	(2)	Purchases	510
(30)	Balance c/d	590	(10)	Purchases	92
		602			602
			(1)	Balance b/d	590

P Lee

(30)	Balance c/d	280	(2)	Purchases	280
			(1)	Balance b/d	280

R James

(17)	Returns	84	(10)	Purchases	870
(26)	Bank	766			
(30)	Balance c/d	20			
		870			870
			(1)	Balance b/d	20

6.1

Cash

(1)	Capital	800	(6)	Rent	180
			(15)	Carriage	38
			(31)	Balance c/d	582
		800			800

Bank

(1)	Capital	2,200	(12)	M Taylor	174
(9)	J Sharpe	340	(12)	J Ward	610
(10)	F Titmus	1,000	(31)	Rent	230
			(31)	Bal c/d	2,526
		3,540			3,540

Capital

			(1)	Cash	800
			(1)	Bank	2,200

Rent

(6)	Cash	180			
(31)	Bank	230			

Purchases

(2)	J Ward	610			
(2)	P Green	214			
(2)	M Taylor	174			
(2)	S Gemmill	345			
(2)	P Tone	542			
(18)	P Green	291			
(18)	S Gemmill	940			

Sales

			(4)	J Sharpe	340
			(4)	G Boycott	720
			(4)	F Titmus	1,152
			(21)	G Boycott	810

G Boycott

(4)	Sales	720			
(21)	Sales	810			

F Titmus

(4)	Sales	1,152	(10)	Bank	1,000

Carriage

(15) Cash	38		

J Ward

(12) Bank	610	(2) Purchases	610

P Green

		(2) Purchases	214
		(18) Purchases	291

M Taylor

(12) Bank	174	(2) Purchases	174

S Gemmill

		(2) Purchases	345
		(18) Purchases	940

P Tone

		(2) Purchases	542

J Sharpe

(4) Sales	340	(9) Bank	340

Trial balance as at 31 May 2008

	Dr	Cr
Cash	582	
Bank	2,526	
Capital		3,000
Rent	410	
Carriage	38	
P Green		505
S Gemmill		1,285
P Tone		542
G Boycott	1,530	
F Titmus	152	
Purchases	3,116	
Sales		3,022
	8,354	8,354

6.2

Bank

(1) Capital	8,000	(17) G Byers	700
(24) B Tyler	845	(21) Stop Ltd	740
		(31) Van	6,250
		(31) Bal c/d	1,155
	8,845		8,845

Cash

(5) Sales	510	(6) Wages	110
(30) G Prince (Loan)	1,000	(9) Purchases	120
		(12) Wages	110
		(31) Bal c/d	1,170
	1,510		1,510

Capital

		(1) Bank	8,000

Van

(31) Bank	6,250		

Wages

(6) Cash	110		
(12) Cash	110		

Shop fixtures

(15) Stop Ltd	740		

G Prince (loan)

		(30) Cash	1,000

J Snow

(7) Sales	295		

Sales

		(5) Cash	510
		(7) J Snow	295
		(7) K Park	360
		(7) B Tyler	640
		(13) K Park	610
		(13) B Tyler	205

Purchases

(2) L Frank	550		
(2) G Byers	290		
(2) P Lee	610		
(9) Cash	120		
(10) G Byers	410		
(10) P Lee	1,240		

Returns outwards

		(18) P Lee	83
		(27) L Frank	18

K Park

(7) Sales	360		
(13) Sales	610		

B Tyler

(7) Sales	640	(24) Bank	845
(13) Sales	205		

L Frank

(27) Returns	18	(2) Purchases	550

G Byers

(17) Bank	700	(2) Purchases	290
		(10) Purchases	410

P Lee

(18) Returns	83	(2) Purchases	610
		(10) Purchases	1,240

Stop Ltd

(21) Bank	740	(15) S. fixtures	740

Trial balance as at 31 March 2008

Bank	1,155	
Cash	1,170	
Capital		8,000
Van	6,250	
Wages	220	
Shop fixtures	740	
G Prince (loan)		1,000
J Snow	295	
K Park	970	
L Frank		532
P Lee		1,767
Sales		2,620
Purchases	3,220	
Returns outwards		101
	14,020	14,020

6.5

Bank

Balance b/d	17,500	Central Council	2,500
Aardvarks	1,500	Klingon Corp	2,800
		Vehicle expenses	10,000
		Balance c/d	3,700
	19,000		19,000
Balance b/d	3,700		

Capital

Balance c/d	49,000	Bank	49,000
	49,000		49,000
		Balance b/d	49,000

Cash

Balance b/d	375.00	Spock	3,016.25
Sales	5,000.00	Balance c/d	2,358.75
	5,375.00		5,375.00
Balance b/d	2,358.75		

Fixtures

Balance b/d	20,000	Balance c/d	23,500
Klingon Corp	3,500		
	23,500		23,500
Balance b/d	23,500		

Inventory

Balance b/d	15,000	Cost of sales	500
Central Council	2,500	Cost of sales	250
		Balance c/d	16,750
	17,500		17,500
Balance b/d	16,750		

Cost of sales

Inventory	500	Balance c/d	750
Inventory	250		
	750		750
Balance b/d	750		

Sales

Balance c/d	6,500	Cash	5,000
		Aardvarks	1,500
	6,500		6,500
		Balance b/d	6,500

Discount received

Balance c/d	858.75	Spock	158.75
		Klingon Corp	700.00
	858.75		858.75
		Balance b/d	858.75

6.5 (*cont'd*)

Spock

Cash	3,016.25	Balance b/d	3,175
Discount	158.75		
	3,175.00		3,175

McCoy

Balance c/d	500	Balance b/d	500
	500		500
		Balance b/d	500

Aardvarks

Sales	1,500	Bank	1,500
	1,500		1,500

Vehicle expenses

Bank	10,000	Balance c/d	10,000
	10,000		10,000
Balance b/d	10,000		

Scott

Balance c/d	200	Balance b/d	200
	200		200
		Balance b/d	200

Central Council

Bank	2,500	Inventory	2,500
	2,500		2,500

Klingon Corp

Bank	2,800	Fixtures	3,500
Discount	700		
	3,500		3,500

USS Enterprise
Trial Balance as at 31 October 2009

	Dr £	Cr £
Bank	3,700	
Capital		49,000
Cash	2,358.75	
Fixtures	23,500	
Inventory	16,750	
Cost of sales	750	
Sales		6,500
Discount received		858.75
Scott		200
McCoy		500
Vehicle expenses	10,000	
	57,058.75	57,058.75

7.1

A Moore
Income statement for the year ended 31 December 2008

Sales		190,576
Less Cost of goods sold:		
Purchases	119,832	
Less Closing inventory	12,408	107,424
Gross profit		83,152
Less Expenses:		
Salaries	56,527	
Motor expenses	2,416	
Rent	1,894	
Insurance	372	
General expenses	85	61,294
Net profit		21,858

7.2

B Lane
Income statement for the year ended 30 June 2008

Sales		265,900
Less Cost of goods sold:		
Purchases	154,870	
Less Closing inventory	16,280	138,590
Gross profit c/d		127,310
Less Expenses:		
Salaries and wages	51,400	
Rent	4,200	
Lighting and heating	530	
Insurance	2,100	
Motor expenses	4,110	
Sundry expenses	412	62,752
Net profit		64,558

7.5

Bank

Bal b/d	5,672	Purchases	800
W Abbot	1,246	Office expenses	100
G Smart	315	Salaries	230
Cash	45	Balance c/d	5,981
	7,278		7,278
Balance b/d	5,981		

Cash

Balance b/d	100	Wages	39
Sales	152	Sundry expenses	73
Sales	94	Wages	39
		Bank	45
		Balance c/d	150
	346		346
Balance b/d	150		

Sales

Balance c/d	1,492	W Abbot	1,246
		Cash	152
		Cash	94
	1,492		1,492
		Balance b/d	1,492

W Abbot

Sales	1,246	Bank	1,246
	1,246		1,246

Wages

Cash	39	Balance c/d	78
Cash	39		
	78		78
Balance b/d	78		

G Smart

Balance b/d	344	Bank	315
		Discount allowed	29
	344		344

Discount allowed

G Smart	29	Balance c/d	29
	29		29
Balance b/d	29		

Sundry expenses

Cash	73	Balance c/d	73
	73		73
Balance b/d	73		

Purchases

Bank	800	Balance c/d	800
	800		800
Balance b/d	800		

J Sanders

Bank	185	Balance b/d	201
Discount received	16		
	201		201

Discount received

Balance c/d	16	J Sanders	16
	16		16
		Balance b/d	16

Office expenses

Bank	100	Balance c/d	100
	100		100
Balance b/d	100		

Salaries

Bank	230	Balance c/d	230
	230		230
Balance b/d	230		

Henry York
Income statement for the month ended 31 March

Sales		1,492
Less: Cost of goods sold – Purchases		800
Gross profit		692
Add: Discount received		16
		708
Less:		
Wages	78	
Discount allowed	29	
Sundry expenses	73	
Office expenses	100	
Salaries	230	510
Net profit		198

8.1

A Moore
Balance sheet as at 31 December 2008

Non-current assets		
Premises	95,420	
Motor vehicles	16,594	112,014
Current assets		
Inventory	12,408	
Accounts receivable	26,740	
Bank	16,519	
Cash	342	56,009
		168,023
Current liabilities		
Accounts payable		16,524
		151,499
Capital		
Balance at 1.1.2008	138,066	
Add Net profit	21,858	
	159,924	
Less Drawings	8,425	151,499

8.2

B Lane
Balance sheet as at 30 June 2008

Non-current assets		
Buildings	85,000	
Fixtures	1,100	
Vans	16,400	102,500
Current assets		
Inventory	16,280	
Accounts receivable	31,300	
Bank	14,590	62,170
		164,670
Less Current liabilities		
Accounts payable		15,910
		148,760
Capital		
Balance at 1.7.2007	114,202	
Add Net profit	64,558	
	178,760	
Less Drawings	30,000	148,760

8.5

G Hope
Balance sheet as at 30 June 2008

Non-current assets		
Premises		76,000
Current assets		
Inventory	24,000	
Accounts receivable	2,800	
Cash and bank	5,400	32,200
		108,200
Current liabilities		
Accounts payable	7,600	
Non-current liability		
Mortgage	50,000	(57,600)
		50,600
Capital		
Balance at 1.07.2007		40,000
Capital introduced		6,000
Net profit		13,600
		59,600
Less Drawings		9,000
		50,600

9.1

J Bell

Trading account part of the income statement for the year ending 31 December 2007

Sales		162,918	
Less Returns in		1,290	161,628
Less Cost of goods sold:			
Purchases	121,437		
Less Returns out	840	120,597	
Carriage inwards		980	
		121,577	
Less Closing inventory		11,320	110,257
Gross profit			51,371

9.3

G Still

Income statement for the year ending 30 September 2009

Sales		380,400	
Less Returns in		1,540	378,860
Less Cost of goods sold:			
Opening inventory		41,600	
Add Purchases	188,430		
Less Returns out	3,410	185,020	
Carriage inwards		3,700	
		230,320	
Less Closing inventory		44,780	185,540
Gross profit			193,320
Less Expenses:			
Salaries and wages		61,400	
Warehouse rent		3,700	
Carriage out		2,100	
Insurance		1,356	
Motor expenses		1,910	
Office expenses		412	
Lighting and heating		894	
General expenses		245	72,017
Net profit			121,303

Balance sheet as at 30 September 2009

Non-current assets		
Premises	92,000	
Fixtures and fittings	1,900	
Motor vehicles	13,400	107,300
Current assets		
Inventory	44,780	
Accounts receivable	42,560	
Bank	5,106	92,446
		199,746
Current liabilities		
Accounts payable		(31,600)
		168,146
Capital		
Balance at 1.10.2008	68,843	
Add Net profit	121,303	
	190,146	
Less Drawings	22,000	168,146

9.4

F Sorley

Income statement for the year ending 30 April 2007

Sales		210,420	
Less Returns in		4,900	205,520
Less Cost of goods sold:			
Opening inventory		9,410	
Add Purchases	108,680		
Less Returns out	3,720	104,960	
Carriage inwards		840	
		115,210	
Less Closing inventory		11,290	103,920
Gross profit			101,600
Less Expenses:			
Salaries and wages		41,800	
Motor expenses		912	
Rent		6,800	
Carriage out		1,115	
Sundry expenses		318	50,945
Net profit			50,655

Balance sheet as at 30 April 2007

Non-current assets		
Fixtures and fittings	912	
Motor vehicles	14,400	15,312
Current assets		
Inventory	11,290	
Accounts receivable	23,200	
Bank	4,100	
Cash	240	38,830
		54,142
Less Current liabilities		
Accounts payable		14,100
		40,042
Capital		
Balance as at 1.5.2006	18,827	
Add Net profit	50,655	
	69,482	
Less Drawings	29,440	40,042

9.7

Capital

			01.05 Bank	1,500
			01.05 Cash	500

Bank

01.05 Capital	1,500	03.05 Fixtures	150
31.05 Cash	2,000	30.05 Wages	450
		31.05 Drawings	500

Purchases

02.05 C Dunn	1,750		
06.05 E Farnham	115		

C Dunn

		02.05 Purchases	1,750

Fixtures and fittings

03.05 Bank	150		

E Farnham

		06.05 Purchases	115

Cash

01.05 Capital	500	10.05 Rent	300
31.05 Sales	2,500	12.05 Stationery	75
		31.05 Bank	2,000

Rent

10.05 Cash	300		

Stationery

12.05 Cash	75		

Sales

		14.05 G. Harlem	125
		31.05 Cash	2,500

G Harlem

14.05 Sales	125		

Van

20.05 I Jumpstart	2,000		

I Jumpstart

		20.05 Van	2,000

Wages

30.05 Bank	450		

Drawings

31.05 Bank	500		

A Baker
Trial balance as at 31 May

Capital		2,000
Bank	2,400	
Purchases	1,865	
C Dunn		1,750
Fixtures and fittings	150	
E Farnham		115
Cash	625	
Rent	300	
Stationery	75	
Sales		2,625
G Harlem	125	
Van	2,000	
I Jumpstart		2,000
Wages	450	
Drawings	500	
	7,490	7,490

Balance sheet as at 31 May

Non-current assets		
Fixtures and fittings		150
Van		2,000
		2,150
Current assets		
Inventory	500	
Accounts receivable	125	
Bank	2,400	
Cash	625	3,650
		5,800
Current liabilities – Accounts payable		
		(3,865)
		1,935
Capital		
Balance at 1 May		2,000
Add: Net profit*		435
		2,435
Less: Drawings		500
		1,935

*2,625 – (1,865 – 500) – (300 + 450 + 75) = 435

9.9 **Kingfire**
Income statement for the year ending 30 June 2008

Sales		35,800
Less Cost of sales		
Purchases	14,525	
Less Closing inventory	3,000	
		11,525
Gross profit		24,275
Less		
Salaries	2,325	
Motor expenses	9,300	
Rent and business rates	1,250	
Insurance – Buildings	750	
– Vehicles	1,200	
		14,825
Net profit		9,450

9.9 *(cont'd)* Balance sheet as at 30 June 2008

Non-current assets			
Motor vehicles			10,000
Fixtures			17,500
			27,500
Current assets			
Inventory		3,000	
Accounts receivable		11,725	
Cash		500	15,225
			42,725
Less Current liabilities			
Accounts payable	9,750		
Bank	1,250	11,000	
Loan		15,000	(26,000)
			16,725
Capital			
Opening balance	19,275		
Net profit	9,450		
	28,725		
Less Drawings	12,000		16,725

10.1
See text.

10.2
See text.

10.3
See text.

10.4
(*a*) See text.
(*b*) The historical cost convention does not make the going concern convention unnecessary. Several instances illustrate this:
(*i*) Non-current assets are depreciated over the useful economic life of the assets. This presupposes that the business will continue to operate during the years of the assumed useful economic life of the assets.
(*ii*) Prepayments also assume that the benefits available in the future will be able to be claimed, because the business is expected to continue.
(*iii*) Inventory is also valued on the basis that it will be disposed of during the future ordinary running of the business.
(*iv*) The accruals concept itself assumes that the business is to continue.
All of this shows that the two complement each other.
(*c*) Shareholders want financial statements so that they can decide what to do with their shareholdings, whether they should sell their shares or hold on to them.
To enable them to decide upon their actions, they would really like to know what is going to happen in the future. To help them in this they would also like information which shows them what happened in the past. Ideally, therefore, they would like both types of report, those on the past and those on the future.
If they had a choice, the logical choice would be to receive a report on the future provided that it could be relied upon.

13.1 Cash book

	Cash	*Bank*		*Cash*	*Bank*
(1) Capital	1,000		(2) Rent	230	
(3) G Broad (Loan)		2,000	(4) J Fine		860
(5) Sales	190		(9) A Moore	92	
(7) F Love		34	(16) Bank ¢	100	
(11) Sales		151	(19) R Onions (Loan)		500
(15) P Hood	96		(26) Motor expenses		75
(16) Cash ¢		100	(30) Cash ¢		200
(22) Sales		122	(31) Wages	320	
(30) Bank ¢	200		(31) Balances c/d	744	772
	1,486	2,407		1,486	2,407

13.3 Cash book

	Disct	*Cash*	*Bank*		*Disct*	*Cash*	*Bank*
(1) Balance b/d		620	7,142	(4) Rent			430
(2) G Slick	13		247	(8) R White	18		702
(2) P Fish	16		304	(8) G Green	24		936
(2) T Old	21		399	(8) L Flip	40		1,560
(6) F Black: loan			5,000	(10) Motor expenses		81	
(12) J Pie	2		88	(15) Wages		580	
(18) A Pony	27		513	(21) Cash			400
(18) B Line & Son	35		665	(24) Drawings		200	
(18) T Owen	26		494	(25) W Peat	5	155	
(21) Bank		400		(29) Fixtures			720
(31) Commission			120	(31) Balances c/d		4	10,224
	140	1,020	14,972		87	1,020	14,972

Discounts received

		(31) Total for month	87

Discounts allowed

(31) Total for month	140		

13.5

Bank

Balance b/d	1,000	Newton & Ridley	4,050
M Baldwin	2,000	J Duckworth	125
G Platt	250		
Balance c/d	925		
	4,175		4,175
		Balance b/d	925

Discounts allowed

M Baldwin	500	Balance c/d	500

M Baldwin

Balance b/d	2,500	Cash	2,000
		Discount	500
	2,500		2,500

G Platt

Balance b/d	250	Cash	250

Discount received

Balance c/d	450	Newton and Ridly	450

A Roberts

Balance b/d	900	Bad debts	900

Newton and Ridley

Cash	4,050	Balance b/d	4,500
Discount	450		
	4,500		4,500

Bad debts

A Roberts	900	Balance c/d	900

J Duckworth

Cash	125	Balance b/d	125

14.1

Sales Day Book

(1) B Hope	310
(3) T Fine	285
(6) L Moore	38
(10) B Hope	74
(17) H Tor	534
(19) J Young	92
(27) T Most	44
(31) R Best	112
	1,489

General Ledger

Sales Account

(31) Total for month	1,489

Sales Ledger

B Hope	
(1) Sales	310
(10) Sales	74
T Fine	
(3) Sales	285
L Moore	
(6) Sales	38
H Tor	
(17) Sales	534
J Young	
(19) *Sales*	92
T Most	
(27) Sales	44
R Best	
(31) Sales	112

14.3

Workings of invoices:

(1) F Gray	3 rolls white tape × 10 =	30		
	5 sheets blue cotton × 6 =	30		
	1 dress length × 20 =	20	80	
	Less trade discount 25%		20	60
(4) A Gray	6 rolls white tape × 10 =	60		
	30 metres green felt × 4 =	120	180	
	Less trade discount 33$^1/_3$%		60	120
(8) E Hines	1 dress length black silk × 20 =			20
(20) M Allen	10 rolls white tape × 10 =	100		
	6 sheets blue cotton × 6 =	36		
	3 dress lengths black silk × 20 =	60		
	11 metres green felt × 4 =	44	240	
	Less trade discount 25%		60	180
(31) B Cooper	12 rolls white tape × 10 =	120		
	14 sheets blue cotton × 6 =	84		
	9 metres green felt × 4 =	36	240	
	Less trade discount 33$^1/_3$%		80	160

Sales Day Book

(1) F Gray	60
(4) A Gray	120
(8) E Hines	20
(20) M Allen	180
(31) B Cooper	160
	540

General Ledger

Sales Account

(31) Total for month	540

Sales Ledger

F Gray	
(1) Sales	60
A Gray	
(4) Sales	120
E Hines	
(8) Sales	20
M Allen	
(20) Sales	180
B Cooper	
(31) Sales	160

15.1

Workings of purchases invoices

(1) D Pope	4 DVDs × 60 =	240		
	3 mini hi-fi units × 240 =	720	960	
	Less trade discount 25%		240	720
(3) F Lloyd	2 washing machines × 280 =	560		
	5 vacuum cleaners × 80 =	400		
	2 dishwashers × 200 =	400	1,360	
	Less trade discount 20%		272	1,088
(15) B Sankey	1 hi-fi unit × 600 =	600		
	2 washing machines × 320 =	640	1,240	
	Less trade discount 25%		310	930
(20) J Wilson	6 CD/radios × 45		270	
	Less trade discount 33$^1/_3$%		90	180
(30) R Freer	4 dishwashers × 240		960	
	Less trade discount 20%		192	768

15.1 *(cont'd)*

Purchases Day Book

(1) D Pope	720
(3) F Lloyd	1,088
(15) J Sankey	930
(20) J Wilson	180
(30) R Freer	768
	3,686

General Ledger

Purchases Account

(31) Total for month	3,686

Purchases Ledger

D Pope	
(1) Purchases	720
F Lloyd	
(3) Purchases	1,088
J Sankey	
(15) Purchases	930
J Wilson	
(20) Purchases	180
R Freer	
(30) Purchases	768

15.3 **Purchases Day Book**

(1) Smith Stores	90
(23) C Kelly	105
(31) J Hamilton	180
	375

Sales Day Book

(8) A Grantley	72
(15) A Henry	240
(24) D Sangster	81
	393

Purchases Ledger

Smith Stores

(1) Purchases 90

C Kelly

(23) Purchases 105

J Hamilton

(31) Purchases 180

Sales Ledger

A Grantley

(8) Sales 72

A Henry

(15) Sales 240

D Sangster

(24) Sales 81

General Ledger

Sales Account

(31) Total for month 393

Purchases Account

(31) Total for month 375

15.5(*a*) **Sales Day Book**

May 1 M Marshall	45
1 R Richards	200
23 T Young	160
	405

Purchases Day Book

May 9 C Clarke	240
16 A Charles	160
31 M Nelson	50
	450

(*b*)

Sales Ledger

M Marshall

May 1 Sales	45		

R Richards

May 1 Sales	200		

T Young

May 23 Sales	160		

Purchases Ledger

C Clarke

		May 9 Purchases	240

A Charles

		May 16 Purchases	160

M Nelson

		May 31 Purchases	50

(*c*)

Sales

		May 31 Credit sales for the month	405

Purchases

May 31 Credit purchases for the month	450		

(*d*) See text.

16.1 **Purchases Day Book**

(1) F Bean	324
(4) A Clerk	216
(4) B Lock	322
(4) F Turner	64
(4) G Rill	130
(10) B Lock	140
(18) J Top	230
(18) I Gray	310
(18) F Low	405
(18) P Able	180
(31) F Turner	174
(31) T Burns	230
	2,725

Returns Outwards Day Book

(7) F Bean	56
(7) A Clerk	28
(25) I Gray	140
(25) B Lock	34
	258

General Ledger

Purchases

(31) Total for month 2,725

Returns Outwards

(31) Total for month 258

Purchases Ledger

F Bean			
(7) Returns	56	(1) Purchases	324
A Clerk			
(7) Returns	28	(4) Purchases	216
B Lock			
(25) Returns	34	(4) Purchases	322
		(10) Purchases	140
F Turner			
		(4) Purchases	64
		(31) Purchases	174
G Rill			
		(4) Purchases	130
J Top			
		(18) Purchases	230
I Gray			
(25) Returns	140	(18) Purchases	310
F Low			
		(18) Purchases	405
P Able			
		(18) Purchases	180
T Burns			
		(31) Purchases	230

16.3

Sales Day Book

(1)	T Thompson	56
(1)	L Rodriguez	148
(1)	K Barton	145
(7)	K Kelly	89
(7)	N Mendes	78
(7)	N Lee	257
(24)	K Mohammed	57
(24)	K Kelly	65
(24)	O Green	112
(31)	N Lee	55
		1,062

Purchases Day Book

(3)	P Potter	144
(3)	H Harris	25
(3)	B Spencer	76
(9)	B Perkins	24
(9)	H Harris	58
(9)	H Miles	123
(17)	H Harris	54
(17)	B Perkins	65
(17)	L Nixon	75
		644

Returns Inwards Day Book

(14)	T Thompson	5
(14)	K Barton	11
(14)	K Kelly	14
(28)	N Mendes	24
		54

Returns Outwards Day Book

(11)	P Potter	12
(11)	B Spencer	22
(20)	B Spencer	14
		48

Sales Ledger

T Thompson

(1)	Sales	56	(14)	Returns	5

L Rodriguez

(1)	Sales	148			

K Barton

(1)	Sales	145	(14)	Returns	11

K Kelly

(7)	Sales	89	(14)	Returns	14
(24)	Sales	65			

N Mendes

(7)	Sales	78	(28)	Returns	24

N Lee

(7)	Sales	257			
(31)	Sales	55			

K Mohammed

(24)	Sales	57			

O Green

(24)	Sales	112			

Purchases Ledger

P Potter

(11)	Returns	12	(3)	Purchases	144

H Harris

			(3)	Purchases	25
			(9)	Purchases	58
			(17)	Purchases	54

B Spencer

(11)	Returns	22	(3)	Purchases	76
(20)	Returns	14			

B Perkins

			(9)	Purchases	24
			(17)	Purchases	65

H Miles

			(9)	Purchases	123

L Nixon

			(17)	Purchases	75

General Ledger

Purchases

(31)	Total for month	644			

Sales

			(31)	Total for month	1,062

Returns Inwards

(31)	Total for month	54			

Returns Outwards

			(31)	Total for month	48

17.1

(*a*)	Van	Dr	5,395	:	Deedon Garage	Cr	5,395
(*b*)	Bad debts	Dr	81	:	P Knight	Cr	81
(*c*)	Timewas Ltd	Dr	610	:	Office furniture	Cr	610
(*d*)	(*i*) Bank	Dr	51	:	R Twig	Cr	51
	(*ii*) Bad debts	Dr	269	:	R Twig	Cr	269
(*e*)	Drawings	Dr	22	:	Purchases	Cr	22
(*f*)	Drawings	Dr	62	:	Insurance	Cr	62
(*g*)	Machinery	Dr	1,260	:	Electrotime Ltd	Cr	1,260

17.3

The Journal

(1)	Premises	34,000	
	Van	5,125	
	Fixtures	810	
	Inventory	6,390	
	Accounts receivable:		
	P Mullen	140	
	F Lane	310	
	Bank	6,240	
	Cash	560	
	Accounts payable:		
	S Hood		215
	J Brown		460
	Capital		52,900
		53,575	53,575
(14)	Van	4,850	
	Abel Motors		4,850

Purchases Day Book

(2)	S Hood	145
(2)	D Main	206
(2)	W Tone	96
(2)	R Foot	66
(22)	L Mole	183
(22)	W Wright	191
		887

Sales Day Book

(3)	J Wilson	112
(3)	T Cole	164
(3)	F Syme	208
(3)	J Allen	91
(3)	P White	242
(3)	F Lane	90
(9)	T Cole	68
(9)	J Fox	131
		1,106

Returns Inwards Day Book

(11)	J Wilson	32
(11)	F Syme	48
		80

Returns Outwards Day Book

(19)	R Foot	6

17.3 *(cont'd)*

Cash Book

	Disct	Cash	Bank		Disct	Cash	Bank
(1) Balances b/d		560	6,240	(1) Storage			40
(16) P Mullen	7		133	(4) Motor expenses		47	
(16) F Lane	20		380	(7) Drawings		150	
(16) J Wilson	4		76	(24) S Hood	18		342
(16) F Syme	8		152	(24) J Brown	23		437
				(24) R Foot	6		54
				(27) Salaries			480
				(30) Business rates			132
				(31) Abel Motors			4,850
				(31) Balance c/d		363	646
	39	560	6,981		47	560	6,981

Trial Balance as at 31 May 2009

	Dr	Cr
D Main		206
W Tone		96
L Mole		183
W Wright		191
T Cole	232	
J Allen	91	
P White	242	
J Fox	131	
Capital		52,900
Storage	40	
Motor expenses	47	
Drawings	150	
Salaries	480	
Business rates	132	
Sales		1,106
Purchases	887	
Returns inwards	80	
Returns outwards		6
Premises	34,000	
Vans	9,975	
Fixtures	810	
Inventory	6,390	
Discounts allowed	39	
Discounts received		47
Bank	646	
Cash	363	
	54,735	54,735

Purchases Ledger

W Wright

		(22) Purchases	191

P Mullen

(1) Balance	140	(16) Bank & disct	140

F Lane

(1) Balance	310	(16) Bank & disct	400
(3) Sales	90		
	400		400

J Wilson

(3) Sales	112	(11) Returns	32
		(16) Bank & disct	80
	112		112

L Mole

		(22) Purchases	183

S Hood

(24) Bank & disc	360	(1) Bal b/d	215
		(2) Purchases	145
	360		360

J Brown

(24) Bank & disct	460	(1) Balance b/d	460

D Main

		(2) Purchases	206

W Tone

		(2) Purchases	96

R Foot

(19) Returns	6	(2) Purchases	66
(24) Bank & disct	60		
	66		66

Sales Ledger

T Cole

(3) Sales	164		
(9) Sales	68		

F Syme

(3) Sales	208	(11) Returns	48
		(16) Bank & disct	160
	208		208

J Allen

(3) Sales	91		

P White

(3) Sales	242		

J Fox

(9) Sales	131		

General Ledger

Capital

		(1) Bal b/d	52,900

Storage

(1) Bank	40		

Motor Expenses

(4) Cash	47		

Drawings

(7) Cash	150		

Salaries

(27) Bank	480		

Business rates

(30) Bank	132		

Sales

		(31) Total for month	1,106

Purchases

(31) Total for month	887		

Returns Inwards

(31) Total for month	80		

Returns Outwards

		(31) Total for month	6

Premises

(1) Bal b/d	34,000		

Vans

(1) Bal b/d	5,125		
(14) Better Motors	4,850		

Fixtures

(1) Bal b/d	810		

Inventory

(1) Bal b/d	6,390		

Discounts Allowed

(31) Total for month	39		

Discounts Received

		(31) Total for month	47

Abel Motors

(31) Bank	4,850	(14) Van	4,850

18.1

(*a*)–(*c*)

Petty Cash Book

Receipts		*Total*	*Cleaning*	*Motor Expenses*	*Postage*	*Stationery*	*Travelling*
300	(1) Balance b/d						
	(2) Postage	18			18		
	(3) Travelling	12					12
	(4) Cleaning	15	15				
	(7) Petrol	22		22			
	(8) Travelling	25					25
	(9) Stationery	17				17	
	(11) Cleaning	18	18				
	(14) Postage	5			5		
	(15) Travelling	8					8
	(18) Stationery	9				9	
	(18) Cleaning	23	23				
	(20) Postage	13			13		
	(24) Motor service	43		43			
	(26) Petrol	18		18			
	(27) Cleaning	21	21				
	(29) Postage	5			5		
	(30) Petrol	14		14			
		286	77	97	41	26	45
286	(31) Cash						
	(31) Balance c/d	300					
586		586					

(*d*) See text.

18.2

(*a*) Briefly: To keep detail out of cash book.
To reduce postings to expense accounts.
To enable petty cash to be kept by someone other than main cashier.

(*b*)

Petty Cash Book

Receipts		*Total*	*Postage and Stationery*	*Travel Expenses*	*Ledger Accounts*
1.13	(1) Balance b/d				
23.87	(2) Cash				
	(4) Postage	8.50	8.50		
	(9) Courtney Bishop	2.35			2.35
	(11) Bus fares	1.72		1.72	
	(17) Envelopes	0.70	0.70		
0.68	(23) Telephone reimbursed				
	(26) Petrol	10.00		10.00	
		23.27	9.20	11.72	2.35
	(30) Balance c/d	2.41			
25.68		25.68			
2.41	(1) Balance b/d				
22.59	(1) Cash				

(*c*)

Postage and Stationery

(30) Petty cash	9.20	

Travel Expenses

(30) Petty cash	11.72	

Courtney Bishop

(9) Petty cash	2.35	

Telephone

	(23) Petty cash	0.68

18.4 Oakhill Printing Cost Ltd

Receipts	Date	Details	Total	Travel	Stationery	Postage	Miscellaneous	Repairs/ Replacement
19.37	May 1	Balance b/d						
60.63	1	Cash						
	1	Bus fares	0.41	0.41				
	2	Stationery	2.35		2.35			
	4	Bus fares	0.30	0.30				
	7	Postage	1.70			1.70		
	7	Trade journal	0.95				0.95	
	8	Bus fares	0.64	0.64				
	11	Tippex	1.29		1.29			
	12	Typewriter ribbons	5.42					5.42
	14	Parcel	3.45			3.45		
	15	Paper-clips	0.42		0.42			
	15	Newspaper	2.00				2.00	
	16	Photocopier repair	16.80					16.80
	19	Postage	1.50			1.50		
	20	Drawing pins	0.38		0.38			
	21	Train fare	5.40	5.40				
	22	Photo-paper	5.63		5.63			
	23	Display decorations	3.07				3.07	
	23	Tippex	1.14		1.14			
	25	Wrapping paper	0.78				0.78	
	27	String	0.61				0.61	
	27	Sellotape	0.75		0.75			
	27	Pens	0.46		0.46			
	28	Typewriter repairs	13.66					13.66
	30	Bus fares	2.09	2.09				
	31	Balance c/d	8.80					
80.00			80.00	8.84	12.42	6.65	7.41	35.88
8.80	June 1	Balance b/d						
71.20	1	Cash						

19.1

(*a*) Style of invoice will vary.

Calculations:	£
3 sets of Tiger Gold Golf Clubs × £810	2,430
150 Rose golf balls at £20 per 10 balls	300
4 Daly golf bags at £270	1,080
	3,810
Less trade discount 33⅓%	1,270
	2,540
Add VAT 10%	254
	2,794

(*b*)

F Marr Ltd Ledger

M Low & Son

Date	Details	£	Date	Details	£
2007					
May 1	Sales	2,794			

M Low & Son Ledger

F Marr Ltd

Date	Details	£	Date	Details	£
			2007		
			May 1	Purchases	2,794

19.3

Sales Day Book

2009		Net	VAT
Aug 1	G Clark Ltd	210	21
8	P Main	430	43
19	W Roy Ltd	120	12
31	F Job	60	6
		820	82

Sales Ledger

G Clark Ltd

(1) Sales	231		

P Main

(8) Sales	473		

W Roy Ltd

(19) Sales	132		

F Job

(31) Sales	66		

General Ledger

Sales

		(31) Credit sales for the month	820

Value Added Tax

		(31) Sales Day Book: VAT content	82

19.4

Sales Day Book

	Net	VAT
(1) A Bell	220	22
(4) D Player and Co	380	38
(16) D Player and Co	80	8
(31) P Green	30	3
	710	71

Purchases Day Book

	Net	VAT
(10) F Loy and Partners	510	51
(10) R Dixon Ltd	270	27
(14) G Melly	90	9
(23) E Flynn	140	14
	1,010	101

Sales Ledger

A Bell and Co

(1) Sales	242		

D Player and Co

(4) Sales	418		
(16) Sales	88		

P Green

(31) Sales	33		

Purchases Ledger

F Loy and Partners

		(10) Purchases	561

R Dixon Ltd

		(10) Purchases	297

G Melly

		(14) Purchases	99

E Flynn

		(23) Purchases	154

General Ledger

Sales

		(31) Credit sales for month	710

Purchases

(31) Credit purchases for month	1,010		

Value Added Tax

(31) VAT content in Purchases Day Book	101	(31) VAT content in Sales Day Book	71
		(31) Balance c/d	30
	101		101

19.6

(*a*)

Sales Day Book

Date	*Name and Details*	*List price less trade discount* £	*p*	*VAT* £	*p*	*Total* £	*p*
2009							
Mar 9	Neville's Electrical	576	–	57	60	633	60
17	Maltby plc	3,000	–	300	–	3,300	–
29	Neville's Electrical	368	–	36	80	404	80
		3,944	–	394	40	4,338	40

(*b*)

Neville's Electrical

2009			
Mar 9	Sales	633.60	
29	Sales	404.80	

Maltby plc

2009			
Mar 17	Sales	3,300.00	

Sales

2009		
Mar 31	Sales Day Book	3,944.00

Value Added Tax

2009		
Mar 31	Sales Day Book	394.40

(*c*)

Trial Balance as at 31 March 2009

	Dr	*Cr*
Neville's Electrical	1,038.40	
Maltby plc	3,300.00	
Sales		3,944.00
Value Added Tax		394.40
	4,338.40	4,338.40

20.1

Columnar Sales Day Book

	Inv No	*Total*	*VAT*	*Music Dept*	*TV Dept*	*Kitchen Dept*
2007						
Feb 1 M Long	403	4,290	390		3,900	
2 F Ray	404	1,210	110	1,100		
3 M Tom	405	1,078	98		980	
5 T John	406	451	41			410
7 F Ray	407	1,826	166		1,660	
7 M Long	408	2,684	244	2,440		
		11,539	1,049	3,540	6,540	410

General Ledger

Sales

	Music	*TV*	*Kitchen*
2007			
Feb 28 Total for month	3,540	6,540	410

Value Added Tax

2007	
Feb 7 Total for week	1,049

M Long

Feb 1 Sales	4,290
7 Sales	2,684

F Ray

Feb 2 Sales	1,210
7 Sales	1,826

M Tom

Feb 3 Sales	1,078

T John

Feb 5 Sales	451

20.2

F Wayne
Purchases Analysis Book

			Total	*Purchases*	*Light & Heat*	*Motor Exps*	*Stationery*	*Carriage Inwards*
2006								
July	1	G Hope	560	560				
	3	B Smith	420	420				
	4	Scottish Gas	91		91			
	5	F Loy	373	373				
	6	Bright Body Shop	192			192		
	8	Light Letters	46				46	
	10	Pope Garage	124			124		
	12	Scottish Gas	88		88			
	15	B Bill	265	265				
	17	G Fyfe	18		18			
	18	T Tully	296	296				
	19	Rapid Flight Ltd	54					54
	21	K Frank	14				14	
	24	F Loy	218	218				
	27	Couriers Ltd	44					44
	31	Pope Garage	104			104		
			2,907	2,132	197	420	60	98

20.3

General ledger: Purchases Dr 2,132; Lighting and heating Dr 197;
Motor expenses Dr 420; Stationery Dr 60;
Carriage inwards Dr 98.

Purchases ledger: Credits in personal accounts should be obvious.

21.1

Gross pay		200
Less: Income tax	27	
National Insurance	16	43
Net pay		157

21.2

Gross pay 40 × 4	160	
5 × 6	30	190
Less: Income tax*	25	
National Insurance	17	42
Net pay		148

*190 − 80 = 110. First 50 × 20% = 10 + (60 × 25%) 15 = total 25.

21.3

Salary		200
Commission		600
Gross pay		800
Less: Income tax*	85	
National Insurance	66	151
Net pay		649

*800 − 450 = 350. First 50 × 20% = 10 + (300 × 25%) 75 = total 85.

21.4

Salary		2,000
Bonus		400
		2,400
Less		
Superannuation	120	
Income tax*	450	
National Insurance	190	760
		1,640

*2,400 − 120 − 430 = 1,850. First 250 × 20% = 50 + (1,600 × 25%) 400 = 450.

22.1
See text.

22.2
See text.

22.3
See text.

23.1
See text.

23.2
See text.

23.3
See text.

23.4
See text.

24.1
(*a*) Per text.
(*b*) Capital: (*i*), (*ii*), machine part of (*v*), (*vi*).
Revenue: (*iii*), (*iv*), drinks part of (*v*).

24.3
Capital: (*a*), (*c*), (*e*), (*g*); Revenue: (*b*), (*d*), (*f*)

24.5
Capital: (*a*), (*b*), (*e*).

24.7
Capital: (*a*), (*c*), (*d*), (*f*), (*j*), (*l*); Revenue: (*b*), (*e*), (*g*), (*h*), (*i*), (*k*).

24.9
(*a*) Per text.
(*b*) PC – acquisition cost

Basic cost	4,000
Installation and testing	340
	4,340
Less 5% discount	217
	4,123
Special wiring	110
Modifications	199
Staff training	990
Total cost	5,422

(*c*) 1. Revenue. 2. Capital. 3. Capital. 4. Revenue. 5. Revenue. 6. Revenue. 7. Capital. 8. Revenue. 9. Capital. 10. Capital.

24.11

Wooden store shed

Balance b/d	850	Wooden store shed disposal	850

Office buildings

Balance b/d	179,500		
Wages	109		
Materials	109		

Office buildings repairs

Wages	181		
Materials	351		

New store

Wooden store shed disposal	100		
Materials	4,750		
Wages	3,510		
Direct expenses	85		

Wooden store shed disposal

Wooden store shed	850	Bank	180
Bank	265	New store	100

24.12

(*a*) *Plant at Cost*

Balance 1 April 2005		372,000
Add Acquisitions during year		96,000
		468,000
Less Disposals (36,000 + 4,000 + 4,400)		44,400
Balance 31 March 2006		423,600

(*b*) *Provision for Depreciation of Plant*

Balance 1 April 2005		205,400
Less Depreciation on disposals (W1)		25,200
		180,200
Add Provision for year 20% × (423,600 – 180,200)		48,680
Balance 31 March 2006		228,880

Plant Sold

Cost: year to 31 March 2002		40,000
Depreciation: year to 31 March 2002	20%	8,000
		32,000
Depreciation: year to 31 March 2003	20%	6,400
		25,600
Addition		4,400
		30,000
Depreciation: year to 31 March 2004	20%	6,000
		24,000
Depreciation: year to 31 March 2005	20%	4,800
		19,200

(W1) Depreciation accumulated: 8,000 + 6,400 + 6,000 + 4,800 = 25,200.

(*c*) *Sale of plant*

Sale of plant		13,700
Less Cost (40,000 + 4,400)	44,400	
Depreciation	25,200	
Book value at date of sale		19,200
Loss on disposal		5,500

24.14

Classifying something as a capital expense rather than a revenue expense increases non-current assets, reduces expenses and so increases net profit (and so also increases capital). This makes the business look more profitable than it would have been had the expenditure been classified instead as revenue expenditure. It also makes it look in a better financial state than it would have been (as non-current assets have increased). Misclassifying revenue expenditure as capital expenditure is misleading to users of the financial statements.

25.1

Bad Debts

2007		2007	
May 31 S Gill & Son	340	Dec 31 Profit and loss	959
Sep 30 H Black Ltd	463		
Nov 30 A Thom	156		
	959		959

Allowance for doubtful debts

		2007	
		Dec 31 Profit and loss	410

Profit and Loss (extracts)

Bad debts	959
Allowance for doubtful debts	410

Balance Sheet as at 31 December 2007 (extract)

Accounts receivable	14,420	
Less: Allowance for doubtful debts	410	
		14,010

25.2

(*a*) *Bad debts*

2008		2008	
Dec 31 Various	680	Dec 31 Profit and loss	680

(*b*) *Allowance for doubtful debts*

Dec 31 Balance c/d	672	Jan 1 Balance b/d	320
		Dec 31 Profit and loss	352
	672		672

(*c*) *Profit and Loss (extracts)*

Bad debts	680
Allowance for doubtful debts	352

(*d*) *Balance Sheet (extract)*

Accounts receivable	16,800	
Less allowance for doubtful debts	672	16,128

25.3

(*i*) *Bad Debts*

2007		2007	
May 31 F Lamb	175	Dec 31 Profit and loss	405
Oct 31 A Clover	230		
	405		405
2008		2008	
Jan 31 D Ray	190	Dec 31 Profit and loss	604
Jun 30 P Clark	75		
Oct 31 J Will	339		
	604		604

25.3 *(cont'd)*

Allowance for Doubtful Debts

2007			2007		
Dec 31	Balance c/d	640	Dec 31	Profit and loss	640
		640			
2008			2008		
Dec 31	Balance c/d	710	Jan 1	Balance b/d	640
			Dec 31	Profit and loss	70
		710			710

(*ii*) *Balance Sheet (extracts)*

	2007		2008	
Debtors	52,400		58,600	
Less Allowance for doubtful debts	640	51,760	710	57,890

25.5

Allowance for Doubtful Debts

2007			2007		
Dec 31	Balance c/d	500	Jan 1	Balance b/d	400
			Dec 31	Profit and loss	100
		500			500
2008			2008		
Dec 31	Balance c/d	600	Jan 1	Balance b/d	500
			Dec 31	Profit and loss	100
		600			600
2009			2009		
Dec 31	Profit and loss	200	Jan 1	Balance b/d	600
Dec 31	Balance c/d	400			
		600			600

Income Statement Extract for the year ending 31 December

2007	
Gross profit	xxx
Less Expenses	
Allowance for doubtful debts	100
Bad debts	420
2008	
Gross profit	xxx
Less Expenses	
Allowance for doubtful debts	100
Bad debts	310
2009	
Gross profit	xxx
Add Reduction in allowance for doubtful debts	200
	xxx
Less Expenses	
Bad debts	580

25.7

(*a*) *Allowance for Doubtful Debts*

2008			2007		
May 31	Profit and loss (W1)	1,390	Jun 1	Balance b/d	2,300
31	Balance c/d	910			
		2,300			2,300
			2008		
			Jun 1	Balance b/d	910

(*b*) *Provision for Discounts Allowed*

2008		
May 31	Profit and loss (W2)	594

Workings

(W1) Provision 1.6.2007			2,300
Less Provision 31.5.2008	1% × 24,000	240	
	2% × 10,000	200	
	4% × 8,000	320	
	5% × 3,000	150	910
Reduction in Provision			1,390
(W2) Accounts receivable liable for discounts		24,000	
Less Allowance for doubtful debts		240	23,760

Provision for discounts allowed $2^1/_2$% × 23,760 = 594

25.9

(days and months omitted)

(*a*) *Bad Debts*

2006 Debtors	1,400	2006 Profit and loss	1,400
2007 Debtors	2,200	2007 Profit and loss	2,200
2008 Debtors	3,800	2008 Profit and loss	3,800

(*b*) *Bad Debts Recovered*

2007 Profit and loss	210	2007 J Sweeny	210
2008 Profit and loss	320	2008 Various accounts receivable	320

(*c*) *Allowance for Doubtful Debts*

2006 Balance c/d	2,600	2006 Profit and loss	2,600
2007 Balance c/d	3,680	2007 Balance b/d	2,600
		Profit and loss	1,080
	3,680		3,680
2008 Profit and loss	80	2008 Balance b/d	3,680
Balance c/d	3,600		
	3,680		3,680

(*d*) *Profit and Loss Account (extracts)*

(2006) Bad debts	1,400		
Allowance for doubtful debts	2,600		
(2007) Bad debts	2,200	(2007) Bad debt recovered	210
Allowance for doubtful debts	1,080		
(2008) Bad debts	3,800	(2008) Reduction in allowance for doubtful debts	80
		Bad debt recovered	320

25.10

(A) See text.
(B) See text.
(C) (1) (*i*)

Allowance for Doubtful Debts

2007			2007		
Dec 31	Profit and loss	33	Jan 1	Balance b/d	750*
	Balance c/d	717**			
		750			750

(*ii*)

Bad Debts

2007			2007		
?	Accounts receivable – A Stewart	900	Dec 31	Profit and loss	3,800
?	Accounts receivable	2,300			
Dec 31	Accounts receivable – J Smith	600			
		3,800			3,800

(2) the net profit will increase by £33.

*3% 25,000 = 750; **3% 23,900

26.1

Straight Line		*Reducing Balance*	
Cost	2,600	Cost	2,600
Yr 1 Depreciation*	600	Yr 1 Depn 45% of 2,600	1,170
	2,000		1,430
Yr 2 Depreciation	600	Yr 2 Depn 45% of 1,430	644**
	1,400		786
Yr 3 Depreciation	600	Yr 3 Depn 45% of 786	354
	800		432
Yr 4 Depreciation	600	Yr 4 Depn 45% of 432	194
	200		238

*2,600 – 200 = 2,400 ÷ 4 = 600 **rounded up from 643.5

26.2

(*a*) *Straight Line*		(*b*) *Reducing Balance*	
Cost	8,000	Cost	8,000
Yr 1 Depreciation*	1,120	Yr 1 Depn 20% of 8,000	1,600
	6,880		6,400
Yr 2 Depreciation	1,120	Yr 2 Depn 20% of 6,400	1,280
	5,760		5,120
Yr 3 Depreciation	1,120	Yr 3 Depn 20% of 5,120	1,024
	4,640		4,096
Yr 4 Depreciation	1,120	Yr 4 Depn 20% of 4,096	819
	3,520		3,277
Yr 5 Depreciation	1,120	Yr 5 Depn 20% of 3,277	655
	2,400		2,622

$^{*}\frac{8,000 - 2,400}{5} = 1,120$

26.3

(*a*) *Reducing Balance*		(*b*) *Straight Line*	
Cost	9,600	Cost	9,600
Yr 1 Depn 35% of 9,600	3,360	Yr 1 Depreciation*	2,333
	6,240		7,267
Yr 2 Depn 35% of 6,240	2,184	Yr 2 Depreciation	2,333
	4,056		4,934
Yr 3 Depn 35% of 4,056	1,420	Yr 3 Depreciation	2,333
	2,636		2,601

$^{*}\frac{9,600 - 2,600}{3} = 2,333$

26.7

			Machines A	B	C
	Bought 1.1.2006		2,000		
2006	Depreciation	15% for 12 months	300		
			1,700		
	Bought 1.9.2007			4,000	
2007	Depreciation	15% × 1,700	255		
	Depreciation	15% for 4 months		200	
			1,445	3,800	
	Bought 1.4.2008				3,000
2008	Depreciation	15% × 1,445	217		
	Depreciation	15% × 3,800		570	
	Depreciation	15% for 8 months			300
			1,662	3,230	2,700

2008 Total depreciation provision 217 + 570 + 300 = 1,087

26.8

Motor Vehicle

2006		
Jan 1	Trucks Ltd	12,000

Accumulated provision for depreciation on motor vehicles

2006			2006		
Dec 31	Balance c/d	3,000	Dec 31	Depreciation	3,000
2007			2007		
Dec 31	Balance c/d	5,250	Jan 1	Balance b/d	3,000
			Dec 31	Depreciation	2,250
		5,250			5,250

26.9

Ivor Innes
Balance Sheet as at 31 March 2008

Non-current assets		
Fixtures (7,600–600)		7,000
Current assets		
Inventory	19,000	
Accounts receivable	4,440	
Bank	8,320	
Cash	700	32,460
		39,460
Current liabilities		
Accounts payable		(8,800)
		30,660
Capital		
Balance at 1 April 2007*		34,900
Capital introduced		18,000
		52,900
Less: Net loss	10,840	
Drawings	11,400	
		22,240
		30,660

*840 + 7,600 + 5,500 + 17,800 + 8,360 − 5,200 = 34,900

26.12

(*a*) Reducing balance. Obsolescence probably very slow and not relevant.
(*b*) Straight line. Obsolescence very slow and probably not relevant.
(*c*) Straight line. Obsolescence depends on the market and growth at the business.
(*d*) Reducing balance (as it is likely to be more efficient in the early years of use and susceptible to obsolescence).
(*e*) Machine hours. Already obsolete.

27.1

Vans

2005			2005	
Jan 1 Bank	13,800		Dec 31 Balance c/d	21,000
Aug 1 Bank	7,200			
	21,000			21,000

Provision for Depreciation: Vans

2005			2005	
Dec 31 Balance c/d	4,200		Dec 31 Profit and loss	4,200*

*13,800 × 25% = £3,450
7,200 × 25% × $^5/_{12}$ = 750
4,200

27.2

(*a*)

Machinery

2003		2003	
Jan 1 Bank	1,400	Dec 31 Balance c/d	1,400
2004		2004	
Jan 1 Balance b/d	1,400	Dec 31 Balance c/d	3,600
Jul 1 Bank	1,200		
Oct 1 Bank	1,000		
	3,600		3,600
2005		2005	
Jan 1 Balance b/d	3,600	Dec 31 Balance c/d	3,600
2006		2006	
Jan 1 Balance b/d	3,600	Dec 31 Balance c/d	4,000
Apr 1 Bank	400		
	4,000		4,000

(*b*)

Provision for Depreciation: Machinery

2003		2003	
Dec 31 Balance c/d	140	Dec 31 Profit and loss	140
2004		2004	
Dec 31 Balance c/d	365	Jan 1 Balance b/d	140
		Dec 31 Profit and loss	225*
	365		365
2005		2005	
Dec 31 Balance c/d	725	Jan 1 Balance b/d	365
		Dec 31 Profit and loss	360
	725		725
2006		2006	
Dec 31 Balance c/d	1,115	Jan 1 Balance b/d	725
		Dec 31 Profit and loss	390**
	1,115		1,115

*1,400 × 10% = 140
1,200 × 10% × $^1/_2$ = 60
1,000 × 10% × $^1/_4$ = 25
225

**3,600 × 10% = 360
400 × 10% × $^3/_4$ = 30
390

(*c*)

Balance Sheet Extracts

31 December 2003			31 December 2005		
Machinery at cost	1,400		Machinery at cost	3,600	
Less Depreciation	140	1,260	*Less* Depreciation to date	725	2,875
31 December 2004			31 December 2006		
Machinery at cost	3,600		Machinery at cost	4,000	
Less Depreciation to date	365	3,235	*Less* Depreciation to date	1,115	2,885

27.4

Plant

2004		2004		
Jan 1 Bank	2,600	Dec 31 Balance c/d	4,700
Oct 1 Bank	2,100		
	4,700		4,700
2006		2006	
Jan 1 Balance b/d	4,700	Dec 31 Balance c/d	7,500
Sep 1 Bank	2,800		
	7,500		7,500
2007		2007	
Jan 1 Balance b/d	7,500	Aug 31 Disposals	2,600
		Dec 31 Balance c/d	4,900
	7,500		7,500

Provision for Depreciation: Plant

2004		2004	
Dec 31 Balance c/d	781	Dec 31 Profit and loss	781*

2,600 × 25% = 650
2,100 × 25% × $^3/_{12}$ = 131.25
781

2005		2005	
Dec 31 Balance c/d	1,956	Jan 1 Balance b/d	781
		Dec 31 Profit and loss	1,175
	1,956		1,956
2006		2006	
Dec 31 Balance c/d	3,364	Jan 1 Balance b/d	1,956
		Dec 31 Profit and loss	1,408*
	3,364		3,364

*4,700 × 25% = 1,175
2,800 × 25% × $^4/_{12}$ = 233.33
1,408

2007		2007	
Sep 30 Plant Disposals	2,383	Jan 1 Balance b/d	3,364
Dec 31 Balance c/d	2,639	Dec 31 Profit and loss	1,658*
	5,022		5,022

*2,600 × 25% × $^8/_{12}$ = 433.33
2,100 × 25% = 525
2,800 × 25% = 700
1,658

Plant Disposals

2007		2007	
Sep 30 Plant	2,600	Sep 30 Provn for depn	2,383
Dec 31 Profit and loss	593	30 Bank	810
	3,193		3,193

Balance Sheets

	2004	2005	2006	2007
Plant at cost	4,700	4,700	7,500	4,900
Less depn to date	781	1,956	3,364	2,639
	3,919	2,744	4,136	2,261

27.5

Machinery

2009		2009	
Jan 1 Balance b/d	94,500	Dec 31 Machinery disposals	1,600
Dec 31 Bank	16,000	31 Balance c/d	108,900
	110,500		110,500

Office Furniture

2009		2009	
Jan 1 Balance b/d	3,200	Dec 31 Balance c/d	3,660
Dec 31 Bank	460		
	3,660		3,660

Provision for Depreciation: Machinery

2009		2009	
Dec 31 Machinery disposals	1,280	Jan 1 Balance b/d	28,350
31 Balance c/d	48,850	Dec 31 Profit and loss	21,780
	50,130		50,130

Provision for Depreciation: Office Furniture

2009		2009	
Dec 31 Balance c/d	1,646	Jan 1 Balance b/d	1,280
		Dec 31 Profit and loss	366
	1,646		1,646

Machinery Disposals

2009		2009	
Dec 31 Machinery	1,600	Dec 31 Provision for depn	1,280
31 Profit and loss: Gain on sale	40	31 Bank	360
	1,640		1,640

Balance Sheet as at 31 December 2009

Machinery at cost	108,900	
Less Depreciation to date	48,850	60,050
Office furniture at cost	3,660	
Less Depreciation to date	1,646	2,014

27.6
£2,500 and £8,500.

27.8

(*a*) (*i*) Time factor (*ii*) Economic factors (*iii*) Deterioration physically (*iv*) Depletion.

(*b*) (*i*) Depletion (*ii*) Physical deterioration (*iii*) Time (*iv*) Not usually subject to depletion, but depends on circumstances (*v*) Economic factors, obsolescence for example (*vi*) Time factor.

(*c*)

Equipment

Balance b/d	135,620	Asset disposals	36,000
Bank	47,800	Balance c/d	147,420
	183,420		183,420
Balance b/d	147,420		

Provision for Depreciation – Equipment

Asset disposals	28,224	Balance b/d	81,374
Balance c/d	90,858	Profit and loss	37,708
	119,082		119,082
		Balance b/d	90,858

Asset Disposals

Equipment	36,000	Provision for depreciation	28,224
		Bank	5,700
		Profit and loss	2,076
	36,000		36,000

27.10

(*a*) (*i*) Straight line depreciation method

Non-current Asset

Year 1 Bank	10,000	Year 3 Asset disposals	10,000

Accumulated Provision for Depreciation

		Year 1 Profit and loss	2,000
Year 2 Balance c/d	4,000	Year 2 Profit and loss	2,000
	4,000		4,000
Year 3 Asset disposals	4,000	Year 3 Balance b/d	4,000

Asset Disposals

Year 3 Non-current asset	10,000	Year 3 Bank	5,000
		Year 3 Acc. provn for depn	4,000
		Year 3 Profit and loss	1,000
	10,000		10,000

(*ii*) Reducing balance method

Non-current Asset

Year 1 Bank	10,000	Year 3 Asset disposals	10,000

Accumulated Provision for Depreciation

		Year 1 Profit and loss	4,000
Year 2 Balance c/d	6,400	Year 2 Profit and loss	2,400
	6,400		6,400
Year 3 Asset disposals	6,400	Year 3 Balance b/d	6,400

Asset Disposals

Year 3 Non-current asset	10,000	Year 3 Bank	5,000
Year 3 Profit and loss	1,400	Year 3 Acc. provn for depn	6,400
	11,400		11,400

(*b*) (*i*) The purpose of depreciation provisions is to apportion the cost of non-current asset over the useful years of its life to the organisation.

The matching concept concerns the matching of costs against the revenues which those costs generate. If the benefit to be gained is equal in each year then the straight line method is to be preferred. If the benefits are greatest in year 1 and then falling year by year, then the reducing balance method would be preferred. The impact of maintenance costs of the non-current asset, if heavier in later years, may also give credence to the reducing balance method.

(*ii*) The net figure at the end of year 2 is the amount of original cost not yet expensed against revenue.

(*c*) The charge in year 1 should be nil in this case. The matching concept concerns matching costs against revenues. There have been no revenues in year 1, therefore there should be no costs.

27.12 Your letter should include the following:

- Depreciation is an expense.
- It allows the expense of an asset to be spread over its useful economic life.
- It is only a book figure and therefore 'real' money is not set aside when you depreciate an asset.
- It is not a reserve, and never can be as there are no assets of the business underpinning it.

27.14

			Dr	*Cr*
(*a*) (*a*)	2001	Machines	15,000	
		XY Manufacturing Co		15,000
	2002	Depreciation	2,000	
		Acc. provn for depn: machine		2,000
	2003	Depreciation	2,000	
		Acc. provn for depn: machine		2,000

(*b*)

Balance Sheet extract as 30 September 2003

Machine	11,000

(*b*) (*a*)

Machine

2004		2004	
Oct 1 Balance b/d	15,000	Oct 1 Machine disposal	15,000

Accumulated Provision for Depreciation: Machine

2004		2004	
Oct 1 Machine disposal	6,000	Oct 1 Balance b/d	6,000

Machine Disposal

2004			2004		
Oct 1	Machine	15,000	Oct 1	Acc. provn for depn	6,000
			1	Cash	7,500
			2005		
			Sept 30	Profit and loss	1,500
		15,000			15,000

(*b*)

Machine Account and Accumulated Provision for Depreciation Account are as in (a)

Machine Disposal

2004			2004		
Oct 1	Machine	15,000	Oct 1	Acc. provn for depn	6,000
			1	Cash	12,000
2005					
Sept 30	Profit and loss	3,000			
		18,000			18,000

27.16

Machinery

2005			2005		
Jan 1	Bank	10,000	Dec 31	Balance c/d	16,000
July 1	Bank	6,000			
		16,000			16,000
2006			2006		
Jan 1	Balance b/d	16,000	Dec 31	Balance c/d	24,000
Mar 31	Bank	8,000			
		24,000			24,000
2007			2007		
Jan 1	Balance b/d	24,000	Oct 7	Machinery disposal	10,000
Nov 5	Bank	12,000	Dec 31	Balance c/d	26,000
		36,000			36,000
2008			2008		
Jan 1	Balance b/d	26,000	Feb 4	Machinery disposal	6,000
Feb 6	Bank	9,000	Oct 11	Machinery disposal	12,000
Oct 11	Machinery disposal	7,000	Dec 31	Balance c/d	24,000
		42,000			42,000

Accumulated provision for depreciation

2005			2005		
Dec 31	Balance c/d	3,200	Dec 31	Depreciation	3,200
2006			2006		
Dec 31	Balance c/d	8,000	Jan 1	Balance b/d	3,200
			Dec 31	Depreciation	4,800
		8,000			8,000
2007			2007		
Oct 7	Machinery disposal	4,000	Jan 1	Balance b/d	8,000
Dec 31	Balance c/d	9,200	Dec 31	Depreciation	5,200
		13,200			13,200
2008			2008		
Feb 4	Machinery disposal	3,600	Jan 1	Balance b/d	9,200
Oct 11	Machinery disposal	2,400	Dec 31	Depreciation	4,800
Dec 31	Balance c/d	7,000			
		13,000			13,000

Machinery Disposal

2007			2007		
Oct 7	Machinery	10,000	Oct 7	Acc. provn for depn	4,000
			7	Bank	5,500
			Dec 31	Profit and loss (loss on sale)	500
		10,000			10,000
2008			2008		
Feb 4	Machinery	6,000	Feb 4	Acc. provn for depn	3,600
Oct 11	Machinery	12,000	4	Bank	3,000
			Oct 11	Acc. provn for depn	2,400
			11	Machinery	7,000
			Dec 31	Profit and loss (loss on disposal)	2,000
		18,000			18,000

X Y Ltd
Balance Sheet extract as at 31 December

2007	
Machinery at cost	26,000
Less: Accumulated depreciation	9,200
	16,800
2008	
Machinery at cost	24,000
Less: Accumulated depreciation	7,000
	17,000

27.18

Plant and machinery

2004			2004		
Jan 1	Balance b/d	180,000	Dec 31	Balance c/d	200,000
Mar 1	Bank	20,000			
		200,000			200,000
2005			2005		
Jan 1	Balance b/d	200,000	Dec 31	Balance c/d	200,000
2006			2006		
Jan 1	Balance b/d	200,000	Jan	Plant and m/c disposal	20,000
			Dec 31	Balance c/d	180,000
		200,000			200,000

27.18 *(cont'd)*

Accumulated provision for depreciation

2004		2004		
Dec 31 Balance c/d	96,000	Jan 1 Balance b/d	70,000	
		Dec 31 Depreciation	26,000	
	96,000		96,000	
2005		2005		
Dec 31 Balance c/d	116,800	Jan 1 Balance b/d	96,000	
		Dec 31 Depreciation	20,800	
	116,800		116,800	
2006		2006		
Jan Plant and m/c disposal**	7,200	Jan 1 Balance b/d	116,800	
Dec 31 Balance c/d	123,067	Dec 31 Depreciation*	13,467	
	130,267		130,267	

*180,000 – (116,800 – 7,200) – 30,000 = 41,400 ÷ 3 = 13,467
**(20,000 × 0.2) + [(20,000 – (20,000 × 0.2) × 0.2)] = 4,000 + 3,200 = 7,200

Plant and Machinery Disposal

2006		2006	
Jan Plant and machinery	20,000	Mar 1 Acc provn for depn	7,200
Dec 31 Profit and loss	1,200	Bank	14,000
	21,200		21,200

27.20

(a) *(i)* Straight line:
Cost £112,000 – trade-in £12,000 = £100,000
Per month £100,000 ÷ 48 = 2,083.33

2006	9 months	=	18,750	
2007	12 months	=	25,000	
2008	12 months	=	25,000	
2009	12 months	=	25,000	
2010	3 months	=	6,250	100,000

(ii) Diminishing (reducing) balance:

Cost	112,000
Depreciation 2006 (40%)	44,800
	67,200
Depreciation 2007	26,880
	40,320
Depreciation 2008	16,128
	24,192
Depreciation 2009	9,677
	14,515
Depreciation 2010	5,806
	8,709

(iii) Units of output (total £100,000):

2006	4,000/20,000	=	20,000
2007	5,000/20,000	=	25,000
2008	5,000/20,000	=	25,000
2009	5,000/20,000	=	25,000
2010	1,000/20,000	=	5,000

(b) *(i)*

Machine

2007		2007	
Jan 1 Balance b/d	112,000	Dec 31 Assets disposal	112,000

(ii)

Provision for Depreciation

2007		2007	
Dec 31 Assets disposal	31,250	Jan 1 Balance b/d	18,750
		Dec 31 Profit and loss	12,500
	31,250		31,250

(iii)

Assets Disposals

2007		2007	
Dec 31 Machine	112,000	Jun 30 Bank	80,000
		Dec 31 Depreciation	31,250
		31 Profit and loss	750
	112,000		112,000

28.1

(a)

Motor Expenses

2006		2006	
Dec 31 Cash and bank	819	Dec 31 Profit and loss	913
31 Owing c/d	94		
	913		913

(b)

Insurance

2006		2006	
Dec 31 Cash and bank	840	Dec 31 Prepaid c/d	68
		31 Profit and loss	772
	840		840

(c)

Stationery

2006		2006	
Dec 31 Cash and bank	370	Jan 1 Owing b/d	110
31 Owing c/d	245	Dec 31 Profit and loss	505
	615		615

(d)

Business Rates

2006		2006	
Jan 1 Prepaid b/d	140	Dec 31 Prepaid c/d	120
Dec 31 Cash and bank	1,654	31 Profit and loss	1,674
	1,794		1,794

(e)

Rent Received

2006		2006	
Jan 1 Owing b/d	175	Dec 31 Cash and bank	1,400
Dec 31 Profit and loss	1,410	31 Owing c/d	185
	1,585		1,585

28.3

Business Rates

2008			2008		
Jan 1	Balance b/d	210	Dec 31	Profit and loss	1,650
Dec 31	Bank	1,920	31	Prepaid c/d	480*
		2,130			2,130

$*1{,}920 \times {}^{3}/_{12} = 480$

Packing Materials

2008			2008		
Jan 1	Balance b/d	740	Dec 31	Profit and loss	3,379
Dec 31	Bank	3,150	31	Cash: Scrap	63
31	Owing c/d	242	31	Stock c/d	690
		4,132			4,132

28.5

(*a*)

Insurance

2010			2010		
Jan 1	Prepaid b/d	562	Dec 31	Profit and loss	1,236
Dec 31	Bank	1,019	31	Prepaid c/d	345
		1,581			1,581
2011					
Jan 1	Prepaid b/d	345			

Wages

2010			2010		
Dec 31	Cash	15,000	Jan 1	Accrued b/d	306
31	Accrued c/d	419	Dec 31	Profit and loss	15,113
		15,419			15,419
			2011		
			Jan 1	Accrued b/d	419

Rent Receivable

2010			2010		
Dec 31	Profit and loss	2,741	Jan 1	In advance b/d	36
			Dec 31	Bank	2,600
			31	Arrears c/d	105
		2,741			2,741
2011					
Jan 1	Arrears b/d	105			

(*b*)

Income Statement (extract)

Insurance	1,236
Wages	15,113
Rent receivable	(2,741)

(*c*) (*i*) Expenses accrued increases the amount charged as expense for that period. It reduces the recorded net profit. It shows as a current liability in the balance sheet.

(*ii*) Income received in advance reduces the revenue to be recorded for that period. It reduces the recorded net profit. It shows as a current liability in the balance sheet.

(*d*) (*i*) To match up expenses charged in the income statement account with the expense cost used up in the period.

(*ii*) To match up revenue credited to the income statement with revenue earned for the period.

28.8

R Giggs

Income Statement for the year ending 28 February 2007

Sales			157,165
Less Cost of goods sold:			
Opening inventory		4,120	
Add Purchases		92,800	
		96,920	
Less Closing inventory		2,400	94,520
Gross profit			62,645
Add Discounts received			160
			62,805
Less Expenses:			
Wages and salaries (31,400 + 340)		31,740	
Rent (3,400 – 230)		3,170	
Discounts allowed		820	
Van running costs (615 + 72)		687	
Bad debts		730	
Doubtful debt allowance		91	
Depreciation:			
Office furniture	380		
Delivery van	1,250	1,630	38,868
Net profit			23,937

Balance Sheet as at 28 February 2007

Non-current assets			
Office furniture		2,900	
Less Depreciation		380	2,520
Delivery van		3,750	
Less Depreciation		1,250	2,500
			5,020
Current assets			
Inventory		2,400	
Accounts receivable	12,316		
Less Allowance for doubtful debts	496	11,820	
Prepaid expenses		230	
Cash at bank		4,100	
Cash in hand		324	18,874
			23,894
Less Current liabilities			
Accounts payable	5,245		
Expenses owing (340 + 72)	412		(5,657)
Net assets			18,237
Financed by:			
Capital			
Balance at 1.3.2006			11,400
Add Net profit			23,937
			35,337
Less Drawings			17,100
			18,237

28.9

Rent

Aug 31 Balance b/d	4,400	Aug 31 Profit and Loss	4,800
31 Accrual c/d	400		
	4,800		4,800
		Sept 1 Accrual b/d	400

Rates

Aug 31 Balance b/d	1,600	Aug 31 Prepaid c/d	300
		31 Profit and loss	1,300
	1,600		1,600
Sept 1 Prepaid b/d	300		

Income Statement for the year ending 31 August 2008

Sales			40,900
Less Cost of goods sold			
Opening inventory		8,200	
Add Purchases		26,000	
		34,200	
Less Closing inventory		9,100	25,100
Gross profit			15,800
Less expenses:			
Rent	4,800		
Business rates	1,300		
Sundry expenses	340		
Depreciation	1,800		8,240
Net profit			7,560

Balance sheet as at 31 August 2008

Non-current assets			
Motor vehicles			9,000
Less Depreciation			3,000
			6,000
Current assets			
Accounts receivable		1,160	
Inventory		9,100	
Prepayment		300	
Bank		1,500	12,060
			18,060
Current liabilities			
Accounts payable	2,100		
Accrual	400		(2,500)
			15,560
Capital			
Opening balance			19,700
Add Net profit			7,560
			27,260
Less Drawings			11,700
			15,560

28.11

John Brown
Income statement for the year ending 31 December 2007

Sales		400,000	
Less Returns in		5,000	395,000
Less Cost of goods sold			
Inventory at 1.1.2007		100,000	
Add Purchases	350,000		
Less Returns out	6,200	343,800	
		443,800	
Less Inventory at 31.12.2007		120,000	323,800
Gross profit			71,200
Less Wages		35,000	
Rates		5,500	
Telephone		1,220	
Bad debts		200	
Allowance for doubtful debts		180	
Depreciation: Shop fittings		4,000	
Van		6,000	52,100
Net profit			19,100

Balance sheet as at 31 December 2007

Non-current assets			
Shop fittings at cost		40,000	
Less Depreciation		4,000	36,000
Van at cost		30,000	
Less Depreciation		6,000	24,000
			60,000
Current assets			
Inventory		120,000	
Accounts receivable	9,800		
Less Provision for doubtful debts	980	8,820	
Prepayments		500	
Bank		3,000	132,320
			192,320
Less Current liabilities			
Accounts payable	7,000		
Expenses accrued	5,220		(12,220)
Net assets			180,100
Financed by:			
Capital			
Balance as at 1.1.2007			179,000
Add Net profit			19,100
			198,100
Less Drawings			18,000
			180,100

28.13

Mr Chai
Income statement for the year ending 30 April 2007

Sales (259,870 – 5,624)		254,246
Less Cost of goods sold		
Inventory 1.5.2006	15,654	
Purchases (135,680 – 13,407)	122,273	
Carriage inwards	11,830	
	149,757	
Less Inventory 30.4.2007	17,750	132,007
Gross profit		122,239
Discounts received		1,750
		123,989
Less Expenses		
Salaries and wages	38,521	
Rent, rates and insurances (25,973 – 1,120 – 5,435)	19,418	
Heating and lighting (11,010 + 1,360)	12,370	
Carriage out	4,562	
Advertising	5,980	
Postage, stationery and telephone	2,410	
Bad debts	2,008	
Allowance for doubtful debts	223	
Discounts allowed	2,306	
Depreciation	12,074	99,872
Net profit		24,117

Balance Sheet as at 30 April 2007

Non-current assets			
Fixtures and fittings at cost		120,740	
Less Depreciation to date		63,020	57,720
Current assets			
Inventory		17,750	
Accounts receivable	24,500		
Less Allowance for doubtful debts	735	23,765	
Prepaid expenses		6,555	
Bank		4,440	
Cash		534	53,044
			110,764
Less Current liabilities			
Accounts payable	19,840		
Expenses accrued	1,360		(21,200)
Net assets			89,564
Financed by:			
Capital: Balance as at 1.5.2006			83,887
Add Net profit			24,117
			108,004
Less Drawings			18,440
			89,564

29.1

(*i*) *FIFO* Closing Inventory 190 × £19 = £3,610

(*ii*) *LIFO*

	Received	*Issued*	*Inventory after each transaction*		
Mar	100 × £16				
			100 × £16		1,600
Sept	220 × £19				
			100 × £16	1,600	
			220 × £19	4,180	5,780
Dec		130 × £24			
			100 × £16	1,600	
			90 × £19	1,710	3,310

(*iii*) *AVCO*

	Received	*Issued*	*Average cost per unit inventory held*	*No. of units in inventory*	*Total value of inventory*
Mar	100 × £16		£16	100	£1,600
Sept	220 × £19		£18.0625	320	£5,780
Dec		130	£18.0625	190	£3,432*

*3,431.875 rounded to nearest £

29.2 **Trading Account for the year ending 31 December 2010**

	FIFO	*LIFO*	*AVCO*
Sales	3,120	3,120	3,120
Less Cost of sales			
Purchases	5,780	5,780	5,780
Less Closing inventory	3,610	3,310	3,432
	(2,170)	(2,470)	(2,348)
Gross profit	950	650	772

29.5

(*a*) (*dates and calculations omitted*)

Cash

Loan: School fund	200.00	Purchases	51.36
Sales	53.50		

Purchases

Cash	51.36		

Sales

		Cash	53.50

(*b*) Inventory valuation:

34	Break × 16p =	5.44
15	Brunch × 12p =	1.80
		7.24

Stock

Trading account	7.24		

(*c*)

Broadway School
Trading Account for the month ending 31 December 2009

Sales		53.50
Less Cost of sales		
Purchases	51.36	
Less Closing inventory	7.24	44.12
Gross profit		9.38

29.5 (*cont'd*)

(*d*)

	Break	*Brunch*
Purchases (units)	240	108
Less Sold	200	90
Inventory should have been	40	18
Actual inventory	34	15
Missing items	6	3

If there have been no arithmetical errors, one can only assume that someone has stolen 6 Breaks and 3 Brunches.

29.6

(This is a brief answer showing the main points to be covered. In the examination the answer should be in report form and elaborated.)

1 For Charles Gray

(*i*) The concept of prudence says that inventory should be valued at lower of cost or net realisable value. As 50% of the retail price £375 is lower than cost £560, then £375 will be taken as net realisable value and used for inventory valuation.

(*ii*) The sale has not taken place by 30 April 2009. The prudence concept does not anticipate profits and therefore the sale will not be assumed. The gun should therefore be included in inventory, at cost price £560.

2 For Jean Kim

It appears that it is doubtful if the business can still be treated as a going concern.

If the final decision is that the business cannot continue, then the inventory valuation should be £510 each, as this is less than cost, with a further overall deduction of auction fees and expenses £300.

3 For Peter Fox

Inventory must be valued at the lower of cost or net realisable value in this case.

The cost to be used is the *cost* for Peter Fox. It is quite irrelevant what the cost may be for other distributors.

It would also be against the convention of consistency to adopt a different method. The consistency applies to Peter Fox, it is not a case of consistency with other businesses. Using selling prices as a basis is not acceptable to the vast majority of businesses.

29.8

(*a*) In one respect the consistency convention is not applied, as at one year end the inventory may be shown at cost whereas the next year end may see inventory valued at net realisable value.

On the other hand, as it is prudent to take the lower of cost or net realisable value, it can be said to be consistently prudent to consistently take the lower figure.

(*b*) Being prudent can be said to be an advantage. For instance, a shareholder can know that inventory is not overvalued: if it were, it would give him a false picture of his investment.

Someone to whom money is owed, such as a creditor, will know that the inventory in the balance sheet is realisable at least at that figure.

It is this knowledge that profits are not recorded because of excessive values placed on inventory that gives outside parties confidence to rely on reported profits.

29.9

Cobden Ltd

Computation of inventory as at 31 May 2009

		Increase	*Decrease*
(*a*)	No adjustment needed Cost lower than net realisable value	–	–
(*b*)	Reduction to net realisable value		130
(*c*)	Arithmetic corrected	72	126
(*d*)	Omitted items	2,010	
(*e*)	Transposition error		9
(*f*)	Goods omitted	638	
(*g*)	Hired item not to be included		347
(*h*)	Samples to be excluded		63
(*i*)	Sale or return items reduced to cost		184
(*j*)	Goods held simply on sale or return		267
		2,720	1,126
	Net increase	1,594	
	Inventory as originally computed	87,612	
		89,206	

30.1

Bank Reconciliation as at 31 December 2006

Cash at bank as per cash book	2,910
Add: Credit transfers	340
Cash at book per balance sheet	3,250
Less: bank lodgements	560
	2,690
Add: impresented cheques	730
Cash at bank per bank statement	3,420

Note for students

Both in theory and in practice you can start with the cash book balance working to the bank statement balance, or you can reverse this method. Many teachers have their preferences, but this is a personal matter only. Examiners sometimes ask for them using one way, sometimes the other. Students should therefore be able to tackle them both ways.

30.3

(*a*)

Cash Book

2009	(Totals so far)	4,129	2009 (Totals so far)	692
Dec 31	T Morris	93	Dec 31 Bank charges	47
			31 Balance c/d	3,483
		4,222		4,222

(*b*) *Bank Reconciliation Statement as on 31 December 2009*

Balance per cash book	3,483
Add Unpresented cheque	209
	3,692
Less Bankings not yet on bank statement (319 + 246)	565
Balance per bank statement	3,127

or

Bank Reconciliation Statement as at 31 December 2009

Balance per bank statement	3,127
Add Bankings not yet on bank statement (319 + 246)	565
	3,692
Less Unpresented cheque	209
Balance per cash book	3,483

30.5

(*a*) *Cash Book (bank columns)*

2008			2008		
Dec 31	Balance b/d	1,500	Dec 31	Bank charges	30
31	Dividends	240	31	RAC	70
31	HM Revenue & Customs	260	31	Loan repayment	200
31	Deposit account	1,400	31	Balance c/d	3,100
		3,400			3,400

(*b*) *Bank Reconciliation Statement as on 31 December 2008*

Balance per cash book	3,100
Add Unpresented cheques (250 + 290)	540
	3,640
Less Bankings not entered on statement	690
Balance per bank statement	2,950

30.7

Cash Book

2006			2006		
	(Totals so far)	853		(Totals so far)	5,048
Mar 31	G Frank	88	Mar 31	TYF	32
31	Balance c/d	4,158	31	Bank charges	19
		5,099			5,099

Bank Reconciliation Statement as at 31 March 2006

Overdraft per cash book	4,158
Add Bankings not yet in bank statement	192
	4,350
Less Unpresented cheques	504
Overdraft per bank statement	3,846

30.9

(a) Balance per Cash Book at 31 October	(554)	
Less: Bank charges	136	
Sundries cheque	44	
Cheque returned – Jones	80	
Rates standing order	150	
Incorrect entry	6	
		(416)
		(970)
Add Dividends received not entered	62	
Error in calculation of opening balance	50	
		112
Corrected Cash Book balance		(858)

George Ltd

(*b*) **Bank Reconciliation Statement as at 31 October**

Balance per bank statement*	(1,353)
Add Outstanding lodgements	762
	(591)
Less Unpresented cheques	(267)
Balance per cash book	(858)

*This is the balancing figure.

31.1

Sales Ledger Control

Balances b/d	23,220	Returns inwards	826
Sales Day Book	14,194	Cheques and cash	17,918
		Discounts allowed	312
		Balances c/d	18,358
	37,414		37,414

31.3

Sales Ledger Control

2009			2009		
March 1	Balances b/d	12,271	March 31	Cash and bank	11,487
31	Sales	9,334	31	Discounts allowed	629
31	Balances c/d	47	31	Set-offs: Purchases ledger	82
			31	Balances c/d	9,454
		21,652			21,652

31.5

Purchases Ledger Control

Returns outwards	1,452	Balances b/d	19,420
Bank	205,419	Purchases Day Book	210,416
Petty cash	62		
Discounts received	1,721		
Set-offs against sales ledger	640		
Balances c/d	20,210		
	*229,504		*229,836

*Difference between two sides 332

Sales Ledger Control

Balances b/d	28,227	Returns inwards	3,618
Sales Day Book	305,824	Bank and cash	287,317
		Discounts allowed	4,102
		Set-offs against Purchase ledger	640
		Balances c/d	38,374
	334,051		334,051

31.6

Accounts Receivable Ledger Control

Balance b/d	46,462	Balance b/d	245
Sales	126,024	Contra	455
Cash	52	Bad debt	1,253
		Discount	746
		Cash	120,464
		Balance c/d	49,375
	172,538		172,538
Balance b/d	49,375		

Accounts Payable Ledger Control

Balance b/d	1,472	Balance b/d	25,465
Returns	2,154	Purchases	76,474
Contra	455		
Discount received	1,942		
Cash	70,476		
Balance c/d	25,440		
	101,939		101,939
		Balance b/d	25,440

31.9

Total Accounts Receivable Account

Balance b/d	26,555	Cash (600,570 – 344,890)	255,680
Credit sales	268,187	Discounts allowed	5,520
		Set-offs (Total accounts receivable)	70
		Bad debts	780
		Returns inwards	4,140
		Balances c/d	28,552
	294,742		294,742
Balances b/d	28,552		

Total Accounts Payable Account

Cash (503,970 – 14,440)	489,530	Balances b/d	43,450
Discounts received	3,510	Credit purchases	496,600
Set-offs (total accounts payable)	70		
Returns outwards	1,480		
Balances c/d	45,460		
	540,050		540,050
		Balances b/d	45,460

Note: the Allowance for doubtful debts does not affect the control accounts.

31.10

(*a*) To ensure an arithmetical check on the accounting records. The agreement of the total of individual accounts payable balances with that of the balance on the control account provides that check.

If the control account and the ledger are kept by separate personnel, then a check on their work and honesty is provided.

(*b*) (*i*) Increase £198 (*ii*) Decrease £100 (*iii*) No effect (*iv*) Decrease £400 (*v*) Decrease £120.

(*c*) A computer will automatically enter two figures in different directions and will then confirm it in total fashion. As such there may seem at first sight to be no need for control accounts.

However, there is still the need to check on the accuracy of data input. It is important that both the skill and the honesty of the programmer are checked.

Accordingly there will still be a need for control accounts.

31.11

(*a*) See Section 31.1.
(*b*) See Section 31.5.

32.1

(*a*) Error of omission – a credit purchase omitted from the books.
(*b*) Error of commission – a credit sale to J Briggs entered in the account of H Briggs.
(*c*) Error of principle – repairs debited to the asset account.
(*d*) Compensating errors – prepayments £15 too high and accruals £15 too high.
(*e*) Errors of original entry – a credit purchase for £100 recorded in the books as £10.
(*f*) Complete reversal of entries – payment of advertising debited to bank and credited to advertising.
(*g*) Transposition error – sales invoice for £263 entered as £236 in both ledger accounts.

32.2

To economise on space, all narratives for journal entries are omitted.

(*a*)	T More	Dr	412	:	T Mone	Cr	412
(*b*)	Machinery	Dr	619	:	J Frank	Cr	619
(*c*)	Computer	Dr	550	:	Office expenses	Cr	550
(*d*)	B Wood	Dr	18	:	Sales	Cr	18
(*e*)	Sales	Dr	164	:	Commissions rec'd	Cr	164
(*f*)	Cash (needs double the amount)	Dr	136	:	T Blair	Cr	136
(*g*)	Purchases	Dr	372	:	Drawings	Cr	372
(*h*)	Discounts allowed	Dr	48	:	Discounts received	Cr	48

32.4

(*a*) 100 units × £1.39 = £139 *not* £1,390.
(*b*) (*i*) Inventory overstated by £1,251 (i.e. 1,390 – 139).
(*ii*) Cost of goods sold understated by £1,251.
(*iii*) Net profit overstated by £1,251.
(*iv*) Current Assets overstated by £1,251.
(*v*) Owner's Capital overstated by £1,251.

32.5

(*a*)	Sales	Dr	5,000	:	Capital	Cr	5,000
(*b*)	Drawings	Dr	72	:	Sundry expenses	Cr	72
(*c*)	Drawings	Dr	191	:	Rent	Cr	191
(*d*)	D Pine	Dr	180	:	Purchases	Cr	180
(*e*)	Bank	Dr	820	:	Cash	Cr	820
(*f*)	Bank	Dr	120	:	Cash	Cr	120
(*g*)	T Young	Dr	195	:	G Will	Cr	195
(*h*)	Office expenses	Dr	100	:	Printer disposals	Cr	100

33.1

Suspense

(*i*) Purchases	20	Balance b/d	40
(*ii*) Accounts payable	9		
(*iii*) Sales	11		
	40		40

33.2

(*a*) **The Journal (narratives omitted)**

	Dr	*Cr*
(*i*) Suspense	200	
Sales		200
(*ii*) T Vantuira	610	
T Ventura		610
(*iii*) Rent	90	
Suspense		90
(*iv*) Suspense	100	
Discounts allowed		100
(*v*) Sales	230	
Computer disposals		230

(*b*) *Suspense Account*

Sales	200	Balance b/d	210
Discounts allowed	100	Rent	90
	300		300

(*c*) Net profit per financial statements		31,400
Add (*i*) Sales undercast	200	
(*iv*) Discounts overcast	100	300
		31,700
Less (*iii*) Rent undercast	90	
(*v*) Reduction in sales	230	320
Corrected net profit		31,380

33.4

Item	*If no effect state 'No'*	*Debit side exceeds credit side by*	*Credit side exceeds debit side by*
(*i*)	No		
(*ii*)	No		
(*iii*)	No		
(*iv*)		£290	
(*v*)			£188
(*vi*)			£317
(*vii*)	No		

33.5 **Trial Balance as at 31 January 2003**

	Dr	*Cr*
Drawings	19,500	
Inventory	8,410	
Accounts receivable (34,517 – 8)	34,509	
Furniture (2,400 + 407)	2,807	
Cash	836	
Returns inwards	2,438	
Business expenses	3,204	
Purchases (72,100 – 407)	71,693	
Discounts allowed	42	
Capital		7,845
Accounts payable (6,890 – 315)		6,575
Sales (127,510 + 90)		127,600
Discounts received		1,419
	143,439	143,439

33.6

(*a*) (*i*) **The Journal**

	Dr	*Cr*
C Thomas	450	
Thomasson Manufacturing Ltd		450
Suspense	100	
Telephone		100
Suspense	2,000	
Sales account		2,000
Machine repairs	390	
Machinery		390
Suspense	1,500	
Rent received*		1,500
Purchases account	765	
P Brooks		765

*Assumed not invoiced to Atlas Ltd

(*ii*) **Computation of Corrected Profit for year ending 31 December 2008**

Profit as originally reported		47,240
Add Telephone expense overstated	100	
Sales understated	2,000	
Rent received omitted	1,500	3,600
		50,840
Less Machinery repairs understated	390	
Purchases omitted	765	1,155
Corrected profit figure		49,685

(*b*) (*i*) Per text (*ii*) Per text

33.8

(*a*) **Difference on Trial Balance Suspense**

Per trial balance	2,513	J Winters	198
Discounts received	324	Wages	2,963
Discounts allowed	324		
	3,161		3,161

(*b*) **Computation of Corrected Net Profit for year ending 30 April 2007**

	–	+	
Net profit per draft accounts			24,760
(*i*) Discounts		648	
(*ii*) Wages	2,963		
(*iv*) Stationery inventory		1,500	
(*vi*) Remittance	3,000		
	5,963	2,148	3,815
Correct net profit			20,945
(*iii*) and (*v*) did not affect profit			

(*c*) Per text

33.11

(*a*) (*i*) Van	6,000	
Motor vehicle expenses		6,000
(*ii*) Fuel	250	
Drawings		250
(*iii*) B Struton	300	
B Burton Ltd		300
(*iv*) Drawings	750	
Business rates		750
(*v*) Drawings	720	
Wages		720
(*vi*) Purchases	500	
K Jarman		500

(*b*) Net profit per draft financial statements		23,120
Add (*i*)	6,000	
(*iv*)	750	
(*v*)	720	
		7,470
		30,590
Less (*ii*)	250	
(*vi*)	500	
		750
		29,840

33.12

(*a*) (*i*) Suspense	10	
Sales		10
(*ii*) Discount allowed	2	
Suspense		2
(*iii*) Discount allowed	140	
Suspense		140
(*iv*) D Bird	10	
Suspense		10
(*v*) Suspense	3	
J Flyn		3

(*b*) The overall effect on the trial balance is that the following changes have been made:

		Dr	*Cr*
(*i*)	Sales		10
(*ii*) and (*iii*)	Discount allowed	142	
(*iv*) and (*v*)	Accounts receivable	7	
(*i*) to (*v*)	Suspense		139

33.14 **Workings**

(*i*)	Purchases	10	
	Suspense		10
(*ii*)	A Supplier	45	
	Suspense		45
(*iii*)	Plant and Machinery	70	
	Repairs		70
(*iv*)	Suspense	20	
	S Kane		20
(*v*)	Sales	300	
	Plant and Machinery disposals		300
(*vi*)	Accounts receivable	60	
	Suspense		60
(*vii*)	Suspense	2	
	B Luckwood		2
(*viii*)	Business rates	45	
	Prepayments		45

(*a*) *Suspense*

Balance	93	(*i*) Purchases	10
(*iv*) S Kane	20	(*ii*) A Supplier	45
(*vii*) B Luckwood	2	(*vi*) Accounts receivable	60
	115		115

(*b*) (*i*) The suspense account is shown in the balance sheet, not the income statement. The following item increases net profit:

(*iii*)		70
The following items reduce net profit:		
(*i*)	10	
(*viii*)	45	
		(55)
Overall, net profit is increased by		15

Note: (*v*) has no effect on net profit. Sales are reduced by 300 and the loss on disposal of the plant and machinery is reduced by 300.

(*ii*) The following items are changed in the balance sheet:

	Dr	*Cr*
Suspense		93
(*ii*) Accounts payable	45	
(*iii*) Plant and Machinery	70	
(*iv*), (*vi*), (*vii*) Accounts receivable	38	
(*viii*) Prepayments		45
Net profit		15
	153	153

Answers to Scenario Questions

SQ1 (*a*)

Picta Simpla

Income Statement for the year ending 30 June 2007

	£	£
Sales		258,100
Less Cost of goods sold		
Opening inventory	19,250	
Purchases	185,850	
	205,100	
Less: Closing inventory	50,150	
		154,950
Gross profit		103,150
Less Expenses		
Wages	14,500	
Advertising	15,500	
Postage and packing	7,250	
Rent	12,000	
Insurance	2,850	
Electricity	3,400	
Depreciation	800	
Stationery	1,350	
Telephone	3,450	
		61,100
Net profit		42,050

(*b*) Your note should explain that the business is a separate entity from him and so the cost of having a holiday has nothing to do with the business, but must be treated as drawings. It should also explain that drawings represent the amount of business assets taken out of the business by the owner for the owner's, not the business's, use. Drawings are *never* an expense of the business.

SQ2

(*a*)

Sleasy Cars

Balance Sheet as at 31 December 2006

	£	£	£	£
Non-current assets				
Land				5,000
Offices			500	
Less Depreciation			100	400
Truck			5,000	
Less Depreciation			2,500	2,500
				7,900
Current assets				
Inventory				
Accounts receivable and prepayments		21,000		
Cash		1,900		
		100		23,000
				30,900
Current liabilities				
Accounts payable and accruals	8,600			
Bank overdraft	6,400			
		15,000		
Non-curret liability		3,000		(18,000)
Net assets				12,900
Capital				
Opening balance*			15,500	
Add Net profit*			8,400	
			23,900	
Less Drawings			11,000	
				12,900

*5,000 + 10,000 + 500 = 15,500
*23,500 – 500 – 100 – 3,000 – 2,500 – 500 – 2,000 – 400 – 5,000 – 1,500 + 400 = 8,400

SQ2 *(cont'd)*

(b)

	Dr	*Cr*
Office overvalued: Net profit	500	
Office		500
Office depreciation: Net profit	100	
Depreciation – Office		100
Land overvalued: Net profit	5,000	
Land		5,000
Provision for long-term liability: Net profit	3,000	
Non-current liability		3,000
Depreciation on truck: Net profit	2,500	
Depreciation – Truck		2,500
Car overvalued: Net profit	500	
Inventory		500
Bad debt: Net profit	2,000	
Accounts receivable		2,000
Accruals: Net profit	400	
Accruals		400
Prepayment: Prepayment	400	
Net profit		400
Car overvalued: Net profit	1,500	
Inventory		1,500

SQ3

Mr Jones

Income Statement for the year ending XXX

	£	£
Sales		430,000
Less Cost of goods sold		
Opening inventory	6,520	
Purchases	305,500	
Carriage in	2,100	
	314,120	
Less Closing inventory	7,000	
		307,120
Gross profit		122,880
Less: Expenses		
Rent	5,350	
Business rates	2,800	
Insurance	400	
Postage	250	
Stationery	1,002	
Advertising	200	
Salaries and wages	10,500	
Bad debts	400	
Allowance for doubtful debts	112	
Depreciation	15,000	
		36,014
Net profit		86,866

Balance Sheet as at XXXX

	£	£	£
Non-current assets			
Equipment			150,000
Less: Depreciation			50,000
			100,000
Current assets			
Inventory		7,000	
Accounts receivable		4,608	
Prepayment		200	
Cash in hand		120	11,928
			111,928
Current liabilities			
Accounts payable	9,600		
Bank overdraft	2,743		
Accrual	366		
			(12,709)
Net assets			99,219
Capital			
Balance			43,353
Net profit			86,866
			130,219
Less Drawings			31,000
			99,219

SQ4

(a)

Mr Try

Income Statement for the year ending 30 June 2007

	£	£
Sales		17,644
Less Expenses		
Repairs	230	
Miscellaneous	110	
Insurance (350 – 50)	300	
Accounting fees (250 – 250 + 275)	275	
Postage and stationery	50	
Depreciation	375	
Allowance for doubtful debts	110	
Bank charges	45	
		1,495
Net profit		16,149

(*b*) *Balance Sheet as at 30 June 2007*

	£	£	£
Non-current assets			
Ladders and equipment			750
Less: Depreciation			375
			375
Current assets			
Cleaning materials and cloths		3,400	
Accounts receivable		110	
Prepayments		50	
Bank		2,345	
Cash		35	5,940
			6,315
Current liabilities			
Accounts payable	100		
Accruals	320		
			(420)
			5,895
Capital			
Balance at 1 July 2006			346
Net profit			16,149
			16,495
Less Drawings			10,600
			5,895

(*c*) Your letter should explain that consumables are items purchased with the intention of using them in the short term, after which they will either have been used up (e.g. printer ink) or no longer usable (e.g. carbon paper). The ladders do not fall into the category of consumables. They were purchased for use in the long term, in this case, more than one accounting period. As such, they are non-current assets and must be depreciated.

SQ5 (*a*) **B's Casuals**

Income Statement for the year ending 30 June 2007

Sales		260,040
Less: Cost of goods sold		
Opening inventory	21,500	
Purchases	68,500	
Carriage in	5,200	
	95,200	
Less: Closing inventory	22,500	
		72,700
		187,340
Gross profit		
Less: Expenses		
Wages	24,500	
Business rates	9,950	
Bad debt	2,000	
Advertising	1,040	
Insurance	2,850	
Electricity	3,400	
Depreciation	15,800	
Stationery	1,350	
Telephone	3,450	
		64,340
		123,000

(*b*) *Balance Sheet as at 30 June 2007*

Non-current assets			
Factory and Machinery	400,000		
Less Depreciation	115,000		285,000
Computer	4,000		
Less Depreciation	2,400		1,600
			286,600
Current assets			
Prepayments:			
Insurance		650	
Telephone		200	
Cash in hand		600	1,450
			288,050
Current liabilities			
Accounts payable	3,500		
Rates Accrual	2,450		
Electricity Accrual	500		
Loan from Mrs Baldwin	600		
			(7,050)
			281,000
Capital			
Balance at 1 July 2006			213,000*
Net profit			123,000
Less Drawings			(55,000)
			281,000

*balancing figure

(c) You need to explain how the accrual system operates and why it is used (see text Section 10.8). You also need to explain that drawings are assets withdrawn from the business for the owner's personal use, which is what his 'wages' and his home cinema system purchase are. Drawings are *never* expenses of a business.

34.1 **G Flynn**

Trading Account part of the Income Statement for the year ending 31 December 2007

Sales			155,880
Less Cost of goods sold:			
Inventory 1.1.2007		19,400	
Add Purchases	(D)	137,160	
	(C)	156,560	
Less Inventory 31.12.2007		26,660	
	(B)		129,900
Gross profit	(A)		25,980

Missing figures found in the order (A) to (D).

(A) Mark-up is 20%. Therefore Margin is 16.67%. Sales are 155,880 so Margin is 16.67% or $^1/_6$; $^1/_6 \times 155,880 = 25,980$ Gross Profit

(B) + (A) = 155,880. Therefore (B) + 25,980 = 155,880 and accordingly (B) is 129,900.

(C) − 26,660 = 129,900. Therefore (C) is 156,560.

(D) + 19,400 = 156,500. Therefore (D) is 137,160.

34.3

(*a*) We know that

$$\frac{\text{Cost of goods sold}}{\text{Average inventory}} = \text{Rate of inventory turnover}$$

Substituting $\frac{x}{16{,}240} = 8$

x = Cost of goods sold = 129,920.

(*b*) If mark-up is 60%, gross profit is 60% of the cost of sales = 77,952.
(*c*) Turnover is (*a*) + (*b*) = 129,920 + 77,952 = 207,872.
(*d*) 70% × 77,952 = 54,566.40.
(*e*) Gross Profit – Expenses = Net Profit = 23,385.60.

34.5

(*a*) Sales = 230,000 + (20% × 230,000) = 276,000.
(*b*) 41,400 – (9% × 271,400) = 16,974.

(*c*) $\frac{230{,}000}{(34{,}000 + 41{,}000) \div 2} = \frac{230{,}000}{37{,}500} = 6.13$

(*d*) Gross profit is 25% × 260,000 = 65,000.
Sales are 260,000 + 65,000 = 325,000.
Expenses are 9% of sales = 29,250.
Net profit = 65,000 – 29,250 = 35,750.

34.7

(*a*)

Capital

Balance c/d	5,000	Bank	5,000
	5,000		5,000
		Balance b/d	5,000

Bank

Capital	5,000	Cash	300
		Van	3,500
		Rent	500
		Balance c/d	700
	5,000		5,000
Balance b/d	700		

Cash

Bank	300	Sundry Expenses	50
Sales	300	Drawings	500
		Balance c/d	50
	600		600
Balance b/d	50		

Van

Bank	3,500	Balance c/d	3,500
	3,500		3,500
Balance b/d	3,500		

Purchases

A Supplier	2,500	Balance c/d	2,500
	2,500		2,500
Balance b/d	2,500		

A. Supplier

Returns	500	Purchases	2,500
Balance c/d	2,000		
	2,500		2,500
		Balance b/d	2,000

Sales

Balance c/d	1,300	Cash	300
		B Safe	1,000
	1,300		1,300
		Balance b/d	1,300

B Safe

Sales	1,000	Balance c/d	1,000
	1,000		1,000
Balance b/d	1,000		

Returns out

Balance c/d	500	A Supplier	500
	500		500
		Balance b/d	500

Sundry Expenses

Cash	50	Balance c/d	50
	50		50
Balance b/d	50		

Rent

Bank	500	Balance c/d	500
	500		500
Balance b/d	500		

Drawings

Cash	500	Balance c/d	500
	500		500
Balance b/d	500		

(*b*)

L Mann
Trial Balance as at 30 April

Bank	700	
Cash	50	
Van	3,500	
Purchases	2,500	
Accounts receivable	1,000	
Sundry expenses	50	
Rent	500	
Drawings	500	
Capital		5,000
Accounts payable		2,000
Sales		1,300
Returns out		500
	8,800	8,800

(*c*) *Income Statement for the month ending 30 April*

Sales		1,300
Purchases	2,500	
– Returns out	500	
	2,000	
– Closing inventory	1,250	
Cost of sales		750
Gross profit		550
Less Expenses		
Sundry expenses	50	
Rent	500	
		550
Net profit		0

(*d*) *Balance Sheet as at 30 April*

Non-current assets		
Van		3,500
Current assets		
Inventory	1,250	
Accounts receivable	1,000	
Bank	700	
Cash	50	3,000
		6,500
Current liabilities		
Accounts payable		(2,000)
		4,500
Capital		5,000
Less Drawings		500
		4,500

(*e*) (*i*) $\frac{550}{1,300} = 42.3\%$

(*ii*) $\frac{0}{5,000} = 0\%$

(*f*) (*i*) As there has been neither a profit nor a loss, the £500 drawings are eating into capital. This is not a good sign. Drawings must not exceed net profit in the long term, or the business will fail.

(*ii*) Working capital is £1,000. The current ratio is 1.5, which ought to be adequate, though this would need to be confirmed by comparison with other businesses operating in the same sector.

34.9 (*a*)

	2007	2008	2009
Opening inventory	10,000	21,000	25,000
Purchases	70,000	86,000	77,000
	80,000	107,000	102,000
Less Closing inventory	21,000	25,000	23,000
Cost of goods sold	(59,000)	(82,000)	(79,000)
Sales	90,000	125,000	120,000
Gross profit	31,000	43,000	41,000

(*b*) (*i*) Gross profit/sales

2007

$\frac{31,000}{90,000} = 34\%$

2008

$\frac{43,000}{125,000} = 34\%$

2009

$\frac{41,000}{120,000} = 34\%$

34.9 *(cont'd)*

(*ii*) $\text{Inventory turnover} = \frac{\text{Cost of goods sold}}{\text{Average inventory}}$

2007

$\frac{59{,}000}{(10{,}000 + 21{,}000) \div 2} = 3.8 \text{ times}$

2008

$\frac{82{,}000}{(21{,}000 + 25{,}000) \div 2} = 3.6 \text{ times}$

2009

$\frac{79{,}000}{(25{,}000 + 23{,}000) \div 2} = 3.3 \text{ times}$

35.1

F Lee

Statement of Affairs as at 31 December 2002

Non-current assets			
Van at cost		6,400	
Less Depreciation		1,600	4,800
Current assets			
Inventory		6,200	
Accounts receivable		15,200	
Prepaid expenses		310	
Bank		33,490	
Cash		270	55,470
			60,270
Less Current liabilities			
Trade accounts payable	7,100		
Expenses owing	640		(7,740)
			52,530
Capital			
Cash introduced			35,000
Add Net profit		(C)	
		(B)	
Less Drawings			20,870
		(A)	

Missing figures (A), (B) and (C) deduced in that order. (A) to balance is 52,530, thus (B) has to be 73,400 and (C) becomes 38,400.

35.2

500 × 4 = 2,000 = Costs
× 5
= 10,000 = Fees

Fees	10,000
Costs	2,000
Profit	8,000

35.4

Workings:

Purchases Bank	67,360	*Sales* Banked	91,190
Cash	4,940	Cash	17,400
	72,300		108,590
– Creditors 31.12.2001	12,700	– Debtors 31.12.2001	21,200
	59,600		87,390
+ Creditors 31.12.2002	14,100	+ Debtors 31.12.2002	19,800
Purchases for 2002	73,700	Sales for 2002	107,190

Opening Capital:	Bank	4,100	
	Inventory	10,800	
	Accounts receivable	21,200	
	Insurance prepaid	420	
	Fixtures	1,800	38,320
	Less Accounts payable	12,700	
	Rent owing	390	13,090
			25,230

Jane

Income Statement for the year ending 31 December 2002

Sales		107,190
Less Cost of goods sold:		
Opening inventory	10,800	
Add Purchases	73,700	
	84,500	
Less Closing inventory	12,200	72,300
Gross profit		34,890
Less Expenses:		
Wages	11,260	
Rent (3,950 – 390)	3,560	
Insurance (1,470 + 420 – 440)	1,450	
Sundry expenses	610	
Depreciation: Fixtures	200	17,080
Net profit		17,810

Balance Sheet as at 31 December 2002

Non-current assets			
Fixtures at valuation		1,800	
Less Depreciation		200	1,600
Current assets			
Inventory		12,200	
Accounts receivable		19,800	
Prepayments		440	32,440
			34,040
Current liabilities			
Trade accounts payable	14,100		
Bank overdraft	6,300		
Net current assets			(20,400)
			13,640
Capital			
Balance at 1.1.2002			25,230
Add Net profit			17,810
			43,040
Less Drawings (1,200 + 28,200)			29,400
			13,640

35.6

Jenny Barnes

Income Statement for the year ending 30 April 2009

Sales*		102,908
Less: Opening inventory	9,500	
Purchases	78,100	
	87,600	
Less: Closing inventory	13,620	
		73,980
Gross profit		28,928
Less: Expenses		
Sales assistants' wages	5,620	
Vehicle running expenses	1,020	
Bad debts	150	
Miscellaneous expenses**	1,370	
Light and heat	940	
Depreciation: Equipment	720	
Vehicles	1,000	10,460
Net profit		18,468

*Sales 96,500 + takings in cash later spent 6,408 (drawings 6,000 + expenses 408)
**Bank 962 + cash 408 = 1,370

35.8

(*a*)

Accounts Payable Control

Bank	101,500	Balances b/d	7,400
Cash	1,800	Drawings: Goods	600
Balances c/d	8,900	Purchases (difference)	104,200
	112,200		112,200

(*b*)

Janet Lambert

Income Statement for the year ending 31 August 2009

Sales (deduced – as margin is 25% = 4 × gross profit)			128,000
Opening inventory		8,600	
Add Purchases		104,200	
		112,800	
Less Closing inventory		16,800	
Cost of goods sold			96,000
Gross profit ($33\frac{1}{3}$% of Cost of goods sold)			32,000
Less:	Casual labour (1,200 + 6,620)	7,820	
	Rent (5,040 + 300 – 420)	4,920	
	Delivery costs	3,000	
	Electricity (1,390 + 160 – 210)	1,340	17,080
Net profit			14,920

Balance Sheet as at 31 August 2009

Current assets		
Inventory	16,800	
Accounts receivable	4,300	
Prepayments	420	
Bank	1,650	
Cash	330	23,500
Current liabilities		
Accounts payable	8,900	
Expenses owing	160	(9,060)
		14,440
Capital:		
Balance as at 1 September 2008 (Workings 1)		7,850
Add Net profit		14,920
		22,770
Less Drawings (Workings 2)		8,330
		14,440

Workings:

(1) Capital as on 1.9.2008. Inventory 8,600 + Accounts receivable 3,900 + Prepaid 300 + Bank 2,300 + Cash 360 = 15,460 – Accounts payable 7,400 – Accruals 210 = 7,850.

(2) Cash drawings. Step (A) find cash received from sales. Accounts receivable b/d 3,900 + Sales 128,000 – Accounts receivable c/d 4,300 = 127,600 cash received.

35.8 *(cont'd)*

Step (B) find cash banked. Balance b/d 2,300 + cash received? – payments 117,550 = balance c/d 1,650. Therefore cash banked? = 116,900. Step (C) draw up cash account:

Balance b/d	360	Labour	1,200
Sales receipts	127,600	Purchases	1,800
		Banked	116,900
		Drawings (difference)	7,730
		Balance c/d	330
	127,960		127,960

(*c*) Per text.

35.10

David Denton

Income Statement for the year ending 31 December 2010

Work done: Credit accounts		29,863	
For cash		3,418	33,281
Less Expenses:			
Materials (9,600 – 580)		9,020	
Secretarial salary		3,000	
Rent		225	
Rates (180 – 45)		135	
Insurance (800 – 200)		600	
Electricity (1,122 + 374 estimated)		1,496	
Motor expenses		912	
General expenses (1,349 + 295)		1,644	
Loan interest (4,000 × 10% × 3/4)		300	
Allowance for doubtful debts		425	
Accounting fee		250	
Amortisation of lease (650 × 3/4)		487	
Depreciation: Equipment	960		
Van	900	1,860	20,354
Net profit			12,927

Balance Sheet as at 31 December 2010

	Cost	Depreciation	
Non-current assets			
Lease	6,500	487	6,013
Equipment	4,800	960	3,840
Vehicle	3,600	900	2,700
	14,900	2,347	12,553
Current assets			
Inventory		580	
Accounts receivable	4,250		
Less Allowance for doubtful debts	425	3,825	
Prepaid expenses (75 + 200)		275	
Bank (see workings)		6,084	
Cash		123	10,887
			23,440
Less Current liabilities			
Trade accounts payable	714		
Interest owing	300		
Accountancy fee owing	250		
Rates owing	135		
Electricity owing	374	1,773	
Net current assets			
Less Loan		4,000	(5,773)
			17,667
Financed by:			
Capital			
Introduced (6,500 + 3,600)			10,100
Add Net profit			12,927
			23,027
Less Drawings (4,680 + 280 + 400)			5,360
			17,667

Workings:

Bank (6,500 + 25,613 + 2,600 + 4,000) = 38,713 – 4,680 – 280 – 6,500 – 300 – 3,000 – 8,886 – 4,800 – 1,122 – 912 – 1,349 – 800 = 6,084

35.11

(*a*)

J Duncan

Capital Account on 1 January 2008

Bank		8,000
Cash		300
Inventory		4,100
Machinery		12,600
Rent prepaid		200
Accounts receivable		6,300
		31,500
Accounts payable	2,400	
Loan	5,000	
		(7,400)
		24,100

(*b*)

J Duncan
Income Statement for the year ending 31 December 2008

Sales			40,450
Less: Sales returns			1,200
			39,250
Less: Cost of Sales			
Opening Inventory at 1 January 2008		4,100	
Add: Purchases		18,950	
		23,050	
Less: Withdrawn by the owner	300		
Less: Closing inventory at 31 December 2008	3,200		
		3,500	
			19,550
Gross profit			19,700
Add: Discount received			350
			20,050
Less: Expenses			
Rent		1,850	
Bad debts written-off		400	
Wages		6,100	
Insurance		1,450	
Loan interest		400	
Depreciation		4,200	
Repairs		300	
Electricity		750	
			15,450
Net profit			4,600

Workings:
Sales 26,000 – 250 + 14,000 + 400 – 6,300 + 5,000 + 1,200 + 400 = 40,450
Purchases 18,500 – 2,400 + 2,500 + 350 = 18,950
Depreciation = balancing figure.

35.12

J Duncan
Balance Sheet as at 31 December 2008

Non-current assets				
Machinery at 1 January 2008			12,600	
Add: Additions			7,500	
			20,100	
Less: Depreciation			4,200	
				15,900
Current assets				
Inventory			3,200	
Accounts receivable			5,000	
Bank			2,600	
Cash			50	10,850
				26,750
Current liabilities				
Accounts payable		2,500		
Accrued charges				
Loan interest	100			
Rent	250			
		350		
			2,850	
Non-current liabilities				
Bank loan 8%			5,000	(7,850)
				18,900
Capital account				
Balance at 1 January 2008			24,100	
Add: Net profit			4,600	
			28,700	
Less: Drawings			9,800	
				18,900

35.15

Inventory value per stocktake on 3 May 2008	124,620
Less Purchases (1,510 – 530)	980
	123,640
Less Sales returns (222 @ 80%)	176
	123,464
Less Obsolete inventory	300
	123,164
Add Inventory sold (2,300 @ 80%)	1,840
Value of inventory on 30 April 2005	125,004

36.1

Downline Rugby Club
Income and Expenditure Account for the year ending 31 December 2006

Income		
Collections at matches		4,218
Profit on refreshments		5,520
		9,738
Less Expenditure		
Rent for pitch (1,600 – 400)	1,200	
Printing and stationery (104 + 25)	129	
Secretary's expenses	220	
Repairs to equipment	210	
Groundsman's wages	6,400	
Miscellaneous expenses	96	
Depreciation of equipment	476	8,731
Surplus of income over expenditure		1,007

Balance Sheet as at 31 December 2006

Non-current assets		
Equipment	2,380	
Less Depreciation	476	1,904
Current assets		
Prepayment	400	
Cash	2,168	2,568
		4,472
Current liabilities		
Expenses owing		(25)
Net assets		4,447
Financed by:		
Accumulated fund		
Balance at 1.1.2006 (2,000 + 1,440)		3,440
Add Surplus of income over expenditure		1,007
		4,447

36.3

(*a*)

The Happy Haddock Angling Club
Income and Expenditure Account for the year ending 31 December 2008

Income:		
Subscriptions		3,500
Visitors' fees		650
Competition fees		820
Snack bar profit (see workings)		1,750
		6,720
Less Expenditure:		
Rent and rates	1,500	
Secretarial expenses	240	
Loan interest	260	
Depreciation on games equipment	400	2,400
Surplus of income over expenditure		4,320

Workings: Snack bar profit: 6,000 – (800 + 3,750 – 900) – 600 = 1,750

(*b*)

Balance Sheet as at 31 December 2008

Non-current assets		
Clubhouse buildings		20,500
Games equipment	2,000	
Less Depreciation	400	1,600
		22,100
Current assets		
Snack bar inventory	900	
Bank	700	1,600
		23,700
Current liabilities		
Subscriptions received in advance	380	
Less Loan from bank	5,500	(5,880)
		17,820
Financed by:		
Accumulated fund		
Balance 1.1.2008 (see workings)	13,500	
Add surplus for year	4,320	17,820

Workings: 200 + 800 + 12,500 = 13,500

36.5

(*a*)

Accumulated fund 1 August 2008

Equipment		975
Inventory of prizes		38
Arrears of subscriptions		65
Cash and bank		210
		1,288
Less Subscriptions in advance	10	
Prizes suppliers	58	68
		1,220

(*b*)

(*i*)

Subscriptions

In arrears b/d	65	In advance b/d	10
In advance c/d	37	Cash	1,987
Income and expenditure	1,980	In arrears c/d	85
	2,082		2,082

(*ii*)

Competition prizes

Inventory b/d	38	Accounts payable b/d	58
Cash	270	Inventory c/d	46
Accounts payable c/d	68	Cost of prizes given	272
	376		376

(*c*) **Miniville Rotary Club**

Income and Expenditure Account for the year ending 31 July 2009

Income			
Subscriptions			1,980
Ticket sales		437	
Less Cost of prizes		272	165
Donations received			177
			2,322
Less Expenditure			
Rent (1,402 – 500)		902	
Visiting speakers' expenses		1,275	
Secretarial expenses		163	
Stationery and printing		179	
Donations to charities		35	
Depreciation		195	2,749
Excess of expenditure over income			427

Balance Sheet as at 31 July 2009

Non-current assets			
Equipment at cost		1,420	
Less Depreciation		640	780
Current assets			
Inventory of prizes		46	
Arrears of subscriptions		85	131
			911
Current liabilities			
Accounts payable for prizes	68		
Advance subscriptions	37		
Bank overdraft	13		(118)
			793
Accumulated fund			
Balance 1.8.2008			1,220
Less Excess of expenditure over income			427
			793

36.7

(*a*)

Café operations:		
Takings		4,660
Less Cost of supplies:		
Opening inventory	800	
Add purchases (1,900 + 80)	1,980	
	2,780	
Less Closing inventory	850	1,930
		2,730
Wages		2,000
Profit		730
Sports equipment:		
Sales		900
Less Cost of goods sold:		
Opening inventory	1,000	
Add Purchases (1,000 × 50%)	500	
	1,500	
Less Closing inventory (*see* note)	900	600
Profit		300

Note: To find closing sports equipment inventory: 900 is sales at 50% on cost profit so cost of sales is 600. By arithmetical deduction closing inventory is found to be 900.

(*b*)

Subscriptions

Owing b/d	60	In advance b/d	120
		Cash: 2007	40
Income and expenditure	1,280	2008	1,100
		2009	80
In advance c/d	80	Owing c/d	80
	1,420		1,420

Life Subscriptions

Income and expenditure (11 × 20)	220	Balance b/d	1,400
		Cash	200
Balance c/d	1,380		
	1,600		1,600

(*c*) **Happy Tickers & Social Club**

Income and Expenditure Account for the year ending 31 December 2008

Income:		
Subscriptions (1,280 + 220)		1,500
Profit on café operations		730
Profit on sports equipment		300
		2,530
Less Expenditure		
Rent	1,200	
Insurance	600	
Repairs to roller ($^1/_2$ × 450)	225	
Sports equipment depreciation (*see* note 1)	486	
Depreciation of roller ($^1/_2$ × 200)	100	2,611
Excess of expenditure over income		81

36.7 *(cont'd)*

Balance Sheet as at 31 December 2008

Non-current assets			
Share in motor roller at cost		1,000	
Less Depreciation to date		500	500
Used sports equipment at valuation			700
			1,200
Current assets			
Inventory of new sports equipment (*see* note 2)		900	
Inventory of café supplies		850	
Subscriptions owing		80	
Carefree Conveyancers: owing for expenses		225	
Prepaid expenses		350	
Cash and bank (note 3)		754	3,159
			4,359
Current liabilities			
Café suppliers	80		
Advance subscriptions	80	160	
Non-current liabilities			
Life subscriptions		1,380	(1,540)
			2,819
Accumulated fund			
Balance at 1.1.2008		2,900	
Less Excess of expenditure		81	
			2,819

Notes:

Used Sports Equipment

1 Inventory b/d	700	Cash	14
Transferred from		Income and expenditure a/c	486
purchases	500	Inventory c/d	700
	1,200		1,200

2 b/d 1,000 + bought (1,000 × $^1/_2$) 500 = 1,500 – sold 600 = 900
3 b/d 1,210 + receipts 6,994 – paid 7,450 = 754

(*d*) To most people probably the best description of the item would be 'deferred income', i.e. income paid in advance for future benefits.

It could, however, be described as a liability of the club. The club in future will have to provide and finance amenities for life members, but those members do not have to pay any more money for them. This is therefore the future liability to provide these services without further payment.

37.1

Loose Tools

2007			2007			
Jan 1 Balance	b/d	2,400	Dec 31 Manufacturing			1,930
Dec 31 Bank		3,800	31 Balance		c/d	5,100
31 Wages		490				
31 Materials		340				
		7,030				7,030
2008			2008			
Jan 1 Balance	b/d	5,100	Dec 31 Manufacturing			2,010
Dec 31 Bank		1,820	31 Balance		c/d	5,940
31 Wages		610				
31 Materials		420				
		7,950				7,950
2009			2009			
Jan 1 Balance	b/d	5,940	Dec 31 Bank: Refund			142
Dec 31 Bank		2,760	31 Manufacturing			3,168
31 Wages		230	31 Balance		c/d	5,990
31 Materials		370				
		9,300				9,300

37.2

Manufacturing and Trading Account for 2003

Sales		202,283
Less: Cost of goods sold		
Opening inventory of raw materials	13,500	
Purchases of raw materials	82,700	
Carriage in of raw materials	4,430	
	100,630	
Closing inventory raw materials	14,100	
Cost of materials consumed	86,530	
Direct expenses		
Salaries and wages (75,674 – 22,700)	52,974	
Factory direct expenses	365	
Prime cost	139,869	
Indirect expenses		
Salaries and wages	22,700	
Rent and rates	1,200	
Light and heat	2,590	
Repairs to machinery	1,527	
Depreciation – machinery	2,700	
Insurance – plant and machinery	440	
	171,026	
Add Work-in-progress at 1 Jan 2003	11,800	
	182,826	
Less Work-in-progress at 31 Dec 2003	11,450	
Production cost of goods produced	171,376	
Add Opening inventory of finished goods	13,400	
	184,776	
Less Closing inventory of finished goods	14,160	
		170,616
Gross profit		31,667

37.4

W Miller
Manufacturing Account and Income Statement
for the year ending 31 December 2003

Inventory raw materials 1.1.2003		25,400
Add Purchases		91,535
Add Carriage inwards		1,960
		118,895
Less Inventory raw materials 31.12.2003		28,900
Cost of raw materials consumed		89,995
Direct labour		84,208
Prime cost		174,203
Factory overhead expenses		
Rent $^{3}/_{4}$	3,900	
Fuel and power	8,120	
Depreciation: Machinery	10,200	22,220
		196,423
Add Work-in-progress 1.1.2003		31,100
		227,523
Less Work-in-progress 31.12.2003		24,600
Production cost of goods completed		202,923
Sales		318,622
Less Cost of goods sold		
Inventory finished goods 1.1.2003	23,260	
Add Production cost of goods completed	202,923	
	226,183	
Less Inventory finished goods 31.12.2003	28,840	197,343
Gross profit		121,279
Less Expenses:		
Office salaries	33,419	
Rent $^{1}/_{4}$	1,300	
Lighting and heating	4,420	
Depreciation: Office equipment	2,300	41,439
Net profit		79,840

37.5

Manufacturing Account and Trading Account part of the Income Statement for
the six months ending 30 September 2005

Raw materials		
Opening inventory		2,990
Purchases		15,630
Carriage in		126
		18,746
Less Closing inventory		4,200
(*a*) *Cost of raw materials consumed*		14,546
Direct wages		48,648
(*b*) *Prime cost of production*		63,194
Indirect expenses		
Factory general expenses	7,048	
Depreciation – Factory equipment	4,200	
Rent and business rates	2,100	
		13,348
		16,542
Add Opening work-in-progress		3,900
		80,442
Less Closing work-in-progress		3,600
(*c*) *Production cost of finished goods*		76,842
Sales		112,410
Less Cost of goods sold		
Opening inventory of finished goods	15,300	
Add Production cost of finished goods	76,842	
	92,142	
Less Closing inventory of finished goods	17,700	
		74,442
Gross profit		37,968

(*d*) Gross profit on sales $= \dfrac{37,968}{112,410} = \underline{\underline{33.8\%}}$

37.7

E Wilson
Manufacturing Account and Income Statement for the year ending 31 December 2002

Inventory of raw materials 1.1.2002		13,260
Add Purchases		57,210
		70,470
Less Inventory of raw materials 31.12.2002		14,510
Cost of raw materials consumed		55,960
Manufacturing wages (72,100 + 550)		72,650
Prime cost		128,610
Factory overhead expenses:		
Factory lighting and heating	7,220	
General expenses: factory	8,100	
Rent of factory	6,100	
Depreciation: Machinery	3,000	24,420
Production cost of goods completed		153,030
Sales		194,800
Less Cost of goods sold:		
Inventory of finished goods 1.1.2002	41,300	
Add Production cost of goods completed	153,030	
	194,330	
Less Inventory of finished goods 31.12.2002	44,490	149,840
Gross profit		44,960
Less Expenses:		
Office salaries	17,740	
General expenses: office	1,940	
Office rent (2,700 – 140)	2,560	
Office heating and lighting	1,490	
Sales reps' commission	11,688	
Delivery van expenses	1,760	
Depreciation: Office equipment	600	
Van	1,200	38,978
Net profit		5,982

Balance Sheet as at 31 December 2002

	Cost	*Depreciation*	*Net*
Non-current assets			
Machinery	40,000	14,400	25,600
Office equipment	9,000	1,400	7,600
Van	6,800	1,800	5,000
	55,800	17,600	38,200
Current assets			
Inventory: Finished goods		44,490	
Raw materials		14,510	
Accounts receivable		34,200	
Prepaid expenses		140	
Bank		16,142	109,482
			147,682
Current liabilities			
Accounts payable	9,400		
Expenses owing	550		(9,950)
Net current assets			137,732
Capital			
Balance 1.1.2002			155,950
Add Net profit			5,982
			161,932
Less Drawings			24,200
			137,732

37.8

Mendip Ltd
Manufacturing Account and Income Statement for the year ending 30 June 2002

Raw materials			
Opening inventory			20,000
Purchases			130,100
			150,100
Less Closing inventory			22,000
Cost of raw materials consumed			128,100
Direct wages (63,000 – 15,700)			47,300
Direct factory expenses			9,100
Prime cost of production			184,500
Factory overheads			
Rates		3,000	
Heat and light		6,500	
Supervision		15,700	
Depreciation: Plant and machinery		10,500	35,700
Production cost of finished goods			220,200
Sales			317,500
Less: Cost of goods sold			
Opening inventory of finished goods		38,000	
Production cost of finished goods		220,200	
		258,200	
Less Closing inventory of finished goods		35,600	222,600
Gross profit			94,900
Less: Office salaries	36,300		
Directors fees	6,700		
Selling expenses	11,000		54,000
Net profit			40,900

Note: The dividends are not charged against revenue in the calculation of net profit. They are an appropriation of profit.

37.10

(*a*)

Jane Seymour
Manufacturing Account and Income Statement for the year ending 31 July 2006

Direct materials purchased	43,000	
Less Inventory 31 July 2006	7,000	36,000
Direct factory wages		39,000
Prime cost		75,000
Factory overhead expenses:		
Indirect factory wages	8,000	
Machinery repairs	1,600	
Rent and insurance (11,600 – 800) × $^2/_3$	7,200	
Light and power (5,000 + 1,000) × $^2/_3$	4,000	
Loose tools (9,000 – 5,000)	4,000	
Motor vehicle running expenses (12,000 × $^1/_2$)	6,000	
Depreciation: Plant and machinery	6,000	
Motor vehicles (7,500 × $^1/_2$)	3,750	40,550
		115,550
Less Work-in-progress 31 July 2006		12,300
		103,250
Transfer of goods manufactured to trading account		95,000
Loss on manufacturing		8,250
Sales		170,000
Less Goods manufactured transferred	95,000	
Inventory at 31 July 2006	10,000	85,000
Gross profit		85,000
Less Administrative staff salaries	31,000	
Administrative expenses	9,000	
Sales and distribution staff salaries	13,000	
Rent and insurance (11,600 – 800) × $^1/_3$	3,600	
Motor vehicle running expenses (12,000 × $^1/_2$)	6,000	
Light and power (5,000 + 1,000) × $^1/_3$	2,000	
Depreciation: Motors (7,500 × $^1/_2$)	3,750	68,350
Net profit in trading		16,650
Loss on manufacturing		8,250
Overall net profit		8,400

(*b*) *Conservatism*. The valuation of inventory or work-in-progress does not include any element of expected future profit.

Matching. All of the prepayments and accruals adjusted for are examples of matching expenses against the time period, as also are the depreciation provisions.

Going Concern. When valuing inventory and work-in-progress, it has been assumed that the business is going to carry on indefinitely, and that they will be sold in the normal course of business rather than being sold because of cessation of activities.

38.1

Fine's Department Store
Departmental Trading Account for the year ending 30 June 2006

		Carpet		*White Goods*		*Music*
Sales		62,400		151,300		94,820
Less Cost of good sold:						
Inventory 1.7.2005	16,100		37,916		31,222	
Add Purchases	43,600		118,260		55,924	
	59,700		156,176		87,146	
Less Inventory 30.6.2006	18,410	41,290	35,119	121,057	40,216	46,930
Gross profit		21,110		30,243		47,890

38.2

J Horner
Departmental Income Statement for the year ending 31 August 2007

	A		*B*	
Sales		75,000		50,000
Less Cost of goods sold:				
Inventory 1.9.2006	1,250		1,000	
Add Purchases	51,000		38,020	
	52,250		39,020	
Less Inventory 31.8.2007	1,410	50,840	912	38,108
Gross profits		24,160		11,892
Less Expenses:				
Wages	7,200		6,800	
Picture framing costs	300		–	
General office salaries	7,920		5,280	
Fire insurance	144		216	
Lighting and heating	248		372	
Repairs to premises	70		105	
Internal telephone	12		18	
Cleaning	72		108	
Accountancy changes	894		596	
General office expenses	306	17,166	204	13,699
Net profits/(losses)		6,994		(1,807)

39.1

F Black
Statement of Cash Flows for the year ending 31 December 2006

Operating activities		
Profit from operations		22,000
Adjustments for:		
Depreciation		4,650
Operating cash flows before movements in working capital		26,650
Decrease in inventory	300	
Decrease in accounts receivable	5,200	
Decrease in accounts payable	(10,400)	
		(4,900)
Cash generated by operations		21,750
Tax paid	–	
Interest paid	–	–
Net cash from operating activities		21,750
Investing activities		
Payments to acquire tangible non-current assets	(6,000)	
Net cash used in investing activities		(6,000)
Financing activities		
Loan received	20,000	
Drawings	(15,000)	
Net cash from financing activities		5,000
Net increase in cash and cash equivalents		20,750
Cash and cash equivalents at beginning of year		(13,650)
		7,100
Cash and cash equivalents at end of year		
Bank balances and cash		7,100

39.3

(*a*)

Malcolm Phillips
Statement of Cash Flows for the year ending 30 April 2009

Operating activities		
Profit from operations		8,500
Adjustments for:		
Depreciation		200
Operating cash flows before movements in working capital		8,700
Increase in inventory	(2,800)	
Increase in accounts payable	200	
Decrease in accounts receivable	500	
		(2,100)
Cash generated by operations		6,600
Tax paid	–	
Interest paid	–	–
Net cash from operating activities		6,600
Investing activities		
Payments to acquire tangible non-current assets	(3,000)	
Net cash used in investing activities		(3,000)
Financing activities		
Capital introduced	2,000	
Drawings	(8,000)	
Net cash used in financing activities		(6,000)
Net decrease in cash and cash equivalents		(2,400)
Cash and cash equivalents at beginning of year		1,500
		(900)
Cash and cash equivalents at end of year		
Bank balances and cash		(900)

(*b*) (*i*) $\frac{7,500}{30,000} \times \frac{100}{1} = 25\%$ (*ii*) $\frac{22,500}{(3,100 + 5,900) \div 2} = \frac{22,500}{4,500} = 5$

39.4

D Duncan
Statement of Cash Flows for the year ending 31 December 2005

Operating activities		
Profit from operations		23,240
Adjustments for		
Depreciation	1,800	
Profit on sale of tangible non-current asset	(620)	
Increase in allowance for doubtful debts	200	
		1,380
Operating cash flows before movements in working capital		24,620
Increase in inventory	(5,400)	
Decrease in accounts receivable (8,800 – 7,700)	1,100	
Increase in accounts payable	1,300	
		(3,000)
Cash generated by operations		21,620
Tax paid	–	
Interest paid	–	–
Net cash from operating activities		21,620
Investing activities		
Receipts from sale of tangible non-current assets	3,820	
Net cash from investing activities		3,820
Financing activities		
Loan repaid to J Fry	(2,500)	
Drawings	(22,630)	
Net cash used in financing activities		(25,130)
Net increase in cash and cash equivalents		310
Cash and cash equivalents at beginning of year		410
		720
Cash and cash equivalents at end of year		
Bank balances and cash		720

40.1

Stanley's Books (dates ignored)
Joint Venture with Barclay

TVs	1,100	Sales	3,100
Repairs	840		
Profit and loss	68		
Balance c/d	1,092		
	3,100		3,100
Cash: to Barclay	1,092	Balance b/d	1,092

Barclay's Books
Joint Venture with Stanley

Office rental	300	Balance c/d	1,092
Advertising	90		
Packaging materials	34		
TV	600		
Profit and loss	68		
	1,092		1,092
Balance b/d	1,092	Cash: from Stanley	1,092

40.1 *(cont'd)*

Memorandum Joint Venture Account

TVs		1,700	Sales	3,100
Repairs		840		
Office rental		300		
Advertising		90		
Packaging materials		34		
Profit on venture				
Stanley $^1/_2$	68			
Barclay $^1/_2$	68	136		
		3,100		3,100

40.3

Bull's Books

Joint Venture with Craig and Finch

Rent	600	Balance c/d	1,503
Labour: Planting	260		
Labour: Fertilising	180		
Sundries	19		
Labour	210		
Fertiliser	74		
Profit and loss	160		
	1,503		1,503
Balance c/d	1,503	Cash: from Finch	1,503

Craig's Books

Joint Venture with Bull and Finch

Plants	510	Balance c/d	639
Motor expenses	49		
Profit and loss	80		
	639		639
Balance b/d	639	Cash: from Finch	639

Finch's Books

Joint Venture with Bull and Craig

Labour: Lifting	416	Sales	2,916
Sale expenses	318		
Profit and loss	40		
Balance c/d	2,142		
	2,916		2,916
Cash: to Bull	1,503	Balance b/d	2,142
Cash: to Craig	639		
	2,142		2,142

Memorandum Joint Venture Account

Rent		600	Sales	2,916
Labour: Planting		260		
Labour: Fertilising		180		
Labour: Sundry		210		
Labour: Lifting		416		
Fertiliser		74		
Motor expenses		49		
Plants		510		
Sale expenses		318		
Sundries		19		
Profit shared: Bull $^4/_7$	160			
Craig $^2/_7$	80			
Finch $^1/_7$	40	280		
		2,916		2,916

41.1

Black, Brown and Cook

Appropriation Account for the year ending 31 July 2002

Net profit b/d			111,000
Less Salaries: Brown	30,000		
Cook	18,000	48,000	
Interest on capitals: Black	3,600		
Brown	2,400		
Cook	1,200	7,200	55,200
Balance of profits			55,800
Shared: Black $^2/_9$		12,400	
Brown $^1/_3$		18,600	
Cook $^4/_9$		24,800	55,800

41.3

I Skip and U Jump

Profit and Loss Appropriation Account 2004

Net profit			30,000
Profit shared	I Skip	15,000	
	U Jump	15,000	30,000

Profit and Loss Appropriation Account 2005

Net profit			38,000
Salaries	I Skip	10,000	
	U Jump	14,000	
Interest on capital	I Skip	5,600	
	U Jump	2,800	
Profit shared	I Skip	2,800	
	U Jump	2,800	
			38,000

Profit and Loss Appropriation Account 2006

Net profit			29,000
Salaries	I Skip	10,000	
	U Jump	14,000	
Interest on capital	I Skip	5,600	
	U Jump	2,800	
Loss shared	I Skip	(1,700)	
	U Jump	(1,700)	
			29,000

Current Account – I Skip

2004		*2004*	
Drawings	8,000	Profit share	15,000
Bal c/d	7,000		
	15,000		15,000
2005		*2005*	
Drawings	13,000	Bal b/d	7,000
Bal c/d	12,400	Salary	10,000
		Interest on capital	5,600
		Profit share	2,800
	25,400		25,400
2006		*2006*	
Loss share	1,700	Bal b/d	12,400
Drawings	12,000	Salary	10,000
Bal c/d	14,300	Interest on capital	5,600
	28,000		28,000
		2007	
		Bal b/d	14,300

Current Account – U Jump

2004		*2004*	
Drawings	9,000	Profit share	15,000
Bal c/d	6,000		
	15,000		15,000
2005		*2005*	
Drawings	17,000	Bal b/d	6,000
Bal c/d	8,600	Salary	14,000
		Interest on capital	2,800
		Profit share	2,800
	25,600		25,600
2006		*2006*	
Loss share	1,700	Bal b/d	8,600
Drawings	20,000	Salary	14,000
Bal c/d	3,700	Interest on capital	2,800
	25,400		25,400
		2007	
		Bal b/d	3,700

41.4

Blair, Short and Steel
Appropriation Account for the year ending 31 December 2007

Net profit b/d				111,100
Add Interest on drawings:	Blair		400	
	Short		300	
	Steel		200	900
				112,000
Less Interest on capitals:	Blair	3,000		
	Short	2,000		
	Steel	1,500	6,500	
Salaries:	Short	20,000		
	Steel	25,000	45,000	51,500
Balance of profits				60,500
Shared: Blair 70%			42,350	
Short 20%			12,100	
Steel 10%			6,050	60,500

Balance Sheet as at 31 March 2008 (extracts)

Capital Accounts: Blair			100,000	
Short			50,000	
Steel			25,000	175,000
Current Accounts:	*Blair*	*Short*	*Steel*	
Balances 1.4.2007	18,600	9,460	8,200	
Add Interest on capital	3,000	2,000	1,500	
Salaries		20,000	25,000	
Share of profits	42,350	12,100	6,050	
	63,950	43,560	40,750	
Less Interest on drawings	400	300	200	
Drawings	39,000	27,100	16,800	
	24,550	16,160	23,750	64,460

41.8

Considerations

(*a*) *Legal position re Partnership Act 1890*: Partners can agree to anything. The main thing is that of mutual agreement. The agreement can either be very formal in a partnership deed drawn up by a lawyer or else it can be evidenced in other ways.

The Act lays down the provisions for profit sharing if agreement has not been reached, written or otherwise.

(*b*) As Bee is not taking an active part in the running of the business he could be registered as a limited partner under the 1907 Limited Partnership Act. This has the advantage that his liability is limited to the amount of capital invested by him; he can lose that but his personal possessions cannot be taken to pay any debts of the firm.

As Bee is a 'sleeping partner' you will have to decide whether his reward should be in the form of a fixed amount, or should vary according to the profits made. In this context you should also bear in mind whether or not he would suffer a share of losses if they occurred.

If he were to have a fixed amount, irrespective as to whether profits had been made or not, then the question arises as to the amount required. This is obviously a more risky investment than, say, government securities. He therefore would naturally expect to get a higher return.

Bee would probably feel aggrieved if the profits rose sharply, but he was still limited to the amounts already described. There could be an arrangement for extra payments if the profits exceeded a given figure.

Cee is the expert conducting the operations of the business. He will consequently expect a major share of the profits.

One possibility would be to give him a salary, similar to his current salary, before dividing whatever profits then remain.

(*c*) Dee is making himself available, as well as bringing in some capital. Because of this active involvement he will affect the profits made. It would seem appropriate to give him a salary commensurate with such work, plus a share of the profits.

(*d*) *Interest on capital*: Whatever is decided about profit sharing, it would seem appropriate for each of the partners to be given interest on their capitals before sharing the balance of the profits.

41.9

Frame and French
Income Statement and Profit and Loss Appropriation Account for the year ending 30 September 2009

Sales			363,111
Less Cost of goods sold:			
Opening inventory		62,740	
Add Purchases		210,000	
		272,740	
Less Closing inventory		74,210	198,530
Gross profit			164,581
Add Reduction in allowance for doubtful debts			150
			164,731
Less Salaries and wages (57,809 + 720)		58,529	
Office expenses (4,760 + 215)		4,975	
Carriage outwards		3,410	
Discounts allowed		620	
Bad debts		1,632	
Loan interest		3,900	
Depreciation: Fixtures	600		
Buildings	5,000	5,600	78,666
Net profit			86,065
Add Interest on drawings: Frame		900	
French		600	1,500
			87,565
Less Interest on capitals: Frame	5,000		
French	3,750	8,750	
Salary: Frame		30,000	38,750
Balance of profits			48,815
Shared: Frame		29,289	
French		19,526	48,815

Balance Sheet as at 30 September 2009

	Cost	*Depn*	*N.B.V.*
Non-current assets			
Buildings	210,000	55,000	155,000
Fixtures	8,200	4,800	3,400
	218,200	59,800	158,400
Current assets			
Inventory		74,210	
Accounts receivable	61,400		
Less Allowance for doubtful debts	1,250	60,150	
Bank		6,130	140,490
Current liabilities			298,890
Accounts payable	26,590		
Expenses owing	935	27,525	
Net current assets			
Non-current liabilities			
Loan from P Prince		65,000	(92,525)
			206,365
Financed by			
Capital Accounts: Frame		100,000	
French		75,000	175,000
Current Accounts	*Frame*	*French*	
Balance 1.10.2008	4,100	1,200	
Add Interest on capital	5,000	3,750	
Salary	30,000	–	
Balance of profit	29,289	19,526	
	68,389	24,476	
Less Drawings	31,800	28,200	
Interest on drawings	900	600	
	35,689	(4,324)	31,365
			206,365

41.11

Sage and Onion
Income Statement and Profit and Loss Appropriation Account for the year ending 31 December 2001

Sales (508,000 – 6,000)			502,000
Opening inventory		75,000	
Purchases (380,000 + 3,000)		383,000	
Carriage in		21,500	
		479,500	
Returns		12,000	
		467,500	
Closing inventory	68,000		
Drawings (500 + 630)	1,130	69,130	398,370
Gross profit			103,630
Discounts received			1,000
			104,630
Expenses			
Salaries (42,000 + 900)		42,900	
Office		7,500	
Carriage out		3,000	
Adverts		5,000	
Discount allowed		1,200	
Repairs and renewals (2,800 – 200)		2,600	
Bad debt		1,400	
Depreciation – Fixtures and fittings		1,500	
Allowance for doubtful debts		400	
			65,500
Net profit			39,130
Add Interest on drawings (360 + 280)			640
Interest on current account			30
			39,800
Less Interest on capital (5,000 + 2,500)		7,500	
Interest on current account		100	
Salaries (12,000 + 8,000)		20,000	27,600
Balance of profits			12,200
Shared: Sage		6,100	
Onion		6,100	
			12,200

Balance Sheet as at 31 December 2001

Non-current assets				
Freehold – Cost				50,000
Fixtures and fittings – Cost			15,000	
– Depreciation			4,500	10,500
				60,500
Current assets				
Inventory			68,000	
Accounts receivable (52,400 – 2,400)			50,000	
Bank			31,600	
Prepayments			200	149,800
				210,300
Current liabilities				
Accounts payable (33,300 + 3,900)		37,200		
VAT		8,700		
				(45,900)
				164,400
Financed by				
Capital Accounts				
Sage		100,000		
Onion		50,000		150,000
Current Accounts	*Sage*	*Onion*		
Balance b/d	2,000	(600)		
Interest on capital	5,000	2,500		
Interest on current account	100	(30)		
Salaries	12,000	8,000		
Profit	6,100	6,100		
Drawings/Int/Goods	(15,860)	(10,910)		
	9,340	5,060		14,400
				164,400

41.13

Reid and Benson
Income Statement for the year ending 31 December 2003

Sales		541,750	
Less Returns		800	540,950
Purchases		291,830	
Less Returns		330	
		291,500	
Carriage inwards		3,150	
		294,650	
Less Closing inventory		1,500	
			293,150
Gross profit			247,800
Less Expenses			
Staff salaries		141,150	
Rent		2,500	
Benson compensation		10,000	
General expenses		9,500	
Bad debts		1,150	
Allowance for doubtful debts		1,500	
Depreciation		7,400	
Insurance		2,350	
			175,550
Net profit transferred to Appropriation Account			72,250

Appropriation Account for the year ending 31 December 2003

Net profit			72,250
Less salary – Reid			18,000
			54,250
Add Interest on Drawings – Reid	1050		
– Benson	550		1,600
			55,850
Less Interest on Capital – Reid	3,750		
– Benson	2,500		6,250
			49,600
Less Interest on Current a/c – Reid	250		
– Benson	200		
			450
Balance of profits			49,150
Shared – Reid		29,490	
– Benson		19,660	49,150

Balance Sheet as at 31 December 2003

Non-current assets			
Fixtures and fittings		74,000	
Less Depreciation		19,400	
			54,600
Current assets			
Inventory		1,500	
Accounts receivable		136,000	
Prepayments		150	
Cash		400	138,050
			192,650
Current liabilities			
Accounts payable			(23,400)
			169,250
Financed by:	*Reid*	*Benson*	
Capital Accounts	75,000	50,000	125,000
Current Accounts			
Balance b/d	5,000	4,000	
Salary	18,000	–	
Interest on drawings	(1,050)	(550)	
Interest on capital a/c	3,750	2,500	
Interest on current a/c	250	200	
Profit	29,490	19,660	
Drawings	(17,000)	(20,000)	
Balance c/d	38,440	5,810	44,250
			169,250

42.1

(*a*)

Balance Sheet as at 31 March 2003

Goodwill	24,000
Other assets	100,000
	124,000
Capitals: Vantuira (30,000 + 7,200)	37,200
Aparecida (20,000 + 4,800)	24,800
Fraga (50,000 + 12,000)	62,000
	124,000

(*b*)

Goodwill Workings

Before			*After*		*Loss or Gain*		*Action needed*	
Vantuira	$^3/_{10}$	7,200	$^1/_2$	12,000	Gain	4,800	Debit Vantuira	4,800
Aparecida	$^1/_5$	4,800	$^1/_8$	3,000	Loss	1,800	Credit Aparecida	1,800
Fraga	$^1/_2$	12,000	$^3/_8$	9,000	Loss	3,000	Credit Fraga	3,000
		24,000		24,000				

Balance Sheet as at 1 April 2003

Net assets	100,000
	100,000
Capitals Vantuira (30,000 – 4,800)	25,200
Aparecida (20,000 + 1,800)	21,800
Fraga (50,000 + 3,000)	53,000
	100,000

42.3

(*a*)

Goodwill	Dr	40,000	
Capitals Black			20,000
Smart			20,000
Cash	Dr	70,000	
Capital King			70,000

(*b*) *Balance Sheet*

Goodwill	40,000
Non-current and current assets (other than cash)	160,000
Cash	71,000
	271,000
Current liabilities	(41,000)
	230,000
Capitals Black	90,000
Smart	70,000
King	70,000
	230,000

(*c*)

Capitals Black	Dr	20,000	
Smart	Dr	7,500	
King	Dr	12,500	
Goodwill			40,000

42.5

(*a*) *Capital Accounts (£000)*

	Wilson	Player	Sharp	Titmus		Wilson	Player	Sharp	Titmus
					Bal b/d	57	76	38	
					Cash				30
Bal c/d	73	108	62	30	Goodwill	16	32	24	
	73	108	62	30		73	108	62	30

(*b*) Goodwill 72,000; Other assets except cash 200,000; Cash 32,000; Capitals as in (*a*); Accounts payable 31,000.

42.6

The senior partner's objection is a correct response. The money does not belong to the new partner once it has been paid.

This is because a new partner becomes an owner of part of the business, and this includes a part of the goodwill. This payment is specifically for that part of the goodwill. The goodwill was created by previous partners, and this is where the new partner buys his share from them. The £10,000 will be credited to the old partners in their old profit sharing ratio.

If C, the new partner, has paid £10,000 for one-fifth of the goodwill, then total goodwill is £50,000. Should the business be sold at a future date, and the goodwill realise £50,000, then C would receive one-fifth of the proceeds, i.e. £10,000, thus getting his money back. This illustrates the fairness of the accounting treatment of his original payment for goodwill. If anything had been credited to his account from this original payment for goodwill then he would have received that in addition. Obviously this would be unfair.

42.7

(*a*) **Stone, Pebble & Brick trading as Bigtime Building Supply Company Profit and Loss Appropriation Account for the year ending 31 March 2009**

		Apr–Dec		*Jan–Mar*
Net profit		27,225		9,075
Less Interest on Stone's loan		–		385
		27,225		8,690
Less Interest on capitals: Stone				250
Pebble				200
Brick				125
Less Salary: Brick				2,125
				5,990
Balance of profits shared:				
Stone	1/3	9,075	1/2	2,995
Pebble	1/3	9,075	3/10	1,797
Brick	1/3	9,075	1/5	1,198
		27,225		5,990

(*b*) *Capitals*

	Stone	Pebble	Brick		Stone	Pebble	Brick
Goodwill adjustment*		2,000	6,000	Balances b/d	26,000	18,000	16,000
Transfer to loan	14,000			Goodwill adjustment*	8,000		
Balances c/d	20,000	16,000	10,000				
	34,000	18,000	16,000		34,000	18,000	16,000

Current Accounts

	Stone	Pebble	Brick		Stone	Pebble	Brick
Drawings	8,200	9,600	7,200	Interest on capital	250	200	125
Balances c/d	4,120	1,472	5,323	Salary			2,125
				Share of profits:			
				Apr–Dec	9,075	9,075	9,075
				Jan–Mar	2,995	1,797	1,198
	12,320	11,072	12,523		12,320	11,072	12,523

42.7 *(cont'd)*

**Note:*

Goodwill:	*Value of goodwill taken over*	*Elimination of goodwill*	*Net effect*
Stone	30,000	22,000	8,000 Cr
Pebble	20,000	22,000	2,000 Dr
Brick	16,000	22,000	6,000 Dr
	66,000	66,000	–

43.1

(a)

Buildings

Balance b/d	80,000	Balance c/d	106,000
Revaluation: Increase	26,000		
	106,000		106,000

Motor Vehicles

Balance b/d	16,500	Revaluation: Reduction	3,500
		Balance c/d	13,000
	16,500		16,500

Inventory

Balance b/d	6,100	Revaluation: Reduction	1,206
		Balance c/d	4,894
	6,100		6,100

Office Fittings

Balance b/d	1,800	Revaluation: Reduction	350
		Balance c/d	1,450
	1,800		1,800

Revaluation

Motor vehicles		3,500	Buildings	26,000
Inventory		1,206		
Office fittings		350		
Profit on revaluation				
Pitt	11,968			
Lamb	5,984			
Soul	2,992	20,944		
		26,000		26,000

Capitals

	Pitt	*Lamb*	*Soul*		*Pitt*	*Lamb*	*Soul*
Balances c/d	71,968	35,984	25,592	Balances b/d	60,000	30,000	22,600
				Profit on revaluation	11,968	5,984	2,992
	71,968	35,984	25,592		71,968	35,984	25,592

(b) *Balance Sheet as at 1 January 2006*

Non-current assets		
Buildings at valuation		106,000
Motor vehicles at valuation		13,000
Office fittings at valuation		1,450
		120,450
Current assets		
Inventory at valuation	4,894	
Accounts receivable	7,400	
Bank	800	13,094
		133,544
Capitals:		
Pitt	71,968	
Lamb	35,984	
Soul	25,592	
		133,544

43.3

(a)

*Revaluation**

Premises		90,000	Premises	120,000
Plant		37,000	Plant	35,000
Inventory		62,379	Inventory	54,179
Allowance for doubtful debts		3,000		
Profit on revaluation				
Alan ½	8,400			
Bob ⅓	5,600			
Charles ⅙	2,800	16,800		
		209,179		209,179

*Just the net increases/decreases could have been recorded. Either method is acceptable.

Goodwill

Goodwill		Goodwill cancelled	
Capitals: Alan ½	21,000	Capitals: Alan 3/7	18,000
Bob ⅓	14,000	Bob 2/7	12,000
Charles ⅙	7,000	Don 2/7	12,000
	42,000		42,000

Capitals

	Alan	*Bob*	*Charles*	*Don*		*Alan*	*Bob*	*Charles*	*Don*
Goodwill	18,000	12,000	–	12,000	Balances b/d	85,000	65,000	35,000	–
Retirement			42,000		Goodwill	21,000	14,000	7,000	–
Cash	21,000				Cash				79,000
Balances b/d	67,000	67,000		67,000					
	106,000	79,000	42,000	79,000		106,000	79,000	42,000	79,000

Current Accounts

	Alan	Bob	Charles	Don		Alan	Bob	Charles	Don
Balance b/d		2,509			Balance b/d	3,714		4,678	
Retirement			7,478		Profit on				
Cash	9,023				Revaluation	8,400	5,600	2,800	
Balances c/d	3,091	3,091		3,091	Cash				3,091
	12,114	5,600	7,478	3,091		12,114	5,600	7,478	3,091

Charles: Retirement

Car	3,900	Capital	42,000
Cash	53,578	Current	7,478
Balance c/d	20,000	Loan	28,000
	77,478		77,478

Bank

Don: Capital	79,000	Balance b/d	4,200
Don: Current	3,091	Retirement – Charles	53,578
Balance c/d	5,710	Repaid Alan – Capital	21,000
		Current	9,023
	87,801		87,801

(*b*) *Balance Sheet (summarised)*:
Non-current assets total 168,100 + Current assets 86,919 – Current liabilities 24,746 – Loan 20,000 = 210,273.
Capitals 67,000 each × 3 + Current accounts 3,091 × 3 = Total 210,273.

43.5

(*a*)

Revaluation

Capital account:		Freehold premises	2,000
Gain on revaluation		Machinery and tools	900
A	4,000	Investments	1,100
B	4,000	Goodwill	8,000
C	4,000		
	12,000		12,000

Bank

Balance b/d	12,100	Capital account: A	18,900
Capital account:		Balance c/d	9,200
B	10,000		
C	6,000		
	28,100		28,100

Capital Accounts

	A	B	C
Balance b/d	20,000	17,000	25,000
Revaluation	4,000	4,000	4,000
New capital		10,000	6,000
Investment	(5,100)		
Bank	(18,900)		
	NIL	31,000	35,000

B and C
Balance Sheet as at 31 December 2007

Goodwill		8,000
Non-current assets		
Freehold premises		18,000
Machinery and tools		16,000
		42,000
Current assets		
Inventory	16,000	
Accounts receivable	12,800	
Bank	9,200	38,000
		80,000
Current liabilities		
Accounts payable		(14,000)
		66,000
Financed by:		
Capital Accounts – B		31,000
– C		35,000
		66,000

44.1

Realisation

Buildings	80,000	Cash: Accounts receivable	8,200
Tools and fixtures	2,900	Buildings	66,000
Accounts receivable	8,400	Tools and fixtures	1,800
Cash: Expenses	400	Discounts	300
		Loss on realisation: Poole	7,700
		Burns	7,700
	91,700		91,700

Capital Accounts

	Poole	Burns		Poole	Burns
Loss on realisation	7,700	7,700	Balance b/d	52,680	35,120
Cash	44,980	27,420			
	52,680	35,120		52,680	35,120

44.1 *(cont'd)*

Cash

Balance b/d	600	Realisation expenses	400
Accounts receivable	8,200	Accounts payable	3,800
Buildings	66,000	Capitals: Poole	44,980
Tools	1,800	Burns	27,420
	76,600		76,600

44.2

(a)

Realisation

Non-current assets	14,000	Bank: Non-current assets		8,000
Inventory	5,000	X: Non-current assets		7,000
Accounts receivable	21,000	Bank: Inventory		4,000
Bank: Dissolution costs	800	Bank: Accounts receivable		3,000
		Discounts on accounts payable		500
		Loss: X 3/6	9,150	
		Y 2/6	6,100	
		Z 1/6	3,050	18,300
	40,800			40,800

(b)

Capital Accounts

	X	Y	Z		X	Y	Z
Non-current assets taken over	7,000			Balances b/d	4,000	4,000	2,000
Loss shared	9,150	6,100	3,050	Deficiency shared:			
Deficiency	525	525		X			525
				Y			525
				Bank to settle	12,675	2,625	
	16,675	6,625	3,050		16,675	6,625	3,050

Bank (as proof only)

Realisation: Non-current assets	8,000	Balance b/d	13,000
Inventory	4,000	Accounts payable	16,500
Accounts receivable	3,000	Realisation: Costs	800
Capital: X	12,675		
Y	2,625		
	30,300		30,300

44.5

(a) (i)

Amis, Lodge and Pym
Income Statement and Profit and Loss Appropriation Account for the year ending 31 March 2008

Sales			404,500
Less Cost of goods sold:			
Opening inventory		30,000	
Add Purchases		225,000	
Add Carriage inwards		4,000	
		259,000	
Less Closing inventory		35,000	224,000
Gross profit			180,500
Add Bank interest		750	
Discounts received		4,530	5,280
			185,780
Less Office expenses (30,400 + 405)		30,805	
Rent, rates, light and heat (8,800 – 1,500)		7,300	
Carriage outwards		12,000	
Discounts allowed		10,000	
Allowance for doubtful debts		295	
Depreciation: Motor		15,000	
Plant		20,000	95,400
Net profit			90,380
Add Interest on current accounts and drawings:			
Amis		1,000	
Lodge		900	
Pym		720	2,620
			93,000
Less Salary – Pym		13,000	
Interest on capitals: Amis	8,000		
Lodge	1,500		
Pym	500	10,000	23,000
Balance of profit			70,000
Shared:			
Amis 50%		35,000	
Lodge 30%		21,000	
Pym 20%		14,000	70,000

(a) (ii)

Current Accounts

	Amis	*Lodge*	*Pym*		*Amis*	*Lodge*	*Pym*
Balances b/d	1,000	500	400	Salary			13,000
Drawings	25,000	22,000	15,000	Interest on capital	8,000	1,500	500
Interest on drawings	1,000	900	720	Balance of profits	35,000	21,000	14,000
Transfer to capital	16,000		11,380	Transfer to capital		900	
	43,000	23,400	27,500		43,000	23,400	27,500

(*b*) (*i*)

Realisation

Motors (80,000 – 35,000)		45,000	Discount on accounts payable	500
Plant (100,000 – 56,600)		43,400	Amis: Motor	5,000
Accounts receivable			Bank: Accounts receivable	12,985
(14,300 – 715)		13,585	Fowles Ltd (75,000 + 63,500)	138,500
Inventory		35,000		
Profit on realisation				
Amis 50%	10,000			
Lodge 30%	6,000			
Pym 20%	4,000	20,000		
		156,985		156,985

(*b*) (*ii*)

Bank

Balance b/d	4,900	Office expenses	405
Realisation: Accounts receivable	12,985	Accounts payable	16,000
Rent rebate	1,500	Capital: Amis	76,000
Fowles Ltd	63,500		
Capitals: Lodge	4,900		
Pym	4,620		
	92,405		92,405

(*b*) (*iii*)

Capital Accounts

	Amis	*Lodge*	*Pym*		*Amis*	*Lodge*	*Pym*
Current a/c		900		Balances b/d	80,000	15,000	5,000
Fowles Ltd				Current a/c	16,000		11,380
Shares	25,000	25,000	25,000				
Realisation:				Profit on			
Motor	5,000			realisation	10,000	6,000	4,000
Bank	76,000			Bank		4,900	4,620
	106,000	25,900	25,000		106,000	25,900	25,000

44.7

(*a*)

Lock, Stock and Barrel
Income Statement for the six months ending February 2007

Sales of completed houses		280,000
Less Costs of completing houses		
Houses in course of construction at start	115,000	
Materials used	35,750	
Land used (75,000 × 1/3)	25,000	
Wages and subcontractors	78,000	253,750
Gross profit		26,250
Less Administration salaries	17,250	
General expenses	12,500	
Depreciation: Freehold land	300	
Plant and equipment (6/12 × 10%)	7,500	
Vehicles (25% × 6/12)	4,500	42,050
Net loss		15,800
Shared: Lock 40%	6,320	
Stock 30%	4,740	
Barrel 30%	4,740	15,800

Capitals

	Lock	*Stock*	*Barrel*		*Lock*	*Stock*	*Barrel*
Drawings	6,000	5,000	4,000	Balances b/d	52,000	26,000	3,500
Loss shared	6,320	4,740	4,740	Balance c/d			5,240
Balances c/d	39,680	16,260					
	52,000	26,000	8,740		52,000	26,000	8,740

Lock, Stock and Barrel
Balance Sheet as at 1 February 2007

	Cost	*Depreciation*	
Non-current tangible assets			
Freehold land and buildings	20,000	3,300	16,700
Plant and equipment	150,000	89,500	60,500
Motor vehicles	36,000	27,500	8,500
	206,000	120,300	85,700
Current assets			
Inventory of land for building		50,000	
Inventory of materials		7,500	
Accounts receivable for completed houses		35,000	92,500
Total assets			188,200
Less Current liabilities			
Trade accounts payable	52,250		
Bank overdraft	75,250		
Total liabilities			(127,500)
Net assets			50,700
Financed by:			
Capitals: Lock			39,680
Stock			16,260
Barrel			(5,240)
			50,700

(*b*) Amounts distributable to partners:
On 28 February there was only (6,200 + 7,000 + 72,500 – 75,250) 10,450 hence there was nowhere near enough to pay off the accounts payable, and so payment to partners could not be made.
On 30 April we treat it as though no more cash will be received.

44.7 *(cont'd)*

(c) First distribution	*Lock*	*Stock*	*Barrel*
Capital balances before dissolution	39,680	16,260	(5,240)
Loss if no further assets realised (85,700 + 92,500 – 6,000 – 6,200 – 7,000 – 72,500 – 35,000 – 50,000) = 1,500			
Loss shared in profit/loss ratios	(600)	(450)	(450)
Cars taken over	(2,000)	(2,000)	(2,000)
	37,080	13,810	(7,690)
Barrel's deficiency shared profit/loss ratio	4,394	3,296	7,690
Paid to partners	32,686	10,514	–
Second and final distribution			
Capital balances before dissolution	39,680	16,260	(5,240)
Profit finally ascertained 100,000 – 1,500 = 98,500			
Shared	39,400	29,550	29,550
	79,080	45,810	24,310
Less Distribution and cars	34,686	12,514	2,000
Final distribution (100,000)	44,394	33,296	22,310

45.1

Flyer Ltd
Statements of Changes in Equity (extract)

(1) For the year ending 31 March 2005

	Retained Profits	*General Reserve*
Opening balance	–	–
Retained profit for the year	90,200	–
Transferred to general reserve	(20,000)	20,000
Preference dividend paid	(5,000)	–
Closing balance	65,200	20,000

(2) For the year ending 31 March 2006

	Retained Profits	*General Reserve*
Opening balance	65,200	20,000
Retained profits for the year	84,600	–
Transferred to general reserve	(15,000)	15,000
Preference dividend paid	(5,000)	–
Ordinary dividend paid	(16,000)	–
Closing balance	113,800	35,000

45.2

Trainsign Ltd
Statements of Changes in Equity

(1) For the year ending 31 December 2002

	Retained Profits	*General Reserve*	*Foreigh Exchange Reserve*
Opening balance	–	–	–
Retained profits for the year	62,400	–	–
Transferred to general reserve	(10,000)	10,000	–
Preference dividend paid	(6,300)	–	–
Closing balance	46,100	10,000	–

(2) For the year ending 31 December 2003

	Retained Profits	*General Reserve*	*Foreigh Exchange Reserve*
Opening balance	46,100	10,000	–
Retained profits for the year	81,900	–	–
Transferred to general reserve	(18,000)	18,000	–
Preference dividend paid	(6,300)	–	–
Ordinary dividend paid	(15,600)	–	–
Closing balance	88,100	28,000	–

(3) For the year ending 31 December 2004

	Retained Profits	*General Reserve*	*Foreigh Exchange Reserve*
Opening balance	88,100	28,000	–
Retained profits for the year	114,190	–	15,000
Transferred foreign exchange reserve	(15,000)	–	–
Preference dividend paid	(6,300)	–	–
Ordinary dividend paid	(20,800)	–	–
Closing balance	160,190	28,000	15,000

45.3

Balance Sheet as at 30 September 2002

	Cost	Depn	
Non-current assets			
Buildings	330,000	40,000	290,000
Motors	74,000	41,000	33,000
Fixtures	9,200	5,100	4,100
	413,200	86,100	327,100
Current assets			
Inventory		21,400	
Accounts receivable		10,300	
Bank (difference)		6,900	38,600
			365,700
Current liabilities			
Accounts payable		13,700	
Loan notes			
Net current assets			
Total assets *less* current liabilities			
Non-current liabilities: repayable 30.9.2006		40,000	(53,700)
			312,000
Capital and reserves			
Called-up share capital			200,000
Non-current assets replacement reserve			30,000
General reserve			50,000
Retained profits			32,000
			312,000

45.4

OK Limited

Statements of Changes in Equity (extract) for the year ending 31 March 2006

	Retained Profits	General Reserve
Opening balance	27,000	30,000
Retained profits for the year	29,000	–
Transfer to general reserve	(10,000)	10,000
Preference dividend paid	(4,000)	–
Ordinary dividend paid	(12,000)	–
Closing balance	30,000	40,000

Balance Sheet as at 31 March 2006

Non-current assets		167
Current assets		
Inventory	52	
Accounts receivable	24	
Bank	14	90
		257
Current liabilities		
Accounts payable		(37)
		220
Share Capital and Reserves		
8% preference share capital		50
Ordinary shares	100	
General reserve	40	
Retained profits	30	
Ordinary shareholder's equity		170
Total shareholder's equity		220

45.6

Select Limited

Profit and Loss Account part of the Income Statement for the year ending 31 March 2010

Gross profit		98,050
Office salaries and expenses	25,000	
Advertising	5,000	
Directors' fees	11,300	
Allowance for doubtful debts	350	
Provision for depreciation	8,000	49,650
Net profit		48,400

Note: the proposed dividend will be shown as a note.

Statement of Changes in Equity (extract) for the year ending 31 March 2010

	Retained Profits	General Reserve	Share Premium
Opening balance	12,000	–	20,000
Retained profits for the year	48,400	–	–
Transferred to general reserve	(25,000)	25,000	–
Closing balance	35,400	25,000	20,000

45.6 *(cont'd)*

Balance Sheet as at 31 March 2010

	Cost	Depreciation	
Non-current assets			
Land and buildings	170,000	–	170,000
Fixtures and fittings	80,000	40,000	40,000
	250,000	40,000	210,000
Current assets			
Inventory		42,000	
Accounts receivable		37,600	
VAT		3,800	
Bank		12,000	95,400
			305,400
Current liabilities			
Sunday accounts payable			(25,000)
			280,400
Share capital			
Authorised; 300,000 ordinary shares of £1			
Allotted, called-up and fully paid			200,000
Reserves			
Share premium		20,000	
General reserve		25,000	
Retained profits		35,400	80,400
			280,400

Balance Sheet as at 31 December 2003

Non-current assets			
Premises		271,000	
Less Depreciation		79,000	192,000
Machinery		84,000	
Less Depreciation		37,800	46,200
			238,200
Current assets			
Inventory		94,300	
Accounts receivable	74,200		
Less Allowance for doubtful debts	1,500	72,700	
Prepayments		700	
Bank		16,200	183,900
			422,100
Current liabilities			
Accounts payable		68,300	
Expenses owing		1,800	(70,100)
			352,000
Financed by:			
Authorised and issued capital			200,000
Retained profits (124,500 + 27,500)			152,000
			352,000

45.8

Tailor Times Ltd
Income Statement for the year ending 31 December 2003

Sales		925,300
Less Cost of goods sold		
Opening inventory	81,900	
Add Purchases	563,700	
	645,600	
Less Closing inventory	94,300	551,300
Gross profit		374,000
Less expenses		
Wages and salaries (179,400 + 1,800)	181,200	
Business rates (6,100 – 700)	5,400	
Electricity	4,800	
Bad debts	1,400	
Allowance for doubtful debts	300	
General expenses	14,600	
Depreciation: Freehold premises	25,000	
Machinery	16,800	249,500
Net profit		124,500

45.10

Partido Ltd
Income Statement for the year ending 31 December 2002

Sales		1,606,086
Less Cost of goods sold		
Opening inventory	290,114	
Add Purchases	810,613	
Add Carriage inwards	2,390	
	1,103,117	
Less Closing inventory	317,426	785,691
Gross profit		820,395
Less Expenses		
Salaries	384,500	
Business rates	16,500	
Carriage outwards	13,410	
Office expenses	9,345	
Sundry expenses	2,360	
Depreciation: Buildings	40,000	
Equipment	48,000	
Directors' remuneration	119,200	633,315
Net profit		187,080

Balance Sheet as at 31 December 2002

	Cost	Depn	Net
Non-current assets			
Buildings	800,000	120,000	680,000
Equipment	320,000	144,000	176,000
	1,120,000	264,000	856,000
Current assets			
Inventory		317,426	
Accounts receivable		321,219	
Bank		8,100	646,745
			1,502,745
Current liabilities			
Accounts payable		237,516	
Expenses owing		1,945	
			(239,461)
			1,263,284
Financed by:			
Share capital: authorised and issued			800,000
Reserves			
Foreign exchange		50,000	
General reserve		190,000	
Retained profits (187,080 + 136,204 – (70,000 + 30,000)		223,284	463,284
			1,263,284

45.12

1 **Burden plc: Computation of corrected net profit**

Recorded net profit		58,070
Add Profit on sale of equipment		500
		58,570
Less Bad debt written off	300	
Inventory reduced to net realisable value	700	1,000
Correct figure of net profit		57,570

2 **Burden plc**
Statement of Changes in Equity (extract) for the year ending 31 May 2009

	Retained Profits	General Reserve	Share Premium
Opening balance	16,200	20,000	25,000
Retained profits for the year	57,570	–	–
Transfer to general reserve	(50,000)	50,000	–
	23,770	70,000	25,000

3 (*i*)

Current assets			
Inventory		17,100	
Accounts receivable		6,540	
Prepayments		760	
		24,400	
Less Current liabilities			
Trade accounts payable	28,500		
Accrued expenses	430		
Bank overdraft	2,400	(31,330)	
Working capital (deficit)			(6,930)

Note: Figures in brackets are negative.

(*ii*)

Capital and reserves	
Ordinary share capital: called up	200,000
Share premium	25,000
General reserve	70,000
Retained profits	23,770
Shareholders' funds	318,770

4 *Examples*:
Issue of shares: + Bank; + Share capital.
Sales of non-current assets: + Bank; – Non-current assets.
Loan notes issued: + Bank; + Loan notes.

45.14

(*a*) See text.

(*b*) The historical cost convention does not make the going concern convention unnecessary. Several instances illustrate this:

(*i*) Non-current assets are depreciated over the useful life of the assets. This presupposes that the business will continue to operate during the years of assumed useful life of the assets.

(*ii*) Prepayments also assume that the benefits available in the future will be able to be claimed, because the business is expected to continue.

(*iii*) Inventory is valued also on the basis that it will be disposed of during the future ordinary running of the business.

(*iv*) The accruals concept itself assumes that the business is to continue.

All of this shows that the two concepts complement each other.

(*c*) Shareholders want financial statements so that they can decide what to do with their shareholding, whether they should sell their shares or hold on to them.

To enable them to decide upon their actions, they would really like to know what is going to happen in the future. To help them in this they would also like information which shows them what happened in the past. Ideally, therefore, they would like both types of report, those on the past and those on the future.

If they had a choice, the logical choice would be to receive a report on the future providing that it could be relied upon.

45.15

Extract 1

(*a*) The amount paid for goodwill.
(*b*) The excess represents share premium.
(*c*) Equity shares generally means ordinary shares.
(*d*) That although issued in 2006 a dividend will not be paid in that year. The first year that dividends *could* be paid is 2007.

Extract 2

(*e*) (*i*) A rate of 8% per annum interest will be paid on them, irrespective of whether profits are made or not.
(*ii*) These are the years within which the loan stock could be redeemed, if the company so wished.
(*f*) (*i*) This is the rate per annum at which preference dividends will be paid, subject to there being sufficient distributable profits.
(*ii*) That the shares could be bought back by the company.
(*g*) Probably because there was currently a lower interest rate prevailing at the time of redemption and the company took advantage of it.
(*h*) Large amounts of both fixed interest and fixed dividend funds have resulted in a raising of the gearing.
(*j*) Debenture interest gets charged before arriving at net profit. Dividends are an appropriation of profits in the period in which they are actually paid.
(*k*) Shareholders are owners and help decide appropriations. Debenture holders are external lenders and interest expense has to be paid.

45.16

(*a*) This is incorrect. The tax portion has to be counted as part of the total cost, which is made up of loan note interest paid plus tax. Holding back payment will merely see legal action taken by the HM Revenue & Customs to collect the tax.
(*b*) This cannot be done. The repainting of the exterior does not improve or enhance the original value of the premises. It cannot therefore be treated as capital expenditure.
(*c*) This is not feasible. Only the profit on the sale of the old machinery, found by deducting net book value from sales proceeds, can be so credited to the profit and loss account. The remainder is a capital receipt and should be treated as such.
(*d*) This is an incorrect view. Although some of the general reserve could, if circumstances allowed it, be transferred back to the retained profits, it could not be shown as affecting the operating profit for 2009. This is because the general reserve was built up over the years before 2009.
(*e*) This is not feasible. The share capital has to be maintained at nominal value as per the Companies Act. A share premium cannot be created in this fashion, and even if it could, it would still have to be credited to the *share premium account* and not the profit and loss account.
(*f*) Incorrect. Although the premises could be revalued the credit for the increase has to be to a capital reserve account. This cannot then be transferred to the credit of the profit and loss account.

45.17

See text. Points to be made include that there must be an expectation that sufficient profits will be made in future to make the loan note interest payments when due; also, there may be cheaper sources of finance available; also, if secured loan notes are to be issued, there must be sufficient assets available to act as security over the issue. Gearing is also an issue to be considered – see text.

46.1 Balance Sheet as at 31 March 2006

	(*a*) *T Malloy*	(*b*) *F Templar*
Goodwill	34,771	23,699
Premises	190,000	205,000
Inventory	39,200	36,100
Accounts receivable	18,417	18,417
Bank	828	–
	283,216	283,216
Accounts payable	(23,216)	(23,216)
	260,000	260,000
Capital	260,000	260,000

46.3

(*a*)

Spectrum Ltd
Balance Sheet as at 1 January 2002

Non-current assets		
Goodwill (note 1)		94,000
Premises (75,000 + 80,000 + 90,000 + 60,000)		305,000
Delivery vans (7,000 + 10,000)		17,000
Furniture and fittings (12,000 + 13,000 + 13,000)		38,000
		454,000
Current assets		
Inventory (8,000 + 7,000 + 12,000)	27,000	
Bank (note 2)	25,000	52,000
		506,000
Current liabilities		
Accounts payable (6,000 + 8,000 + 7,000)		(21,000)
Net current assets		485,000
Equity		
Share capital		
Authorised 700,000 shares £1	700,000	
Issued 500,000 shares £1		500,000
Reserves		
Retained profits		(15,000)
		485,000

Notes:

1 Goodwill: Red – paid		120,000	
Net assets taken over 75,000 + 7,000 + 12,000 + 8,000 – 6,000 =		96,000	24,000
Yellow – paid		130,000	
Net assets taken over 80,000 + 13,000 + 7,000 – 8,000 =		92,000	38,000
Blue – paid		150,000	
Net assets taken over 90,000 + 10,000 + 13,000 + 12,000 – 7,000 =		118,000	32,000
			94,000
2 Bank: Shares issued		500,000	
Less: Preliminary expenses	15,000		
Warehouse	60,000		
Red	120,000		
Yellow	130,000		
Blue	150,000	475,000	25,000

(*b*) Spectrum Ltd can issue part or the remainder of the authorised capital, i.e. 700,000 – 500,000 = £200,000. £100,000 will buy the business but some extra Net current assets is also needed.

46.4

(*a*)

Dinho and Manueli
Realisation Account

Property	290,000	Accounts payable	85,800
Equipment	65,000	Bank	56,700
Inventory	143,500	Loan	160,000
Accounts receivable	121,000	Bin Ltd	304,000
		Loss: Dinho	6,500
		Manueli	6,500
	619,500		619,500

(*b*)

Bin Ltd

Goodwill [write-downs (30,000 + 5,000) – realisation loss (13,000)]	22,000
Property	260,000
Equipment	65,000
Inventory	143,500
Accounts receivable	116,000
Bank (120,000 – 56,700)	63,300
Accounts payable	(85,800)
	584,000
Loan	160,000
	424,000
Ordinary Share Capital	300,000
10% Preference shares (D = 87,500; M = 16,500; P = 20,000)	124,000

(*c*) (salary as before, therefore not relevant); earnings on savings were 120,000 @ 6% = 7,200; preference dividend will be 20,000 @ 10% = 2,000, therefore 5,200 needed from profit after preference dividend. Profit must be 3 × 5,200 = 15,600 + the total preference dividend of 12,400 = 28,000.

47.1

(*a*)

		X	Y
(*i*)	Gross profit as % of sales	$\frac{315,000}{555,000} \times \frac{100}{1} = 56.8\%$	$\frac{420,000}{750,000} \times \frac{100}{1} = 56\%$
(*ii*)	Net profit as % of sales	$\frac{100,000}{555,000} \times \frac{100}{1} = 18\%$	$\frac{150,000}{750,000} \times \frac{100}{1} = 20\%$
(*iii*)	Expenses as % of sales	$\frac{215,000}{555,000} \times \frac{100}{1} = 38.7\%$	$\frac{270,000}{750,000} \times \frac{100}{1} = 36\%$
(*iv*)	Inventory turnover	$\frac{240,000}{(100,000 + 60,000) \div 2}$ = 3 times	$\frac{330,000}{(80,000 + 70,000) \div 2}$ = 4.4 times
(*v*)	Rate of return	$\frac{100,000}{(76,000 + 116,000) \div 2} \times \frac{100}{1}$ = 104.2%	$\frac{150,000}{(72,000 + 152,000) \div 2} \times \frac{100}{1}$ = 133.9%

47.1 (*cont'd*)

		X	Y
(*vi*)	Current ratio	$\frac{210,000}{104,000} = 2.02$	$\frac{182,500}{100,500} = 1.82$
(*vii*)	Acid test ratio	$\frac{145,000}{104,000} = 1.39$	$\frac{112,500}{100,500} = 1.12$
(*viii*)	Accounts receivable/sales ratio	$\frac{125,000}{555,000} \times 12 = 2.7$ months	$\frac{100,000}{750,000} \times 12 = 1.6$ months
(*ix*)	Accounts payable/purchases ratio	$\frac{104,000}{200,000} \times 12$ = 6.24 months	$\frac{100,500}{320,000} \times 12$ = 3.77 months

(*b*) Business Y is the most profitable, both in terms of actual net profit, £150,000 compared to £100,000, but also in terms of capital employed; Y has managed to achieve a return of £133.90 for every £100 invested compared with £104.20 for X. Reasons – possibly only – as not until you know more about the business could you give a definite answer:

(*i*) Possibly managed to sell far more merchandise because of lower prices, but the margins are so similar (56.8% v. 56%) that this is unlikely.

(*ii*) Maybe more efficient use of mechanised means in the business. Note that Y has more equipment and, perhaps as a consequence, kept other expenses down to £35,000 as compared with X's £45,000.

(*iii*) Did not have as much inventory lying idle. Turned over inventory 4.4 times in the year as compared with 3 for X.

(*iv*) X's current ratio of 2.02 is not much higher than Y's (1.82) so it is unlikely that this has contributed significantly to the difference in profitability through money sitting around doing nothing to increase profits.

(*v*) Following on from (*iv*) the Acid Test ratio for X may be higher than necessary.

(*vi*) Part of the reason for (*v*) is that X waited (on average) 2.7 months to be paid by customers. Y managed to collect them on average in 1.6 months. Money represented by debts is money lying idle.

(*vii*) Another reason for (*v*) is that X took almost twice as long to pay its creditors (6.24 months v. 3.77). However, this may be a 'good' sign for X as long as suppliers do not object and start refusing to sell to X.

Put all these factors together, and it appears that Y may be being run more efficiently, and is more profitable as a consequence.

47.3

(*a*)

Durham Limited
Statement of Changes in Equity (extract) for the year ending 30.4.2009

	Retained Profits	*General Reserve*
Opening balance	14,500	4,000
Retained profits for the year	16,500	–
Transferred to general reserve	(5,000)	5,000
Preference dividend paid	(2,000)	–
	24,000	9,000

(*b*)

Balance Sheet as at 30.4.2009

Non-current assets			
Premises at cost		86,000	
Machinery and plant at cost	60,000		
Less Depreciation	40,000	20,000	106,000
Current assets			
Inventory		60,000	
Accounts receivable	20,000		
Less Allowance for doubtful debts	4,000	16,000	
Prepayments		900	
Bank		13,100	90,000
			196,000
Current liabilities			
Accounts payable		12,900	
Expenses owing		100	(13,000)
			183,000
Equity			
8% preference shares		50,000	
Ordinary shares		100,000	150,000
General reserve			9,000
Retained profits			24,000
Shareholders' funds			183,000

(*c*) (*i*) *Return on Capital Employed (ROCE)*
This is the amount of profit earned compared with the amount of capital employed to earn it. Calculated:

$$\frac{\text{Net profit}}{\text{Average of shareholders' funds}} \times \frac{100}{1} = \frac{16,500}{(168,500 + 183,000) \div 2} \times \frac{100}{1}$$
$$= 9.39\%$$

(*ii*) *Current Ratio*
This calculates how well the current assets can finance current liabilities. Calculated:

$$\frac{\text{Current assets}}{\text{Current liabilities}} = \frac{90,000}{13,000} = 6.9 : 1$$

Acid Test Ratio
This calculates whether the business has sufficient liquid resources to meet its current liabilities. Calculated:

$$\frac{\text{Current assets} - \text{Inventory}}{\text{Current liabilities}} = \frac{30,000}{13,000} = 2.3 : 1$$

(*d*) ROCE. The return of 9.39% would appear to be adequate, but we cannot really comment further without more information.
Current Ratio. A figure of 2 : 1 is often reckoned as adequate. In this case a 6.9 : 1 figure is more than adequate.
Acid Test Ratio. All current liabilities can be met and the return is therefore adequate.

(*e*) 1 Previous years' figures.
2 We would need to know ratios for other similar businesses.

47.4

(*a*) (*i*) Gross profit: Sales

2008: $\frac{50}{200} \times \frac{100}{1} = 25\%$

2009: $\frac{70}{280} \times \frac{100}{1} = 25\%$

(*ii*) Inventory turnover

2008: $\frac{150}{(50 + 20) \div 2} = 4.29$

2009: $\frac{210}{(20 + 30) \div 2} = 8.4$

(*iii*) Net profit: Sales

2008: $\frac{12}{200} \times \frac{100}{1} = 6\%$

2009: $\frac{20}{280} \times \frac{100}{1} = 7.14\%$

(*iv*) Quick ratio

2008: $\frac{25}{25} = 1$

2009: $\frac{33}{12} = 2.75$

(*v*) Working capital (current ratio)

2008: $\frac{45}{25} = 1.8$

2009: $\frac{63}{12} = 5.25$

(*vi*) Net profit: Capital employed

2008: $\frac{12}{130} \times \frac{100}{1} = 9.23\%$

2009: $\frac{20}{191} \times \frac{100}{1} = 10.47\%$

(*b*) (Brief answer, but you should expand in an exam)

(*i*) No change.

(*ii*) Increase caused by lowering average inventory; also probably better sales management.

(*iii*) An increase in sales, without a larger increase in expenses, has led to a better return.

(*iv*) Issue of loan notes has improved the cash situation and therefore the quick ratio.

(*v*) Net current assets have increased largely due to issue of debentures, although partly offset by non-current assets bought.

(*vi*) Increasing sales and better inventory turnover brought about better ROCE.

47.7

(*a*)

Joan Street

Income Statement for the year ending 31 March 2008

Sales			(W3)	240,000
Cost of sales				
Opening inventory		21,000		
Add Purchases	(W6)	174,000		
	(W7)	195,000		
Less Closing inventory		15,000	(W1)	180,000
Gross profit			(W2)	60,000
Sundry expenses			(W5)	38,400
Net profit			(W4)	21,600

Balance Sheet as at 31 March 2008

Non-current assets			(W9)	108,000
Current assets				
Inventory		15,000		
Accounts receivable	(W8)	24,000		
Bank	(W14)	9,000	(W13)	48,000
				156,000
Current liabilities			(W13)	12,000
Net assets			(W12)	144,000
Financed by:				
Capital:				
Balance at 1.4.2007			(W11)	122,400
Add Net profit				21,600
			(W10)	144,000

Workings (could possibly find alternatives)

(W1) As average inventory 21,000 + 15,000 ÷ 2 = 18,000 and inventory turnover is 10, this means that cost of sales = 18,000 × 10 = 180,000

(W2) As gross profit is 25% of sales, it must therefore be $33\frac{1}{3}\%$ of cost of sales

(W3) As (W1) is 180,000 and (W2) is 60,000 therefore sales = (W1) + (W2) = 240,000

(W4) Net profit = 9% of sales = 21,600

(W5) Missing figure, found by arithmetical deduction

(W6) and (W7) Missing figures – found by arithmetical deduction

(W8) $\frac{\text{Accounts receivable (?)} \times 365}{\text{Sales}} = 36\frac{1}{2}$, i.e.

$\frac{? \times 365}{240,000} = 36\frac{1}{2}$, by arithmetic

Accounts receivable = 24,000. Proof $\frac{24,000 \times 365}{240,000} = 36\frac{1}{2}$

47.7 (*cont'd*)

(W9) 45% × 240,000 = 108,000

(W10) Knowing that net profit 21,600 is 15% of W10, so W10 = 21,600 × 100/15 = 144,000

(W11) Missing figure

(W12) Put in after (W11)

(W13) If Net current assets ratio is 4, it means a factor of current assets 4, current liabilities 1 = Net current assets 3 which is (W12 – W9) = 36,000, current assets therefore:
4/3 × 36,000 = 48,000
and current liabilities
1/3 × 36,000 = 12,000

(W14) Is new missing figure.

(*b*) Question asked for two favourable aspects and two unfavourable aspects but four of each are given here
Favourable: Inventory turnover, liquidity, net current assets, net profit on sales
Unfavourable: Gross profit to sales, accounts receivable collection, return on capital employed, turnover to net capital employed.

(*c*) Drawbacks include:
- (*i*) No access to trends over recent years.
- (*ii*) No future plans etc. given.
- (*iii*) Each business is often somewhat different.
- (*iv*) Size of businesses not known.

47.9

(*a*)
- (*i*) Current ratio: by dividing current assets by current liabilities.
- (*ii*) Quick assets ratio: by dividing current assets less inventory by current liabilities.
- (*iii*) Return on capital employed (ROCE): can have more than one meaning. One in common use is net profit divided by capital plus long-term liabilities (e.g. loans), and shown as a percentage.
- (*iv*) Return on shareholders' funds (ROSF): net profit divided by capital, shown as a percentage.
- (*v*) Accounts receivable turnover: Sales divided by average accounts receivable, expressed in days or months.
- (*vi*) Accounts payable turnover: Purchases divided by average accounts payable, expressed in days or months.
- (*vii*) Gross profit percentage: Gross profit divided by sales, expressed as a percentage.
- (*viii*) Net profit percentage: Net profit divided by sales.
- (*ix*) Inventory turnover: Cost of goods sold, divided by average inventory, expressed in days.

(*b*) (This part of the question tests your ability to be able to deduce some conclusions from the information given. You have to use your imagination.)

First, an assumption, we do not know relative sizes of these two businesses. We will assume that they are approximately of the same size.

A has a higher current ratio, 2 to 1.5, but the quick assets ratio shows a much greater disparity, 1.7 to 0.7. As inventory is not included in the quick assets ratio, it can be deduced that B has relatively greater inventory. Expected also from these ratios is that A has high amounts of accounts receivable, this being seen because accounts receivable turnover is three times as great for A as for B.

The return on shareholders' funds (ROSF) is much greater for A than for B, 30% to 18%, but the ROCE is not that different, 20% to 17%. This shows that A has far more in long-term borrowings than B. The ROCE indicates that A is somewhat more efficient than B, but not by a considerable amount.

Gross profit percentage is far greater for A than B, but net profit percentage is the same. Obviously A has extremely high operating expenses per £100 of sales.

The last ratio shows that inventory in A lies unsold for twice as long a period as for B.

A summary of the above shows that A has lower inventory, a higher figure for accounts receivable, sells at a slower rate, and has high operating expenses. B has more inventory, and sells its goods much quicker but at lower prices as shown by the gross profit percentage.

All the evidence points to A being a firm which gives emphasis to personal service to its customers. B on the other hand emphasises cheap prices and high turnover, with not as much concentration on personal service.

47.11

(There is no set answer. In addition, as a large number of points could be mentioned, the examiner cannot expect every aspect to be covered.)

The main points which could be covered are:

- (*i*) The financial statements are for last year whereas, in fact, the bank is more interested in what might happen to the business in the future.
- (*ii*) The financial statements are usually prepared on a historic cost basis. These therefore do not reflect current values.
- (*iii*) The bank manager would want a cash budget to be drawn up for the ensuing periods. This would give the manager an indication as to whether or not the business will be able to meet its commitments as they fall due.
- (*iv*) The bank manager wants to ensure that bank charges and interest can be paid promptly, also that a bank loan or overdraft will be able to be paid off. He will want to see that these commitments can still be met if the business has to cease operations. This means that the market value of assets on cessation, rather than the cost of them, is of much more interest to the bank manager.

To say that the financial statements are 'not good enough' is misleading. What the manager is saying is that the financial statements do not provide him with what he would really like to know. One could argue that there should be other types of financial statements drawn up in addition to those drawn up on a historic basis.

47.12

(*a*) The basis on which financial statements are prepared is that of 'accruals'. By this it is meant that the recognition of revenue and expenditure takes place not at the point when cash is received or paid out, but instead at the point when the revenue is earned or the expenditure is incurred.

To establish the point of recognition of a sale, several criteria are necessary:
- (*i*) The product, or the service, must have been supplied to the customer.
- (*ii*) The buyer must have indicated willingness to pay for the product or services and have accepted liability to do so.

(*iii*) A monetary value of the goods or services must have been agreed to by the buyer.
(*iv*) Ownership of the goods must have passed to the buyer.

(*b*) (*i*) This cannot be recognised as a sale. It does not comply with any of the four criteria above.
(*ii*) This also cannot be recognised as a sale. Neither criterion (*i*) nor (*iv*) has been covered.
(*iii*) If this was a cash sale, all of the above criteria would probably be achieved on delivery, and therefore it could be appropriate to recognise the sale.

If it was a credit sale, if the invoice was sent with the goods and a delivery note stating satisfaction by the customer is signed, then it would also probably be appropriate to recognise the sale.
(*iv*) Usually takes place after the four criteria have been satisfied. If so, the sale should be recognised.
(*v*) In the case of cash sales this would be the point of recognition.

In the case of credit sales it would depend on whether or not criteria (*a*) (*i*) and (*iv*) had also been satisfied.
(*vi*) This would only influence recognition of sales if there was serious doubt about the ability of the customer to pay his/her debts.

47.13

Obviously there is no set answer to this question. However, the following may well be typical:

(*a*) If the business is going to carry on operating, then the going concern concept comes into operation. Consequently, non-current assets are valued at cost, less depreciation to date. Inventory is valued at lower of cost or net realisable value. The 'net realisable value' will be that based on the business realising stock through normal operations.

(*b*) Should the business be deemed as a case for cessation, then the going concern concept could not be used. The values on non-current assets and inventory will be their disposal values. This should be affected by whether or not the business could be sold as a whole or whether it would have to be broken up. Similarly, figures would be affected by whether or not assets had to be sold off very quickly at low prices, or sold only when reasonable prices could be achieved.

It is not only the balance sheet that would be affected, as the income statement would reflect the changes in values.

47.14

(*a*) See text, Chapter 10.

(*b*) Various illustrations are possible, but the following are examples:
(*i*) Apportionment of expenses between one period and another. For instance, very rarely would very small inventories of stationery be valued at the year end. This means that the stationery gets charged against one year's profits even though it may not all have been used up in that year.
(*ii*) Items expensed instead of being capitalised. Small items which are, in theory, capital expenditure will often be charged up to an expense account.
(*iii*) The value of assets approximated, instead of being measured with absolute precision.

(*c*) (*i*) An illustration could be made under (*b*) (*iii*). An inventory of oil could well be estimated; the true figure, if known, might be one or two litres out. The cost of precise measurement would probably not be worth the benefit of having such information.
(*ii*) What is material in one company may not be material in another.

47.15

No set answer. Question is of a general nature rather than being specific. A variety of answers is therefore acceptable.

The examiner might expect to see the following covered (this is not a model answer):

(*a*) Different reports needed by different outside parties, as they have to meet different requirements. Might find they therefore include:
(*i*) for bankers – accounts based on 'break-up' value of the assets if they have to be sold off to repay loans or overdrafts;
(*ii*) for investors – to include how business has fared against budgets set for that year to see how successful business is at meeting targets;
(*iii*) for employees – include details of number of employees, wages and salaries paid, effect on pension funds;
(*iv*) for local community – to include reports showing amounts spent on pollution control, etc.

And any similar instances.

(*b*) The characteristics of useful information have been stated in *The Framework for the Preparation and Presentation of Financial Statements*, and the accounting reports should be measured against this.

(*c*) Presentation (additional) in form of pie charts, bar charts, etc., as these are often more easily understood by readers.

47.16

(*a*) Accountants follow the realisation concept when deciding when to recognise revenue on any particular transaction. This states that profit is normally regarded as being earned at the time when the goods or services are passed to the customer and he/she incurs liability for them. For a service business it means when the services have been performed.

(*b*) The stage at which revenue is recognised could be either F or G. The normal rule is that the goods have been despatched, not delivered. For instance the goods may be shipped to Australia and take several weeks to get there.

Exactly where this fits in with F or G in the question cannot be stipulated without further information.

(*c*) If F is accepted as point of recognition, then £130 will be gross profit. If G is accepted as point of recognition the gross profit recognised will be £120.

(*d*) The argument that can be advanced is to take the prudence concept to its final conclusion, in that the debtor should pay for the goods before the profit can be recognised.

Until H is reached there is always the possibility that the goods will not be paid for, or might be returned because of faults in the goods.

(*e*) If the goods are almost certain to be sold, it could give a better picture of the progress of the firm up to a particular point in time if profit could be recognised in successive amounts at stages B, C and D.

47.17

(*a*) A 'provision' is an amount written off or retained by way of providing for depreciation, renewals or diminution in value of assets, or retained by way of providing for any known liability of which the amount cannot be determined with 'substantial' accuracy. This therefore covers such items as provisions for depreciation. A 'liability' is an amount owing which can be determined with substantial accuracy.

Sometimes, therefore, the difference between a provision and a liability hinges around what is meant by 'substantial' accuracy. Rent owing at the end of the financial year would normally be known with precision; this would obviously be a liability. Legal charges for a court case which has been heard, but for which the lawyers have not yet submitted their bill, would be a provision.

Accrued expenses are those accruing from one day to another, but not paid at the year end. Such items as rates, electricity, telephone charges will come under this heading.

Accounts payable represent persons to whom money is owed for goods and services.

Reserves consist of either undistributed profits, or else sums that have been allocated originally from such profits or have been created to comply with the law. An example of the first kind is a *general reserve*, whilst a *share premium account* is of the second type.

Provisions, accrued expenses and accounts payable would all be taken into account before calculating net profit. Reserves do not interfere with the calculation of net profit, as they are appropriations of profit or, as in the case of capital reserves, do not pass through the profit and loss account.

(*b*) (*i*) Provision made for £21,000. Charge to profit and loss and show in balance sheet under current liabilities.

(*ii*) Accrued expenses, $^{2}/_{12}$ £6,000 = £1,000. Charge in profit and loss account and show as current liability in balance sheet.

(*iii*) Account payable £2,500. Bring into purchases in trading account and show as current liability in balance sheet.

(*iv*) Reserve £5,000. Transfer from retained profits to plant replacement reserve and show the transfer in the statement of changes in equity and in the balance sheet under *reserves*.

47.18

(*a*) *The bank*

The bank will be interested in two main aspects. The first is the ability to repay the loan as and when it falls due. The second is the ability to pay interest on the due dates.

Mr Whitehall

He will be interested in the expected return on his investment. This means that recent performance of the company and its plans will be important to him. In addition the possible capital growth of his investment would be desirable.

(*b*) *Note*: For your information; more than four ratios for bank are given below despite you having being asked for four.

Bank

Long-term ability to repay loan

(*i*) Members' equity/Total assets
(*ii*) Loan capital/Members' equity
(*iii*) Total liabilities/Members' equity
(*iv*) Operating profit/Loan interest.

Short-term liquidity

(*i*) Liquid assets/Current liabilities.
(*ii*) Current assets/Current liabilities.

Mr Whitehall

Return on investment

(*i*) Price per share/Earnings per share
(*ii*) Trends of (*i*) for past few years.
(*iii*) Net profit – Preference dividend/Ordinary dividend.
(*iv*) Trends of (*iii*) for past few years.

47.19

See text.

48.1

See text.

48.2

See text.

48.3

See text.

48.4

See text.

48.5

See text.

ppendix 2

Answers to multiple choice questions

Set 1 (pages 64–7)

1	(C)	**2**	(D)	**3**	(B)	**4**	(C)	**5**	(A)
6	(C)	**7**	(C)	**8**	(A)	**9**	(C)	**10**	(A)
11	(B)	**12**	(D)	**13**	(B)	**14**	(D)	**15**	(B)
16	(C)	**17**	(C)	**18**	(A)	**19**	(D)	**20**	(C)

Set 2 (pages 149–52)

21	(A)	**22**	(B)	**23**	(A)	**24**	(D)	**25**	(C)
26	(A)	**27**	(D)	**28**	(A)	**29**	(C)	**30**	(A)
31	(C)	**32**	(D)	**33**	(C)	**34**	(C)	**35**	(D)
36	(B)	**37**	(A)	**38**	(B)	**39**	(C)	**40**	(C)

Set 3 (pages 310–13)

41	(A)	**42**	(C)	**43**	(A)	**44**	(D)	**45**	(A)
46	(A)	**47**	(B)	**48**	(C)	**49**	(D)	**50**	(C)
51	(A)	**52**	(D)	**53**	(C)	**54**	(C)	**55**	(D)
56	(C)	**57**	(A)	**58**	(A)	**59**	(B)	**60**	(C)

Set 4 (pages 400–3)

61	(B)	**62**	(A)	**63**	(D)	**64**	(A)	**65**	(C)
66	(A)	**67**	(D)	**68**	(D)	**69**	(B)	**70**	(A)
71	(D)	**72**	(C)	**73**	(D)	**74**	(B)	**75**	(B)
76	(C)	**77**	(D)	**78**	(A)	**79**	(B)	**80**	(C)

Set 5 (pages 594–7)

81	(B)	**82**	(B)	**83**	(C)	**84**	(D)	**85**	(A)
86	(B)	**87**	(A)	**88**	(C)	**89**	(C)	**90**	(A)
91	(C)	**92**	(B)	**93**	(B)	**94**	(D)	**95**	(C)
96	(B)	**97**	(C)	**98**	(B)	**99**	(D)	**100**	(B)

appendix 3

Glossary

Absorption costing (Chapter 48): The method of allocating all factory indirect expenses to products. (All fixed costs are allocated to cost units.)

Account (Chapter 2): Part of double entry records, containing details of transactions for a specific item.

Account codes (Chapter 23): The computerised equivalent of the folio references used in a manual accounting system, whereby each ledger account is given a unique number.

Account payable (or **Creditor**) (Chapter 1): A person to whom money in owed for goods or services.

Account receivable (or **Debtor**) (Chapter 1): A person who owes money to a business for goods or services supplied.

Accounting (Chapter 28): The process of identifying, measuring and communicating economic information to permit informed judgements and decisions by users of the information.

Accounting cycle (Chapter 17): The sequence in which data is recorded and processed until it becomes part of the financial statements at the end of the period.

Accounting information system (AIS) (Chapter 23): The total suite of components that, together, comprise all the inputs, storage, transformation processing, collating and reporting of financial transaction data. It is, in effect, the infrastructure that supports the production and delivery of accounting information.

Accounting policies (Chapter 47): Those principles, bases, conventions, rules and practices applied by an entity that specify how the effects of transactions and other events are to be reflected in its financial statements.

Accounts (or **final accounts**) (Chapter 9): This is a term previously used to refer to statements produced at the end of accounting periods, such as the income statement and the balance sheet. Nowadays, the term 'financial statements' is more commonly used.

Accounts payable/purchases ratio (Chapter 47): A ratio assessing how long a business takes to pay creditors.

Accounts receivable/sales ratio (Chapter 47): A ratio assessing how long it takes debtors to pay their debts.

Accruals basis (or **Accruals concept**) (Chapter 10): The concept that profit is the difference between revenue and the expenses incurred in generating that revenue.

Accrued expense (Chapter 28): An expense for which the benefit has been received but which has not been paid for by the end of the period. It is included in the balance sheet under current liabilities as 'accruals'.

Accrued income (Chapter 28): Income (normally) from a source other than the main source of business income, such as rent receivable on an unused office in the company headquarters, that was due to be received by the end of the period but which has not been received by that date. It is added to accounts receivable in the balance sheet.

Accumulated depreciation account (Chapter 27): The account where depreciation is accumulated for balance sheet purposes. It is used in order to leave the cost (or valuation) figure as the balance in the non-current asset account. (It is sometimes confusingly referred to as the 'provision for depreciation account'.)

Accumulated fund (Chapter 36): A form of capital account for a non-profit-oriented organisation.

Acid test ratio (Chapter 47): A ratio comparing current assets less inventory with current liabilities.

Allowance for doubtful debts (Chapter 25): An account representing an estimate of the expected amount of debts at the balance sheet date which may not be paid.

Amortisation (Chapter 26): A term used instead of 'depreciation' when assets are used up simply because of the passing of time.

Assets (Chapter 1): Resources owned by a business.

AVCO (Chapter 29): A method by which goods used are priced out at average cost.

Bad debt (Chapter 25): A debt that a business will not be able to collect.

Balance brought down (Chapter 5): The difference between both sides of an account that is entered below the totals on the opposite side to the one on which the balance carried down was entered. (This is normally abbreviated to 'balance b/d'.)

Balance carried down (Chapter 5): The difference between both sides of an account that is entered above the totals and makes the total of both sides equal each other. (This is normally abbreviated to 'balance c/d'.)

Balance sheet (Chapter 1): A statement showing the assets, liabilities and capital of a business.

Balance-off the account (Chapter 5): Insert the difference (called a 'balance') between the two sides of an account and then total and rule off the account. This is normally done at the end of a period (usually a month, a quarter or a year).

Bank cash book (Chapter 18): A cash book that only contains entries relating to payments into and out of the bank.

Bank giro credit (Chapter 12): A type of pay-in slip usually used when the payment is into an account held in a different bank. The two types of form are virtually identical – a bank giro credit can be used instead of a pay-in slip, but not the other way around, as the details of the other bank need to be entered on the bank giro credit.

Bank loan (Chapter 12): An amount of money advanced by a bank that has a fixed rate of interest that is charged on the full amount and is repayable on a specified future date.

Bank reconciliation statement (Chapter 30): A calculation comparing the cash book balance with the bank statement balance.

Bank statement (Chapter 13): A copy issued by a bank to a customer showing the customer's current account maintained at the bank.

Bookkeeping (Chapter 1): The process of recording data relating to accounting transactions in the accounting books.

Books of original entry (Chapter 11): Books where the first entry recording a transaction is made. (These are sometimes referred to as 'books of prime entry'.)

Bought ledger (Chapter 20): A variant of a purchases ledger where the individual accounts of the creditors, whether they be for goods or for expenses such as stationery or motor expenses, can be kept together in a single ledger.

Budget (Chapters 1 and 48): A plan quantified in monetary terms in advance of a defined time period – usually showing planned income and expenditure and the capital employed to achieve a given objective.

Business entity concept (Chapter 10): Assumption that only transactions that affect the firm, and not the owner's private transactions, will be recorded.

Capital (Chapter 1): The total of resources invested and left in a business by its owner.

Capital expenditure (Chapter 24): When a business spends money to buy or add value to a non-current asset.

Capital reserve (Chapter 46): An account that can be used by sole traders and partnerships to place the amount by which the total purchase price paid for a business is less than the valuation of the net assets acquired. Limited companies cannot use a capital reserve for this purpose. Sole traders and partnerships can instead, if they wish, record the shortfall as negative goodwill.

Carriage inwards (Chapter 9): Cost of transport of goods into a business.

Carriage outwards (Chapter 9): Cost of transport of goods out to the customers of a business.

Cash (Chapter 39): Cash balances and bank balances, plus funds invested in 'cash equivalents'.

Cash book (Chapter 11): A book of original entry for cash and bank receipts and payments.

Cash equivalents (Chapter 39): Temporary investments of cash not required at present by the business, such as funds put on short-term deposit with a bank. Such investments must be readily convertible into cash, or available as cash within three months.

Casting (Chapter 32): Adding up figures.

Charge card (Chapter 12): A payment card that requires the cardholder to settle the account in full at the end of a specified period, e.g. American Express and Diners cards. Holders have to pay an annual fee for the card. (Compare this to a credit card.)

Chart of accounts (Chapter 23): The list of account codes used in a computerised accounting system.

Cheque book (Chapter 12): Book containing forms (cheques) used to pay money out of a current account.

Clearing (Chapter 12): The process by which amounts paid by cheque from an account in one bank are transferred to the bank account of the payee.

Close off the account (Chapter 5): Totalling and ruling off an account on which there is no outstanding balance.

Columnar purchases day book (Chapter 20): A purchases day book used to record all items obtained on credit. It has analysis columns so that the various types of expenditure can be grouped together in a column. Also called a purchases analysis book.

Columnar sales day book (Chapter 20): A sales day book used to show the sales for a period organised in analysis columns according to how the information recorded is to be analysed. Also called a sales analysis book.

Compensating error (Chapter 32): Where two errors of equal amounts, but on opposite sides of the accounts, cancel each other out.

Consistency (Chapter 10): Keeping to the same method of recording and processing transactions.

Contra (Chapter 13): A contra, for cash book items, is where both the debit and the credit entries are shown in the cash book, such as when cash is paid into the bank.

Contribution (Chapter 38): The surplus of revenue over direct costs allocated to a section of a business.

Control account (Chapter 31): An account which checks the arithmetical accuracy of a ledger.

Cost centre (Chapter 48): A production or service location, function, activity or item of equipment whose costs may be attributed to cost units.

Cost unit (Chapter 48): A unit of product or service in relation to which costs are ascertained.

Credit (Chapter 2): The right-hand side of the accounts in double entry.

Credit card (Chapter 12): A card enabling the holder to make purchases and to draw cash up to a prearranged limit. The credit granted in a period can be settled in full or in part by the end of a specified period. Many credit cards carry no annual fee. (Compare this to a charge card.)

Credit note (Chapter 16): A document sent to a customer showing allowance given by a supplier in respect of unsatisfactory goods.

Creditor (or **Accounts Payable**) (Chapter 1): A person to whom money is owed for goods or services.

Current account (Chapter 12): A bank account used for regular payments in and out of the bank.

Current assets (Chapter 8): Assets consisting of cash, goods for resale or items having a short life.

Current liabilities (Chapter 8): Liabilities to be paid for within a year of the balance sheet date.

Current ratio (Chapter 47): A ratio comparing current assets with current liabilities.

Day books (Chapter 11): Books in which credit sales, purchases, and returns inwards and outwards of goods are first recorded. The details are then posted from the day books to the ledger accounts.

Debit (Chapter 2): The left-hand side of the accounts in double entry.

Debit card (Chapter 12): A card linked to a bank or building society account and used to pay for goods and services by debiting the holder's account. Debit cards are usually combined with other facilities such as ATM and cheque guarantee functions.

Debit note (Chapter 16): A document sent to a supplier showing allowance to be given for unsatisfactory goods.

Debtor (or **Accounts Receivable**) (Chapter 1): A person who owes money to a business for goods or services supplied to him.

Depletion (Chapter 26): The wasting away of an asset as it is used up.

Deposit account (Chapter 12): A bank account for money to be kept in for a long time.

Depreciation (Chapter 26): The part of the cost of a non-current asset consumed during its period of use by the firm. It represents an estimate of how much of the overall economic usefulness of a non-current asset has been used up in each accounting period. It is charged as a debit to profit and loss and a credit against non-current asset accounts in the general ledger.

Direct costs (Chapter 37): Costs that can be traced to the item being manufactured.

Direct debit (Chapter 12): A medium used to enable payments to be made automatically into a bank account for whatever amount the recipient requests.

Directors (Chapter 45): Officials appointed by shareholders to manage the company for them.

Discounts allowed (Chapter 13): A deduction from the amount due given to customers who pay their accounts within the time allowed.

Discounts received (Chapter 13): A deduction from the amount due given to a business by a supplier when their account is paid before the time allowed has elapsed. It appears as income in the profit and loss part of the trading and profit and loss account.

Dishonoured cheque (Chapter 30): A cheque which the writer's bank has refused to make payment upon.

Dissolution (Chapter 44): When a partnership firm ceases operations and its assets are disposed of.

Dividends (Chapter 45): The amount given to shareholders as their share of the profits of the company.

Double entry bookkeeping (or **Double entry**) (Chapter 2): A system where each transaction is entered twice, once on the debit side and once on the credit side.

Drawer (Chapter 12): The person making out a cheque and using it for payment.

Drawings (Chapter 4): Funds or goods taken out of a business by the owners for their private use.

Dual aspect concept (Chapter 10): The concept of dealing with both aspects of a transaction.

Dumb terminal (Chapter 22): A computer screen with a keyboard and/or mouse, which has no processing power of its own but uses the processing power of a central computer to carry out tasks involving the data held on that central computer.

Endorsement (Chapter 12): A means by which someone may pass the right to collect money due on a cheque.

Equity (Chapter 1): Another name for the capital of the owner.

Error of commission (Chapter 32): Where a correct amount is entered, but in the wrong person's account.

Error of omission (Chapter 32): Where a transaction is completely omitted from the books.

Error of original entry (Chapter 32): Where an item is entered, but both the debit and credit entries are of the same incorrect amount.

Error of principle (Chapter 32): Where an item is entered in the wrong type of account, e.g. a fixed asset in an expense account.

Estimation techniques (Chapter 47): The methods adopted in order to arrive at estimated monetary amounts for items that appear in the financial statements.

Exception reporting (Chapter 23): A process of issuing a warning message to decision-makers when something unexpected is happening: for example, when expenditure against a budget is higher than it should be.

Exempted businesses (Chapter 19): Businesses which do not have to add VAT to the price of goods and services supplied to them. They cannot obtain a refund of VAT paid on goods and services purchased by them.

Expenses (Chapter 4): The value of all the assets that have been used up to obtain revenues.

Extranet (Chapter 22): A network based on Internet technologies where data and information private to the business is made available to a specific group of outsiders, such as suppliers.

Factoring (Chapter 16): Selling the rights to the amounts owing by debtors to a finance company for an agreed amount (which is less than the figure at which they are recorded in the accounting books because the finance company needs to be paid for providing the service).

FIFO (Chapter 29): A method by which the first items to be received are said to be the first to be sold.

Final accounts (or **accounts**) (Chapter 9): This is a term previously used to refer to statements produced at the end of accounting periods, such as the income statement and the balance sheet. Nowadays, the term 'financial statements' is more commonly used.

Financial modelling (Chapter 22): Manipulating accounting data to generate forecasts and perform sensitivity analysis.

Financial statements (Chapter 9): The more common term used to refer to statements produced at the end of accounting periods, such as the income statement and the balance sheet (sometimes referred to as 'final accounts' or simply 'the accounts').

Fixed capital accounts (Chapter 41): Capital accounts which consist only of the amounts of capital actually paid into the partnership.

Fixed costs (Chapter 47): Expenses which remain constant whether activity rises or falls, within a given range of activity.

Float (Chapter 18): The amount at which the petty cash starts each period.

Fluctuating capital accounts (Chapter 41): Capital accounts the balances of which change from one period to the next.

Folio columns (Chapter 13): Columns used for entering reference numbers.

Forecasting (Chapter 22): Taking present data and expected future trends, such as growth of a market and anticipated changes in price levels and demand, in order to arrive at a view of what the likely economic position of a business will be at some future date.

***Garner* v *Murray* rule** (Chapter 44): If one partner is unable to make good a deficit on his/her capital account, the remaining partners will share the loss in proportion to their last agreed capitals, not in the profit/loss sharing ratio.

Gearing (Chapter 47): The ratio of long-term loans and preference shares shown as a percentage of total shareholders' funds, long-term loans, and preference shares.

General ledger (Chapter 11): A ledger for all accounts other than those for customers and suppliers.

Going concern concept (Chapter 10): The assumption that a business is to continue for the foreseeable future.

Goodwill (Chapter 42): An amount representing the added value to a business of such factors as customer loyalty, reputation, market penetration and expertise.

Gross loss (Chapter 7): Where the cost of goods sold exceeds the sales revenue.

Gross profit (Chapter 7): Where the sales revenue exceeds the cost of goods sold.

Historical cost concept (Chapter 10): Assets are normally shown at cost price.

Impersonal accounts (Chapter 11): All accounts other than debtors' and creditors' accounts.

Imprest system (Chapter 18): A system where a refund is made of the total paid out in a period in order to restore the float to its agreed level.

Income and expenditure account (Chapter 36): An account for a non-profit-oriented organisation to find the surplus or loss made during a period.

Income statement (Chapter 7): The financial statement in which the calculations of gross profit and then net profit are presented.

Indirect manufacturing costs (Chapter 37): Costs relating to manufacture that cannot be economically traced to the item being manufactured (also known as 'indirect costs' and, sometimes, as 'factory overhead expenses').

Input tax (Chapter 19): VAT added to the net price of inputs (i.e. purchases).

Inputs (Chapter 19): Purchases of goods and services.

Intangible asset (Chapter 42): An asset, such as goodwill, that has no physical existence.

Interest on capital (Chapter 41): An amount at an agreed rate of interest which is credited to a partner based on the amount of capital contributed by him/her.

Interest on drawings (Chapter 41): An amount at an agreed rate of interest, based on the drawings taken out, which is debited to the partners.

Intranet (Chapter 22): A network based on Internet technologies where data and information private to the business is made available to employees of the business.

Inventory (Chapter 1): Goods in which the business normally deals that are held with the intention of resale. They may be finished goods, partly finished goods or raw materials awaiting conversion into finished goods which will then be sold.

Inventory turnover (Chapter 34): The number of times inventory is sold in an accounting period. (Also known as 'stockturn'.)

Job costing (Chapter 48): A costing system that is applied when goods or services are produced in discrete jobs, either one item at a time, or in batches.

Joint ventures (Chapter 40): Business agreements under which two businesses join together for a set of activities and agree to share the profits.

Journal (Chapter 11): A book of original entry for all items not contained in the other books of original entry.

Liabilities (Chapter 1): Total of funds owed for assets supplied to a business or expenses incurred not yet paid.

LIFO (Chapter 29): A method by which goods sold are said to have come from the last lot of goods received.

Limited company (Chapter 45): An organisation owned by its shareholders, whose liability is limited to their share capital.

Limited partner (Chapter 41): A partner whose liability is limited to the capital he or she has put into the firm.

Liquidity ratios (Chapter 47): Those ratios that relate to the cash position in an organisation and hence its ability to pay liabilities when due.

Local area network (LAN) (Chapter 22): A group of workstations linked together locally through wires.

Loan note (Chapter 45): Loan made to a company for which a formal certificate has been issued to the leader by the company.

Loss (Chapter 3): The result of selling goods for less than they cost.

Manufacturing account (Chapter 37): An account in which production cost is calculated.

Margin (Chapter 34): Profit shown as a percentage or fraction of selling price.

Marginal costing (Chapter 48): An approach to costing that takes account of the variable cost of products rather than the full production cost. It is particularly useful when considering utilisation of spare capacity.

Mark-up (Chapter 34): Profit shown as a percentage or fraction of cost price.

Materiality (Chapter 10): That something should only be included in the financial statements if it would be of interest to the stakeholders, i.e. to those people who make use of financial accounting statements. It need not be material to every stakeholder, but it must be material to a stakeholder before it merits inclusion.

Measurement basis (Chapter 47): The monetary aspects of the items in the financial statements, such as the basis of the inventory valuation, say FIFO or LIFO.

Memorandum joint venture account (Chapter 40): A memorandum account outside the double entry system where the information contained in all the joint venture accounts held by the parties to the joint ventures are collated, the joint venture profit is calculated and the share of profit of each party is recorded in order to close off the account.

Money measurement concept (Chapter 10): The concept that accounting is concerned only with facts measurable in monetary terms, and for which purpose measurements can be used that obtain general agreement as to their suitability.

Narrative (Chapter 17): A description and explanation of the transaction recorded in the journal.

Negative contribution (Chapter 38): The excess of direct costs allocated to a section of a business over the revenue from that section.

Negative goodwill (Chapter 46): The name given to the amount by which the total purchase price for a business a limited company has taken over is less than the valuation of the assets at that time. The amount is entered at the top of the non-current assets in the balance sheet as a negative amount. (Sole traders and partnerships can use this approach instead of a capital reserve.)

Net current assets (Chapter 28): Current assets minus current liabilities. The figure represents the amount of resources the business has in a form that is readily convertible into cash. Same as working capital.

Net loss (Chapter 7): Where the cost of goods sold plus expenses is greater than the revenue.

Net profit (Chapter 7): Where sales revenue plus other income, such as rent received, exceeds the sum of cost of goods sold plus other expenses.

Net realisable value (Chapter 29): The value of goods calculated as their selling price less expenses before sale.

Nominal accounts (Chapter 11): Accounts in which expenses, revenue and capital are recorded.

Nominal ledger (Chapter 11): Another name for the general ledger.

Non-current assets (Chapter 8): Assets which have a long life bought with the intention to use them in the business and not with the intention to simply resell them.

Non-current liabilities (Chapter 8): Liabilities that do not have to be paid within twelve months of the balance sheet date.

Objectivity (Chapter 10): Using a method that everyone can agree to based on some clear and indisputable fact.

Obsolescence (Chapter 26): Becoming out-of-date.

Ordinary shares (Chapter 45): Shares entitled to dividends after the preference shareholders have been paid their dividends.

Output tax (Chapter 19): VAT added to the net price of outputs (i.e. sales).

Outputs (Chapter 19): Sales of goods and services.

Overdraft (Chapter 12): A facility granted by a bank that allows a customer holding a current account with the bank to spend more than the funds in the account. Interest is charged daily on the amount of the overdraft on that date and the overdraft is repayable at any time upon request from the bank.

Partnership (Chapter 41): A business in which two or more people are working together as owners with a view to making profits.

Partnership salaries (Chapter 41): Agreed amounts payable to partners in respect of duties undertaken by them.

PAYE (Pay As You Earn) (Chapter 21): The system whereby income tax is deducted from wages and salaries by employers and sent to HM Customs and Revenue.

Payee (Chapter 12): The person to whom a cheque is paid.

Pay-in slip (Chapter 12): A form used for paying money into a bank account with the same bank.

Personal accounts (Chapter 11): Accounts for creditors and debtors.

Personal allowances (Chapter 21): Amounts each person may subtract from income in order to arrive at taxable income. The value of each allowance is set by Parliament following the Budget each year.

Personal Identification Number or **PIN** (Chapter 12): A secret number issued by a bank to a customer so that the customer may use a debit card in an ATM.

Petty cash book (Chapter 18): A cash book for small payments.

Plastic card (Chapter 12): The generic name for the range of payment-related cards.

Posting (Chapter 13): The act of transferring information into ledger accounts from books of original entry.

Preference shares (Chapter 45): Shares that are entitled to an agreed rate of dividend before the ordinary shareholders receive anything.

Preliminary expenses (Chapter 45): All the costs that are incurred when a company is formed.

Prepaid expense (Chapter 28): An expense which has been paid in advance, the benefits from which will be received in the next period. It is included in the balance sheet under current assets as 'prepayments'.

Prime cost (Chapter 37): Direct materials plus direct labour plus direct expenses.

Private company (Chapter 45): A limited company that must issue its shares privately.

Private ledger (Chapter 11): A ledger for capital and drawings accounts.

Process costing (Chapter 48): A costing system that is applied when goods or services are produced in a continuous flow.

Production cost (Chapter 37): Prime cost plus indirect manufacturing costs.

Profit (Chapter 3): The result of selling goods or services for more than they cost.

Profit and loss account (Chapter 7): An account in which net profit is calculated that is summarised and included in a separate edition of the income statement.

Prudence (Chapter 10): Ensuring that profit is not shown as being too high, not that assets are shown at too high a value and that the financial statements are neutral: that is, that neither gains nor losses are understated or overstated.

Public company (Chapter 45): A company that can issue its shares publicly, and for which there is no maximum number of shareholders.

Purchased goodwill (Chapter 42): The difference between the amount paid to acquire a part or the whole of a business as a going concern and the value of the net assets owned by the business.

Purchases (Chapter 3): Goods bought by the business for the prime purpose of selling them again.

Purchases day book (Chapter 11): Book of original entry for credit purchases. Also called the purchases journal.

Purchases invoice (Chapter 15): A document received by a purchaser showing details of goods bought and their prices.

Purchases ledger (Chapter 11): A ledger for suppliers' personal accounts.

Real accounts (Chapter 11): Accounts in which property of all kinds is recorded.

Realisation concept (Chapter 10): Only profits and gains realised at the balance sheet date should be included in the income statement. For a gain to be realised, it must be possible to be reasonably certain that it exists and that it can be measured with sufficient reliability.

Receipts and payments account (Chapter 36): A summary of the cash book of a non-profit-oriented organisation.

Reduced rate (of VAT) (Chapter 19): A lower VAT rate applicable to certain goods and services.

Reducing balance method (Chapter 26): A method of calculating depreciation based on the principle that you calculate annual depreciation as a percentage of the net-of-depreciation-to-date balance brought forward at the start of the period on a non-current asset.

Registered business (Chapter 19): A business that has registered for VAT. It must account for VAT and submit a VAT Return at the end of every VAT tax period.

Reserves (Chapter 45): Accounts to which profits are transferred for use in future years.

Residual value (Chapter 26): The net amount receivable when a non-current asset is put out of use by the business.

Return on capital employed (Chapter 47): Net profit as a percentage of capital employed, often abbreviated as ROCE.

Return on owners' equity (Chapter 47): Net profit as a percentage of ordinary share capital plus all reserves, often abbreviated as ROOE. The more common term in use for this is 'return on shareholders' funds'.

Return on shareholders' funds (Chapter 47): Net profit as a percentage of ordinary share capital plus all reserves, often abbreviated as ROSF and more commonly used than the alternative term, return on owners' equity.

Returns inwards (Chapter 9): Goods returned by customers. (Also known as 'sales returns'.)

Returns inwards day book (Chapter 11): Book of original entry for goods returned by customers. Also called the returns inwards journal or the sales returns book.

Returns outwards (Chapter 9): Goods returned to suppliers. (Also known as 'purchases returns'.)

Returns outwards day book (Chapter 11): Book of original entry for goods returned to suppliers. Also called the returns outwards journal or the purchases returns book.

Revaluation account (Chapter 43): An account used to record gains and losses when assets are revalued.

Revenue (Chapter 4): The financial value of goods and services sold to customers.

Revenue expenditure (Chapter 24): Expenses needed for the day-to-day running of the business.

Sale or return (Chapter 29): Goods passed to a customer on the understanding that a sale will not occur until they are paid for. As a result, these goods continue to belong to the seller.

Sales (Chapter 3): Goods sold by the business in which it normally deals which were bought with the prime intention of resale.

Sales day book (Chapter 11): Book of original entry for credit sales. Also called the sales journal.

Sales invoice (Chapter 14): A document showing details of goods sold and the prices of those goods.

Sales ledger (Chapter 11): A ledger for customers' personal accounts.

Sensitivity analysis (Chapter 22): Altering volumes and amounts so as to see what would be likely to happen if they were changed. For example, a company may wish to know the financial effects of cutting its selling price by £1 a unit. Also called 'what if' analysis.

Separate determination concept (Chapter 10): The amount of each asset or liability should be determined separately.

Shareholders (Chapter 45): Individuals or entities holding are or more share in a company.

Shares (Chapter 45): The division of the capital of a limited company into parts.

Smart card (Chapter 12): A card that holds details on a computer chip instead of a magnetic stripe.

Stakeholdes (Chapter 7): Those goups, entities and individuals who base decisions upon financial statements and other information relating to the entity of which they are stakeholders.

Standard cost (Chapter 29): What you would expect something to cost.

Standard rate (of VAT) (Chapter 19): The VAT rate usually used.

Standard-rated business (Chapter 19): A business that charges VAT at the standard rate on its sales.

Standing order (Chapter 12): A medium used to enable payments to be made automatically at given dates into a bank account for an amount agreed by the payer.

Statement (Chapter 16): A copy of a customer's personal account taken from the supplier's books.

Statement of affairs (Chapter 35): A statement from which the capital of the owner can be found by estimating assets and liabilities. Then Capital = Assets – Liabilities. It is the equivalent of the balance sheet.

Statement of cash flows (Chapter 39): A statement showing how cash has been generated and disposed of by an organisation. The layout is regulated by IAS 7.

Statement of changes in Equity (Chapter 45): A statement reconciling the opening and closing carrying amounts at each class and type of equity.

Stocktaking (Chapter 29): The process of physically identifying the inventory on hand at a given point in time.

Straight line method (Chapter 26): A method of calculating depreciation that involves deducting the same amount every accounting period from the original cost of a non-current asset.

Subjectivity (Chapter 10): Using a method that other people may not agree to, derived from one's own personal preferences.

Substance over form (Chapter 10): Where real substance takes precedence over legal form.

Super profits (Chapter 42): Net profit less the opportunity costs of alternative earnings and alternative returns on capital invested that have been foregone.

Suspense account (Chapter 33): An account in which you can enter the amount equal to the difference in the trial balance while you try to find the cause of the error(s) that resulted in the failure of the trial balance to balance.

Switch (Chapter 12): A system that allows a debit card to be used to pay for goods and services in the UK. In effect, it is the electronic version of paying by cheque.

T-account (Chapter 2): The layout of accounts in the accounting books.

Tax code (Chapter 21): The number found by adding up an individual's personal allowances which is used to calculate that individual's tax liability.

Time interval concept (Chapter 10): Financial statements are prepared at regular intervals.

Total cost (Chapter 37): Production cost plus administration, selling and distribution expenses and finance expenses.

Trade discount (Chapter 14): A deduction in price given to a trade customer when calculating the price to be charged to that customer for some goods. It does not appear anywhere in the accounting books and so does not appear anywhere in the financial statements.

Trading account (Chapter 7): An account in which gross profit is calculated that is part of the income statement.

Transposition error (Chapter 32): Where the characters within a number are entered in the wrong sequence.

Trial balance (Chapter 6): A list of account titles and their balances in the ledgers, on a specific date, shown in debit and credit columns.

True and fair view (Chapter 45): The expression that is used by auditors to indicate whether, in their opinion, the financial statements fairly represent the state of affairs and financial performance of a company.

Unpresented cheque (Chapter 30): A cheque which has been given to a creditor but which has not yet been received and processed by the writer's bank.

Unregistered business (Chapter 19): A business that ignores VAT and treats it as part of the cost of purchases. It does not charge VAT on its outputs. It does not need to maintain any record of VAT paid.

Value Added Tax (VAT) (Chapter 19): A tax charged on the supply of most goods and services.

Variable costs (Chapter 47): Expenses which change in response to changes in the level of activity.

Website (of a business) (Chapter 22): A location on the Internet where businesses place information for the use of anyone who happens to want to look at it. In many cases, a business website contains copies of the latest financial statements of the business and a part of the website is devoted to promoting and selling goods and services.

'What if' analysis (Chapter 22): Altering volumes and amounts so as to see what would be likely to happen if they were changed. For example, a company may wish to know the financial effects of cutting its selling price by £1 a unit. Also called sensitivity analysis.

Wide area network (WAN) (Chapter 22): A group of workstations, not all of which are based locally, that are linked together by wires and over telephone lines.

Working capital (Chapter 28): Current assets minus current liabilities. The figure represents the amount of resources the business has in a form that is readily convertible into cash. Same as net current assets.

Work-in-progress (Chapter 37): Items not completed at the end of a period.

Workstation (Chapter 22): A dumb terminal or a PC that is used to access data held in a database on a central computer.

Zero rate (of VAT) (Chapter 19): The VAT rate (of zero) that applies to supply of certain goods and services.

Zero-rated business (Chapter 19): A business that only supplies zero-rated goods and services. It does not charge VAT to its customers but it receives a refund of VAT on goods and services it purchases.

Index

Note: Page references in bold relate to entries in the glossary.